Tel Akko Area H

Harvard Museum of the Ancient Near East Publications

Director of Publications

Michael D. Coogan

Editorial Board

Gojko Barjamovic (Harvard University)
Aaron A. Burke (University of California, Los Angeles)
Alejandro Botta (Boston University)
Katrien De Graef (Ghent University)
Paul Delnero (Johns Hopkins University)
Steven E. Fassberg (Hebrew University, Jerusalem)
Uri Gabbay (Hebrew University, Jerusalem)
W. Randall Garr (University of California, Santa Barbara)
Jonathan Greer (Cornerstone University)
Rebecca Hasselbach-Andee (University of Chicago)
Robert S. Homsher (Harvard University)
Jeremy M. Hutton (University of Wisconsin, Madison)

Enrique Jiménez (Ludwig-Maximilians-Universität München)
Dan'el Kahn (University of Haifa)
Na'ama Pat-El (University of Texas, Austin)
Sara Milstein (University of British Columbia)
Francesca Rochberg (University of California, Berkeley)
Aaron Rubin (Pennsylvania State University)
Hervé Reculeau (University of Chicago)
Piotr Steinkeller (Harvard University)
Joshua Walton (Capital University)
Mark Weeden (University of London)
Christopher Woods (University of Pennsylvania)

Studies in the Archaeology and History of the Levant

VOLUME 10

The titles published in this series are listed at *brill.com/sahl*

Tel Akko Area H

From the Middle Bronze Age to the Crusader Period

By

Aaron Brody
Michal Artzy

With contributions by

Jennie Ebeling
Jeffrey Rose
Edward Maher
Ragna Stidsing

BRILL

LEIDEN | BOSTON

The Library of Congress Cataloging-in-Publication Data

Names: Artzy, Michal, 1943- editor, author. | Brody, Aaron Jed, editor, author.
Title: Tel Akko area H : from the middle Bronze Age to the Crusader period / edited by Aaron Brody, Michal Artzy ; with contributions by Jennie Ebeling, Jeffrey Rose, Edward Maher, Ragna Stidsing.
Description: Leiden ; Boston : Brill, [2023] | Series: Studies in the archaeology and history of the Levant, 2589-2495 ; volume 10 | Includes bibliographical references.
Identifiers: LCCN 2023002182 (print) | LCCN 2023002183 (ebook) | ISBN 9789004522985 (hardback) | ISBN 9789004523531 (ebook)
Subjects: LCSH: Acre (Israel—Antiquities. | Excavations (Archaeology)—Israel—Acre. | Harbors—Israel—Acre—History.
Classification: LCC DS110.A3 T45 2023 (print) | LCC DS110.A3 (ebook) | DDC 933/.4—dc23/eng/20230125
LC record available at https://lccn.loc.gov/2023002182
LC ebook record available at https://lccn.loc.gov/2023002183

Typeface for the Latin, Greek, and Cyrillic scripts: "Brill". See and download: brill.com/brill-typeface.

ISSN 2589-2495
ISBN 978-90-04-52298-5 (hardback)
ISBN 978-90-04-52353-1 (e-book)

Copyright 2023 by President and Fellows of Harvard College. Published by Koninklijke Brill NV, Leiden, The Netherlands.
Koninklijke Brill NV incorporates the imprints Brill, Brill Nijhoff, Brill Hotei, Brill Schöningh, Brill Fink, Brill mentis, Vandenhoeck & Ruprecht, Böhlau, V&R unipress and Wageningen Academic.
All rights reserved. No part of this publication may be reproduced, translated, stored in a retrieval system, or transmitted in any form or by any means, electronic, mechanical, photocopying, recording or otherwise, without prior written permission from the publisher. Requests for re-use and/or translations must be addressed to Koninklijke Brill NV via brill.com or copyright.com.

This book is printed on acid-free paper and produced in a sustainable manner.

This volume is dedicated to the memory of two unwaivering patrons of the coastal and underwater archaeology of Israel, Leon Levy and Sir Maurice Hatter. Without their support, this publication would not have been possible.

Contents

Acknowledgements IX

1 Introduction, Excavation Strategies, and Methodologies 1
   Michal Artzy and Aaron Brody

2 The Stratigraphy and Architecture of Area H 15
   Aaron Brody, Michal Artzy and Ragna Stidsing

3 The Pottery of Stratum 7 (MB IIA) 218
   Aaron Brody and Michal Artzy

4 The Pottery and Other Material Culture of Stratum 6 (MB IIB–IIC) 266
   Aaron Brody and Michal Artzy

5 The Pottery of Stratum 5 (LB IIB–Iron IA Transition, or LB IIC) 344
   Michal Artzy, Aaron Brody, and Ragna Stidsing

6 The Pottery of Stratum 4 (Iron IIA–IIB Transition) 441
   Aaron Brody and Michal Artzy

7 Discussion and Conclusions 583
   Michal Artzy and Aaron Brody

Appendix 1: The Ground Stone Artifacts from Area H, Akko 597
   Jennie R. Ebeling

Appendix 2: Analysis of the Lithic Assemblage from Area H at Tel Akko 617
   Jeffrey Rose

Appendix 3: Middle Bronze Age Mortuary Animal Offerings from Akko 629
   Edward F. Maher

Bibliography 635
Index 651

Acknowledgements

The research and compilation of the manuscript for this final publication were made possible through a generous grant from the Shelby White–Leon Levy Program for Archaeological Publications. We would like to thank the committee for providing us with the support to work on the dormant material from Tel Akko, especially Lawrence Stager, Philip King, and James Wiseman who have encouraged us at every step along the way of this project. We would especially like to thank the fund's benefactors, Shelby White and Leon Levy, for their vision and backing, which has made this program and project possible. The wider ramifications and importance of Shelby White's and Leon Levy's contributions to the field of eastern Mediterranean archaeology have been revealed as the fruits of their program have come to bear, and have had a tremendous impact on the publication of archaeological materials in the 21st century and on the field in general. Leon Levy passed away during the preparation of this volume, a tragic loss to archaeology of an unwavering patron. In a small way this volume is a tribute to Leon Levy's legacy of philanthropy and the continued support of Shelby White. Larry Stager also died quite suddenly before we had finished formatting the illustrations for this final report; we hope that its publication stands as a testament to the memory of his dedication to the field of southern Levantine archaeology and the Bronze and Iron Age archaeology of the region.

During the long years since excavation, the processing of materials and manuscript preparation was carried out at the Sir Maurice and Lady Irene Hatter Laboratory at the University of Haifa. Sir Maurice and the Hatter Foundation kindly supported the research carried out as part of students' training in the Department of Maritime Civilizations at the University of Haifa. Grants from the Israel Science Foundation were instrumental in the original processing of the data. The excavation was financed by kind help from the Dorot Foundation, Tribute to the Danes Foundation and the late Rabbi B. Melchior, Den danske Israel-komite and the late editor of Politiken, H. Pundik, Knud Højgaards Fond and the University of Copenhagen Humanities Faculty. Thanks are due to the students in the Near Eastern and Classical Archaeology Department (now Carsten Niebuhr Institute).

This volume would not have come to fruition without the constant help and diligent work of Ragna Stidsing, both through her insights in the stratigraphy, illustrations and photos and their preparation for publication, compilation and analyses, and through taking on the role as an intermediary between the two authors and the publisher's format, not a simple set of tasks in the least. Christin Engstrom aided with the initial digitizing of the architectural drawings. Catherine Painter Foster initially formatted many of the illustrations for publication, making sense of many bits and pieces. We have enjoyed interacting with numerous archaeology students at the University of Haifa, who have helped in immeasurable ways with the organization and cataloguing of the dormant Tel Akko materials.

Brody would like to thank the Breitstein family for inviting him into their home for so many wonderful Shabbat and holiday meals while in Haifa, and his colleague, and friend, Ezra Marcus, for welcoming him back to Haifa and for his support and intellectual stimulation. He wishes to thank his wife, Christina Kahrl Brody, for her patience and gentle urges to move forward and wrap up this large and complex project through numerous moves and the birth and growth of our two sons, Noah James and Nathaniel Alan Brody. It's finally out of our house!

He would also like to acknowledge the unwaivering support of his parents, Richard Alan Brody and Marjorie Jean Brody, throughout his career. Richard (Dick) passed away close to the completion of the volume; may his memory continue to be a blessing.

Brody would like to thank Michal Artzy for giving him access to the Area H materials. He hopes that this work serves as a small commemoration of her fieldwork, teaching, mentoring of students, research, publications, and career in Israeli and eastern Mediterranean archaeology. Her research in NAA testing and material science approaches to understanding the maritime exchange of ceramics and other goods was pioneering, as has been her work as one of the few female dig directors in Israel through her excavations at Tel Nami, Tell Abu Hawam, and now back at Tel Akko's Total Archaeology Project. Michal is truly a "woman of valor," an inspiration, and an unwaivering mentor, colleague, and friend.

Artzy would like to thank the late Sir Maurice and Lady Hatter and the Hatter Foundation as well as the members of the Sir Maurice and Lady Irene Hatter Laboratory for Coastal and Underwater Archaeology, especially Ragna Stidsing and the Recanati Institute for Maritime Studies at the University of Haifa and its staff. Thanks are also due to former students and lecturers participating in the excavation in Area H. They hearken from the Near Eastern and Classics Departments at the University of Copenhagen, University of Haifa, Evergreen College and University of California, Berkeley. In charge of some of the squares were: Bo Dahl-Hermansen, Maria Jacobsen, Stephen Lumsden, Mette Qvistorff Lumsden, Ragna Stidsing, and Aage Westenholz. Special thanks to Yael, who as a toddler in Area H never fell from the balks into the squares.

CHAPTER 1

Introduction, Excavation Strategies, and Methodologies

Michal Artzy and Aaron Brody

Introduction

The multiperiod site of Tel Akko (Tell el-Fukhar) is located on the northern Mediterranean coast of modern Israel at a confluence of ancient terrestrial and maritime trade routes (fig. 1.1). As a gateway city, Akko was central in connecting the northern region of the southern Levant to exchange networks stretching overseas to the Aegean, Cyprus, the central and northern Levantine coast, the Egyptian Delta, and overland from Egypt to Mesopotamia. More localized, dendritic networks placed Akko as a maritime outlet for regional products coming from the Akko Plain, the Galilee hills, and the Jezreel and Jordan Valleys. The city's strategic position, on the northern side of the Haifa/Akko bay, one of the few bays along the southern Levantine littoral, the Na'aman River estuary, and agricultural hinterland, rendered Tel Akko as a natural location of continual habitation from at least the beginning of the Middle Bronze Age through the Hellenistic period. During the Hellenistic period, the settlement at Tel Akko began to extend off the tell to its present position on the bay and harbor, under the area named the Old City of modern Akko (photo 1.1), which has been continually inhabited from the Hellenistic period until today (Artzy and Beeri 2010; Gambash 2012; Artzy 2013; 2015; 2016; Morhange et al. 2016; Giaime et al. 2018).

From 1973 to 1989, over twelve seasons of excavation, nine areas were excavated on the mound of Akko under the directorship of Moshe Dothan (photo 1.2; fig. 1.2; table 2.1), through the auspices first of the Israel Antiquities Authority (then the Israel Antiquities Service) and later of the Center (now Institute) for Maritime Studies at the University of Haifa in Israel (M. Dothan 1993). Following the death of Dothan, M. Artzy initiated a renewal of the publication of the material of Areas A, AB, B, G, H, and PH. R. Beeri researched the Middle and Late Bronze strata from Areas A, AB, and B for his PhD thesis, and S. Zagorski worked on the LB strata from Area PH in her MA thesis (Zagorski 2004). In 1999, an educational excavation of the Departments of Archaeology and Maritime Civilizations directed by M. Artzy and A. Killebrew took place.

Since 2010, a renewed project on the tell, directed by A. Killebrew and M. Artzy, called the Tel Akko "Total Archaeology" Project, has been undertaken.

This renewed excavation is centered in Area A, partially excavated by Dothan and extending to the south and north toward Dothan's Area AB. The excavation is a combined effort in which several universities and individual scholars are involved, among them T. Schneider and G. Gilbert from McKenna, Claremont; M. Risser from Trinity College, Hartford; M. Sugerman from SUNY Binghamton and Washington State University; A. Brody from Pacific School of Religion, Berkeley; Jamie Quartermaine from Oxford Archaeology North, Great Britain; Jane Skinner from Yale University; and Jolanta Mlynarczyk from University of Warsaw. Ragna Stidsing, from the Hatter Laboratory, RIMS at the University of Haifa, is the coordinator of data. The goal is to further understand and refine Dothan's unpublished stratigraphy and chronology in Area A and AB, as well as understand the ecological and coastal changes and their influence on the site's habitation patterns. This project includes a search for possible landlocked locations of the anchorages and proto-harbors on the southwestern areas below the tell proper. Field testing has included Electric Resistivity Tomography headed by P. Bauman and his team from Worley-Parsons Company, Canada; Ground Penetrating Radar headed by H. Jol and students from the University of Wisconsin at Eau Claire, USA, and Y. Salmon from the Hatter Laboratory at the University of Haifa and the Technion, Israel Technology Institute; Optical Stimulation Luminescence by G. López, CENIEH–Centro Nacional de Investigación sobre la Evolución Humana in Spain; geophysical work was carried out by C. Morhange and his students, from Aix-Marseille University in France followed by M. Giaime, Morhange's former student and a post-doctorate at the Hatter Laboratory at the Recanati Institute for Maritime Studies at the University of Haifa; and pollen analysis and climatic changes by D. Kaniewski from Université Paul Sabatier-Toulouse 3, France (Kaniewski et al. 2013; Kaniewski et al. 2014; Morhange et al. 2016; Giaime et al. 2018). In 2017, Artzy and Jol received a Binational Science Foundation Grant to further the research. Analyses are being carried out on the dormant Area K materials, the late D. Conrad's project, presently being prepared for publication by M. Peilstöker and W. Zwickel. Areas F and P, excavated under the direction of A. Raban, are being prepared for publication by E. Marcus. In addition, several salvage excavations were carried out around the tell by the Israel Antiquities Authority (Abu Hamid 2016; Artzy 2012).

Area H, the topic of this study, is located in the midst of the northern side of Tel Akko (fig. 1.2, photo 1.4). The area is situated between the massive rampart extending from the summit of the tell (Area AB, B) to the east, and Area F, where a gate, named the "Sea Gate" and dating to the MB IIA, was excavated (M. Dothan and Raban 1980). Graves of the MB IIB–IIC periods found in

Area H were positioned in such a manner as to negate the presence of a defensive wall on the northern rampart, as was envisioned by Dothan. He had hoped to find a wall in Area H in accordance with the Egyptian depiction of Akko in the Karnak reliefs. The graves, while dating more or less to concurrent periods in the MB IIB–IIC, seemed to have been utilized by different cultural entities, and there is a clear distinction in the manner of burial and the material goods found in them (see chapter 4). The earliest habitation levels in Area H, or signs of human occupational presence besides the graves, are dated at the earliest to the end of the 13th and the very start of the 12th centuries BCE (Artzy 2006b). These remains included pits, as well as a cultic area in which an altar was found. On the southern part of the area most of the building materials were robbed out in antiquity. According to ancient written sources, the site was named Toron (Artzy and Quartermaine 2014; Artzy 2016). All in all, this part of Area H underwent three major stone robbing incidents, during the Persian period, the Crusader period (Artzy 2015), and another by builders for the reconstruction of the peninsula site to the west during the 15th century CE. The area was thus replete with leveling fills from the 13th century CE, or with soil fills in the areas robbed of their architecture in earlier periods.

The excavation of Area H took place from 1978 to 1982. It was supported financially by the Tribute to the Danes Foundation, Rabbi B. Melchior, and the Politiken newspaper in Copenhagen and its editor, H. Pundik. Students from the Near Eastern and Classical Archaeology Department and the Carsten Niebuhr Institute at the University of Copenhagen participated in the excavation (photo 1.3).

What follows is the publication of the excavation strategies and methods for Dothan's project in general, the stratigraphy and modified Harris matrices for the seven defined phases in Area H, and the Bronze and Iron Age ceramics and other material cultural remains from Area H. Area H has three phases from the later Persian and Hellenistic periods; however, the presentation of the pottery and other material culture from the Persian and Hellenistic layers is beyond the scope of the present study. Work by specialists on the ground stone and chipped stone industries, and the faunal remains from MB IIB–IIC tombs are included in appendixes to the main work.

Excavation Strategies and Methodology

Before the start of excavations, in 1973, the area of the tell was divided into 100 meter squares, which M. Dothan refers to as Master Grid Squares (fig. 1.3; M. Dothan 1976: 5, 17, 23, 34). These Master Grid Squares are oriented to the directions of the compass, and are coordinated within the Israeli mapping system for the entire region, which has divided the country into 20 km squares. These 100 meter squares, or Master Grid Squares, were subdivided into 5 m squares, numbered 1 to 20 from south to north, and lettered A to U from west to east; each square was named by the coordinates of its southwestern corner (note that the letter I was not used, so the sequence of letters skips from H to J). Typically a .50 m wide balk was left on each side of the excavation square, reducing the excavated area to 4 square meters. Sometimes these balks were recorded and excavated; in other instances they were left untouched. In the beginning of the project, areas of excavation were lettered according to the sequence in which they were begun. These lettered excavation areas were located both on the tell and off the site, in rescue excavations in areas of building and road construction in, and near, the modern city of Akko. From the Dothan project there were ten areas of excavation on the tell: A, AB, B, C, F, G, H, K, P, PH (fig. 1.2). The area named Area S was part of a survey of the southern part of the site, and a pit found in this survey was excavated; later projects included Areas T and TD (fig. 1.2).

The method of recording consisted of a field diary, with a record of pottery buckets and sketch top plans of the excavated squares, and separate personal notebooks for daily notes of the square supervisors. For some of the areas there are also locus summary sheets and pottery cards. For some of the squares, section drawings were produced at the end of the season (fig. 2.1–4). In addition to the notebook sketches, architectural features were drawn by project architects. Typically these drawings include several strata (phases) of buildings in the same drawing.

The method of excavation followed the standard Israeli methodology of the time: major features, such as walls, floors, tombs, pits, tabuns (bread/food ovens), were given sequential wall or locus numbers. Intermediate layers were left unnumbered, and were excavated using the pottery basket system. When excavating a feature, the locus number was included on the pottery basket; when digging a layer there was no locus number. Thus, it is difficult to determine the stratigraphic separation between pottery baskets, although they were changed daily and in transitions between different layers. Architectural features were generally not removed, if possible, when continuing to earlier strata. Thus the area of excavation within a given square diminished as the depth increased, as earlier debris layers were left in place to support later architectural features. This system was pioneered in the 1950s and 60s at the Israeli-led excavations at Hazor, directed by Y. Yadin, and Ramat Rachel, directed by Y. Aharoni (Mazar 1988).

The collection of artifacts and ecofacts seems to have differed by excavation area and preferences of the area supervisors. From the present material culture stored at the University of Haifa, it is apparent that ceramics, flaked stone, ground stone, metals, and glass were collected. Animal bones and charred seeds/grain were preserved by the excavators.[1] Little dry or wet sifting was performed. Ceramics were "read" and sorted during the field seasons, and only diagnostic pottery (based primarily the ability to ascertain the vessel's type and not on the fabric of the ceramic) was stored for future study.

Given these methods of retrieval and sorting, approaches to stratigraphic reconstruction and pottery analysis are limited. The deposition in Area H (chapter 2 below) has been reconstructed pottery basket by basket in relation to architectural features with the aid of a system of modified Harris matrices (figs. 2.18–2.42). With the goal of more accurately representing archaeological stratigraphy, Edward Harris developed the use of matrices to present the superimposition of the different layers and features that make up an archaeological site (Harris 1975; 1989). Harris's system was designed specifically with the goal of portraying the fourth dimension, or the process of time, which is typically lacking in a straightforward drawing of a section: balk drawings may show stratigraphy; however, they are not represented as phased (Harris 1975: 119). The matrix was conceived, in essence, as a vertical phase plan, a concept in keeping with the practice of phasing horizontal top plans, or architectural phase plans. As developed by Harris, for his work in England on an Iron Age fortress site, the matrix was a simple flow chart with rectangular boxes depicting an individual archaeological layer or feature. Unlike a section drawing that only represents the loci that interface with it, matrices could include every layer or feature excavated in a given square regardless of whether or not they intersected with the balk (Harris 1975: 112).

The initial flow chart matrix designed by Harris has been modified slightly to incorporate further capabilities to visually display the stratigraphy of a given site. Further addition of various symbols to represent different categories of loci was developed for the excavation of Tell el-Maskhuta, on the Wadi Tumilat in Egypt, and for Mayan sites in Belize (Paice 1991; Hammond 1993). Harris's use of a simple rectangle to represent all types of loci thus has been replaced by a system where a circle may equal a pit, a hexagon a tabun, etc. (fig. 2.18). The distinction in the use of symbols provides a visual cue to those viewing the matrix. For instance an architectural unit with associated features, represented in the modified matrix by a set of symbols in relationship to one another, stands out dramatically from the fill layers used to level the area before its construction. In practical terms the modified Harris matrix also allows for a quick and easy separation between more and less meaningful loci. Material culture remains

---

[1] Unfortunately the majority of these samples were not located for analysis.

associated with well-stratified loci can be identified in relation to those of less importance, or those like fills which are tertiary in terms of information they provide.

By working through the daily notes, field diaries, locus cards, top plans, and photographs from Area H, each individual pottery basket could be placed in its relative stratigraphic sequence. In many ways the pottery baskets are representative of the layers of the site. Typically, it was possible to establish if these were superimposed based on the descriptions of the makeup of the layers provided in the daily notes, checked against the absolute height of each pottery basket recorded in the field diaries. When pottery baskets were assigned to individual loci they were placed in the matrix in different shapes coded for different types of loci: thus baskets from pits were placed in circles, pottery from walls were recorded in rhomboids, and materials attributed to surfaces were placed in rectangles with lines at each end (see chapter 2 below; figs. 2.18–2.42). Lines were inserted between the various shapes of loci to indicate direct relationships: "on top of" or "beneath" is indicated with a vertical line; contemporaneity is marked by horizontal lines connecting loci or layers; horizontal connecting lines can also represent the fact that two loci are connected physically. Each shape on the matrix, corresponding to a reconstituted layer or a locus, was filled with information corresponding to the date of the seasons excavated ('79 = 1979, '80 = 1980, etc.), numbers of the pottery baskets it contained (i.e., b.612 = pottery basket 612), its relative top and bottom height (i.e., 21.73/21.63 = top height/bottom height in meters above sea level), the range of time periods indicated by preliminary pottery readings (i.e., LB II–Iron I, Pers.–Hell., etc.), and a short description if it was a distinctive feature (surface, column base, pit, etc.).

It should be noted that the modified Harris matrix is used to represent temporal relationships in a given excavation area. It is not meant, however, to convey spatial relationships. Occasionally physical positions of given loci can be mimicked with the placement of their corresponding markers in the matrix; however, this is not always possible given the attempt to represent three-dimensional archaeological remains on a two-dimensional matrix. Associations such as "cut by" or "contiguous with" are not represented on the matrix, regardless of their stratigraphic significance.

The outcome of this first stage was a set of matrices somewhat akin to Harris's original matrix type, although he used only rectangles to represent his layers and features while we employed various shapes. These represented a fairly straightforward flow chart that primarily depicted which loci were superimposed one above the other. The next stage was to manipulate the flow chart according to phases, since even within a 5 × 5 m square the different sequences of matrices produced did not necessarily match up in terms of visual presentation. We coded the representative time periods based on the preliminary pottery readings in the field diaries: these included Middle Bronze Age, Late Bronze–Early Iron I transition, Iron Age II, Persian, Hellenistic, and surface finds. Through further stratigraphic and ceramic analysis, it was determined that the Middle Bronze and Hellenistic levels should be further divided into two phases each (see chapter 2 below). This greater stratigraphic refinement, reflecting seven occupational phases in Area H, is not represented in the matrices.

Based on the modified Harris matrices, it was possible to phase each of the flow chart sequences within a given square, and thus to relate contemporary loci for each excavation square. In turn the matrices allowed for greater ease of phasing between squares, thus providing a picture of the makeup of different strata throughout Area H. These matrices will also aid in the comparison of different phases between areas excavated on the site that have no physical links, and provide researchers interested in the ceramics of the Persian and Hellenistic phases in Area H, which are beyond the scope of this study, with a guide to promising loci.

Ceramic studies of the Bronze and Iron Age phases in Area H (chs. 3–6) are limited methodologically; statistical approaches could not be used since collection of ceramics was not performed with numeric analysis in mind. Seriation could not be used because of the gaps in the depositional sequence in Area H, as presented in chapter 2, a situation which is typical of other areas of excavations at Tel Akko. A traditional approach in ceramic analysis will thus be utilized: pottery will be presented first as it was originally found, grouped together by pottery basket (as locus designations were not universal); and a typology of ceramic material will then be developed for each of the Bronze and Iron Age phases in Area H. Ceramic types at Akko will then be compared with pottery from corresponding strata at relevant sites to aid in the chronological phasing of the levels in Area H.[2] When possible, absolute dates will be assigned to the phases in Area H based on finds from the excavation. As the chronology for the region of the southern Levant is in flux, it is preferable to wait for the excavations at Akko, presently being carried out by the Total Archaeology Project, and a planned program of collection and analysis of ^{14}C and OSL samples in order to reconstruct the range of absolute dates for the multiple strata of the tell. Until such research is completed, comparative absolute dates will be presented in the conclusions to this study.

---

2 The authors acknowledge that the research and writing of the ceramic chapters was completed prior to the publication of Seymour Gitin's edited volumes in the series *The Ancient Pottery of Israel and Its Neighbors*, see Artzy 2019; Gilboa 2015; and Lehmann 2015 for relevant comparsions unfortunately not considered in chapters 3–6 of this work.

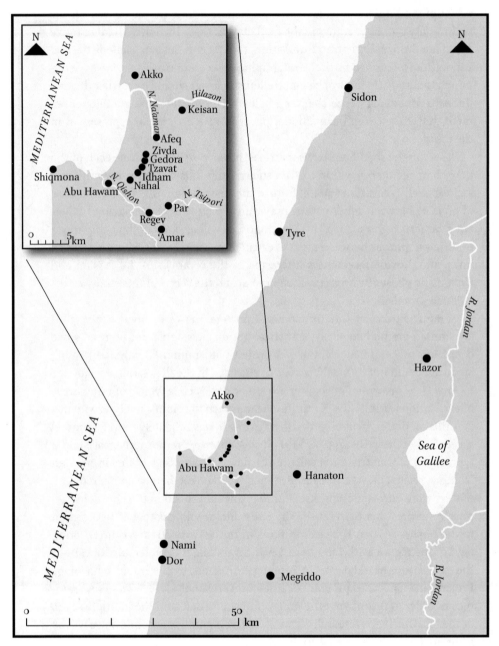
FIGURE 1.1   Map of sites in the Akko Plain and surrounding regions

INTRODUCTION, EXCAVATION STRATEGIES, AND METHODOLOGIES 9

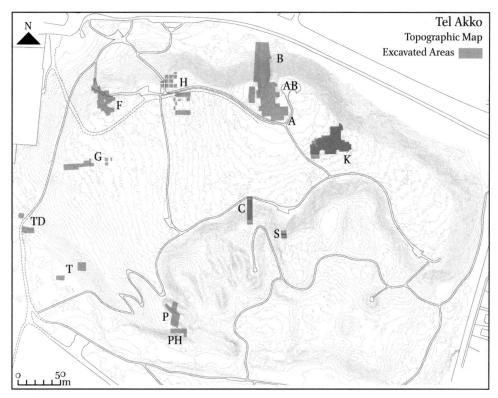

FIGURE 1.2 Tel Akko topographic map with excavated areas
PREPARED BY: J. QUARTERMAINE

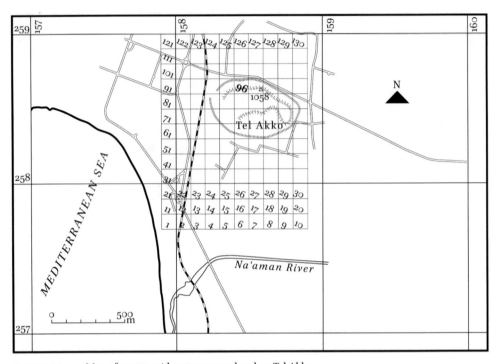

FIGURE 1.3   Map of master grid system around and on Tel Akko

INTRODUCTION, EXCAVATION STRATEGIES, AND METHODOLOGIES

PHOTO 1.1 Tel Akko, Acre old city and the sea from ENE
PHOTO: M. ARTZY

PHOTO 1.2   Moshe Dothan in Area A at Tel Akko, ca. 1974
PHOTO: MOTI FRIEDMAN

PHOTO 1.3 Area H archaeologists and volunteers in 1983
PHOTO: ELLA EGERT

PHOTO 1.4   Area H 1983, view from east
PHOTO: M. ARTZY

CHAPTER 2

The Stratigraphy and Architecture of Area H

Aaron Brody, Michal Artzy and Ragna Stidsing

Area H (photo 1.4), in the northwestern area of the mound, Master Grid #96, was excavated under the direction of its area supervisor, M. Artzy, for five seasons: 1979, 1980, 1982–84 (figs. 1.2–1.3, 2.5). Initially the area was chosen for exploration because M. Dothan thought that it had potential for revealing remains of the Late Bronze Age city wall, as depicted in the reliefs of the Egyptian Pharaoh Ramses II (M. Dothan 1979: 228; 1993: 21).

Area H, however, produced few remains from the Late Bronze Age. Its stratigraphy consists of MB IIA fills from the outer slope of the later phases of the city rampart (Stratum 7); MB IIB and MB IIB–IIC tombs cut into the rampart (Stratum 6; fig. 2.11); LB IIB–early Iron I transition period pits and floors (Stratum 5; fig. 2.10); a few Iron IIA–IIB transition period domestic remains (Stratum 4; fig. 2.9); "Persian period pits" (see below), human and dog burials (Stratum 3; fig. 2.8); and two phases of Hellenistic domestic architecture (Strata 2 and 1; figs. 2.6, 2.7).[1] These strata were not numbered in the original excavations, so we are labeling them strata 1–7, localized to Area H with Stratum 1 being the latest and Stratum 7 the earliest. Following the general practice employed in the excavations at Akko, the two Middle Bronze Age and Hellenistic phases in Area H are given separate stratum numbers, since in previous reports a stratum is essentially equal to an architectural phase rather than an entire cultural period.

Area H Stratum 7, the Rampart

The earliest stratum in Area H consists of sloping levels of the final phase of the city's Middle Bronze Age rampart. This is best seen in section drawings from Square M/9, from the 1984 season, which clearly show large fill layers of the rampart, sloping downward toward the north (fig. 2.1) and from Square P/5

---

[1] In squares N/1 and O/1 remains of a large medieval element were noted. A cannon trailer wheel dated to the Napoleonic era was found in Area H on the path leading to the site from the north, and there were remains of 1940s army trenches, bringing the phasing of the excavation area into our modern era.

where the rampart's declining slope inward is clearly seen in the eastern balk of the square (fig. 2.4). The rampart was noted in several squares, for instance in Square P/4 where the rampart and the slope appear both on the northern and eastern balks (photos 2.1 and 2.2), and Squares M/3 and O/5 (figs. 2.2–2.3). Pottery from these fill levels is typical of the MB IIA (chapter 3). This supports the finding in earlier preliminary reports that the final phases of Akko's Middle Bronze Age ramparts were constructed in the MB IIA, with patch repairs occurring in the MB IIB–IIC, which was based on excavations of the rampart in Areas B and F (table 2.1; M. Dothan 1976: 7–14; Raban 1991). An MB IIA date for Stratum 7 is further confirmed by the fact that this outer slope of the rampart in Area H became a burial ground in Stratum 6, with one grave dating to the MB IIB and two to the MB IIB–IIC, all cut into the upper layers of the rampart. The final layers of rampart construction thus predated these MB IIB–IIC tomb cuts, created for disposal of the dead in the city's IIB–IIC phases of Middle Bronze occupation.

Area H Stratum 6, Burials

Three graves were excavated in Area H that date from the MB IIB and MB IIB–IIC periods. Two were located in Square L/9 and a third in Square P/5 (photo 2.3–4, 2.6; fig. 2.11). There is a possible grave in Square O/5 so badly robbed in antiquity, either by looters or later builders, that it is difficult to determine whether the structure was used for burial or domestic purposes. The location of Middle Bronze and Late Bronze Age burials varied throughout the region of the southern Levant: they are found primarily in extramural cemeteries, but tombs are also frequently placed on the outer slopes of tell sites, and in several instances, there are intramural Middle and Late Bronze I burials (Gonen 1992a; Hallote 1995; Ilan 1996; Van den Brink 1982). The location of these tombs at Akko, cut into the outer slope of the MB IIA rampart in Area H, is thus not unusual for Middle to Late Bronze Age funereal practices, and is especially common at nearby Megiddo (Guy 1938: 3, fig. 2).

A pit, Locus 913, was found, cut into the rampart layers. It is somewhat difficult to establish this pit's stratigraphy, since its remains (photo 4.14) appear to be later than those in the rampart layers, but earlier than those found in the tombs. It seems that the pit was cut after the final phase of the rampart in Area H, but before the area was used as a cemetery.

Pit Locus 913
Locale: Area H, Square M/9.

Type: pit.

Stratigraphy (fig. 2.34): elevation 24.53/24.17; locus above is 905, a large, well built, east-west running stone wall from the late Hellenistic period (Stratum 1); the locus below is the Stratum 7 MB IIA rampart into which Locus 913 is cut.

Dimensions: unknown.

Pit contents: three platter bowls (photo 4.14; fig. 4.6.1–3), storage jar [?], and animal bones.

Preliminary date: transition from MB IIA–IIB.

The pit, Locus 913, was found in Square M/9 (fig. 2.34). It contained intact pottery vessels and the remains of animal bones. It was found at the bottom of a probe excavated to the north of the Hellenistic, Stratum 1 wall, Locus 905, so the full dimensions of the pit and its exact relationship to the rampart layers into which it was cut are not clearly discerned. The finds in Locus 913 include three platter bowls with features typical of the transitional phase from the MB IIA to the MB IIB (fig. 4.6.1–3). It is possible that these vessels were buried in the rampart as an offering; otherwise we are at a loss to explain their high degree of preservation.

Burial, Locus 727
Locale:[2] Area H, Square L/9 (fig. 2.11).

Type: cist.

Stratigraphy (fig. 2.27): elevation 25.15/24.92; loci above include 728, a floor from Stratum 5, the Late Bronze–Early Iron I transition (LB IIC) phase, and 813, a pit from the same phase which cuts the

---

2 This trait list follows that which David Ilan developed for his study of Middle Bronze Age burials at Tel Dan (1996).

northeastern corner of the burial; the locus below is the Stratum 7 MB IIA rampart into which Locus 727 is cut.

Dimensions: .43 × 1.30 m, depth .17 m

Orientation: the grave is cut in a west-east direction, with the skulls of the interred bodies positioned toward the east.

Human skeletal remains: two articulated, primary burials, one adult and one child.

Burial goods: two ceramic vessels, one bronze toggle pin, and one bronze earring.

Preliminary date: MB IIB

Locus 727, Square L/9, is the earliest of the three graves in Area H (fig. 2.11). It is a double burial of an adult and child in a grave cut into the rampart (photo 2.3; fig. 2.12). According to the excavator, Guy Grainger,[3] "the adult was supine, though turned slightly on its right side with the knees raised and the legs as a result somewhat contracted. The arms were placed on the chest. The child was laid on top of the right side of the adult. The child lay on its right side with the legs flexed and one arm straight behind the trunk. The adult was not holding the child." Both the adult and child, and the cist in which they are interred, are oriented toward the east, and the adult's head is facing up. The child's skull was not preserved well enough to determine which way it faced.

Grainger describes the osteology of each individual: "Adult burial: the skeleton was in poor condition; all of the bones being broken and generally extremely friable. The skull was badly damaged and later activities removed the knees. Molar attrition indicates that this individual was about twenty-five years old.[4] Periodontal disease and dental hypoplasia were both present to a slight degree. Slight deposits of dental calculus were seen on the upper and lower incisors with traces of calculus being found on most of the other teeth as well. Slight bony protuberances on the lingual surfaces of the mandible, resembling Tori Mandibularis, were present. The right upper third molar was much reduced in size being peg-like in appearance and the right upper second incisor had a shovel-shaped crown. Associated grave goods indicated (suggested)

---

[3] Quotations taken from field notebook.
[4] *R* 8765\\21 \2345678 *L*8765432\ 1234\\\\ This information is provided by G. Grainger in his preliminary osteological work on the burial.

that this individual was female. This is in accord with the limited osteological evidence, noticed during excavation. The skeleton was a wide hipped female with gracile long bones. The skull was four to five mm thick."

Grainger further calculated the height of the adult individual: "Stature was calculated using Trotter and Glesers' regression equations for certain bones that were measured in situ.[5] From these measurements it is suggested that this individual was between 160–161 cm tall."

The child was buried on top of the adult female (fig. 2.12). Grainger describes the burial thus: "The skeleton was in very poor condition with the bones being fragmented and eroded. Two teeth were recovered: a permanent upper left first incisor, partially formed, and the upper left deciduous canine with some wear on it. These teeth, together with the size of the bones indicate that the child was four years old."

Grave goods in Locus 727 include two complete vessels, a dipper juglet and cylindrical juglet, both dated to the MB IIB, a bronze pin, and a bronze earring (fig. 2.12). The dipper juglet was placed close to the child's left shoulder, with its spout pointing in the direction of the adult's head and the back of the child's skull (although the skull is largely missing). This positioning of vessels near children's heads has been noted by Ilan for burials at Tel Dan and elsewhere in the southern Levant. It was also present in several Middle Bronze Age child burials at Tell el-Dabᶜa, and an LB I child's tomb from Tel Ashkelon (Ilan 1996: 179, 183; Bietak 1991: 134, 202, 210, 229, 252, 274; Brody 2008). It is possible that the placement of containers near children's heads and specifically their mouths suggests aid in "feeding" these children after their death, specifically in their journey to the Canaanite netherworld (Brody 2008). The cylindrical juglet, with double-strand handle, appears to have been placed to the south of the child's feet and above the left femur of the adult burial (figs. 2.12 and 4.1.1; photo 2.3). Perhaps it was nestled in the area between her pelvis and raised left leg, though after decomposition of the body's flesh the vessel has settled and pushed up against the adult's left femur. A bronze pin was likely associated with clothing of the adult individual. It is difficult to assess its exact original position before decomposition, but it appears to have been on the individual's upper right side. Part of a bronze earring is also noted, closest to the area of the adult's left shoulder.

---

5 Right fibula = 34.8 cm long: estimated stature = 160.6 cm
    Left radius = 21.9 cm long: estimated stature = 158.7 cm
    Left ulna = 24.0 cm long: estimated stature = 161.2 cm
    After Grainger.

Burial, Locus 829 (fig. 2.13.1–12)
Locale: Area H, Squares L/9–M/9 (fig. 2.11).

Type: built chamber tomb.

Stratigraphy (figs. 2.27, 2.34): elevation 25.21/23.75; entrance threshold 24.71, first step 24.38; loci above include 814 in L/9, a stone lined pit from Stratum 5, the Late Bronze–Early Iron I transition phase, which cuts the northwest corner of the tomb, and 930 in L/9–M/9, a Stratum 3 Persian period burial which cuts the top of the eastern end of the structure (figs. 2.13.12; 2.16.2); the locus below is the Stratum 7 MB IIA rampart into which Locus 829 is cut (photo 2.4). Dimensions: interior 2.92 × 1.78 m (base level), 2.78 × .86 m (top level); exterior 3.92 × 2.26 m (base level), 3.93 × 1.98 m (top level); depth 1.14–1.46 m (fig. 2.13.1).

Orientation: the rectangular base of the structure is laid out west-east (fig. 2.13.1), with the position of one articulated body directed west (fig. 2.13.3); entrance on the west side of the tomb.

Human skeletal remains: one articulated, primary burial (fig. 2.13.3); many disarticulated human remains (fig. 2.13.4–6); minimum of five individuals.

Burial goods (fig. 2.13.7–11): thirty ceramic vessels (figs. 4.1.2–4.2.10); bronze balance pans and hematite weights (photo 4.6; fig. 4.3.1–2, 4.3.16–19); gold earrings, rings (fig. 4.3.4–9); beads made from bone, semiprecious stone, bronze, and gold, and what appear to be bead blanks (fig. 4.5.10–24); four steatite scarabs (photo 4.12), two plain amethyst scarabs, one plain and one inscribed amethyst scarab set in gold bezels with silver rings, one inscribed amethyst scarab in a gold bezel (photo 4.11; scarabs in fig. 4.5.1–9); a grinding stone and large limestone mortar (photo 4.9; fig. 4.3.20), flint scrapers and flakes; alabaster vessels (photo 4.7; fig. 4.3.10–15); worked bone inlays (fig. 4.4.1–26); ocher; animal and fish bones; olive pits.

Preliminary date: MB IIB–IIC.

In the northeastern corner of Square L/9 and stretching across the balk into M/9, a built chamber tomb, Locus 829, was excavated which dates to the

MB IIB–IIC (fig. 2.13.1).[6] The tomb structure is rectangular and corbelled, constructed from fieldstones built up in ever narrowing courses (figs. 2.13.12, 2.15). The bottom of the tomb's interior is 2.92 × 1.78 m, and is oriented, more or less, to the cardinal directions with the shorter ends of the tomb on the west and east sides. The walls of the structure are .54–.58 m wide toward the bottom of the tomb, and remain within that range of width to the top of the tomb. At the very top the southern wall broadens to .72 m. This wider portion appears to be the only preserved area of roofing, the rest having been cut out or robbed in antiquity. The original floor of the tomb is at 23.75 m above sea level, and the tomb is between 1.14–1.46 m deep. This is not quite its full depth as the roof of the structure was almost totally removed by later pitting and a Persian period tomb, Locus 930 (photo 2.4), which cut the top of Locus 829 (figs. 2.13.12, 2.16.2). The angle of the corbelling of the northern and southern walls of the tomb is approximately 74–75°. The entrance to the tomb was from the western side, as is indicated by a threshold and step located in the northern half of the western wall of the structure (fig. 2.13.1). It is not clear if there was a shaft leading down to the tomb, because later building activities robbed out the northwest area above the tomb where one would expect a shaft leading to the entrance. It is possible that there was no shaft as this burial was outside the area of contemporary settlement and may have been situated so its roof was exposed at the surface of the tell. A strange configuration of wall stones in the westernmost part of the northern wall of the structure may indicate an area where roofing stones were removed and replaced to gain access to the tomb entrance (fig. 2.13.1), but this is far from certain and must remain a conjecture. The area just west of the threshold and step was never excavated, and might conceal the remnants of a stone lined shaft, as is evident from a similar structural tomb in neighboring Area A on the acropolis of Akko and from the plans of comparable built chamber tombs at Kabri, Megiddo, and Tel Dan (M. Dothan 1993: 20; Kempinski 2002: 51; Gonen 1992b: 154–55; Ilan 1996: 173).

There appear to have been a minimum of five individuals buried in Locus 829, as indicated by the presence of five skulls (fig. 2.13.3–6). The original positioning of each of the interred is not always clear as defleshed bones and grave goods were pushed to the sides of the structure in antiquity, presumably to make room for further interment. This is indicated by clustering of disarticulated human remains and material culture along the sides of the tomb. Thin, water-borne mud layers also indicate the presence of water in the bounded space of the tomb, which likely disturbed the original position of both skeletal and material cultural remains, as vessels and skulls filled with air are buoyant

---

6 Excavation of this square was supervised by Maria Jacobsen of the University of Copenhagen.

and are likely to float and move around with a flow of water. Though not in their original, articulated position, all five skulls were found in the eastern half of the tomb while the majority of pottery offerings were in the western half. One individual, labeled skeleton A, was partially articulated, and this may be one of the earliest to be interred in the corbelled tomb as it lay on the lowest floor associated with the structure (fig. 2.13.3). The body, missing its skull and arms, appears to have been laid out on its back parallel to the northern wall of the tomb. Thus, it is oriented west-east, with both legs extending straight out from the hips. This is comparable to the positioning of contemporary burials in another nearby structural tomb, Locus 932, located in Area H, Square P/5, discussed below. Skeleton A remained in partial articulation due to the fact that it appears to have been covered over by a matrix of what the excavators described as "loose, mixed, sandy material." This sounds like naturally deposited sand common at coastal sites, which blows in during winter storms and then is carried around by rainwater. Structural tombs cut into open areas of the tell would have formed natural low spots, and acted like sumps attracting water and water-borne sediments.[7] As long as a tomb was unattended by the living it would begin to fill up. On top of the .10 m thick sandy matrix covering skeleton A was a different matrix described as "a hard packed layer," made of "mixed soil and plaster." This surface as described by the excavator is likely a deliberate fill, created by activities of the living so that further bodies could be laid to rest in the tomb, and the majority of the finds in Locus 829 occur above this second floor level.

Grave goods discovered in the tomb, Locus 829, include an abundance of pottery vessels, such as platters (photo 4.2) and open-mouthed juglets; artifacts of metal and stone, such as a balance scale and weights (photo 4.6); worked bone inlays (photo 4.10); beads and scarabs (photos 4.11–4.13). Ecofacts were in Locus 829 as well, such as animal and fish bones, olive pits, charcoal, and ocher (figs. 4.1.2–4.5.24). While the grave goods could be simply grouped into categories of personal possession or adornment, it is possible that the finds also indicate that this was a tomb of a merchant family with Egyptian contacts. Items related to food and food preparation, consumption, and storage (animal and fish bones, olive pits, a stone mortar and grinding stone, flint tools, open

---

7   A similar natural buildup occurs in courtyards found in buildings at coastal sites, which are open, bounded areas. They are typified by alternating layers of wind and water-borne sand and mud. Similar sand and mud layers filled human made cave tombs, dating to the MB IIA–LB IIB, which were cut into the kurkar bedrock at Ashkelon. Brody supervised their excavation over the 1996–97 seasons of the Leon Levy Expedition to Ashkelon, and it was clear that once these tombs were no longer cared for in antiquity they quickly filled with alternating layers of sand and mud.

and closed vessels) were also found in the grave. These grave goods are further described below in chapter 4.

Partial Animal Burial Locus 934, Outside of Burial Locus 829
Locale: Area H, Square M/10 (fig. 2.11).

Type: burial of part of an animal.

Stratigraphy (fig. 2.35): elevation 25.13/25.11; locus above is 929, a plaster floor from the LB IIB–early Iron transition period (Stratum 5); the locus below is the Stratum 7 MB IIA rampart into which Locus 934 is cut.

Dimensions: unknown.

Burial contents: three lower limbs of a quadruped animal.

Preliminary date: MB II (likely MB IIB–IIC).

A pit located approximately .40 m north of the northeastern corner of Tomb 829, in the southwestern corner of Square M/10, and around .60 m northwest of Pit 913 contained the remains of three lower limbs of an animal. No detailed description is provided in the notes, but judging from a photograph of Locus 934 these may be a radius and two tibia of a large quadruped (photo 2.5). In addition, one of the tibias has its accompanying fibula in articulation, and the second tibia has two lower bones in articulation, perhaps the calcaneus and metacarpus. It is possible that these are the lower limbs of an equid, offered in conjunction with a burial in nearby Tomb 829. A comparable equid burial was found in Area AB (Beeri et al. 2020). The absolute height of animal burial Locus 934, 25.13/15.11, corresponds with those of the built chamber tomb, Locus 829, and the animal burial is in close proximity to the northeastern, outside corner of the chamber. The pottery finds accompanying the animal bones in Locus 934 are datable to Middle Bronze Age, and it is therefore likely that Locus 934 is contemporaneous with Tomb 829.

Burial, Locus 932
Locale: Area H, Square P/5 (fig. 2.11).

Type: built chamber tomb.

Stratigraphy (fig. 2.42): elevation 25.90/25.26; possible entrance threshold 25.84, first step or bench 25.62; loci above include walls

811 from the late Hellenistic phase (Stratum 1) and 820 from the early Hellenistic period (Stratum 2), the building of which leveled and robbed out most of the superstructure of the chamber tomb Locus 932; its northern wall was also largely removed by Stratum 2 period pitting; the locus below is the Stratum 7 MB IIA rampart into which Locus 932 is cut.

Dimensions: interior 2.50 m × 1.62–1.75 m (base level); exterior 3.24 × 2.52–2.53 m (base level); tomb deposit height .50–55 m, tomb architecture height .58–.64 m (greatly truncated by later leveling activity).

Orientation: the slightly obtuse, rectangular structure is laid out west-east (fig. 2.17.1), with the position of one articulated body directed west and that of a second directed east (fig. 2.17.2–3); the entrance of the tomb is possibly in the western end of the southern wall, as is indicated by a feature in this wall which may be a step or a bench.

Human skeletal remains: two articulated, primary burials; one partially articulated burial; many disarticulated human remains; minimum of nine to ten individuals (fig. 2.17.2–3).[8]

Burial goods: sixteen ceramic vessels (figs. 2.17.5, 4.6.4–4.8.4); fired ceramic loom weight (fig. 4.8.5); mudbrick; bronze axe head (fig. 4.8.6), bronze blade fragments (fig. 4.8.7–4.8.8), bronze ring/earring; bronze crescent-shaped object (pendant?), silver ring fragment (fig. 4.8.9); large, water rounded stones (ballast stones; fig. 4.9.1–3); two alabaster vessels (fig. 4.8.10); a flint; worked bone (fig. 4.9.4–6); a faience bead fragment; two scarabs (fig. 4.9.7–8); painted plaster; an ostrich eggshell (fig. 4.9.9); two astragali; animal and fish bones, seeds, charcoal, and ocher (for locations of small finds see fig. 2.17.4).

---

8   All human remains were delivered for analysis but were unfortunately misplaced and lost by the research lab.

Preliminary date: MB IIB–IIC.

Locus 932 (photo 2.6), a built chamber tomb dated to the MB IIB–IIC period is located in the north central area of Square P/5 (fig. 2.11).[9] The structure of the chamber tomb is a slightly obtuse rectangle, since the southern wall is not quite perpendicular to the west and east walls, constructed from fieldstones (fig. 2.17.1). The tomb's interior dimensions are 2.50 m in width by 1.62 m in breadth on the west, and 1.75 m on the east. Its exterior dimensions are 3.24 m in width by 2.52–.53 in breadth (with a reconstructed width of .22 m for the largely missing northern wall). The width of the western wall is .32 m, the eastern wall is .36 m, and the southern wall varies from .68 to .56 m. The interior faces of all four walls of Tomb 932, even the small remnant of the northern wall, are plastered with white plaster. This plaster slopes down the walls and lips over the floor of the tomb, extending typically 20 cm around the outside edge of the floor but not continuing in to the center of the surface. The floor of the tomb, which is described as hard packed, reddish clay with inclusions of small pieces of charcoal and white plaster, is at 25.30–.35 m above sea level, and the tomb deposit goes up to 25.85 m, yielding a height of .55–.50 m. The excavators noted three relatively distinct levels of remains and grave goods within this deposit at 25.30–34, 25.40–44, and 25.50–55 (fig. 2.17.4–5). The tomb's walls are a bit deeper and higher than this deposit, from 25.90/25.26, 25.89/25.31, and 25.87/25.29, to a height of .58–.64 m. The tomb's walls, however, are only preserved to two courses as they were badly cut, leveled, and robbed out by pitting and building activity in the Persian, Hellenistic, and possibly Crusader periods. A step or bench, 1.22 × .34 m and .22 m deep, is located in the eastern half of the southern wall of the tomb's structure (fig. 2.17.1). It is possible that this represents the location of the bottom step of the original entrance to Locus 932 in its southeastern corner. It is also possible that this feature was utilized solely as a bench in the southern wall and that the tomb entrance has been completely removed by later building activities.

A minimum of nine to ten individuals were buried in Locus 932, as is shown by the discovery of nine or ten skulls (the number is not definite since it was not clear if fragmentary skulls were originally from the same individual; fig. 2.17.2–3). All but two of these individuals were discovered in piles of disarticulated bones, which clearly represented the defleshed remains of earlier interments pushed to the sides of the structure to make room for further burial. This is demonstrated by clustering of disarticulated human remains and material culture in the corners and along the sides of Tomb 932 (photo 2.6). Fewer

---

9 Steven Lumsden of the University of California at Berkeley supervised its excavation, assisted by Mette Qvistorff Lumsden of the University of Copenhagen.

indications of water-borne mud layers are found in Locus 932 than in Locus 829, although the excavators noted the presence of water-borne soil at the very top of the tomb deposit. This means that the movement of remains and finds in Tomb 932 was mainly due to anthropogenic and not hydrokinetic causes. The matrix in which the individuals and goods were buried below this thin, water-borne layer is described as very hard packed, reddish soil with many ash and charcoal inclusions. Flakes of white plaster are often described mixed into this matrix, which is not surprising given the fact that the interior walls of the tomb were plastered. A majority of the disarticulated skulls, six in total, were found with many other disarticulated human bones pushed into the southwest corner of Tomb 932 (fig. 2.17.3). Three articulated, or partially articulated, skeletons were uncovered which were labeled skeleton A, B, and C (fig. 2.17.2). Skeleton A was laid out on its back along the southern wall of Tomb 932, with its head to the west and body laid out straight to the east. The skull was not preserved well enough to establish its orientation, but it appears that the head and neck rested on a smooth, granite stone, almost like a headrest or pillow (photo 2.6). The granite stones of the Cypriot Trodos mountains, tumbled smooth by, and originating from, the Kouris River, were likely used as ballast aboard ships on their way to Tel Akko. The skeleton's left, upper arm runs along the left side of its torso, then the lower arm is crossed across the body on top of the lower torso area. Skeleton A's right arm is positioned so that the upper arm runs down along the right side of the torso, and the lower arm is completely flexed back along the upper arm so that the hand touches the right shoulder.[10] Many of the ribs of skeleton A are missing, which is not surprising given the high salinity of the soil on the tell. The legs are both extended straight down from the pelvis, and are resting on earlier, disarticulated remains that had been piled up in the southeast corner of the structure. Skeleton B is also laid out straight, but along the northern wall of the tomb, with its head to the east (fig. 2.17.2). Skeleton B is placed on its stomach, its skull turned slightly to face the south. The right arm is flexed down and away from the shoulder, with the lower arm bent back underneath the torso. The left upper arm is largely missing but the part preserved by the shoulder is flexed down and away from the left side of the body, with the lower arm bent back toward the left hip and left hand resting beside the left side of the pelvis. The right leg extends straight down from the hip, with right foot turned to the inside; the left upper leg also extends straight down but the lower leg is largely missing, likely cut by later Persian pitting and Hellenistic building activities. It is important to note that

---

10   This observation is taken from the daily notes and is not terribly obvious in the drawings of skeleton A.

a sherd of Cypriot Red-on-Black ware was found underneath skeleton B in a sandier matrix (fig. 4.6.8), which means that the body was laid out in the MB IIC.[11] Skeleton C was highly disturbed by later cutting and building, and only its badly deteriorated skull, articulated left arm, and one vertebra remains. From this meager evidence, it appears that skeleton C is stratigraphically below skeleton A, also placed along the southern wall of the tomb, underneath the legs of skeleton A. The head seems to be face down, the left upper arm flexed up and away from where the shoulder would have been, the lower arm is bent slightly back toward the head with the hand palm down, fingers spread out.

Grave goods in Tomb 932 include local and imported ceramics (photo 4.15 and 4.16; figs. 2.17.5, 4.6.4–4.8.4); gypsum/alabaster juglets; artifacts of metal (photo 4.17), stone, worked bone (photo 4.18), scarabs (photo 4.19), and an ostrich eggshell; and ecofacts, such as animal and fish bones, seeds, charcoal, and ocher (figs. 2.17.4, 4.8.5–4.9.9). The grave goods are described in further detail in chapter 4.

Area H Stratum 5, the Transition from LB IIB to Iron IA (LB IIC)

Following the MB IIB–IIC burials of Stratum 6, Area H has a gap in occupation lasting the majority of the Late Bronze Age. Remains of the Late Bronze Age have been found on the tell, but have been few and far between. Multiple phases are reported from the step trench, Area C, excavated in the first season (table 2.1; Dothan 1976: 17–23). Area C is directly south of the acropolis of the site (fig. 1.2; Areas A and AB) and may represent a location in the Bronze Age lower city. It is currently at the edge of the midway point of the C-shaped area of the southern portion of the site; this area of the tell was mined during the British Mandate period to fill nearby swamps, and has since suffered from further erosion. A newer study established that the "banana/crescent" shape existed in antiquity (Artzy and Quartermaine 2014). The original boundary of the site in the Bronze Age is still unknown. The relative dearth of Late Bronze Age material from the areas excavated on the tell suggests that the Late Bronze city, known from various contemporary textual references such as the Amarna letters, Egyptian conquest lists, and an Egyptian pictorial representation of the city's destruction at the hands of Ramses II, lies within the area of the mound

---

11   Cypriot Red-on-Black ware is traditionally dated to the MB IIC–LB I. Since the majority of pottery forms in Tomb 932 are of the MB IIB–IIC family, the presence of this Red-on-Black sherd would suggest a later point in this range, therefore the MB IIC, at least for the latest burials in the tomb that still remain in their original articulation.

bounded by previous excavation areas. Some pottery baskets in Area H, preliminarily dated to the Late Bronze Age, represent material washed in to the area during the use of the city in the Late Bronze Age or fills in secondary or tertiary use brought in by later builders to level out parts of the area. Regardless, the remains consist solely of layers, without any corresponding features, and thus do not represent a true stratum; see a similar gap at Tel Qiri (Ben-Tor and Portugali 1987: 5). This phenomenon is found in other areas excavated around the Akko rampart, namely AB and PH, where a Late Bronze Age hiatus was also noted (Artzy 2006b).

The remains, following the MB IIB–IIC tombs, local Stratum 5, reveal a poor settlement phase dated to the transition from the very end of the LB IIB to the beginning of the Iron IA, which may be characterized as the LB IIC (Martín Garcia and Artzy 2018). Despite its ephemeral nature, the features of Stratum 5 are found scattered over a fairly broad area, west-east from Squares K/7–K/8 to O/5 and south-north from M/4 to M/10, though they do not form any kind of coherent plan (fig. 2.10). Stratum 5 remains consist primarily of stone lined pits (photo 2.7), one possible hearth, and a few beaten earth floors. A similar situation is found in Akko's Area AB and PH, where stone lined pits, cut into the MB rampart, have been excavated (Artzy 2006b). This ephemeral settlement pattern is typical for the region in LB IIC and Iron IA phases, and is found at the nearby sites of Sarepta (Area II, Y, Stratum G–F, Anderson 1988: 380–90; Area II, X, period IV–V, Khalifeh 1988: 88–113), Tyre (Stratum XIV, Bikai 1978: 8, 68), and Tel Dan (Stratum VIIA–VI, Biran 1989: 95, fig. 4.25; Ilan 1999: 51–52). Similar stone lined pits are also recorded at Tell Abu Hawam in Hamilton's early excavations, although it is difficult to determine contemporaneity as they are slightly earlier than the ones at Tel Akko (Stratum V, Hamilton 1935: Stratum V plan). A possible cultic area in Area H Stratum 5 was also designated by the excavator, M. Artzy, based on the discovery of a stone mortar-like object (photo 2.8, 5.2; fig. 5.3.1) in which three large pebbles were found (photo 5.3; fig. 5.3.2–4). Two of the pebbles are decorated: one, quartz, with a boat, a depiction of three people, and a fish swimming below; and another with a depiction of a Tuna-like fish. The mortar-like object was interpreted as a portable altar (Artzy 1984; 1987; 2003). The discovery of graffiti of ships on this object led Artzy to suggest that the altar had been used aboard a seagoing vessel before its final deposition on land at the harbor site of Akko (photo 5.1).

The material remains from Stratum 5 of Area H are scanty, with a preponderance of small, worn sherds and worn pebbles. It is possible that this is due to postdepositional water flow; in other words, the stone lined pits of Stratum 5 acted like sumps attracting the water runoff or seepage from later strata in Area H. The presence of Aegean-style pottery in Stratum 5 will be discussed with other ceramics from this phase in chapter 5. Older stylistic and scientific analysis of Aegean-style sherds found in this phase have produced mixed results. One example was thought by Dothan to be as an import of Late Helladic IIIC:1b from Cyprus (M. Dothan 1989: 60; Sherratt 1998: 304 n. 24; D'Agata et al. 2005: 371–79), although a renewed examination of the sherd demonstrated it to be of an earlier Late Helladic II period mixed in with other Stratum 5 ceramics (Stockhammer, personal communication).

Stratum 5 Features

J/6: Square J/6 was investigated in a limited probe. Pottery attributed to Stratum 5 was uncovered in several superimposed pottery baskets (fig. 2.19). A fieldstone wall, Wall 1061 is mentioned in the daily notes as having toppled from the south toward the north. No further details of Wall 1061, or any drawings of the feature, were preserved.

K/8 (fig. 2.23): In Square K/8, in the northwestern part of the area intersecting the western balk, is a stone lined pit, Locus 937 (fig. 2.23.d). The pit, Locus 937, is cut into layers of the Middle Bronze Age rampart, and is lined with fieldstones, comprising four courses .35 m deep from 24.78/24.43 (to the top of the stones lining the pit's bottom). It can be phased to Stratum 5 based on the preliminary reading of the pottery it contains and the general presence of stone lined pits from this stratum. The locus is .54 m in diameter, measuring to the outside of the lining stones, and .34 m inside of the stones. The matrix inside the pit is described as an ash layer, which may indicate that some burning took place within Locus 937.

K/7: In Square K/7, in the eastern central part of the square intersecting the eastern balk, is another stone lined pit, Locus 753 (fig. 2.22). Locus 753 was discovered at the bottom of a probe, which was never expanded; therefore it is difficult to determine its exact phasing, but based on the preliminary pottery readings from the locus and its construction the pit may be phased to Stratum 5. The bottom of the pit showed evidence of having been cut into a reddish sand layer of the Stratum 7 MB IIA rampart. Locus 753 is ringed by fieldstones, except for an area the north of the feature which was robbed of its lining stones, likely during the construction of later walls which appear to cut Pit 753. Locus 753 is .64 m deep, from 23.88/23.24, and its inside diameter averages approximately .85 m, while the diameter including the width of the lining stones averages approximately 1.23 m (the pit is more ovoid than round, so we have calculated its average diameter based on its greatest and smallest diameters, both inside and outside its stone lining). No details pertaining to the matrix inside the pit are provided.

L/7 (fig. 2.25): In Square L/7 are several features associated with Stratum 5, in close proximity across the balk from Square K/7's Locus 753. The area excavated is located stratigraphically below and spatially next to Wall 729, Wall 730, and an installation of the lower body of a storage jar attributed to Stratum 2 (fig. 2.25.b). In the postexcavation evaluation of the pottery from Locus 731, originally defined as a surface contemporary with Wall 730, it became clear that the locus should be divided, using the daily pottery baskets, into three horizons, Locus 731a from the absolute height of 25.21/24.87, Locus 731b at the height of 24.87/24.60, and Locus 731c at the height of 24.60 (fig. 2.25.b).[12]

In the southern part of Square L/7, a stone lined pit, Locus 750 (photo 2.7), was found beneath the floor buildup, or occupational debris, Locus 731b, and is contemporary with beaten earth surface Floor 731c (figs. 2.10, 2.25.b). Locus 750 is likely contemporaneous with the other stone lined pits from this stratum in Area H, based on the similarity of these features and their contents. The pit, Locus 750, was only partially lined with fieldstones, which are concentrated in the northern and western sides of the pit, and the bottom of pit was also lined with stones (photo 2.7). It is noted that the bottom of Locus 750 is cut into Stratum 7 MB IIA rampart layers. Pit 750 is 1.08 m in depth, with an absolute height of 24.66/23.58, its inside diameter is 1.00 m, and its diameter including the width of the rock lining is 1.50 m. The matrix inside of the pit, Locus 750, included worn pebbles, worn ceramic sherds, and one sherd described by Dothan as Late Helladic IIIC:Ib; however, it is more likely an Aegeanized type sherd of local production (fig. 5.2.4).

Abutting the northern edge of stone lined pit Locus 750, and within the layer of Locus 731b, at 24.87/24.60, was a carved limestone object (photo 5.2; fig. 5.3.1) identified as a portable altar (Artzy 1984; 1987; 2003). Inside the

---

12   Locus 731 was originally excavated as a single 0.60 thick layer with no clear or apparent differences in the matrix or color between the top and the bottom of the layer. The absolute height of the locus was 25.21/24.60 m above sea level. In a postexcavation evaluation of the locus and the pottery from it, the layer was divided into three horizons, named Locus 731a, Locus 731b, and Locus 731c from top to bottom. The upper part of the locus, Locus 731a from absolute height of 25.21/24.87 meters above sea level includes primarily pottery from the LB II/Iron Age I transitional period, but also sporadic sherds from later periods including the Iron Age II, Persian and Hellenistic periods. This part of the layer was disturbed by the later preparation of the area for the constructions of Wall 729 and Wall 730 and the installation of the associated storage jar. Locus 731b with absolute heights of 24.87/24.60 m above sea level represents the preceding 0.27 m of Locus 731 below Locus 731a. This part of Locus 731 is believed to represent a floor buildup or other occupational debris on the beaten earth floor on which the ship altar was found. Locus 731b includes pottery from the LB II/Iron I transitional period only. Locus 731c at the absolute height of 24.60 represents the beaten earth floor associated with the altar.

hollowed bowl-like top of the altar were visible traces of burning, three large pebbles, including a quartz pebble with a ship and indications of three persons, a fish swimming below it and a possible bird above. Another stone has a fish, possibly a tuna (photo 5.3; fig. 5.3.2–4). One of the stones from the lining of Pit 750 which abutted the stone altar is described as covered with lime. Whether this lime was discarded from use of the altar is not clear. The altar is located on a beaten earth floor, Locus 731c, representing one of the few surfaces from this transitional period (fig. 2.25.b). The floor's absolute height is 24.60 above sea level. The full dimensions of this surface are not clear because of later pitting; it appears to extend to the balks in both the southern portion of the square, beyond the northern balk, and perhaps to the western balk in the area below Wall 729 and Wall 730.

L/9: Two squares north of L/7 is Square L/9, which contains several features attributed to Stratum 5. There appear to be two phases of occupation in Stratum 5 of Square L/9, consisting of an upper phase made up of a beaten earth surface and a stone lined pit, and a lower phase comprising two pits (fig. 2.10). Beaten earth floor, Locus 728, is preserved in the eastern half of the square directly over parts of the Stratum 6 tombs 727 and 829, and was badly cut by later pitting and Hellenistic construction. What remained of Floor 728, nevertheless, was approximately 3.50 m long and 2.25 m wide, and was between .13–.10 m thick (absolute height 25.35–25.28/25.22–25.18). The matrix of the floor is said to have been light gray in color. Because of comparable absolute heights, we would phase the stone lined pit, Locus 814, together with Floor 728. Locus 814 is cut into red sandy layers of the Stratum 7 MB IIA rampart, and also into the northwestern corner of the Stratum 6, MB IIB–IIC Tomb 829 (obscuring what was likely the original entranceway into Tomb 829), and intersects the northern balk of Square L/9. The lining of Pit 814 is at least three courses of fieldstones, and may have been higher since Locus 814 was cut by later construction. The pit is .51 m deep, 25.31/24.80, and has a diameter of .60 m measured to the inside of the stone lining, and .86 m measured to the outside of the fieldstones. The matrix within Pit 814 is noted as an ash layer, gray in color, which changes toward the bottom of the pit where there is a shift to the reddish, sandy matrix of the rampart layers the pit cuts.

The earlier phase of Stratum 5 in L/9 consists of two pits. The first of these pits, Locus 813, is located in the southeastern corner of the square and is covered over by Floor 728; thus it is earlier than the Stratum 5 surface described above. Pit 813 is cut into the Stratum 7 MB IIA rampart layers and cuts the northeastern corner of the Stratum 6, MB IIB tomb 727. It also intersects the eastern balk of Square L/9. The pit is .62 m deep, 24.98/24.36, and approximately 1.45 m in diameter. The matrix of the pit is noted as containing numerous waterworn pebbles, very few pottery sherds, many small pieces of charcoal, a grinding stone, and murex shells. In the southwestern part of Square L/9 is a second pit, Locus 17, which we would phase as contemporary with Locus 813, primarily based on absolute heights. Pit 17 is .61 m deep, 25.05/24.44, and is 1.30 m in diameter. It is one of the few features from Stratum 5 to contain an assemblage of complete ceramics, consisting of two storage jars placed on top of a krater and two amphariskoi (photos 2.9, 2.10, 2.16). It is noted that a very hard, blackish material was discovered beneath the smashed storage jars, and above the group of the krater and amphariskoi. The five vessels are typical of the transition from the LB IIB to the early Iron IA at sites in the northern valleys, as is the phenomenon of finding pits filled with whole vessels, which occurs frequently in more or less contemporary strata at Tel Dan VIIA–VI and Hazor XII (Biran 1989: 71–83; Ilan 1999: 51–52; Ben-Ami 2001: 151–56), although it should be emphasized that Akko is a coastal site.

M/10: A surface, Locus 929, was excavated in a probe in the southern half of Square M/10 which has been phased to Stratum 5 based on the preliminary pottery reading of ceramics found on the floor (figs. 2.10, 2.35.b). The surface stretched across the entire 4.00 × 2.00 m probe, and was partially disturbed by a later pit and by rock fall that damaged the surface and broke through its plaster in places. Floor 929 is .16 m thick, with an absolute height of 25.36/25.20. This is almost identical to Floor 728, kitty corner to Locus 929, in Square L/9 (fig. 2.10). It is likely that 929 represents a continuation of the same surface, Locus 728, from Square M/10 to L/9, separated by dividing balks, although it is not clear if 728 was plastered as was 929. There is no evidence of a similar surface in Square M/9, but the area excavated in the eastern half of M/9 was cut by a Stratum 3 Persian period grave, Locus 930, which may have destroyed any continuation of this surface into Square M/9.

M/7: In the southeastern corner of Square M/7, a stone lined pit (no locus number) was excavated, 5 m to the east of the contemporary Stratum 5 features in Square L/7 (figs. 2.10, 2.33.b). The pit was cut into Stratum 7 MB IIA rampart layers, and intersects both the southern and eastern balks of Square L/7. The pit was excavated to a depth of .37 m, 24.42/24.05, and may continue even deeper. Its projected inside diameter, based on the quarter or so of the pit not covered by balks, is around 1.00 m, the fieldstones lining the pit might add another .50 m to the diameter of the pit if measured to the outside of the stones. It is noted that the sherds from this pit were covered with a greenish film. This is possibly due to the later flow of water and organics down through this stone lined pit.

M/4: In a probe in the western half of Square M/4, a stone lined pit, Locus 744, was excavated which has been phased to Stratum 5 based on pottery readings and on the reoccurrence of stone lined pits in this stratum (figs. 2.10, 2.31). Locus 744 was cut into Middle Bronze Age rampart layers, and partially lined with fieldstones. It is not clear how deep Pit 744 is; the top of the feature is at around 23.10 above sea level and its diameter is around .90 m.

N/5: In the southwestern area of Square N/5, an installation was uncovered, Locus 1054, which was described by the excavators as a hearth, and has been phased to Stratum 5 (fig. 2.10; 2.38). Locus 1054 was partially cut into layers of the Stratum 7 MB IIA rampart, and intersected the western balk of the square, although the balk was excavated to reveal the entire feature. Locus 1054 is .66 m deep, 25.21/24.55, has small fieldstones lining its bottom, and has a .40 m inside diameter and .50 m outside diameter. Its sides were constructed from large body sherds of a broken pithos. It is not noted whether the matrix contained within Locus 1054 was ashy, or if ash lenses were scattered around the feature, thus leading to the excavator's interpretation of the installation as a hearth. Given the small stones lining the bottom of the feature and high, protective walls, this seems like an accurate attribution.

Area H Stratum 4, Iron IIA–IIB Transition

Once again there is a gap in Area H, as there is no Iron IB phase following Stratum 5. The stratum dates to the transition from the end of the Iron IIA to the beginning of the Iron IIB (see chapter 6). The remains of Stratum 4 in Area H are very limited, and are clustered in the southern squares of the excavation area (fig. 2.9). The few features that were uncovered, primarily walls and floors, appear to be domestic in nature, although any firmer conclusions must await a much broader exposure of this stratum. The richness of the material cultural finds and architectural remains in Square O/1, and contemporary finds from the Areas A, AB, B, C, and K, suggests that the majority of the Iron II city is situated to the south and east of the excavations in Area H (M. Dothan 1976; 1993).

Stratum 4 Features

M/4: Square M/4 was only excavated in a probe in its western half. In the southern part of this probe a single feature from Stratum 4, mudbrick floor Locus 742, was noted at a height of 24.00 (fig. 2.31). The exact dimensions of Floor 742 are not clear, but the feature appears to extend 2.0 × 4.0 m across the western half of the square, and was constructed over the Stratum 7 MB IIA rampart and the Stratum 5 pit, Locus 744. The matrix above Floor 742 is .50 m of melted mudbrick, 24.50/24.00, and is likely from the destruction or abandonment of the building associated with the floor. No contemporary walls, however, were uncovered. Pottery basket 184, from the matrix above Floor 742, included an almost complete Phoenician jug (fig. 6.2.12), and beneath Floor 742 a nearly complete Cypriot barrel jug in basket 178 (fig. 6.1.12, Photo 6.1). It is possible that this barrel jug was deposited in an undistinguished pit cut into Floor 742.

M/3: Just to the south of Square M/4, a probe was excavated in the eastern half of Square M/3 (fig. 2.30). One feature from Stratum 4, Wall 743, was revealed in the southeastern portion of the probe. Wall 743 was founded above the Stratum 7 MB IIA rampart, the slope of which is nicely illustrated in the drawing of Square M/3's western balk (fig. 2.2). The layers excavated below Wall 743, pottery baskets 200, 201, 206, show a mixture of Middle Bronze and Iron II pottery, denoting the transition from Stratum 7 to Stratum 4. Only the western end of Wall 743, running west-southeast, was uncovered, the eastern extent of the feature continues into the square's eastern balk. What is visible of Wall 743 is fieldstone construction with its uppermost course at a height of 24.35, its two rows are .50 m wide, and 1.00 m of the wall's length is exposed before it intersects the balk (fig. 2.9). It is likely that Wall 743 is contemporary with Floor 742 in Square M/4, especially given the correspondence of absolute heights (the top of the wall is at 24.35 while the top of the floor is at 24.00; unfortunately we do not have a bottom height for the wall). It is possible that these features were from the same architectural unit, although this is difficult to demonstrate since both were revealed in separate probes.

O/1: Square O/1, at the very southern extent of Area H, had the most substantial remains from Stratum 4 (fig. 2.9). The concentration of Iron II material culture in this square and Squares M/3 and M/4 suggest a northwestern boundary for the Stratum 4 city approximately 30–50 m from the current northern edge of the tell. The architectural features from Stratum 4 in O/1 consist of a lime plaster floor, Locus 833, and three walls, 830–32 (fig. 2.39.c–d). Above these features was an accumulation of over .80 m of layers that contained mainly Iron II pottery, without late intrusions and very few earlier ceramics mixed in with the Iron II diagnostics (fig. 2.39.d). This suggests that these layers represent the destroyed remains of the Stratum 4 habitation in the area.

Locus 833, a lime plaster floor, was revealed in the northwestern part of the square (figs. 2.9, 2.39.c). The greatest extent of the floor measures 1.25 × 1.25 m, despite the fact that Locus 833 is covered over by a Stratum 2 Hellenistic wall, Wall 817, on its west side; is covered by fallen fieldstones and mudbrick detritus on its north, likely from the destruction of a wall to the north; and ends abruptly in the south, likely due to later disturbances or pitting. The plaster floor is .06 m thick, 22.28/22.22, and it was noted that Iron II sherds were lying flat on its surface.

To the south of this floor is a contemporary wall, 830 (figs. 2.9, 2.39.c). Wall 830 extends from the southern balk to the northeast, for a length of .55 m. The wall is made up of one row of fieldstones, .30 m in width, and is only one course high, with a top height of 22.48. This corresponds nicely with the absolute height of Floor 833, whose top is at 22.28, some .20 m below the highest extent of Wall 830. It was noted that there was no foundation trench for Wall 830.

To the east of Wall 830 and Floor 833 are two more contemporary architectural features, Walls 831 and 832, which are joined to form the corner of a room (fig. 2.9). Unfortunately, both of these walls extend into the eastern subsidiary balk of Square O/1, which leaves much of the suggested room unexcavated. Wall 831 runs northeast-southwest for a length of 1.00 m before it intersects the eastern subsidiary balk (fig. 2.39.c). 831 is constructed from one row of oblong, loaf-shaped stones which are .20 m wide, and appear to be laid widthwise in a very uniform fashion. Two courses of Wall 831 are preserved to a height of .18 m, 22.45/22.27, and no accompanying foundation trench could be discerned. Stones were discovered to the west of 831, which were likely fall from further courses of the wall that tumbled in the destruction or collapse of the building. Wall 832 corners with 831, running lengthwise in a northwest-southeasterly direction for .38 m before extending into the eastern subsidiary balk (fig. 2.9). Wall 832 is constructed from oblong stones very similar to those of 831, but 832 consists of two rows of these stones laid out lengthwise, with a width of .15 m. Thus, both walls were constructed with their building stones oriented in the same direction. Wall 832 also has two courses preserved, to a height of .15 m, 22.44/22.29, with no foundation trench. A complete Iron II globular juglet, pottery basket 354, was discovered on the southern side of Wall 832 close to the eastern subsidiary balk, at an absolute height of 22.39/22.33 (fig. 6.7.1). It is possible that this find signals the presence of a floor between Walls 830 and 832, or could represent an item stored on a shelf connected to Wall 832 or stored in a second story that reached its present depositional level in the collapse of the building. Further excavation of the eastern part of Square O/1, or investigations in surrounding squares might approach solving some of these questions.

Area H, Stratum 3: Persian Period Remains

The remains of Stratum 3 in Area H are fairly limited, and are spread out in the northwestern and eastern squares of the excavation area (fig. 2.8). The features uncovered were of a mixed nature, including human and animal burials, isolated pits/fills and floors, and the remains of domestic structures in P/4. The concentration of architectural remains in Square P/4 suggests that the Persian period site, like its Iron II predecessor, lies to the south and east of the excavations in Area H, while the burials in Squares L/9 and M/9 likely demarcate the northern boundary of the site in this stratum.

Stratum 3 Features

K/8: A plaster floor, Locus 935, was excavated in the northeastern part of Square K/8 that has been assigned to Stratum 3 (figs. 2.8, 2.23.d). The floor lay over a series of fill layers, dated to the Persian period and the Iron II, which in turn were over a red sandy layer of the Stratum 7 MB IIA rampart. Locus 935 was revealed in a probe in the northern half of Square K/8; thus we do not have its full extent as it intersects the north, east, and south subsidiary balks. The plaster floor is preserved to 2.30 m in width, before it extends into the eastern balk, and spans the 2.00 m of length between the north and south subsidiary balks. Locus 935 is .08 m high, 25.08/25.00, and two complete bowls were discovered lying flat on its surface (pottery basket 1256). A stone bowl was found underneath the floor at a height of 24.92, in pottery basket 1274, which may be indicative of an earlier floor beneath Locus 935, or may represent an object that settled during its depositional history. Near the stone bowl, in the same pottery basket, a lead weight was discovered. Just west of the floor, in an area where the plaster of 935 has been disturbed, several restorable storage jars were excavated (pottery baskets 1264 and 1272). We would associate these jars with the use of Floor 935, though they lie somewhat below it at 24.80/24.71, perhaps in a pit. Although we have no walls in the area that are contemporary, the items associated with Floor 935, ceramic bowls, storage jars, a stone bowl or mortar, and a lead weight, suggest the remains of a domestic structure.

L/9–M/9: A structural chamber tomb phased to Stratum 3 was uncovered in the northern end of the balk between Squares L/9 and M/9 (figs. 2.8, 2.16.1). A trait list follows similar to that used above to describe the burials in Stratum 6.

Burial, Locus 930

Locale: Area H, Squares L/9–M/9.

Type: built chamber tomb.

Stratigraphy: elevation 25.29/24.66; cist cut for tomb 25.67/24.66; the locus above is the Stratum 1 Wall 905 in M/9 (figs. 2.14, 2.15, 2.34.a), a fieldstone wall whose foundation cut the roof of the tomb; the locus below is the Stratum 6, MB IIB–IIC, Tomb 829 whose top was cut by the cist excavated for Locus 930 (fig. 2.13.12), and whose south and east walls were reused in the construction of Locus 930.

Dimensions: interior 1.44 × .44 m; exterior 1.72 × 1.00 m; depth of tomb .63 m; depth of cist 1.01 m.

Orientation (fig. 2.16.1): the rectangular form of the structure is laid out with a slight northwest-southeast orientation, with the position of the articulated body directed east; entrance was likely through the roof of the structure (now largely missing).

Human skeletal remains: one articulated, primary burial (fig. 2.16.1).

Burial goods: none.

Preliminary date: Persian period.

Locus 930 is a built chamber tomb (fig. 2.16.1). The tomb was constructed from fieldstones and capped with large slab stones, still preserved at the eastern and southern ends of the locus but missing from the center of the structure. The north wall of the chamber is three courses, .63 m, high and one row, .20–.30 m, wide; the south and east walls were originally part of the earlier Stratum 6 Tomb 829 that were reused in the structure of Tomb 930; the west wall appears to have only been one course high, matching the uppermost course of the north wall. The orientation of the tomb is northwest-southeast, just slightly off of the west-east line.

Tomb 930 contained one primary inhumation, in a loose sandy matrix (photo 2.11; fig. 2.16.1). The articulated body was positioned on its back, with its head toward the east; the orientation of the head is not clear from the remains. The skeleton's right arm is extended straight down from its shoulder along its side, and parallel to the inside of the northern wall of the tomb. The left arm similarly extends straight down the skeleton's left side, except the lower left arm is not preserved. Both legs are extended straight down from the pelvis.

No grave goods were left in Tomb 930. The feature can be phased to Stratum 3 based on the Persian period pottery readings from the fill in the cist cut for the tomb's construction, and from the fill within, above, and below the tomb itself.[13]

---

13   For parallels see Stern 2001: 471–72 and Wolff 2002: 134, 136.

M/9: Two further burials phased to Stratum 3 were uncovered near Tomb 930, Locus 1062 is in the northeast of Square M/9 and Locus 1063 is in its southeast corner (figs. 2.8, 2.34.a, 2.34.b). Locus 1062 is described as a tomb with scattered bones, but no further details are provided. Locus 1063, described as a cist grave, intersects the eastern balk of the square. The depth of the cist cut for burial 1063 is .23 m, 25.30/25.07. The articulated remains appear to be on their left side, with the lower legs flexed up toward the torso. Given the small measurements of the skeletal remains, 1.00 m in length from ribs to ankle, and .35 m in width, it is possible that this was the burial of a child or an animal. This discrepancy is not clarified in the notes, and it will be shown that there were two dog burials from this same stratum in Square P/4. Interpreting Locus 1063 as an animal burial, thus, is possible, though one must consider the proximity of the human burial in Locus 930, 3.50 m to the northwest of burial 1063. Note that the absolute heights of Locus 930 and 1063 are virtually identical, 25.29 and 25.30, which suggests contemporaneity between the two burials if not some sort of further link.

M/5: Four squares south of the burials in M/9, a pit was excavated which is phased to Stratum 3 (fig. 2.8). Locus 749 is a Persian period pit discovered in a probe in the eastern half of Square M/5, and intersects the east and south balk of the square (fig. 2.32). The pit is cut into fine yellow sand layer of the Stratum 7 MB IIA rampart, and is approximately 1.50 m in diameter. Pit 749 is .90 m deep, 24.80/23.90.

P/4: To the east and down one square from M/5, architectural features and dog burials from Stratum 3 were uncovered in Square P/4 (figs. 2.8, 2.41.c, 2.41.d). In the northwest corner of the square, an east-west wall, Wall 936, stretches for 1.85 m in length before it intersects the west balk. It appears that Wall 936 (photo 2.12) was founded in a sand layer of the Stratum 7 rampart, and is cut by a later Stratum 2 Hellenistic wall, 922 (photo 2.12). The construction of Wall 936 comprises either one or two rows of fieldstones, .60 m in width, and its three courses are .62 m in height, 25.71/25.09. At its eastern end, Wall 936 was cut by a later Hellenistic robber's trench. This trench extends north-south from Wall 936, likely representing the outlines of a contemporary corner wall to 936 that was robbed out for later Hellenistic construction. The trench stretches for 1.20 m in length before intersecting the north balk, and is .55 m wide and .40 m deep (25.64/25.24). Its width is similar to that of Wall 936, and it is possible that the easternmost stone attributed to 936 is more appropriately the final remnant of the north-south wall, the rest of which was taken out in antiquity.

In the southeast of Square P/4 is another east-west wall, Wall 924, phased to Stratum 3 (fig. 2.41.c). Wall 924 is constructed from ashlar masonry, laid out in header stretcher fashion. Each ashlar block is approximately .42–.44 m long, .22 m wide, and .23–.24 m high. Wall 924 is .55 m long before it intersects the east balk, and is .79 m wide. The southern face of the wall is three courses high, .65 m from 25.14 to 25.79, while the northern face comprises only two courses, .50 m high from 25.29 to 25.79. It is not clear why an extra course was included along the southern face of Wall 924, but it may have to do with issues of structural stability. A plaster floor was noted to the south of Wall 924, at a height of 25.60. This floor extends 1.50 m from the southern face of Wall 924 to the south balk, and is 1.30 m in width before intersecting the east balk. The makeup of the floor, before its plastered surface, is .18–.24 m thick and is a grayish matrix.

Into the grayish matrix of this plaster floor, a pit was cut for the burial of a dog (fig. 2.8, 2.41.d, photo 2.13). This dog burial, Locus 928, is located in the southeastern corner of the square, and intersects the south balk. The skeleton of the dog is articulated, with the rear legs flexed up toward the body. The head is under the balk; the front legs and all of the paws are missing. The orientation of the animal is with its head toward the west. Small pieces of copper were discovered in front of the knees of the hind legs of the skeleton. The full extent of the pit cut for the burial of the animal is not apparent because it intersects the balk; however, it is at least .33 m in diameter, and is a rather shallow .07 m deep (25.64/25.57).

Nearby to the north and west of dog burial 928, a second burial of an animal, a dog, was discovered in Square P/4 (figs. 2.8, 2.41.d). The pit for the second animal burial, Locus 914 (photo 2.14), was cut into a layer described as hard packed red clay. This second animal burial was not as well preserved as the first, but what remains seems to have been laid out in a similar position with its rear legs flexed up toward the body. Again, there are no remnants of the animal's paws. The head and a better part of the body are not preserved; however, what remains of the lower part of the skeleton appears to have been oriented toward the northwest. The lower part of a Persian period storage jar was discovered just east of the skeleton, associated with the same matrix into which Locus 914 was cut. The pit for animal burial 914 is at least .35 m in diameter, and .15 m deep (25.68/25.53).

It is not totally clear how these two animal burials are associated with the Stratum 3 architectural features in Square P/4. It is possible, given the relative heights of the burials at 25.64–25.68, that they represent a phase slightly later than the use of Wall 924 and the floor that intersects its southern face, whose height is 25.60, especially since the pit for burial 928 seems to have cut this surface. It is possible, however, that these burials were made during the use of the Stratum 3 buildings and coexisted with the habitation of the structures.[14]

---

14   Parallels for dog burials have been uncovered at Beirut, Dor, and in great number at Ashkelon in the Persian period (Stern 2001: 487).

Area H, Stratum 2: Early Hellenistic Period Remains

The remains of Stratum 2 in Area H are extensive and are found in most squares opened in the excavation area (fig. 2.7). The hallmark of this phase is rectilinear architecture with an orientation approximately 3–18° off of true north or east. The Hellenistic phase above Stratum 2, Stratum 1, has a marked shift in the orientation of its architecture to the cardinal directions (fig. 2.6).

Stratum 2 Features

J/7: Two perpendicular walls and a column base have been phased to Stratum 2 in Square J/7 (figs. 2.7, 2.20). Wall 11 is a north-south fieldstone wall (12° off of true north) that is cut at its northern end by the Stratum 1 Wall 16. Wall 11 is 2.56 m long, with its southern end intersecting the south balk, and is .45 m wide. Its two courses are .33 m high, 25.40/25.07. Toward the southern end of Wall 11 is a perpendicular, east-west cross wall (no locus number), with a similar orientation slightly off of true east-west. This perpendicular wall, constructed from fieldstones, is .90 m long, .45 m wide, and is covered at its western end by a later Phase 1 wall, Wall 8. A kurkar column base was uncovered to the west of Wall 11 and north of the matching perpendicular wall. The column base is at an absolute height of 25.13, and is oval in shape .30–.25 m in diameter.

K/7: Very few traces of Stratum 2 were present in Square K/7 (figs. 2.7, 2.22). One small north-south wall, Wall 751, was uncovered on the last days of the 1980 dig season. The two rows of fieldstones which make up Wall 751 are .28 m in width, and only .24 m of the length of the wall are preserved before it intersects the north balk of the square. There is no apparent continuation of this north-south wall in Square K/8.

K/8: Several features in Square K/8 are phased to Stratum 2, notably several architectural elements which are 10° off of true east-west (figs. 2.7, 2.23.a, 2.23.b). Wall 5 is an east-west fieldstone wall with ashlar blocks at its western end, which likely formed one side of an entryway as matching ashlar blocks were discovered in line with the wall after a .75 m opening. Wall 5 is stratigraphically below the Stratum 1 pit, Locus 3. The wall stretches for 2.10 m in length before intersecting the east balk and is .60–.65 m in width. A parallel east-west wall, Wall 18, is just .70 m south of Wall 5, and is also 10° off of true east-west. Wall 18 is 1.45 m long before it intersects with the east balk and, like Wall 5, is .60 m wide. A tabun, Locus 19, was discovered in the southeast corner of the square that abuts the southern face of Wall 18. As Locus 19 intersects both the south and east balk it is difficult to determine its exact dimensions; however, a projected diameter for the tabun is 1.15 m. A floor, of sorts, was associated with this tabun because of the ash and charcoal discovered scattered on its surface from the cleaning of the tabun in antiquity. This surface is at a height of 25.25, its dimensions are 2.35 × 2.10 m as it is bounded to the north by Wall 5, peters out toward the west where stones were uncovered which may be a pillar base, and intersects both the south and east balk. A second tabun, Locus 10, was uncovered at 25.42 on the west side of the square. Tabun Locus 10 is 1.00 m in diameter and intersects the west balk. It is just southwest of the entranceway between the ashlar blocks of Wall 5 and the matching, lone ashlar. It appears that the architectural unit made up of Walls 5 and 18 had two tabuns, although it is not clear whether these were associated with inside or outside space.

K/9: Two substantial walls and a floor are phased in Square K/9 to Stratum 2 (figs. 2.7, 2.24). Wall 6, a north-south fieldstone wall 16° off of true north, is partially covered by a Stratum 1 feature, Wall 2. Wall 6 is 3.00 m long, with its northern end intersecting the north balk of the square. The full width of Wall 6 is not known as its eastern side is covered by the later Stratum 1 Wall 2 and by the east balk; however, from its partial exposure the wall is at minimum 1.50 m wide. Wall 6 is preserved to a height of .39 m, from 25.50/25.11. The southern end of Wall 6 abuts a perpendicular east-west wall (no locus number), which is 7° off of true west. This cross wall is covered by Wall 4 from the later Stratum 1, and is 3.20 m long before it intersects the east balk. The width of the wall is difficult to determine since it is largely covered by the Stratum 1 Wall 4; however, .75 m of the wall's width is exposed. The height of the wall is undetermined, although its top is 25.24 above sea level. An earthen floor (no locus number) is noted running up to the western face of Wall 6, made from the local iron rich soil, hamra. This hamra surface is .09 m thick, 25.34/25.25; its other dimensions are not recorded.

L/9: One square east, in L/9, several more Stratum 2 features were uncovered (figs. 2.7, 2.27). Wall 12 is a north-south fieldstone wall, 14° off of true north. It is stratigraphically above two pits from Stratum 5, Locus 17 and 814. The wall is 1.85 m long before it intersects the north balk, and .80 m wide, although this measurement is only partial since the wall's west side is underneath the west balk of the square. The preserved height of Wall 12 is .30 m, 25.52/25.22. Just .65 m to the east of Wall 12 is another north-south wall constructed at a similar angle off of true north. This parallel wall (no locus number) is constructed from fieldstones, is 1.70 m long before it intersects the north balk, and is .40 m wide. Its top height is recorded at 25.49, similar to that of Wall 12. A pit (no locus number) was excavated between these two walls that is contemporary with their use. The pit is .60 m in diameter, with its top height at 25.29, which may be indicative of the relative height of a surface to match these walls. Another north-south wall, 723, is located in the southern part of the square, and is 10°

off of true north. Wall 723 covers over the western part of the earlier Stratum 5 surface, Locus 728, and the Stratum 6 burial, Locus 727. The fieldstone wall is 3.30 m long, including its southern end that extends into Square L/8. Wall 723 is .85–.95 m wide and .42 m high, from 25.76/25.34.

L/8: Besides the southernmost extension of Wall 723, described above, Square L/8 contains several Stratum 2 features (figs. 2.7, 2.26). Wall 15, an east-west wall made from fieldstones, is a continuation of Wall 5 from Square K/8. The later Stratum 1 pit, Locus 13, cuts it. Within Square L/8, Wall 15 is 1.75 m long before intersecting the west balk and continuing into Square K/8; the overall length of the wall is 4.85 m including the section covered by the balk. Wall 15 is .60 m in width. A plaster floor (no locus number) extends from the southern side of Wall 15 for 1.60 m until it intersects the south balk, and from the west balk runs for 1.60 m before meeting the west face of a wall perpendicular to Wall 15. This perpendicular wall is the continuation of north-south Wall 729 in Square L/7, and protrudes from the south balk for a length of .40 m and is .50 m wide. A fragment of a stone basin was discovered in the northeast corner of the square and has been phased to Stratum 2.

L/7: Several features are attributed to Stratum 2 in Square L/7 (figs. 2.7, 2.25). They were, at least partly, laid on top of and partially dug into the upper ca. 0.30 m of Locus 731, equivalent to Locus 731a, attributed to the LB II/Early Iron I Stratum 5 but containing later Iron II–Hellenistic sherds.

Wall 729 is a fieldstone wall oriented north-south, 14° off of true north (fig. 2.7). Wall 729 is comprised of one or two rows of fieldstones, and is only one course high, with its top at 25.50–25.34 above sea level. Wall 729 is .50 m wide and 2.05 m long, but runs into the north balk continuing .40 m further north in Square L/8, for a total length of 3.45 m. The wall extends over Wall 730 and thus forms a slightly later addition. Wall 730 is four rows wide and only one .18 m course high, with an absolute height of 25.35/25.17. The wall is 1.10 m wide and is 1.25 m long, but intersects the northern balk and may continue north in Square L/8. Given its unusual shape it is possible that the fieldstones that comprise Wall 730 were actually flagstones of a pavement, and not the foundation stones for a higher wall. Within the borders of Wall 729 and Wall 730 the bottom portion of a storage jar was placed upright in the debris layer of Locus 731a,[15] the top of the walls of the vessel reaching to 25.21. The storage jar portion was filled with waterworn stones, pottery sherds, and fragments of burned animal bones, described in general by the excavator as "domestic rubbish." It is not clear if this portion of a storage jar acted as some sort of installation.

---

15 See note 12 above.

Two pits have been assigned to Stratum 2, Locus 740 and 741, both of which cut into the Stratum 5 debris, Locus 731a–c. Pit 740, in the southeast corner of the square and intersecting both the south and east balk, is 1.10 m in diameter and .22 m deep, 24.71/24.49. Pit 741, in the northeast part of the square intersecting the east balk, is 1.60 m in projected diameter (as it is mostly covered by the balk) and .67 m deep, 25.00/24.33. W730 borders the western edge of Pit 741.

M/7: A Stratum 2 Wall (no locus number) is located in the southeast corner of Square M/7 (figs. 2.7, 2.33). The wall runs north-south, 13° off of true north, and is stratigraphically above a Stratum 5 stone lined pit in the square. The fieldstone wall intersects both the south and east balks, but at least 1.25 m in length was exposed and .48 m in width. The top height of the wall is 25.69.

N/5: The squares excavated in the southern part of Area H included features from Stratum 2 as well. Two consecutive floors and a pit can be assigned to this phase in Square N/5 (figs. 2.7, 2.38). The plaster floor, Locus 1051, appears to be a rebuild directly on top of another Stratum 2 surface, Locus 1052, and is cut by a later Stratum 1 pit, Locus 1053. The upper floor, 1051, is highly disturbed, but what remains is 3.15 m long, 1.05 m wide, and .05 m thick (25.65/25.60). Surface 1051 intersects the south balk toward its middle. The plaster floor underneath 1051, Locus 1052, is much better preserved. The later Stratum 1 pit, Locus 1053, also cuts Locus 1052. The floor stretches almost the entire length of the square, measuring 4.9 m, but is only preserved 1.00 m in width. The thickness of Floor 1052 is a substantial .15 m, 25.59/25.44. A pit (no locus number) just east of surface 1052 appears to be contemporaneous with this floor level. The pit is 2.00 m in diameter and .15 m deep, the same height as Floor 1052, 25.59/25.44.

O/5: Several features in Square O/5 are phased to Stratum 2 (figs. 2.7, 2.40). Wall 827 (= Wall 906) is an east-west fieldstone wall, 12° off of true east. Its two rows are .75 m wide, although the north balk masks the full width, and the wall is 2.00 m long before it intersects the west and north balks. The top of Wall 827 is at 25.82. A drainage channel separates the east end of Wall 827 from a perpendicular, north-south wall, Wall 903. Wall 903 is stratigraphically above the Stratum 6 disturbed burial whose walls are numbered 933 and 939. Wall 903 is a fieldstone wall comprising two rows of stones, .50 m in width. The wall is .90 m long before intersecting the north balk, and is .47 m high, 26.05/25.58. A plastered surface, Locus 825, runs from the southern face of Wall 827, eventually meeting up with the west end of another Stratum 2 wall, Wall 821. Locus 827 is stratigraphically above the Stratum 6 disturbed burial described above. The surface, Locus 827, was made up of a series of plaster washes, which may have been created by runoff from the drainage channel between Walls 827 and 903. A concentration of murex shells was noted in conjunction with the excavation of Locus 827, which is 3.00 m wide, 2.75 m long, and .27 m thick (25.94/25.67). Further plaster washes with crushed murex shells were discovered under the drainage channel, at a height of 25.52/25.50, which may indicate slightly earlier activities along the same lines as those that created Locus 827. An ashy pile, Locus 901, was noted 1.50 m south of Wall 827, and ashy pits are recorded between Locus 901 and 827. This concentration of ash is likely further indication of industry associated with the architectural unit comprising Walls 827 and 903. It seems likely that this industry was taking place further to the north, in an area as yet unexcavated, and that the waste and runoff collected in Square O/5. The remains of murex shells, whole and crushed, make it likely that this activity area was related to the production of purple dye.

The final Stratum 2 feature in Square O/5 is an east-west wall, Wall 821, to the southeast of this industrial area. Wall 821 is 16° off of true east, and runs for 6.25 m in length, well into the neighboring Square P/5. Wall 821 is .55 m wide, comprising two or three rows of fieldstones, and .53 m high, 26.41/25.88. Contemporary features will be described below, as these are located in Square P/5.

P/5: Several features are phased to Stratum 2 in Square P/5 (figs. 2.7, 2.42). Wall 820 (=Wall 910) is the perpendicular cross wall to 821, described above. Wall 820 is covered by the Stratum 1 Wall 805, and in turn cuts through part of the earlier Stratum 6 tomb, Locus 932. 820 is a north-south wall, 13° off of true north, constructed primarily of fieldstones but incorporating several ashlars, as well. Its two rows are .55 m wide, and the wall stretches the length of the square, some 4.85 m. Wall 820 is two to three courses high, measuring .70 m from 26.62/25.92. In the southeastern part of the square, a plaster floor and drain, Locus 816, are associated with the east end of Wall 821. Floor 816 was founded on Stratum 7 layers of the Middle Bronze Age rampart. The floor is preserved to 2.80 m in width and 1.20 m in length, and is .10 m high (26.24/26.14). The drainage channel runs north-south through the center of the plaster floor, and slopes toward the south. This is very similar to the drain associated with Walls 827 and 903 in Square O/5, described above.

A pit was excavated to the north of Floor 816 that appears to be contemporary with the floor and other Stratum 2 features. The pit (no locus number) is in the northeast corner of the square and cuts the northeast corner of Stratum 6 tomb, Locus 932. This pit's diameter is difficult to determine, as its extent is masked by both the north and east balks, but can be approximated at around 2.00 m. Its depth is .36 m, 25.97/25.61.

In the northwestern part of Square P/5 is an ashlar wall, 809, associated with the Stratum 2 walls 827 and 903 in Square O/5 by proximity. Wall 809 cuts the northwest corner of the Stratum 6 tomb, Locus 932. The ashlars are laid in a header stretcher fashion, the width of the wall is .55 m, but may be partially masked by its intersection with the north balk. The length of Wall 809, including part that continues into O/5, is 2.00 m, and its four courses are 1.12 m high from 26.64/25.52. A surface, Locus 806, consisting of small pebbles and sherds stretches from the southern face of Wall 809. Surface 806 is preserved to 2.00 m in length and 1.35 m in width, and is .20 m thick, 26.46/26.26.

P/4: In the square just south, several more features are phased to Stratum 2 (figs. 2.7, 2.41). Wall 920 is a north-south wall constructed from ashlars, 3° off of true north. 920 is stratigraphically above the Stratum 3 Wall 924. Wall 920 is 1.75 m long, and its north end intersects the north balk. The full width of the wall is not known, since it is largely underneath the east balk with only .20 m exposed. Wall 920 is one to two courses high, .47 m from 26.39/25.92. A parallel north-south wall, Wall 921, is just to the west. Wall 921 is constructed from a mix of ashlars and fieldstones. Its length of .80 m is partially masked by the north balk, its width is .45 m, and its height is between .21–.25 m (26.51–26.38/26.30–26.13). Wall 922, a third parallel north-south wall, 7° off of true north, is located slightly further west in the square. Wall 922 is built directly over the Stratum 3 Wall 936. Its length is 1.30 m, its two rows of ashlars are .50 m, and five to six courses are 1.05 m in height (26.33/25.28). It is possible that Wall 922 is the southern extension of Wall 820 in Square P/5; however, any direct correlation between these two features is masked by the north balk. At the northern end of Wall 922 is an east-west ashlar wall, Wall 923, largely covered by the north balk. Wall 923 is 9° off of true east, stretches for 1.35 m in length, and its width is mostly contained within the balk although .25 m protrudes. Its two courses measure .60 m in height from 26.46 to 25.86. Another east-west ashlar wall (no locus number) is located in the southern part of the square. Its full extent is masked by a Stratum 1 north-south wall that runs over it, and by the south balk. The wall, however, is at least 1.00 m in length, and .25 m wide, with the majority of the width covered by the south balk.

Three floors are contemporary with this Stratum 2 architecture. Locus 828, a plaster and ceramic sherd floor, runs from the west face of Wall 922 to the west and north balks. Floor 828 is .90 m wide before it intersects the west balk, .80 long before disappearing in to the north balk, and is .26 m thick from 26.50/26.24. On the east face of Wall 922 is another floor, Locus 826, which runs all the way to the west face of Wall 921. In total, Floor 826 is 1.75 m wide and 1.20 m long before it intersects the north balk. Floor 826 is .23 m thick, from 26.36/26.13, and lies directly over a second floor, Locus 925. Floor 925 (photo 2.15) is made from small cobblestones and plaster .46 m thick. Given this unusual thickness for a surface, it is possible that Locus 925 was the underbedding or subfloor fill for Floor 826.

N/4: The southern half of Square N/4 was excavated in a probe, and a few Stratum 2 features were uncovered (figs. 2.7, 2.37). Wall 1057 appears to be wall fall, comprising ashlar masonry and fieldstones. It was covered over by a later Stratum 1 plaster floor, Locus 1055. When cleared, it appears that the east balk mostly covers the in situ stones of Wall 1057. Wall fall, likely from Wall 1057, lies directly on top of a very thick plaster floor, Locus 1059, which is contemporaneous with the in situ portions of Wall 1057. The Stratum 1 floor, Locus 1055, also covers Floor 1059. The plaster floor, 1059, extends almost the entire area of the probe, 3.25 m in width, 2.00 m long, and is .45 m thick (25.56/25.11).

O/1: Several features in Square O/1 are phased to Stratum 2 (figs. 2.7, 2.39). Wall 817, a north-south wall 18° off of true north, is located in the northwest corner of the square and intersects both the west and north balks. The wall is underneath the Stratum 1 Wall 807, and is above the Stratum 4 floor, Locus 833. Like other Stratum 2 walls, 817 is constructed from both ashlar masonry and fieldstones. 2.15 m in length is exposed before both ends intersect balks, and Wall 817's two rows of stones are between .55–.60 m wide. One or two courses of the wall are preserved to a height of .69 m, from 24.79 to 24.10. In the small space between the western face of Wall 817 and the northwest corner of the square a floor, Locus 834, was uncovered. Floor 834 is underneath Stratum 1 Wall 807. The floor is .50 m wide and .90 m long; however, it intersects both the west and north balk and presumably continues in either direction. Floor 834 is .33 m thick, 24.57/24.24, and is made up of fist-sized stones. These cobble stones may indicate an outdoor, courtyard surface. A second surface, Locus 819, was discovered in the northeastern part of the square. Rubble indicated on top of this surface is most likely wall fall from the destruction of contemporary architectural features. Floor 819 is 1.75 m wide before intersecting the east balk, 1.6 m long before intersecting the north balk, and is .27 m thick, from 24.61/24.34. Three complete storage jars are also noted in the northeast (basket 170), center (basket 156), and southeast (basket 185) of the square, likely associated with the destruction of the building. One jar, basket 170, was found upside down in the rubble on top of Floor 819, perhaps indicating it was on a shelf, hung on a wall, or was in an upper story when the collapse took place.

Area H, Stratum 1: Late Hellenistic Period and Later Remains

The remains of Stratum 1 in Area H are extensive, although they were heavily damaged by later use of the tell (fig. 2.6). Despite all of the later disturbances, detailed below, the uppermost phase of architecture on the site is preserved well enough to discern that Stratum 1 walls are typically alligned with the cardinal directions (fig. 2.6). This shows a shift in orientation from the buildings in Stratum 2.

Stratum 1 Features

J/7: Two walls in Square J/7 have been phased to Stratum 1 (figs. 2.6, 2.20). Wall 8 is a north-south wall, which is built directly above a Stratum 2 east-west wall (no locus number). Wall 8 is 2.54 m long before it intersects the south balk, and its three rows of fieldstones are .60 m wide. The top of Wall 8 is at 25.50. An east-west cross wall, Wall 16, abuts the north end of Wall 8. Wall 16 is directly above the north end of Stratum 2 Wall 11. The fieldstone wall runs for 2.00 m in length before ending on its east side with an ashlar. This ashlar likely represents the side of an entryway; however, this cannot be demonstrated as the east balk of the square blocks it. Wall 16 is constructed similarly to Wall 8, with three rows of fieldstones, .60 m wide.

K/7: Just to the east in Square K/7 is a possible continuation of J/7's Wall 16 (figs. 2.6, 2.22). Wall 747 is an east-west fieldstone wall that is in line with Wall 16. Again, if there is an entranceway between the two walls it is largely masked by the balk that runs between the two squares. The wall is directly above the Stratum 5 stone lined pit, Locus 753. Wall 747 is 3.00 m long, with its west end intersecting the west balk, and its two to three rows of fieldstones are .60–.70 m wide. The height of the wall is .41 m, from 25.12 to 24.71. In the northeast corner of the square is a Stratum 1 wall, Wall 748, perpendicular to Wall 747. Wall 748 is directly above Locus 753, the stone lined pit from Stratum 5. Walls 747 and 748 do not intersect, but as they are only .25–.50 m apart it is likely that the eastern end of 747 was robbed out. Wall 748 is made from fieldstones, stretches 1.60 m in length before intersecting the north balk, and is .45–.60 m wide, although the east balk masks its full width. A parallel north-south wall, Wall 745, is to the west of Wall 748 and north of Wall 747. The north balk largely masks the wall; however, .50 m of its length is exposed, and its three rows of fieldstones are .90 m wide. The top of Wall 745 is at 25.29.

K/8: Only one feature in Square K/8 is phased to Stratum 1 (figs. 2.6, 2.23). Locus 3 is a large pit in the northeastern corner of the square, and is stratigraphically above Stratum 2 Wall 5. Although it intersects both the north and east balks, the diameter can be reconstructed somewhere between 3.30–3.70 m. Pit 3 is fairly shallow, measuring only .20 m in depth, from 25.90 to 25.70. Pit 3 can be placed in a late phase of Stratum 1, as its continuation in Square K/9, Locus 1,[16] cuts the Stratum 1 Wall 4.

---

16 There is no drawing of Locus 1 available. Information regarding this continuation of Locus 3 to the north is based on its verbal description in the fieldnotes.

K/9: Locus 1, the continuation of the late phase of the Stratum 1 pit, Locus 3, in K/8, cuts the earlier Stratum 1 east-west wall, Wall 4 (figs. 2.6, 2.24). Wall 4 is directly on top of the Stratum 2 Wall 6. It is made of two to three rows of fieldstones, .80 m wide. Wall 4 stretches for 3.20 m in length within the square, and continues to the east across the balk as Wall 14 in Square L/9, for a total of 6.80 m. The top height of Wall 4 is 25.60. A perpendicular north-south cross wall, Wall 2, abuts Wall 4 near the east balk. Wall 2 is directly above the Stratum 2 Wall 6, and runs for 3.00 m in length before intersecting the north balk. Most of the width of Wall 2 is hidden beneath the balk, with only .15 m exposed. No continuation of the wall is visible across the balk in Square L/9.

L/9: A large pit in the southern half of Square L/9, Locus 9, belongs to the late phase of Stratum 1 as it cuts an earlier Stratum 1 wall (figs. 2.6, 2.27). This wall, east-west Wall 14, is the continuation of Wall 4 in K/9, described above. Wall 14 is directly above Wall 723 in Stratum 2, and the Stratum 5 pit, Locus 17. A surface is described running north from the north face of Wall 14, but no details are provided. This floor is directly above Locus 17 in Stratum 5. An east-west wall fragment was uncovered in the northeastern part of the square that is largely covered by the eastern balk.

L/8: Two pits, Locus 13 and 16, are phased to Stratum 1 in Square L/8 (figs. 2.6, 2.26). Both pits are stratigraphically above the Stratum 2 Wall 15 and its contemporary plaster floor. It is not clear whether these two pits should be placed in the late phase of Stratum 1, matching the pits from surrounding squares. No details of the shape or exact location of either pit is provided.

L/7: One feature, Wall 724, can be phased to Stratum 1 in Square L/7 (figs. 2.6, 2.25). Because the west balk largely covers it, it is not clear which direction Wall 724 runs, and it is possible that it is actually a pillar base since there is no continuation in Square K/7. Wall 724 is stratigraphically above the Stratum 5 pit, Locus 750. What is exposed of Wall 724 is comprised of three ashlars, .80 m wide and .65 m long. The one course of Wall 724 is .30 m high, from 25.68 to 25.38. Surrounding Wall 724 is a cobblestone surface (no locus number), which runs from the south balk 2.20 m in length and 1.5 m in width. This surface is .20 m thick, 25.38/25.18, and abuts the bottom of Wall 724.

M/9: One Stratum 1 feature is present in Square M/9, only the western half of which was excavated (figs. 2.6, 2.34). Wall 905 is an east-west fieldstone wall in the northern part of the half square. It is constructed directly above the Stratum 3, Persian period burial, Locus 930. The wall runs for a length of 3.60 m, from the east subsidiary balk through the west balk, revealed when the balk was removed. The western end of Wall 905 just barely protrudes into Square L/9. Wall 905's three rows of fieldstones are 1.00 m in width, and the wall is preserved to .52 m in height, 26.16/25.64.

M/10: Several features are phased to Stratum 1 in Square M/10, which was only excavated in its southern half (figs. 2.6, 2.35). A fragment of a north-south wall, Wall 931, was revealed in the eastern part of the half square. 931 is stratigraphically above the Stratum 5 floor, Locus 929. It is likely that Wall 931 was a corner wall to Wall 905 in M/9, but any definite connection was robbed out in antiquity or lies underneath the unexcavated southeastern corner of Square M/9. Wall 905 is comprised of three rows of fieldstones, 1.00 m wide, and only 1.00 m of length is exposed before Wall 931 intersects the north subsidiary balk. The height of Wall 931 is 1.44 m, from 25.46 to 24.02. Two superimposed floors, Locus 1058 and 1060, meet the western face of Wall 931. Both floors stretch 2.35 m in width, from 931 to the west balk, and are 2.00 m in length, from the south balk to the north subsidiary balk. Floor 1058 is .06 m thick, 24.18/24.12, and is directly on top of Floor 1060, which is .10 m thick, 24.12/24.02. Floor 1060 is stratigraphically above the Stratum 6 (or Stratum 7) animal burial, Locus 934.

P/5: Several architectural features are phased to Stratum 1 in Square P/5 (figs. 2.6, 2.42). An east-west wall, Wall 805, is located in the southwestern part of the square. It is directly on top of the Stratum 2 walls 820 and 821. Wall 805's two rows of fieldstones are .95 m wide, and the wall is 2.20 m long before it intersects the west balk. The wall is preserved only to a height of .15 m, 26.56/26.43, likely representing the lowest foundation course. A perpendicular north-south wall, Wall 811, is located northeast of 805. Wall 811 is stratigraphically above the Stratum 2 Wall 820, and directly above the Stratum 6 tomb, Locus 932. 811 is constructed from ashlars laid in a header stretcher fashion, .95 m wide and 1.15 m long. The wall is preserved to a height of .77 m, 26.87/26.10. It is possible that 811 was a pier or column base, or that it was a wall that was robbed out when the site was quarried for building materials. A cobblestone and pebble floor, Locus 806, stretches from the northern side of Wall 805 to the western face of Wall 811. Locus 806 is directly above Stratum 2 walls 820 and 809 and Floor 806. The cobbled surface is 3.00 m wide, intersecting the west balk, and 3.10 m long intersecting the north balk. Its .60 m thickness, 26.71/26.11, likely includes the subsurface makeup. It is probable that Locus 806 is the floor of an outside courtyard given its cobbled surface.

P/4: One north-south wall is phased to Stratum 1 in Square P/4 (figs. 2.6, 2.41). This wall (no locus number) is directly on top of a Stratum 2 east-west wall (no locus number). The Stratum 1 wall is constructed from ashlars placed end to end, and fieldstones; it is .35 m in width and .60 m long before it intersects the south balk. Its top height is 26.98.

N/4: To the west in Square N/4 is a surface, Locus 1055, phased to Stratum 1 (figs. 2.6, 2.37). Floor 1055 is directly over Wall 1057 and Floor 1059, both of which are Stratum 2 features. Surface 1055 is a plaster floor located in the southeast corner of the southern half square excavated in N/4. It is 1.70 m wide before intersecting the east balk, and 1.45 m long before being covered by the south balk. Locus 1055 is .25 m thick, 25.82/25.57.

M/4: In the southern part of the west half square that was excavated in M/4 is a Stratum 1 east-west wall, Wall 732 (figs. 2.6, 2.31). This wall is stratigraphically above the Stratum 4 mudbrick floor, Locus 742. Wall 732 is 1.52 m long, before intersecting the east subsidiary balk, and .40 m wide. Its top height is 25.89.

O/1: Two features in Square O/1 are phased to Stratum 1 (figs. 2.6, 2.39). The east-west Wall 807 is stratigraphically above Floor 819 in Stratum 2. Wall 807 is made from fieldstones, it is 3.05 m long before intersecting the east balk and .85 m wide, and may be more extensive as its full width is masked by the south balk. A fragmentary plaster floor (no locus number) runs from the north face of Wall 807. The floor is stratigraphically above Stratum 2 Floor 819. It stretches for 1.10 m in width before intersecting the east balk, and is 1.15 m long. The plaster of the floor is .08 m thick, 25.07/24.99.

Area H Post-Stratum 1 Remains

A Templar castle was constructed on the tell in Area H. Some of the stones from earlier periods of settlement were robbed and utilized for the construction of Toron, as the castle was known (Artzy 2015). The Templar castle's foundations were found in at least Squares M/1 (photo 2.17), O/1, and P/1. It is likely that the area was flattened in preparation for the construction of the fortress, and contemporary gardens and vineyards. Later builders of the walls and buildings in 'Akka/Acre, situated on the peninsula to the west of the tell, in turn, robbed the stones of the Crusader building, leaving only the ceramics of the previous periods. Historical records of the Crusaders, published by Rey (1889: 10–13) mention, besides the Templar's Toron, orchards extending from the northern banks of the Na'aman River to the southern outskirts of the tell, which were cultivated by the Genoese. The Crusader sherds found in the tree root negatives remain from this cultivation (Artzy 2015). Tell el-Fukhar, the Arabic name for the site meaning the mound of ceramics, indicates the unusual amounts of sherds found on the tell.

Despite the fact that Tel Akko is called "Napoleon's Hill" today by locals, Napoleon's army was not stationed on the tell, but in its vicinity. The tell was under control of the Ottoman army. During the Mandate period, British engineers mined a part of the southern section of the tell and used the soil to dry the swampy areas of the Na'aman (Belos) River in the Akko Plain. Their endeavor, however, did not completely change the unusual shape of the tell as present studies indicate (Artzy and Quartermaine 2014). Trenches associated with the Israeli army's 1948 conquest of the city were also found in Area H. Remains dating to the period include spent bullets. The abandoned tell site was farmed and, in the last years before 1972, was plowed by mechanical plows to the depth of 30–40 cms, at which time Moshe Dothan decided to undertake an excavation. Dothan's project was first conducted under the auspices of the then Israel Department of Antiquities and eventually under the then Center for Maritime Studies at the University of Haifa.

Summary

Area H is located in the northwestern area of Tel Akko, and was chosen for excavation because it was considered the likely area of a Late Bronze Age gate depicted in an Egyptian representation of the city being conquered by Pharaoh Ramses II. After five seasons of excavation and the discovery of seven distinct strata in Area H, no LB phases were discerned. The earliest phase, Stratum 7, consists of sloping layers of rampart construction that are dated to the MB IIA. In the following phase, Stratum 6, the rampart becomes a place of burial as is evidenced by a cist tomb and two structural tombs dating to the MB IIB–IIC cut into the older rampart layers (fig. 2.11). Area H was abandoned until the period of transition from the end of the LB IIB to the beginning of the Iron IA (LB IIC), when a poor settlement phase, Stratum 5, is marked by beaten earth floors and stone lined pits (fig. 2.10). Another gap ensues after Stratum 5, followed by the remains of domestic architecture located in the furthest southeastern corner of the excavation area, phased to Stratum 4 and dated to the end of the Iron IIA/beginning of the Iron IIB (fig. 2.9). The area was abandoned in the Iron IIC, and later used by the Persian army, as the numerous amphoras and storage jars found in the new Total Archaeology Project indicates. A burial of a human and several dogs from the Persian period, Stratum 3 were noted (fig. 2.8). Two Hellenistic phases of domestic settlement follow in Stratum 2 and Stratum 1, with a marked shift in the orientation of dwellings between these final two phases in Area H (figs. 2.7, 2.6). The features called "Persian pits" in preliminary field notes are, to a large extent, filled with the ceramics left by the robbing of walls over the millennia, fills for the Crusaders' vineyards, and pits prepared for the disposal of stones and sherds during the modern tilling of the tell.

In Area G, which is situated to the southwest of Area H, the last datable coin is of Antiochus IV Epiphanes, from the first third of the 2nd century BCE, giving a terminus post quem for the late Hellenistic phase on the tell. The architectural remains from the Iron Age in this Area, as well as in other trenches, such as Area H Square M/1, which was excavated in 1980, are spotty since this part of the tell underwent major construction and stone robbing activities in various later periods. Due to later disturbances, ceramics from later periods, such as those from the Persian and Hellenistic periods, were found in lower levels in Area G, albeit not under the spotty parts of floors. Not surprising, some Crusader ceramics dating to the 13th century CE were found there as well, witness of later activity in this area.

TABLE 2.1 Comparative local phasing of Akko excavation areas

Time Period	Area H: Local Phase	Area A: Local Phase	Area C: Local Phase	Area B: Local Phase
Crusader	Stratum 0	Stratum 1	Stratum 1	
Hellenistic	Stratum 1	Stratum 2	Stratum 2	
Hellenistic	Stratum 2	Stratum 3	Stratum 3	
Persian, late		Stratum 4	Stratum 4	
Persian, early	Stratum 3—later phase	Stratum 5	Stratum 5	
Persian, early	Stratum 3	Stratum 6		
Iron IIC		Stratum 7	Stratum 6	
Iron IIA–IIB	Stratum 4	Stratum 8	Stratum 7	
Iron IB				
LB IIB–Iron IA	Stratum 5		Stratum 8	
LB II			Stratum 9	
LB II			Stratum 10	
LB IB/LB IIA			Stratum 11	
LB I			Stratum 12	
MB IIC	Stratum 6—later phase		Stratum 13	Rampart 6
MB IIB	Stratum 6			Rampart 5
MB IIA				Rampart 4
MB IIA	Stratum 7			Rampart 3
MB IIA				Rampart 2
MB IIA				Rampart 1

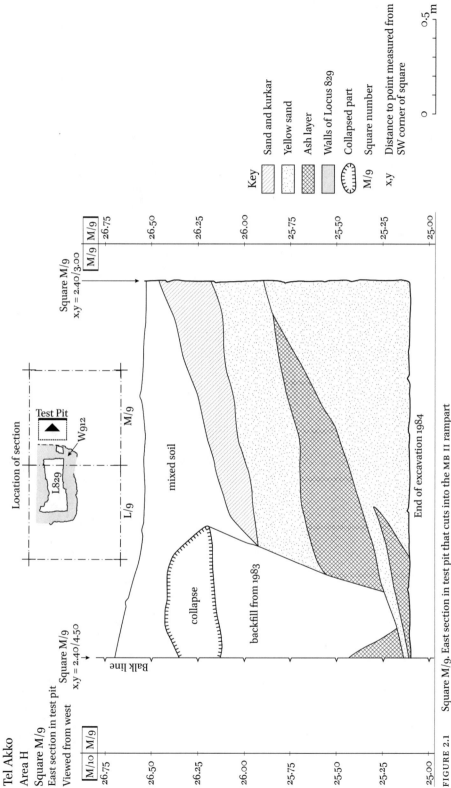

FIGURE 2.1   Square M/9. East section in test pit that cuts into the MB II rampart

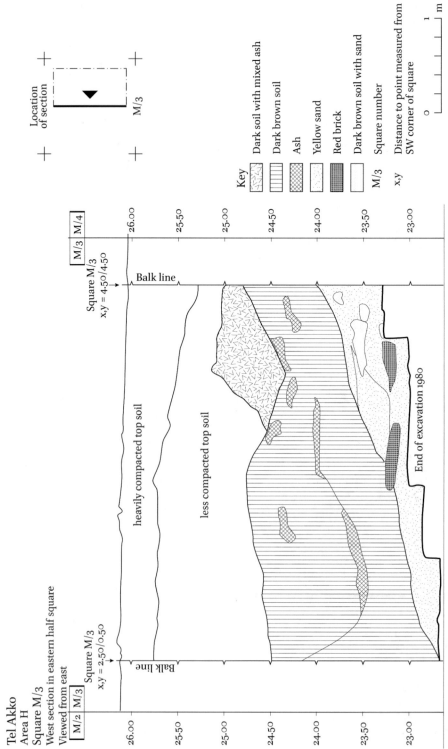

FIGURE 2.2 Square M/3. West section in the eastern half-square that cuts into the MB II rampart

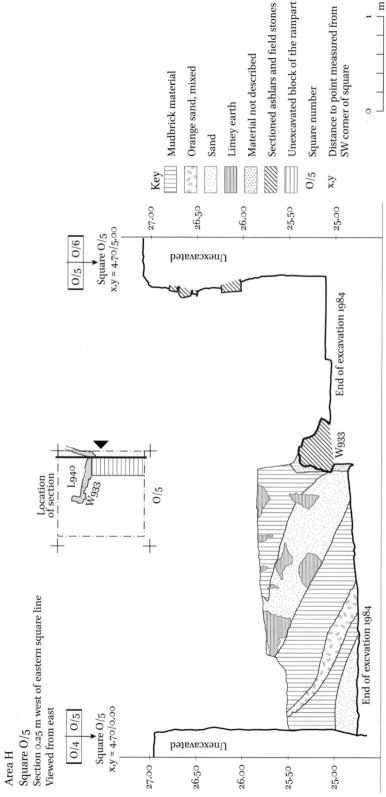

FIGURE 2.3 Square O/5, Section cutting the MB II rampart 0.25 m west of eastern square-boundary

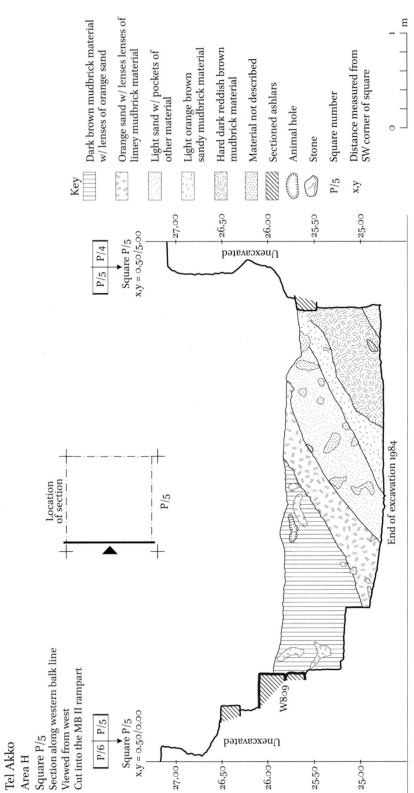

FIGURE 2.4   Square P/5. Section cutting the MB II rampart along the western balk

THE STRATIGRAPHY AND ARCHITECTURE OF AREA H

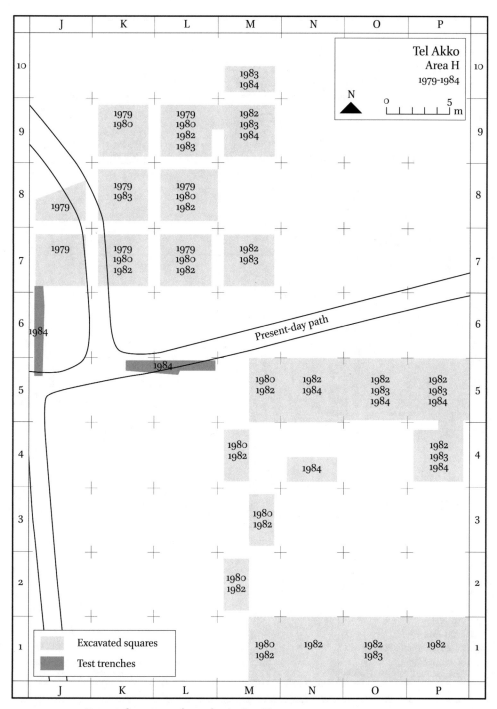

FIGURE 2.5   Excavated squares and trenches in Area H

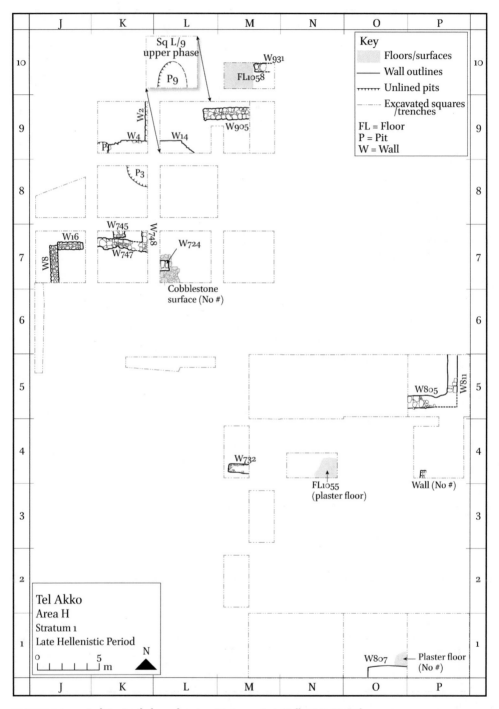

FIGURE 2.6 Architectural phase drawing, Stratum 1, Late Hellenistic Period

THE STRATIGRAPHY AND ARCHITECTURE OF AREA H

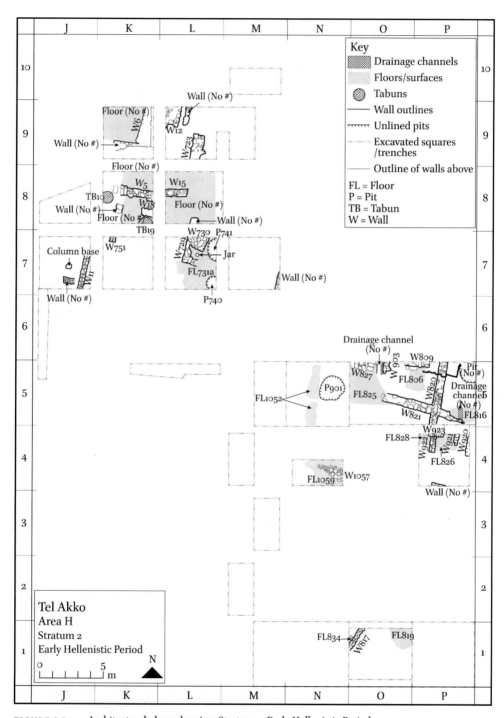

FIGURE 2.7   Architectural phase drawing, Stratum 2, Early Hellenistic Period

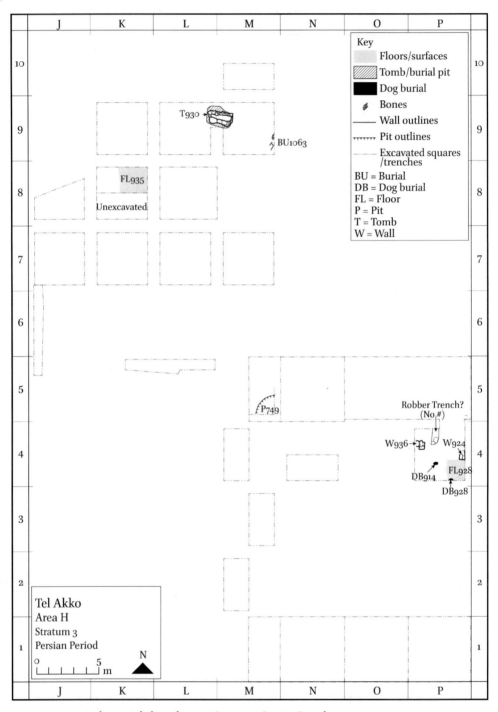

FIGURE 2.8 Architectural phase drawing, Stratum 3, Persian Period

THE STRATIGRAPHY AND ARCHITECTURE OF AREA H

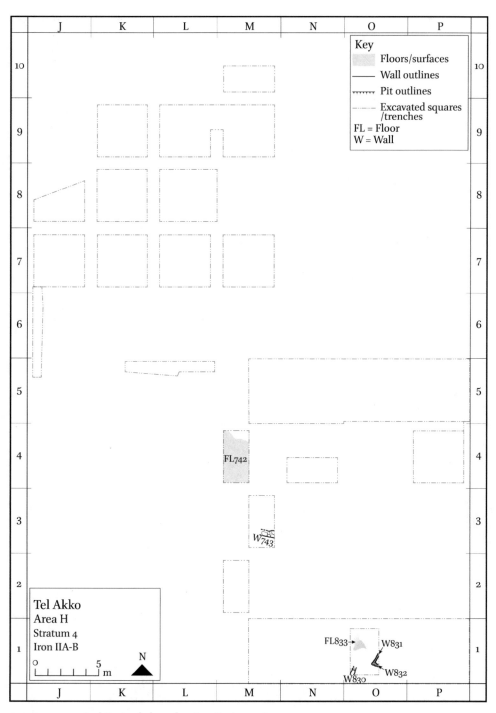

FIGURE 2.9   Architectural phase drawing, Stratum 4, Iron IIA–B

62 BRODY, ET AL.

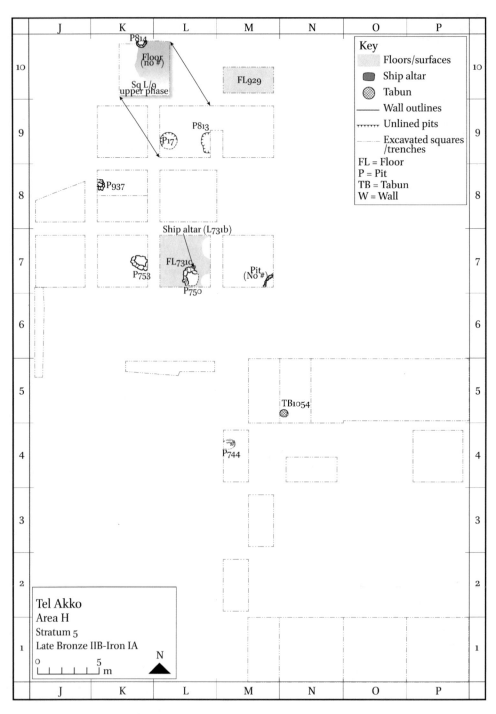

FIGURE 2.10   Architectural phase drawing, Stratum 5, Late Bronze IIB–Iron IA

THE STRATIGRAPHY AND ARCHITECTURE OF AREA H

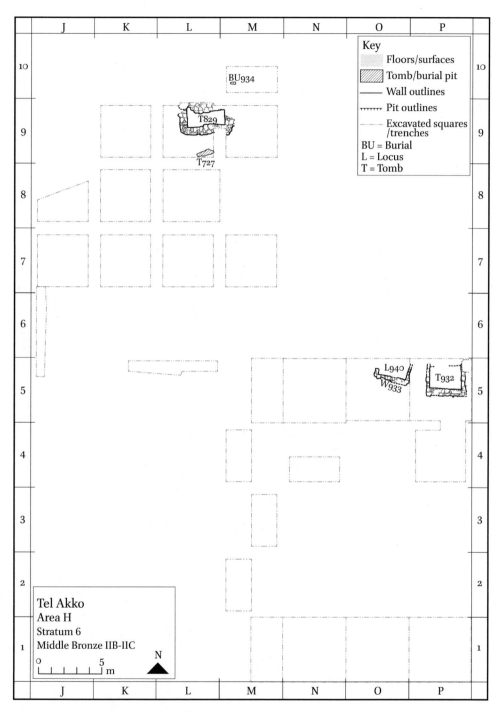

FIGURE 2.11   Architectural phase drawing, Stratum 6, Middle Bronze IIB–C

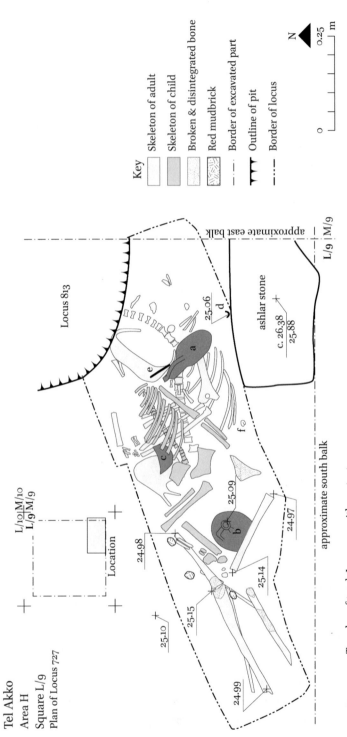

FIGURE 2.12   Top plan of tomb Locus 727 with contents

Figure 2.12 Top plan of tomb Locus 727 with contents

No.	Object	Reg. no.	Top height	Bottom height	Figure
a	Dipper juglet (lost)	AK VII 1980, b. 202/1			
b	Cylindrical juglet	AK VII 1980, b. 216/1	25/09		4.1.1
c	Pottery sherd (lost)	Unknown			
d	Bronze earring (lost)	Unknown	25.06		
e	Bronze pin (lost)	Unknown			
f	Cowry shell bead (lost)	Unknown			

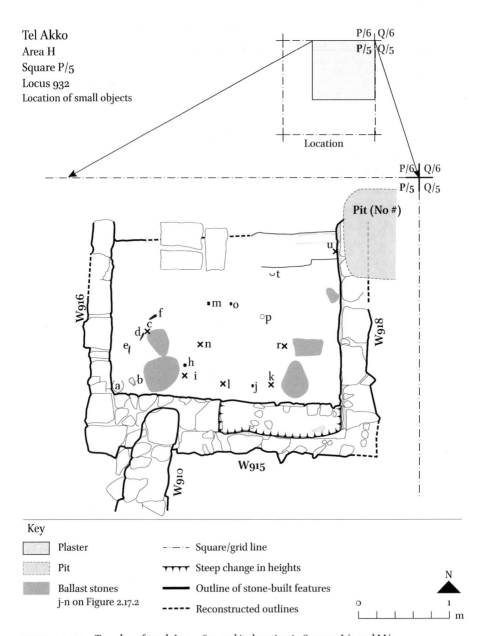

FIGURE 2.13.1   Top plan of tomb Locus 829 and its location in Squares L/9 and M/9 and adjacent loci

THE STRATIGRAPHY AND ARCHITECTURE OF AREA H

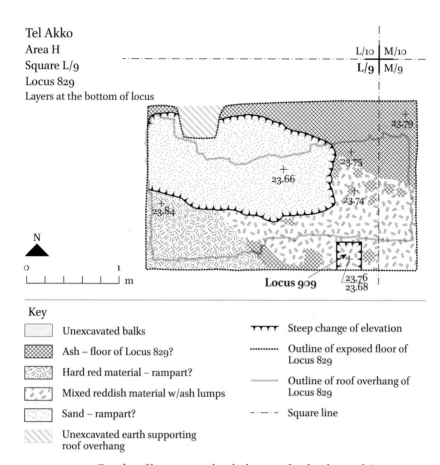

FIGURE 2.13.2   Top plan of layers exposed at the bottom of and within tomb Locus 829

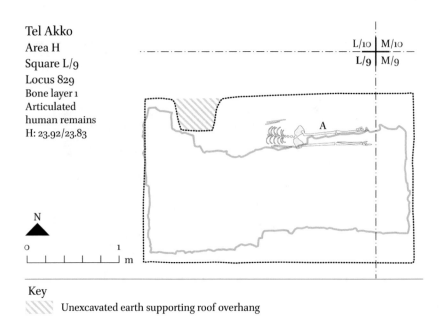

FIGURE 2.13.3   Top Plan of tomb Locus 829. Bone layer 1 with articulated human remains at heights between 23.92–23.83

Figure 2.13.3 Top plan of tomb Locus 829. Bone layer 1 with articulated human remains at heights between 23.92–23.83

No.	Object	Reg. no.	Top height	Bottom height
A	Headless human skeleton	AK IX 1983, b. 1315	23.92	23.83

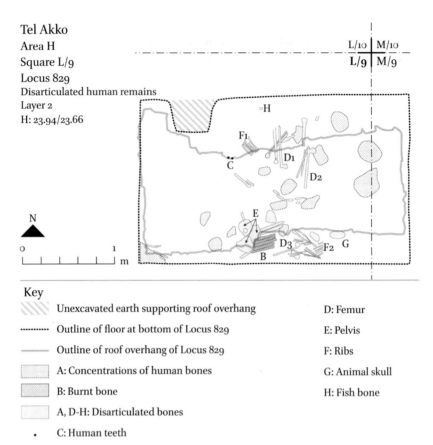

FIGURE 2.13.4   Top plan of tomb Locus 829. Bone layer 2 with disarticulated human remains at heights between 23.94–23.66

Figure 2.13.4 Top plan of tomb Locus 829. Bone layer 2 with disarticulated human remains at heights between 23.94–23.66

No.	Object	Reg. no.	Top height	Bottom height
A	Bone concentrations	AK IX 1983, b. 1103	23.94	23.83
B	Larger parallel bones, powdery, possibly burnt(?)	AK IX 1983, b. 1229/B, K	23.93	23.88
C	2 human teeth	AK IX 1983, b. 1271/D	23.85	23.66
D1	Femur	AK IX 1983, b. 1229/B, K	23.92	23.86
D2	Femur	AK IX 1983, b. 1229/B, K	23.92	23.86
D3	Femur	AK IX 1983, b. 1229/B, K	23.92	23.86
E	Pelvis	AK IX 1983, b. 1229/B, K	23.92	23.86
F1	Ribs	AK IX 1983, b. 1229/B, K	23.92	23.86
F2	Ribs	AK IX 1983, b. 1229/B, K	23.92	23.86
G	Pieces of animal skull	AK IX 1983, b. 1307/B	23.92	23.86
H	Fish bone	AK IX 1983, b. 1271/D	23.85	23.66

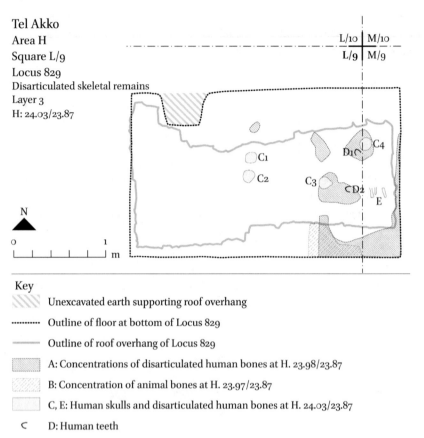

FIGURE 2.13.5 Top plan of tomb Locus 829. Bone layer 3 with disarticulated human remains at heights between 24.03–23.87

Figure 2.13.5 Top plan of tomb Locus 829. Bone layer 3 with disarticulated human remains at heights between 24.03–23.87

No.	Object	Reg. no.	Top height	Bottom height
A	Concentrations of human bones	AK IX 1983, b. 1302/I	23.98	23.87
B	Concentration of animal bones	AK IX 1983, b. 1302/I	23.97	23.87
C1	Skull II and bones around it	AK IX 1983, b. 1109/B	24.00	23.87
C2	Skull III, possibly of a child(?) and bones around it	AK IX 1983, b. 1109/A	24.00	23.87
C3	Skull IV	AK IX 1983, b. 1302/B	24.00	23.88
C4	Skull V	AK IX 1983, b. 1302/C	24.03	23.90
D1	Human teeth	AK IX 1983, b. 1302/C	23.90	
D2	Human teeth	AK IX 1983, b. 1302/G	23.92	
D3	Human teeth	AK IX 1983, b. 1293/D	24.09	23.98
E	Disarticulated human bones	AK IX 1983, b. 1285	23.99	

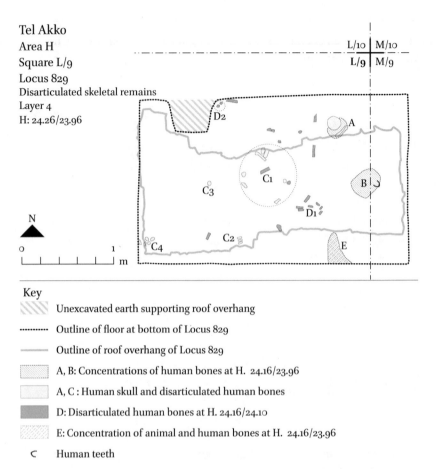

FIGURE 2.13.6 Top plan of tomb Locus 829. Bone layer 4 with disarticulated human remains at heights between 24.26–23.96

Figure 2.13.6 Top plan of tomb Locus 829. Bone layer 4 with disarticulated human remains at heights between 24.26–23.96

No.	Object	Reg. no.	Top height	Bottom height
A	Skull I and concentrations of disarticulated human bones around it	AK IX 1983, b. 1293/B	24.16	23.96
B	Concentrations of disarticulated human bones and teeth	AK IX 1983, b. 1293/C	24.16	23.96
C1	Disarticulated human bones	AK IX 1983, b. 1074/B	24.26	24.00
C2	Human ribs	AK VIII 1982, b. 340	24.08	
C3	Human toe bone	AK VIII 1982, b. 333	24.25	24.11
C4	Toe bones	AK VIII 1982, b. 350	24.09	
D1	Human ribs	AK IX 1983, b. 1094/B	24.16	24.10
D2	Toe bones	AK IX 1983, b. 1094/B	24.16	24.10
E	Concentration of human and animal bones	AK IX 1983, b. 1293/c	24.16	23.96

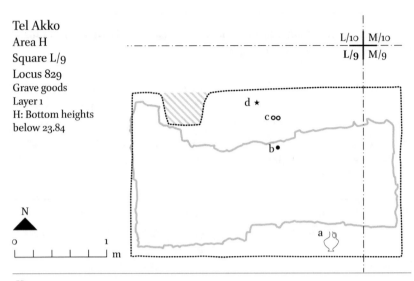

FIGURE 2.13.7   Top plan of tomb Locus 829. Layer 1 of grave goods at heights below 23.84

Figure 2.13.7 Top plan of tomb Locus 829. Layer 1 of grave goods at heights below 23.84

No.	Object	Reg. no.	Top height	Bottom height	Figure
a	Gold Braid holders	AK IX 1983, b. 1271/1–2	23.85	23.66	4.3.6–7
b	Gold bead	AK IX 1983, b. 1271/3	23.85	23.66	4.5.10
c	Ochre	AK IX 1983, b. 1271/D	23.85	23.66	
d	Jug	AK IX 1983, b. 1340	23.76	23.68	4.2.6
	2 Bone inlays (not on plan)	AK IX 1983, b. 1271/4–5	23.85	23.66	4.4.24–25
	Bone inlay (not on plan)	AK IX 1983, b. 1277/1	23.85	23.83	4.5.26

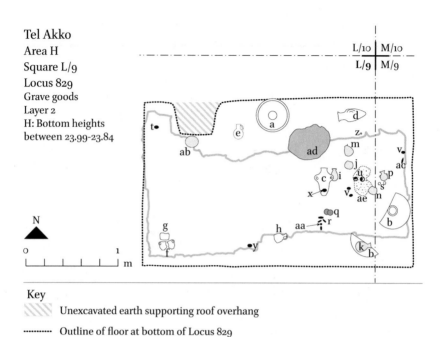

FIGURE 2.13.8   Top plan of tomb Locus 829. Layer 2 of grave goods at bottom heights between 23.99–23.84

THE STRATIGRAPHY AND ARCHITECTURE OF AREA H

Figure 2.13.8 Locus 829. Top plan of tomb Locus 829. Layer 2 of grave goods at bottom heights between 23.99–23.84

No.	Object	Reg. no.	Top height	Bottom height	Figure
a	Bowl	AK IX 1983, b. 1251/1229	23.95	23.87	4.1.3
b	Bowl	AK IX 1983, b. 1081/3 +1303	23.95	23.87	4.1.4
c	Amphoriskos	AK IX 1983, b. 1228	24.04	23.85	4.2.2
d	Amphoriskos	AK IX 1983, b. 1289	24.06	23.95	4.2.1
e	Tankard (lost)	AK VIII 1982, b. 349	24.20	23.96	
f	Juglet	AK VIII 1982, b. 350/1	24.05	23.99	4.2.5
f	Juglet	AK VIII 1982, b. 350/4	24.00	23.95	4.2.4
g	Juglet	AK IX 1983, b. 1101	24.00		4.2.10
h	Juglet	AK IX 1983, b. 1102	24.00	23.94	4.2.9
i	Alabaster jar	AK IX 1983, b. 1229/1	23.92	23.86	4.3.12
j	Alabaster jar	AK IX 1983, b. 1229/10	23.92	23.86	4.3.15
k	Alabaster jar	AK IX 1983, b. 1293	24.09	23.98	4.3.10
m	Alabaster jar	AK IX 1983, b. 1302/7	23.98	23.87	4.3.11
n	Alabaster jar	AK IX 1983, b. 1302/8	23.98	23.87	4.3.14
p	Alabaster jar	AK IX 1983, b. 1302/10	23.98	23.87	4.3.13
q	Bronze scales	AK IX 1983, b. 1229/6a+b	23.92	23.86	4.3.1–2

Figure 2.13.8 Locus 829. Top plan of tomb Locus 829. Layer 2 of grave goods at bottom heights between 23.99–23.84

No.	Object	Reg. no.	Top height	Bottom height	Figure
r	4 Weights, hematite	AK IX 1983, b. 1307/1–4	23.97	23.87	4.3.16–19
s	2 gold earrings	AK IX 1983, b. 1293/2–3	24.09	23.98	4.3.4–5
t	Scarab, steatite	AK IX 1983, b. 1104/2	-	23.94	4.5.1
u	Scarab ring, amethyst/gold/silver	AK IX 1983, b. 1302/1	23.98	23.87	4.5.5, 4.3.8
u	Scarab ring, amethyst/gold/silver	AK IX 1983, b. 1302/2	23.98	23.87	4.5.7, 4.3.9
v	Scarab, amethyst/gold	AK IX 1983, b. 1302/3	23.98	23.87	4.5.6
v	3 Scarabs, steatite	AK IX 1983, b. 1302/4, 5, 9	23.98	23.87	4.5.2–4
	Scarab (not on plan)	AK IX 1983, b. 1302/4	23.98	23.87	4.5.2
x	Scarab, amethyst (inside amphoriskos)	AK IX 1983, b. 1228/2	24.04	23.85	4.5.9
y	Scarab, amethyst	AK IX 1983, b. 1229/5	23.92	23.86	4.5.8
	5 bone inlays (not on plan)	AK VIII 1982, b. 350/2			4.5.63–67
	Bone inlay (not on plan)	AK IX 1983, b. 1201/1	23.92	23.86	4.4.9
	5 bone inlays (not on plan)	AK IX 1983, b. 1218/1–5	23.92	23.86	4.4.10–14
	9 bone inlays (not on plan)	AK IX 1983, b. 1229/7–15	23.92	23.86	4.4.15–23
	Bead, rock crystal (not on plan)	AK IX 1983, b. 1201/2	23.91	23.86	4.5.13
z	Bead, amethyst	AK IX 1983, b. 1307/5	23.97	23.87	4.5.12

THE STRATIGRAPHY AND ARCHITECTURE OF AREA H 81

Figure 2.13.8 Locus 829. Top plan of tomb Locus 829. Layer 2 of grave goods at bottom heights between 23.99–23.84

No.	Object	Reg. no.	Top height	Bottom height	Figure
aa	Pebble	AK IX 1983, b. 1307/6	23.97	23.87	4.5.24
ab	Bead, bronze (approximate location)	AK IX 1983, b. 1196/1	23.91	23.84	4.5.11
ab	Bead, rock crystal (approximate location)	AK IX 1983, b. 1196/2	23.91	23.84	4.5.14
ab	Pellet, lead (approximate location)	AK IX 1983, b. 1196/3	23.91	23.84	4.3.3
ab	Game piece (approximate location)	AK IX 1983, b. 1196/4	23.91	23.84	4.5.22
ab	3 Pebbles (approximate location)	AK IX 1983, b. 1196/5–7	23.91	23.84	4.5.18–20
ab	Garnet (approximate location)	AK IX 1983, b. 1196/8	23.91	23.84	4.5.21
ab	Pebble (approximate location)	AK IX 1983, b. 1196/9	23.91	23.84	4.5.23
ac	Bronze object (lost)	AK IX 1983, b. 1302/j	23.98	23.87	
ad	Stone mortar found upside down		24.30	23.91	4.3.20
ae	Area with glittering flakes in the soil (gold(?)) (not collected/ sampled in the excavation)		23.87		

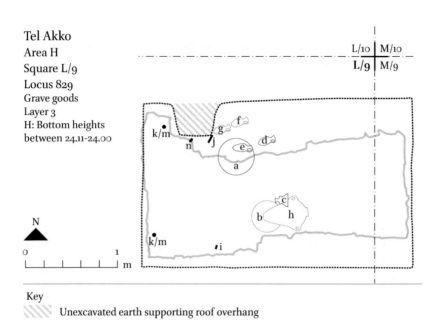

FIGURE 2.13.9   Top plan of tomb Locus 829. Layer 3 of grave goods at bottom heights between 24.11–24.00

THE STRATIGRAPHY AND ARCHITECTURE OF AREA H

Figure 2.13.9 Top plan of tomb Locus 829. Layer 3 of grave goods at bottom heights between 24.11–24.00

No.	Object	Reg. no.	Top height	Bottom height	Figure
a	Bowl	AK IX 1983, b. 1082	24.08	24.05	4.1.6
b	Plate (not found)	AK VIII 1982, b. 339/1	24.14	24.02	
c	Chalice	AK VIII 1982, b. 337/1	24.15	24.09	4.1.7
d	Juglet	AK VIII 1982, b. 321/1	24.13	24.07	4.2.7
e	Juglet	AK VIII 1982, b. 333/4	24.16	24.11	4.2.8
f	Juglet (not found)	AK VIII 1982, b. 348	24.19	24.08	
g	Juglet (not found)	AK IX 1983, b. 1073/B	24.10		
h	Storage jar (not found)	AK VIII 1982, b. 339	24.30	24.02	
	Bone inlay	AK VIII 1982, b. 333/2	24.25	24.11	4.4.61
i	Bone inlay	AK VIII 1982, b. 340/1	24.09	24.00	4.4.60
j	Bone Inlay	AK IX 1983, b. 1094	24.16	24.10	4.4.62
k	Bead	AK IX 1983, b. 1094/2	24.16	24.10	4.5.15
m	Bead (not found)	AK IX 1983, b. 1094	24.16	24.10	
	Shell pendant(?)	AK IX 1983, b. 1094/3	24.16	24.10	4.5.16
	Shell pendant(?)	AK IX 1983, b. 1094/4	24.16	24.10	4.5.17
n	Flint Flake (not found)	AK IX 1983, b. 1094/D	24.16	24.10	

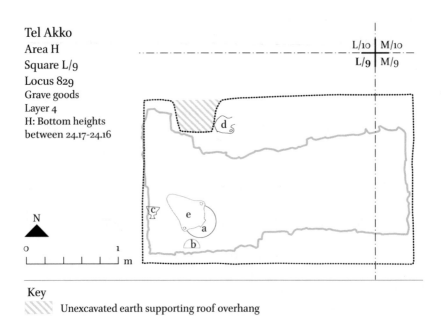

FIGURE 2.13.10 Top plan of tomb Locus 829. Layer 4 of grave goods at bottom heights between 24.17–24.16

Figure 2.13.10 Top plan of tomb Locus 829. Layer 4 of grave goods at bottom heights between 24.17–24.16

No.	Object	Reg. no.	Top height	Bottom height	Figure
a	Plate	AK VIII 1982, b. 310	24.41	24.17	4.1.2
b	Bowl (not found)	AK VIII 1982, b. 338	24.23	24.16	
c	Chalice	AK VIII 1982, b. 350/3	24.24	24.16	4.1.8
d	Jug	AK VIII 1982, b. 344	24.43	24.16	4.2.3
e	Storage Jar (not found)	AK VIII 1982, b. 310	24.41	24.17	

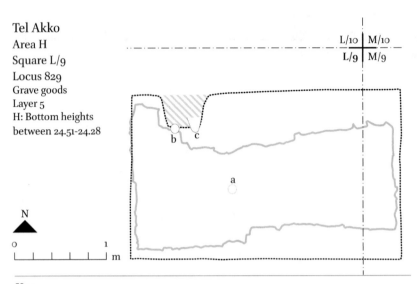

FIGURE 2.13.11   Top plan of tomb Locus 829. Layer 5 of grave goods at bottom heights between 24.51–24.28

Figure 2.13.11. Top plan of Locus 829. Layer 5 of grave goods at bottom heights between 24.51–24.28

No.	Object	Reg. no.	Top height	Bottom height	Figure
a	Vessel of unknown form (not found)	AK VIII 1982, b. 239	24.54		
b	Vessel of unknown form (not found)	AK VIII 1982, b. 255	24.65	24.51	
c	Jar, lower part (not found)	AK VIII 1982, b. 343	24.49	24.28	

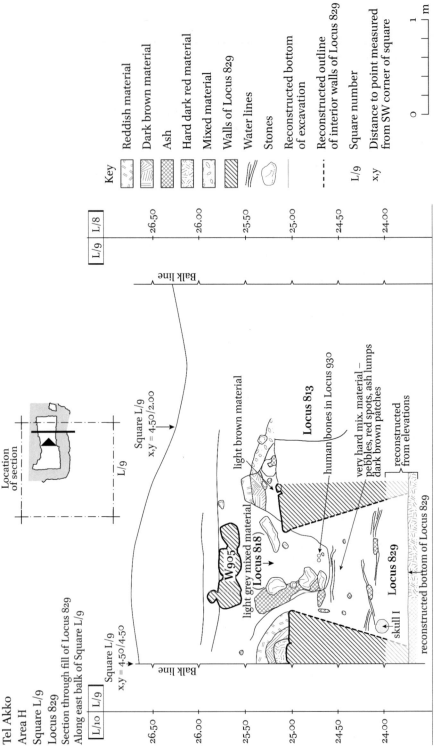

FIGURE 2.13.12 Section along east balk of Square L/9 through the fill in tomb Locus 829

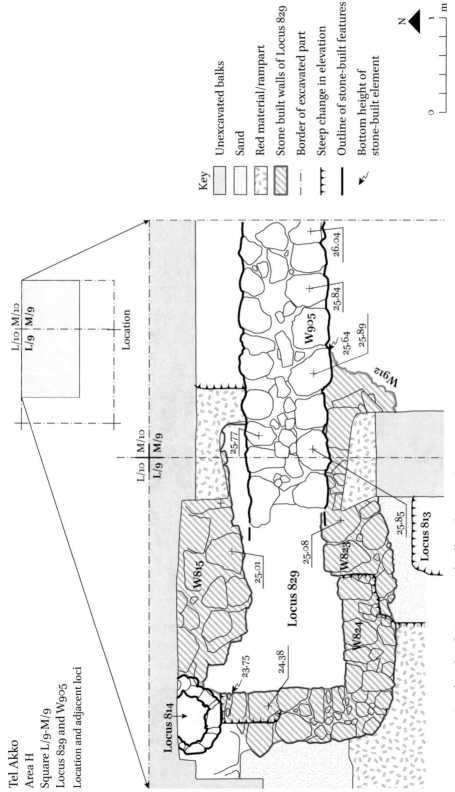

FIGURE 2.14   Top plan of tomb Locus 829 and Wall 905 (Stratum 1)

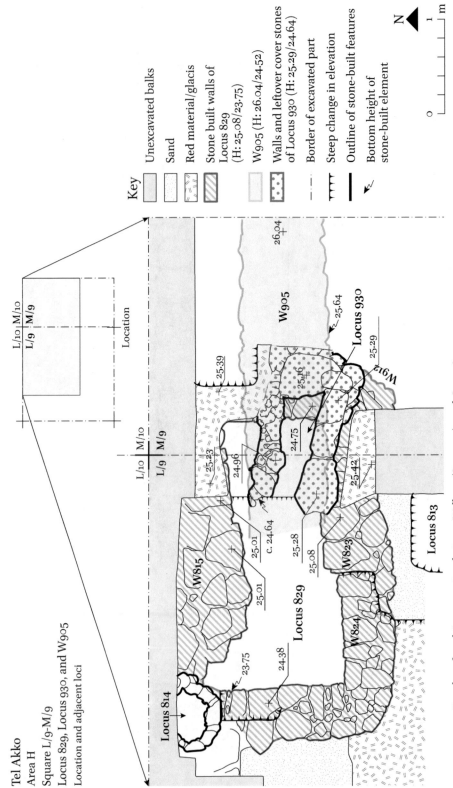

FIGURE 2.15 Top plan of tomb Locus 930 in relation to Wall 905 (Stratum 1), tomb Locus 829 (Stratum 6), and other adjacent loci from various strata

THE STRATIGRAPHY AND ARCHITECTURE OF AREA H

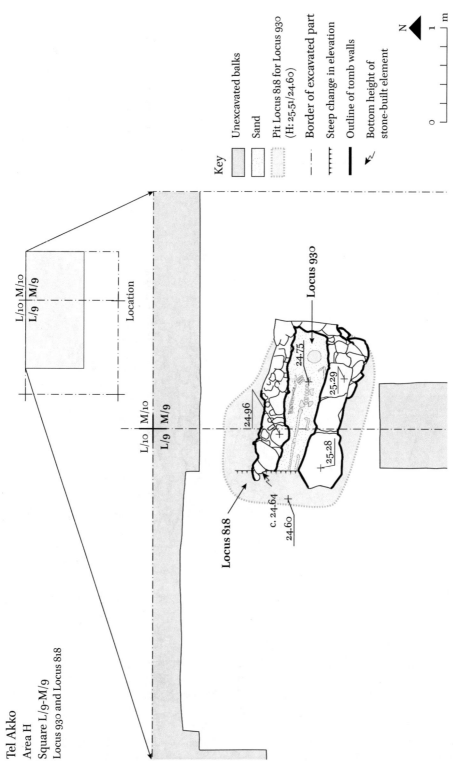

FIGURE 2.16.1   Top plan of pit Locus 818 and tomb Locus 930 with skeleton

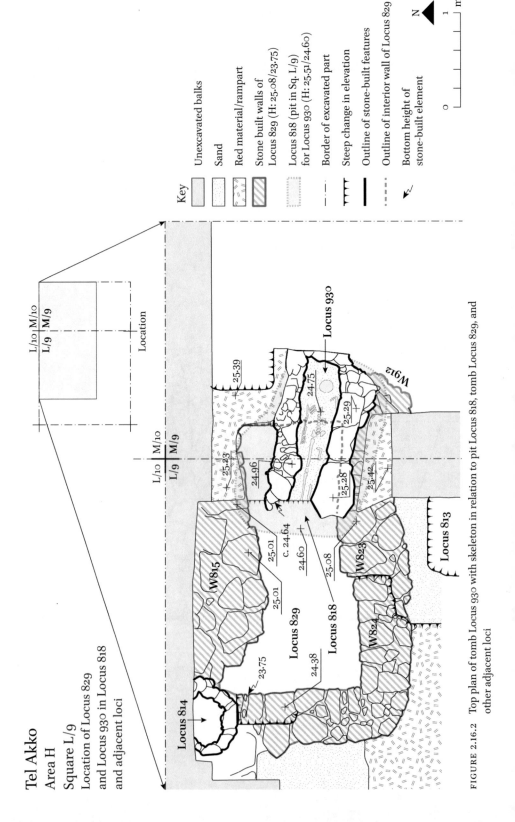

FIGURE 2.16.2 Top plan of tomb Locus 930 with skeleton in relation to pit Locus 818, tomb Locus 829, and other adjacent loci

THE STRATIGRAPHY AND ARCHITECTURE OF AREA H

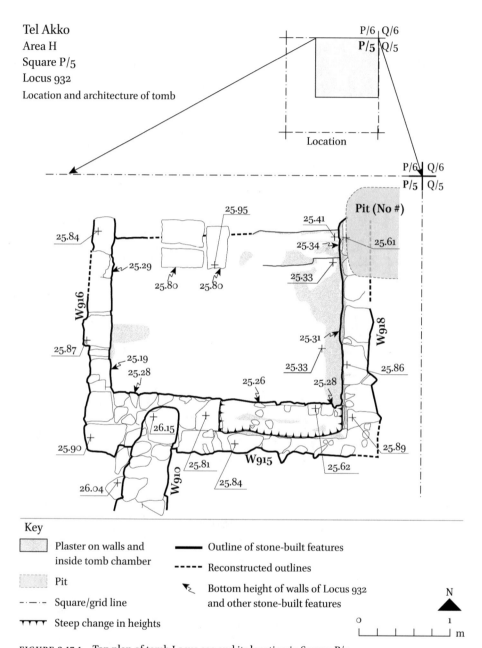

FIGURE 2.17.1   Top plan of tomb Locus 932 and its location in Square P/5

94

BRODY, ET AL.

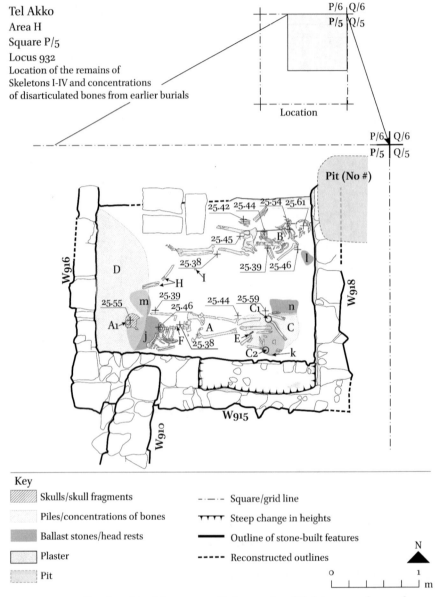

FIGURE 2.17.2   Top plan of tomb Locus 932 with the remains of Skeletons I–IV, heaps of bones pushed aside from earlier burials, and ballast stones used as possible head rests

THE STRATIGRAPHY AND ARCHITECTURE OF AREA H 95

Figure 2.17.2 Top plan of tomb Locus 932 with the remains of Skeletons I – IV, heaps of bones pushed aside from earlier burials, and ballast stones used as possible head rests

No.	Object	Reg. no.	Top height	Bottom height	Figure
A	Complete skeleton (Skeleton I) lying on back	AK IX 1983, b. 1291, 1322/D	25.59	25.39	
A1	Skull of Skeleton I	AK IX 1983, b. 1291	25.59		
B	Complete skeleton (Skeleton II) lying on stomach	AK IX 1983, b. 1295/B, 1308/B, 1317/B, 1322/C	25.6	25.44	
C	Heap of human bones w/ two skulls (C1 & C2) of two complete(?) skeletons (Skeleton III and IV) pushed aside from earlier burials	AK IX 1983, b. 1322/D	25.65	25.4	
C1	Skull of a child (Skeleton III)	AK IX 1983, b. 1322/D			
C2	Skull of a young adult(?) (Skeleton IV)	AK IX 1983, b. 1322/D			
D	Concentration of disarticulated bones pushed aside from earlier burials (see also M on plan in fig. 2.17.2)	AK IX 1983, b. 1305/B, 1310/E, 1318/B, 1331/C – E	25.53	25.30–25.28	
E	Human teeth	AK IX 1983, b. 1310/A	25.42		
F	Human tooth (not belonging to Skeleton I)	AK IX 1983, b. 1291/B	25.38		

Figure 2.17.2 Top plan of tomb Locus 932 with the remains of Skeletons I – IV, heaps of bones pushed aside from earlier burials, and ballast stones used as possible head rests

No.	Object	Reg. no.	Top height	Bottom height	Figure
G	Arm bone		25.29		
H	Arm bones	AK IX 1983, b. 13.28/B		25.30–35.34	
I	Knuckle bone	AK IX 1983, b. 1296/B		25.42	
j	Ballast stone (head rest)	AK IX 1983, b. 1328/5	25.56	25.33	4.9.1
k	Ballast stone (head rest)	AK IX 1983, b. 1326/1	25.56	25.37–25.31	4.9.2
l	Ballast stone (head rest)	AK IX 1983, b. 1222/2	25.56	25.42	4.9.3
m	Ballast stone (head rest)	Not saved	25.5	25.3	
n	Ballast stone (head rest)	Not saved	25.54	25.32	

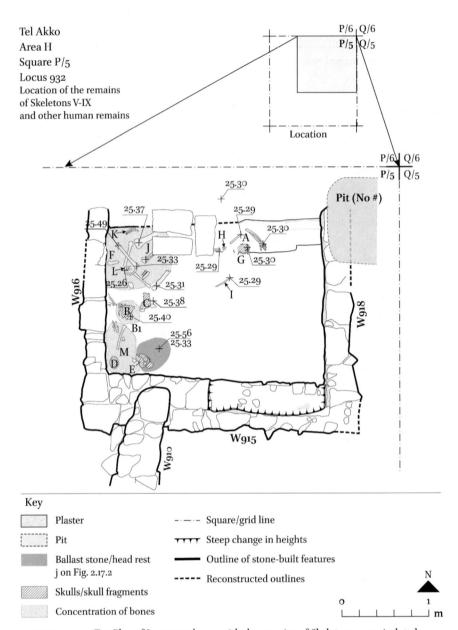

FIGURE 2.17.3   Top Plan of Locus tomb. 932 with the remains of Skeletons V–IX, isolated disarticulated bones, and heaps of bones pushed aside from earlier burials

Figure 2.17.3 Top Plan of tomb Locus 932 with the remains of Skeletons V – IX, isolated disarticulated bones, and heaps of bones pushed aside from earlier burials

No.	Object	Reg. no.	Top height	Bottom height	Figure
A	Remains of Skeleton V	AK IX 1983, b. 1315	23.92	25.83	
B	Remains of child Skeleton VI w/ unworn teeth	AK IX 1983, b. 1328/B	25.40	25.36	
C	Fragmented skull, possibly child's(?) (Skeleton VII)	AK IX 1983, b. 1328(?)		25.38	
D	Fragments of skull (Skeleton VIII)	AK IX 1983, b. 1328(?)	25.53	25.30	
E	Fragments of skull (Skeleton IX)	AK IX 1983, b. 1328/C	25.53	25.30	
F	Dense mass of disarticulated bones including at least five large bones from adult and some ribs. Possibly lower part of bone-heap D on Plan 2	AK IX 1983, b. 1331/E, 1337/B	c. 25.47– c. 25.31	25.28	
G	Half a skull lying sideways, badly disintegrated (from Skeleton V(?))	AK IX 1983, b. 1338/B	25.30		
H	Vertebra	AK IX 1983, b. 1315(?)	25.26		
I	Arm bone(?)	AK IX 1983, b. 1315(?)	25.29		
J	Two very large bones (animal(?))	AK IX 1983, b. 1337/B	25.35– 25.37		
K	Ribs	AK IX 1983, b. 1337/B	from c. 25.47– c. 25.31		
L	Vertebra	AK IX 1983, b. 1337/B	25.26		
M	Concentration of bones (possibly deeper part of bone heap D on Plan 2.17.2)	AK IX 1983, b. 1328(?), 1331/B(?)	25.53	c. 25.31	

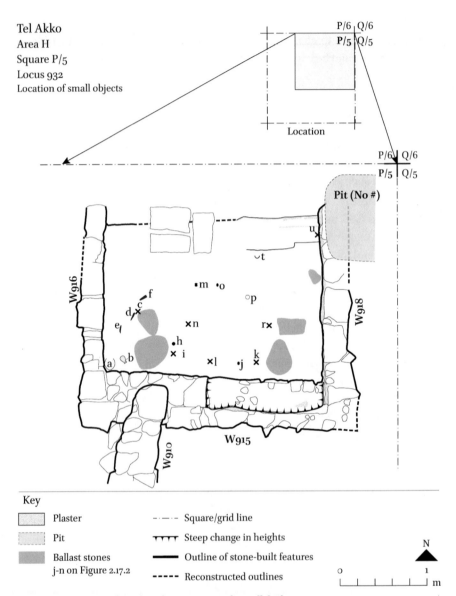

FIGURE 2.17.4   Top plan of tomb Locus 932 with small finds

THE STRATIGRAPHY AND ARCHITECTURE OF AREA H 101

Figure 2.17.4 Top plan of Locus 932 with small finds

No.	Object	Reg. no.	Top height	Bottom height	Figure
a	Ostrich egg	AK IX 1983, b. 1116/1	c. 25.80(?)	25.6	4.9.9
b	Alabaster vessel	AK IX 1983, b. 1328/2	25.48	25.40	4.8.10
c	Piece of bronze handle (not found)	AK IX 1983, b. 1291/C		Between 25.50–25.45(?)	
d	Dagger blade	AK IX 1983, b. 1328/1		25.28	4.8.7
e	Bronze blade	AK IX 1983, b. 1310/1		25.42	4.8.8
f	Bronze axe head	AK IX 1983, b. 1331/1		25.30	4.8.6
g	Silver ring fragment	AK IX 1983, b. 1331/2		Between 25.34–25.28(?)	4.8.9
h	Piece of faience bead(?) (not found)	AK IX 1983, b. 1291/B		c. 25.40(?)	
i	Piece of bronze object (not found)	AK IX 1983, b. 1291/B		c. 25.40(?)	
j	Scarab, steatite	AK IX 1983, b. 1222/1		25.40	4.9.7
k, l	Pieces of bone inlay	AK IX 1983, b. 1222/B (not found), 1231/1–3		Between 25.56–25.40(?)	4.9.4–6
m	Knuckle bone	AK IX 1983, b. 1296/B		25.42	
n	Piece of bronze blade(?) (not found)	AK IX 1983, b. 1309/B		25.35	
o	Scarab, steatite	AK IX 1983, b. 1332/1		25.34	4.9.8
p	Loom weight	AK IX 1983, b. 1249/1		25.43	4.8.5
q	Piece of bronze ring(?)	AK IX 1983, b. 1151/B		Between 25.76–25.59	

Figure 2.17.4 Top plan of Locus 932 with small finds

No.	Object	Reg. no.	Top height	Bottom height	Figure
r	Piece of ochre	AK IX 1983, b. 1249/B		25.41	
s	Knuckle bone(?)	AK IX 1983, b. 1322/B		Between 25.65–25.36	
t	Bronze crescent shaped object (not found)	AK IX 1983, b. 1234/B		25.49	
u	Piece of ochre	AK IX 1983, b. 1267/B		25.51	

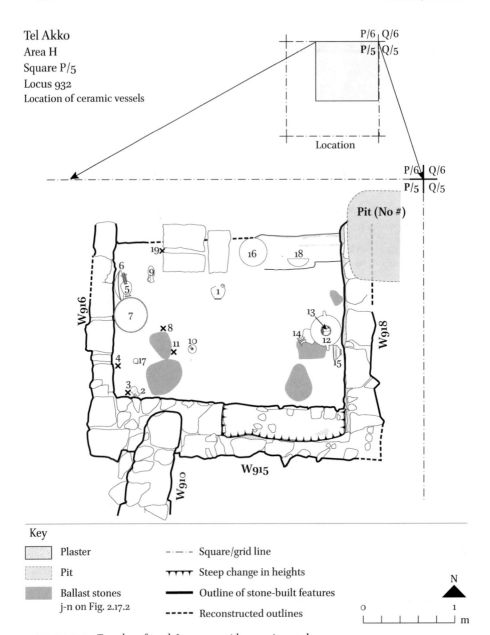

FIGURE 2.17.5   Top plan of tomb Locus 932 with ceramic vessels

Figure 2.17.5 Top plan of Locus 932 with ceramic vessels

No.	Object	Reg. no.	Top height	Bottom height	Figure
1	Jug (approximate location on plan)	AK IX 1983, b. 1189/1	25.58	25.47	4.7.2
2	Juglet, Cypriot White Painted family of Middle Cypriot pottery	AK IX 1983, b. 1164/1	25.63	25.54	4.8.3
3	Handle and part of Cypriot White Slip bowl (not found)	AK IX 1983, b. 1164/B	c. 25.60		
4	Fine 'fish – bowl' (not found)	AK IX 1983, b. 1179/B	25.56	25.51	
5	Jug with 5 – strand handle	AK IX 1983, b. 1305/1	25.48		4.7.4
6	Bowl	AK IX 1983, b. 1305/2	25.57	25.32	4.6.5
7	Bowl	AK IX 1983, b. 1310/3	25.51	25.32	4.6.6
8	Dipper Juglet	AK IX 1983, b. 1309/1	25.39	25.32	4.8.1
9	Handled globular jug (not found)	AK IX 1983, b. 1337/C (possibly 1189/1(?))	25.37	25.30	
10	Cylindrical juglet	AK IX 1983, b. 1296/1, 1221/B, 1232/B	25.39	25.35	4.8.2
11	Handled globular jug (not found)	AK IX 1983, b. 1309/C	25.47	25.28	
12	Storage Jar	AK IX 1983, b. 1177/2	25.76	25.32	4.7.1
13	Chalice in Storage Jar	AK IX 1983, b. 1319/1	25.76–25.52	25.44	4.6.9
14	Jug, Anatolian	AK IX 1983, b. 1177/1	25.67	25.48	4.7.3

Figure 2.17.5 Top plan of Locus 932 with ceramic vessels

No.	Object	Reg. no.	Top height	Bottom height	Figure
15	Bowl, carinated	AK IX 1983, b. 1248/1	25.64	25.47	4.6.7
16	Bowl	AK IX 1983, b. 1250/1	25.47	25.39	4.6.4
17	Lamp	AK IX 1983, b. 1318/1	25.52	25.42	4.8.4
18	Bowl, Cypriot Black-on-Red Ware (approximate location)	AK IX 1983, b. 1308/1	?	25.46	4.6.8
19	Jug with double-strand handle (not found)	AK IX 1983, b. 1337/1341	25.40	25.11	

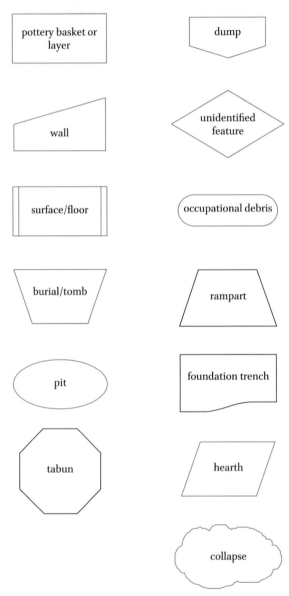

FIGURE 2.18   Key to the symbols used in the Harris' matrices

THE STRATIGRAPHY AND ARCHITECTURE OF AREA H

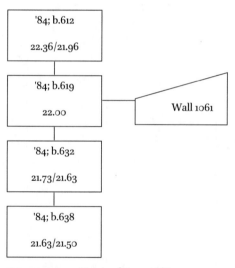

FIGURE 2.19   Matrix of Square J/6

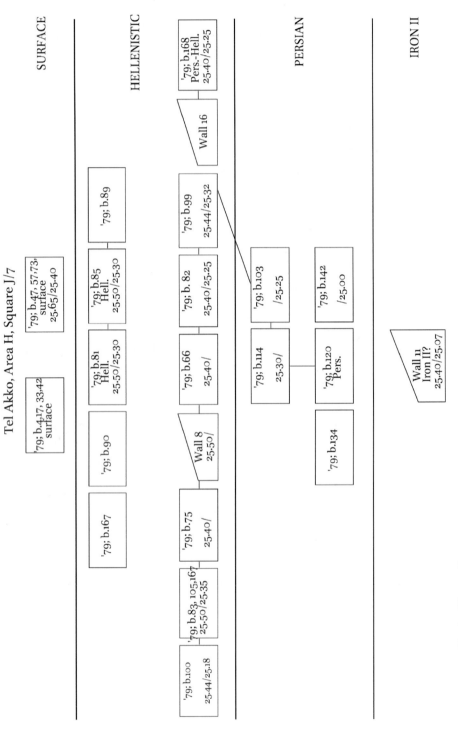

FIGURE 2.20 Matrix of Square J/7

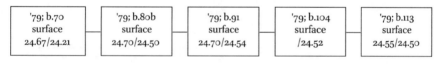

FIGURE 2.21   Matrix of Square J/8

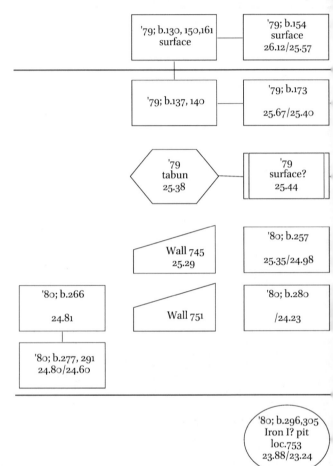

FIGURE 2.22   Matrix of Square K/7

, Square K/7

```
'82; b.24,46                         SURFACE

'79; b.180
25.67/25.25

'80; b.240-42, 252,265,
       279
       pit                           HELLENISTIC
   25.40/24.51

Wall 747        grey layer
25.12/24.71       floor?              Wall 748

'80; b.310
```

LATE BRONZE-EARLY IRON I
TRANSITION

THE STRATIGRAPHY AND ARCHITECTURE OF AREA H

Division key for Square K/8 matrix

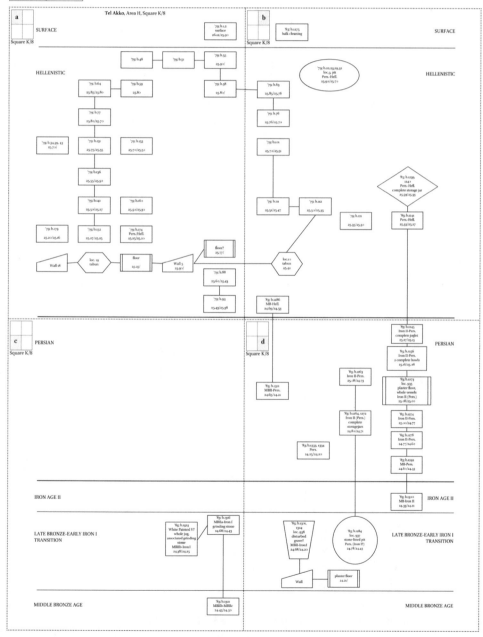

FIGURE 2.23 Division key for the matrix of Square K/8

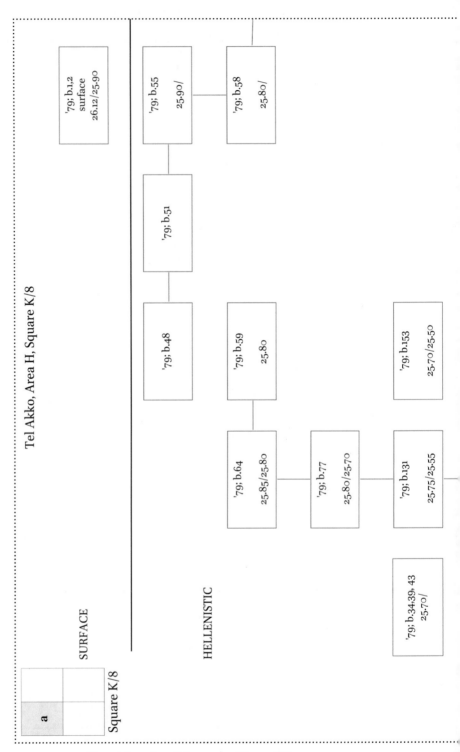

FIGURE 2.23.A Upper left section of the matrix of Square K/8

THE STRATIGRAPHY AND ARCHITECTURE OF AREA H

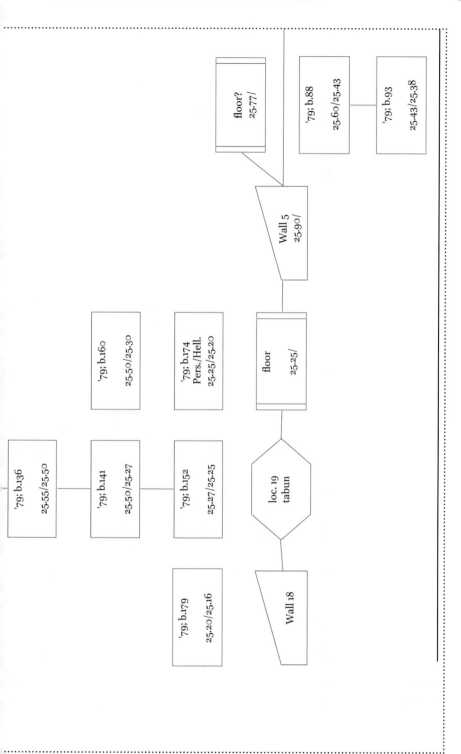

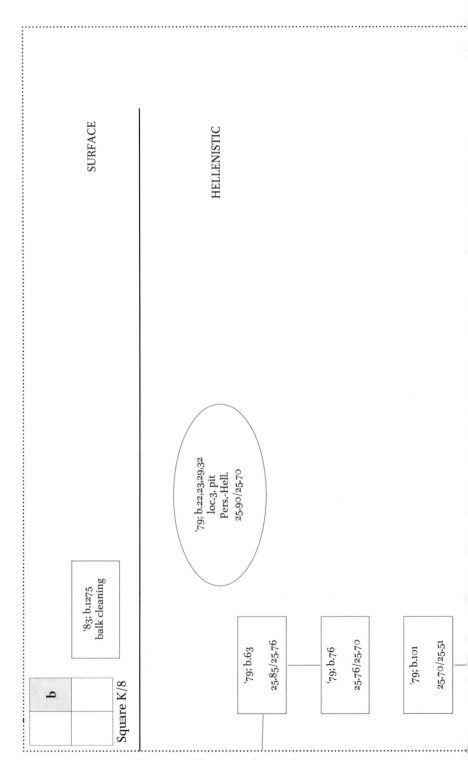

FIGURE 2.23.B Upper right section of the matrix of Square K/8

THE STRATIGRAPHY AND ARCHITECTURE OF AREA H

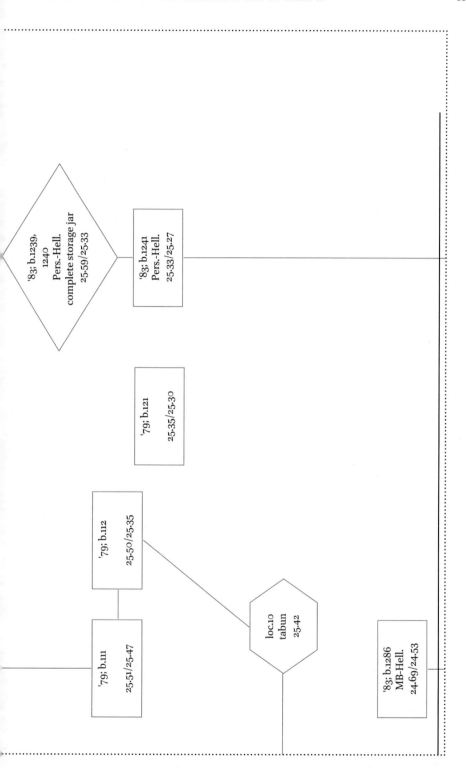

FIGURE 2.23.C Lower left section of the matrix of Square K/8

THE STRATIGRAPHY AND ARCHITECTURE OF AREA H

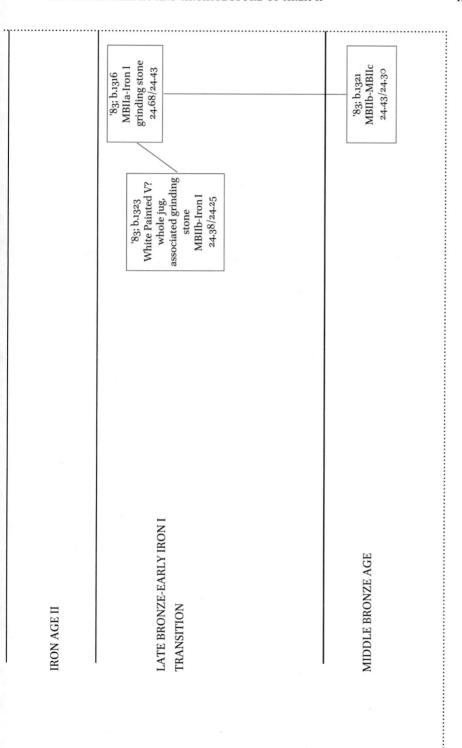

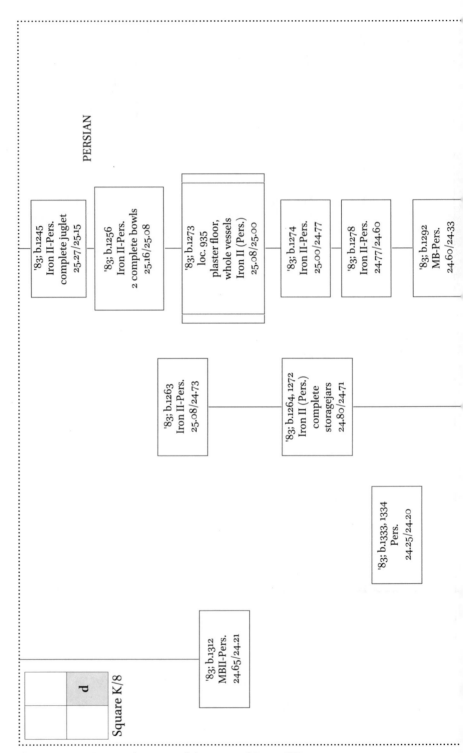

FIGURE 2.23.D Lower right section of the matrix of Square K/8

THE STRATIGRAPHY AND ARCHITECTURE OF AREA H

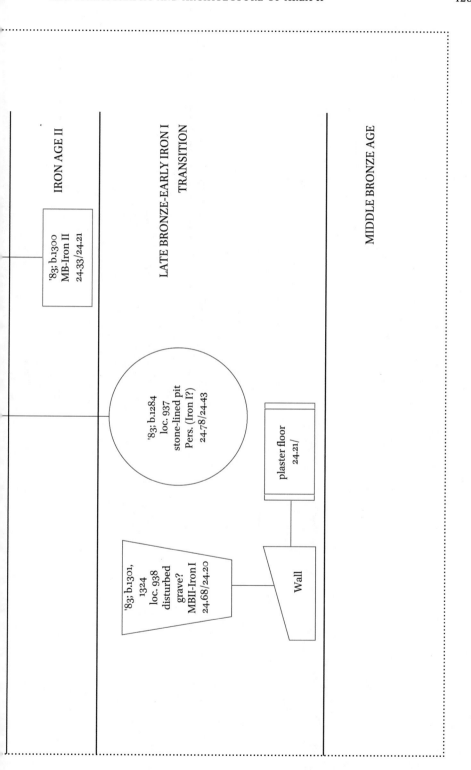

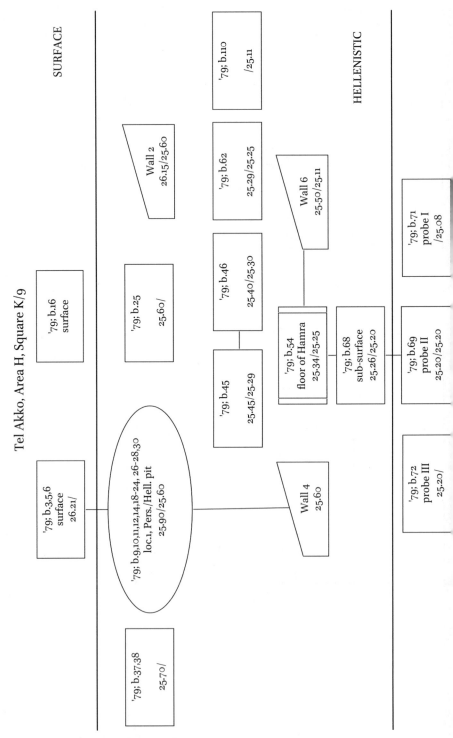

FIGURE 2.24   Matrix of Square K/9

THE STRATIGRAPHY AND ARCHITECTURE OF AREA H

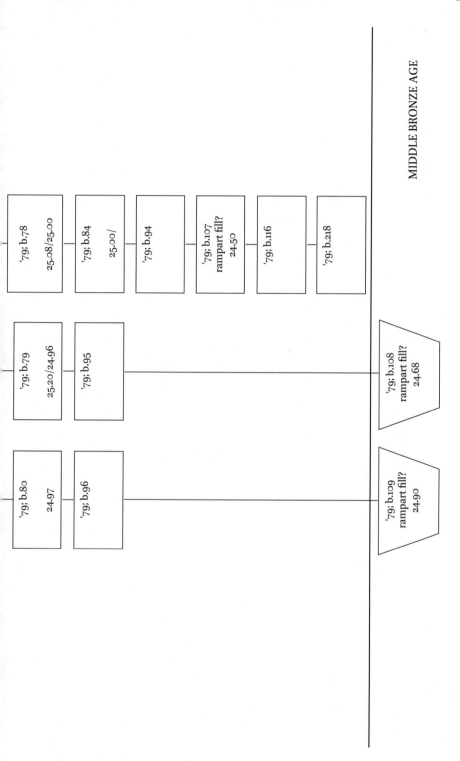

Division key for Square L/7 matrix

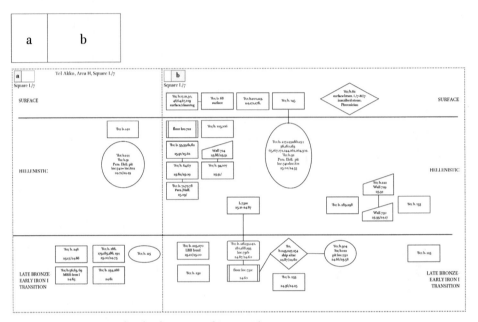

FIGURE 2.25   Division key for the matrix of Square L/7

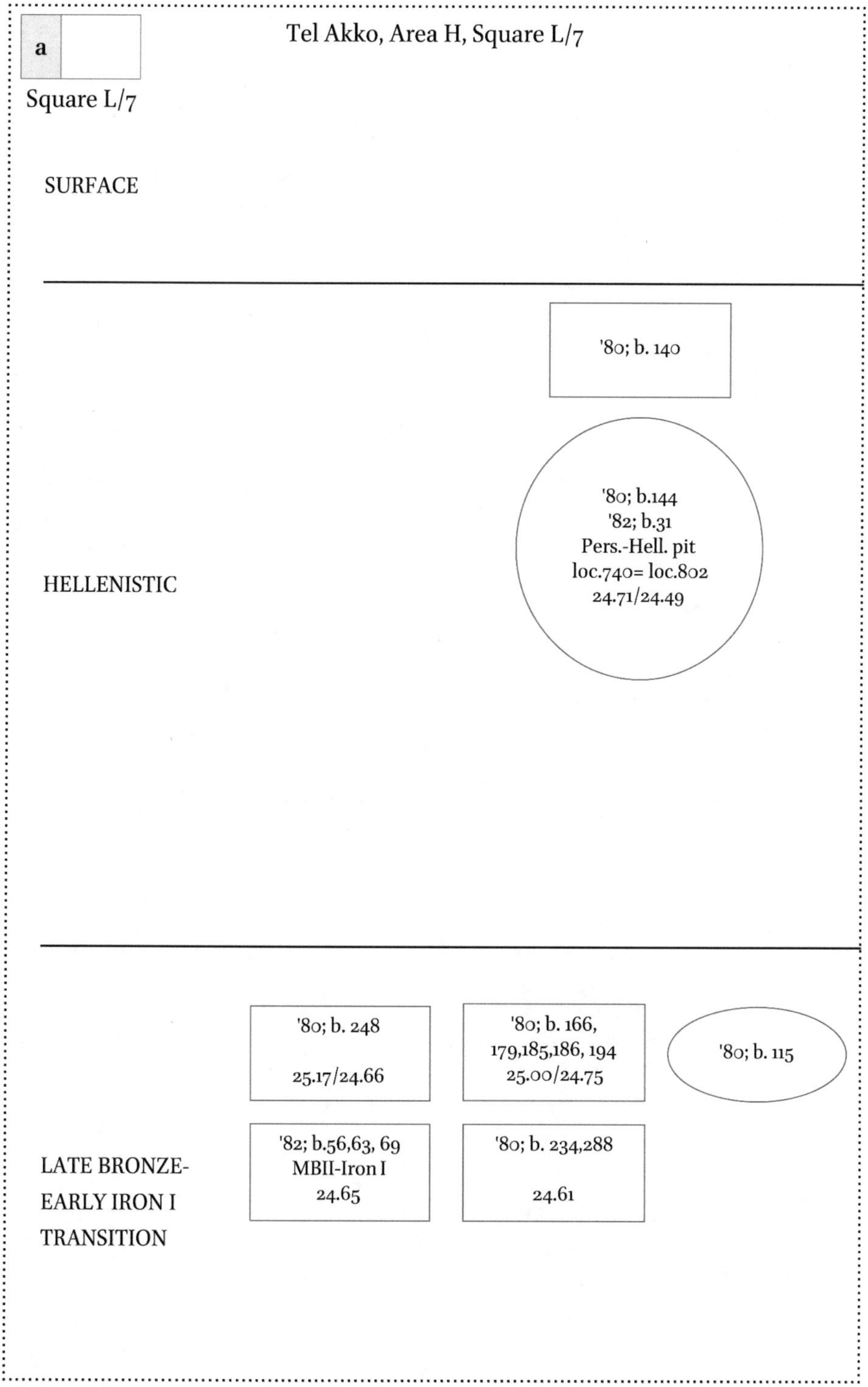

THE STRATIGRAPHY AND ARCHITECTURE OF AREA H 127

Tel Akko, Area H, Square L/7

a Square L/7

SURFACE

HELLENISTIC

'80; b. 140

'80; b.144
'82; b.31
Pers.-Hell. pit
loc.740= loc.802
24.71/24.49

LATE BRONZE-
EARLY IRON I
TRANSITION

'80; b. 248

25.17/24.66

'80; b. 166,
179,185,186, 194
25.00/24.75

'80; b. 115

'82; b.56,63, 69
MBII-Iron I
24.65

'80; b. 234,288

24.61

FIGURE 2.25.A Left section of the matrix of Square L/7

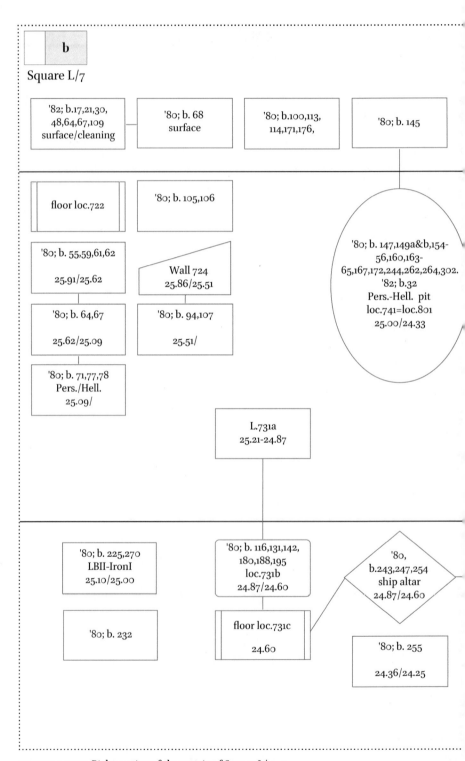

FIGURE 2.25.B Right section of the matrix of Square L/7

THE STRATIGRAPHY AND ARCHITECTURE OF AREA H

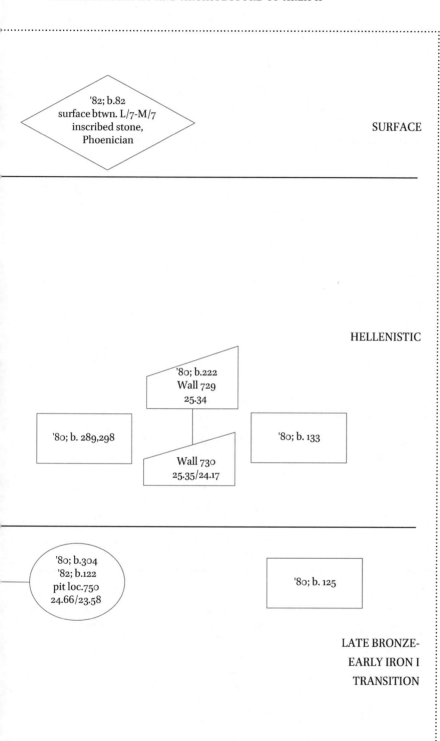

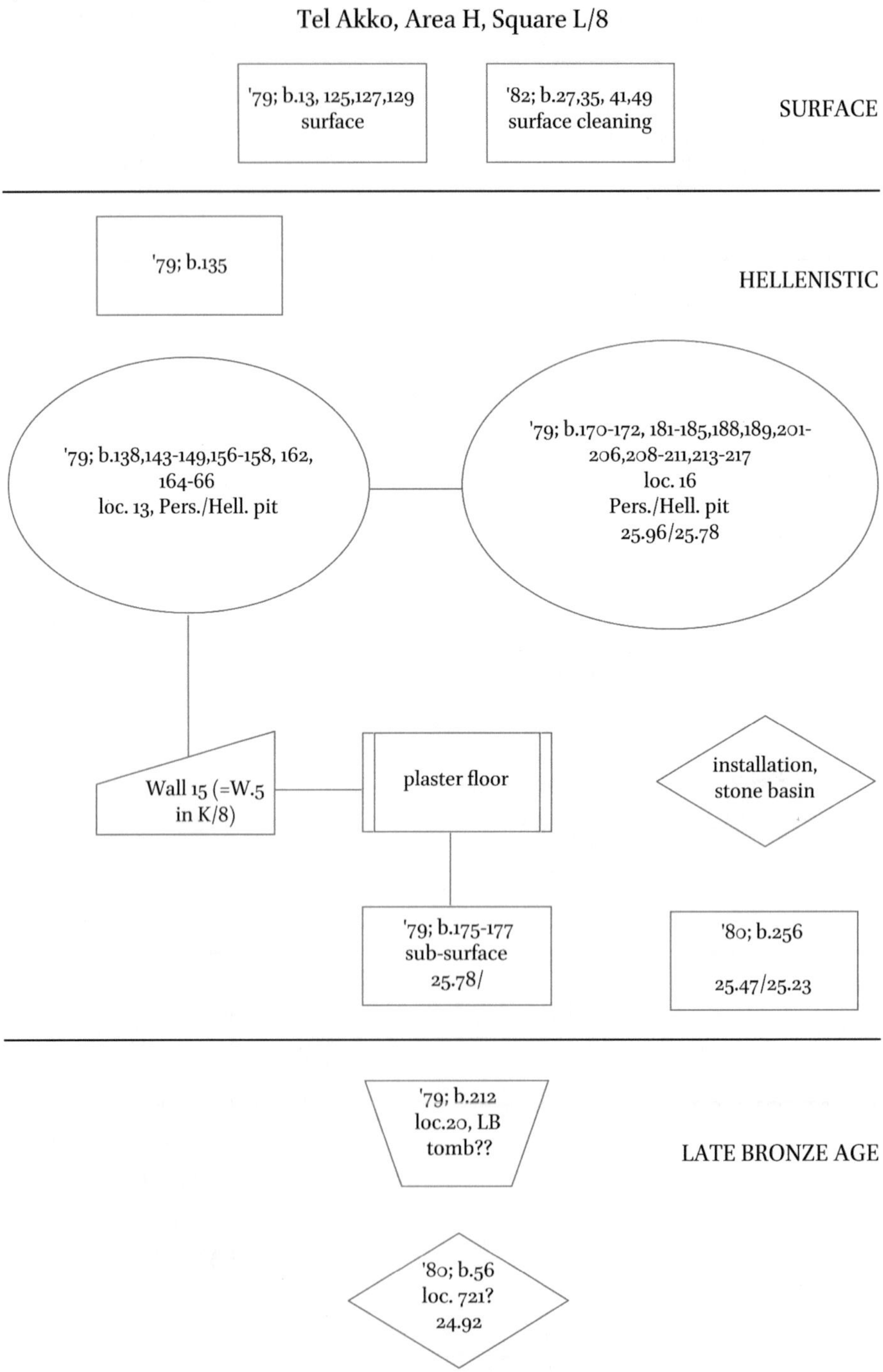

Tel Akko, Area H, Square L/8

'79; b.13, 125,127,129
surface

'82; b.27,35, 41,49
surface cleaning

SURFACE

'79; b.135

HELLENISTIC

'79; b.138,143-149,156-158, 162,
164-66
loc. 13, Pers./Hell. pit

'79; b.170-172, 181-185,188,189,201-
206,208-211,213-217
loc. 16
Pers./Hell. pit
25.96/25.78

Wall 15 (=W.5
in K/8)

plaster floor

installation,
stone basin

'79; b.175-177
sub-surface
25.78/

'80; b.256

25.47/25.23

'79; b.212
loc.20, LB
tomb??

LATE BRONZE AGE

'80; b.56
loc. 721?
24.92

FIGURE 2.26 Matrix of Square L/8

THE STRATIGRAPHY AND ARCHITECTURE OF AREA H

Division key for Square L/9 matrix

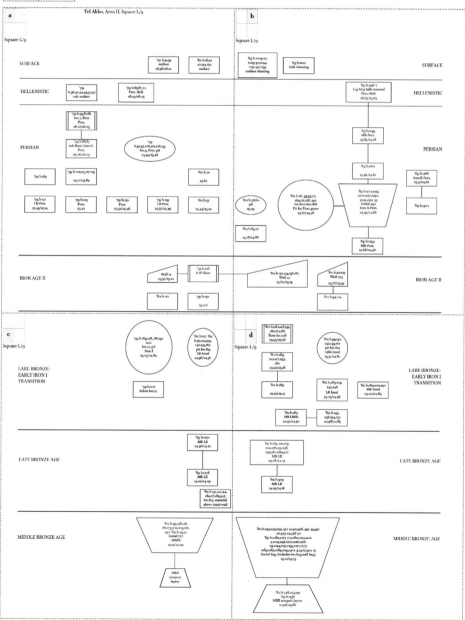

FIGURE 2.27   Division key for the matrix of Square L/9

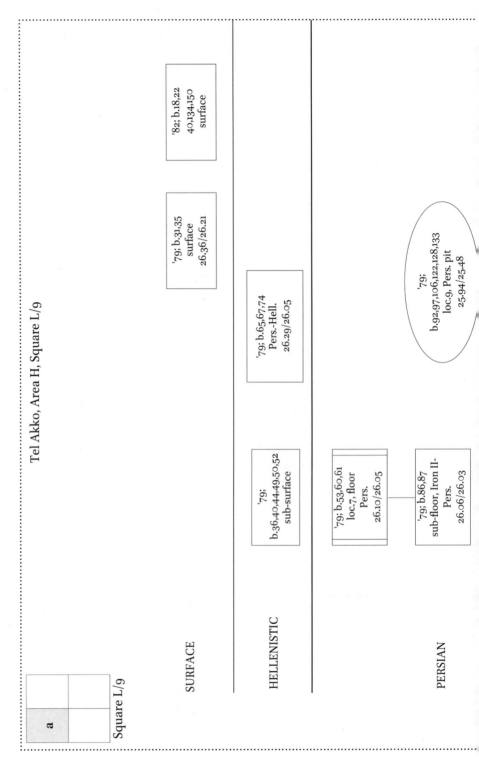

FIGURE 2.27.A Upper left section of the matrix of Square L/9

THE STRATIGRAPHY AND ARCHITECTURE OF AREA H

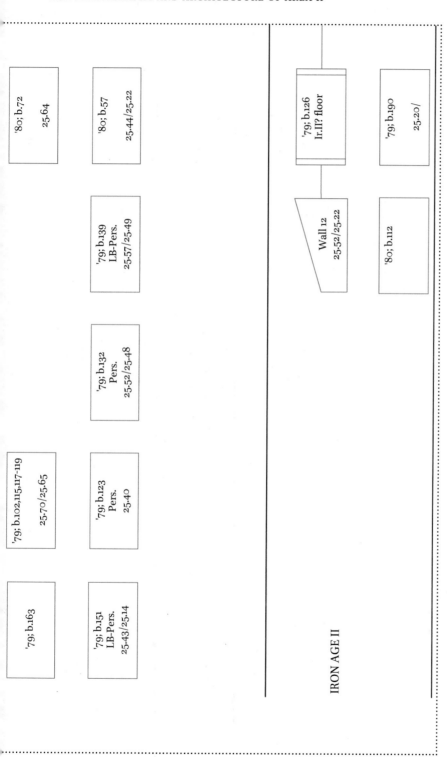

IRON AGE II

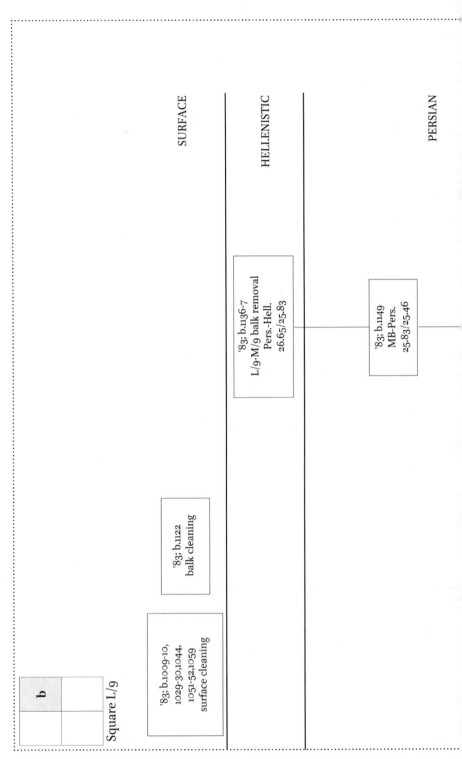

FIGURE 2.27.B Upper right section of the matrix of Square L/9

THE STRATIGRAPHY AND ARCHITECTURE OF AREA H

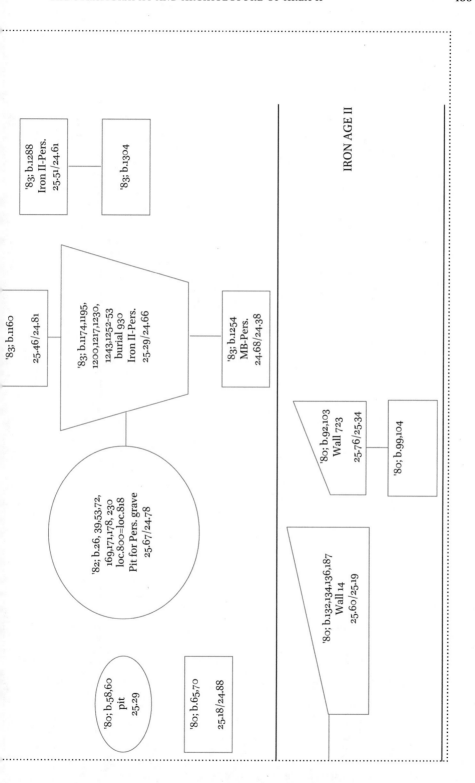

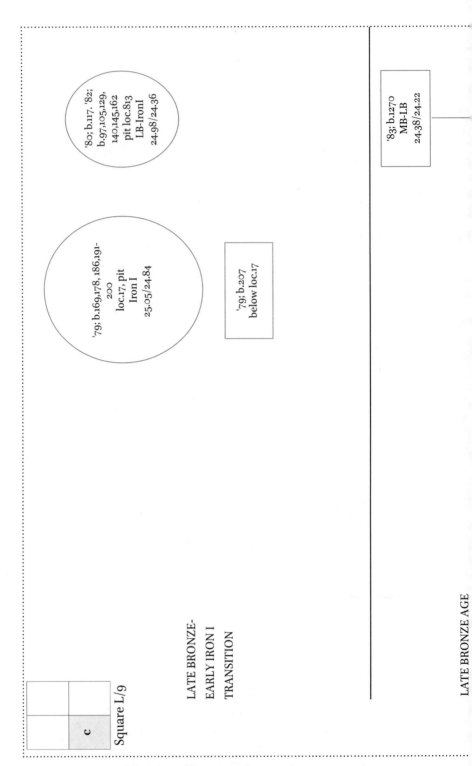

FIGURE 2.27.C Lower left section of the matrix of Square L/9

THE STRATIGRAPHY AND ARCHITECTURE OF AREA H 137

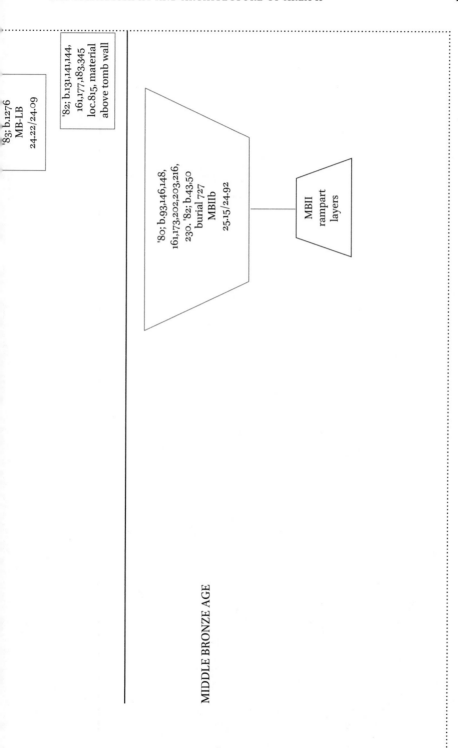

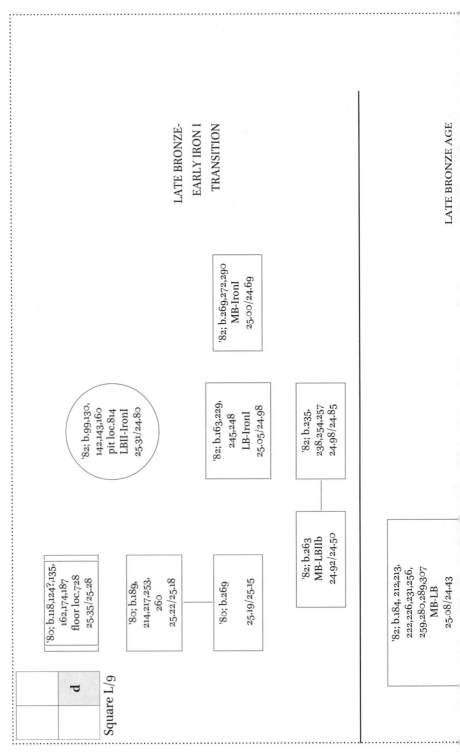

FIGURE 2.27.D Lower right section of the matrix of Square L/9

THE STRATIGRAPHY AND ARCHITECTURE OF AREA H

MIDDLE BRONZE AGE

'82; b.309
MB-LB
24.25/24.18

'82; b.239,255,299, 310-12,321,326, 332-33,337-40,343-44,348-50
'83; b.1062,1072-74,1082,1094,1101-4,1109,1196,1201,1218,1228-29,1244,1251,1255,1271,1277,1283,1285,1289,1293,1302-3,1307,1314-15
burial 829 (includes loc.823,wall 824)
25-21/23-75

'82; b.246,273,291
'83; b.1336
MBII rampart layers
24.96/23.68

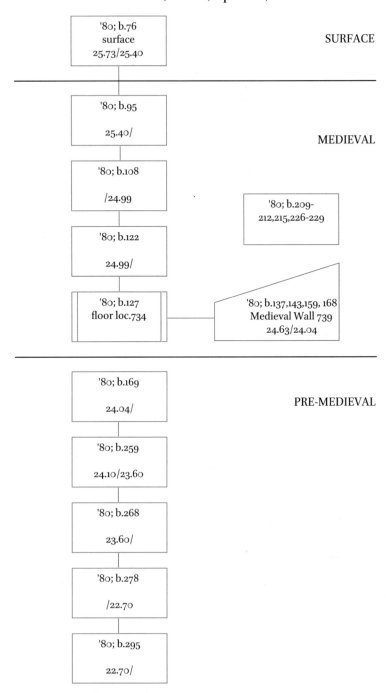

FIGURE 2.28   Matrix of Square M/1

THE STRATIGRAPHY AND ARCHITECTURE OF AREA H

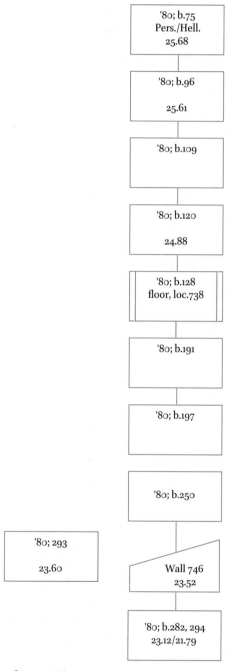

FIGURE 2.29   Matrix of Square M/2

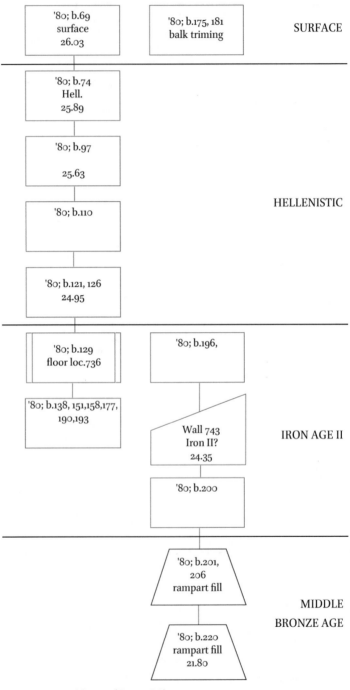

FIGURE 2.30   Matrix of Square M/3

THE STRATIGRAPHY AND ARCHITECTURE OF AREA H

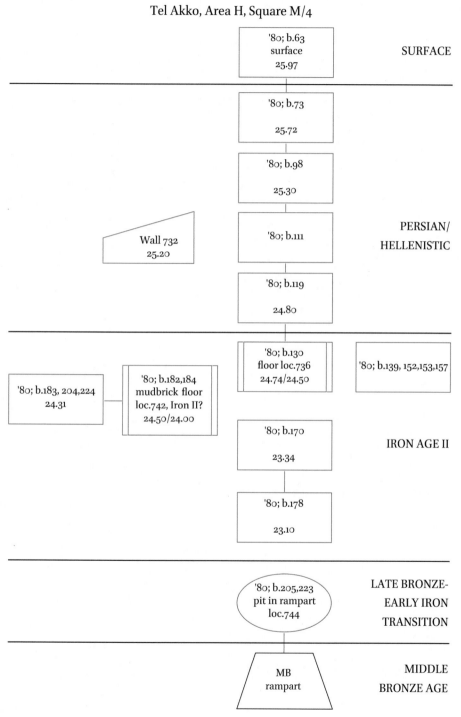

FIGURE 2.31   Matrix of Square M/4

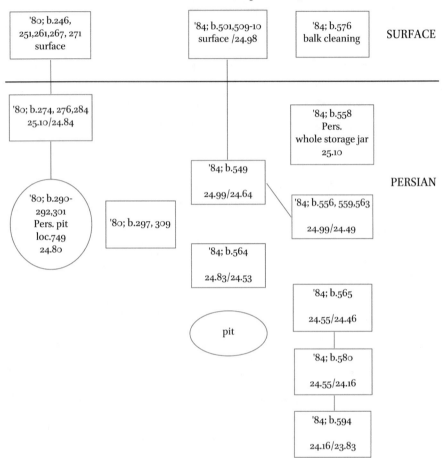

FIGURE 2.32   Matrix of Square M/5

THE STRATIGRAPHY AND ARCHITECTURE OF AREA H

Division key for Square M/7 matrix

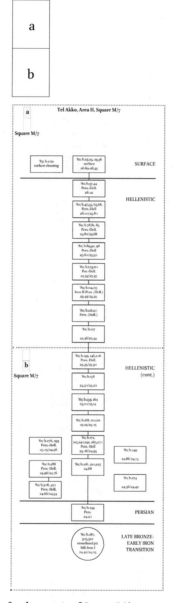

FIGURE 2.33   Division key for the matrix of Square M/7

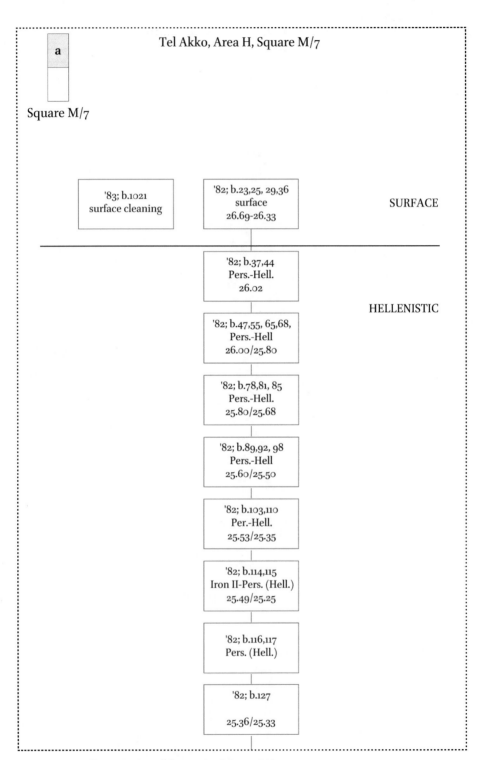

FIGURE 2.33.A Upper section of the matrix of Square M/7

THE STRATIGRAPHY AND ARCHITECTURE OF AREA H

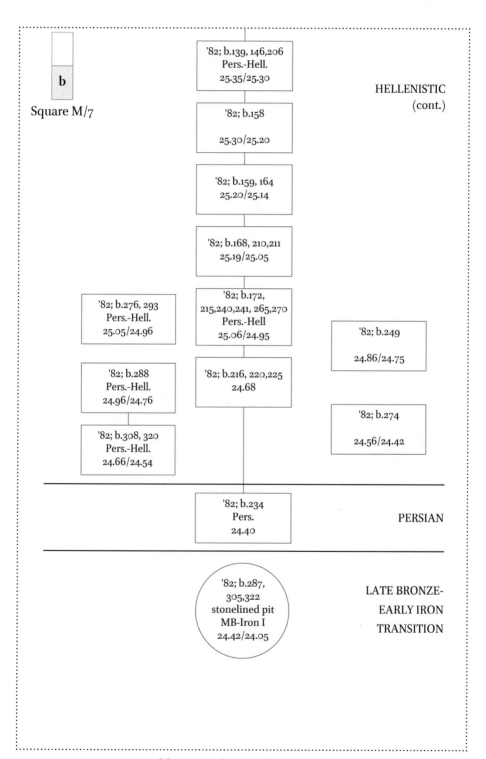

FIGURE 2.33.B Lower section of the matrix of Square M/7

THE STRATIGRAPHY AND ARCHITECTURE OF AREA H 149

Division key for Square M/9 matrix

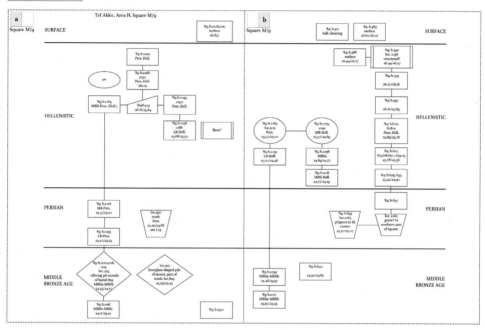

FIGURE 2.34   Division key for the matrix of Square M/9

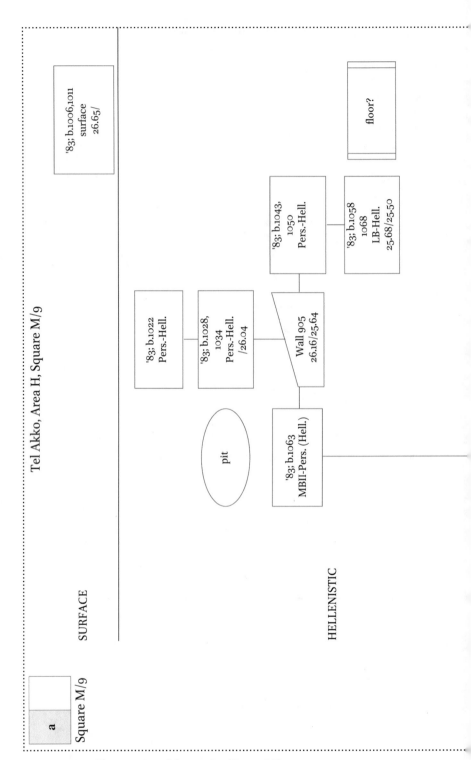

FIGURE 2.34.A Upper section of the matrix of Square M/9

THE STRATIGRAPHY AND ARCHITECTURE OF AREA H

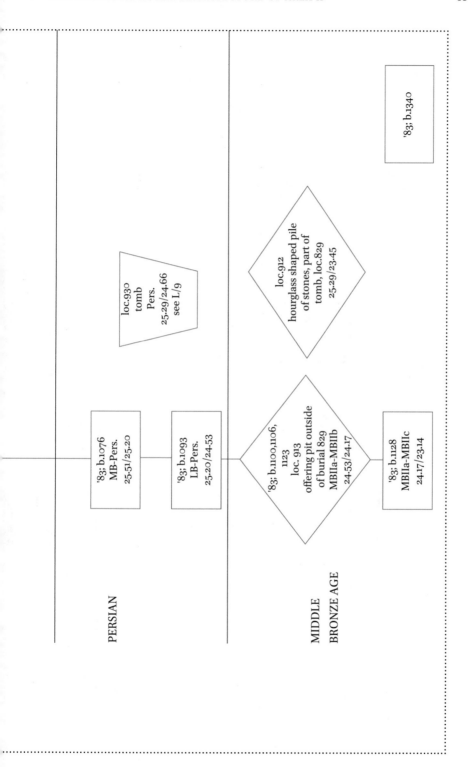

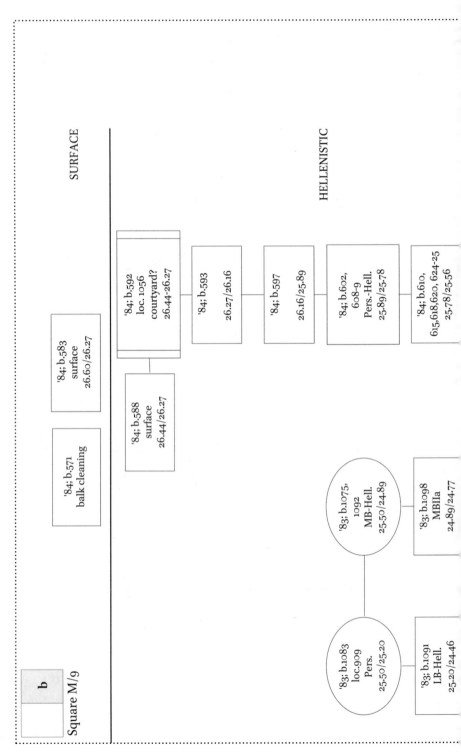

FIGURE 2.34.B Lower section of the matrix of Square M/9

THE STRATIGRAPHY AND ARCHITECTURE OF AREA H 153

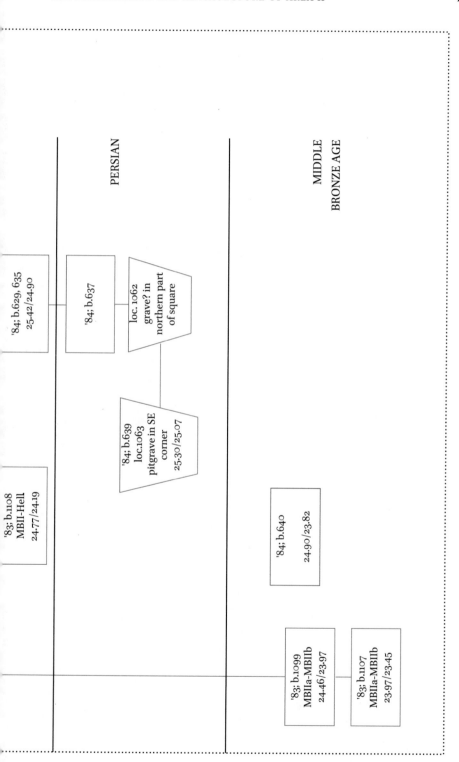

THE STRATIGRAPHY AND ARCHITECTURE OF AREA H

Division key for Square M/10 matrix

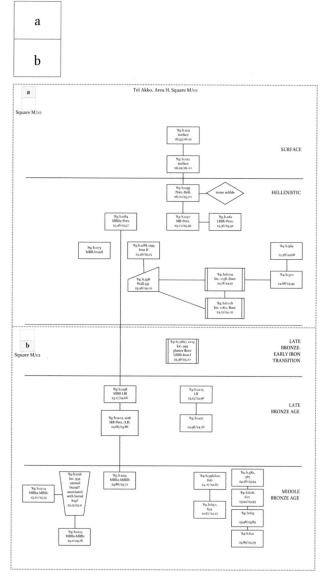

FIGURE 2.35   Division key for the matrix of Square M/10

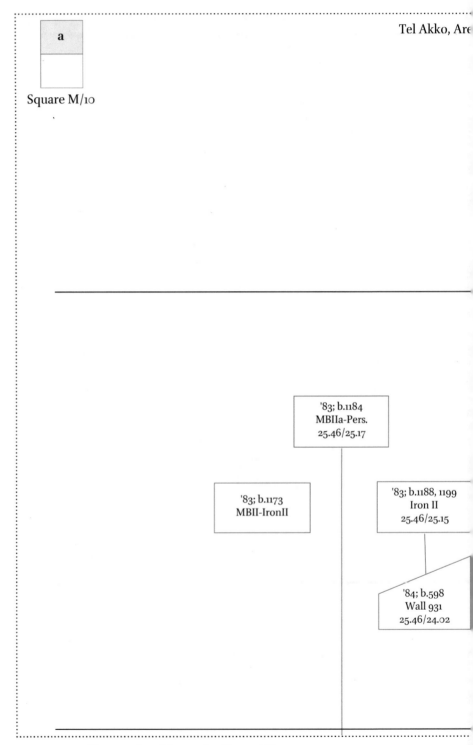

FIGURE 2.35.A Upper section of the matrix of Square M/10

THE STRATIGRAPHY AND ARCHITECTURE OF AREA H

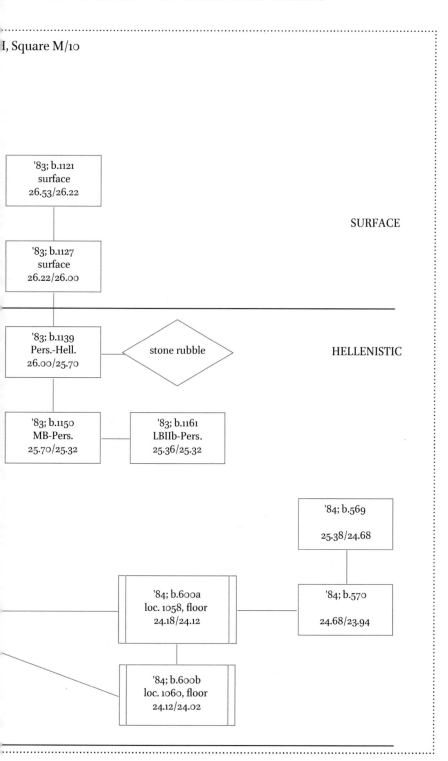

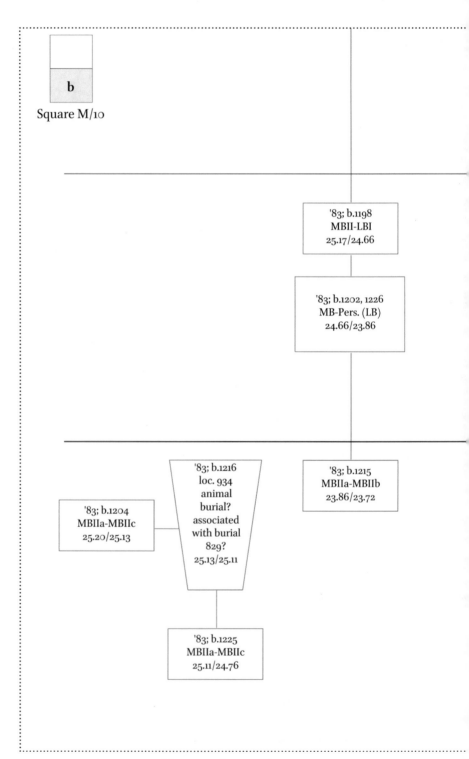

FIGURE 2.35.B Lower section of the matrix of Square M/10

THE STRATIGRAPHY AND ARCHITECTURE OF AREA H

LATE BRONZE–
EARLY IRON
TRANSITION

LATE
BRONZE AGE

MIDDLE
BRONZE AGE

Tel Akko, Area H, Square N/1

'82; b.28,34, 45,52
surface

FIGURE 2.36
Matrix of Square N/1

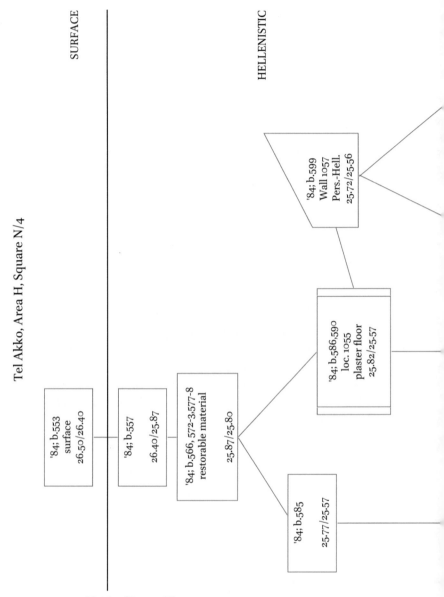

FIGURE 2.37   Matrix of Square N/4

THE STRATIGRAPHY AND ARCHITECTURE OF AREA H 163

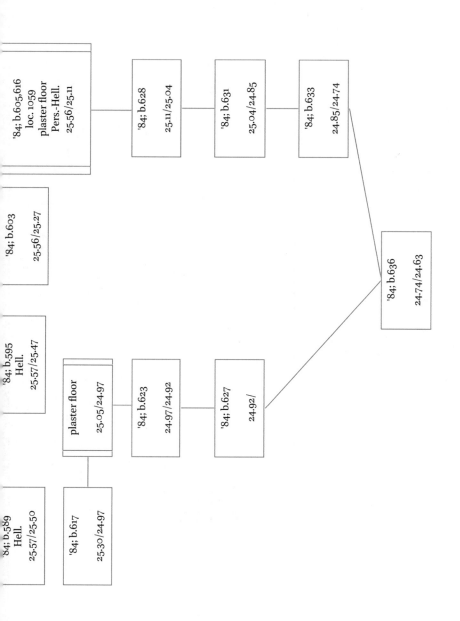

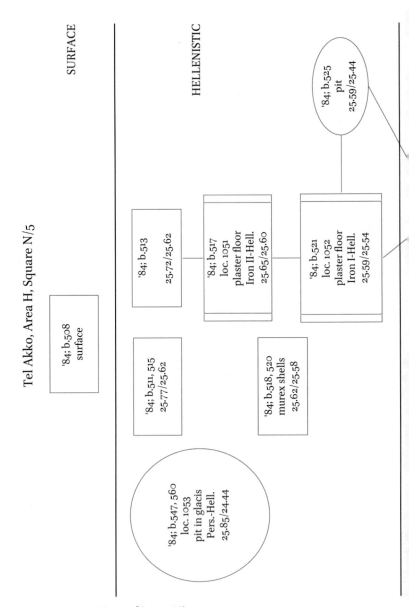

FIGURE 2.38   Matrix of Square N/5

THE STRATIGRAPHY AND ARCHITECTURE OF AREA H

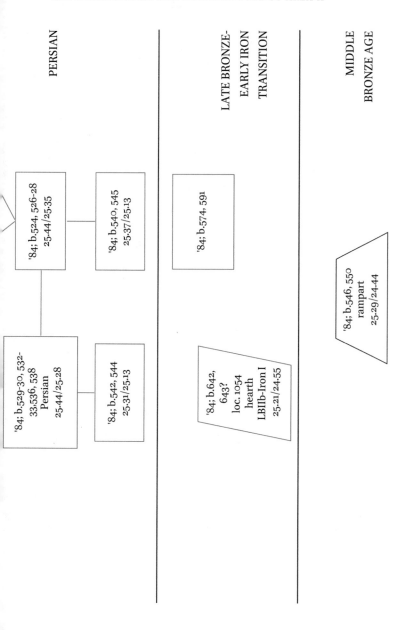

THE STRATIGRAPHY AND ARCHITECTURE OF AREA H

Division key for Square O/1 matrix

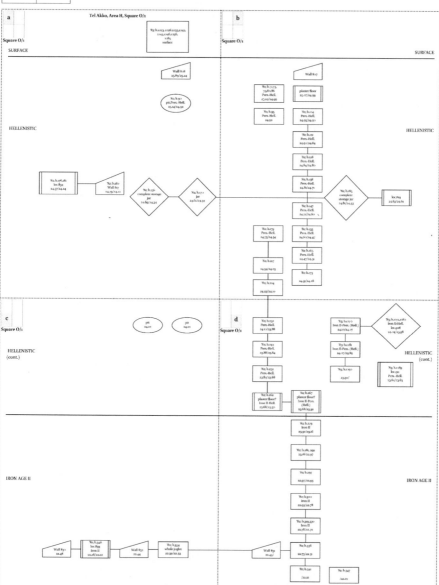

FIGURE 2.39   Division key for the matrix of Square O/1

168 BRODY, ET AL.

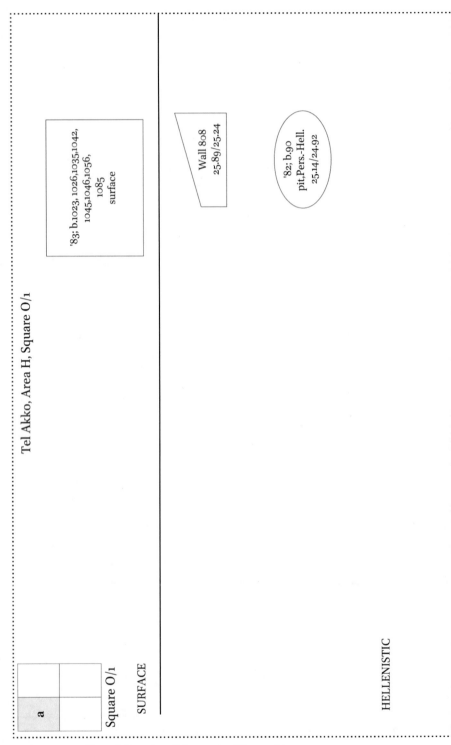

FIGURE 2.39.A Upper left section of the matrix of Square O/1

THE STRATIGRAPHY AND ARCHITECTURE OF AREA H 169

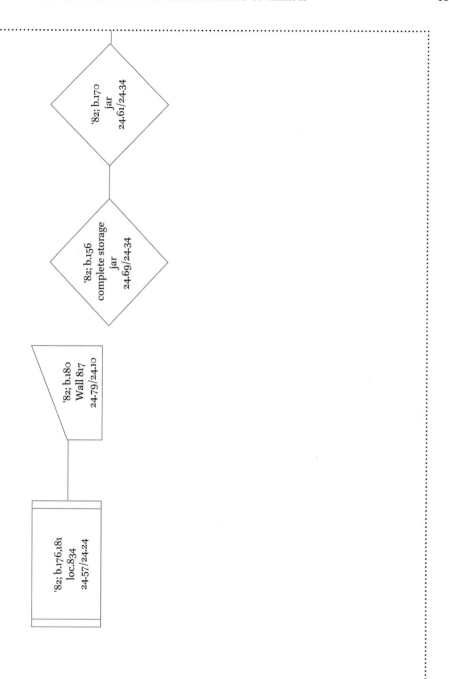

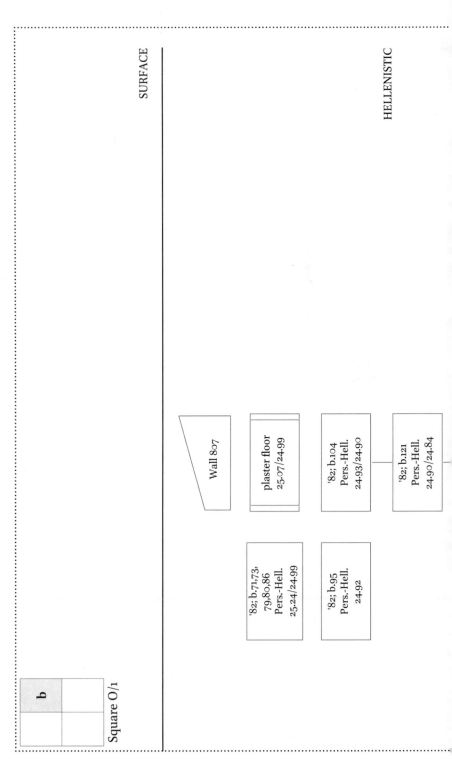

FIGURE 2.39.B Upper right section of the matrix of Square O/1

THE STRATIGRAPHY AND ARCHITECTURE OF AREA H

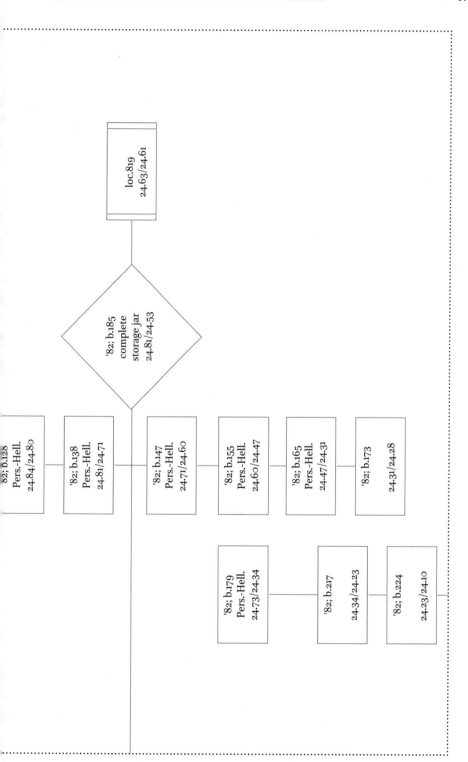

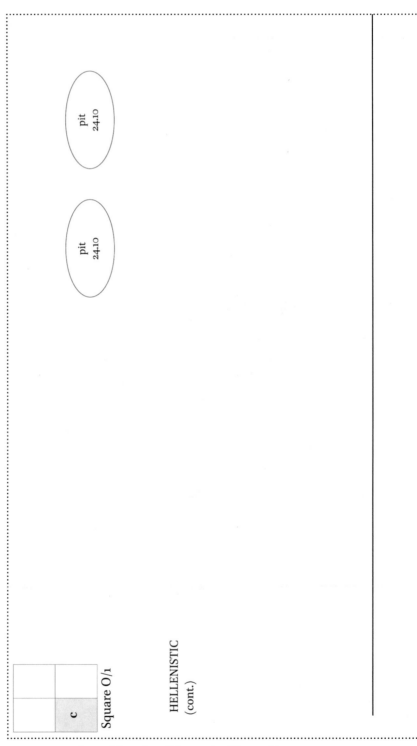

FIGURE 2.39.C Lower left section of the matrix of Square O/1

THE STRATIGRAPHY AND ARCHITECTURE OF AREA H 173

'82; b.354
whole juglet
22.39/22.33

Wall 832
22.44

'82; b.346
loc.833
Iron II
22.28/22.22

Wall 830
22.48

IRON AGE II

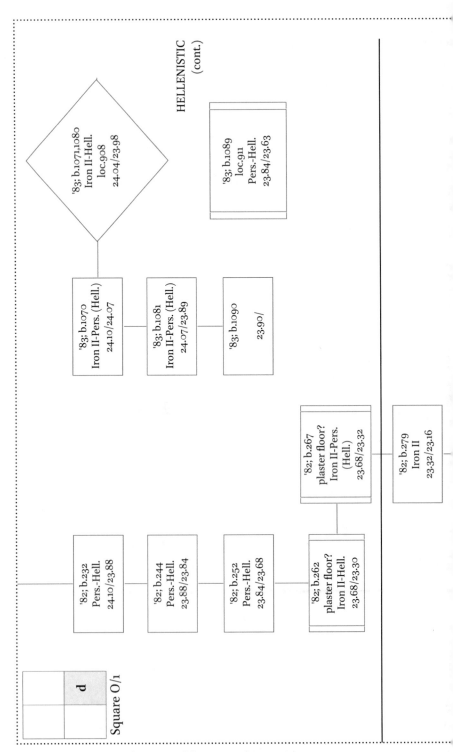

FIGURE 2.39.D Lower right section of the matrix of Square O/1

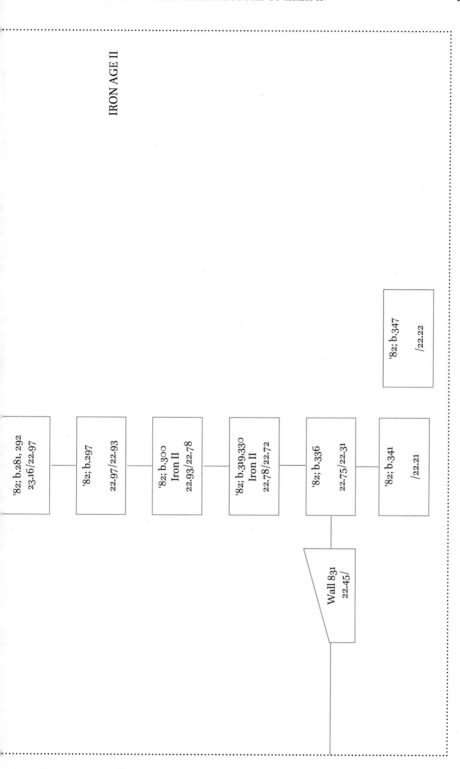

THE STRATIGRAPHY AND ARCHITECTURE OF AREA H 177

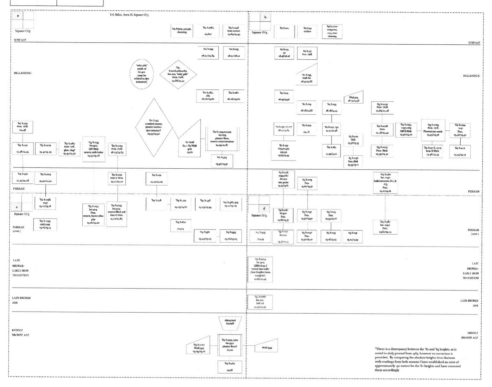

FIGURE 2.40   Division key for the matrix of Square O/5

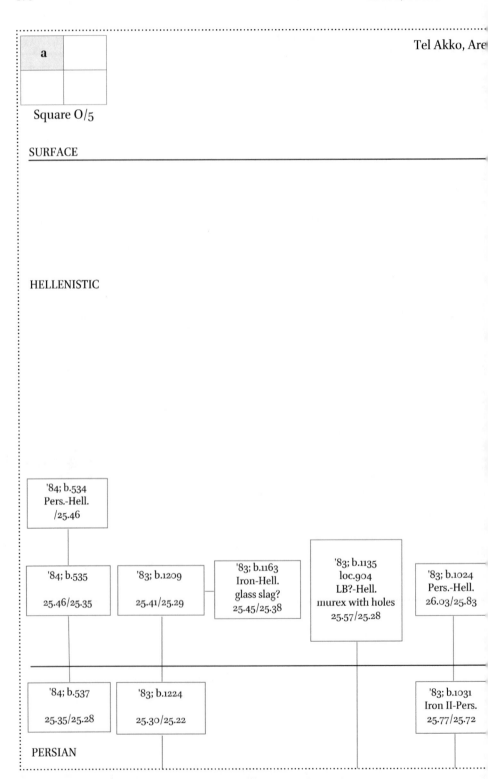

FIGURE 2.40.A Upper left section of the matrix of Square O/5

THE STRATIGRAPHY AND ARCHITECTURE OF AREA H

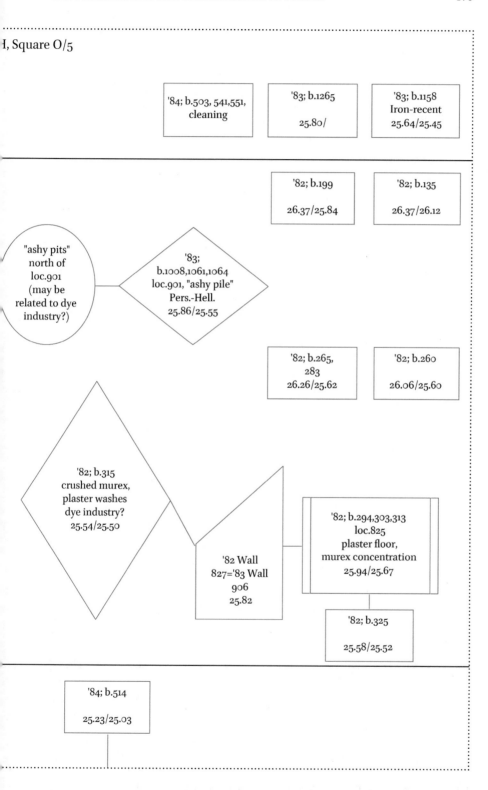

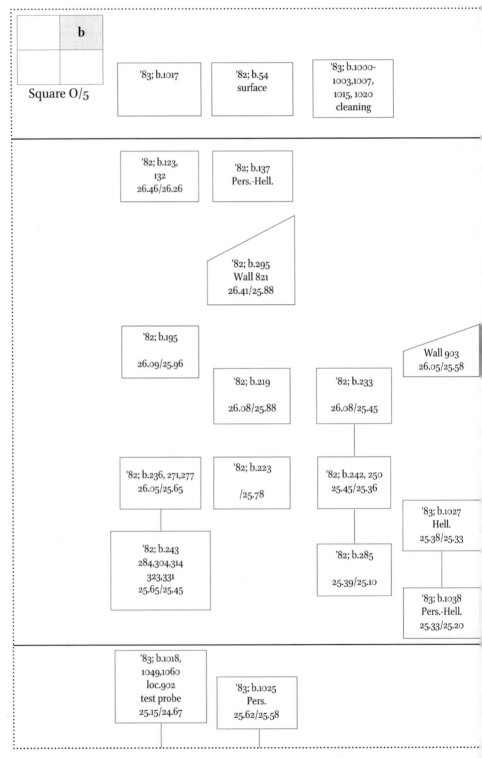

FIGURE 2.40.B Upper right section of the matrix of Square O/5

THE STRATIGRAPHY AND ARCHITECTURE OF AREA H

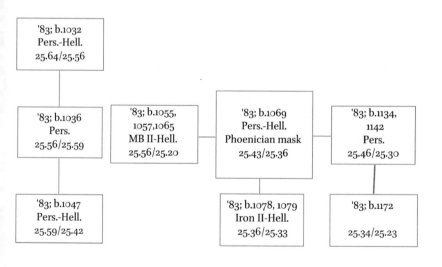

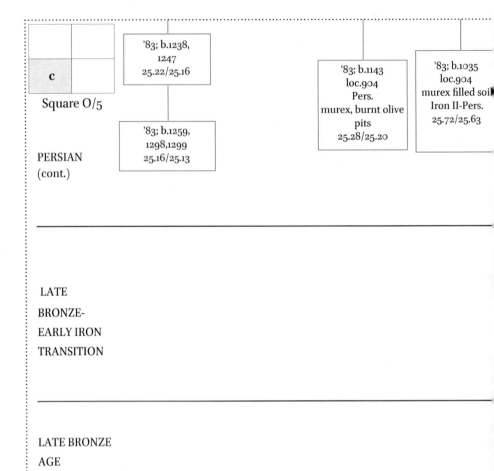

FIGURE 2.40.C Lower left section of the matrix of Square O/5

THE STRATIGRAPHY AND ARCHITECTURE OF AREA H 183

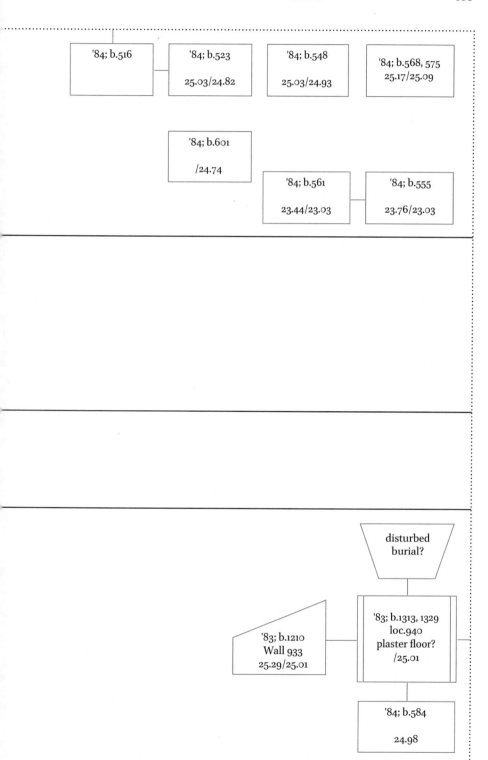

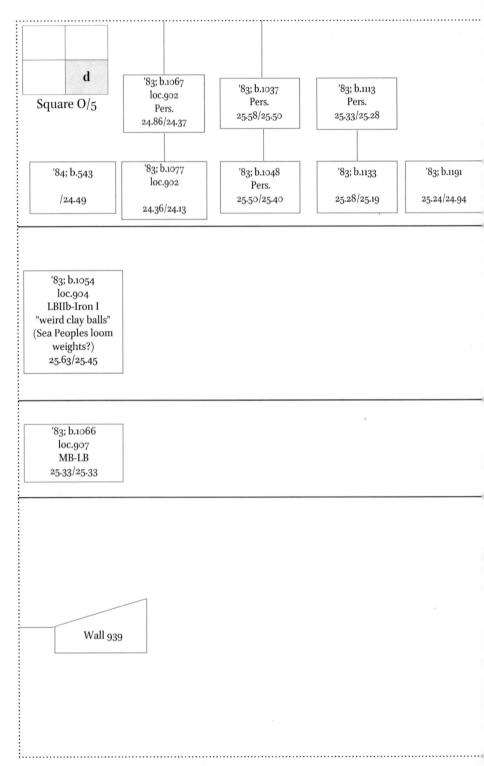

FIGURE 2.40.D Lower right section of the matrix of Square O/5

THE STRATIGRAPHY AND ARCHITECTURE OF AREA H 185

'84; b.567
loc. 1050
Pers.
24.81/24.75

PERSIAN
(cont.)

LATE
BRONZE-
EARLY IRON
TRANSITION

LATE BRONZE
AGE

MIDDLE
BRONZE AGE

*There is a discrepancy between the '82 and '83 heights, as is noted in daily journal from 1983, however no correction is provided. By comparing the absolute heights from features with readings from both seasons I have established an error of approximately .92 meters for the '82 heights and have corrected them accordingly

THE STRATIGRAPHY AND ARCHITECTURE OF AREA H 187

Division key for Square P/4 Matrix

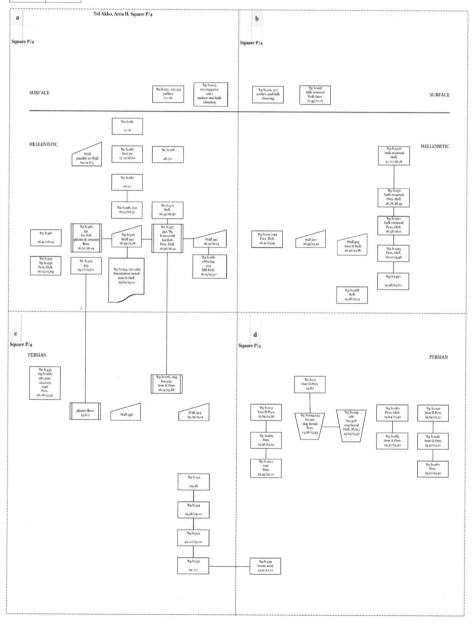

FIGURE 2.41   Division key for the matrix of Square P/4

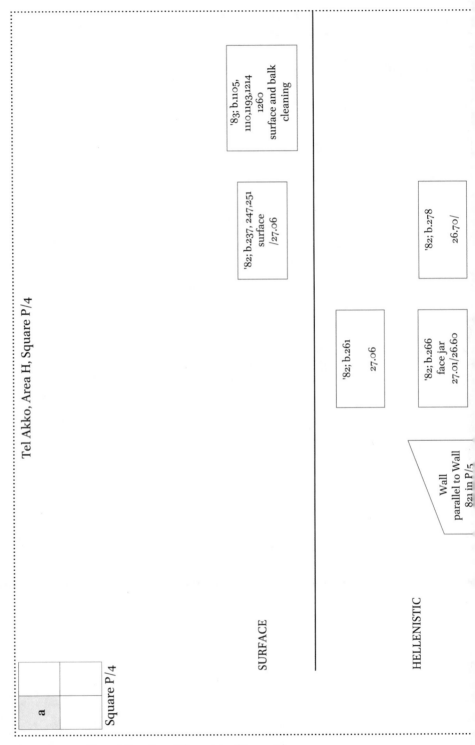

FIGURE 2.41.A Upper left section of the matrix of Square P/4

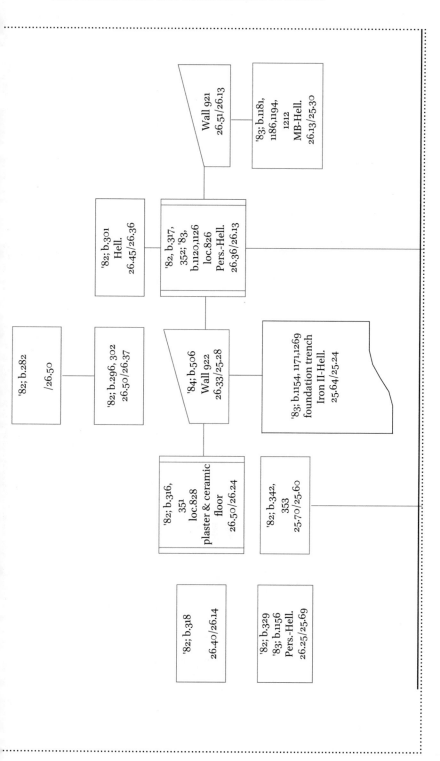

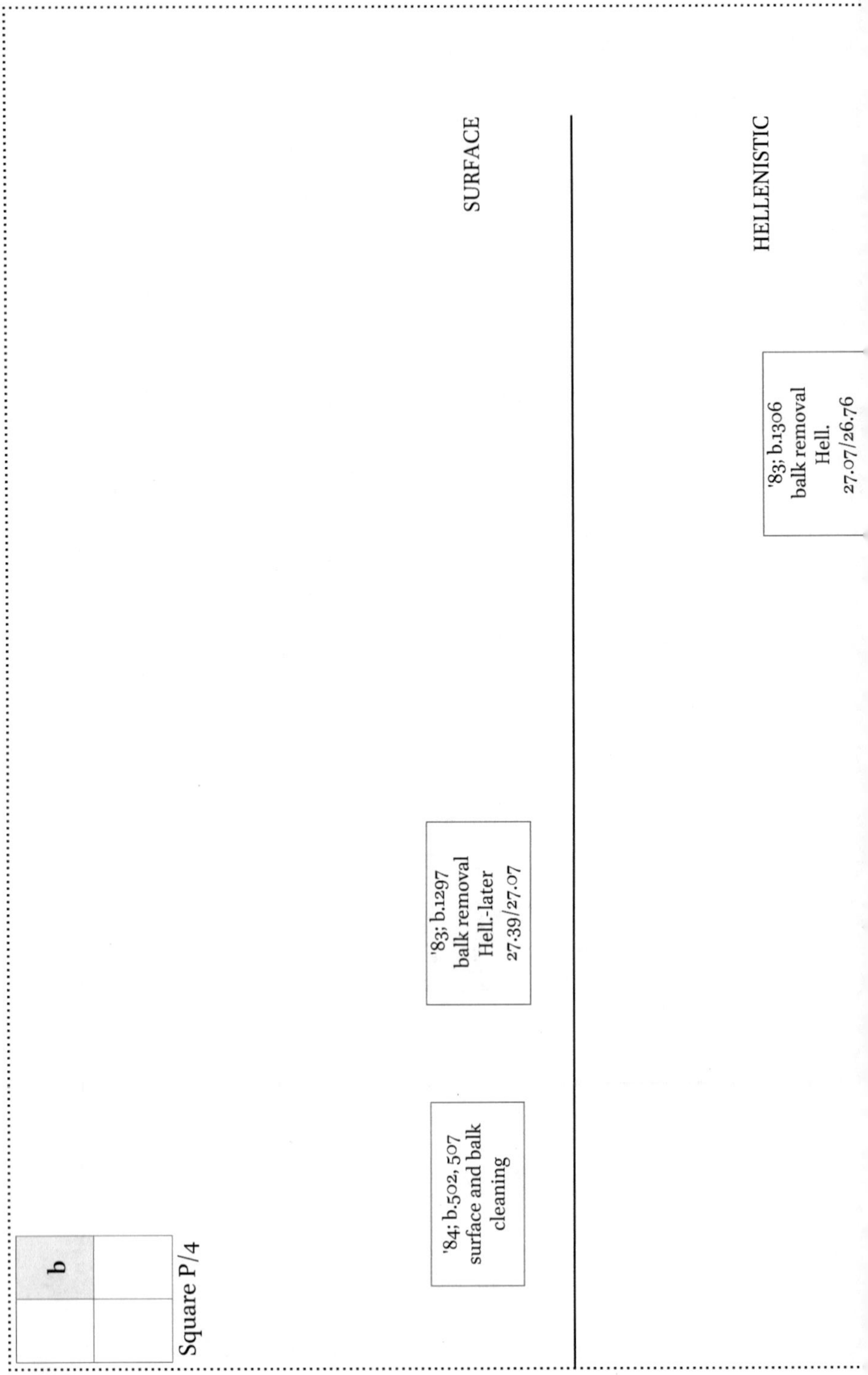

SURFACE

HELLENISTIC

'83; b.1306
balk removal
Hell.
27.07/26.76

'83; b.1297
balk removal
Hell.-later
27.39/27.07

'84; b.502, 507
surface and balk
cleaning

Square P/4

FIGURE 2.41.B   Upper right section of the matrix of Square P/4

THE STRATIGRAPHY AND ARCHITECTURE OF AREA H 191

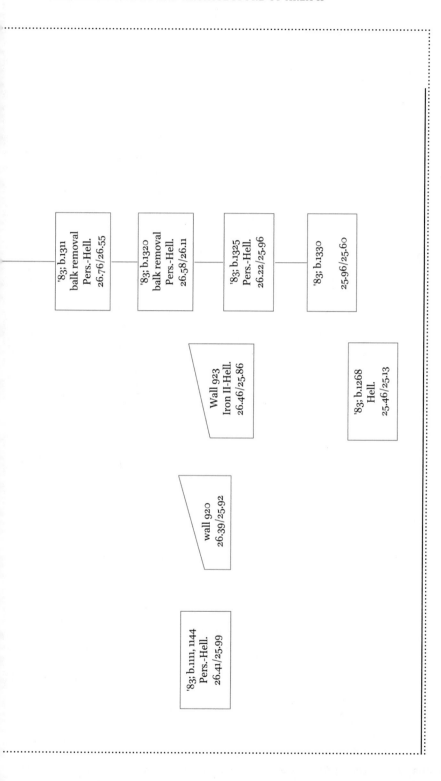

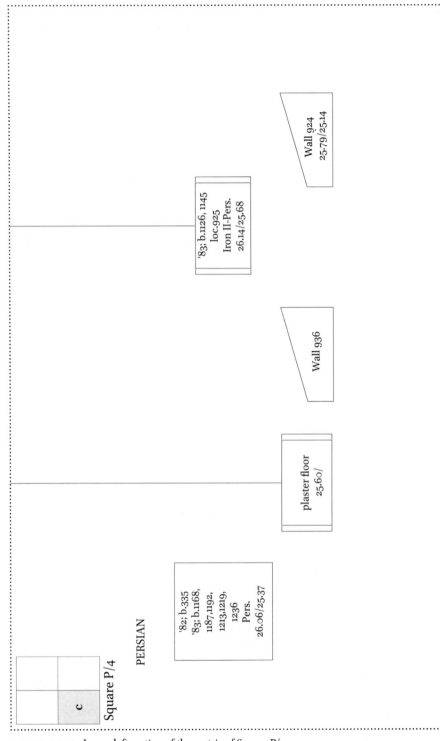

FIGURE 2.41.C Lower left section of the matrix of Square P/4

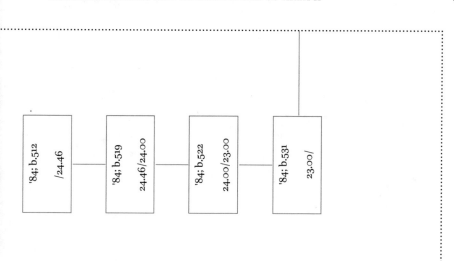

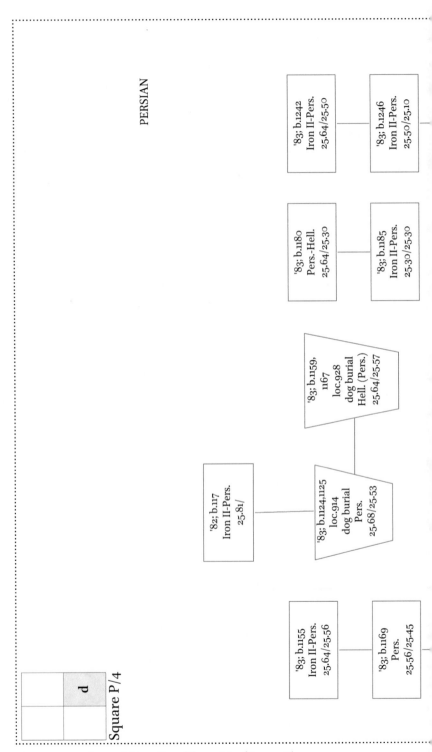

FIGURE 2.41.D   Lower right section of the matrix of Square P/4

'83; b.1280
Pers.
25.50/23.40

'83; b.1220,
1237
Pers.
25.45/25.00

'84; b.539
burnt seed
23.12/22.72

Division key for Square P/5 Matrix

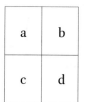

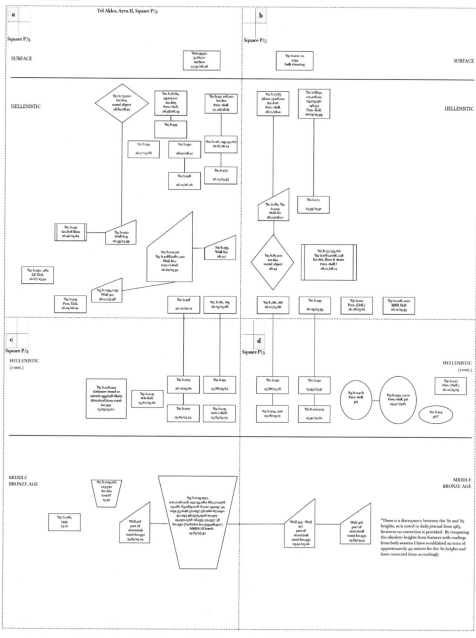

FIGURE 2.42   Division key for the matrix of Square P/5

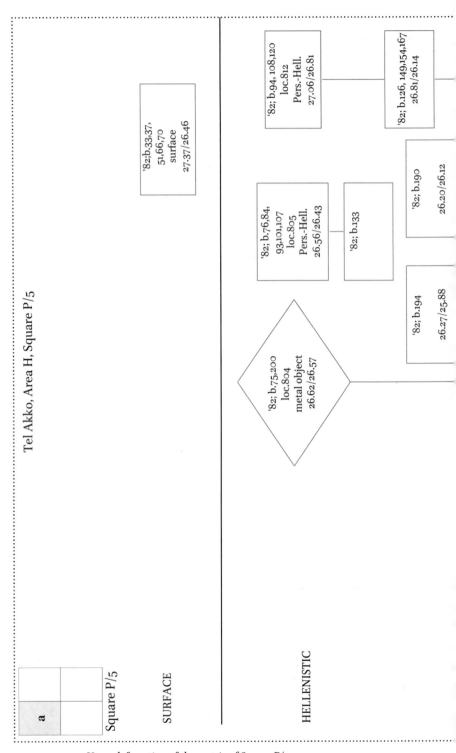

FIGURE 2.42.A Upper left section of the matrix of Square P/5

THE STRATIGRAPHY AND ARCHITECTURE OF AREA H

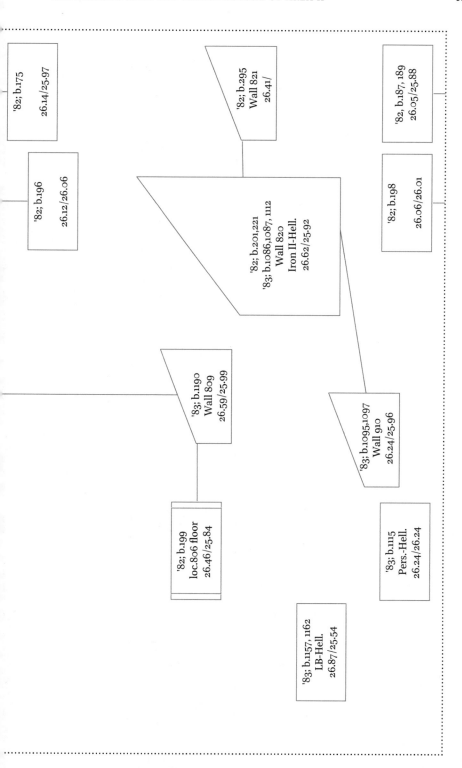

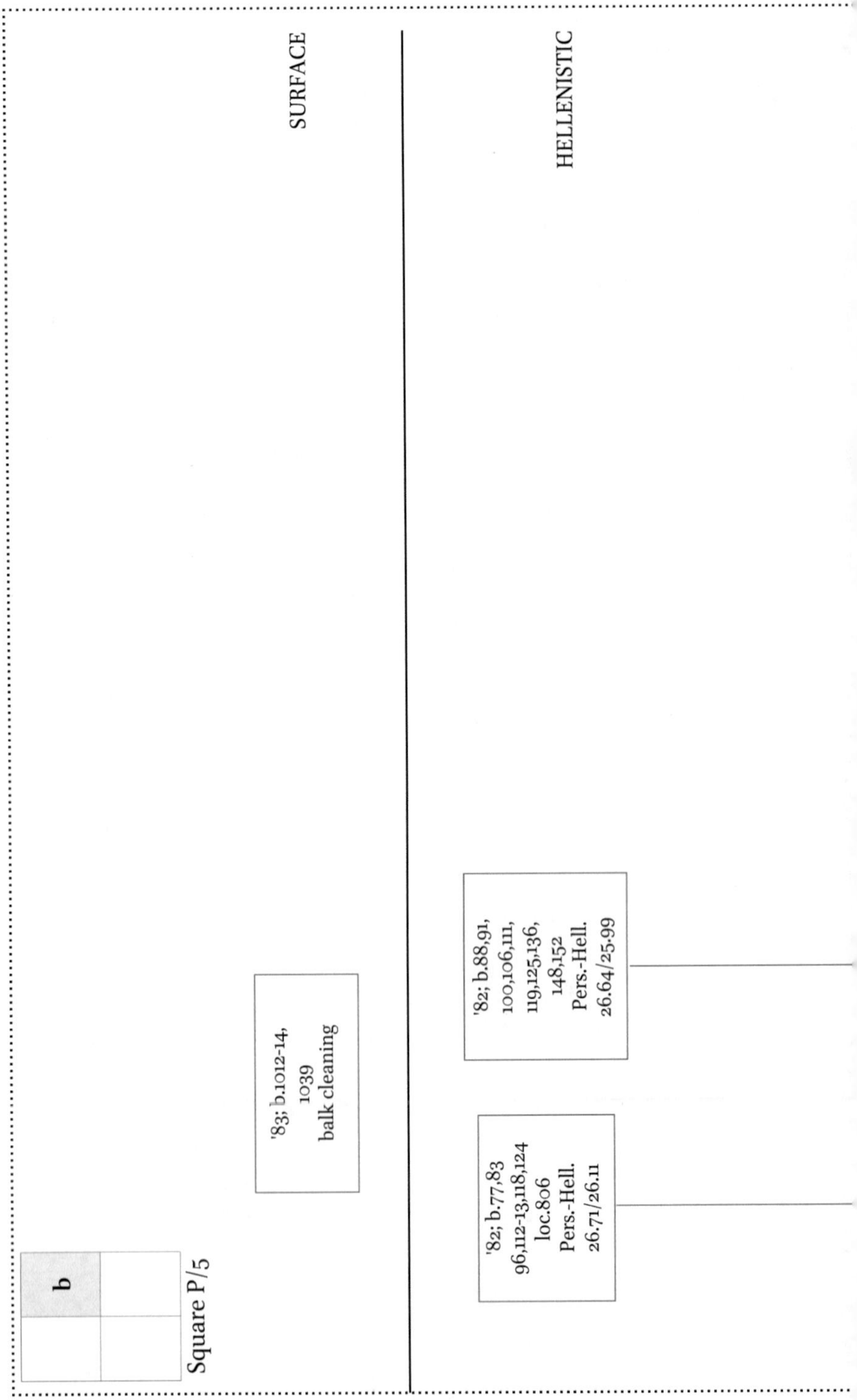

SURFACE | HELLENISTIC

'83; b.1012-14,
1039
balk cleaning

'82; b.88,91,
100,106,111,
119,125,136,
148,152
Pers.-Hell.
26.64/25.99

'82; b.77,83
96,112-13,118,124
loc.806
Pers.-Hell.
26.71/26.11

Square P/5

FIGURE 2.42.B Upper right section of the matrix of Square P/5

THE STRATIGRAPHY AND ARCHITECTURE OF AREA H

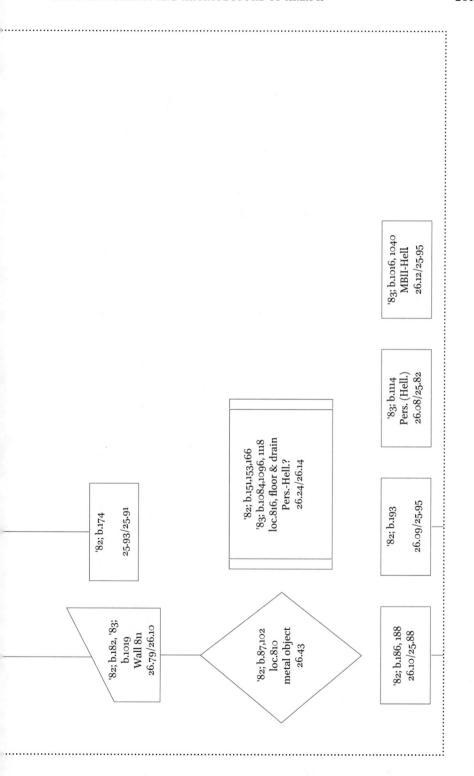

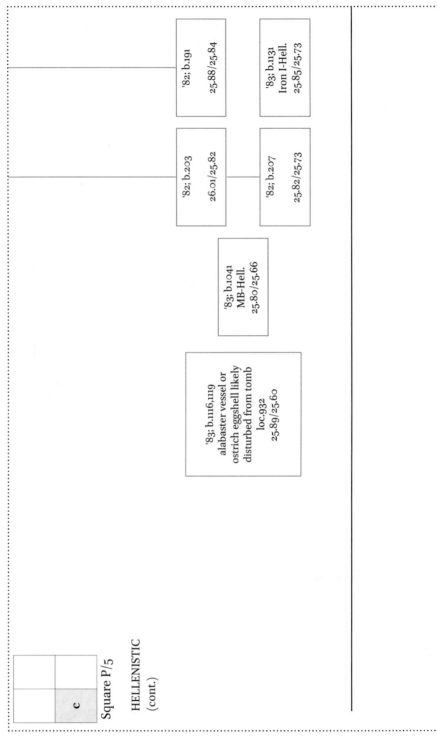

FIGURE 2.42.C Lower left section of the matrix of Square P/5

THE STRATIGRAPHY AND ARCHITECTURE OF AREA H

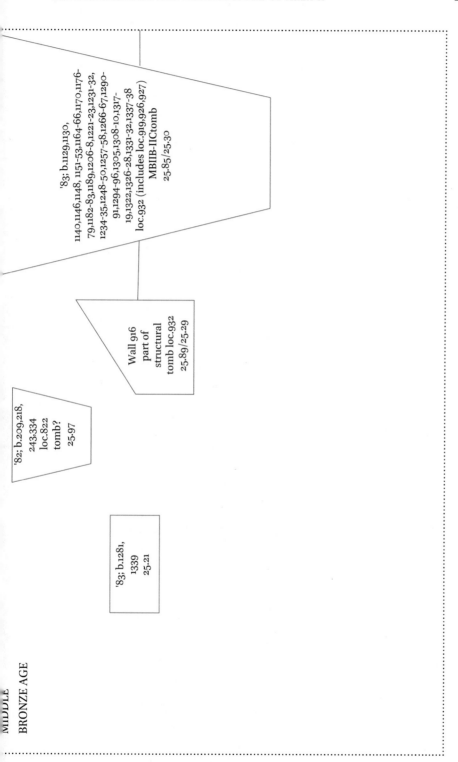

MIDDLE
BRONZE AGE

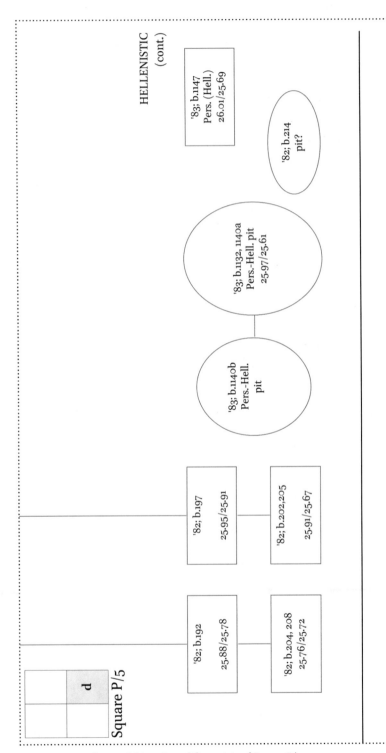

FIGURE 2.42.D Lower right section of the matrix of Square P/5

THE STRATIGRAPHY AND ARCHITECTURE OF AREA H

MIDDLE BRONZE AGE

*There is a discrepancy between the '82 and '83 heights, as is noted in daily journal from 1983, however no correction is provided. By comparing the absolute heights from features with readings from both seasons I have established an error of approximately .92 meters for the '82 heights and have corrected them accordingly

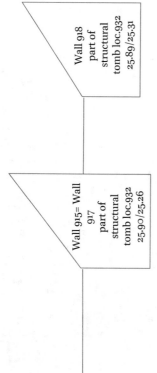

Wall 918 part of structural tomb loc.932
25.89/25.31

Wall 915= Wall 917 part of structural tomb loc.932
25.90/25.26

PHOTO 2.1   Stratum 7, Square P/4, north balk: sloping layers of MBIIA rampart; view from south
PHOTO: M. ARTZY

PHOTO 2.2   Stratum 7, Square P/4, east balk: sloping layer of MBIIA rampart; view from west
PHOTO: M. ARTZY

THE STRATIGRAPHY AND ARCHITECTURE OF AREA H

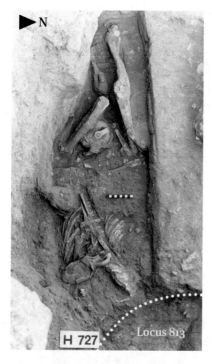

PHOTO 2.3
Stratum 6, Square L/7, tomb Locus 727, view from the east
PHOTO: G. GRAINGER

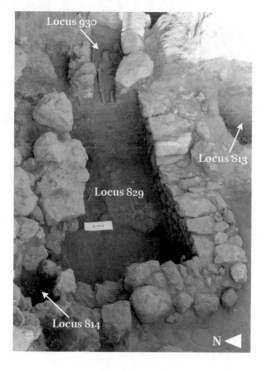

PHOTO 2.4
Stratum 6, Square L/9, tomb Locus 829; view from the west
PHOTO: M. ARTZY

PHOTO 2.5   Stratum 6, Square M/10, animal burial Locus 934
            PHOTO: M. ARTZY

PHOTO 2.6   Stratum 6, Square O/5, tomb Locus 932, Skeletons A and B, granite headrests;
            view from west
            PHOTO: M. ARTZY

PHOTO 2.7   Stratum 5, Square L/7, stone lined pit Locus 750; view from west
PHOTO: M. ARTZY

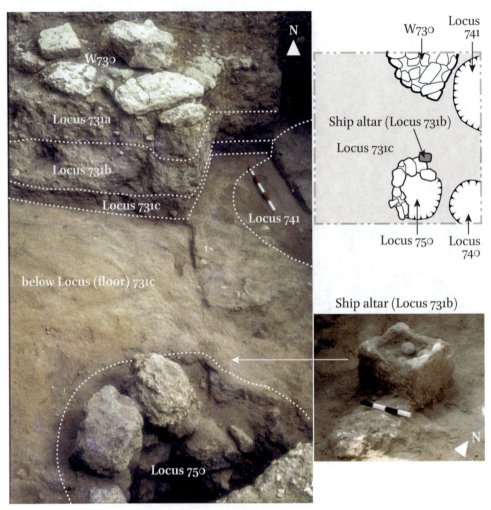

PHOTO 2.8   Stratum 5, Square L/7 Locus 731 a, b, and c (floor) and inserts with '*in situ*' ship altar and its surrounding; views from south and south-west
PHOTOS: M. ARTZY, NAVA BEN SHIMON

THE STRATIGRAPHY AND ARCHITECTURE OF AREA H

PHOTO 2.9   Stratum 5, Square L/9, pit Locus 17, broken and complete ceramic vessels; view from east
PHOTO: M. ARTZY

PHOTO 2.10   Stratum 5, Square L/9, pit Locus 17, krater and two *amphoriscoi* below broken storage jars; view from east north-east
PHOTO: M. ARTZY

PHOTO 2.11   Stratum 3, Square L/9–L/10, grave Locus 930; view from north
PHOTO: M. ARTZY

THE STRATIGRAPHY AND ARCHITECTURE OF AREA H 213

PHOTO 2.12   Strata 3 and 2, Square P/4 Walls 936, 922 (Stratum 3) and 923 (Stratum 2); view from south
PHOTO: M. ARTZY

PHOTO 2.13   Stratum 3, Square P/4, dog burial Locus 928; view from north
PHOTO: M. ARTZY

PHOTO 2.14   Stratum 3, Square P/4, dog burial Locus 914; view from south
PHOTO: M. ARTZY

PHOTO 2.15   Stratum 2, Square O/5, Walls 923 and 921 and floor Locus 925; view from south
PHOTO: M. ARTZY

PHOTO 2.16   Strata 1 and 5, Square L/9, Wall 14 above pit Locus 17; view from north
PHOTO: M. ARTZY

PHOTO 2.17 Square M/1, foundation/basement Crusader period; view from west
PHOTO: M. ARTZY

CHAPTER 3

The Pottery of Stratum 7 (MB IIA)

Aaron Brody and Michal Artzy

Stratum 7 consists of layers from different phases of the ramparts that appear in the northern and part of the eastern, the western, and southern borders of the urbanized Middle Bronze Age city.[1] The rampart layers in the northern side of the tell, where Area H is located, are considerably more substantial than those on the tell's southern side. Excavation of the rampart in Area H clearly distinguished several layers in the rampart (photo 2.1), although the research goals in Area H did not deal with the question of the phasing of the Middle Bronze Age rampart, and a study combining data from all the excavated areas is yet to be undertaken. This is one reason why there are no truly primary, sealed, loci from Stratum 7. Ceramic finds are typically represented by sherds, which may or may not be in their original positions. The homogeneity of the pottery in these layers, however, suggests that there has been very little disturbance or movement after primary deposition in the early fortification of the city. Some of the ceramics in the rampart layers are of stratigraphic significance because these layers were cut by the Stratum 6 tombs or are sealed underneath layers associated with Stratum 5, so they can be related both spatially and chronologically to these significant benchmarks for Area H. Typically, however, the excavation was halted once the rampart layers were reached and identified, since their investigation was not a main research goal for Area H.

A small sequence of superimposed pottery baskets was excavated in Square M/10 on the northeastern edge of the excavation area, and it is with these baskets that the discussion of the pottery of Stratum 7 begins. It will be continued by a discussion of the relevant pottery baskets from neighboring Square M/9, which also revealed Stratum 7 ceramics, and from Square L/9, where several baskets were excavated beneath a Stratum 6 tomb. The initial discussion of pottery will be presented by basket in an attempt to best represent the "locus unit" or pottery assemblage in as unbiased a form as possible. Discussion of a typology of the ceramics will follow, and will utilize the arrangement of types developed by R. Amiran, presenting open vessels first, followed by closed

---

1 Most of the southern side of the site bordered the coast and the Na'aman River during that time (Morhange et al. 2016). The construction of the rampart was associated with clear ecological changes due to human intervention in the general area of the site (Kaniewski et al. 2013).

THE POTTERY OF STRATUM 7 (MB IIA) 219

vessels and imports (1969: 15). The typology of the ceramic sequence includes a search for parallels from well-stratified contemporary sites in order to better phase this material from Tel Akko's Area H and place the material in a larger, regional context.

Stratum 7 Pottery Sequences

Square M/10: The lowest basket in Square M/10 is number 634 (fig. 2.35). Its diagnostic sherds are typical of the MB IIA, with a variety of open vessels including fragments of platter bowls with both direct and incurving rims and a disk base fragment (fig. 3.1.1–4). Two small bowls are also present; one is the slightly flaring rim and neck of either a necked bowl or a high-necked flaring bowl of a well-levigated ware (fig. 3.1.5), and the other is a carinated bowl with red burnished decoration down to its carination (fig. 3.1.6). Basket 634 contained a fragment from a wheel-made cooking pot (fig. 3.1.7). Closed vessels include a thick body sherd with patterned combing from a pithos or storage jar (fig. 3.1.8); storage jars represented by several different rim types, flared and slightly everted (fig. 3.1.9–11); a body fragment from a small jar (fig. 3.1.12); and the base of a large dipper juglet (fig. 3.1.13). Decorated sherds include four fragments of handmade Cypriot White Painted wares (fig. 3.1.14–17). One sherd has been nicely worked into a circular shape, perhaps to be used as a jar stopper, although the beginning of drilling in the center of one side may indicate that this piece was being fashioned into a spindle whirl that was never completed (fig. 3.1.18).

Pottery basket 630 was excavated above 634 and has similar ceramic remains. Open vessels include three platter bowls with direct and incurving rims, decorated with interior radial burnishing or red slip and burnish on the interior of the bowl and just over the outside lip, and two fragments of disk bases, which are likely from large bowls (fig. 3.2.1–5). A wide variety of carinated bowls with flared and direct rims were present, decorated with red slip and burnish typically on the exterior of the bowls down to the carination and on the interior just beyond the incurve of the rim (fig. 3.2.6–12). One plain bowl (fig. 3.2.13), one krater with an everted depressed rim (fig. 3.2.14), and the rim of a wheel-made cooking pot (fig. 3.2.15) complete the variety of open vessel types. Closed vessels in pottery basket 630 include three fragments of storage jars with slightly flared rims with a ridge (fig. 3.2.16–18) and two upright rims which are difficult to identify but may be from a type of jug (fig. 3.2.19–20); two body fragments from dipper juglets, both with red slip and burnish on the outside, one made from a cream-colored fabric not local to the Akko region (fig. 3.2.21–22); the handle of a juglet with a single line, or potter's mark, scratched where the handle joined the body of the vessel (fig. 3.2.23), and a ring base which may have been from a jug (fig. 3.2.24). One body sherd, perhaps from a storage jar, was decorated with a combed design (fig. 3.2.25).

In the next basket, basket 626 above basket 630, are open vessels represented by a disk base of a large platter bowl (fig. 3.3.1) and fragments of three carinated bowls, all with a dark brown slip and burnish (fig. 3.3.2–4). On one vessel, the area below the carination has a white slip (fig. 3.3.4). There are also two kraters, one with an upright depressed rim and cream-colored slip on its shoulder down to the gentle carination which is burnished with decorative horizontal strokes (fig. 3.3.5), and another with a gently everted rim (fig. 3.3.6). The last open vessel is a fragment of a wheel-made cooking pot with a gutter rim (fig. 3.3.7). Closed vessels include the flared rim of a storage jar that ends in a ridge, and a body fragment of a storage jar with a raised band at the juncture of its neck and shoulders (fig. 3.3.8–9). A body fragment of an early Tell el-Yahudiyeh ware juglet, associated with the Middle Bronze IIA, was also found in basket 626 (fig. 3.3.10). It preserves the remnants of a double-strand loop handle and incised decorations of stipples and bands both of which have no trace of white inclusions. The sherd is similar to those found in the excavations of the kiln in 'Afula (Zevulun 1990; Artzy and Asaro 1979), although a possible origin from a coastal site can also be entertained (Kaplan et al. 1982). The rectangular handle of a Cypriot jug was also discovered, with red painted stripes and two small oval indentations (fig. 3.3.11).

Pottery basket 622 originates above basket 626, containing similar ceramics. The open vessels include several variations of the carinated bowl with red or brown slip and burnishing, and flared or upright rims (fig. 3.4.1–3), one fragmentary example of a small carinated S profiled bowl with a flared rim made from a plain buff ware (fig. 3.4.4); and a body sherd, red slipped and burnished on its exterior, which may have been from a large bowl (fig. 3.4.5). A thick walled krater with an upturned rim (fig. 3.4.6) was found alongside a small body sherd which may have belonged to a krater with a raised band and an incised chevron design (fig. 3.4.7). Closed vessels include the simple, upright rim of a storage jar (fig. 3.4.8), a body sherd from the shoulder of a storage jar decorated with small half moon indentations (fig. 3.4.9), and the fragmentary rim of a handmade vessel possibly from a cooking pot (fig. 3.4.10). There are two small fragments of imported Cypriot vessels, both with dark brown stripes on a buff background (fig. 3.4.11–12). One of the fragments has two parallel lines scratched on its interior. It has a postfiring slipped surface. Two jar stoppers are also among the ceramic finds (fig. 3.4.13–14).

The uppermost basket in this sequence of superimposed baskets from square M/10 is 596, with only two diagnostic sherds. One is of a small carinated

THE POTTERY OF STRATUM 7 (MB IIA) 221

bowl with a flared rim, red slip and burnished decoration (fig. 3.5.1). The other is a button base of a thin dipper juglet with red slip and burnish on its exterior (fig. 3.5.2).

A separate sequence of superimposed pottery baskets was excavated in square M/10 just to the east of the series of baskets described above (fig. 2.35.b). The lowest basket, 621, contained only one diagnostic body sherd of a handmade Cypriot White Painted III vessel, perhaps a fragment from the neck of a jug, with dark brown painted stripes (fig. 3.5.3). Basket 613 was directly above basket 621. Open vessels from 613 consist of three typical platter bowls with incurving or inverted rims (fig. 3.5.4–6). Smaller bowls include three examples of carinated bowls with flared rims and red slipped and burnished decoration on their exteriors, which extends just inside the lip of each bowl (fig. 3.5.7–9); and two plain bowls, one hemispheric bowl with an upright rim made from a buff ware (fig. 3.5.10), and a second slightly larger bowl with a flared rim (fig. 3.5.11). A fragment of a wheel-made cooking pot with a gutter rim was also present in basket 613 (fig. 3.5.12). Closed vessels include a rim fragment of a pithos (fig. 3.5.13), the profiled rim and shoulder of a large storage jar (fig. 3.5.14), and the upright rim of a storage jar with a slightly raised collar (fig. 3.5.15). A concave disk base may have belonged to a jug (fig. 3.5.16). One fragmentary handle from a Cypriot White Painted Ware vessel with dark brown painted stripes was found in basket 613, and three ceramic jar stoppers (fig. 3.5.17–20).

Pottery basket 606 is above basket 613, and contains similar ceramic remains. Two examples of platter bowls have red burnished decoration; one bowl with an upturned rim has the decorative slip and burnishing on its interior and exterior applied in a band which only covers the top half of the vessel (fig. 3.6.1), while the second bowl has the slip and burnish only in its interior (fig. 3.6.2). This may be due to the fact that only its base is preserved. One flat disk base may also belong to a platter bowl (fig. 3.6.3), although it is difficult to be certain due to the fragmentary nature of the sherd. Rim fragments of three carinated bowls were found in basket 606, one plain and two with red slip and burnish decoration (fig. 3.6.4–6). Closed vessels include the vertical loop handle from a storage jar (fig. 3.6.7) and a body sherd with heavy combing which may have been from a storage jar (fig. 3.6.8). A fragment of an upright rim is difficult to identify but may be from a jug (fig. 3.6.9), two ring bases may be from jars or jugs (fig. 3.6.10–11), and a smaller body sherd with red slipped and burnished exterior is from a small dipper juglet (fig. 3.6.12). One body sherd from a handmade White Painted Cypriot vessel with three red stripes was discovered along with two jar stoppers (fig. 3.6.13–15).

Next in the sequence is basket 587 and finally basket 582. Basket 587 contained only two diagnostic sherds, the flared rim of a small bowl and a juglet's vertical loop handle (fig. 3.7.1–2). The pottery in basket 582 is slightly more varied. It contained a very unusual carinated bowl with a brown slipped and burnished exterior (fig. 3.7.3), which may be a type imported from the Lebanese coast; however, this visual identification has not been established through material science testing. A wheel-made cooking pot with a gutter rim and globular body was also found alongside rim fragments from two storage jars (fig. 3.7.4–6).

All of the pottery baskets so far described were excavated in two neighboring sequences in the 1984 season in Square M/10. One basket from the previous, 1983, season reached comparable rampart levels (based on relative heights and pottery comparisons), and warrants description. Basket 1215 contained similar forms to the finds in M/10 from the 1984 season: the open vessels include an incurving rim fragment from a platter bowl; the flared rim fragments of two carinated bowls, one decorated with red slip and burnish and the other simply burnished; a flared rimmed, globular krater; and a gutter-rimmed, wheel-made cooking pot (fig. 3.7.7–11). Closed vessels are highly fragmentary: the stub of a vertical loop handle from a storage jar, a handle stub possibly from a jar, a loop handle from a dipper juglet, and a red slipped and burnished body fragment from another dipper juglet (fig. 3.7.12–15).

Square M/9: Square M/9 is just south of Square M/10. It is, however, difficult to posit the exact relationship of its Stratum 7 pottery since individual layers were not necessarily differentiated during excavation. The absolute heights of the Stratum 7 baskets in each of the two squares is comparable, yet this is a less than desirable indication for establishing a stratigraphic relationship. Two flared rim fragments from carinated bowls were found in basket 1099, one with red slip (fig. 3.8.1) and one with brown slip (fig. 3.8.2); both are highly burnished. Basket 640 contained several diagnostic sherds: the flared rim of a small, globular bowl of buff fabric, not local to the Akko region; an upright rim fragment from a storage jar with a very slight collar on the neck; a small fragment of an upright rim of the spout of a red burnished dipper juglet; and part of the rim from an oil lamp (fig. 3.8.3–6).

Square L/9: Just west of M/9 is the contiguous Square L/9, in which a few remains of Stratum 7 ceramics were found. Again, the exact stratigraphic relationship between Stratum 7 pottery in L/9 and that of either M/9 or M/10 is hard to establish. Although the pottery baskets are comparable in absolute heights, this, as we have mentioned above, is a less than desirable mode for comparison. In the case of L/9, the diagnostic ceramics from the two baskets, described here, are more important because of their vertical stratigraphic relationship. They are both physically and temporally below the sealed locus of burial 829 of Stratum 6, which is dated to the MB IIB–IIC (see detailed description of this burial and its contents in chapter 4). Basket 291 contained only two diagnostic sherds, a small incurved rim fragment from a red slipped and burnished platter bowl, and the collared shoulder of a sherd from a storage jar (fig. 3.8.7–8). Above basket 291 was basket 273, which contained a flat disk base of a platter bowl (fig. 3.8.9) and a flared rim fragment from a red slipped and burnished carinated bowl (fig. 3.8.10). Basket 273 also held a body sherd from a Cypriot handmade White Painted jug (fig. 3.8.11) decorated with dark brown stripes on a burnished buff-colored body.

Cypriot pottery from later contexts: Two fragments of White Painted Ware pottery were discovered in later strata (fig. 3.15.7, 12). The sherds represent pieces from typical forms exported from Cyprus in the MB IIA, which are relatively rare in southern Levantine contexts (Artzy and Marcus 1993).

Stratum 7 Typology

The repertoire of Stratum 7 pottery types is fairly limited, consisting primarily of large platter bowls, small carinated bowls, cooking pots, storage jars, and juglets. Very few kraters, straight walled handmade cooking pots, pithoi, jugs, or lamps are represented; Tell el-Yahudiyeh ware is rare, limited to a single fragment; and there are only a handful of Cypriot imports. Missing are examples of goblets and chalices; handless jars, and any form of Levantine Painted Wares. This is most likely due to the primary context from this phase excavated in Area H, which is rampart fills. Presumably domestic contexts within the city, elite structures, and burials would fill out the missing pottery forms and expand the existing typology. Comparisons will mainly be drawn with the best stratified MB IIA sites thus far published, Tel Aphek-Antipatris and Tell el-Ifshar, but material from Megiddo will also be referenced given the site's importance and proximity to Tel Akko. The order of presentation of the various forms follows that developed by R. Amiran (1969: 15).

Platter bowls: The platter bowls from Area H fit the characteristics of the MB IIA period already distinguished by Amiran primarily from examples from Megiddo (1969: 91). There are no major distinctions among the platter bowls from the area in their vertical sequence described above. Therefore the examples will be treated as a group which most likely originate from the same rampart layer or at least layers within a single phase of the rampart's construction.

Typically, the platter bowls from the rampart layers have incurving or direct rims (fig. 3.9.1–12). In only one instance is a fragment preserved from rim to base (fig. 3.9.11), and this example has a disk base. Other fragments lacking rims show similar disk bases (fig. 3.9.13–15), while other fragments of bases are disks slightly concave in the center (fig. 3.9.16–18) or are ring bases (fig. 3.9.19). Conjecturing variation of the style of bases of platter bowls based on incomplete forms is rather risky, so we must leave this question open until further, more complete samples are published from other areas already excavated at Akko or from future excavation. Decoration on the platter bowls include radial burnishing (fig. 3.9.9, 11) and red slip and burnish, to varying levels on both the interior and exterior of our examples (fig. 3.9.1–4); and a red painted X (photo 4.14).

These decorative features, radial burnishing and red slip and burnish, along with the incurved or direct rim and disk base, are best paralleled by examples from the Area A Palace phase at Tel Aphek (table 3.1; Stratum A XIVb–a, Beck 2000a: 194). Similar features appear in Pre-Palace phase examples, but are less frequent than in examples from the Palace phase (Beck 2000a: 175); in Post-Palace phases, platter bowls (open bowls) lose both their radial burnishing and are typically not slipped and burnished (Beck 2000a: 213). This distinction agrees with the phases distinguished by Gerstenblith for the MB IIA at Megiddo, all four of which have platter bowls with combinations of the following features: radial burnishing, red slip and burnish, and incurved rims (Gerstenblith 1983: figs. 10.6; 11.3, 6, 11; 12.3, 19; 13.6, 11, 14; 14.2; 15.10; 17.14). Despite the proximity to Megiddo, however, it should be borne in mind that Akko is a coastal site. We rely on the stratigraphy from Aphek and await further results in stratigraphic refinement of the MB IIA at Megiddo, from the current Tel Aviv University excavations, and especially the fine tuned sequence from Tell el-Ifshar. So far, no good parallels have been illustrated from Tell el-Ifshar; however, the excavators (Marcus, personal communication) describe red slip and burnish decoration on bowls starting in phase C/C (A being the earliest phase of the MB IIA in Area C, and H the latest) and becoming typical by phases C/E–C/H (Paley and Porat 1997: 373).

Carinated bowls: The carinated bowls from Area H are representative of the typical variety of rim types, body shapes, and decorative schema of MB IIA carinated bowls (fig. 3.10). The sample of twenty-six bowl fragments does not appear to show any major typological differences over its vertical sequencing detailed above, and so will be treated here as a group. Several rim types typify the carinated bowls: upright, slightly flared, and gutter rim. The angle of the carination varies and can be either gentle or sharp. Unfortunately, not a single base was preserved in any of our twenty-six examples. Red slip and burnish decoration is found on eighteen vessels in the group, and varies considerably: on the outside of the bowls the slip and burnish sometimes covers the whole vessel, extends just to the carination, or just covers the lip; on the interior of the bowls the slip and burnish typically extends down to the inside of the lip or just beyond. Six examples are decorated with brown slip and burnish (fig. 3.10.4, 5, 8, 9, 23, 24), which may simply have been red slip that turned a slight variation in color during firing. It is also possible that this color difference was intentional, but we must wait for further investigation and publication of MB IIA pottery from the site. One of these brown slipped bowls is decorated with white slip and is burnished on its exterior below the line of the carination (fig. 3.10.5). Of the three remaining bowls, two show slight traces of burnishing without any slipping on their exteriors (fig. 3.10.1–2) and one lacks any decoration (fig. 3.10.15).

Comparative evidence for carinated bowls is not helpful for differentiating potential phases within the MB IIA. The features of the Area H carinated bowls are paralleled at Aphek in Area A Pre-Palace, Palace, and Post-Palace phases (table 3.1; Beck 2000a: 174, 193, 213). A similar continuity is shown among the carinated bowls of all four phases of MB IIA differentiated by Gerstenblith for Megiddo (1983: 26–28). As with platter bowls no good parallels of carinated bowls are illustrated from Tell el-Ifshar; however, given the excavators' description of red slip and burnish decoration beginning in phase C/C and dominating from phase C/E to C/H, it would appear that the Akko carinated bowls would be best matched somewhere in these later phases (Paley and Porat 1997: 373; Marcus et al. 2008). At least we can say that red slip and burnish decoration is not robustly paralleled in the earliest MB IIA phases C/A and C/B at Tell el-Ifshar, where carinated bowls are primarily decorated with combing (Paley and Porat 1997: 373); although a further study of the ceramics from these earliest MB IIA phases at Tell el-Ifshar details very limited use of slip and burnish (Marcus et al. 2008: 231, 237–38).

Hemispheric bowls: Only one example of a hemispheric bowl was uncovered in Area H. This one fragment has a typical upright rim and hemispheric curve to its body, the base is missing and the vessel is undecorated (fig. 3.11.1).

Hemispheric bowls excavated at Aphek are most frequent in the Pre-Palace phase from Area A (table 3.1; Beck 2000a: 174), although they continue into the Palace phase as well. They are also found in Aphek's Area X, whose levels are equivalent to Area A's Pre-Palace phase (Beck 1985: 183, 190–92). Examples of hemispheric bowls from Megiddo have deeper bodies, often have a decorative red stripe around their lip, and span all four phases of the MB IIA (Gerstenblith 1983: figs. 11.4, 13.4, 15.12, 17.4, 18.24).

S-profiled bowls: Three examples of this bowl type were discovered in Area H (fig. 3.11.2–4). All have slightly everted rims and globular bodies, and are missing their base. Two of the bowls are not decorated; one has red slip and burnish on its exterior and on the interior of its lip. Although fragmentary, this decorated bowl is differentiated from carinated bowls, described above, by the roundness of its shoulders and presumed globular-shaped body (fig. 3.11.4).

Similar S-profiled bowls were found in the Palace Phase of Area A at Tel Aphek (table 3.1; Beck 2000a: 192). This bowl type seems to be limited to this phase only at Aphek. At Megiddo we could only find parallels in the phase 4 repertoire of pottery (Gerstenblith 1983: fig. 16.3–5, 14), which is generally considered equivalent to Aphek's Area A Post-Palace phase.

Flaring carinated bowls and necked bowls?: Four remaining bowl fragments were uncovered in Stratum 7 levels of Area H. The high flaring neck and shallow carinated body of what may be termed a flaring carinated bowl, with a dark brown slipped and highly burnished exterior, was discovered in the uppermost basket of one of our sequences (fig. 3.11.5). The surface treatment, well-levigated clay, and high firing of this vessel is similar to that of a spouted "tea pot" from Area H's Stratum 6 Tomb 932. Two of the remaining fragments have gently flaring necks and upright rims (fig. 3.11.6–7), which may have been of the flaring carinated bowl or the necked bowl type; however, since the body of these bowls are missing it is impossible to differentiate. The final plain bowl is too fragmentary to determine its type (fig. 3.11.8).

Flaring carinated bowls are rare in MB IIA contexts. They are absent from the Aphek repertoire, and we could find only one example from Megiddo in phase 4 of the MB IIA (Gerstenblith 1983: fig. 16.20). Typically, these vessels are representative of the MB IIB–IIC, especially the IIC phases (Ilan 1996: 217–18). Whether or not this highly burnished example is intrusive in Stratum 7, especially given its insecure context at the very top of the sequence of pottery baskets, remains to be seen through further investigation of the Middle Bronze Age pottery and levels at Akko. Necked bowls are limited to Post-Palace phases at Aphek (Beck 2000a: 213). However, given the fragmentary nature of our one possible example it is best not to use this piece for stratigraphic comparison.

Kraters: Several krater types were found in Area H forming a very small sample of six fragmentary vessels. Two of these are variations of a krater type defined at Tel Aphek as "inward slanting rims, sometimes with gutter" (Beck 2000b: 113); one has a very gently inward slanting rim (or perhaps more appropriately, slightly everted rim); the second has a more pronounced everted rim with a much thicker, oval rim profile, closer in shape but not in stance to the rim on the holemouth krater types from Aphek (Beck 2000b:

fig. 3.11.12–13). Another krater rim fragment, with an upturned rim, is harder to categorize (fig. 3.11.9). Two examples have upright or everted depressed rims (fig. 3.11.10–11), one preserving the contours of a hemispherical body nicely decorated with cream-colored slip from the lip to its gentle carination, and burnished with horizontal strokes. This vessel could also be categorized as a large bowl; it is unusual and rare and may be an imported vessel (fig. 3.11.10). The final fragment is a body sherd with a raised band decorated with an incised chevron pattern, typical on kraters from Aphek (Beck 2000b: 129; fig. 3.11.14). No bases were preserved with our few examples of krater rims.

The best comparative material for kraters with inward slanting or gutter rims are from Tel Aphek's Areas B and A in Pre-Palace phases (table 3.1; Beck 2000b: 113, 175). We have not been able to find good parallels for our one example with the upturned rim, and have found only one match for our krater type with the upright depressed rim in phase 4 at Megiddo, where it is referred to as a large bowl (Gerstenblith 1983: 18.10).

Cooking pots: All of the fragments of cooking pots from Area H are of the MB IIA wheel-made variety (fig. 3.12.1–6), except for one that may have been from a handmade vessel (fig. 3.12.7). Most of the examples have variations of the gutter rim. Bases are missing as are bodies, except preserved shoulders hint at the typical globular body of these vessels, which vary in size. The gutter rimmed, wheel-made, cooking pot is a *fossile directeur* of the MB IIA (Kempinski 1992: 166). One example (fig. 3.12.1) has a slightly everted triangular rim, which may be the ancestor of the type which Amiran calls the most common in the MB IIB–IIC (1969: 102, pl. 30:5) and has a parallel in Pre-Palace levels at Aphek (Beck 2000a: fig. 10.1.22).

Comparative evidence is best found at Aphek. In Area A and B wheel-made cooking pots were far more common than their handmade counterparts (Beck 2000a: 192; 2000b: 113), and were found in both Pre-Palace and Palace phases (table 3.1). The counterparts from Aphek show similar variations in size, rim shape, and stance of the rim. Handmade and wheel-made cooking pots are prevalent in the MB IIA sequence at Tell el-Ifshar, where gutter rims on wheel-made examples eventually change to tube or folded rims; however, the phasing of this transition is not detailed (Paley and Porat 1997: 373).

Pithoi: Of the few fragments that we have attributed to the category of pithoi, one is a body fragment with patterned combing (fig. 3.12.9). This piece has been judged as coming from a pithos because of the thickness of the sherd, but it could also have belonged to a large storage jar. Neither Amiran nor Beck fully differentiate between pithoi and storage jars for the MB IIA (Amiran 1969: 102–103; Beck 2000a; 2000b). We also place one rim fragment (fig. 3.12.8), in the pithos category due to the width of its mouth and general stance and shape of its direct rim and concave neck (based on a very small portion of the neck preserved).

The best stratified comparison for this pithos type is found at Tel Aphek (table 3.1). Beck has categorized the type among storage jars, her SJ4B "pithos, molded rim" (2000a: 233). These pithoi or large, handless storage jars were found in Palace and Post-Palace phases in Area A at Aphek (Beck 2000a: 193, 213).

Storage jars: The remnants of storage jars from MB IIA layers in Area H are fragmentary and varied. Rim forms are typically slightly flared and end with a ridge (fig. 3.13.1–8). Two examples from Area H, 582/4 and 613/1, are from a larger jar type with a heavier flared rim that ends in a pronounced ridge (fig. 3.13.12–13). The final rim type is a direct rim on a vertical neck (fig. 3.13.10–11), and one example in which the neck is slightly flared (fig. 3.13.9). Two storage jars neck fragments with raised relief bands (fig. 3.13.14–15) and several storage jar vertical loop handles of varying sizes have been preserved (fig. 3.13.16–17). No bases of storage jars were found. Several body sherds with combed or impressed decoration are likely of storage jars, although they may have been from pithoi (fig. 3.12.10–12).

The best comparisons for MB IIA storage jars come from the sequence at Tel Aphek (table 3.1). The rim profile that is slightly flared and ends in a ridge is identified with Aphek's SJ2 storage jar type (Beck 2000a: 177–78). The examples from Aphek are as varied as the ones in the small sample from Area H at Akko, and come from all three main phases of the MB IIA at the site of Aphek. The larger jar form with heavier flared rim belongs to Aphek's SJ1 type (Beck 2000a: 177), with nice parallels in two examples from Area B, Stratum BVc (Beck 2000b: fig. 8.12.27–28), which is equated with Pre-Palace levels in Area A. The SJ1 type is prevalent in Area A's Pre-Palace and Palace phases (Beck 2000a: 233). The direct rim type for storage jars at Akko does not appear to be paralleled at Aphek, but is matched by one example from the MB IIA pottery from Achziv (Oren 1975: fig. 3.57). Decorative features, such as the relief band around the neck, combing, or punctated designs, are abundant on storage jars from Aphek (Beck 1985: 192; 2000b: 129).

Jugs: The jug sherds identified are highly fragmentary, thus making a firm attribution difficult. Three direct rims are a bit of a mystery (fig. 3.14.1–3) as it is hard to pinpoint exactly what type of vessel they belonged to originally. Their identification as fragments of a jug form is open. One example's dark gray fabric differs from the local fabrics and is reminiscent of the gray fabric of Tell el-Yahudiyeh ware (fig. 3.14.2). There are several examples of ring bases (fig. 3.14.5–7) and a concave disk base (fig. 3.14.4) whose body fragments are too sharply angled to belong to platter bowls, and we are attributing these to a form of jug with a globular or ovoid body, although this attribution is tenuous.

We were not able to find good parallels for the direct rims, possibly from jugs, described above (fig. 3.14.1–3). There are examples of globular jugs with ring bases from Megiddo in phases 1/2 and 3 (Gerstenblith 1983: fig. 10.3; 13.1; 14.4). At Aphek, ring bases on jugs do not appear until the equivalent of Area A Palace phase (table 3.1; Beck 2000b: 114).

Juglets: The remains of juglets in Area H are quite fragmentary. All of these fragments appear to have been from dipper juglets (fig. 3.14.8–14) except for one piece from a Tell el-Yahudiyeh ware juglet (fig. 3.14.15), which was most likely piriform in shape similar to the those found in a kiln in Afula (Zevulon 1990). It has preserved the stumps of the double-strap handle and parts of punctated and incised circular designs. Only one rim fragment was preserved from the spouted mouth of a small dipper juglet (fig. 3.14.14). Two dipper juglet bases were uncovered (fig. 3.14.8–9); both are pointed and one has a ring base attached slightly above the point. Three vertical handles from dipper juglets were found in Area H: two with round cross sections (fig. 3.14.16–17); and one oval in section from a large dipper juglet, bearing an incised potter's mark where the handle joined the shoulder of the vessel (fig. 3.14.18). The remaining fragments are sherds from the bodies of dipper juglets (fig. 3.14.10–13), showing slight variations in the size and angle of the shape of the juglets' bodies. Most of the fragments from dipper juglets are decorated with red slip and burnish on their exterior, although several examples are plain.

Dipper juglets with similar attributes are found in all four phases of the MB IIA at Megiddo (Gerstenblith 1983). They are also represented in all of the three major MB IIA phases at Aphek (table 3.1; Beck 2000a: 235). Tell el-Yehudiyeh ware is absent from the MB IIA levels at our comparative stratified sites; however, it has been found elsewhere in good MB IIA contexts (Amiran 1969: 120; Zevulun 1990).

Lamps: Only one small fragment of a lamp was found in the Stratum 7 levels of Area H (fig. 3.14.19). It does not exhibit any diagnostic attributes, and so cannot be used for comparative purposes.

Cypriot imports: Several fragments of imported Cypriot pottery were found in Stratum 7 levels of Area H alongside local pottery from the MB IIA. All of the sherds originated from handmade White Painted III vessels. No rims or bases were preserved; only gently curving body sherds from globular jugs were noted (fig. 3.15.1–7). A neck fragment was found (fig. 3.15.8), alongside two fragmentary handles also from jugs (fig. 3.15.10–11). One body sherd could be assigned to a bowl (fig. 3.15.9). One typical thrust-through handle fragment was found in a later mixed context (fig. 3.15.12). Each one of these sherds is easily distinguishable from local pottery by its painted decoration and its ware. Stripes, cross lines, pendent lines, and squiggles were applied in either red or dark brown paint. Although highly fragmentary, the pieces appear to be of the Cypriot White Painted III family and are of the Cross Line and Pendent Line Style (Åström 1957). One bowl fragment (fig. 3.15.9) is likely from a Composite Ware family. The identification is not easily made since the sherd is small. It is, however, a different style from the Cross Line and Pendent Line examples. Similar fragments of Cypriot White Painted and Composite Ware have been published from the rampart layers in Area B at Akko (M. Dothan 1976: 9), just east of Area H. Neutron Activation Analysis conducted on samples from Area B demonstrated that they came from sources in eastern Cyprus (Yellin 1984: 93).

Cypriot imported pottery is not present in the MB IIA sequences at either Aphek or Tell el-Ifshar. Gerstenblith has isolated Cypriot imports to her final phase, Phase 4, of the MB IIA at Megiddo (1983: 28). Later excavations of stratified habitation levels at Tel Nami, a coastal site north of Tel Dor and south of Atlit, have produced several fragments of Cypriot pottery in well-stratified MB IIA contexts (table 3.1; Artzy and Marcus 1992). The terminal MB IIA phase at Nami has been equated with the Area A Palace phase at Aphek (Artzy and Marcus 1992: 105), which means that Nami's Cypriot pottery must have arrived in a time frame equivalent to Aphek's Area A Palace phase or earlier.

Typological Conclusions

Although initially presented sequentially by pottery basket, a close examination of the Stratum 7 pottery in Area H has shown the homogeneity of types within the internal vertical sequence. Therefore, we suggest it all originated from the same phase of rampart construction in Area H, and all dates typologically to the MB IIA.

From the broad ceramic categories detailed above and presented in table 3.1, the Akko Area H carinated bowls, storage jars, and juglets have parallels in all three major phases at Aphek. Akko platter bowls, hemispherical bowls, and cooking pots match best with types in the Pre-palace and Palace phases at Aphek. Akko's S-profiled bowls and jugs from Area H cluster around Aphek's Palace phase. The few examples of pithoi fragments from Akko span the Palace and Post-palace phases at Aphek. The only Akko pottery type whose paralleled span at Aphek does not include a component in the Palace phase is the krater type with inward slanting rim (see p. 227). All other types are found in Aphek's Palace phase repertoire, whether or not they began earlier or continue later;

THE POTTERY OF STRATUM 7 (MB IIA)

therefore, we would equate the final rampart phase in Area H with the Palace phase (Area A's Palace II, which site-wide is referred to as Phase 3) at Aphek.

Six phases of rampart construction have been identified for Tel Akko in Area B, in the vicinity of the site's acropolis (table 2.1; Raban 1991: 20*). The four earliest phases are dated to the MB IIA, the fifth to the MB IIB, and the sixth and final phase to the MB IIC (Raban 1991: 20*). In Area F, the city's western gate, named the "Sea Gate," has been shown to span of time of the earliest two MB IIA ramparts (Raban 1991: 25*). The latest material in the gate has been attributed by Raban with Aphek's Palace I phase 2 (which is equated with the Pre-palace phase in Aphek Area A). Following the gate's demise, it was covered by Akko's third rampart, and it is this third MB IIA rampart phase that appears to be the final rampart in Area H at Tel Akko (see table 2.1 above). From the position of Area H vis-à-vis Areas F (the gate) and Area AB, we venture to infer that the uppermost levels of the rampart were a part of the "acropolis" of the tell. The layers of the different ramparts can be seen in photos 2.1 and 2.2.

TABLE 3.1   Comparison of Area H Stratum 7 ceramic types with Aphek Area A phasing

	Aphek Area A Pre-Palace Phase	Aphek Area A Palace Phase	Aphek Area A Post-Palace Phase
Platter bowls			
Carinated bowls			
Hemispheric bowls			
S-profiled bowls			
Kraters			
Cooking pots, wheel-made			
Pithoi			
Storage jars with flared rim & ridge			
Storage jars with heavier flared rim			
Jugs with ring bases			
Dipper juglets			
Cypriot imports		finds from Tel Nami	finds from Phase 4 Megiddo

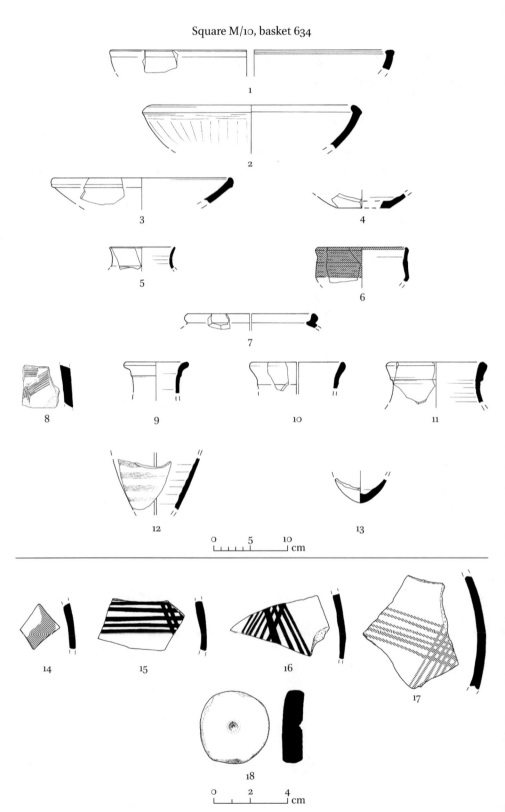

FIGURE 3.1

THE POTTERY OF STRATUM 7 (MB IIA)

Figure No.	Shape/ object	Reg. No.	Locus/ Pottery Basket	Description (color of exterior/interior/core; inclusions; decorations; etc.)
3.1.1	Bowl	AK X 1984 H M/10 b. 634/1	634/1	Pink/pink/pink; many small white, grey, and miniscule brown inclusions
3.1.2	Bowl	AK X 1984 H M/10 b. 634/33	634/33	Pink to dark brown/pink/pink to red; many small to medium sized white and grey, and miniscule brown inclusions
3.1.3	Bowl	AK X 1984 H M/10 b. 634/2	634/2	Pink/pink/pink to light grey; medium amount of small white and small grey inclusions and voids
3.1.4	Bowl	AK X 1984 H M/10 b. 634/8	634/8	Pink/pink/pink; few small white inclusions and voids
3.1.5	Bowl	AK X 1984 H M/10 b. 634/9	634/9	Pink/pink/pink; very few small white inclusions
3.1.6	Bowl	AK X 1984 H M/10 b. 634/15	634/15	Pink/pink/pink to buff; medium amount of small white and grey, miniscule brown, inclusions; red slip and burnished on exterior from carination and on interior from middle of rim
3.1.7	Cooking pot	AK X 1984 H M/10 b. 634/14	634/14	Dark brown/buff/dark brown to light brown; large amount of small white inclusions
3.1.8	Pithos or storage jar	AK X 1984 H M/10 b. 634/7	634/7	Pink/pink/light grey; medium amount of small white and small brown inclusions; patterned combing
3.1.9	Storage jar	AK X 1984 H M/10 b. 634/4	634/4	Pink/pink/red; large number of small to large white and grey inclusions
3.1.10	Storage jar	AK X 1984 H M/10 b. 634/5	634/5	Red/red/red; many small white and few medium sized grey inclusions
3.1.11	Storage jar	AK X 1984 H M/10 b. 634/6	634/6	Pink/pink/pink; few small white, few small grey, many miniscule brown inclusions
3.1.12	Jar	AK X 1984 H M/10 b. 634/10	634/10	Buff/light grey/light grey; many small to medium sized white and miniscule brown inclusions
3.1.13	Juglet	AK X 1984 H M/10 b. 634/13	634/13	Pink/pink/pink to red; few small white and miniscule brown inclusions
3.1.14	Body sherd	AK X 1984 H M/10 b. 634/20	634/20	Buff/buff/buff; few miniscule brown inclusions; few miniscule brown and micaceous inclusions; red painted stipe on exterior; Cypriot White Painted III Ware
3.1.15	Jug	AK X 1984 H M/10 b. 634/21	634/21	Dark buff/buff/buff; very small amount of miniscule brown and micaceous inclusions; dark brown painted stripes on exterior; Cypriot White Painted III Ware
3.1.16	Jug	AK X 1984 H M/10 b. 634/22	634/22	Pink/pink/pink; small amount of miniscule white, miniscule brown, and small micaceous inclusions; dark red stripes on exterior; Cypriot White Painted III Ware
3.1.17	Jug	AK X 1984 H M/10 b. 634/23	634/23	Buff/buff/buff; small amount of miniscule brown inclusions; dark brown stripes on exterior; Cypriot White Painted III Ware
3.1.18	Stopper	AK X 1984 H M/10 b. 634/12	634/12	Brown to pink/buff/light grey; indentation from drilling in center (does not go all the way through)

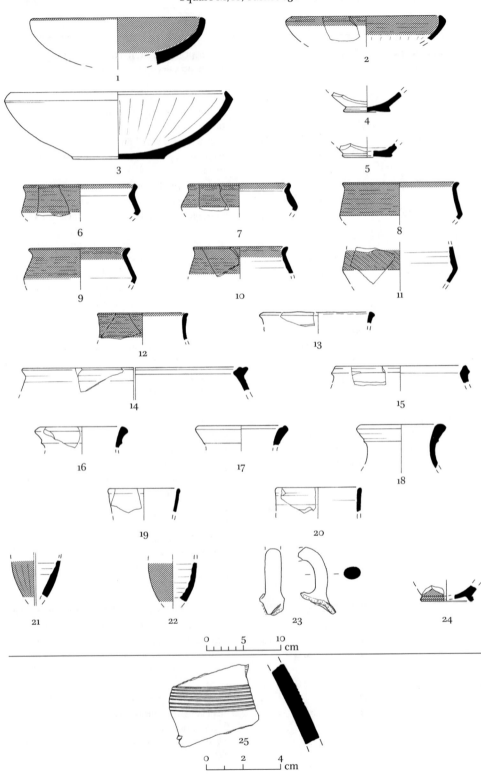

FIGURE 3.2

THE POTTERY OF STRATUM 7 (MB IIA)

Figure No.	Shape/ object	Reg. No.	Locus/ Pottery Basket	Description (color of exterior/interior/core; inclusions; decorations; etc.)
3.2.1	Bowl	AK X 1984 H M/10 b. 630/24	630/24	Buff/buff/light grey; few small white inclusions; red slip and burnished interior and lip
3.2.2	Bowl	AK X 1984 H M/10 b. 630/2	630/2	Pink/pink/pink; small amount of small to medium sized white and grey inclusions; red slip and burnished on exterior from below rim and on interior
3.2.3	Bowl	AK X 1984 H M/10 b. 630/15	630/15	Pink/pink/pink to light grey; few small white and medium grey inclusions; radial burnishing on interior
3.2.4	Bowl	AK X 1984 H M/10 b. 630/16	630/16	Pink/pink/light grey; large amount of small to large white inclusions
3.2.5	Bowl	AK X 1984 H M/10 b. 630/18	630/18	Buff/red to grey/light grey; medium amount of small white inclusions
3.2.6	Bowl	AK X 1984 H M/10 b. 630/7	630/7	Pink/pink/pink to buff; medium amount of small to medium sized white inclusions; brown slip and burnished from carination on exterior and middle of rim on interior
3.2.7	Bowl	AK X 1984 H M/10 b. 630/3	630/3	Pink/pink/light grey; few small white and miniscule brown inclusions; red slip and burnished on exterior from carination and from middle of rim on interior
3.2.8	Bowl	AK X 1984 H M/10 b. 630/8	630/8	Pink/pink/pink to buff; medium amount of small white inclusions; red slip and burnished on exterior from carination and on interior from bottom of rim
3.2.9	Bowl	AK X 1984 H M/10 b. 630/9	630/9	Pink/pink/pink; medium amount of small white inclusions; red slip and burnished on exterior from carination and on interior from below rim
3.2.10	Bowl	AK X 1984 H M/10 b. 630/6	630/6	Pink/pink/pink to light grey; few medium sized white inclusions; red slip and burnished on exterior and on interior from below rim
3.2.11	Bowl	AK X 1984 H M/10 b. 630/4	630/4	Pink/pink/pink; few small white and miniscule brown inclusions; red slip and burnished on exterior from carination
3.2.12	Bowl	AK X 1984 H M/10 b. 630/5	630/5	Light brown/light brown/light brown; few small white inclusions; red slip and burnished on exterior and on interior from bottom of rim
3.2.13	Bowl	AK X 1984 H M/10 b. 630/20	630/20	Buff/buff/buff; few small white inclusions
3.2.14	Krater	AK X 1984 H M/10 b. 630/14	630/14	Pink/pink/pink; few small white and miniscule brown inclusions
3.2.15	Cooking pot	AK X 1984 H M/10 b. 630/23	630/23	Brown/brown/dark grey; medium amount of small white inclusions
3.2.16	Storage jar	AK X 1984 H M/10 b. 630/11	630/11	Pink/pink/pink; few small white inclusions
3.2.17	Storage jar	AK X 1984 H M/10 b. 630/12	630/12	Pink/pink/light grey; large amount of medium sized white inclusions
3.2.18	Storage jar	AK X 1984 H M/10 b. 630/17	630/17	Pink/pink/light grey; few small to medium sized white and medium sized grey inclusions

Figure No.	Shape/object	Reg. No.	Locus/Pottery Basket	Description (color of exterior/interior/core; inclusions; decorations; etc.)
3.2.19	Jug?	AK X 1984 H M/10 b. 630/21	630/21	Dark grey/dark grey/dark grey; medium amount of small to medium sized white inclusions
3.2.20	Jug?	AK X 1984 H M/10 b. 630/22	630/22	Pink/pink/red; medium amount of small to medium sized white and grey inclusions
3.2.21	Juglet	AK X 1984 H M/10 b. 630/10	630/10	Pink/pink/pink; medium amount of small to large white inclusions; red slip and burnished on exterior
3.2.22	Juglet	AK X 1984 H M/10 b. 630/19	630/19	Cream/cream/cream; few small to medium sized grey inclusions; traces of red slip on exterior
3.2.23	Juglet	AK X 1984 H M/10 b. 630/25	630/25	Buff/buff/light grey; many small to medium sized white and large dark grey inclusions; possible potter's mark on exterior below handle
3.2.24	Jug?	AK X 1984 H M/10 b. 630/1	630/1	Pink/pink/light grey; medium amount of small to medium sized white and grey inclusions; red slip and burnished exterior
3.2.25	Storage jar	AK X 1984 H M/10 b. 630/13	630/13	Buff/buff/light grey; medium amount of medium sized grey and small white inclusions; combed decoration

Square M/10, basket 626

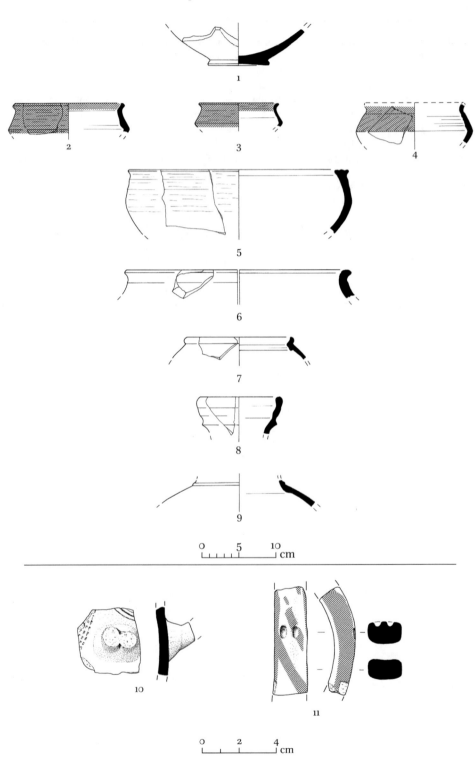

FIGURE 3.3

Figure No.	Shape/ object	Reg. No.	Locus/ Pottery Basket	Description (color of exterior/interior/core; inclusions; decorations; etc.)
3.3.1	Bowl	AK X 1984 H M/10 b. 626/11	626/11	Buff/buff/buff to light grey; few small white inclusions;
3.3.2	Bowl	AK X 1984 H M/10 b. 626/8	626/8	Pink/pink/pink; few small to medium sized white inclusions; brown slip and burnished exterior to carination and interior from bottom of rim
3.3.3	Bowl	AK X 1984 H M/10 b. 626/9	626/9	Pink/pink/pink to grey; few small white inclusions; brown slip and burnished exterior to carination and interior from bottom of rim
3.3.4	Bowl	AK X 1984 H M/10 b. 626/7	626/7	Buff/pink/pink to brown; few small to medium sized white to light grey inclusions; brown slip and burnished on exterior above carination, white slip on exterior below carination
3.3.5	Krater	AK X 1984 H M/10 b. 626/6	626/6	Buff/buff/light grey; medium amount of small to medium sized white inclusions; ivory-colored slip and burnished exterior and top of rim
3.3.6	Krater	AK X 1984 H M/10 b. 626/10	626/10	Pink/pink/light grey; few small to medium sized white inclusions
3.3.7	Cooking pot	AK X 1984 H M/10 b. 626/2	626/2	Brown/reddish brown/brown; medium amount of small white inclusions
3.3.8	Storage jar	AK X 1984 H M/10 b. 626/4	626/4	Pink/pink/pink; medium amount of small to medium sized white and light grey inclusions
3.3.9	Storage jar	AK X 1984 H M/10 b. 626/1	626/1	Pink/pink/light grey; few small white inclusions
3.3.10	Juglet	AK X 1984 H M/10 b. 626/3	626/3	Light grey/light grey/light grey; medium amount of small brown and dark grey inclusions; Tell el-Yahudiyeh Ware
3.3.11	Jug	AK X 1984 H M/10 b. 626/5	626/5	Pink/pink/grey brown; few small white inclusions; red painted stripes and two oval indentations on handle; Cypriot White Painted III Ware

Square M/10, Locus 1060, basket 622

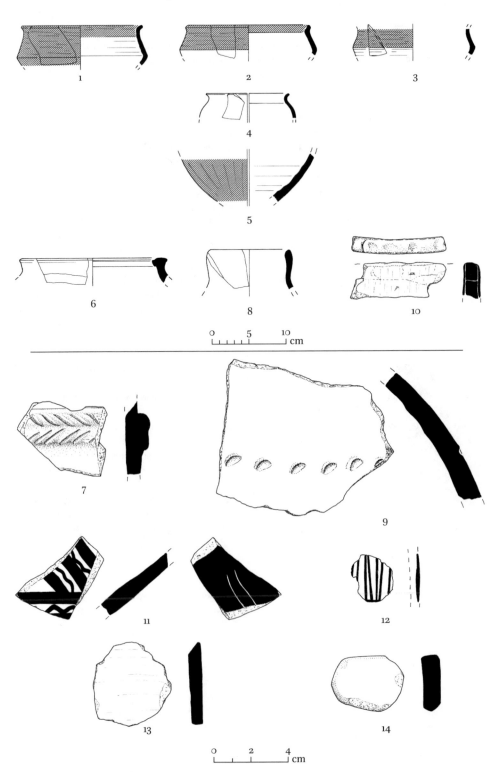

FIGURE 3.4

Figure No.	Shape/ object	Reg. No.	Locus/ Pottery Basket	Description (color of exterior/interior/core; inclusions; decorations; etc.)
3.4.1	Bowl	AK X 1984 H M/10 b. 622/2	622/2	Pink/pink/pink; few small white inclusions; red slip and burnished exterior and interior from below lip
3.4.2	Bowl	AK X 1984 H M/10 b. 622/3	622/3	Pink/pink/pink; few small to medium sized white inclusions; red slip and burnished exterior from carination to rim and interior from below lip
3.4.3	Bowl	AK X 1984 H M/10 b. 622/1	622/1	Pink/pink/pink to light grey; few small white inclusions; red slip and burnished exterior above carination
3.4.4	Bowl	AK X 1984 H M/10 b. 622/4	622/4	Buff/buff/buff; few small brown inclusions
3.4.5	Bowl?	AK X 1984 H M/10 b. 622/10	622/10	Pink/pink/pink; few small white inclusions; red slip and burnished exterior
3.4.6	Krater	AK X 1984 H M/10 b. 622/7	622/7	Pink buff/pink/light grey; large amount of small to large white and miniscule dark brown inclusions
3.4.7	Krater?	AK X 1984 H M/10 b. 622/5	622/5	Pink/pink/pink to grey; few small white inclusions; raised band with an incised chevron design
3.4.8	Storage jar	AK X 1984 H M/10 b. 622/11	622/11	Pink/pink/light grey; small number of small to medium sized white inclusions
3.4.9	Storage jar	AK X 1984 H M/10 b. 622/14	622/14	Pink/light grey/red to light grey; medium number of medium sized white and occasional small dark brown inclusions; wheel combed, small half-moon indentations
3.4.10	Cooking pot?	AK X 1984 H M/10 b. 622/6	622/6	Light brown/dark brown/light brown; few small white inclusions
3.4.11	Body fragment	AK X 1984 H M/10 b. 622/12	622/12	Buff/buff/buff; small number of small brown inclusions; burnished interior with dark brown painted designs, dark brown slipped exterior; Cypriot White Painted Ware
3.4.12	Body fragment (chip)	AK X 1984 H M/10 b. 622/13	622/13	Buff/interior not visible/buff; small number of small brown inclusions; dark brown stripes on exterior; Cypriot
3.4.13	Stopper	AK X 1984 H M/10 b. 622/8	622/8	Pink/pink/light pink; large amount of small to medium sized white and light grey inclusions
3.4.14	Stopper	AK X 1984 H M/10 b. 622/9	622/9	Pink/pink/light grey

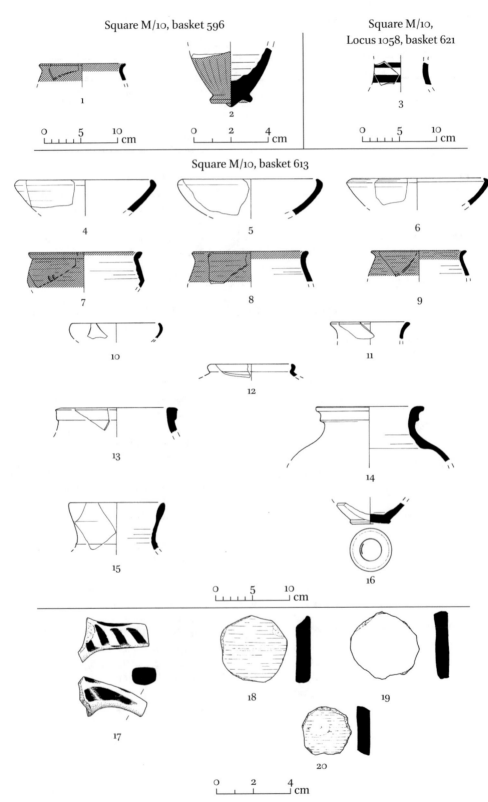

FIGURE 3.5

THE POTTERY OF STRATUM 7 (MB IIA)

Figure No.	Shape/ object	Reg. No.	Locus/ Pottery Basket	Description (color of exterior/interior/core; inclusions; decorations; etc.)
3.5.1	Bowl	AK X 1984 H M/10 b. 596/2	596/2	Pink/pink/pink; medium amount of small to medium sized white and medium sized dark grey inclusions; red slip and burnished exterior and interior from bottom of rim
3.5.2	Juglet	AK X 1984 H M/10 b. 596/1	596/1	Cream/light grey/cream to light grey; few small dark brown inclusions; red slip and burnished exterior
3.5.3	Jug?	AK X 1984 H M/10 b. 621/1	621/1	Greenish buff/buff/pink; many small dark brown inclusions; dark brown painted stripes on exterior; Cypriot White Painted III Ware
3.5.4	Bowl	AK X 1984 H M/10 b. 613/8	613/8	Pink/pink/reddish pink; few small white inclusions
3.5.5	Bowl	AK X 1984 H M/10 b. 613/6 + 10	613/6 + 10	Pink/pink/dark grey; few small to medium sized white inclusions
3.5.6	Bowl	AK X 1984 H M/10 b. 613/9	613/9	Pinkish buff/pinkish buff/reddish pink; few small white inclusions
3.5.7	Bowl	AK X 1984 H M/10 b. 613/14	613/14	Pink/pink/pink to light grey; few small white and miniscule dark brown inclusions; red slip and burnished exterior and interior from middle of rim
3.5.8	Bowl	AK X 1984 H M/10 b. 613/15	613/15	Pink/pink/pink; few small white and miniscule brown inclusions; red slip and burnished exterior and interior from beginning of rim
3.5.9	Bowl	AK X 1984 H M/10 b. 613/18	613/18	Pink/pink/pink; few small white and miniscule dark brown inclusions; red slip and burnished exterior and interior from beginning of rim
3.5.10	Bowl	AK X 1984 H M/10 b. 613/7	613/7	Buff/buff/buff; few small white inclusions
3.5.11	Bowl	AK X 1984 H M/10 b. 613/21	613/21	Pink/pink/pink; few medium sized light grey inclusions
3.5.12	Cooking pot	AK X 1984 H M/10 b. 613/23	613/23	Brown/dark brown/dark brown; many small to medium white and light grey inclusions
3.5.13	Pithos	AK X 1984 H M/10 b. 613/4	613/4	Pink/pink/pink; few small white inclusions
3.5.14	Storage jar	AK X 1984 H M/10 b. 613/2	613/2	Pink/pink/pink to grey; medium amount of small to large white inclusions
3.5.15	Storage jar	AK X 1984 H M/10 b. 613/3	613/3	Pink/pink/red pink; few large white inclusions
3.5.16	Jug?	AK X 1984 H M/10 b. 613/5	613/5	Pink/pink/reddish pink; few small white inclusions
3.5.17	Jug	AK X 1984 H M/10 b. 613/1	613/1	Greenish buff/buff/buff; few miniscule dark brown inclusions; red painted stripes on exterior; Cypriot White Painted III Ware
3.5.18	Stopper	AK X 1984 H M/10 b. 613/13	613/13	Pink/pink/light grey
3.5.19	Stopper	AK X 1984 H M/10 b. 613/12	613/12	Pink/pink/light grey
3.5.20	Stopper	AK X 1984 H M/10 b. 613/11	613/11	Pink/pink/light grey

Square M/10, basket 606

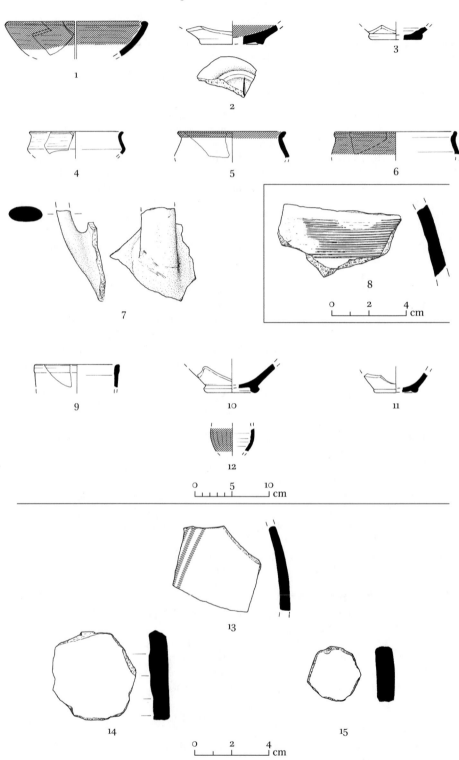

FIGURE 3.6

THE POTTERY OF STRATUM 7 (MB IIA)

Figure No.	Shape/ object	Reg. No.	Locus/ Pottery Basket	Description (color of exterior/interior/core; inclusions; decorations; etc.)
3.6.1	Bowl	AK X 1984 H M/10 b. 606/20 + 23	606/20 + 23	Pink/pink/pink; medium amount of small to medium white inclusions; red slip and burnished exterior and interior
3.6.2	Bowl	AK X 1984 H M/10 b. 606/5	606/5	Pink/pink/pink to light grey; few small white inclusions; red slip and burnished interior
3.6.3	Bowl?	AK X 1984 H M/10 b. 606/6	606/6	Buff/buff/buff; few small white inclusions
3.6.4	Bowl	AK X 1984 H M/10 b. 606/11	606/11	Buff/buff/buff; medium amount of small white and miniscule brown inclusions
3.6.5	Bowl	AK X 1984 H M/10 b. 606/10	606/10	Pink/pink/pink; few small white and grey and miniscule brown inclusions; brown slipped and burnished exterior and interior from beginning of rim
3.6.6	Bowl	AK X 1984 H M/10 b. 606/9	606/9	Red/red/red; many small white and miniscule brown inclusions; red slip and burnished exterior
3.6.7	Storage jar	AK X 1984 H M/10 b. 606/2	606/2	Pink/pink/light grey; few small white inclusions
3.6.8	Storage jar	AK X 1984 H M/10 b. 606/17	606/17	Pink/pink/pink; few small to large white inclusions; patterned combing on body sherd
3.6.9	Jug?	AK X 1984 H M/10 b. 606/12	606/12	Pink/pink/pink; few small white, one large grey, inclusions
3.6.10	Jar or jug	AK X 1984 H M/10 b. 606/8	606/8	Buff/buff/buff to light grey; few small white inclusions
3.6.11	Jar or jug	AK X 1984 H M/10 b. 606/7	606/7	Pink/pink/pink; few small white inclusions
3.6.12	Juglet	AK X 1984 H M/10 b. 606/22	606/22	Buff/buff/buff; medium amount of miniscule brown inclusions; red slip and burnished exterior
3.6.13	Jug	AK X 1984 H M/10 b. 606/19	606/19	Pink/pink/pink; many miniscule white and brown inclusions; red painted stripes on exterior; Cypriot White Painted III Ware
3.6.14	Stopper	AK X 1984 H M/10 b. 606/4	606/4	Pink/light grey/light grey
3.6.15	Stopper	AK X 1984 H M/10 b. 606/3	606/3	Pink/pink/pink

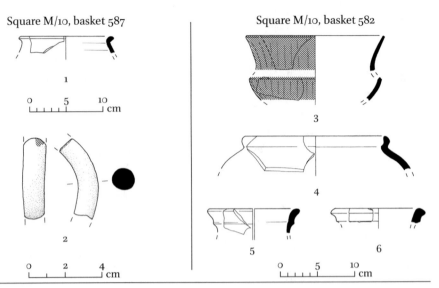
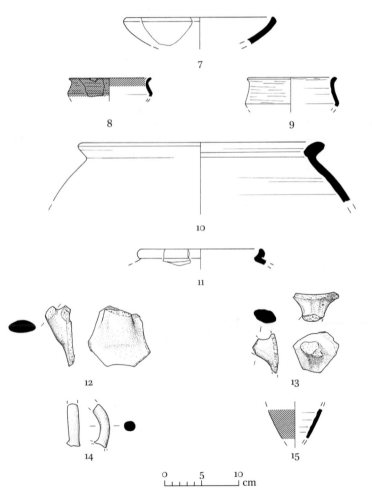

FIGURE 3.7

THE POTTERY OF STRATUM 7 (MB IIA)

Figure No.	Shape/ object	Reg. No.	Locus/ Pottery Basket	Description (color of exterior/interior/core; inclusions; decorations; etc.)
3.7.1	Bowl	AK X 1984 H M/10 b. 587/2	587/2	Buff/buff/buff; few medium sized white inclusions and voids
3.7.2	Juglet	AK X 1984 H M/10 b. 587/1	587/1	Pink/pink/pink; medium amount of small white and miniscule brown inclusions
3.7.3	Bowl	AK X 1984 H M/10 b. 582/2, 598	582/2	Brown/brown/pink to dark grey; few small black inclusions; brown slipped and burnished exterior
3.7.4	Cooking pot	AK X 1984 H M/10 b. 582/1	582/1	Brown/brown/brown to light grey; medium amount of small white and miniscule brown inclusions
3.7.5	Storage jar	AK X 1984 H M/10 b. 582/3	582/3	Pink/pink/pink; few small white inclusions
3.7.6	Storage jar	AK X 1984 H M/10 b. 582/4	582/4	Pink/pink/pink; few small white inclusions
3.7.7	Bowl	AK IX 1983 H M/10 b. 1215/2	1215/2	Light grey/dark grey/light grey; few small white inclusions
3.7.8	Bowl	AK IX 1983 H M/10 b. 1215/8	1215/8	Pink/pink/pink; many small to medium sized white and miniscule brown inclusions; red slip and burnished exterior and interior from bottom of rim
3.7.9	Bowl	AK IX 1983 H M/10 b. 1215/6	1215/6	Tan/tan/tan; medium amount of medium sized white and grey, and miniscule brown, inclusions; burnished exterior and interior from middle of rim
3.7.10	Krater	AK IX 1983 H M/10 b. 1215/1	1215/1	Buff green/buff green/red to pink; many small grey and white inclusions
3.7.11	Cooking pot	AK IX 1983 H M/10 b. 1215/5	1215/5	Brown/reddish brown/reddish brown; many small white and light grey inclusions
3.7.12	Storage jar	AK IX 1983 H M/10 b. 1215/3	1215/3	Pink/pink/light grey; medium amount of small to medium sized white and light grey inclusions
3.7.13	Jar?	AK IX 1983 H M/10 b. 1215/4	1215/4	Pink/pink/pink to grey; few small white inclusions
3.7.14	Juglet	AK IX 1983 H M/10 b. 1215/7	1215/7	Pink/pink/reddish pink; medium amount of small white and grey inclusions
3.7.15	Juglet	AK IX 1983 H M/10 b. 1215/10	1215/10	Pink/pink/pink; few miniscule brown inclusions; red slip and burnished exterior

Square M/9, basket 1099

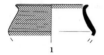 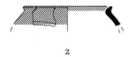

1 2

Square M/9, basket 640

 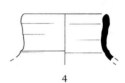

3 4

 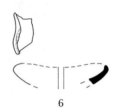

5 6

Square L/9, Locus 749, basket 291

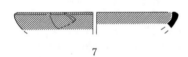 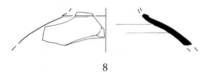

7 8

Square L/9, Locus 728, basket 273

 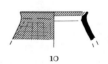

9 10

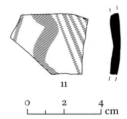

11

FIGURE 3.8

THE POTTERY OF STRATUM 7 (MB IIA)

Figure No.	Shape/object	Reg. No.	Locus/Pottery Basket	Description (color of exterior/interior/core; inclusions; decorations; etc.)
3.8.1	Bowl	AK IX 1983 H M/9 b. 1099/2	1099/2	Buff/buff/buff; small amount of small brown and small white inclusions; brown slip and burnished from just below carination to over the lip
3.8.2	Bowl	AK IX 1983 H M/9 b. 1099/1	1099/1	Pink/pink/pink to light grey; red slip and burnished exterior and interior
3.8.3	Bowl	AK X 1984 H M/9 b. 640/2	640/2	Buff/buff/buff; medium amount of small dark brown inclusions
3.8.4	Storage jar	AK X 1984 H M/9 b. 640/1	640/1	Pink/pink/grey; medium amount of small white inclusions
3.8.5	Juglet	AK X 1984 H M/9 b. 640/7	640/7	Pink/pink/pink; few small white inclusions; red slip and burnished exterior and interior from bottom of rim
3.8.6	Lamp	AK X 1984 H M/9 b. 640/3	640/3	Pink/pink/red to pink; medium amount of small white and grey inclusions
3.8.7	Bowl	AK VIII 1982 H L/9 b. 291/1	291/1	Pink/pink/pink; small amount of small brown inclusions; red slip and burnished exterior and interior
3.8.8	Storage jar	AK VIII 1982 H L/9 b. 291/2	291/2	Pink/pink/buff; medium amount of small to medium sized white inclusions; raised collar on shoulder
3.8.9	Bowl	AK VIII 1982 H L/9 b. 273/2	273/2	Pink/pink/pink; small number of small white inclusions; possible remnants of red slip on interior
3.8.10	Bowl	AK VIII 1982 H L/9 b. 273/3	273/3	Pink/pink/pink; medium number of small white and small dark grey inclusions; red slip and burnished exterior and just over lip on interior
3.8.11	Jug	AK VIII 1982 H L/9 b. 273/1	273/1	Buff/buff/buff; large number of small dark brown and a few mica inclusions; burnished exterior with dark brown painted stripes; Cypriot White Painted Wares

MB IIA typology
Platter bowls

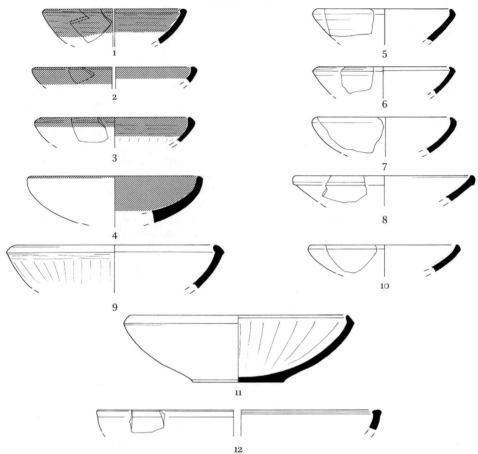

Platter bowl bases

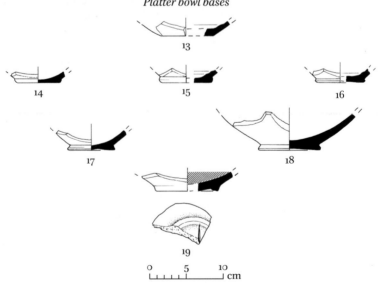

FIGURE 3.9

THE POTTERY OF STRATUM 7 (MB IIA)

Figure No.	Shape/ object	Reg. No.	Locus/ Pottery Basket	Description (color of exterior/interior/core; inclusions; decorations; etc.)
3.9.1	Platter Bowl	AK X 1984 H M/10 b. 606/20 + 23	606/20 + 23	Pink/pink/pink; medium amount of small to medium white inclusions; red slip and burnished exterior and interior
3.9.2	Platter Bowl	AK VIII 1982 H L/9 b. 291/1	291/1	Pink/pink/pink; small amount of small brown inclusions; red slip and burnished exterior and interior
3.9.3	Platter Bowl	AK X 1984 H M/10 b. 630/15	630/15	Pink/pink/pink; small amount of small to medium sized white and grey inclusions; red slip and burnished on exterior from below rim and on interior
3.9.4	Platter Bowl	AK X 1984 H M/10 b. 630/24	630/24	Buff/buff/light grey; few small white inclusions; red slip and burnished interior and lip
3.9.5	Platter Bowl	AK X 1984 H M/10 b. 613/8	613/8	Pink/pink/reddish pink; few small white inclusions
3.9.6	Platter Bowl	AK X 1984 H M/10 b. 613/9	613/9	Pinkish buff/pinkish buff/reddish pink; few small white inclusions
3.9.7	Platter Bowl	AK X 1984 H M/10 b. 613/6 + 10	613/6 + 10	Pink/pink/dark grey; few small to medium sized white inclusions
3.9.8	Platter Bowl	AK X 1984 H M/10 b. 634/2	634/2	Pink/pink/pink to light grey; medium amount of small white and small grey inclusions and voids
3.9.9	Platter Bowl	AK X 1984 H M/10 b. 634/3	634/3	Pink to dark brown/pink/pink to red; many small to medium sized white and grey, and miniscule brown inclusions
3.9.10	Platter Bowl	AK IX 1983 H M/10 b. 1215/2	1215/2	Light grey/dark grey/light grey; few small white inclusions
3.9.11	Platter Bowl	AK X 1984 H M/10 b. 630/2	630/2	Pink/pink/pink to light grey; few small white and medium grey inclusions; radial burnishing on interior
3.9.12	Platter Bowl	AK X 1984 H M/10 b. 634/1	634/1	Pink/pink/pink; many small white, grey, and miniscule brown inclusions
3.9.13	Platter Bowl	AK X 1984 H M/10 b. 634/8	634/8	Pink/pink/pink; few small white inclusions and voids
3.9.14	Platter Bowl	AK VIII 1982 H L/9 b. 273/2	273/2	Pink/pink/pink; small number of small white inclusions; possible remnants of red slip on interior
3.9.15	Platter Bowl?	AK X 1984 H M/10 b. 606/6	606/6	Buff/buff/buff; few small white inclusions
3.9.16	Platter Bowl	AK X 1984 H M/10 b. 630/18	630/18	Buff/red to grey/light grey; medium amount of small white inclusions
3.9.17	Platter Bowl	AK X 1984 H M/10 b. 630/16	630/16	Pink/pink/light grey; large amount of small to large white inclusions
3.9.18	Platter Bowl	AK X 1984 H M/10 b. 626/11	626/11	Buff/buff/buff to light grey; few small white inclusions;
3.9.19	Platter Bowl	AK X 1984 H M/10 b. 606/5	606/5	Pink/pink/pink to light grey; few small white inclusions; red slip and burnished interior

MB IIA typology (cont.)

Carinated bowls

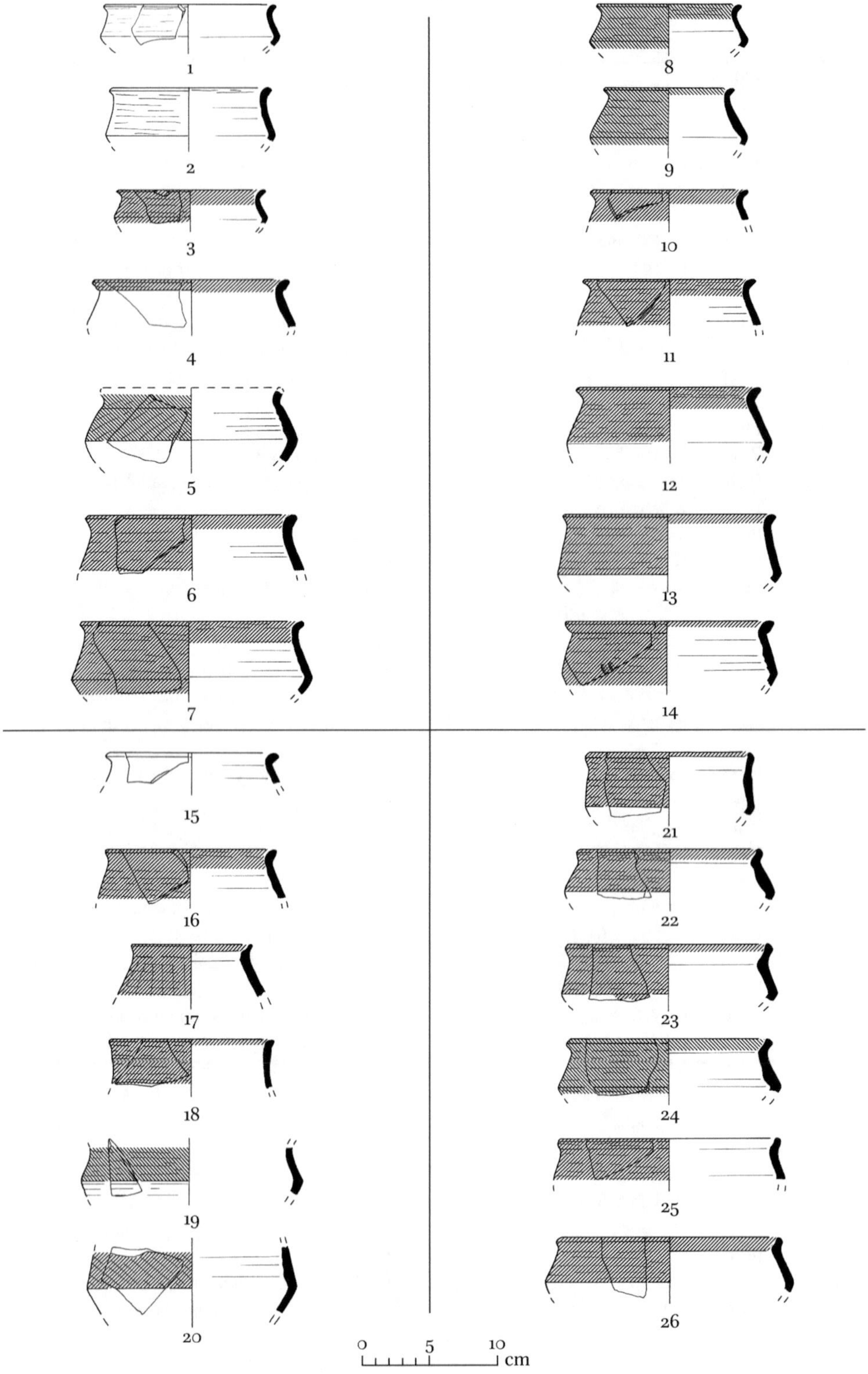

FIGURE 3.10

THE POTTERY OF STRATUM 7 (MB IIA)

Figure No.	Shape/ object	Reg. No.	Locus/ Pottery Basket	Description (color of exterior/interior/core; inclusions; decorations; etc.)
3.10.1	Carinated bowl	AK X 1984 H M/10 b. 606/11	606/11	Buff/buff/buff; medium amount of small white and miniscule brown inclusions
3.10.2	Carinated bowl	AK IX 1983 H M/10 b. 1215/6	1215/6	Tan/tan/tan; medium amount of medium sized white and grey, and miniscule brown, inclusions; burnished exterior and interior from middle of rim
3.10.3	Carinated bowl	AK IX 1983 H M/10 b. 1215/8	1215/8	Pink/pink/pink; many small to medium sized white and miniscule brown inclusions; red slip and burnished exterior and interior from bottom of rim
3.10.4	Carinated bowl	AK X 1984 H M/10 b. 606/10	606/10	Pink/pink/pink; few small white and grey and miniscule brown inclusions; brown slipped and burnished exterior and interior from beginning of rim
3.10.5	Carinated bowl	AK X 1984 H M/10 b. 626/7	626/7	Buff/pink/pink to brown; few small to medium sized white to light grey inclusions; brown slip and burnished on exterior above carination, white slip on exterior below carination
3.10.6	Carinated bowl	AK X 1984 H M/10 b. 613/15	613/15	Pink/pink/pink; few small white and miniscule brown inclusions; red slip and burnished exterior and interior from beginning of rim
3.10.7	Carinated bowl	AK X 1984 H M/10 b. 622/3	622/3	Pink/pink/pink; few small to medium sized white inclusions; red slip and burnished exterior from carination to rim and interior from below lip
3.10.8	Carinated bowl	AK X 1984 H M/10 b. 626/9	626/9	Pink/pink/pink to grey; few small white inclusions; brown slip and burnished exterior to carination and interior from bottom of rim
3.10.9	Carinated bowl	AK IX 1983 H M/9 b. 1099/2	1099/2	Buff/buff/buff; small amount of small brown and small white inclusions; brown slip and burnished from just below carination to over the lip
3.10.10	Carinated bowl	AK X 1984 H M/10 b. 596/2	596/2	Pink/pink/pink; medium amount of small to medium sized white and medium sized dark grey inclusions; red slip and burnished exterior and interior from bottom of rim
3.10.11	Carinated bowl	AK X 1984 H M/10 b. 613/18	613/18	Pink/pink/pink; few small white and miniscule dark brown inclusions; red slip and burnished exterior and interior from beginning of rim
3.10.12	Carinated bowl	AK X 1984 H M/10 b. 630/9	630/9	Pink/pink/pink; medium amount of small white inclusions; red slip and burnished on exterior from carination and on interior from below rim
3.10.13	Carinated bowl	AK X 1984 H M/10 b. 630/8	630/8	Pink/pink/pink to buff; medium amount of small white inclusions; red slip and burnished on exterior from carination and on interior from bottom of rim
3.10.14	Carinated bowl	AK X 1984 H M/10 b. 613/14	613/14	Pink/pink/pink to light grey; few small white and miniscule dark brown inclusions; red slip and burnished exterior and interior from middle of rim

Figure No.	Shape/object	Reg. No.	Locus/Pottery Basket	Description (color of exterior/interior/core; inclusions; decorations; etc.)
3.10.15	Carinated bowl	AK X 1984 H M/10 b. 587/2	587/2	Buff/buff/buff; few medium sized white inclusions and voids
3.10.16	Carinated bowl	AK X 1984 H M/10 b. 630/6	630/6	Pink/pink/pink to light grey; few medium sized white inclusions; red slip and burnished on exterior and on interior from below rim
3.10.17	Carinated bowl	AK VIII 1982 H L/9 b. 273/3	273/3	Pink/pink/pink; medium number of small white and small dark grey inclusions; red slip and burnished exterior and just over lip on interior
3.10.18	Carinated bowl	AK X 1984 H M/10 b. 630/5	630/5	Light brown/light brown/light brown; few small white inclusions; red slip and burnished on exterior and on interior from bottom of rim
3.10.19	Carinated bowl	AK X 1984 H M/10 b. 622/2	622/2	Pink/pink/pink; few small white inclusions; red slip and burnished exterior and interior from below lip
3.10.20	Carinated bowl	AK X 1984 H M/10 b. 630/4	630/4	Pink/pink/pink; few small white and miniscule brown inclusions; red slip and burnished on exterior from carination
3.10.21	Carinated bowl	AK X 1984 H M/10 b. 634/15	634/15	Pink/pink/pink to buff; medium amount of small white and grey, miniscule brown, inclusions; red slip and burnished on exterior from carination and on interior from middle of rim
3.10.22	Carinated bowl	AK X 1984 H M/10 b. 630/25	630/25	Pink/pink/light grey; few small white and miniscule brown inclusions ; red slip and burnished on exterior from carination and from middle of rim on interior
3.10.23	Carinated bowl	AK X 1984 H M/10 b. 630/7	630/7	Pink/pink/pink to buff; medium amount of small to medium sized white inclusions; brown slip and burnished from carination on exterior and middle of rim on interior
3.10.24	Carinated bowl	AK X 1984 H M/10 b. 626/8	626/8	Pink/pink/pink; few small to medium sized white inclusions; brown slip and burnished exterior to carination and interior from bottom of rim
3.10.25	Carinated bowl	AK X 1984 H M/10 b. 606/9	606/9	Red/red/red; many small white and miniscule brown inclusions; red slip and burnished exterior
3.10.26	Carinated bowl	AK X 1984 H M/10 b. 622/1	622/1	Pink/pink/pink to light grey; few small white inclusions; red slip and burnished exterior above carination

MB IIA typology (cont.)
Hemispheric, S-profiled, flaring carinated, and necked bowls

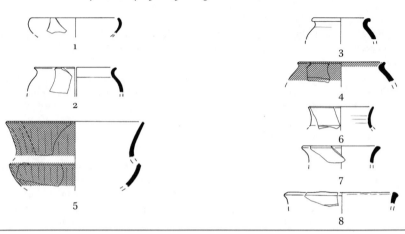

Kraters

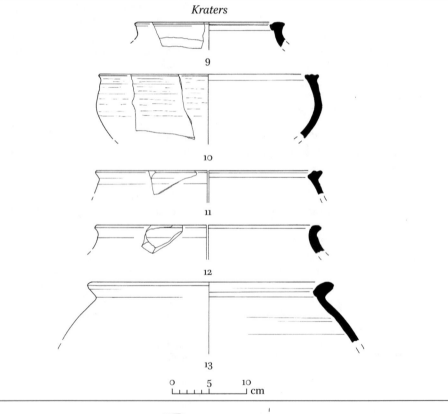

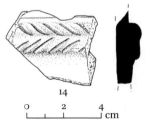

FIGURE 3.11

THE POTTERY OF STRATUM 7 (MB IIA)

Figure No.	Shape/ object	Reg. No.	Locus/ Pottery Basket	Description (color of exterior/interior/core; inclusions; decorations; etc.)
3.11.1	Bowl	AK X 1984 H M/10 b. 613/7	613/7	Buff/buff/buff; few small white inclusions
3.11.2	Bowl	AK X 1984 H M/10 b. 622/4	622/4	Buff/buff/buff; few small brown inclusions
3.11.3	Bowl	AK X 1984 H M/9 b. 640/2	640/2	Buff/buff/buff; medium amount of small dark brown inclusions
3.11.4	Bowl	AK IX 1983 H M/9 b. 1099/1	1099/1	Pink/pink/pink to light grey; red slip and burnished exterior and interior
3.11.5	Bowl	AK X 1984 H M/10 b. 582/2, 598	582/2	Brown/brown/pink to dark grey; few small black inclusions; brown slipped and burnished exterior
3.11.6	Bowl	AK X 1984 H M/10 b. 634/9	634/9	Pink/pink/pink; very few small white inclusions
3.11.7	Bowl	AK X 1984 H M/10 b. 613/21	613/21	Pink/pink/pink; few medium sized light grey inclusions
3.11.8	Bowl	AK X 1984 H M/10 b. 630/20	630/20	Buff/buff/buff; few small white inclusions
3.11.9	Krater	AK X 1984 H M/10 b. 622/7	622/7	Pink buff/pink/light grey; large amount of small to large white and miniscule dark brown inclusions
3.11.10	Krater	AK X 1984 H M/10 b. 626/6	626/6	Buff/buff/light grey; medium amount of small to medium sized white inclusions; ivory-colored slip and burnished exterior and top of rim
3.11.11	Krater	AK X 1984 H M/10 b. 630/14	630/14	Pink/pink/pink; few small white and miniscule brown inclusions
3.11.12	Krater	AK X 1984 H M/10 b. 626/10	626/10	Pink/pink/light grey; few small to medium sized white inclusions
3.11.13	Krater	AK IX 1983 H M/10 b. 1215/1	1215/1	Buff green/buff green/red to pink; many small grey and white inclusions
3.11.14	Krater?	AK X 1984 H M/10 b. 622/5	622/5	Pink/pink/pink to grey; few small white inclusions; raised band with an incised chevron design

MB IIA typology (cont.)

Cooking pots

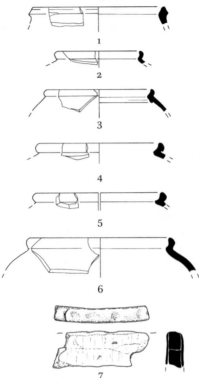

Pithoi

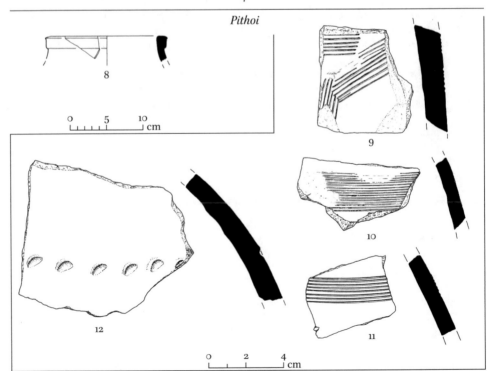

FIGURE 3.12

THE POTTERY OF STRATUM 7 (MB IIA)

Figure No.	Shape/ object	Reg. No.	Locus/ Pottery Basket	Description (color of exterior/interior/ core; inclusions; decorations; etc.)
3.12.1	Cooking pot	AK X 1984 H M/10 b. 630/23	630/23	Brown/brown/dark grey; medium amount of small white inclusions
3.12.2	Cooking pot	AK X 1984 H M/10 b. 613/23	613/23	Brown/dark brown/dark brown; many small to medium white and light grey inclusions
3.12.3	Cooking pot	AK X 1984 H M/10 b. 626/2	626/2	Brown/reddish brown/brown; medium amount of small white inclusions
3.12.4	Cooking pot	AK IX 1983 H M/10 b. 1215/5	1215/5	Brown/reddish brown/reddish brown; many small white and light grey inclusions
3.12.5	Cooking pot	AK X 1984 H M/10 b. 634/14	634/14	Dark brown/buff/dark brown to light brown; large amount of small white inclusions
3.12.6	Cooking pot	AK X 1984 H M/10 b. 582/1	582/1	Brown/brown/brown to light grey; medium amount of small white and miniscule brown inclusions
3.12.7	Cooking pot?	AK X 1984 H M/10 b. 622/6	622/6	Light brown/dark brown/light brown; few small white inclusions
3.12.8	Pithos	AK X 1984 H M/10 b. 613/4	613/4	Pink/pink/pink; few small white inclusions
3.12.9	Pithos or storage jar	AK X 1984 H M/10 b. 634/7	634/7	Pink/pink/light grey; medium amount of small white and small brown inclusions; patterned combing
3.12.10	Pithos or storage jar	AK X 1984 H M/10 b. 606/17	606/17	Pink/pink/pink; few small to large white inclusions; patterned combing on body sherd
3.12.11	Pithos or storage jar	AK X 1984 H M/10 b. 630/13	630/13	Buff/buff/light grey; medium amount of medium sized grey and small white inclusions; combed decoration
3.12.12	Pithos or storage jar	AK X 1984 H M/10 b. 622/14	622/14	Pink/light grey/red to light grey; medium number of medium sized white and occasional small dark brown inclusions; wheel combed, small half-moon indentations

MB IIA typology (cont.)
Storage jars

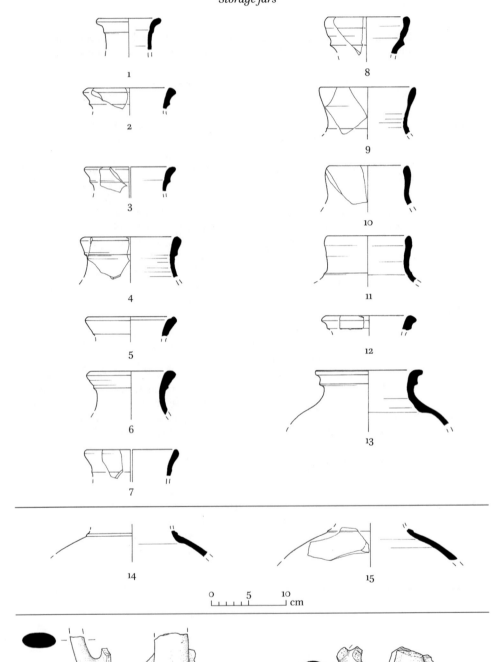

FIGURE 3.13

Figure No.	Shape/object	Reg. No.	Locus/ Pottery Basket	Description (color of exterior/interior/core; inclusions; decorations; etc.)
3.13.1	Storage jar	AK X 1984 H M/10 b. 634/4	634/4	Pink/pink/red; large number of small to large white and grey inclusions
3.13.2	Storage jar	AK X 1984 H M/10 b. 630/11	630/11	Pink/pink/pink; few small white inclusions
3.13.3	Storage jar	AK X 1984 H M/10 b. 582/3	582/3	Pink/pink/pink; few small white inclusions
3.13.4	Storage jar	AK X 1984 H M/10 b. 634/6	634/6	Pink/pink/pink; few small white, few small grey, many miniscule brown inclusions
3.13.5	Storage jar	AK X 1984 H M/10 b. 630/12	630/12	Pink/pink/light grey; large amount of medium sized white inclusions
3.13.6	Storage jar	AK X 1984 H M/10 b. 630/17	630/17	Pink/pink/light grey; few small to medium sized white and medium sized grey inclusions
3.13.7	Storage jar	AK X 1984 H M/10 b. 634/5	634/5	Red/red/red; many small white and few medium sized grey inclusions
3.13.8	Storage jar	AK X 1984 H M/10 b. 626/4	626/4	Pink/pink/pink; medium amount of small to medium sized white and light grey inclusions
3.13.9	Storage jar	AK X 1984 H M/10 b. 613/3	613/3	Pink/pink/red pink; few large white inclusions
3.13.10	Storage jar	AK X 1984 H M/10 b. 622/11	622/11	Pink/pink/light grey; small number of small to medium sized white inclusions
3.13.11	Storage jar	AK X 1984 H M/9 b. 640/1	640/1	Pink/pink/grey; medium amount of small white inclusions
3.13.12	Storage jar	AK X 1984 H M/10 b. 582/4	582/4	Pink/pink/pink; few small white inclusions
3.13.13	Storage jar	AK X 1984 H M/10 b. 613/1	613/1	Pink/pink/pink to grey; medium amount of small to large white inclusions
3.13.14	Storage jar	AK X 1984 H M/10 b. 626/1	626/1	Pink/pink/light grey; few small white inclusions
3.13.15	Storage jar	AK VIII 1982 H L/9 b. 291/2	291/2	Pink/pink/buff; medium amount of small to medium sized white inclusions; raised collar on shoulder
3.13.16	Storage jar	AK X 1984 H M/10 b. 606/2	606/2	Pink/pink/light grey; few small white inclusions
3.13.17	Storage jar	AK IX 1983 H M/10 b. 1215/3	1215/3	Pink/pink/light grey; medium amount of small to medium sized white and light grey inclusions

MB IIA typology (cont.)

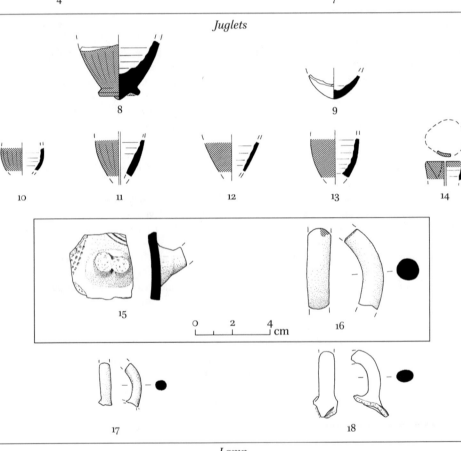

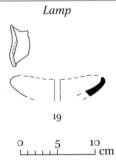

FIGURE 3.14

THE POTTERY OF STRATUM 7 (MB IIA) 263

Figure No.	Shape/ object	Reg. No.	Locus/ Pottery Basket	Description (color of exterior/interior/core; inclusions; decorations; etc.)
3.14.1	Jug?	AK X 1984 H M/10 b. 606/12	606/12	Pink/pink/pink; few small white, one large grey, inclusions
3.14.2	Jug?	AK X 1984 H M/10 b. 630/21	630/21	Dark grey/dark grey/dark grey; medium amount of small to medium sized white inclusions
3.14.3	Jug?	AK X 1984 H M/10 b. 630/22	630/22	Pink/pink/red; medium amount of small to medium sized white and grey inclusions
3.14.4	Jug?	AK X 1984 H M/10 b. 613/5	613/5	Pink/pink/reddish pink; few small white inclusions
3.14.5	Jug?	AK X 1984 H M/10 b. 630/1	630/1	Pink/pink/light grey; medium amount of small to medium sized white and grey inclusions; red slip and burnished exterior
3.14.6	Jar or jug	AK X 1984 H M/10 b. 606/8	606/8	Buff/buff/buff to light grey; few small white inclusions
3.14.7	Jar or jug	AK X 1984 H M/10 b. 606/7	606/7	Pink/pink/pink; few small white inclusions
3.14.8	Juglet	AK X 1984 H M/10 b. 596/1	596/1	Cream/light grey/cream to light grey; few small dark brown inclusions; red slip and burnished exterior
3.14.9	Juglet	AK X 1984 H M/10 b. 634/13	634/13	Pink/pink/pink to red; few small white and miniscule brown inclusions
3.14.10	Juglet	AK X 1984 H M/10 b. 606/22	606/22	Buff/buff/buff; medium amount of miniscule brown inclusions; red slip and burnished exterior
3.14.11	Juglet	AK X 1984 H M/10 b. 630/10	630/10	Pink/pink/pink; medium amount of small to large white inclusions; red slip and burnished on exterior
3.14.12	Juglet	AK IX 1983 H M/10 b. 1215/10	1215/10	Pink/pink/pink; few miniscule brown inclusions; red slip and burnished exterior
3.14.13	Juglet	AK X 1984 H M/10 b. 630/19	630/19	Cream/cream/cream; few small to medium sized grey inclusions; traces of red slip on exterior
3.14.14	Juglet	AK X 1984 H M/9 b. 640/7	640/7	Pink/pink/pink; few small white inclusions; red slip and burnished exterior and interior from bottom of rim
3.14.15	Juglet	AK X 1984 H M/10 b. 626/3	626/3	Light grey/light grey/light grey; medium amount of small brown and dark grey inclusions; Tell el-Yahudiyeh Ware
3.14.16	Juglet	AK X 1984 H M/10 b. 587/1	587/1	Pink/pink/pink; medium amount of small white and miniscule brown inclusions
3.14.17	Juglet	AK IX 1983 H M/10 b. 1215/7	1215/7	Pink/pink/reddish pink; medium amount of small white and grey inclusions
3.14.18	Juglet	AK X 1984 H M/10 b. 630/3	630/3	Buff/buff/light grey; many small to medium sized white and large dark grey inclusions; possible potter's mark on exterior below handle
3.14.19	Lamp	AK X 1984 H M/9 b. 640/3	640/3	Pink/pink/red to pink; medium amount of small white and grey inclusions

MB IIA typology (cont.)
Cypriot imports

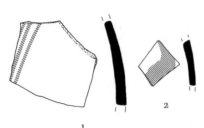
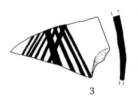
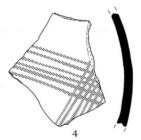

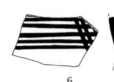

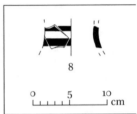

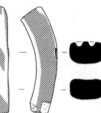

FIGURE 3.15

THE POTTERY OF STRATUM 7 (MB IIA)

Figure No.	Shape/ object	Reg. No.	Locus/ Pottery Basket	Description (color of exterior/interior/core; inclusions; decorations; etc.)
3.15.1	Jug	AK X 1984 H M/10 b. 606/19	606/19	Pink/pink/pink; many miniscule white and brown inclusions; red painted stripes on exterior; Cypriot White Painted III Ware
3.15.2	Body sherd	AK X 1984 H M/10 b. 634/20	634/20	Buff/buff/buff; few miniscule brown inclusions; few miniscule brown and micaceous inclusions; red painted stipe on exterior; Cypriot White Painted III Ware
3.15.3	Jug	AK X 1984 H M/10 b. 634/23	634/23	Buff/buff/buff; small amount of miniscule brown inclusions; dark brown stripes on exterior; Cypriot White Painted III Ware
3.15.4	Jug	AK X 1984 H M/10 b. 634/22	634/22	Pink/pink/pink; small amount of miniscule white, miniscule brown, and small micaceous inclusions; dark red stripes on exterior; Cypriot White Painted III Ware
3.15.5	Body fragment (chip)	AK X 1984 H M/10 b. 622/13	622/13	Buff/interior not visible/buff; small number of small brown inclusions; dark brown stripes on exterior; Cypriot
3.15.6	Jug	AK X 1984 H M/10 b. 634/21	634/21	Dark buff/buff/buff; very small amount of miniscule brown and micaceous inclusions; dark brown painted stripes on exterior; Cypriot White Painted III Ware
3.15.7	Jug	AK VIII 1982 H L/9 b. 273/1	273/1	Buff/buff/buff; large number of small dark brown and a few mica inclusions; burnished exterior with dark brown painted stripes; Cypriot White Painted Wares
3.15.8	Jug?	AK X 1984 H M/10 b. 621/1	621/1	Greenish buff/buff/pink; many small dark brown inclusions; dark brown painted stripes on exterior; Cypriot White Painted III Ware
3.15.9	Body fragment	AK X 1984 H M/10 b. 622/12	622/12	Buff/buff/buff; small number of small brown inclusions; burnished interior with dark brown painted designs, dark brown slipped exterior; Cypriot White Painted Ware
3.15.10	Jug	AK X 1984 H M/10 b. 613/1	613/1	Greenish buff/buff/buff; few miniscule dark brown inclusions; red painted stripes on exterior; Cypriot White Painted III Ware
3.15.11	Jug	AK X 1984 H M/10 b. 626/5	626/5	Pink/pink/grey brown; few small white inclusions; red painted stripes and two oval indentations on handle; Cypriot White Painted III Ware
3.15.12	Juglet?	AK IX 1983 H M/10 b. 1203/1	1203/1	Buff/buff/buff; small amount of miniscule brown inclusions; painted brown stripes on exterior; Cypriot White Painted Ware

CHAPTER 4

The Pottery and Other Material Culture of Stratum 6 (MB IIB–IIC)

Aaron Brody and Michal Artzy

Several burials were placed in cuts in the rampart, one cist burial and two multiburial chamber tombs that have been attributed to Stratum 6 (fig. 2.11). While the two chamber tombs, Tomb 829 and Tomb 932, are less than 20 meters apart from one another they were located in two different contexts of the site, which is an important facet in the understanding of the Middle and Late Bronze fortification system at Tel Akko. Tomb 829 was dug into the MB IIA rampart summit near its edge and was later partially disturbed by a Persian period burial (photo 2.4; fig. 2.13.12). Tomb 932 was located southeast of Tomb 829 and was placed on sand and kurkar (sand stone). It was disturbed by Persian/Hellenistic walls, most of which were robbed during a later period. The lower two-thirds of the structure of Tomb 829 remained intact; the stones of its roof were robbed, although it is hard to point to the period in which this took place. From the remaining top part of the tomb's walls, it seems to have been a false arch tomb, similar in type to those found in Ugarit.

The local ceramic repertoire from the Stratum 6 tombs (photo 4.4) is typical for burials of the MB IIB–IIC period (MB III or MB IIB–LB IA). While imported ceramics are few in number, their origins are varied and indicate the widespread commercial networks of the end of the Middle Bronze Age eastern Mediterranean. The Syro-Anatolian coast is the most likely source of one dark brown, highly burnished, spouted jug from Tomb 932 (fig. 4.7.3). The origin of a ceramic jug imitating a metal form has not been established (photo 4.16; fig. 4.7.4). Two Middle Cypriot vessels were also uncovered in Tomb 932, a Red-on-Black bowl and a White Painted VI juglet, clear indicators of the nascent maritime trade of the period (figs. 4.6.8, 4.8.3). Regional and long distance interaction is further indicated by other material cultural finds from the tombs. Alabaster vessels in each tomb may have originated from a source near Beth Shean in the Jordan Valley, although some are true alabaster imports from Egypt. Connections to Egypt are shown in the sources of the materials used to manufacture weights, beads, and scarabs, such as hematite, amethyst, white steatite, and rock crystal. Egypt is likely the original source for the gold used to make jewelry found in Tomb 829. A turquoise bead and cone shell bead come from the Sinai/Red Sea region (photo 4.13). It is probable that a disk-shaped loom weight from Tomb 932 is either Cypriot or Minoan (fig. 4.8.5).

Personal items from the tombs, such as bronze balance pans and the hematite weight set in Tomb 829 (photo 4.6), and ballast stones of Cypriot origin in Tomb 932 (photo 2.6), are likely indicators that each of the extended families represented by the tombs were directly involved in regional or long distance trade. The port of Akko, after all, is situated at a key juncture between sea routes leading to Cyprus, the Aegean, the Egyptian Delta, and the Lebanese and north Syrian coasts, and overland routes leading through the Jezreel Valley to the Jordan Valley and beyond. These networks seem to have been exploited by the wealthy merchant families of Middle Bronze Age Akko buried in Area H. Other burials of the period, found in Area AB on the tell's summit, were not as wealthy (M. Dothan 1993: 20; Beeri 2003). Each tomb was discussed above in chapter 2 with regard to its phasing, stratigraphy, orientation, and skeletal remains. What follows is a detailed presentation of the ceramics and material culture from each tomb, followed by a typology of the pottery and chronological conclusions.

Material Culture from 727, Stratum 6 Cist Tomb

The burials of an adult and child in the same cist tomb were accompanied by few grave goods (fig. 2.12). The juglets, bronze pin, and bronze earring from the tomb suggest that those interred were of modest means (photo 2.3).

Closed Vessels in 727
Juglets: Two juglets were discovered in Tomb 727. It is apparent from photographs and drawings of the tomb that the dipper juglet was large. The second juglet is cylindrical with a flared rim, short neck, flat base, and a double-strand handle (fig. 4.1.1).

Small Finds in 727, Artifacts
A bronze pin and a bronze earring were also found in the cist grave. These were not located; however, from the drawing it appears that the pin was a straight pin (fig. 2.12). It was found near the upper vertebrae and upper ribs of the adult skeleton, suggesting that it was used for holding the interred's garment. Part of a bronze earring was uncovered close to the left shoulder of the adult. It appears to be a simple hoop earring.

Material Culture from Tomb 829, Stratum 6 Built Chamber Tomb

Of the thirty vessels recorded from the tomb eleven are open forms and nineteen are closed. Besides ceramics, Tomb 829 contained a wide variety of material cultural remains and several types of ecofacts.

Open Vessels in Tombs 829

Platter bowls: Five platter bowls were uncovered in the excavation of the built chamber tomb, 829. All five examples have ring bases and simple rims (fig. 4.1.2–6). Their ware is pink to pinky-cream in color; where the core of the vessels is visible it shows almost no difference in color with the surface. Four out of five of these platter bowls have light radial burnishing on the interior of the bowl, but are not slipped (photo 4.2).

Chalices: Two carinated chalices (also called "goblets") were found in the tomb (fig. 4.1.7–8). This vessel type is a hallmark of the MB IIB–IIC in northern Palestine (Kempinski 1992: 180). Both examples have similar high, trumpet bases and simple rims. The ware is typical of a class of different vessel types; its buff or pale yellow fabric is well levigated and the vessels are very thin walled, as is true for our two chalices. The core of each vessel is identical in color to its surface. The cups of the chalices are highly carinated, which is a general characteristic of globular/carinated bowls in the later MB IIB and MB IIC, and likely copy a metal prototype (photo 4.3).[1]

Closed Vessels in Tomb 829

Storage jars: Three storage jars were recorded in the excavation of 829. Unfortunately we have not been able to locate these jars for further description.

Amphoriskoi: Two jars were excavated which can be considered amphoriskoi. The larger of the two has a flaring rim and wide neck; this rests on an ovoid body typical for Bronze Age jars (fig. 4.2.1). Two protruding loop handles are attached to the ovoid body of the vessel just at the shoulder, and the base is rounded, both of which are also typical for jars of the period. The ware is pink with large inclusions visible on the surface; the core is not visible. It is possible that this shape represents a hybrid of an Egyptian style neck and rim on a storage jar type body with clearly local stylistic affinities. The second amphoriskos is smaller in size, and appears to have a much narrower neck (fig. 4.2.2). It has a direct rim with a profiled cross section. The body is ovoid with a flattened base.

---

1 The gold chalice discovered on the Uluburun shipwreck is a good parallel despite its later LB II date.

A pair of small loop handles is attached just below the shoulder of the vessel. Its ware is brown in color, with a similar core that has small, white inclusions.

Jugs: Three jugs were uncovered in the excavation of Tomb 829. The first is a large jug with missing rim (fig. 4.2.3). The body of the vessel is globular, one loop handle is attached to its shoulder, and the base is disk-shaped. The ware of the vessel is pink with small white inclusions; its core is not visible. Two small jugs were also discovered in the tomb, which are really miniature pitchers (fig. 4.2.4–5). Both have trefoil mouths, loop handles on their shoulders, globular bodies, and disk bases (photo 4.5). The vessels are both reddish brown in color, one shows some indications of slip and burnish (fig. 4.2.5); neither vessel's core is visible. Some see this vessel type's development from globular necked bowls (Ilan 1996: 224), but given its clear pouring function indicated by the trefoil mouth we would keep it under the category of jugs, a type whose main function is to hold and pour liquids (Hunt 1987: 197).

A jug was found in a probe just east of the tomb. It is not clear whether this almost intact vessel (fig. 4.2.6), an MB IIB–IIC jug with a high trumpet base and double-strand handle, should be viewed as an offering placed outside of the tomb, as it is comes from a context in one of the layers of the city rampart. If not, why would an almost whole vessel be found in the rampart? The rim of the vessel is unfortunately missing, but given the elaborated treatment of its base (Cole 1984: 142) and the finely-levigated, buff fabric with a buff interior, it is clearly from the same family of pottery as the carinated chalices discovered inside Tomb 829. Although attributed at first to the Middle Bronze rampart layers, given the narrow excavation area in which it was uncovered, we view this vessel as related to the burials in Tomb 829.

Juglets: Four juglets were found in 829, two dipper and two cylindrical juglets (photo 4.1). Both dipper juglets have pinched mouths, round handles from rim to shoulder, and tapering bodies (fig. 4.2.7–8). One is pink in color (basket 321/1) with a buff slip and burnished; its core is not visible. The second is buff with a buff core. The best preserved cylindrical juglet has an everted rim thickened and rounded, a strap handle from its neck to shoulder, and a slightly rounded base (fig. 4.2.9). Its ware is reddish brown with a cream-colored slip; its core is light brown. The second cylindrical juglet is fragmentary, with only the body of the vessel preserved showing a slightly rounded base (fig. 4.2.10). Its ware is pinkish buff; its core is identical in color with small white inclusions.

Small Finds in Tomb 829, Artifacts

Small finds from the tomb include metal, stone, and bone artifacts; and scarabs, weights, and beads of various materials.

Bronze objects: The only bronze find was a pair of round, slightly concave pans (fig. 4.3.1–2, photo 4.6). One pan is 7.0 cm in diameter, the other is 7.1, and both are 2.5 mm thick. These were clearly used together as a balance scale, as is indicated by the three small holes in each which would have allowed a thin cord or string to support each pan from a balance arm. The holes are at only three out of four cardinal points of each pan, allowing for a space in the front of each scale free of any interference from the supporting cord. The identification of these bronze pans as part of a balance scale seems even more likely given the set of weights discovered in the tomb, described below. Traces of bronze flakes adhere to the inside of the holes on either end of an amethyst scarab (photo 4.11, furthest left scarab), suggesting an original bronze ring that has since disappeared.

Lead object: One lead object was discovered in 829 (fig. 4.3.3). It is small, approximately 1.4 cm in diameter, and bun-shaped with a flat bottom. It weighs 8.12 g. It is not clear that this lead piece functioned as a weight, although hematite weights described below were also found in the tomb. In addition, there are similarly shaped colored stones and a frit gaming piece, all found in the same pottery basket, which may mean the lead object was used as a gaming piece or token (fig. 4.5.18–24; photo 4.13).

Gold objects: Several gold objects were found in the tomb, including a pair of plain, loop earrings (fig. 4.3.4–5). The loops are 12 mm from top to bottom, and 1 mm in diameter at their thickest point at the bottom of the loop. Each tapers down below 1 mm in diameter as the loop continues upward, in order to fit the pierced ear. Virtually identical, the earrings must have been worn as a pair (photo 4.8). Two small bands of flattened sheet gold, or gold foil are harder to interpret (fig. 4.3.6–7). One band is 16 × 7 mm, the other 11 × 6 mm; however, it is likely that each was originally more circular before being crushed in the tomb context. It is most likely that these bands were worn as rings or as some sort of ornament. Other gold finds included bezels for scarab rings and a bead, described in greater detail below (fig. 4.5.5–7, 10).

Silver objects: Two silver rings were found in Tomb 829. One, partially preserved, measures 21 mm from end to end and is 2 mm wide (fig. 4.3.9); the second is 32 mm from one twisted end to its other (fig. 4.3.8). The twisting forms a mount to fit into the holes in the gold bezel of a signet scarab, and is 3 mm wide. Two of the rings were discovered with the gold bezeled, amethyst scarabs that formed a signet (photo 4.11; fig. 4.5.5, 7).

Worked stone objects: Worked stone artifacts in 829 include alabaster/gypsum vessels, hematite weights, flints, a grinding stone, and a large stone mortar.

Gypsum vessels: Six gypsum vessels were found in the tomb; three are ovoid with rounded bases (photo 4.7; fig. 4.3.10–12). One of these vessels has an everted, rolled rim (fig. 4.3.10); the second is broken and missing its rim entirely (fig. 4.3.11); the third and smallest vessel has a flaring rim (fig. 4.3.12). The three remaining vessels are baggy-shaped with rounded or slightly rounded bases. One has a direct rim (fig. 4.3.13), the other has a plain rim (4.3.14), and the third example has no rim preserved (fig. 4.3.15). These baggy-shaped gypsum vessels' surfaces are badly corroded, likely affected by coastal humidity and water in the tombs. The poor preservation of these vessels makes it impossible to judge whether their interiors were hollowed through drilling or chiseling, although a circular indentation at the bottom of the interior of vessel 1302/10 may be left from drilling (fig. 4.3.13). The baggy-shaped form with a flat bottom is the most common in Palestine in the MB II (Ben-Dor 1945: 101). The type was manufactured both in Egypt and locally from gypsum deposits in the Jordan Valley. Ben-Dor emphasizes that the local gypsum is much softer than the Egyptian; therefore the local stone is much more susceptible to corrosion (Dor 1945: 94), which means these three baggy-shaped vessels were most likely manufactured in, or near, Beth Shean, although the possible drill mark in the interior of 1302/10 suggests an Egyptian origin for this vessel (Dor 1945: 96, 98). Regardless of their origin, Egypt or the Jordan Valley, they are either indicators of regional trade from the Jordan Valley through the Jezreel to the Akko Plain, or international imports arriving via terrestrial or maritime routes from Egypt.

Hematite weights: Four hematite weights were found in Tomb 829, and seem to be part of a set with the bronze balance pans (photo 4.6). The largest weight, 34 × 15 mm is an ovoid, truncated on both ends and flattened on one side (fig. 4.3.16). It weighs 18.1–18.2 g. Two other weights are similar in shape, truncated ovoids with flattened bottoms, but are much smaller (fig. 4.3.17–18): the lightest is 17 × 7.5 mm and weighs 2.2–2.3 g, and the second lightest is 15 × 8 mm and weighs 2.9–3.0 g. The fourth weight is shaped like a tapering cylinder, 19 × 9 mm, and seems to have stood on its flat base (fig. 4.3.19). It weighs 3.8–3.9 g. The source of the hematite is likely Egypt (Lucas and Harris 1962: 395), but the metrology points to local standards and local manufacture.

Flaked stone artifacts: The finds in the tomb include a flint scraper, a worked flake, and some debitage. For further details see J. Rose's appendix on the flaked stone finds from Area H below. A small hammer stone was discovered in 829. It is a river pebble, approximately 4.35 cm in rough diameter and 2.3 cm thick, with peck marks along one edge. These marks indicate that this small stone was utilized as a tool.

Groundstones: The groundstones from Tomb 829 include a basalt grinding stone and a large limestone mortar (photo 4.9; fig. 4.3.20). The mortar is 48 cm long, 34 cm wide, and 26 cm high. The grinding bowl in its middle is 19 cm in diameter and 7 cm deep. The bowl is quite smooth, but there are numerous flake scars around the bowl's outer edge that testify to a rough chipping out of the interior of the bowl before it was polished smooth. Further "polishing" likely took place through use of the bowl as well. For further details see J. Ebeling's appendix on groundstone material from Area H below. Remaining finds made out of stone are beads and what we would call bead "blanks" which we will discuss below with beads of different materials.

Worked bone: Numerous examples of incised bone inlay strips and two bone silhouettes of birds were found in Tomb 829 (fig. 4.4, photo 4.10). It is difficult to determine how many objects, most likely wooden boxes, these examples of worked bone decorated. Because of the human and water-borne disturbances to the tomb the decorative bone was not found in concentrations that would indicate that certain pieces were grouped together belonging to decomposed wooden boxes. The finds, however, were concentrated in the northwestern area of Tomb 829. There are several geometric motifs carved in bone, standard types of MB II Palestinian repertoire (fig. 4.4.1–22, 25–26; Liebowitz 1977: 92–93): ten examples of strips with longitudinal lines; three with diagonal lines, and four fragments; three with chevron designs; and three with oblique crosses, two small and one large, plus one large fragment. In addition, two examples of the silhouettes of birds, facing in opposite directions, were uncovered (fig. 4.4.23–24). This is one of the major forms of silhouette design in Middle Bronze Age bone carving traditions (Liebowitz 1977: 92, 95).

Scarabs: Six inscribed scarabs and scarab rings from Tomb 829 have been published (Keel 1997: 622–25, nos. 259–60, 262–63, 265–66). Four of these scarabs (photo 4.12) are carved from white steatite (fig. 4.5.1–4) and the other two, both set in gold bezels one with a silver ring described above, are amethyst (fig. 4.5.5–6, photo 4.11). Both of these types of stone come from quarries in Egypt, although their carving may have taken place locally in Palestine (Lucas and Harris 1962: 388–89, 421). All six scarabs are dated by Keel to the 13th or 15th Egyptian royal dynasties, or a period in between. Following Keel's absolute chronology, this provides a broad range between 1759–1522 BCE, which corresponds nicely with our provisional dating of the tomb to the MB IIB–IIC periods. The tomb contained multiple burials, as is detailed above in chapter 2, and may have been in use over several generations. Three uninscribed scarabs, not catalogued by Keel, were also found in Tomb 829. All three are amethyst. One has a gold bezel and silver ring (fig. 4.5.7), the other two (fig. 4.5.8–9) may have been worn as beads strung together with a plain, globular amethyst bead, described below (photo 4.13).

Beads: Beads made from metal, colored stones, and seashells were discovered in Tomb 829. One gold bead was found near skeleton A in the northwest part of the tomb, along with other gold jewelry described above. The gold bead is nicely crafted with a rimmed, cylindrical tube forming a large string hole on either side of the globular body of the bead with raised, horizontal ribbing (fig. 4.5.10). A large bronze bead was uncovered in the western half of the tomb, clustered together with several other beads and objects which may be bead blanks or gaming pieces (all from pottery basket 1196) described below. The bronze bead, like the gold, has a globular body with less pronounced horizontal ribbing (fig. 4.5.11). Inside the string hole is the remnant of copper or bronze wire. One small, globular amethyst bead was found in the eastern part of the tomb (fig. 4.5.12), and may have been grouped with uninscribed amethyst scarabs on a necklace. Amethyst is relatively common in Middle Bronze Palestine, demonstrating trade contacts with the Wadi el-Hudi, in Upper Egypt southeast of Aswan, known as the source of the semi-precious stone's mining during the Middle Kingdom (Lucas and Harris 1962: 338–39). Two fragments of thin, round, translucent rock crystal beads were also found, one from the cache in basket 1196 (fig. 4.5.13–14). The source of rock crystal is also Upper Egypt (Lucas and Harris 1962: 402–403). The one small, globular turquoise bead was uncovered in the western half of the tomb with two shell beads (fig. 4.5.15). The primary source of turquoise for the region is in the Sinai Peninsula (Lucas and Harris 1962: 404).

Of the two shell beads, one is from the common bivalve still found all along the eastern Mediterranean coast (fig. 4.5.16). D. S. Reese identifies the specimen as a "waterworn Glycymeris (dog-cockle). The hole is made by a carnivorous/boring gastropod, not by man (photo 4.13). It was picked up on the beach and was likely used as a pendant" The second shell bead is made from a "waterworn Conus mediterraneus (cone shell). Naturally holed at the apex, also a beach specimen, likely used as a pendant" (fig. 4.5.17).[2] There are a large number of beads discovered on the Cape Gelidonya and Uluburun shipwrecks, both from the LB II (hundreds from Gelidonya, thousands from Uluburun, see Fitzgerald 1997: 431; Pulak 1997: 85). While postdating our tomb, they indicate the predilection for stowing these easily transportable items for maritime trade. This may be interpreted as a form of "trinket trade" or "sailor's trade," as named by Artzy (2001: 116), in the Bronze Age. Beads would also be easily

---

2   These identifications were made by Dr. David S. Reese of the Peabody Museum of Natural History, Yale University, based on drawings of the two shells. The quotations are taken from a letter of Reese's from April 17, 2003. Brody would also like to thank Reese for taking time from his own research to discuss these two shell beads with him at the Albright Institute, summer 1999.

transportable overland by pack animal or carried by humans, as they easily fill crevices alongside larger items of exchange in panniers or sacks.

Bead blanks and/or gaming pieces: Several colored stones were discovered in pottery basket 1196, along with the bronze, amethyst, and rock crystal beads described above, which show clear signs of having been polished flat on one side. They are relatively uniform in size and are all bun-shaped, with their bottoms flattened (fig. 4.5.18–20). Two are a translucent caramel color, perhaps some sort of colored quartz or local chert, and the third is rock crystal. It is not clear if these colored stones are bead blanks, with only the one side worked, or perhaps were used as gaming pieces or small weights. One multifaceted garnet, a dark red to purple semi-precious stone, came from the same cluster of objects from basket 1196 (fig. 4.5.21). The garnet was not worked, the facets are natural, and may also have been a "blank" ready to be cut into a bead. The source of garnet, like the amethyst and rock crystal described above, is Upper Egypt (Lucas and Harris 1962: 394–95). One white frit conical gaming piece also originated in basket 1196 alongside the lead piece, described above (fig. 4.5.22). Altogether, this grouping of two beads, several partially worked colored stones, an unworked garnet, a frit gaming piece, and a lead object form a confusing group (photo 4.13). They are all very small objects and may have been collected together in a wooden box or a bag, long since disintegrated, to collected by occupants of the tomb who may have been merchants involved in trade of gold and semi-precious stones, as might be indicated by the scale weights and balance pans found in the tomb.

Small Finds in Tomb 829, Ecofacts

Several different types of ecofacts are detailed in the daily notes from the excavation of Tomb 829. These include animal and fish bones, burned olive pits, small pieces of charcoal, and small pieces of ocher. The animal and fish bones are fairly fragmentary; see E. Maher's report on the bones from the tomb in his appendix below for further details. Eight whole and fourteen fragmentary olive pits were preserved because they were burned.

It is not clear why several small pieces of red ocher were present in the tomb. Whether they were used for some sort of coloring purposes is not immediately obvious. Although there is prehistoric tradition for the use of ocher in burials it is not widely reported in Middle Bronze Age burials. A few fragments of white plaster colored red on their surface were discovered in the neighboring tomb, Tomb 932, along with pieces of ocher, described below. This ocher may have been used to decorate the inside of Tomb 932; however, no remains of painted plaster were found in Tomb 829.

Material Culture from 913, Pit

Bowls: Pit 913, located just outside the northeast wall of Tomb 829, contained three platter bowls from the transition phase of the MB IIA–IIB (fig. 4.6.1–3). All three bowls have convex disk bases, typical for the period, and incurved or simple, rounded rims. Two of the bowls have fairly straight side-walls, while one is gently rounded. The interior of 1123/1 is decorated with a red slipped and burnished cross, remnants of which are still preserved (photo 4.14; fig. 4.6.3). Their ware is pink in color, and cores, where visible, are pink to pink-buff.

Storage jar?: Possible pieces of a storage jar are mentioned in the field notes as coming from pottery basket 1106 in 913. We have not been able to locate this storage jar, so further details are not available.

Bones: The notes also mention bones being discovered in conjunction with the pottery vessels. The bones are said to be articulated; however, it is not detailed whether they are animal or human. It is possible that they were animal bones, left as an external offering connected with the burials in Tomb 829, as is true for contemporary burials at Dan, Megiddo, Tell el-'Ajjul, Tell el-Maskhuta, and Tell el-Dab'a (Boessneck 1976: 9–18; Horwitz 1996).

Material Culture from Tomb 932, Stratum 6 Built Chamber Tomb

Of the sixteen vessels found in Tomb 932, seven are open forms, eight are closed, and one is a lamp (photo 4.15). In addition, the tomb contained a rich assortment of artifacts and ecofacts that testify to the wealth of individuals buried therein.

Open Vessels in 932

Platter bowls: Three platter bowls were found in 932. All three have ring bases and simple rims (fig. 4.6.4–6). The ware of two of the vessels is pink in color (fig. 4.6.5–6); one shows a core with almost no difference in color to its surface but has small, reddish brown inclusions (fig. 4.6.6). One of these platter bowls (fig. 4.6.4) has well-levigated, buff ware, similar to that used in the manufacture of the carinated chalices found in Tomb 829 and the one example from 932, described below.

Bowls: A small carinated bowl with a convex disk base and everted, straight rim was discovered in Tomb 932 (fig. 4.6.7). Its ware and core is pink. A portion of a Cypriot Red-on-Black ware bowl, with a simple rim and its base missing was also found among the tomb offerings (fig. 4.6.8). This example shows the characteristic handmade, thin, well-levigated fabric. The exterior of the fabric is buff in color, with its core the identical color with occasional small, white inclusions. Although almost all of the slip is gone it is apparent in several small patches on the piece, as are the typical deep red stripes and cross hatchings (fig. 4.6.8.a–b).

Chalices: One carinated chalice was found in Tomb 932, similar in style, manufacture, and fabric to the two from Tomb 829. The example from Tomb 932 has a high, trumpet base and simple rim (photo 4.3; fig. 4.6.9). The ware is the same as that of the chalices from Tomb 829: the fabric is buff in color and is well levigated; the walls of the vessel are very thin. The core of this particular chalice is not visible. The chalice is highly carinated; the carination has a slight curve.

Closed Vessels in 932

Storage jar: A single storage jar was found in 932. This storage jar has a slightly incurved rim, standard vertical loop handles the tops of which begin at the shoulder of the vessel, and a flattened base (fig. 4.7.1).

Jugs: There are three jugs in the tomb; two are unusual examples of spouted jugs (photo 4.16). The first jug (fig. 4.7.2) has a ring base; its neck and rim are missing. The body of this jug is carinated, with a double-strand handle on its shoulder. Its ware is buff, and core is identical in color; the fabric is similar to that of the carinated chalices from this same tomb and Tomb 829. Identical fabric was used in the manufacture of the second jug, one of two spouted jugs. This unique example has a ring base, the elaborated foot of which is identical to the bases of the above-mentioned carinated chalices (fig. 4.7.4). A handle made of six strands meets the flaring rim; the uppermost strand splits into two opposed spirals where it attaches to the shoulder of the vessel. This is a feature typically found in the decoration of handles on metal vessels (Gershuny 1985: figs. 120, 128, 129, 131). A spout is attached to the opposite shoulder from the handle, but is broken and largely missing. The body of the jug is ovoid, and the ware is our familiar buff, with well-levigated buff core, again similar to our chalices, the above-mentioned carinated jug from the same tomb, and the jug discovered outside of Tomb 829 near to the likely offering Pit 913. This vessel has been called "Syrian" in the preliminary publications, but appears both stylistically and in fabric to belong to the group of buff ware vessels found in Canaan.

The third jug from Tomb 932 is also a spouted jug; however it is quite different from the other spouted jug from the same feature (fig. 4.7.3, photo 4.16). This third vessel has a ring base and a flaring rim; a three-strand handle attaches from the rim to its shoulder. The spout extends as high as the rim of the jug, from the area of the shoulder opposite the handle. The body is gently carinated; the fabric is dark brown with an identical core that has small white inclusions. The vessel is covered with a dark brown slip that is highly burnished (polished), a characteristic of the MB IIA or transition MB IIA–IIB period. Parallels come mainly from Byblos, but also are found at Megiddo, Tell el-ʿAjjul, and Jericho (Salles 1980: 52). It is likely that these ceramic jugs are imitating contemporary silver spouted jugs discovered in the royal tombs at Byblos (Jidejian 1968: 27, figs. 40–41). Although they are not exactly identical in typology they share many features in common, and it is possible that the pottery vessels were manufactured in Byblos itself and exported along the Levantine coast. Perhaps the dark brown color of the slip was chosen by the potter to reference the tarnished silver of the more expensive metal versions.

Juglets: There are three juglets among the finds from Tomb 932. One is the typical, small dipper juglet with ovoid body, very common in the MB IIB–IIC (fig. 4.8.1). Its fabric is reddish-brown with small white inclusions. The second is a cylindrical juglet (fig. 4.8.2), with slightly rounded base and an everted, thickened and rounded rim. Its ware is pink in color with traces of a cream slip applied to the surface. The third juglet is Cypriot (fig. 4.8.3; photo 4.16), of the White Painted family of Middle Cypriot pottery (Amiran 1969: 121–23; Artzy 2019). It is handmade, with a trefoil mouth and globular body (photo 4.16). Its handle is attached from the rim of the vessel to its shoulder in the typical Cypriot fashion, with a central dart from the handle pierced through a hole made in the shoulder. The ware is salmon in color with a buff slip; red to brown horizontal stripes decorate the rim, neck, and body of the vessel, with one vertical stripe painted along the handle. This White Painted juglet and the Red-on-Black bowl, the only Cypriot imports discovered in the tombs in Area H, are both from Tomb 932. Tomb 829 has a wider repertoire of pottery offerings, but they are mainly local vessels, or at least from the greater region of northern Palestine, as the buff wares are not local to the Akko Plain (photo 4.3).

Lamp: One lamp was discovered in Tomb 932 (fig. 4.8.4). Its slightly pinched mouth fits typologically with the MB IIB–IIC dating of this multiple burial (Amiran 1969: 190).

Small Finds in 932, Artifacts

Small finds from the tomb include ceramic, metal, stone, and bone artifacts, and scarabs and beads of various materials.

Ceramic loom weight: A single ceramic loom weight was found among the artifacts in Tomb 932 (fig. 4.8.5; photo 4.15). It is round, 7.5 cm in diameter, with an ovoid profile. A round string hole pierces the weight toward its top, 1.3 cm in diameter; there is no evidence of wear around the string hole nor impressions from the string in the surface of the clay. This is not surprising since the loom weight is highly fired. The weight of the object is 323.2 g. Typologically, this style of loom weight is not common in Bronze Age Palestine (Friend 1996: 8, 71–75). Parallels are found on Crete and Kythera (Barber 1991: 104–105); and on the Anatolian coast at Miletus, a Minoan outpost (Niemeier 1998: 27). It is possible that our example is actually a Minoan disk-shaped loom weight, brought from Crete to Akko.

Bronze objects: Three bronze weapons (photo 4.17) were uncovered in Tomb 932. The first is an axe head, shaped like an elongated trapezoid (fig. 4.8.6). It was found in the northwest part of the tomb, and was not associated with any specific skeletal remains. A slightly curved, single-edged knife's blade was found among remains heaped up in the southwestern corner of the tomb (fig. 4.8.7). It has three bronze rivets to hold on its handle, which must have been made from organic material, but did not survive. A bronze blade was found pushed up against the tomb's western wall (fig. 4.8.8). This blade is not well preserved, and it is not clear whether the blade was a double-edged dagger or a spear point.

Silver objects: A fragment of a silver ring was discovered nearby the bronze axe head. The ring is 9 mm from one twisted end to its other, which is broken, and is 3.5 mm in diameter (fig. 4.8.9). This silver ring was found separate from its ornament, presumably one of the white steatite scarabs in the tomb, described below.

Worked Stone objects: Stone artifacts in Tomb 932 include an alabaster vessel and a flint tool. The alabaster vessel was found in the southwest corner of the tomb. It has an ovoid body, round base, and slightly flared rim (fig. 4.8.10). The inside of the vessel has been smoothed to the extent that no tool marks are visible. Thus it is not possible to determine whether it was manufactured in Egypt or in the Jordan Valley through visual inspection (Ben-Dor 1945). The flaked stone artifact from the tomb is a flint tool, further detailed in J. Rose's report on the flaked stone finds from Tel Akko below.

Unworked stone objects (ballast stones): Five unworked stones were discovered in Tomb 932, which have been interpreted by M. Artzy as having been used as ballast stones before their final deposition in the tomb (fig. 4.9.1–3, photo 2.6). The stones are not local, and appear to be a type of light gray-green granite from the Troodos mountains on Cyprus. No visible signs of human alteration appear on any of the stones. Three of the stones are water worn, as if they were chosen from a riverbed. Two of these worn stones are quite large, and very heavy (fig. 4.9.1–2). The two large stones were found in the tomb with skeleton's necks and heads resting on them, used as pillows or headrests for the deceased (photo 2.6). Another stone is not worn as smooth, and has marine encrustations on its surface, an indication that it once was utilized as ballast in the hold of a ship. The inclusion of the Cypriot ballast stones in this particular tomb is of interest. Since two of the stones were found as head rests of the skeletons, it seems likely that the others were moved to the side of the tomb alongside the bones of the individuals buried earlier. These and the other grave goods might well point to a northern origin of the occupants of the tomb.

Worked bone: Fewer remains of worked bone were uncovered in Tomb 932 than in Tomb 829. Of the three examples, two are incised bone inlay strips and one is a bone silhouette of a bird (fig. 4.9.4–6). The decorative designs on the bone strips are diagonal lines for the first example, and dotted circles with diagonal lines for our second (photo 4.18). The bird silhouette differs in style and execution from the two discovered in Tomb 829, the example from Tomb 932 is smaller in shape and has two etched lines across the body of the bird (fig. 4.9.5). Perhaps this mixed repertoire of inlay strips and bird silhouette decorated a single wooden box deposited in Tomb 932, long since decomposed.

Scarabs: The two scarabs from Tomb 932 (fig. 4.9.7–8, photo 4.19) are both white steatite, and both have been dated by O. Keel to a period between the 13th Dynasty and the beginning of the 15th Dynasty (1997: 624–25, nos. 261, 264). Following Keel's absolute dating, this is a range from 1759–1600 BCE. Like the scarabs in Tomb 829, this date agrees nicely with the preliminary dating of Tomb 932 to the MB IIB–IIC. The source of the steatite is in Egypt (Lucas and Harris 1962: 421).

Painted plaster: Several small pieces of painted plaster were found among the remains in Tomb 932. The plaster is white; its surface is smooth and is painted a deep red color. It is not clear whether this plaster was originally on storage jars or was on the walls of the tomb. The plaster that remained in situ on the lower courses of the walls of the tomb is plain white. It is possible that the fragments of red ocher, detailed below under ecofacts, were used in the coloring of this plaster.

Ostrich eggshell: One ostrich eggshell was found among the burials in Tomb 932 (fig. 4.9.9). The top of the eggshell is not preserved, so it is not possible to determine whether it had been carved for use as a drinking vessel. This was most likely the case, as is apparent from numerous parallels from other Middle Bronze Age burials in the southern Levant and contemporary Canaanite burials in the Egyptian Delta (Van den Brink 1982).

Small Finds in Tomb 932, Ecofacts

Similar types of ecofacts were found in Tomb 932 as in Tomb 829. These include animal and fish bones, burned grape seeds, small pieces of charcoal, and small pieces of ocher. For details on the animal and fish bones see E. Maher's report below in Appendix 3. Several small pieces of red ocher originate from the tomb, but like those from Tomb 829 their use or purpose is not obvious.

Square O/5

Some noteworthy MB IIB–IIC pottery was uncovered in Square O/5, adding to the Stratum 6 tombs in Area H types already described. The context for this pottery is not secure; however, it could be associated with a possible disturbed burial, Locus 940, detailed above in chapter 2. In the test pit survey carried out by the Total Archaeology Project, at least one ballast stone of Cypriot Troodos Mountain origin was located in a disturbed area in the vicinity of Square O/5. It could well have originated from an MB burial like the examples from Tomb 932 detailed above. Pottery basket 514 included a burnished platter bowl (fig. 4.10.1) and the rim fragment of a Chocolate-on-White bowl or goblet (fig. 4.10.2). This fragment is defined as Chocolate-on-White because of its thick highly burnished creamy white slip, over well-fired light gray ware. The piece does not include any of the chocolate-colored painted decoration typical of the pottery family, but there are types from the family that are not painted, especially examples of footed bowls (Amiran 1969: 158–59, pl. 49:1–4). Closed forms from basket 514 include the rims of two jars or storage jars (fig. 4.10.3, 5). Below this basket was pottery basket 516 which included a fragment of a Cypriot Red-on-Red bowl (fig. 4.10.4), with its hallmark red stripes painted on both its interior and exterior over a red slip, which is burnished on the inside of the vessel.

Special Finds from Later Contexts, Associated with Stratum 6

Only one fragment of a Cypriot Bichrome Ware vessel, the rim of a large krater, was found in Area H. It originated, unfortunately, from a later context. The vessel has an everted rim, and is decorated with dark brown and red painted stripes on a buff-colored slip (fig. 4.10.6). We are describing it here alongside the Stratum 6 materials as this is most likely its original phase, although it may just as likely have been washed in or brought in from another part of the tell. Several sherds of Cypriot Red-on-Black ware bowls were also found in later contexts in the area.

Large portions of a Cypriot White Painted IV–VI jar were uncovered in a later, mixed context (fig. 4.16.4). The jar is of the typical Cypriot tan-colored fabric, with a cream-colored self-slip, burnished and with dark brown painted stripes on its exterior. One of its thrust-through handles is preserved.

A sherd from a large MB IIB–IIC bowl was found in a later context (fig. 4.10.7) from a type otherwise not represented so far. The bowl has an elaborate rim and a collar on its shoulder, and its buff fabric along with these features would place it in the family of pottery that includes the buff chalices and jugs described above.

Finally, a fragment of a figurine with upturned arms was discovered in a basket associated with burial 829 (fig. 4.10.8), which is quite unusual. It must be noted that several later sherds were found in this basket, dating to the Persian–Hellenistic periods, so it is clearly from a contaminated context, although the majority of the pottery finds date to the MB IIB–IIC or earlier. It is also unlikely that the multiple burial is the original context of this figurine, as one would expect to find a whole piece, or at least a more complete figure, associated with a tomb context. Several features of the fragment are significant: the body of the figurine was thrown on the wheel, as is evident from concentric wheel marks visible on the inside of the fragment; the figurine is made from well-levigated, highly fired gray ware with its surface covered in a pink slip which is burnished; the figurine is female, as the remnant of the left breast is still extant, applied to the body of the figure; faint evidence of red and dark brown painting remains, indicating a necklace (also represented partially by thin band of applied clay) and strands of long hair; it is not clear what the dark brown stripes on the shoulder of the figurine, nor the small patch of red paint under the raised arm, represent. The figurine is definitely imported, and is of the "goddess with upraised arms" type popular on Crete. The figurine type later became popular on Cyprus in the 11th century BCE (Karageorghis 2003: 217). Its original context at Akko and its use, however, are impossible to determine.

Typology of Pottery Vessels from the Tombs and Comparative Material

The tombs, as more or less sealed loci, are the best representatives of finds for Area H's Stratum 6. One does have to bear in mind that Tombs 829 and 932 had multiple burials, and may have been in use for several generations. There are indications that after each tomb went out of use it gradually filled with debris washed or blown into whatever air space was left open, these natural processes could have brought with them intrusive material; although limited in size. Both tombs were also disturbed by later construction in the area, which may have also introduced some intrusive material, but from much later periods. On the whole, however, the assemblages from each tomb are homogenous and contemporary. The best comparable ceramics are from the tombs at Tel Dan (Ilan 1996), the stratified levels at Shechem (Cole 1984), and the restratified tomb groups from Megiddo (Kenyon 1969). The Akko tombs are different in that they are situated in a coastal Levantine milieu.

Platter bowls: The platter bowls from Tomb 829 all have plain, direct rims, although two examples (fig. 4.11.6, 11) show just a slight hint toward incurving. All have ring bases and fairly large bodies; four of the examples show traces of patterned burnishing on their interiors (fig. 4.11.5–7, 11), though it is faint, and one additionally has some burnishing on its exterior (fig. 4.11.5). None of these burnished vessels is slipped. The three platter bowls from Tomb 932 show similar features: plain, direct rims; ring bases; and large bodies (fig. 4.11.8–10). These bowls lack any signs of burnishing. The well-levigated, buff-colored fabric of one of these bowls (fig. 4.11.8), plus its thinner walls and higher, finer ring base point to a slightly different tradition. This bowl may be a regional import, and appears to belong to the family of pottery marked by other examples from our tombs such as the trumpet-based chalices from Tomb 829 and 932, as well as one of the spouted jugs from Tomb 932.

Comparative studies of contemporary platter bowls are quite informative (table 4.1). The plain, direct rim type is a distinctive feature for the differentiation of MB IIC from IIB at Dan, Shechem, and Megiddo. At Dan, the MB IIB platter bowl types have rims with "thickened profile(s)," often times inverted, whereas the Stratum IX MB IIC examples have plain, direct rims (Ilan 1996: 213, fig. 4.77). Also examples from Dan's Stratum IX, MB IIC, have uneven bodies, hinting at the speed of manufacture, matched by several of the Akko examples from Tomb 829. At Shechem, the parallel bowl type is labeled Bp.11 by Cole (1984: 41). It makes up only 6 percent of the repertoire of platter bowls from the six phases of the MB IIB at the site, but it is the most frequent rim type represented in the MB IIC levels making up 19 percent of the sample from these later phases (Cole 1984: 41, fig. 1). This differentiation is also marked in the platter bowls in the tombs from Megiddo, which by Group F (MB IIC) are dominated by plain, direct rim types (Kenyon 1969: 34). The same plain, direct rims on platter bowls are found in Group E and Group G at Megiddo, also phased to the MB IIC (Kenyon 1969: fig. 8 and 14; for comparative phasing placing Kenyon's Groups E, F, and G in the MB IIC see Ilan 1996: 243, table 4.6).

The Area H platter bowls from Stratum 6 Tombs 829 and 932 show marked differences with those from the rampart layers of the earlier Stratum 7 (see above chapter 3). The Stratum 7 bowls were typified by sharply incurving rims, disk or slightly raised disk bases, and red slipped and burnished decoration. Stratum 6 bowls have plain, direct rims, ring bases, and for the most part lack decoration. The slight burnishing of several of the platter bowls from Tomb 829 may place these earlier in the sequence than the undecorated counterparts in Tomb 932. This differentiation is based on only a few examples so future excavation of the MB habitation levels of the site and further publication of the MB material from Area F might help to distinguish the variation in morphologies of pottery types from the MB IIA through the MB IIC at Tel Akko. So far only ceramics originating in graves at Tel Akko from Areas A and AB have been studied (Beeri 2003).

The three platter bowls from 913 have typological features differentiating them slightly from those typified by the examples presented so far from the tombs from Stratum 6. Two of the 913 bowls have straight side-walls (fig. 4.11.1, 3) and all three have concave disk bases (fig. 4.11.1–3), both features Amiran attributes to the MB IIB–IIC (1969: 91). The red slipped and burnished cross (fig. 4.11.1), however, is a decoration typical of the MB IIA, or the transition phase from the MB IIA to IIB. These bowls are different of those found in Tombs 829 and 932, which are almost double their size in diameter and have ring bases. It is most likely that Locus 913 was a pit cut into the rampart layers in a period of transition between the MB IIA and MB IIB, which is chronologically somewhere between Stratum 7 and 6, or a part of a later repair to the Stratum 7 rampart.

Carinated bowl: A single carinated bowl was revealed in the graves in Area H (fig. 4.12.1). The bowl has a direct rim, a gentle carination, a concave disk base, and is undecorated.

The best parallel for this bowl comes from a Stratum IX, MB IIC, tomb at Tel Dan (Ilan 1996: fig. 4.99.9). In the typology Ilan has developed for carinated bowls from the tombs at Dan, ring bases from transitional Stratum X–IX tombs tend to give way to more solid disk and concave disk bases (Ilan 1996: fig. 4.78). This observation, however, is based on few examples, and awaits future excavation and publication of the habitation levels at the site. The bowl is similar to Cole's Bc A.11 group defined for the MB IIB material at Shechem (1984: 55–56). The example from Akko, while similar in rim and carination, appears to have a shallower bowl, an attribute Cole links with MB IIC levels at Shechem as well as late MB IIB–MB IIC Groups III–V at Jericho (1984: 56; for comparative phasing of Jericho tomb groups see Ilan 1996: table 4.6; table 4.1).

Chalices: Three chalices or goblets, originated from two of the graves, Tomb 829 and Tomb 932 in Area H. The two examples from Tomb 829 have direct rims, sharp carinations, and high ring (also called pedestal or trumpet) bases (fig. 4.12.2–3). The one example from Tomb 932 has a direct rim, more curved carination, and a high ring (pedestal/trumpet) base (fig. 4.12.4). All three are made from a buff-colored, well-levigated fabric, reminiscent of Eggshell Ware.

Comparable chalices were found in Stratum X and Stratum IX tombs at Tel Dan (Ilan 1996: 218). The one example from the Stratum IX, MB IIC, Tomb 8096 (Ilan 1996: fig. 4.99.16) is closer in form and fabric to our parallel vessels at Akko than the earlier Stratum X chalice. Cole has presented an elaborate schema for the development of the chalice form from the MB IIA–IIC based on examples from Shechem and comparative material from other sites in the southern Levant (1984: 58–59). He notes that the latest examples from Shechem's MB IIC phases have deep cups, a more rounded profile, and "high pedestal bases" (Cole 1984: 58, fig. 13:f). Our chalice from Tomb 932 best parallels this combination of features. The Tomb 829 chalices from Akko corresponds well with Cole's vessels in Figure 13:e and d, which are MB IIB and transitional MB IIB to IIC (1984: 58, fig. 13:e, d). These chalices are marked by sharper carinations, have deep cups, and high pedestal bases, similar to the features of the chalices from Akko Tomb 829. As Ilan warns, this evolutionary schema must be used with caution (1996: 218–20), and the MB IIB examples Cole publishes are covered with red slip and burnished (1984: plate 19: Bf C:a–c), decorations not found on the Akko chalices. If the buff fabric wares are indeed regional imports, a hypothesis which requires further scientific fabric analysis, perhaps these Shechem examples are local copies as is the Stratum X example from Tel Dan, or perhaps the buff wares are copying a Palestinian prototype? These suggestions require refinement from further stratigraphic excavations of MB IIB–IIC habitation levels and further fabric analyses on MB IIB–IIC ware types. In Kenyon's reanalysis of the Megiddo material, goblets parallel to those from Akko appear as a new type in her Group F assemblage, and continue into Group G (1969: 34, fig. 12.8, fig. 14.10). Group F and G have been phased by Ilan to the MB IIC and late MB IIB (1996: table 4.6). Following Amiran's typology, this particular chalice form does not extend into the LB I pottery repertoire (1969: 129, 134; table 4.1).

Storage jars: The hallmarks of the storage jar from Tomb 932 are an incurved rim, slightly protruded base, ovoid body, and two vertical loop handles beginning at the shoulder of the vessel (fig. 4.12.5).

The ovoid body of storage jars is noted by Amiran as the most typical aspect shared among MB IIB–IIC examples (1969: 103; table 4.1). The ovoid-shaped body is nicely paralleled by Akko's Tomb 932 example. At Shechem comparisons are rare. Based on rim types, the Tomb 932 jar would fall under Cole's JJ.5 "high collared rim" category for small jars (storage jars as opposed to pithoi), a type with examples only appearing in Strata XIXs–XVIIIs, the middle phases of the MB IIB sequence (1984: 78, fig. 23). The chronological extent of this storage jar type, likely tied to maritime commerce, would be better served by a good sequence for the MB IIB–IIC from sites in the coastal plain or inland valleys if one was available. The Middle Bronze Age sequences from the excavations of Tel Mevorakh and Tel Michal are limited, unfortunately (Stern 1984: fig. 17). Very few storage jars from Megiddo are represented in Kenyon's resequencing of the site; however, there is a good match for the Tomb 932 jar in her Group

E, MB IIC, assemblage (1969: fig. 11.1). This storage jar type is absent from the tombs at Dan, while the squatter jar type with a globular body and frequent painted decoration, is abundant (Ilan 1996: 221–23). It is possible that the differentiation Amiran made for the Late Bronze Age between "commercial jars" and "domestic jars" (1969: 140–42), reflecting utilization in maritime transport containers versus terrestrial transport, was already present in the MB IIB–IIC.

Amphoriskoi: The two amphoriskoi from Stratum 6 were both found in Tomb 829. Their rim types are quite different, one displaying a simple flared rim (fig. 4.13.1) while the other has a direct rim with a profiled cross section (fig. 4.13.2). The neck on the example with the flared rim is much thicker than its companion's; the ovoid bodies are similar though that of 1228/7 is a little less curvy and borders on an inverted conical shape with a slightly rounded base about twice as big as 1289's. Both have vertical loop handles beginning at the shoulders of the vessel. These handles and the body types in general are miniature forms of contemporary storage jar shapes.

No good comparisons for these amphoriskoi were found in the publications in either Dan or Shechem. It may be the case that these types represent a coastal ceramic tradition, while inland or hill country amphoriskoi were much more ovoid in body shape, verging on globular (Cole 1984: 76–77). Kenyon's tomb material from Megiddo also lacks good parallels; however, the original publication of the Bronze Age strata at Megiddo contains representative types. Our Akko example 1289 is best paralleled by Jar type 75 at Megiddo, although the Megiddo example has a more rounded shoulder and a slightly incurving rim; the jar from Tomb 3137 is placed in Stratum XII (Loud 1948: pl. 27.4). Akko's 1228/7 best matches Megiddo's Jar 71, which is dated by the excavator to Stratum XII–X and is from tomb 5067 (Loud 1948: pl. 26.20). Kenyon's restratification of the Megiddo tombs places Tomb 3137 in her Group A, early MB IIB, and Tomb 5067 in Group B, MB IIB (1969: 31). In Ilan's comparative chronology for the Middle Bronze Age, Megiddo Stratum XII–X covers from early MB IIB (Stratum XII) all through the MB IIC (Stratum X) (1996: table 4.6). Thus it is difficult to use the Megiddo material to pinpoint comparative phasing; however, Akko's 1289 may best be placed in the MB IIB while 1228/7 perhaps spans the MB IIB through the MB IIC (table 4.1).

Jugs: The seven jugs attributed to Stratum 6 can be roughly separated into four different jug types. The first type is represented by two whole examples from Tomb 829 and is really a pitcher. It is placed with the jugs because it follows Amiran's schema (1969: 112, pl. 34:2–3) and we see no benefit in creating a separate category. Our Area H examples (fig. 4.13.3–4) have the characteristic trefoil mouth, wide neck, inverted conical body, disk base, vertical loop handle attached at the lip and just above the shoulder, and relatively small size.

The second type of jug has a distinct loop handle on its shoulder. There are two examples of shoulder-handled jugs in the tombs, one from Tomb 932 (fig. 4.14.2) and another from Tomb 829 (fig. 4.14.3). The rims are missing on both of them. They have inverted conical bodies, and double-strand or ovoid loop handles on their shoulders. The shoulder-handled jug from Tomb 932 has a ring base (fig. 4.14.2), while the one from Tomb 829 has a disk base (fig. 4.14.3).

There is only one example of the third type (fig. 4.14.5), it is from Locus 909, a feature associated with Tomb 829. This jug, like the shoulder-handled jugs, is missing its rim and most of its neck, which can be reconstructed as being relatively long and thin. The vessel has an inverted conical body and a high ring base, also called a pedestal or trumpet base (see parallel base described above for the chalice base from this phase). A double-strand handle is connected from the neck to its shoulder.

The fourth jug type is the spouted jug. The two examples are both from Tomb 932, but their fabric differs and they differ stylistically (as detailed above; fig. 4.14.1, 4). They both have flaring rims, however, and relatively narrow necks, large bodies for holding liquids, ring bases, sturdy handles attached from the rim to the shoulder of each vessel, and spouts for pouring.

The first jug type, the small pitcher-jug, is not found in MB IIA assemblages; it begins in the MB IIB and continues in use through the LB I (Amiran 1969: 112; table 4.1). Ilan prefers to typologize the example from the Dan tombs with the globular necked and globular flaring-necked bowls (1996: 217, 224). He tentatively places the pitcher in Dan's Stratum XI (early MB IIB), because of fragmentary parallels from the Dan stratified sequence in Area B (Ilan 1996: 224). It should be noted, however, that the majority of finds from the tomb containing this pitcher, Tomb 8096b, were dated to Stratum IX (MB IIC). At Megiddo, the same type has a range from Strata XII–IX (MB IIB early–LB I) (Cole 1984: 73). This basically agrees with Kenyon's reworking of the phasing of Bronze Age Megiddo, as presented in the presence of these pitchers in her Groups A–G (MB IIB early–MB IIC/LB I) (1969). Parallels are present in MB IIB Shechem but without the trefoil mouth (Cole 1984: 72–73).

The shoulder-handled jug type appears first in the MB IIA and continues in use throughout the LB IIA (Amiran 1969: 112, 146; table 4.1). Amiran's observations of the vessel's wide range finds support in its appearance in a Stratum XII (MB IIA) tomb at Tel Dan (Ilan 1996: fig. 4.82), and in the ubiquity of the type in the phasing groups of Megiddo as defined by Kenyon (from her MB I = MB IIA, to her Group G = MB IIC/LB I) (1969).

No good parallels for either the third type of jug, with its high ring base and long thin neck, nor the spouted jug with the six-strand handle were found. The fabric of both vessels is buff ware, which are placed in the same family with the trumpet-based chalices found in Tombs 829 and 932. The buff ware jugs are thus tentatively dated to the same period as the related chalice type, the MB IIC (table 4.1). Without stratified parallels and a better understanding of the buff ware "family" of ceramics we stress that this phasing is extremely preliminary.

The final spouted jug, 1177/1, is an unusual piece. It is a rare type and has very few parallels in Palestine: one example from Megiddo, two from Tell el-'Ajjul, and one from Jericho (Salles 1980: 52). The overwhelming majority of this type of jug were reported from the Byblian tombs. Six originated from two of the royal tombs and nineteen from the group of chamber tombs referred to as Necropolis "K" (Salles 1980). Several silver spouted jugs, the clear ancestor of the ceramic imitation, have also been found in the excavations at Byblos (Salles 1980). Most of these spouted jugs are from well-dated MB IIA contexts, although a few have been placed in the MB IIB–IIC (Salles 1980). It is feasible that this spouted jug is an heirloom; however, it is just as likely that the vessel should be dated to the MB IIB–IIC and is contemporary with the rest of the tombs' ceramics (table 4.1). Differentiation based on generational tombs is notoriously difficult.

Juglets: Two juglet types are represented in the pottery assemblage of Stratum 6, dipper juglets and cylindrical juglets.

Dipper juglets were uncovered in all three tombs. Unfortunately we have only been able to identify the type in 727 from photographs and a drawing of the burial, and have not been able to locate the dipper juglet itself. Those from Tombs 829 and 932 have pinched mouths, ovoid bodies, and vertical handles beginning just under the rim and ending just above the shoulder of each vessel (fig. 4.15.1–3). Two of these handles are rectangular-shaped in cross section, while the third is circular.

The repertoire of cylindrical juglets is small and with slight variations. Of the three examples with their rims preserved, two are flared (fig. 4.15.4, 6) and one is upright (fig. 4.15.5). One has a slightly more elongated neck than the other two; two have more or less even cylindrical bodies while one body tapers up slightly and the final example tapers down slightly. One base is flat, while the other two (one vessel is missing its base) is slightly rounded. Two of the preserved strap handles are connected just below the rim to right above the shoulder, while the third begins further down the neck. One of the handles is a double-strand handle.

These juglet types provide no additional data to narrowing the chronology of this type. With some variations in form and decoration, the dipper juglet type continues from the MB IIA to the LB II period (Amiran 1969: 112, 146; table 4.1). It occurs in all of the Middle Bronze Age phases at Tel Dan, where the biggest difference is in the red slip and burnish appearing on earlier, MB IIA examples. Dipper juglets are more rare in the MB IIB and IIC at Tel Dan (Ilan 1996: 229). They are present in Kenyon's rephasing of Megiddo from her MB I (=MB IIA) through Group E (MB IIC) (1969). Cole noted that double-strand handles first appear on dipper juglets in the MB IIC phases at Shechem and Jericho; however, he also notes that the double handles are found in MB IIB tombs at Gibeon (1984: 69). The lack of double-strand handles on the Akko Area H dipper juglets does not provide any indication of phasing since the simpler handle types occur in every subperiod of the Middle and Late Bronze Age.

Cylindrical juglets also appear over a long time. The type was introduced in the MB IIA and continues throughout the LB I (Amiran 1969: 112, 146; table 4.1). They occur in all of the Middle Bronze Age strata at Tel Dan with little typological differences, although the form does tend to increase in size and frequency from Stratum XII (MB IIA) to Stratum IX (MB IIC) (1996: 226–29). The increase in frequency of cylindrical juglets in later phases of the Middle Bronze Age and into the LB I (Group E–Group H) was also detailed by Kenyon for the tombs at Megiddo (1969: 33–35). Cole notes a difference between the coast and hill country stating that cylindrical juglets appear already by the MB IIA in coastal settlements, while the type does not occur in the initial MB IIB phases at Shechem and is rare in the middle IIB phases, increasing in frequency by the late IIB and MB IIC phases (1984: 71–72).

Lamps: Only one lamp was found in the three graves in Stratum 6 (fig. 4.15.8). It has a well-defined pinched mouth and is relatively shallow with a rounded base. Following Amiran, this type first appears in the MB IIB–IIC and continues in use into the LB I (1969: 190; table 4.1). The type developed from an MB IIA predecessor with a more open mouth, and lead to the highly pinched mouthed lamp of the LB II and early Iron Age (Amiran 1969: 190). This evolutionary schema has been challenged by Kenyon and Holland based on the lamps found in Jericho (1982: 440–47). Publication of the tomb material from Tel Dan, unfortunately, did not resolve the issue (Ilan 1996: 220–21).

Cypriot imports: Two well-stratified Cypriot imports were found in Tomb 932. The first is a fragmentary bowl of Red-on-Black Ware and the second is a juglet, a White Painted V–VI ceramic, with a typical thrust-through handle, a hallmark of Cypriot Bronze Age handmade pottery (fig. 4.16.1, 3). It is decorated with a broad, horizontal reddish-brown painted stripes on its rim, neck, and halfway down its body, with one vertical stripe running the length of the handle.

The import of Red-on-Black Ware vessels to Palestine begins in the MB IIB, and continues throughout the LB I (Amiran 1969: 121, 173; Johnson 1982: 66; table 4.1). The form of the Akko trefoil mouth juglet is best matched by a White Painted IV Cross Line Style juglet found at Megiddo (Amiran 1969: pl. 37.12; Johnson 1982, fig. 3.N13). The Megiddo juglet is from a Stratum XI, late

MB IIB, burial, Tomb 4109. The painted design on the juglet from Akko, however, lacks crossed lines and is more reminiscent of the decoration on White Painted V vessels, such as a rattle from Enkomi (Dikaios 1969: 224, pl. 53.18). White Painted V Wares have been found in limited quantities in MB IIB–IIC contexts at Megiddo and Tel Mevorakh, and out of context in later LB I fills at Tel Michal (Saltz 1984: 58–59; Negbi 1989: 50). The form of the Akko White Painted juglet is also paralleled by an example from Athienou on Cyprus (Merrillees 1983: 32, fig. 4.4). Merrillees attributes this juglet to the White Painted VI Coarse Linear Style family. The Athienou example, unfortunately, was found in a mixed fill, Stratum post-II/pre-I, and thus is not in its primary context. The vessel has thicker walls than the Akko counterpart, and once again the decoration differs as it is much simpler on the Akko juglet.

Two unstratified Cypriot vessels were uncovered in Area H, along with several small body sherds of Red-on-Black Ware bowls that were found in later contexts. The Cypriot Bichrome krater (fig. 4.16.2) and White Painted IV–VI jar (fig. 4.16.4) are worth highlighting, despite the fact that they originate in later phases, because of the paucity of Cypriot wares in the Stratum 6 burials. Rarely found outside of Cyprus, the White Painted IV–VI storage jar has a close parallel from MB IIB Stratum XIII at Tel Mevorakh (Saltz 1984: 58–59, fig. 17.4, pl. 44.1).

Typological Conclusions

As is typical of tomb assemblages, many ceramic types are missing from the repertoire in Area H's Stratum 6. We have no representations of kraters, cooking pots, pithoi, or jars from this phase. Yet the ceramic types that are present form a fairly coherent group, which can be dated to the MB IIB–IIC through comparative analysis (table 4.1). Despite the diachronic range of time periods for some of the pottery forms, all of ceramics cluster in the MB IIB and MB IIC.

As is clear from table 4.1, the clustering by period leans more toward the MB IIC as all of the forms have MB IIC parallels. Since Tombs 829 and 932 were multiple burials, however, it is likely that they were each used over a span of time, perhaps beginning in the later part of the MB IIB and continuing well into the MB IIC. Given the nature of family tombs, often used for generations, it is not possible to establish a more refined phasing. Judging by the ceramic finds, cist Tomb 727 dates to the MB IIB. As many Syro-Palestinian archaeologists do not distinguish between the MB IIB and the MB IIC, and since it is impossible to do so based primarily on multiple-use burials, we place Stratum 6 in the MB IIB–IIC, or as some archaeologists prefer, MB IIB–LB IA. The three platter bowls from Pit 913 were not included, since they are not directly associated with the tombs in Area H and typologically could be associated to a period between Stratum 7 and Stratum 6, as is detailed above.

The dates of the ceramics agrees well with the dates associated to the scarabs from Tombs 829 and 932, the Egyptian 13–15th Dynasties. Following Keel's chronology this dynastic range is between 1759–1522 BCE (1997: 624–25, nos. 261, 264). They provide Area H's only direct evidence for absolute dates, corresponding with the standard absolute dates for the MB IIB–IIC.

TABLE 4.1   Comparison of Area H Stratum 6 ceramic types with presence in comparative MB–LB phasing

	MB IIA	MB IIB	MB IIC	LB I	LB IIA
Platter bowls with plain direct rims and ring bases			■		
Carinated Bowls with direct rim and concave disk base		■	■		
Chalices with trumpet base			■		
Storage jars with incurved rim			■		
Amphoriskoi		■	■		
Pitcher jugs			■		
Shoulder-handled jugs	■	■	■		
Spouted jugs with 6 strand handle			■		
Burnished spouted jug	■	■	■		
Dipper juglets	■	■	■	■	■
Cylindrical juglets		■	■		
Lamps with pinched mouth and rounded base		■	■	■	■
Cypriot Black-on-Red Wares		■	■	■	■
Cypriot White Painted juglets		■	■		

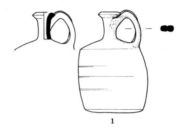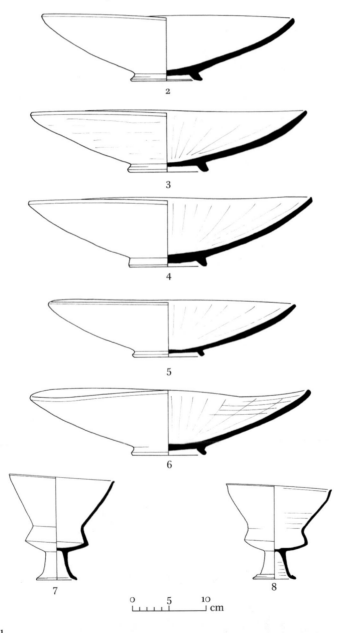

FIGURE 4.1

Figure No.	Shape/ object	Reg. No.	Locus/ Pottery Basket	Description (color of exterior/interior/ core; inclusions; decorations; etc.)
4.1.1	Juglet	AK VII 1980 H L/9 b. 216/1 Hecht Museum# 86-60	Loc. 727	Buff/buff/buff to grey; pink slipped exterior
4.1.2	Bowl	AK VIII 1982 H L/9 b. 310 Hecht Museum# 86-47	Loc. 829	Pink cream/pink cream/core not visible
4.1.3	Bowl	AK IX 1983 H L/9 b. 1251/1 + 1229 Hecht Museum# 86-50	Loc. 829	Pink cream/pink cream/pink; radial burnished interior
4.1.4	Bowl	AK IX 1983 H L/9 b. 1303, 1081/1 Hecht Museum# 86-51	Loc. 829	Pink cream/pink cream/core not visible; radial burnished interior
4.1.5	Bowl	AK IX 1983 H L/9 b. 1229 Hecht Museum# 86-48	Loc. 829	Pink cream/pink cream/core not visible; radial burnished interior
4.1.6	Bowl	AK IX 1983 H L/9 b. 1082/2 Hecht Museum# 86-49	Loc. 829	Pink/pink/pink; radial burnished interior
4.1.7	Chalice	AK VIII 1982 H L/9 b. 337/1 Hecht Museum# 86-56	Loc. 829	Buff/buff/buff
4.1.8	Chalice	AK VIII 1982 H L/9 b. 350/3 Hecht Museum# 86-54	Loc. 829	Buff/buff/buff

Squares L/9-M/9, Locus 829 (cont.)

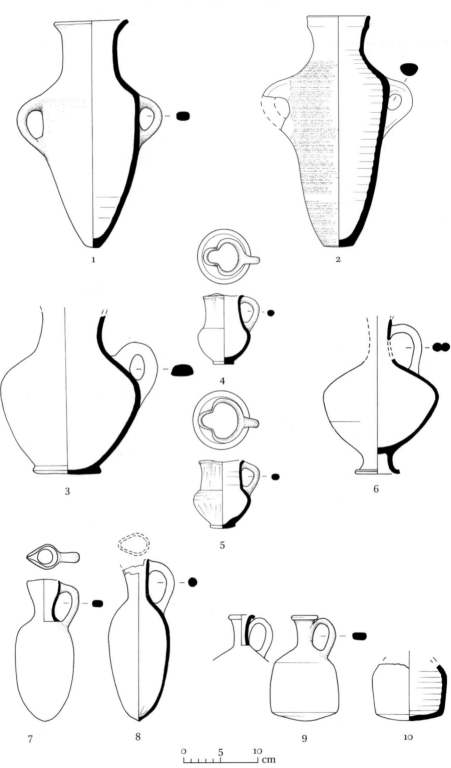

FIGURE 4.2

Figure No.	Shape/ object	Reg. No.	Locus/ Pottery Basket	Description (color of exterior/ interior/core; inclusions; decorations; etc.)
4.2.1	Amphoriskos	AK IX 1983 H L/9 b. 1289 Hecht Museum# 86-66	Loc. 829	Pink/pink/core not visible
4.2.2	Amphoriskos	AK IX 1983 H L/9 b. 1228	Loc. 829	Brown/brown/brown; small white inclusions
4.2.3	Jug	AK VIII 1982 H L/9 b. 344	Loc. 829	Pink/pink/pink
4.2.4	Jug	AK VIII 1982 H L/9 b. 350/1 Hecht Museum# 86-58	Loc. 829	Reddish brown/reddish brown/core not visible
4.2.5	Jug	AK VIII 1982 H L/9 b. 350/4 Hecht Museum# 86-57	Loc. 829	Reddish brown/reddish brown/core not visible; slipped and burnished exterior
4.2.6	Jug	AK IX 1983 H M/9 b. 1340/1	Loc. 909	Buff/buff/buff
4.2.7	Juglet	AK VIII 1982 H L/9 b. 321/1 Hecht Museum# 86-63	Loc. 829	Pink/pink/pink; buff slipped and burnished exterior
4.2.8	Juglet	AK VIII 1982 H L/9 b. 333/4	Loc. 829	Buff/buff/buff
4.2.9	Juglet	AK IX 1983 H L/9 b. 1102 Hecht Museum# 86-64	Loc. 829	Reddish brown/reddish brown/light brown; cream slipped exterior
4.2.10	Juglet	AK IX 1983 H L/9 b. 1101	Loc. 829	Pinkish buff/pinkish buff/pinkish buff; small number of small white inclusions

Squares L/9-M/9, Locus 829 (cont.)

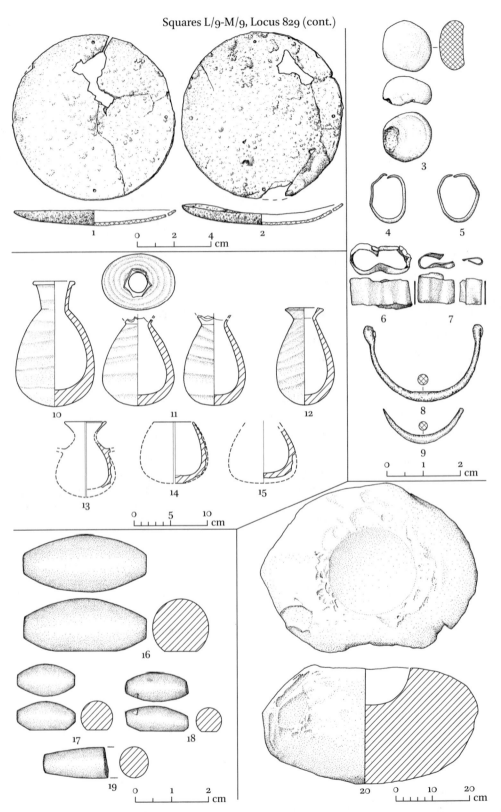

FIGURE 4.3

Figure No.	Shape/ object	Reg. No.	Locus/ Pottery Basket	Description (color of exterior/interior/ core; inclusions; decorations; etc.)
4.3.1	Scale pan	AK IX 1983 H L/9 b. 1229/6a	Loc. 829	Bronze; 3 string holes
4.3.2	Scale pan	AK IX 1983 H L/9 b. 1229/6b	Loc. 829	Bronze; 3 string holes
4.3.3	Weight or gaming piece	AK IX 1983 H L/9 b. 1196/3	Loc. 829	Lead weight or gaming piece; bun-shaped with flat bottom; 8.12 grams
4.3.4	Earring	AK IX 1983 H L/9 b. 1293/2 Hecht Museum# 86-143	Loc. 829	Gold loop earring
4.3.5	Earring	AK IX 1983 H L/9 b. 1293/3 Hecht Museum# 86-143	Loc. 829	Gold loop earring
4.3.6	Band	AK IX 1983 H L/9 b. 1271/1 Hecht Museum# 86-140	Loc. 829	Gold foil band
4.3.7	Band	AK IX 1983 H L/9 b. 1271/2 Hecht Museum# 86-142	Loc. 829	Gold foil band, in 2 pieces
4.3.8	Ring for scarab	AK IX 1983 H L/9 b. 1302/1a Hecht Museum# 86-153	Loc. 829	Silver ring; goes with purple amethyst scarab in gold bezel (pl. 4.5.5)
4.3.9	Ring for scarab	AK IX 1983 H L/9 b. 1302/2a Hecht Museum# 86-151	Loc. 829	Silver ring; goes with purple amethyst scarab in gold bezel (pl. 4.5.7)
4.3.10	Alabaster vessel	AK IX 1983 H L/9 b. 1293/1 Hecht Museum# 86-69	Loc. 829	Creamy yellow
4.3.11	Alabaster vessel	AK IX 1983 H L/9 b. 1302/7 Hecht Museum# 86-71	Loc. 829	Creamy yellow
4.3.12	Alabaster vessel	AK IX 1983 H L/9 b. 1229/1	Loc. 829	Creamy yellow
4.3.13	Alabaster vessel	AK IX 1983 H L/9 b. 1302/10	Loc. 829	Creamy yellow
4.3.14	Alabaster vessel	AK IX 1983 H L/9 b. 1302/8	Loc. 829	Creamy yellow

Figure No.	Shape/ object	Reg. No.	Locus/ Pottery Basket	Description (color of exterior/interior/ core; inclusions; decorations; etc.)
4.3.15	Alabaster vessel	AK IX 1983 H L/9 b. 1229/16	Loc. 829	Creamy yellow
4.3.16	Weight	AK IX 1983 H L/9 b. 1307/1 Hecht Museum# 86-158	Loc. 829	Hematite; truncated ovoid shape with flat bottom; 18.1–18.2 g.
4.3.17	Weight	AK IX 1983 H L/9 b. 1307/2 Hecht Museum# 86-156	Loc. 829	Hematite; truncated ovoid shape with flat bottom; 2.9–3.0 g.
4.3.18	Weight	AK IX 1983 H L/9 b. 1307/3 Hecht Museum# 86-157	Loc. 829	Hematite; truncated ovoid shape with flat bottom; 2.2–2.3 g.
4.3.19	Weight	AK IX 1983 H L/9 b. 1307/4 Hecht Museum# 86-159	Loc. 829	Hematite; tapering cylinder; 3.8–3.9 g.
4.3.20	Mortar	AK IX 1983 H L/9	Loc. 829	Large groundstone mortar; limestone

Squares L/9-M/9, Locus 829 (cont.)

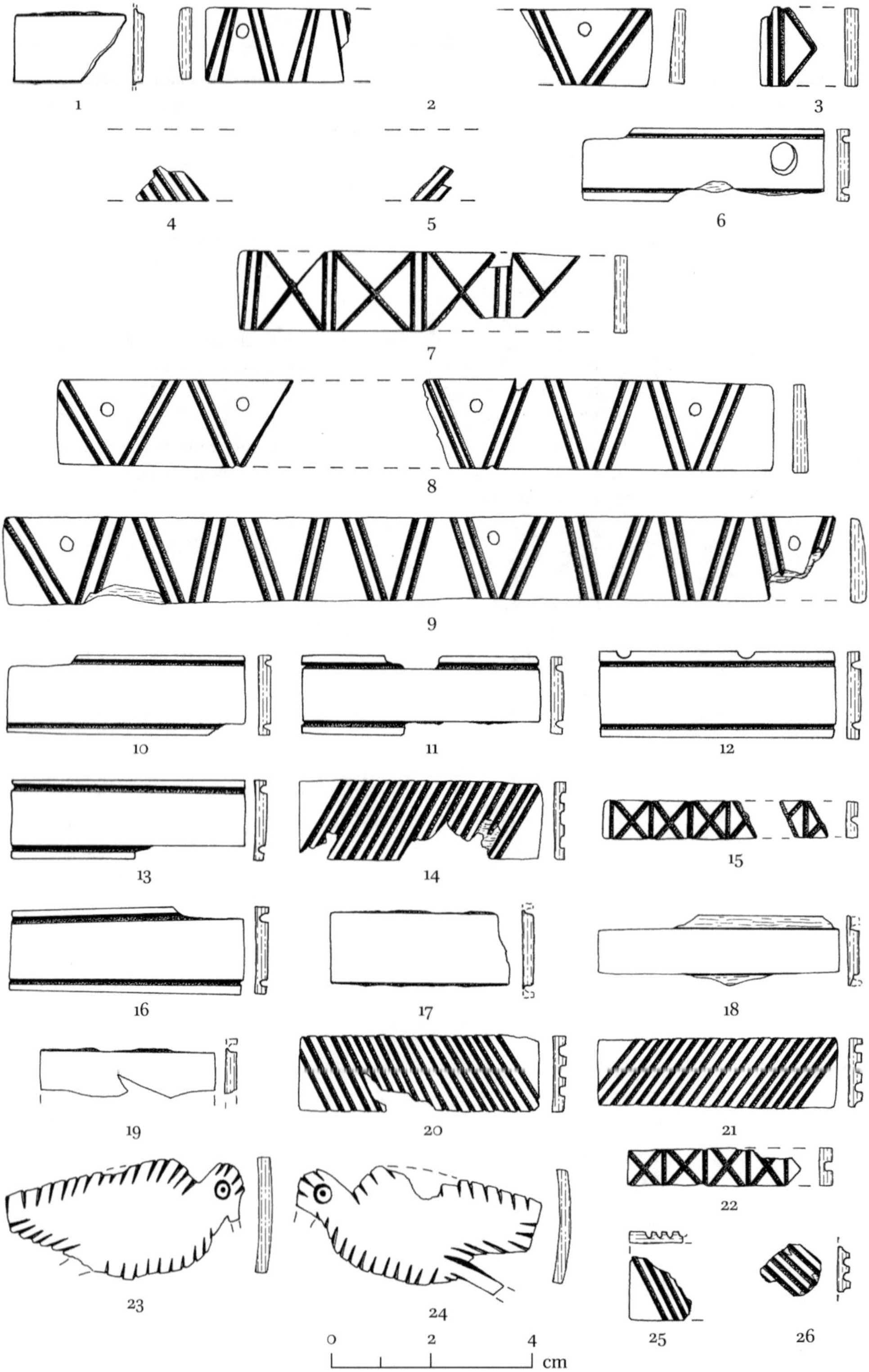

FIGURE 4.4

Figure No.	Shape/ object	Reg. No.	Locus/ Pottery Basket	Description (color of exterior/interior/core; inclusions; decorations; etc.)
4.4.1	Bone inlay	AK IX 1983 H L/9 b. 1271/4	Loc. 829	Worked bone inlay with incised longitudinal lines
4.4.2	Bone inlay	AK VIII 1982 H L/9 b. 333/2	Loc. 829	Worked bone inlay with incised chevron design
4.4.3	Bone inlay	AK VIII 1982 H L/9 b. 340/1	Loc. 829	Highly fragmentary; partial incised oblique cross and vertical parallel lines, likely portion of strip with similar design b. 350/5.
4.4.4	Bone inlay	AK VIII 1982 H L/9 b. 350/7	Loc. 829	Worked bone inlay with incised diagonal parallel lines
4.4.5	Bone inlay	AK VIII 1982 H L/9 b. 350/8	Loc. 829	Worked bone inlay with incised diagonal parallel lines
4.4.6	Bone inlay	AK VIII 1982 H L/9 b. 350/6	Loc. 829	Worked bone inlay with incised longitudinal lines and attachment hole
4.4.7	Bone inlay	AK VIII 1982 H L/9 b. 350/5	Loc. 829	Worked bone inlay with incised oblique crosses divided by vertical parallel lines
4.4.8	Bone inlay	AK VIII 1982 H L/9 b. 350/2	Loc. 829	Worked bone inlay with incised chevron design
4.4.9	Bone inlay	AK IX 1983 H L/9 b. 1094/1	Loc. 829	Worked bone inlay with incised chevron design
4.4.10	Bone inlay	AK IX 1983 H L/9 b. 1201/1	Loc. 829	Worked bone inlay with incised longitudinal lines
4.4.11	Bone inlay	AK IX 1983 H L/9 b. 1218/3	Loc. 829	Worked bone inlay with incised longitudinal lines
4.4.12	Bone inlay	AK IX 1983 H L/9 b. 1218/2	Loc. 829	Worked bone inlay with incised longitudinal lines
4.4.13	Bone inlay	AK IX 1983 H L/9 b. 1218/1	Loc. 829	Worked bone inlay with incised longitudinal lines
4.4.14	Bone inlay	AK IX 1983 H L/9 b. 1218/5	Loc. 829	Worked bone inlay with diagonal parallel lines
4.4.15	Bone inlay	AK IX 1983 H L/9 b. 1218/4	Loc. 829	Worked bone inlay with incised oblique crosses divided by vertical parallel lines
4.4.16	Bone inlay	AK IX 1983 H L/9 b. 1229/7	Loc. 829	Worked bone inlay with incised longitudinal lines
4.4.17	Bone inlay	AK IX 1983 H L/9 b. 1229/9	Loc. 829	Worked bone inlay with incised longitudinal lines
4.4.18	Bone inlay	AK IX 1983 H L/9 b. 1229/8	Loc. 829	Worked bone inlay with incised longitudinal lines
4.4.19	Bone inlay	AK IX 1983 H L/9 b. 1229/10	Loc. 829	Worked bone inlay with incised longitudinal lines
4.4.20	Bone inlay	AK IX 1983 H L/9 b. 1229/11	Loc. 829	Worked bone inlay with incised diagonal parallel lines
4.4.21	Bone inlay	AK IX 1983 H L/9 b. 1229/12	Loc. 829	Worked bone inlay with incised diagonal parallel lines

Figure No.	Shape/ object	Reg. No.	Locus/ Pottery Basket	Description (color of exterior/interior/core; inclusions; decorations; etc.)
4.4.22	Bone inlay	AK IX 1983 H L/9 b. 1229/13	Loc. 829	Worked bone inlay with incised oblique crosses divided by vertical parallel lines
4.4.23	Bone inlay	AK IX 1983 H L/9 b. 1229/14	Loc. 829	Worked bone inlay bird with incised lines and eye
4.4.24	Bone inlay	AK IX 1983 H L/9 b. 1229/15	Loc. 829	Worked bone inlay bird with incised lines and eye
4.4.25	Bone inlay	AK IX 1983 H L/9 b. 1271/5	Loc. 829	Worked bone inlay with incised diagonal parallel lines
4.4.26	Bone inlay	AK IX 1983 H L/9 b. 1277/1	Loc. 829	Worked bone inlay with incised diagonal parallel lines

Squares L/9-M/9, Locus 829 (cont.)

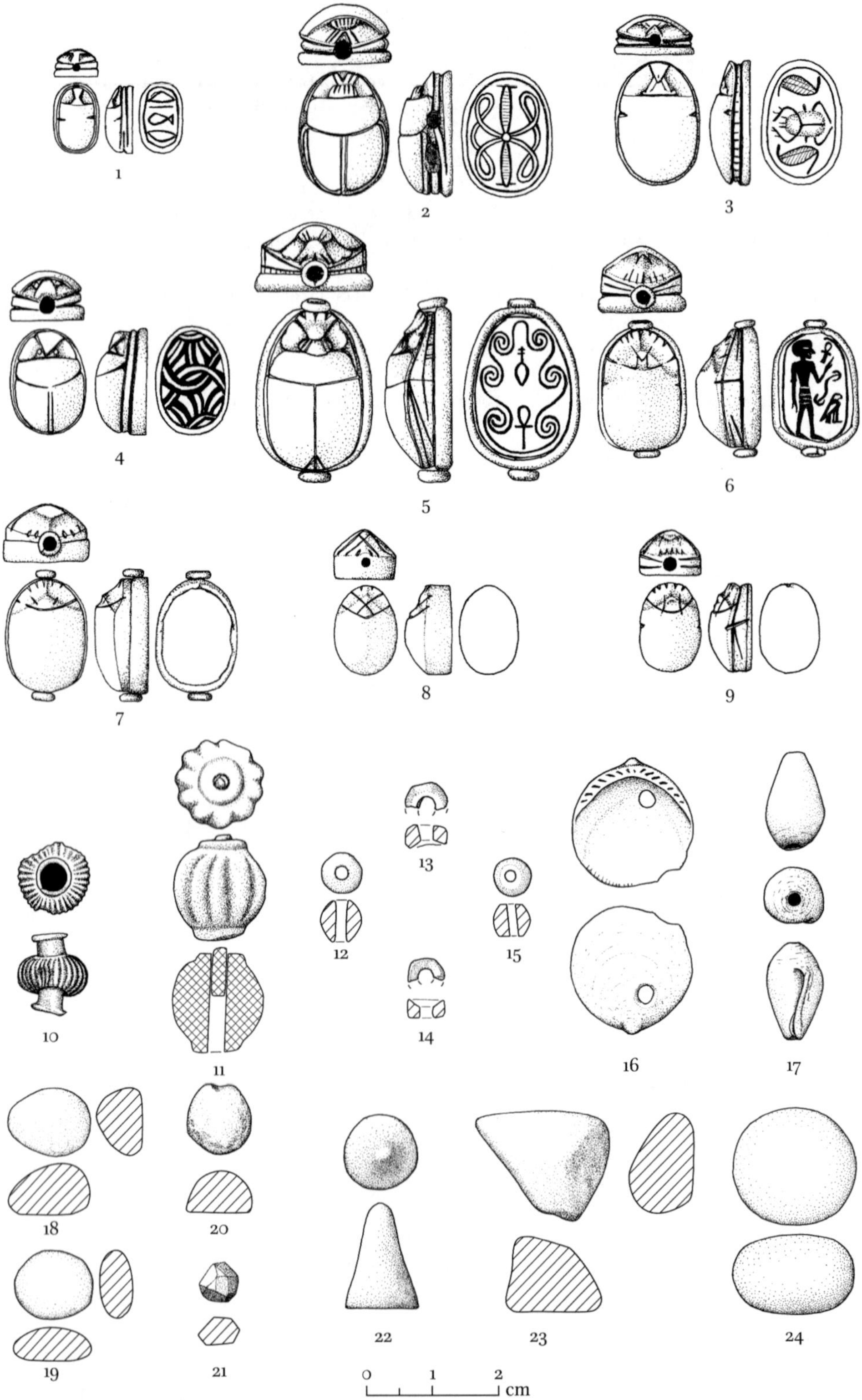

FIGURE 4.5

Figure No.	Shape/ object	Reg. No.	Locus/ Pottery Basket	Description (color of exterior/interior/ core; inclusions; decorations; etc.)
4.5.1	Scarab	AK IX 1983 H L/9 b. 1104/2 Hecht Museum# 86-148	Loc. 829	White steatite
4.5.2	Scarab	AK IX 1983 H L/9 b. 1302/4 Hecht Museum# 86-144	Loc. 829	White steatite
4.5.3	Scarab	AK IX 1983 H L/9 b. 1302/9 Hecht Museum# 86-145	Loc. 829	White steatite
4.5.4	Scarab	AK IX 1983 H L/9 b. 1302/5 Hecht Museum# 86-147	Loc. 829	White steatite
4.5.5	Scarab ring	AK IX 1983 H L/9 b. 1302/1 Hecht Museum# 86-153	Loc. 829	Deep purple amethyst scarab in gold bezel and silver ring (4.3.8)
4.5.6	Scarab in bezel	AK IX 1983 H L/9 b. 1302/3 Hecht Museum# 86-152	Loc. 829	Smokey purple amethyst scarab in gold bezel
4.5.7	Scarab ring	AK IX 1983 H L/9 b. 1302/2 Hecht Museum# 86-151	Loc. 829	Purple amethyst scarab with gold bezel and fragmentary silver ring (4.3.9)
4.5.8	Scarab	AK IX 1983 H L/9 b. 1229/5 Hecht Museum# 86-154	Loc. 829	Purple amethyst scarab; no carvings on bottom
4.5.9	Scarab	AK IX 1983 H L/9 b. 1228/2 Hecht Museum# 86-150	Loc. 829	Purple amethyst scarab; no carvings on bottom; remnants of bronze ring in holes
4.5.10	Bead	AK IX 1983 H L/9 b. 1271/3 Hecht Museum# 86-141	Loc. 829	Gold bead; rimmed, cylindrical tube on either side of globular body with raised, horizontal ribbing
4.5.11	Bead	AK IX 1983 H L/9 b. 1196/1	Loc. 829	Bronze bead with horizontal ribbing; copper or bronze wire in string hole

Figure No.	Shape/ object	Reg. No.	Locus/ Pottery Basket	Description (color of exterior/interior/ core; inclusions; decorations; etc.)
4.5.12	Bead	AK IX 1983 H L/9 b. 1307/5	Loc. 829	Amethyst globular bead
4.5.13	Bead	AK IX 1983 H L/9 b. 1201/2	Loc. 829	Clear crystal bead fragment
4.5.14	Bead	AK IX 1983 H L/9 b. 1196/2	Loc. 829	Clear crystal bead fragment
4.5.15	Bead	AK IX 1983 H L/9 b. 1094/2	Loc. 829	Turquoise globular bead
4.5.16	Beads	AK IX 1983 H L/9 b. 1094/3	Loc. 829	Shell bead, Glycymeris (dog-cockle) with natural hole
4.5.17	Beads	AK IX 1983 H L/9 b. 1094/4	Loc. 829	Shell bead, Conus mediterraneus (cone shell) with natural hole
4.5.18	Bead blank or gaming piece	AK IX 1983 H L/9 b. 1196/5	Loc. 829	Rock crystal; clear; bun-shaped
4.5.19	Bead blank or gaming piece	AK IX 1983 H L/9 b. 1196/6	Loc. 829	Light caramel-colored stone; quartz or polished chert? bun-shaped with flat bottom
4.5.20	Bead blank or gaming piece	AK IX 1983 H L/9 b. 1196/7	Loc. 829	Caramel-colored stone; quartz or polished chert? bun-shaped with flat bottom
4.5.21	Bead blank	AK IX 1983 H L/9 b. 1196/8	Loc. 829	Purple, semi-precious stone, likely garnet
4.5.22	Gaming piece	AK IX 1983 H L/9 b. 1196/4	Loc. 829	Frit conical gaming piece, white
4.5.23	Pebble	AK IX 1983 H L/9 b. 1196/9	Loc. 829	Pebble
4.5.24	Pebble	AK IX 1983 H L/9 b. 1307/6	Loc. 829	Pebble

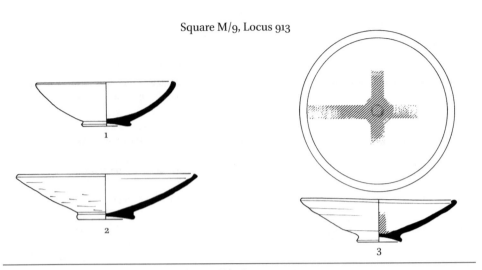
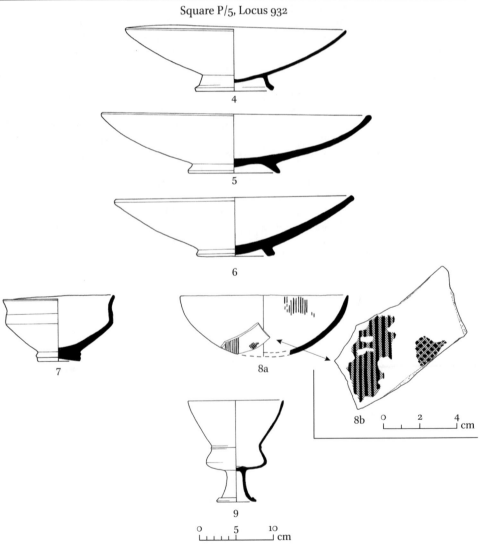

FIGURE 4.6

Figure No.	Shape/ object	Reg. No.	Locus/ Pottery Basket	Description (color of exterior/ interior/core; inclusions; decorations; etc.)
4.6.1	Bowl	AK IX 1983 H M/9 b. 1100/1	Loc. 913	Pink/pink/core not visible
4.6.2	Bowl	AK IX 1983 H M/9 b. 1123/2	Loc. 913	Pink/pink/pink buff
4.6.3	Bowl	AK IX 1983 H M/9 b. 1123/1	Loc. 913	Pink/pink/pink buff; remnants of a red slip and burnished cross in interior
4.6.4	Bowl	AK IX 1983 H P/5 b. 1250/1 Hecht Museum# 86-52	Loc. 932	Buff/buff/core not visible
4.6.5	Bowl	AK IX 1983 H P/5 b. 1305/2	Loc. 932	Pink/pink/core not visible
4.6.6	Bowl	AK IX 1983 H P/5 b. 1310/3	Loc. 932	Pink/pink/pink; small reddish brown inclusions
4.6.7	Bowl	AK IX 1983 H P/5 b. 1248/1	Loc. 932	Pink/pink/pink
4.6.8	Bowl	AK IX 1983 H P/5 b. 1308/1 + 1317	1308/1	Buff/buff/buff; small amount of small white inclusions; red painted stripes on black painted background (not much decoration remaining); Cypriot Black-on-Red Ware
4.6.9	Chalice	AK IX 1983 H P/5 b. 1319/1 Hecht Museum# 86-55	Loc. 932	Buff/buff/buff

Square P/5, Locus 932 (cont.)

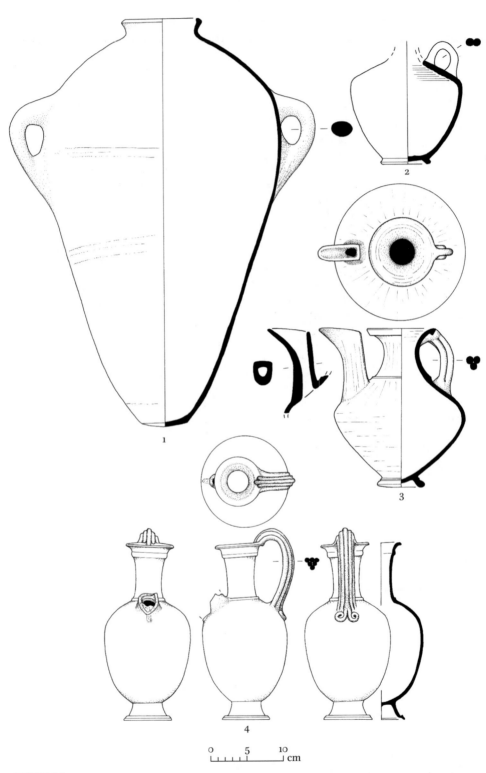

FIGURE 4.7

Figure No.	Shape/ object	Reg. No.	Locus/ Pottery Basket	Description (color of exterior/interior/ core; inclusions; decorations; etc.)
4.7.1	Storage jar	AK IX 1983 H P/5 b. 1177/2	Loc. 932	Pink/pink/grey; small white inclusions
4.7.2	Jug	AK IX 1983 H P/5 b. 1189/1	Loc. 932	Buff/buff/buff
4.7.3	Jug	AK IX 1983 H P/5 b. 1177/1 Hecht Museum# 86-46	Loc. 932	Brown/brown/brown; small white inclusions; brown slipped and highly burnished, or polished, exterior
4.7.4	Jug	AK IX 1983 H P/5 b. 1305/1 Hecht Museum# 86-45	Loc. 932	Buff/buff/buff; well levigated, very few small inclusions

Square P/5, Locus 932 (cont.)

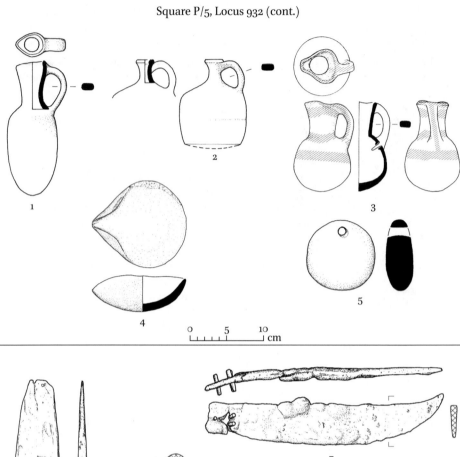
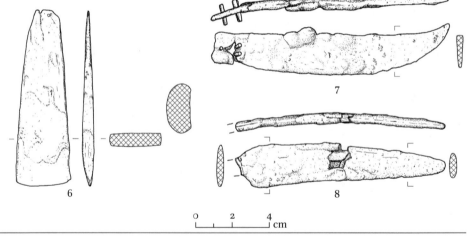
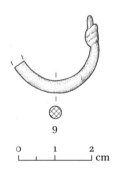
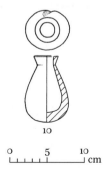

FIGURE 4.8

Figure No.	Shape/ object	Reg. No.	Locus/ Pottery Basket	Description (color of exterior/interior/ core; inclusions; decorations; etc.)
4.8.1	Juglet	AK IX 1983 H P/5 b. 1309/1 Hecht Museum# 86-65	Loc. 932	Reddish brown/reddish brown/core not visible
4.8.2	Juglet	AK IX 1983 H P/5 1296/1 Hecht Museum# 86-61	Loc. 932	Pink/pink/core not visible; cream slipped exterior
4.8.3	Juglet	AK IX 1983 H P/5 b. 1164/1 Hecht Museum# 86-59	Loc. 932	Salmon pink/salmon pink/core not visible; buff slip on outside, red to brown painted stripes; Cypriot White Painted family of Middle Cypriot pottery
4.8.4	Lamp	AK IX 1983 H P/5 b. 1318/1	Loc. 932	Pink/pink/dark grey; many small white inclusions
4.8.5	Loom weight	AK IX 1983 H P/5 b. 1249/1	Loc. 932	No fabric description; hard fired clay; 323.2 grams; Minoan or Cypriot
4.8.6	Axe head	AK IX 1983 H P/5 b. 1331/1 Hecht Museum# 86-72	Loc. 932	Copper alloy
4.8.7	Dagger blade	AK IX 1983 H P/5 b. 1328/1	Loc. 932	Bronze, single edged dagger; 3 rivets for handle
4.8.8	Blade	AK IX 1983 H P/5 b. 1310/1	Loc. 932	Bronze blade; double-edged dagger or spear point
4.8.9	Ring	AK IX 1983 H P/5 b. 1331/2	Loc. 932	Silver ring fragment; end designed to hold bezeled scarab or scarab
4.8.10	Alabaster vessel	AK IX 1983 H P/5 b. 1328/2 Hecht Museum# 86-68	Loc. 932	Creamy yellow

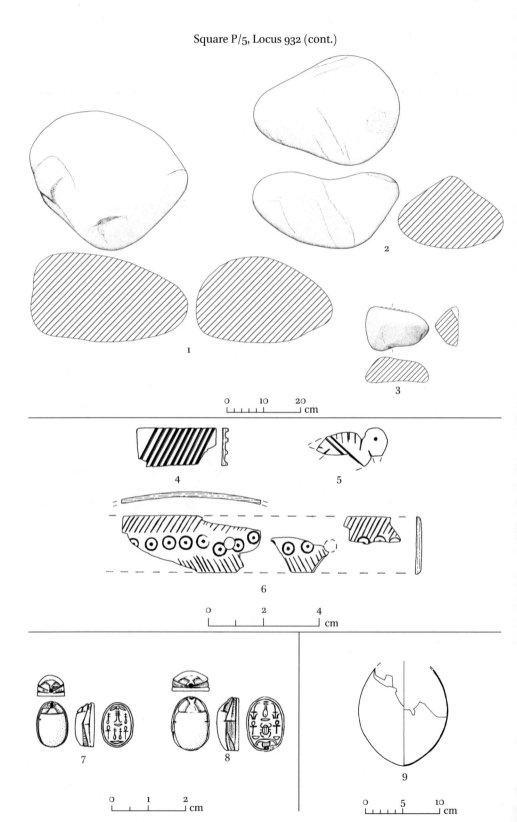

FIGURE 4.9

Figure No.	Shape/ object	Reg. No.	Locus/ Pottery Basket	Description (color of exterior/interior/ core; inclusions; decorations; etc.)
4.9.1	Ballast stone	AK IX 1983 H P/5 b. 1328/5	Loc. 932	Dark green stone; Cypriot
4.9.2	Ballast stone	AK IX 1983 H P/5 b. 1326/1	Loc. 932	Dark green stone; Cypriot
4.9.3	Ballast stone	AK IX 1983 H P/5 b. 1222/2	Loc. 932	Dark green stone; Cypriot
4.9.4	Bone inlay	AK IX 1983 H P/5 b. 1231/1	Loc. 932	Worked bone inlay with incised diagonal parallel lines
4.9.5	Bone inlay	AK IX 1983 H P/5 b. 1231/2	Loc. 932	Worked bone inlay bird with incised lines and eye
4.9.6	Bone inlay	AK IX 1983 H P/5 b. 1231/3	Loc. 932	with incised hatching and circle and dot designs
4.9.7	Scarab	AK IX 1983 H P/5 b. 1332/1 Hecht Museum# 86-149	Loc. 932	White steatite
4.9.8	Scarab	AK IX 1983 H P/5 b. 1222/1 Hecht Museum# 86-146	Loc. 932	White steatite
4.9.9	Ostrich eggshell	AK IX 1983 H P/5 b. 1116/1	Loc. 919 = Loc. 932	Creamy white

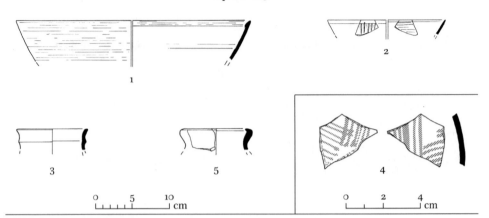
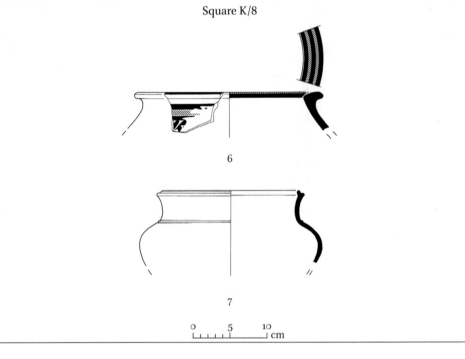
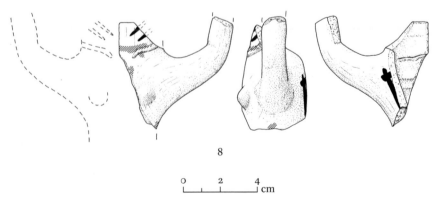

FIGURE 4.10

Figure No.	Shape/ object	Reg. No.	Locus/ Pottery Basket	Description (color of exterior/interior/ core; inclusions; decorations; etc.)
4.10.1	Bowl	AK X 1984 H O/5 b. 514/1, some fragments in b. 516	Loc. 914	Buff/buff/buff; few small white and small brown inclusions; burnished exterior
4.10.2	Bowl or goblet	AK X 1984 H O/5 b. 514/2	Loc. 914	Light grey/light grey/light grey; small dark grey inclusions; creamy white slip and burnished exterior and interior; Chocolate on White Ware
4.10.3	Jar or storage jar	AK X 1984 H O/5 b. 514/3	Loc. 914	Pink/pink/pink; small amount of small white and large grey inclusions
4.10.4	Bowl	AK X 1984 H O/5 b. 516/1	516/1	Red/red/pink; small amount of small micaceous inclusions; red stripes on exterior and interior, interior burnished; Cypriot Red-on-Red Ware
4.10.5	Jar or storage jar	AK X 1984 H O/5 b. 514/4	Loc. 914	Buff/buff/buff; small amount of miniscule brown and occasional medium sized grey inclusions
4.10.6	Krater	AK IX 1983 H K/8 b. 1316/2	1316/2	Buff/buff/pink to light grey; small amount of miniscule brown inclusions; painted dark brown and red stripes on buff slip on top of rim and vessel exterior; Cypriot Bichrome Ware
4.10.7	Bowl	AK IX 1983 H M/10 b. 1204/1	Loc. 934	Buff/buff/buff; few small white inclusions
4.10.8	Figurine	AK IX 1983 H L/9 b. 1251/0	Loc. 829	Grey/grey/grey; well levigated; pink slip and burnished exterior; dark brown and red painted stripes; Minoan or Cypriot

MB IIA-MB IIB-IIC typology
Platter bowls

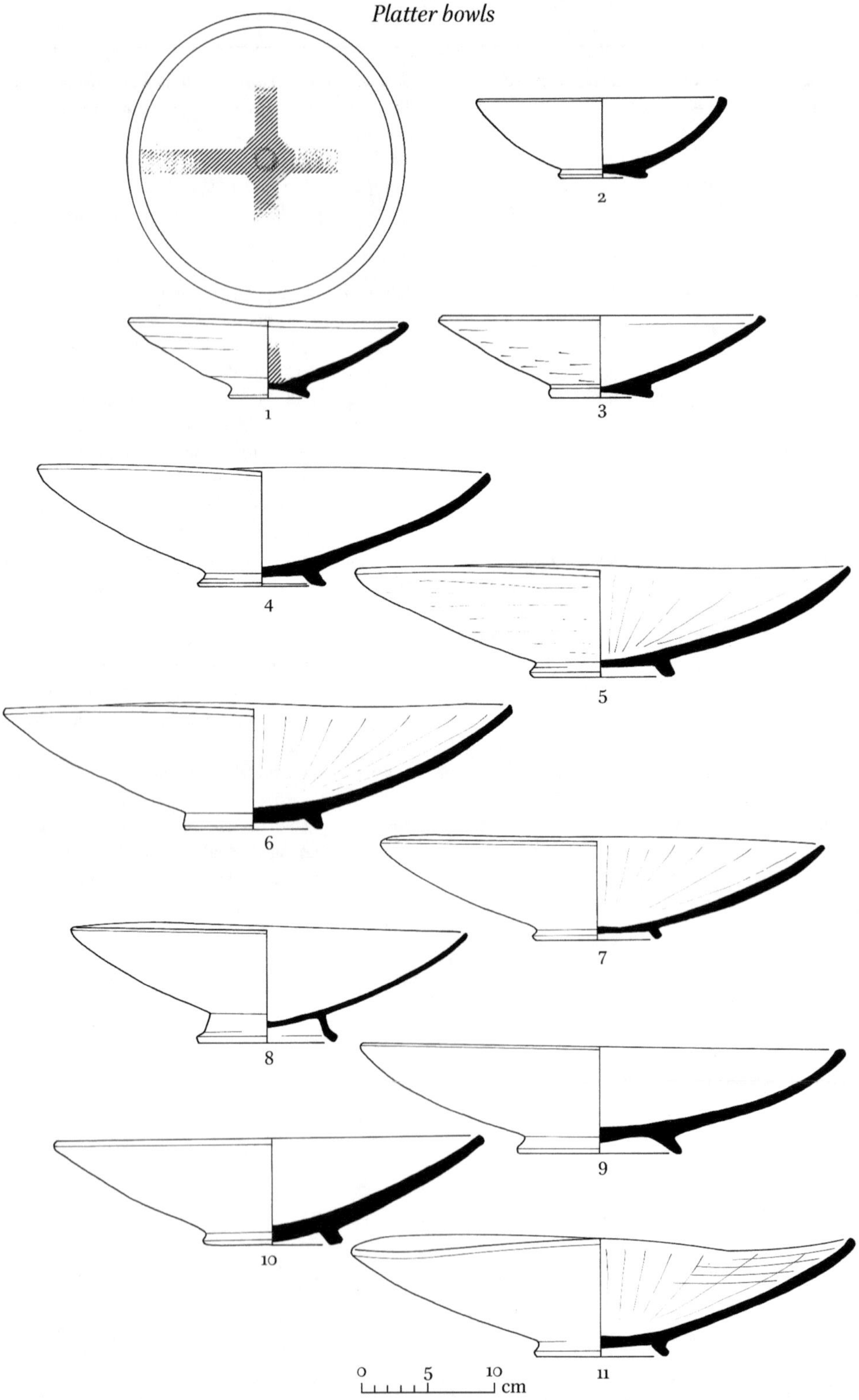

FIGURE 4.11

Figure No.	Shape/ object	Reg. No.	Locus/ Pottery Basket	Description (color of exterior/interior/ core; inclusions; decorations; etc.)
4.11.1	Bowl	AK IX 1983 H M/9 b. 1123/1	Loc. 913	Pink/pink/pink buff; remnants of a red slip and burnished cross in interior
4.11.2	Bowl	AK IX 1983 H M/9 b. 1100/1	Loc. 913	Pink/pink/core not visible
4.11.3	Bowl	AK IX 1983 H M/9 b. 1123/2	Loc. 913	Pink/pink/pink buff
4.11.4	Bowl	AK VIII 1982 H L/9 b. 310 Hecht Museum# 86-47	Loc. 829	Pink cream/pink cream/core not visible
4.11.5	Bowl	AK IX 1983 H L/9 b. 1251/1 +1229 Hecht Museum# 86-50	Loc. 829	Pink cream/pink cream/pink; radial burnished interior
4.11.6	Bowl	AK IX 1983 H L/9 b. 1303, 1081/1 Hecht Museum# 86-51	Loc. 829	Pink cream/pink cream/core not visible; radial burnished interior
4.11.7	Bowl	AK IX 1983 H L/9 b. 1229 Hecht Museum# 86-48	Loc. 829	Pink cream/pink cream/core not visible; radial burnished interior
4.11.8	Bowl	AK IX 1983 H P/5 b. 1250/1 Hecht Museum# 86-52	Loc. 932	Buff/buff/core not visible
4.11.9	Bowl	AK IX 1983 H P/5 b. 1305/2	Loc. 932	Pink/pink/core not visible
4.11.10	Bowl	AK IX 1983 H P/5 b. 1310/3	Loc. 932	Pink/pink/pink; small reddish brown inclusions
4.11.11	Bowl	AK IX 1983 H L/9 b. 1082/2 Hecht Museum# 86-49	Loc. 829	Pink/pink/pink; radial burnished interior

MB IIB-IIC typology

Small carinated bowl

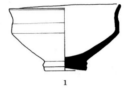

1

Chalices

2 3 4

Storage jar

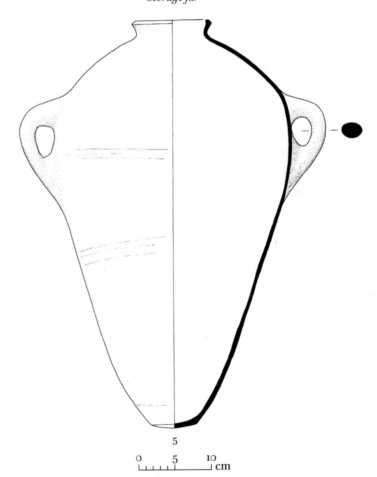

5

FIGURE 4.12

Figure No.	Shape/ object	Reg. No.	Locus/ Pottery Basket	Description (color of exterior/ interior/core; inclusions; decorations; etc.)
4.12.1	Bowl	AK IX 1983 H P/5 b. 1248/1	Loc. 932	Pink/pink/pink
4.12.2	Chalice	AK VIII 1982 H L/9 b. 337/1 Hecht Museum# 86-56	Loc. 829	Buff/buff/buff
4.12.3	Chalice	AK VIII 1982 H L/9 b. 350/3 Hecht Museum# 86-54	Loc. 829	Buff/buff/buff
4.12.4	Chalice	AK IX 1983 H P/5 b. 1319/1 Hecht Museum# 86-55	Loc. 932	Buff/buff/buff
4.12.5	Storage jar	AK IX 1983 H P/5 b. 1177/2	Loc. 932	Pink/pink/grey; small white inclusions

MB IIB-IIC typology (cont.)
Amphoriskoi

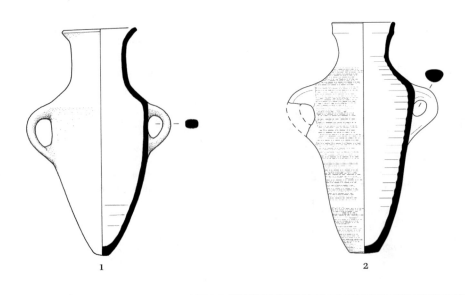

Miniature pitchers

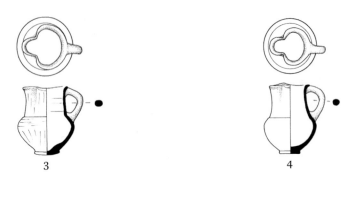

FIGURE 4.13

Figure No.	Shape/ object	Reg. No.	Locus/ Pottery Basket	Description (color of exterior/ interior/core; inclusions; decorations; etc.)
4.13.1	Amphoriskos	AK IX 1983 H L/9 b. 1289 Hecht Museum# 86-66	Loc. 829	Pink/pink/core not visible
4.13.2	Amphoriskos	AK IX 1983 H L/9 b. 1228	Loc. 829	Brown/brown/brown; small white inclusions
4.13.3	Jug	AK VIII 1982 H L/9 b. 350/4 Hecht Museum# 86-57	Loc. 829	Reddish brown/reddish brown/core not visible; slipped and burnished exterior
4.13.4	Jug	AK VIII 1982 H L/9 b. 350/1 Hecht Museum# 86-58	Loc. 829	Reddish brown/reddish brown/core not visible

MB IIB-IIC typology (cont.)

Jugs

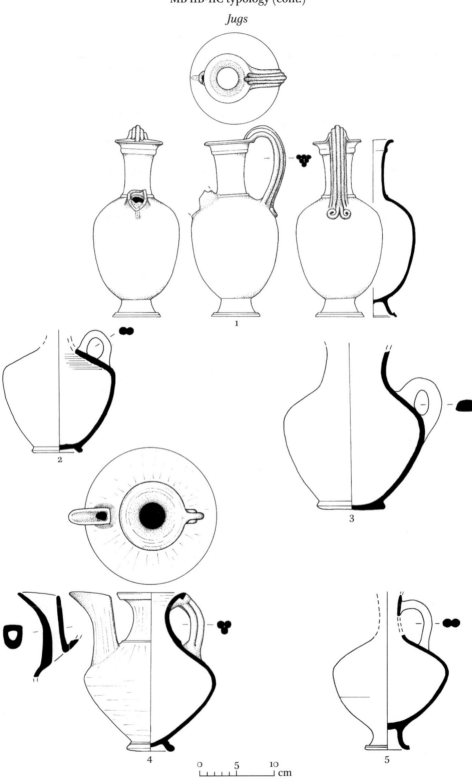

FIGURE 4.14

Figure No.	Shape/object	Reg. No.	Locus/Pottery Basket	Description (color of exterior/interior/core; inclusions; decorations; etc.)
4.14.1	Jug	AK IX 1983 H P/5 b. 1305/1 Hecht Museum# 86-45	Loc. 932	Buff/buff/buff; well levigated, very few small inclusions
4.14.2	Jug	AK IX 1983 H P/5 b. 1189/1	Loc. 932	Buff/buff/buff
4.14.3	Jug	AK VIII 1982 H L/9 b. 344	Loc. 829	Pink/pink/pink
4.14.4	Jug	AK IX 1983 H P/5 b. 1177/1 Hecht Museum# 86-46	Loc. 932	Brown/brown/brown; small white inclusions; brown slipped and highly burnished, or polished, exterior
4.14.5	Jug	AK IX 1983 H M/9 b. 1340/1	Loc. 909	Buff/buff/buff

MB IIB-IIC typology (cont.)
Juglets

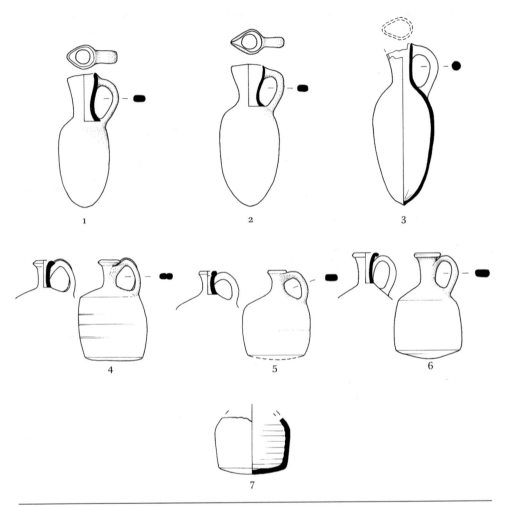

Lamp

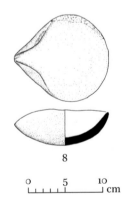

FIGURE 4.15

Figure No.	Shape/ object	Reg. No.	Locus/ Pottery Basket	Description (color of exterior/ interior/core; inclusions; decorations; etc.)
4.15.1	Juglet	AK IX 1983 H P/5 b. 1309/1 Hecht Museum# 86-65	Loc. 932	Reddish brown/reddish brown/core not visible
4.15.2	Juglet	AK VIII 1982 H L/9 b. 321/1 Hecht Museum# 86-63	Loc. 829	Pink/pink/pink; buff slipped and burnished exterior
4.15.3	Juglet	AK VIII 1982 H L/9 b. 333/4	Loc. 829	Buff/buff/buff
4.15.4	Juglet	AK VII 1980 H L/9 b. 216/1 Hecht Museum# 86-60	Loc. 727	Buff/buff/buff to grey; pink slipped exterior
4.15.5	Juglet	AK IX 1983 H P/5 1296/1 Hecht Museum# 86-61	Loc. 932	Pink/pink/core not visible; cream slipped exterior
4.15.6	Juglet	AK IX 1983 H L/9 b. 1102 Hecht Museum# 86-64	Loc. 829	Reddish brown/reddish brown/light brown; cream slipped exterior
4.15.7	Juglet	AK IX 1983 H L/9 b. 1101	Loc. 829	Pinkish buff/pinkish buff/pinkish buff; small number of small white inclusions
4.15.8	Lamp	AK IX 1983 H P/5 b. 1318/1	Loc. 932	Pink/pink/dark grey; many small white inclusions

MB IIB-IIC typology (cont.)

Cypriot imports

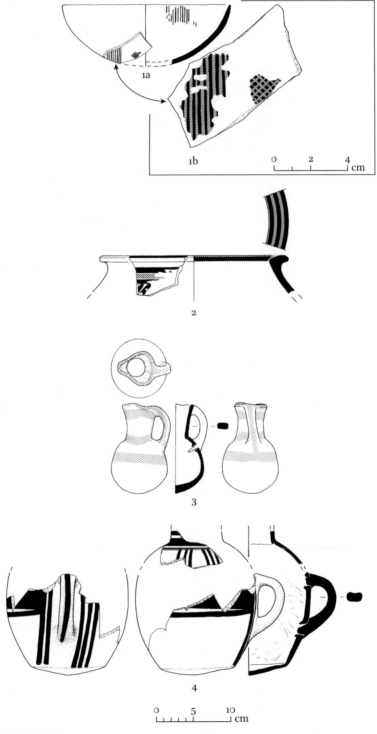

FIGURE 4.16

Figure No.	Shape/object	Reg. No.	Locus/Pottery Basket	Description (color of exterior/interior/core; inclusions; decorations; etc.)
4.16.1	Bowl	AK IX 1983 H P/5 b. 1308/1 + 1317	Loc. 932	Buff/buff/buff; small amount of small white inclusions; red painted stripes on black painted background (not much decoration remaining); Cypriot Black-on-Red Ware
4.16.2	Krater	AK IX 1983 H K/8 b. 1316/2	1316/2	Buff/buff/pink to light grey; small amount of miniscule brown inclusions; painted dark brown and red stripes on buff slip on top of rim and vessel exterior; Cypriot Bichrome Ware
4.16.3	Juglet	AK IX 1983 H P/5 b. 1164/1 Hecht Museum# 86-59	Loc. 932	Salmon pink/salmon pink/core not visible; buff slip on outside, red to brown painted stripes; Cypriot White Painted family of Middle Cypriot pottery
4.16.4	Jar	AK IX 1983 H K/8 b. 1321, 1323	Loc. 937	Tan/tan/tan; many small brown inclusions; cream (to green) slipped on exterior, dark brown painted stripes; Cypriot White Painted IV–VI

PHOTO 4.1   Locus 727 (b), Locus 829 (a, d) and Locus 932 (c, e), dipper and cylindrical juglets
PHOTO: R. STIDSING

PHOTO 4.2   Tomb Locus 829, platter bowls
PHOTO: R. STIDSING

THE POTTERY AND OTHER MATERIAL CULTURE OF STRATUM 6

PHOTO 4.3   Tomb Locus 829 (a, b) and Tomb Locus 932, chalices
PHOTO: M. ARTZY

PHOTO 4.4   Tomb Locus 829, ceramic grave goods
PHOTO: R. STIDSING

PHOTO 4.5   Tomb Locus 829, juglets
PHOTO: M. ARTZY

PHOTO 4.6   Tomb Locus, bronze scales and hematite weights
PHOTO: R. STIDSING

PHOTO 4.7   Four alabaster vessels from tomb Locus 829 and one alabaster vessel (lower right front) from tomb Locus 932
PHOTO: M. ARTZY

THE POTTERY AND OTHER MATERIAL CULTURE OF STRATUM 6

PHOTO 4.8 Tomb Locus 829, gold bead, earrings and scrap
PHOTO: R. STIDSING

PHOTO 4.9 Tomb Locus 829, limestone mortar
PHOTO: R. STIDSING

THE POTTERY AND OTHER MATERIAL CULTURE OF STRATUM 6

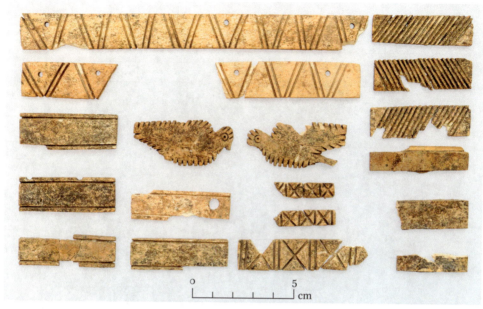

PHOTO 4.10   Tomb Locus 829, decorated bone inlays
              PHOTO: R. STIDSING

PHOTO 4.11   Tomb Locus 829, amethyst scarabs
              PHOTO: R. STIDSING

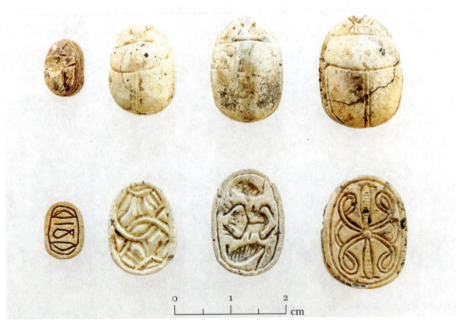

PHOTO 4.12 Tomb Locus 829, steatite scarabs
PHOTO: R. STIDSING

THE POTTERY AND OTHER MATERIAL CULTURE OF STRATUM 6 339

PHOTO 4.13   Tomb Locus 829, bronze, amethyst, turquoise, rock crystal beads, shells, blanks/game pieces
PHOTO: R. STIDSING

PHOTO 4.14   Locus 913, platter and shallow bowls
PHOTO: R. STIDSING

PHOTO 4.15　　Tomb Locus 932, ceramic grave goods
　　　　　　　PHOTO: R. STIDSING

THE POTTERY AND OTHER MATERIAL CULTURE OF STRATUM 6

PHOTO 4.16 Tomb Locus 932, jugs and juglet
PHOTO: R. STIDSING

PHOTO 4.17 Tomb Locus 932, bronze axe and knives
PHOTO: R. STIDSING

THE POTTERY AND OTHER MATERIAL CULTURE OF STRATUM 6

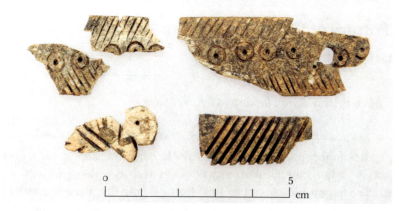

PHOTO 4.18   Tomb Locus 932, bone inlays
PHOTO: R. STIDSING

PHOTO 4.19   Tomb Locus 932, steatite scarabs
PHOTO: R. STIDSING

CHAPTER 5

The Pottery of Stratum 5 (LB IIB–Iron IA Transition, or LB IIC)

Michal Artzy, Aaron Brody and Ragna Stidsing

Stratum 5 is a rather ephemeral phase in Area H, consisting almost entirely of pits, some stone lined, and beaten earth floors, as described above in chapter 2 (fig. 2.10). The impoverished nature of the features from this phase is matched by the scrappy nature of the pottery remains. There is no rich assemblage of ceramics crushed in situ on any of the floor levels. Fortunately one pit preserved a cache of whole vessels; otherwise the ceramic assemblage consisted of sherds and many of these were worn.[1] Small sherds of Cypriot White Slip and Base Ring wares, and even a few fragments of Anatolian vessels, also occur in this phase, alongside some Aegean-style pottery and local late LB IIB–early Iron IA wares.[2] The transition from the LB IIB to Iron IA on the coast, namely

---

1 Artzy posits the worn pottery sherds and worn stones common to this phase became worn through use as tools utilized in burnishing, polishing, or rubbing. Brody suggests that these objects became worn through the natural process of water draining though the layers, especially in stone lined pits that would act as natural sumps during the duration of the phase and possibly for later phases as well.

2 Aegean-style pottery in the southern Levant has been given many labels, including Mycenaean (Myc.) IIIC:1, Late Helladic (LH) IIIC:1, Philistine Monochrome, and Sea Peoples Monochrome wares. Past studies of these ceramic types from Akko labeled them as "Shardanu" (M. Dothan 1986; 1989), in association with the group of Sea Peoples thought to have conquered the settlement at end of the Late Bronze Age. Since then it has been shown that there was no overall destruction at Tel Akko during that period. We prefer to utilize the more neutral term Aegean-style (see Killebrew 1998: 168–69) as it has been shown through fabric analysis on samples from similar forms from other excavation areas at Akko, as well as a stirrup jar found in the neighboring Tell Keisan, that Aegean-style ceramics were made both on Cyprus and locally (Gunneweg and Perlman 1994; Burdajewicz 1995; D'Agata et al. 2005; Artzy and Zagorski 2012). Among the group of Akko LH IIIC sherds analyzed by D'Agata et al. at least some, if not all, of these vessels were attributed to Cyprus. We would like to call attention to yet another problem associated with the samples from Akko, not necessarily only from Area H but from stratigraphically contemporary areas. M. Dothan attributed several sherds to this family, which he called LH IIIC, found in several areas of excavations at Akko. These, however, were a mixed bag. They were not all of the same family, neither in ware nor in decoration. In addition, the so called "ceramic kiln" in Area AB that he associated with a Shardanu sherd (M. Dothan 1993), was actually a furnace for recycling metal, as is evident by the discovery of crucibles with metal remains found in association with this feature. But this is not the only problem associated with this question. Following analyses, both by INAA

the northern coast of modern Israel, is being dealt with in association with the Carmel Coast (Artzy 2006a; 2013; Gilboa et al. 2015) and while LB III has been suggested as terminology for this period in the past (Ussishkin 1985; 1995; Finkelstein 1996; 2003), we prefer to call it coastal LB IIC (Martín Garcia and Artzy 2018). During this period, imports waned, yet continued to appear in sparse numbers (Artzy 2006a). A publication by J. Millek enumerates the sites which have remains from this period and evidence of continuation or destruction between the Late Bronze IIB and the beginning of the Iron Age have been dealt with in the study, although questions still remain (Millek 2019).

This phenomenon, a transition phase with handmade Cypriot Bronze Age pottery such as Base Ring II and White Slip II and III Wares; limited number of Aegean type wares, likely of local or Cypriot production; found alongside early Iron Age local materials, showing great typological continuity with LB II types, has been noted in contemporaneous levels at Tyre Stratum XIV; Sidon Area II, Y Stratum F; and Megiddo Stratum VIIA (Bikai 1978: 65–66; Anderson 1988: 389–90, T. Dothan 1982: 70–76; Artzy and Zagorski 2012). This transitional, regional phase also includes the appearance of Cypriot pithoi, locally made Cypriot-style pithoi, and Plain White Wheel Made (PWWM) wares similar to those of Tell Abu Hawam and Tel Nami in the LB IIB and LB IIC (Artzy 2005; 2006a; 2016; 2019), as well as Tel Dor's IR IA horizon (Gilboa and Sharon 2003: table 5; Gilboa 2005: 54–55). Base Ring and White Slip Wares, traditionally viewed as the hallmarks of LC II pottery on the island of Cyprus, are recognized in numerous contexts in LC IIIA settlements, while earlier they were treated as intrusive in the LC IIIA phase (Kling 1991: 182).

Stratum 5 Pottery

The majority of the pottery from Stratum 5 in Area H was found in Squares L/7 and L/9, although other examples were found in neighboring squares. They

---

and thin section petrography, some of the divisions between wares became clear. Thus, a group associated with Cyprus, often mistaken as a true Myc. IIIA2–B, was called Myc. IIIB by the excavators (Artzy and Zagorski 2012). Again, this group is very different from the Cypriot imports defined as Myc. IIIC/LH IIIC, or as S. Sherratt called them White Painted Wheelmade III Ware (Sherratt 1992). In addition there were clearly sherds which were grouped as Myc. IIIC but were produced locally. At least one sherd assigned, following analysis, to the Aegean, is actually a Myc. II type and is not Myc. IIIC as published by D'Agata et al. (Stockhammer, personal communication). Another decorated sherd of which only a drawing was located for this study, had a porous ware and appears, from the rather blurred line drawing, unlikely to have been Aegean or Cypriot. Stockhammer (forthcoming) has addressed the problem of the nomenclature and identification of the types and ware as an Aegean specialist who now studies wares of the period in the Levant.

are described below in the order in which the stratigraphy is detailed above in chapter 2. For each square, the descriptions are of the diagnostic ceramics from the lowest levels to the upper ones within the phase.

Square J/6: Although not from primary loci, three superimposed baskets from Square J/6 produced diagnostic vessels (fig. 2.19). The lowest of these baskets, basket 632, contained three pieces: the upright rim of a bowl, covered with a self-slip[3] both inside and out (fig. 5.1.1); the everted rim of a krater, with its rim and outside covered in a self-slip (fig. 5.1.2); and a self-slip vertical loop handle, perhaps from a storage jar (fig. 5.1.3). Immediately above this was basket 619 which contained the flared rim of a small bowl (fig. 5.1.4); the ring base of a large bowl or krater (fig. 5.1.5); a self-slipped body fragment decorated on its exterior with a horizontal red painted stripe, possibly a krater (fig. 5.1.6); the upright triangular rim of a cooking pot (fig. 5.1.7); a small piece of the spout from a strainer-spout jug with red painted decoration (fig. 5.1.8); and a small body sherd, a light gray fragment of an Anatolian Grey Ware vessel with micaceous inclusions, burnished inside and out, with incised horizontal and wavy decorations (fig. 5.1.9). Basket 619 also contained fragments of Cypriot White Slip and Monochrome bowls which are too small to illustrate. The uppermost basket in the square is basket 612, containing a fragment of a small carinated bowl with a flared rim decorated with a red stripe, possibly imported Anatolian Tan Ware (fig. 5.1.10), and a body sherd from a Cypriot White Slip bowl (fig. 5.1.11).

Square K/8: No diagnostic pottery from this phase was found in the one excavated feature, a stone lined pit, Locus 937 (fig. 2.23).

Square K/7: One feature was attributed to this phase in a probe in Square K/7 (fig. 2.22). This stone lined pit, Locus 753, contained only one diagnostic sherd: the upright rim of a jar, covered with a self-slip on its interior and exterior and decorated with a single brown stripe on its rim (fig. 5.1.12).

Square L/7: Remains in this square are probably part of an open courtyard, in which cultic elements were noted. The stone lined pit, Locus 750, contained very few diagnostic sherds as the matrix within the pit produced mainly worn sherds and worn pebbles. Basket 304 from Locus 750 had the rims of a small bowl and a krater and the handle of what may have been a Cypriot vessel (fig. 5.2.1–3). In basket 308, which also came from the fill in Pit 750, the shoulder of a monochrome decorated, Aegean-style stirrup jar was discovered with

---

3   What we are defining as a self-slip is not a true slip but a coloration on the surface of the ceramics caused by a purposeful reduction of oxygen in the kiln during firing or addition of salt in the production. For a detailed study on the use of this coloring technique in the manufacture of Cypriot Iron Age pottery see Hocking (2001: 133–39) or Tschegg et al. (2009), for its use on earlier Cypriot wares.

painted stripes and rhomboids with net filled decorations (fig. 5.2.4).[4] This is the vessel attributed by M. Dothan to the Shardanu (1986: 106–107). While it is tempting to call it Myc. IIIC,[5] Artzy views it as quite different from parallel vessels we know from either Cyprus or the southern coast, Philistia. Whether one can assign it to any particular "ethnic" group or not, it is of a type with counterparts in other areas of Akko, Area B and F (M. Dothan: 106–107). A limestone artifact identified by Artzy as a portable ship's altar was discovered connected to a line of stones, some covered in lime, which were in turn connected partially to the stone lined pit, Locus 750, (fig. 5.3.1; Artzy 1984, 1987, 2003). The limestone rectangular altar, ca. 24 × 26 × 30 cm, bears incised decorations of boats on one of its long sides (photos 5.1, 5.2) and indiscernible incised motifs on its short sides. It was most likely utilized aboard a ship as its lower parts were hewn and designed in a way to fit firmly between the planks of a vessel to avoid movement. Inside the bowl of the altar three rather large pebbles were found embedded in ash (fig. 5.3.2–4). Of the three pebbles, at least two bore decorations: one, a quartz foreign to the general area of Akko and the coastal area, has a boat and a fish, among other motifs (fig. 5.3.2); and another stone has a likeness of a fish (photo 5.3), probably a tuna fish (Artzy 2003: 239, fig. 10). Three large body sherds from storage jars and two diagnostic sherds were also discovered in the bowl of the altar: the vertical loop handle from a vessel, perhaps a jug or a storage jar, and the flared ring base of a much smaller vessel, a juglet (fig. 5.3.5–6). Two baskets, nos. 289 and 298, were excavated above Pit 750, which contained examples of Aegean-style pottery, as well as worn sherds, pebbles, and shell fragments. The body sherd of a large monochrome, Aegean-style krater (fig. 5.2.5) was decorated with a fish and a circle with a cross and dots and the remnants of a stripe on the carination of the

---

4 Unfortunately, this sherd, published by M. Dothan (1986: 106–107, fig. 8.5), disappeared, although Artzy remembers its ware, which was neither Aegean nor Cypriot.
5 The nomenclature is a problem. While there seems to be, a partial, standardized division when these wares are found in the Aegean in the eastern Mediterranean there is very little standard agreement as to their name when they appear in the Levant. While we use Aegean-style as an overall name for the LB II/Iron IA painted wares, originally imported from the Aegean, originating mostly in Mycenae/Berbati; the terms "Mycenaean" (Myc.) or "Late Helladic" (LH) are also utilized in the literature. So, LH IIIC or Myc. IIIC, are employed. In the eastern Mediterranean and in our case, the last of the imports from the Aegean are the type named Myc. IIIA2–B1, as are the majority of the imports to Tell Abu Hawam, the other anchorage on the Haifa/Akko Bay. At Akko they are mostly from robbed graves with no clear stratigraphy. Myc.-like sherds found at Akko, ones we named Myc. IIIB, were found to have originated on Cyprus, especially in the southwestern part of the island (Artzy and Zagorski 2012). These were different from the ones produced in the eastern part of Cyprus found at Tel Nami (Artzy 2006a) and can easily be distinguished from those called LH/Myc. IIIC1b.

vessel, all painted in a dark brown color. No slip was apparent on this vessel. The shoulder of a stirrup jar was found in Basket 298, the surface of which was covered in a cream-colored slip, with stripes in both brown and red paint, and a brown circle with a cross (fig. 5.2.6). The uppermost part of a triangle or rhomboid, painted in brown, is preserved just under the stripes on the vessel's shoulder. A jar stopper, made from a sherd from the base of a bowl, was also found in basket 289 (fig. 5.2.7) together with a very small fragment of a body sherd of a Cypriot White Slip bowl (too small to illustrate).

Basket 255 produced some diagnostic pottery. The relationship of these finds to Pit 750 is not completely clear except that basket 255 was excavated outside of the pit but in its vicinity. Basket 255 was next to the stone ship's altar as the pottery bucket sequentially follows the latest basket from inside the altar and its absolute height is lower. Open vessels in basket 255 include the direct rim of a simple bowl (fig. 5.4.1) and the flared rim of a krater (fig. 5.4.2). Closed vessels include the rim and neck of a large mouthed jar (fig. 5.4.3), and fragments of two vertical loop handles from storage jars (fig. 5.4.4–5). A body sherd (fig. 5.4.6) was uncovered with dark brown stripes on a cream-colored fabric, its fragmentary nature makes an attribution of vessel type difficult; however, the fabric is not local. The fragment of the tip of a wishbone handle is definitely Cypriot, its dark brown fabric suggesting White Slip Ware, although any decorative slip has been worn off (fig. 5.4.7).[6] Finally, the rim and neck of a jug (fig. 5.4.8) is preserved with a self-slip on its exterior and interior, over a pink fabric. It is possibly from the Cypriot PWWM family of ceramics (Kling 1991; Artzy 2006a, 2016).

The other main feature in Square L/7 was beaten earth floor Locus 731c. It was on this floor that the portable ship's altar was placed, and large amounts of ash were noted beside and above the altar, associated with Locus 731b that is buildup or occupational debris on Floor 731c. Several baskets could be attributed to the use of the floor. A bowl fragment with a dark brown stripe painted along the top of the rim and slightly over to the interior of the vessel is from an Aegean-style bowl (fig. 5.4.9). The fabric of this bowl is cream-colored on its interior, exterior, and its core, which most likely identifies it as a Cypriot import. Another flared rim fragment from a small carinated bowl came from the same basket (fig. 5.4.10), it is undecorated with an unusual fabric buff-pink on its exterior and interior and buff to light grey at its core, with a few small dark brown inclusions. It is likely an import from western Anatolia, likely

---

6   This sherd is likely of a White Slip II late bowl. These appeared at Tel Nami, assigned to the LB IIC. Their origin is likely in Sanidha (Karageorghis 2001; Artzy 2013).

Anatolian Tan Ware. Two fragments of Cypriot bowls, one White Slip and one Base Ring with a wishbone handle, were also found in Locus 731b (fig. 5.4.11–12).

A basket excavated directly below Floor 731c produced some noteworthy diagnostics: the circular, folded rim of a large krater-pithos (fig. 5.4.13), and two flared rim fragments from large pithoi (fig. 5.4.14–15). The other remains from basket 270 included a rim and handle from storage jars (fig. 5.4.16–17).

Several baskets excavated at an absolute height slightly lower than that of Floor 731c, baskets 69 and 288, contained diagnostic sherds assigned to the stratum. Yet, the exact relationship of this material to the features in this stratum, Floor 731c and Pit 750, is not fully clear. Basket 69 included the everted rim of a jar (fig. 5.4.18), the direct rim of a storage jar that is covered, both in and outside, with a self-slip (fig. 5.4.19), and a small body fragment of a Myc. IIIB vessel (fig. 5.25.8). Basket 288 contained the loop handle of a storage jar (fig. 5.4.20). Both of these baskets, however, are mixed with ceramics dating to the Persian and Hellenistic periods.

Square L/9: We will begin by describing the pottery from the two features, both pits, in the lower phase of this stratum in L/9 and then will move on to the pottery from the features of the upper phase. Included are ceramics from surrounding baskets when available and informative.

Locus 17, a pit from the lower phase of the stratum, preserved the majority of complete vessels for the level in Area H (photos 5.4, 5.5). A large krater (192/1) with an everted rim, ring base, and vertical, ovoid handles attached from the rim of the vessel to its shoulders was the only complete open vessel discovered in Pit 17 (fig. 5.5.1). Two identical storage jars with upright rims, angled carinated shoulders, piriform bodies, and vertical loop handles also came from Pit 17 (fig. 5.5.2–3), along with a pair of small jars or amphoriskoi with upright rims, pointed bases, pronounced angular shoulders, and vertical loop handles that begin at a type of carination found on the vessels' shoulders (fig. 5.6.1–2). Another amphoriskos of a slightly different type was found in Pit 17 (197/1). It lacks the angular shoulder of the amophoriskoi described above (fig. 5.6.3). This vessel is missing several of its diagnostic features: the rim is missing, and only stubs remain of both its vertical loop handles. The body, however, is a nice ovoid shape, unlike the pair of small jars or amphoriskoi found complete, and the vessel has a flattened base.

In three other baskets from Pit 17 (169, 190, and 200), diagnostic sherds of types different from the whole or restorable vessels, so far described, were found. These are obviously less secure than the whole vessels. Open vessels include rim sherds from several different types of small bowls (fig. 5.7.1–5) with varying rim types, body profiles, and fabrics. Several other small bowl types are represented, of varied rim types, body shapes, and fabrics, all covered with a self-slip on their interior and exterior (fig. 5.7.6–10). In basket 200 (fig. 5.7.11–13) rims of three cooking pots were found, two of pendent type and one inverted. Closed vessels include a pithos rim (5.7.14), covered inside and out with a self-slip; the upright rims of a storage jar and two jars (fig. 5.7.15–17); a handle of an Aegean-style stirrup jar, painted with a red stripe (fig. 5.7.18); the flat bases of two jugs, one of which is string cut (fig. 5.7.19), the other remnant (fig. 5.7.20) having some red slip on its outside and faint remnants of burn marks on one part of its broken edge suggesting that this was reused as a lamp;[7] two body sherds decorated with a cream-colored slip and red stripes (fig. 5.7.21–22); and a large pilgrim flask body fragment, decorated with red concentric stripes (fig. 5.7.23).

The other feature in the lower phase of Stratum 5 in Square L/9 is a second pit, Locus 813. Unlike Pit 17, no complete or restorable vessels were found in this feature. Included in the locus are open vessels such as rim fragments of several types of small bowls (fig. 5.8.1–4); the flared rim of a bowl with self-slip on its interior and exterior (fig. 5.8.5); the flared rim of a krater (fig. 5.8.6); and an everted triangular rim of a cooking pot (fig. 5.8.7). Fragments from closed vessels include the base of a large storage jar or pithos with a self-slip on its exterior (fig. 5.8.8); rims from storage jars (fig. 5.8.9–10); the flared rim and neck of a small juglet with the unusual addition of red slip inside of the vessel (fig. 5.8.11); and two handle fragments of jugs or jars (fig. 5.8.12–13), one of which is self-slipped and decorated with red stripes.

In the upper phase of this stratum are two features: a beaten earth floor, Locus 728, and a stone lined pit, Locus 814. Floor 728 suffered from later Persian and Hellenistic pitting. Two complete vessels were discovered associated with the floor, a bowl with a gentle carination and a severe tilt to its stance (fig. 5.8.14), and a chalice with an "X" incised inside its bowl (fig. 5.8.15)[8] The bowl of the chalice has a slight tilt, and the vessel is covered on the outside and inside its bowl with a self-slip. Very few diagnostic sherds were retrieved from the baskets from the stone lined Pit 814, and include the rim from a small carinated bowl with self-slip both outside and inside (fig. 5.9.1); a body sherd from a closed vessel, with a self-slip on its outside and a single red painted stripe decoration (fig. 5.9.2); and the upright rim of a storage jar (fig. 5.9.3).

The remaining diagnostic ceramics from this level in Square L/9 originate from baskets unassociated with features, and therefore of less secure stratigraphy. The description starts with the baskets lowest in the matrix representing

---

7   It is feasible that this red slipped jug fragment is an MB IIA type reused as a crude lamp in this later phase.
8   On display in the Hecht Museum at the University of Haifa.

THE POTTERY OF STRATUM 5

the stratigraphy of this square upward. In general, most of these baskets were both physically and stratigraphically below Floor 728 and Pit 814. They include baskets 306 + 331/1 with an almost complete undecorated bell-shaped bowl, of Aegean-style (fig. 5.9.4). The vessel has the typical slightly everted, rounded rim; ring base; rounded off carination to the body; and two horizontal handles. The fabric appears local. Baskets 238 and 254 (1982 L/9) contained the rim of a pithos (fig. 5.9.5), a jar or storage jar (fig. 5.9.6), and the flared rim and stub of a jug's handle (fig. 5.9.7), covered with a self-slip both inside and out. Baskets 269 and 290 are grouped together and produced diagnostic ceramics: a fragment of the upright rim of a small bowl with a red painted band around the rim, and burnishing on the interior (fig. 5.9.8); an everted triangular rim of a cooking pot (fig. 5.9.9); a fragment from the spout of a lamp, covered both on its interior and exterior with a self-slip (fig. 5.9.10). Imports include a fragment of a Cypriot White Slip II bowl wishbone handle (fig. 5.9.11); the rim of a clearly non-local cooking pot whose fabric is cream-colored throughout and contains numerous small dark brown and white grits (fig. 5.9.12), a body sherd of very similar fabric decorated with a single band of red paint (fig. 5.9.14); and a body sherd of a Myc. IIIB vessel (fig. 5.9.13), likely of Cypriot provenance.

Baskets 163, 212, 226, 229, and 245 are grouped together as part of the same matrix, and the diagnostic pottery from them will be presented as a group. Open vessels include the shoulder and loop handle of a biconical amphora-krater decorated with brown painted stripes (fig. 5.10.1), a similar painted body sherd (fig. 5.10.2), an almost complete biconical amphora-krater with a flared, folded rim, biconical body, and disk base (fig. 5.10.3), and a cooking pot with a slightly flared rim (fig. 5.10.4). Closed vessels include the base and several rim types from storage jars (fig. 5.10.5–7), including one rim fragment with a self-slip on its exterior (fig. 5.10.8). Imported wares include a Cypriot Base Ring II carinated bowl rim fragment (fig. 5.10.9); the upright rim of a self-slipped PWWM bowl of Cypriot origin (fig. 5.10.10); and a body sherd of a small carinated bowl whose dark gray fabric may be Anatolian Grey Ware (fig. 5.10.11).

The ceramics in basket 269 (1980) are reminiscent of several fabric types or treatments already detailed. Two of the vessels are the self-slipped rims of two jars (fig. 5.11.1–2). The other two diagnostic pieces from the basket are a rim fragment of a large bowl and the flared rim of a jar (fig. 5.11.3–4) with a light fabric, likely Cypriot PWWM. Directly above this was basket 189, with the ring base of a large bowl or krater (fig. 5.11.5), the everted rim of a cooking pot (fig. 5.11.6), the upright rim and handle of a juglet (fig. 5.11.8), and the rim and part of a wishbone handle of a Cypriot Base Ring II bowl (fig. 5.11.7).

Square M/7: Only one feature in Square M/7 could be attributed to Stratum 5, a stone lined pit (no locus number; fig. 2.10). As we have seen from other squares, this pit contained a concentration of worn pebbles and worn pottery sherds. Fortunately, a nice array of diagnostic sherds was also preserved, although some intrusive Middle Bronze pottery was in the pit as it was cut into layers of the city's rampart. Open vessels include several varieties of mainly carinated small bowls, both shallow and deep, (fig. 5.11.9–11); one example is covered, both inside and out, with a self-slip (fig. 5.11.12); and there are two fragments of Aegean/Cypriot-style small bowls, one everted rim fragment with a red stripe painted just on the inside of its lip (fig. 5.11.13), and a body fragment which is most likely from a small bowl that has a self-slip on its exterior and interior and fragmentary remains of concentric red painted stripes in its interior (fig. 5.11.14). Large bowls are represented by a fragment of the upright rim of a carinated vessel (fig. 5.11.15). A decorated body sherd most likely from a krater is covered with a self-slip and scant remnants of red painted stripes on its exterior (fig. 5.11.16). Closed vessels from the pit include the flat base of a large pithos (figs. 5.11.17, 5.18.14), fragments of an angled base (fig. 5.11.18) and upright rims (fig. 5.11.19–21) from storage jars, and the shoulder and stump of a vertical loop handle from a juglet (fig. 5.11.22), possibly a wheel-made local imitation of a White Shaved juglet.

Square M/4: Only one feature in Square M/4 was attributed to Stratum 5, a stone lined pit, Locus 744, which was cut into the Middle Bronze rampart layers (fig. 2.10). Pit 744 contained very few diagnostic sherds: the upright, triangular rim of a cooking pot (fig. 5.12.1); the upright rim of a storage jar (fig. 5.12.2); and the vertical loop handle of a storage jar (fig. 5.12.3).

Square N/5: No diagnostic pottery was found in the one feature, hearth Locus 1054, from this phase in Square N/5.

Stratum 5 Pottery from Later Contexts or Stratigraphically Floating Baskets

Occasionally diagnostic sherds from the transition period of the end of the LB IIB to the beginning of the Iron IA were discovered in later period contexts. In this section we are also including material from baskets belonging to Stratum 5 that were not from primary features, or could not be easily associated with or related stratigraphically to primary features. Thus this material, even though originating in the right phase, is not well-stratified. Several categories are represented: plain wares; vessels with a self-slip; local painted pottery; Myc. IIIB vessels; an Egyptian import; Cypriot White Slip, Base Ring, and Monochrome wares; and a fragment, possibly, from a figurine.

Plain wares include small bowls with simple and folded rims, a "cyma" profile, and a carinated bowl (figs. 5.8.16–18, 5.12.4); the rim and carinated shoulder of storage jars (figs. 5.8.19, 5.12.5) and rim of a jug (fig. 5.12.6). Self-slipped vessels include a small carinated bowl with the slip outside and inside (fig. 5.12.7), and the squared off ring base likely of a bell-shaped bowl with self-slip on its exterior (fig. 5.12.8). Local painted pottery is represented by part of a handle of a storage jar covered with a self-slip and decorated with red painted stripes (fig. 5.12.9); and a spout from a jug, with a cream slip covering the inside of the spout and red painted stripes along the edge of it (this may be a later Iron I form) (fig. 5.12.10).

Only a few examples of Myc. IIIB pottery were found in the later contexts in Area H. One body sherd is from the body of a globular pilgrim flask (fig. 5.13.1), and another may be from the body of a stirrup jar (fig. 5.13.2), likely of Cypriot manufacture.

A rim fragment from an Egyptian imported jar (fig. 5.13.3) was identified. It has an upright thickened rim and a broad cylindrical neck, perhaps from a wide-necked handleless ovoid jar (Killebrew 1998: 151–53). The fabric is dark brown and red at the edges with many small white inclusions, likely of Nile silt clay, Egyptian Marl D ware. The vessel is decorated with a cream-colored slip on its exterior and interior, and a red brown paint on the outside of the jar. Comparable Egyptianized vessels, or locally manufactured pottery made in Egyptian form, are known from other sites in the north, in LB II Hazor and Megiddo, and LB II–Iron I Beth Shean (Martin 2004), although this particular sherd is of Egyptian origin.

Cypriot pottery found in poorly stratified contexts in Stratum 5 include a typical repertoire of White Slip II, Base Ring II and Monochrome bowls (figs. 5.8.20, 5.13.4–12). Similar finds of White Slip, Base Ring, and Monochrome wares come from later contexts in Area H (fig. 5.13.13–22). A horn from a Base Ring II bull vessel was also discovered in a later context, decorated with white painted chevrons (fig. 5.13.23).

A piece from a later context is what may be the upraised arm or wing from an Aegean-style figurine (figs. 5.13.24, 5.25.14). It is triangular-shaped and made by hand, with parallel vertical grooves etched on one side and two red painted spots on the opposite side. The interior edge does not appear to be broken, but rather is finished in a rough semi-circular shape. It must have been attached before firing, however, as a light gray core is apparent on this semi-circular edge, which suggests this piece was not fired separately from the body of the figurine.

Stratum 5 Typology

Although the ceramic finds are mostly fragmentary, the assemblage of types from this phase in Area H is fairly rich. Given the diversity of sites during this transitional period we will turn to the comprehensive typology compiled by

A. Killebrew for the basic categories for dividing the corpus, where appropriate, and for the majority of comparisons (1998: 78–186).[9] We will also utilize the pottery studies from Tyre (Bikai 1978), Sarepta (Anderson 1988), Tel Qiri (Hunt 1987), and Tel Qasile (Mazar 1985), and a preliminary copy of the chapter on the pottery from the early Iron Age phases 13–10 of Tell Keisan (Burdajewicz 1995).[10] We have to bear in mind, however, that the diversity of sites is, to a large extent, the result of continuity and change in the geo-political and geo-economics of the region. Studies of sites along the Carmel Coast, such as Dor, Tel Nami, Tell Abu Hawam, and further excavation areas at Akko, show a different development than that of southern coastal sites, especially those in Philistia.

Bowls

The division of the bowl types is based, primarily, on the form of the body and rim of the vessels, and eventually the base and decoration. This suits the prevalence of rim sherds in the assemblage from Area H, and the fragmentary nature of the ceramics from this phase.

Rounded Semi-Hemispherical Bowls with Simple Rims: Several versions of this bowl type were present in the repertoire from Area H at Akko. The overall size of these bowls varies widely as does the depth of the semi-hemispheric body of the bowl (fig. 5.14.1–9). The majority of the rims are simple and upright; some do show a bit of thickening. The angle of their rims and walls are varied. None of the examples from Area H has a preserved base. Three of these bowls (fig. 5.14.1, 4, 7) were covered with a self-slip on their exterior and interior surfaces.

These bowls belong to Killebrew's CA2 bowl type (1998: 83). Following Killebrew's study, the rounded bowl is a Canaanite form common at sites from the LB II through the Iron I (table 5.1). The type is widely distributed throughout southern Palestine, and has antecedents going all the way back to the Middle Bronze Age (Killebrew 1998: 83). At Sarepta this bowl form is best matched by Anderson's types X-27 and X-29 (1988: 160–61). They have a stratigraphic range from Stratum J–D2 and G1–B, or the LB IIA–Iron IIB and LB IIB–Persian period (Anderson 1988: 471).

---

9   The authors would like to thank A. Killebrew for kindly providing a copy of her dissertation.

10 The authors would like to thank M. Burdajewicz for kindly providing a copy of his very relevant chapter on the Iron I ceramics at neighboring Tell Keisan. Burdajewicz's work on the earliest Iron Age ceramics will be more readily available in the future in the second final report on the excavations at Tell Keisan.

Shallow to Semi-Hemispherical Bowls with Folded Rims: This bowl type is relatively rare in Area H, and is marked by a range in size, depth of body, and the treatment of the incurved rim from very slight to well pronounced (fig. 5.14.10–13). No bases are preserved. The smallest bowl, 190/2 (fig. 5.14.10), is covered on its exterior and interior with a self-slip, and 290/2 has a red painted stripe around its rim and burnishing on its interior (fig. 5.14.11).

This bowl type, Killebrew's CA1, is well represented throughout the LB II and transitional LB IIB–Iron IA in Palestine (Killebrew 1998: 82; table 5.1). It is a Canaanite form with an ancestry going back to the Middle Bronze Age, with a distribution throughout the greater region (Killebrew 1998: 82). At Tyre this bowl type, Bikai's Plate (bowl) 11, has a long history of use from Stratum XVII through Stratum IV (1978: 21, table 3B). The peak of its appearance is from Stratum XIV through VII, or the Iron IA through the Iron II (Bikai 1978: 68). At Sarepta, Anderson has divided this bowl form into two types, X-15 and X-18 (1988: 152–53, 155). Bowl X-15 spans Sarepta Stratum J–C1, or the LB IIA–Iron IIC, while X-18 appears in Stratum G2 and ends in D2, approximately the LB IIB–Iron IIA (Anderson 1988: 470–71).

Semi-Hemispherical Bowls with Flared Rim: This bowl type is represented by the sherds from four vessels in Area H. They vary in diameter and size, but all have shallow, semi-hemispherical bodies and slightly flared rims (fig. 5.14.14–17). No bases are preserved. One example, 116/11 (fig. 5.14.14), is decorated with a dark brown stripe painted on the top of its rim, and has thinner walls than our other bowls in this group. This painted bowl is made from a cream-colored fabric not local to the Akko region, and is likely an import to the site.

Killebrew does not categorize the local bowl type in her break down of small bowl shapes for the LB II–Iron I (1998: 81–89); however, the painted bowl is represented in her Aegean-style Form AS 1 (1998: 170). Killebrew distinguishes two styles of rim for her AS 1 bowl form, one of which is "a flattened everted (flared) rim." This bowl type is popular on Cyprus and the Aegean, and is well represented in early Iron I phases at Tel Miqne. The use of matt painting, as on our example, is a hallmark of the LH IIIC tradition on Cyprus and in Philistia, while equivalents in the Aegean retain the Mycenaean tradition of decoration with glossy paint (Killebrew 1998: 171). Local semi-hemispherical bowls with flared rims are present at both Tyre and Sarepta in multiple phases (table 5.1); thus it is possible that this is a northern coastal type. At Tyre, the form is matched by Bikai's Plate (bowl) 14, which is present in Strata XVI–XIV (1978: 21, table 3B, 25). These phases at Tyre correspond chronologically to the LB II–Iron I in Palestine (1978: 68). The type corresponds to Anderson's X-7 bowl form in his typology of pottery from Area II, Y at Sarepta (1988: 148). Bowl type x-7 has a range from Stratum K–F, which can be equated with the LB I–Iron IA in Palestine (1988: 422–23, 472).

Semi-Hemispherical Bowls with "Cyma" Profile: The five examples of this bowl type in Area H are all approximately the same diameter and depth of body (fig. 5.14.18–22). All exhibit similar gently everted rims creating the typical "S"-shaped profile of this bowl type; some rims are slightly thickened while others are the same thickness as the walls of the vessel. None of the bowls fragments of this type have their base preserved. Two of the bowls are covered inside and outside with a self-slip (190/1 & 509/1). It is possible that some of these shallow bowls belong to chalices, as one complete chalice was preserved from Stratum 5 in Area H and it has a "cyma" profile (see details below).

In Killebrew's study this bowl type is labeled CA 7 (1998: 87–89). She points out a wide distribution of these shallow bowls throughout Canaan, with a relative absence in the hill country and in Iron I sites in Philistia where "Aegeanized" bowls replace the "cyma" type. Killebrew defines the chronological range for CA 7 bowls from the end of the LB IIB to the Iron I (table 5.1). At Sarepta this ceramic type, Anderson's x-6 bowl (1988: 147–48), starts to appear a bit earlier. Anderson charts this bowl's range from Stratum K–D2; however, there is only one example of the type in both K and D2 (1988: 470). Removing these outliers, the main body of the battleship curve appears from Stratum J–E, or the LB IIA–Iron IB.

Carinated Semi-Hemispherical Bowl: Three examples of carinated semi-hemispherical bowls were found in Stratum 5 of Area H (fig. 5.15.1, 5.15.4–5.15.5). All have direct simple rims; the location of the carination is about halfway down the vessel on 1304/1 (fig. 5.15.1), while it is very high on 169/5 and 104/1 (fig. 5.15.4–5). One disk base is preserved on bowl 104/1, a vessel that also has an uneven slant to its profile (fig. 5.15.5). Bowl 169/5 is decorated with a self-slip on its interior and exterior (fig. 5.15.4).

This bowl type is termed CA 4 in Killebrew's schema (1998: 84). Descended from the carinated bowls of the Middle Bronze Age, these small carinated bowls are found at sites throughout Canaan in the LB I–II (table 5.1), and are especially popular at sites in the north of the region (Killebrew 1998: 84). Anderson breaks down the parallel bowls into two types, x-24 with the lower carination like Area H's 1304/1 and x-28 with a high line of carination similar to Akko's 169/5 and 104/1 (1988: 158–61). At Sarepta these bowl types have a longer span than in Palestine, as the x-24 type ranges from Stratum K–F and x-28 from Stratum G2–D1, approximately the LB I–Iron IA and LB IIB–Iron IIB in Palestinian chronological terms (Anderson 1988: 471).

Carinated Shallow Bowl: The three examples from Area H all have slightly flared rims and shallow bodies, but fall into two groups based on the angularity of their carination and treatment of their rims (fig. 5.15.2–3, 6). Bowls 169/4 and 190/3 have gentle "S"-shaped carinations and a rounded rim, neither base is preserved (fig. 5.15.2–3). Decorations include a self-slip covering the inside and outside of bowl 190/3 (fig. 5.15.3).

Carinated shallow bowls are Killebrew's type CA 5 (1998: 85). They appear toward the end of the LB IIB, but are primarily an Iron I type (table 5.1), with a distribution mostly at sites in the coastal plain, inland valleys, and southern hill country (Killebrew 1998: 85). Carinated shallow bowls are not well represented at either Tyre or Sarepta. At Tyre a parallel for our more rounded type appears in Stratum XV, the LB IIB (1978: pl. XLII.8). At Sarepta the rounded carinated bowl is type X-23 (Anderson 1988: 157–58). It has a span from Stratum G2–E, or the LB IIB–Iron IB (Anderson 1988: 471). The more angular carinated shallow bowl type with tapering flared rim is not present at these Lebanese coastal sites.

Carinated Deep Bowl: Our one definite example of a large carinated bowl has a simple upright rim and a gentle carination (fig. 5.15.7). Its base is missing. This type is rare, and may be regional to northern Palestine. It is not defined in Killebrew's typology, but is detailed by Amiran as an Iron I type based on examples from Hazor XII and Megiddo VI (1969: 192). These bowls, however, have flared or everted rims. It is likely that the rim fragment 145/1 is from this type of deep bowl; however, it is impossible to be certain since it is such a small piece of the original vessel. Carinated deep bowls are well represented in the multiple Iron IA–IB phases at Tell Keisan. Burdajewicz defines the deep bowl type as Type BC III, which includes examples with upright, direct, and flared rims (1995: 39). Parallels from Tell Keisan with upright rims are found in Levels 12a, 11, and 9, while the general type spans Levels 13–9.

Hemispherical ("Bell-Shaped") Bowls: This bowl type is distinguished by its hemispherical body shape, gently flared simple rim that forms an "S" curve with the body of the vessel, ring base, and horizontal handles (fig. 5.15.8–15). The few examples discovered in Area H show several variations on these generalities: the rim on our one nearly complete example is not uniform from one side to the next, from gently flared to a slight gutter shape (fig. 5.15.8); the angle of the horizontal handles on our two preserved examples varies from almost completely vertical to about 45° (fig. 5.15.8–9). Self-slip appears on the interior and exterior of 129/1 and 200/4, and the exterior of 549/2 (fig. 5.15.10–11, 14); the same colored slip is found on the inside and outside of the bowl fragment 258/1 (fig. 5.15.15) together with two concentric lines which were part of a spiral painted in red. Bowl 322/4 is not slipped but is decorated with a red stripe on the lip of its rim (fig. 5.15.12).

This Aegean-style bowl form is Killebrew's type AS 4 (1998: 174). It is broadly distributed at sites in the Aegean and Cyprus, as well as at sites in the Levant from Cilicia in the north to all of the major Philistine sites in the southern coastal plain (Killebrew 1998: 175–76). Its chronological range varies depending on location: Iron I for Canaan, Late Cypriot IIC–IIIB on Cyprus, and Late Helladic IIIB–IIIC in the Aegean (the comparisons we will make will only be to bowls in the LH IIIC tradition) (Killebrew 1998; table 5.1). A bell-shaped bowl has been identified as an Aegean LH IIIC import by Bikai in Stratum XIV at Tyre (1978: 65). A less decorated bell-shaped bowl is also represented in Tyre's Stratum XIV, painted with both black and deep red colors (Bikai 1978: pl. XXXIX.14). Bikai does not identify this bowl as imported, and thus it may be a local imitation of an imported LH IIIC type. Two Aegean-style, LH IIIC hemispherical bowls were discovered at Sarepta in Area II,Y, one each in Stratum G1 and F, equivalent to the LB IIB–Iron IA in southern Palestine (Anderson 1988: 273). Ten more fragments of Aegean-style hemispherical bowls were found in Area II, X at Sarepta, although not all of these are properly stratified (Koehl 1985: 119–122). LH IIIC pottery in Area II,X has been phased to Period IV–V, which is contemporary with Area II,Y Stratum G–F (Khalifeh 1988: 101, 112). It is Khalifeh's opinion, however, that the LH IIIC sherds in Area II,X's Period IV are intrusive and that LH IIIC fits more properly in Period V (Khalifeh 1988: 101). The bell-shaped bowl is much more common at Tell Keisan than at Tyre or Sarepta. In Burdajewicz's study of the early Iron Age pottery at Tell Keisan he defines the shape as the Type IV bowl, noting its presence in Level 13–8c at the site which span all the phases of the Iron I into the Iron IIA (1995: 48–49). The variations of rim type, decoration or lack there of, and angle of horizontal handles noted above for the few examples from Area H are paralleled by the variety represented in this family of bowls from Keisan. At Tel Dor the vessel type is labled BL 1, it is rare and is found in the IrIa(early)–IrIb horizons (Gilboa and Sharon 2003: table 2; Gilboa 2005: 56–57, fig. 2).

Chalices

Chalice: The one chalice we have preserved in this phase in Area H has a slightly flared rim and a shallow semi-hemispherical bowl, which is of the "cyma" type and would be easily misidentified if none of the chalice's foot was preserved (fig. 5.16.1). The carination of the bowl is close to the rim and is gentle. The chalice's foot is high and stepped. The inside of the bowl of the chalice is marked with a symbol that resembles an "X," and the vessel is covered both on its exterior and the interior of its bowl with a self-slip.

None of the chalices, which Killebrew discusses in her type CA 14, is a good parallel for our Akko chalice (1998: 96–97). This is especially true as her primary examples do not have their foot preserved, and the stepped foot is a useful typological distinction according to Amiran (1969: 213). Following Amiran's study, the stepped foot on chalices is not an LB II feature; it comes into use in the Iron I and continues through the Iron IIB, disappearing by the Iron IIC (table 5.1). Hunt's study of the Iron Age pottery from Tel Qiri shows that the chalice with a slightly flared rim and gentle carination, type CH II/a, is found in all of the Iron Age phases at the site and is the most common chalice type (1987: 198). It should be noted that Hunt's study is mostly based on differentiation of rim types; thus he does not discuss the possible significance of the step profile of the foot which may have helped narrow the range of this type within the Iron Age strata at Qiri. At Tell Keisan this chalice form, Burdajewicz's type Cl III, is found in Iron I Levels 12, 10, and 9 (1995: 57). Stepped feet from chalices separate from their bowls are also found in Levels 8 and 7 at Keisan, Iron IIA–IIB phases at the site (Briend and Humbert 1980: pls. 51.13, 56.13). The stepped foot does appear earlier at coastal sites, however, such as at Tell Abu Hawam (Yoselevich 2004).

Kraters

High-Neck Krater with Everted Rim: One complete example and one rim fragment was preserved of this krater type (fig. 5.16.2–3). The characteristics of this form are the everted rim, high neck, ovoid low carinated body, ring base, and two prominent vertical handles attached from the rim of the vessel to its shoulder.

This exact type is not characterized in Killebrew's study, although the related "carinated krater jar with bulging neck," form CA 11, is detailed (1998: 93). The main differences are in the neck that bulges outward, while in the high-neck krater like the example from Area H the cylindrical neck is slightly incurved; and in the pedestal base, as compared to the high ring base. In Bikai's study of the pottery from Tyre, this form is the only one she defines as a true krater (although there are several examples of deep bowls) (1978: 32). The Tyrian krater was found in Stratum XV–V (Bikai 1978: 31), roughly the LB IIB–Iron IIB in southern Levantine chronological terms (table 5.1). At Sarepta this form is best matched by Anderson's type K-6 krater with everted rim and high neck (1988: 178). Type K-6 is found in Stratum G1–C1, the LB IIB–Iron IIC (Anderson 1988: 483; table 5.1).

Krater Bowl: One very small rim fragment of a krater bowl was found in Area H's Stratum 5 (fig. 5.16.6). The vessel is of a type with a simple flared rim. None of the body is preserved, but presumably this example is related to Killebrew's krater bowl type 9c, with a flared rim, high carination, and large semi-hemispherical bowl (1998: 91). According to Killebrew, this form stems from a preceding MB II–LB I type that reaches its greatest popularity in the LB IIB–Iron I (table 5.1), and is found throughout Canaan. This form is not prevalent enough to be categorized as a deep bowl or krater type at either Tyre or Sarepta, which helps define it as a southern Levantine or a Palestinian vessel type. It appears at neighboring Tell Keisan in virtually every phase of the Iron I, Levels 13/12b–9, defined by Burdajewicz as type BC III (1995: 39). It is relatively rare at Keisan, comprising only seven percent of the collection of deep bowls/kraters (Burdajewicz 1995: 39), and the form is not present at Tel Qiri.

Circular Rimmed Krater-Pithos: The folded, more or less circular rim, and the weight and size of the form mark this vessel (fig. 5.17.1). No direct parallels were found, but the rim type and general angle of the shoulder matches smaller examples from the circular rim krater type at Tel Qiri, Hunt's Crater I (1987: 194). Killebrew has defined a family of vessels: "very large kraters ... which are not easily movable," which she calls krater-pithoi (1998: 122). The family is based on several of these vessel types in the LB IIB–Iron I phases at Beth Shean, Hazor, and Tel Dan, and as such is defined by Killebrew as a northern vessel family (1998: 122–24; table 5.1). We would place the example from Akko in this krater-pithos family, with a relation to the circular rim krater of the Iron I.

Biconical Amphora-Kraters: One shoulder fragment and an almost complete example were discovered of this unusual vessel type. The shoulder fragment preserves one of the two vertical loop handles of the vessel, which are just below the wide, high necks of this vessel type (fig. 5.17.2). Fragments of the linear design in dark brown paint remain on the shoulder, while the handle is decorated with a stripe down its center and numerous perpendicular cross lines. The other, reconstructable vessel has a flared, folded rim, biconical body, and disk base (fig. 5.17.3). Based on parallels, it is likely that there was a handle or pair of handles on the shoulder of the vessel; however, none remained. The exterior of the krater is covered with a self-slip, and is decorated above the carination with red painted, parallel, horizontal stripes that form three zones. The uppermost zone is filled with angled cross line decoration, the middle zone has stylized trees separated by crisscross patterns, and the lowest zone has three horizontal stripes. A few stripes are painted in dark brown, descending vertically from this lowest zone toward the base of the vessel.

The best discussion of this family of vessels is in Amiran's typology (1969: 147). There are three forms within the family: the jug, krater, and amphora (Amiran links these last two types together as amphora-kraters), all grouped together based on the biconical shape of their body and common painted designs. Our shoulder fragment with the painted handle is best paralleled by biconical amphoras from Lachish Tomb 571, while the krater has affinities with a vessel from Megiddo Stratum VIIB (Amiran 1969: pl. 47.11–13). These forms span the LB I–II (table 5.1).

Hemispherical ("Bell-Shaped") Kraters: Three fragments of this krater type were found in Stratum 5 contexts. Two examples, 255/2 and 632/1, preserve their everted rim, which are quite rectangular in section (fig. 5.17.4–5). One body sherd preserves the gentle carination of this type (fig. 5.17.6). It may be the case that the high ring base 619/2 belongs to this type of vessel (fig. 5.16.4). Decoration includes a self-slip on the lip and outside of 632/1 (fig. 5.17.5); and a fish, a circle with a cross and dots, and a stripe on the carination all painted in dark brown (fig. 5.17.6).

Killebrew defines this krater form as an Aegean-style vessel type (Form AS 5), which is readily apparent when compared with the local krater forms so far discussed (1998: 176–78). Its ancestry lies in the Aegean, where similarly shaped kraters span the LH IIIB–IIIC, and it is found in LC IIC–IIIB contexts on Cyprus (Killebrew 1998: 176–78). The decoration on our Akko example has parallels later in either the LH or LC sequences, since the matt slip and monochrome painted designs are in the LH IIIC, not the IIIB, tradition. Artzy views the decoration as most reminiscent of Cypriot Rude Style Ware, and notes another found in Akko's Area K that is also decorated with a fish (Buchholz 1993: 41–55). In the Levant, LH IIIC pottery is found at sites on the Syrian coast, but is mostly concentrated in Philistia, the southern coastal plain, in Iron I phases (Killebrew 1998: 178; table 5.1). Neighboring sites with parallels include Tel Qiri, where monochrome and bichrome kraters were discovered out of their original context (Hunt 1987: 200–201); Tell Keisan Level 9c, a late phase of the Iron I, which has a bichrome example with a thickened rim (Briend and Humbert 1980: pl. 80.12); and Megiddo, where this krater type is found in Stratum VIIA–VIA, multiple phases of the Iron I (T. Dothan 1982: 70–80). The motif of the fish (or dolphin) is found on several different vessel types of Aegean-style Philistine pottery, as well as LH IIIC pottery from Cyprus (T. Dothan 1982: 203–204). Ultimately the fish motif is derived from Late Minoan III predecessors (T. Dothan 1982: 204).

Cooking Pots

Cooking Pot with Everted Rim: One fragment of a cooking pot with an everted rim was found in Stratum 5 (fig. 5.18.1). This corresponds to Killebrew's Form CA 18b, which she dates to the LB II–Iron I (table 5.1), noting its distribution primarily in southern Canaan (1998: 104–105). This may explain its relative rarity at Akko.

Cooking Pot with Vertical to Inverted Triangular Rims: Seven fragments of this cooking pot type were found in Area H (fig. 5.18.2–8). The overall size of the vessel varies, as does the positioning of the rim and the treatment of its triangular profile. Killebrew has noted this variety for her parallel vessel type CA 19a (1998: 107–108). She dates the form to the Iron I and details its distribution throughout Canaan (table 5.1). At Tel Qiri, this cooking pot type, CP Ia, is the most frequent in the Iron I levels of the site (Hunt 1987: 182). It corresponds to Type MII at Tell Keisan, which is found in Levels 12–9, multiple phases of the Iron I (Burdajewicz 1995: 32–33). Note the absence of this popular form of cooking pot at both Tyre and Sarepta.

Low-Necked Cooking Jar: One simple flared rim fragment from a low-necked cooking jar completes the variety of cooking pots (fig. 5.18.9). Although quite different stylistically from the cooking pots so far discussed, this vessel fragment clearly functioned as cookware as its fabric is very similar to that of the cooking pots with vertical or indented triangular rims. This is especially noticeable in the fabric's typical small white quartz inclusions, used as temper in all cooking pots to aid the vessels in withstanding the variations in temperature they were exposed to in daily use (Hunt 1987: 181).

Parallels for the low-necked cooking jar are found at Tel Qiri, where Hunt defines the form as his type CP IVb (1987: 182). Cooking jars are rare in the assemblage at Qiri, making up only seven percent of the repertoire of cooking pots; however, they do appear throughout the Iron I and II phases at the site (Hunt 1987: 182; table 5.1). The form is also found at Tell Keisan, where it is categorized as type M IV (Burdajewicz 1995: 33–34). At Tell Keisan cooking jars make up 12.39 percent of the of cooking pots, and are found in all phases of the Iron I, Levels 13–9 (Burdajewicz 1995: 30, 33–34). Similar low-necked cooking jars were found in Area PH at Tel Akko (Zagorski 2004), and in the Tell Abu Hawam anchorage, which went out of use before the end of the 13th century BCE. Given the stylistic difference with the typical Canaanite LB–early Iron Age cooking pot, and the sudden appearance of the cooking jug at sites like Akko, Qiri, and Tell Keisan in the early Iron Age, we wonder about influences and possible connections of this vessel type to Cyprus or Philistia. Killebrew's work has been fundamental in defining what she terms the "globular cooking jug," Form AS 10, as an Aegean-style cooking vessel found primarily in Philistia and sites in the southern coastal plain in the Iron I period (1998: 183–84). This intrusive form has its best parallels from sites on Cyprus and Cilicia, and is markedly different from preceding LB IIB and contemporary Canaanite forms in Philistia and the greater southern coastal region. Given the variation in form, especially with the high-necked cooking jars from Qiri (Hunt 1987: fig. 34.3–4), it is more likely that these cooking jars in the northern valleys and coastal plain were influenced by the Aegean-style cooking jugs rather than representing imported pottery from Cyprus or Philistia.

Pithoi

Pithos with Flared Thickened Rim: The flared thickened rim of a pithos was found in Stratum 5 (fig. 5.18.10). The long cylindrical neck of this vessel is also preserved; unfortunately, none of the rest of this vessel remained.

This pithos is one of the types defined as northern in the Iron I assemblage (table 5.1). The best parallels come from Tel Dan, where this type spans Stratum VI–IVB or the Iron I–IIA (Biran 1989: 74–82; 1994: 129, 142). A similar form with a more triangular profile is defined at Sarepta as type RR-1 (Anderson 1988: 186). This pithos type at Sarepta has a range from Stratum H–E, or the LB IIA–Iron IB (Anderson 1988: 487). Unfortunately, not enough detailed drawings of type RR-1 pithoi are provided to determine if the type may be defined as a Late Bronze ancestor of the northern pithos, as have Late Bronze pithoi from Hazor and Tel Dan (Biran 1989: 82).

Pithoi with Upright Externally Thickened Rims: The two fragments of this pithos type are both highly fragmentary. Our first example, 270/5, does not have the interior profile of its rim preserved; therefore, it is difficult to properly define (fig. 5.18.11). The thick upright rim, however, is typical of some forms of northern pithoi, so one can conjecture that the rim may have had a heel, or interior projection, balancing out the exterior thickening (Biran 1989: fig. 4.16.9). Our second example, 270/2, has a much reduced thickening of its upright rim and shows little sign of interior projection (fig. 5.18.12). Both examples have very wide mouths, and presumably had long cylindrical necks.

Like the flared rim pithos described above, the best parallels for pithoi with upright externally thickened rims come from Tel Dan (Biran 1989; 1994: 129–42). This form is also part of the group of Galilean pithoi, and is found in Tel Dan Stratum VI–IVB, phases of the Iron I–IIA (Biran 1994: 129–142). This pithos type is defined by Anderson as Pithos RR-2 at Sarepta (1988: 186–87). Type RR-2 spans from Stratum J/H to D1, the LB IIA–Iron IIA; however, the majority of the form is concentrated in Stratum G2–E, or the LB IIB–Iron IB (Anderson 1988: 487; table 5.1).

Pithos with Upright Profiled Rim: The small fragment that remains of this vessel, a rim sherd showing an upright stance and a profiled cross section, makes it difficult to identify (fig. 5.18.13). The piece is covered on its interior and exterior with a self-slip.

Given the thickness of the walls of the rim and the broad diameter of its mouth, it is clear that we are dealing with a large vessel. Parallels exist among pithoi uncovered in the Iron I levels from the excavations at Hazor (Ben-Ami 2001: 162–63, fig. 7.7–8; table 5.1). The examples from Hazor, however, have a thickened profiled rim and no slip is detailed. It is possible that this rim fragment belonged to a type of krater-pithos. These types were also found in the

Tell Abu Hawam anchorage excavation. Many are of Cypriot manufacture, although some were produced locally in the hinterland of Tell Abu Hawam, which is ca. 10 kms from Tel Akko.

Storage Jars and Jars
Handled Piriform-Shaped Storage Jars with Carinated Shoulders: Two almost complete storage jars of the type were discovered, smashed in a pit, Locus 17 (fig. 5.19.1–2). The vessels' rims are upright, with thickening on the interior. The neck of each jar is of medium height, projecting from a gently carinated shoulder. The bodies of the vessels are piriform. Two vertical loop handles are on each jar, with the top of the handle attached to the shoulder of the vessel and the loop of the handle projecting slightly above the upper point of attachment. The toe of each vessel is missing, but from comparative evidence it appears that it would have been knobbed.

In a very general sense these storage jars fit in Killebrew's Form CA 22, the source of the description for the category of this jar type (1998: 113–114). Killebrew presents the very broad evidence for this version of the Canaanite Jar, or commercial transport jar, with dates ranging in the 14–12th century BCE and a distribution throughout the eastern Mediterranean (table 5.1). Looking at the evidence from Sarepta the period can be narrowed. Based mainly on the rim type, our form matches Anderson's Type SJ-8, which is found in Stratum H–D2, or the LB IIA–Iron IIA (1988: 193–94, 488). Following Anderson's table 9A, the vast majority of examples of storage jar SJ-8 are found in Stratum G1–E, or the LB IIB–Iron IB. Very similar storage jars, based not only on the rim type, but on the height of the neck, angle of the shoulder carination, shape of body, and the placement and stance of the handles are found in Tyre Stratum XIII, Tell Keisan Level 9a–b, and Tel Qasile X (Bikai 1978: pl. XXXV.13; Briend and Humbert 1980: pl. 59.5–6, 60.2–3; Mazar 1985: 56, fig. 48.1). All of these contexts are in later phases of the Iron I, or the Iron IB, at Tyre, Keisan, and Qasile, which does not agree with the period associated with Stratum 5 in Area H.

Varying Rim Types from Storage Jars: The variety of storage jar rim types attributed to this phase in Area H is typical for the period (fig. 5.20.1–20); the same phenomenon was noted for the anchorage of Tell Abu Hawam situated on the same bay and only a few kilometers south of Akko (Artzy 2016). Only one rim sherd, 162/1 & 3, matches the type described above with interior thickening (fig. 5.20.8). Given the variation of rim types attributed to Killebrew's storage jar CA 21 (1998: 110–111), let alone the differences among her three other forms, CA 22–24, it is not possible to link a specific storage jar body type to a given shape of rim. It is most likely, however, that all four basic storage jar types were present in Stratum 5 at Akko, especially given the typical northern provenience of Killebrew's globular to oval-shaped storage jars, Forms CA 23 and 24 (1998: 115–16).

Storage Jar Handles and Decoration: Several fragments of vertical loop handles from storage jars also preserve the carination where the shoulder met the body of the vessel (fig. 5.20.21–24, 27). Almost by definition these come from Killebrew's storage jar type CA 22, which is categorized by its carinated shoulder (1998: 113–14). Two of these handle fragments are decorated with a cream-colored slip and red painted stripes (fig. 5.20.27–28), following in the Canaanite tradition of painted storage jars (Killebrew 1998: 112, 114). There is a storage jar rim from Area H, with a self-slip on its interior and exterior and a painted brown stripe on top of its lip (fig. 5.20.7), and the neck of a jar decorated with a self-slip and four parallel red painted stripes (fig. 5.21.4). Very similar painted storage jar and jar fragments are found at Tell Keisan in various Iron I phases (Burdajewicz 1995; table 5.1).

Jars: Three rim fragments are from various types of jars. A flared thickened rim on a high neck, 169/2 (fig. 5.21.1), is smaller in diameter than storage jars and may be from a necked jar. It is also possible that this fragment is from a jug; however, we are missing the diagnostic handle (Killebrew 1998, Ill. III.6.4).

The flared pendent rim of jar 69/1 is unusual (fig. 5.21.2). The remnant of the neck indicates that it was short and wide. A possible parallel is found in a handless vessel uncovered in the excavations at Tel Beth Shean in a Level VII, LB IIB destruction layer (Killebrew 1998, Ill. II.70.6; table 5.1). Killebrew calls the vessel form a krater-pithos (1998: 66). We prefer to call it a jar, but believe these are comparable vessels at both sites despite the preference in terminology that is relatively subjective.

Our final jar fragment, 255/6, has a slightly flared rim on a wide, incurving neck (fig. 5.21.3). A parallel is found at Tell Keisan in Level 13/12b, an early phase of the Iron IA (Burdajewicz 1995: pl. 14.3a; table 5.1).

Stirrup Jars: There are three fragments of stirrup jars in Stratum 5. The first is the decorated shoulder and lower part of the spout of the vessel (fig. 5.21.8). Parallel stripes border the upper register, which is filled with linked rhomboids or lozenges decorated with cross hatching. Further decoration is visible next to the spout, but is unidentifiable. A handle of a stirrup jar, 169/3 (fig. 5.21.9), would have been attached from the false spout to the shoulder of the vessel. It is ovoid in cross section and decorated with a broad stripe in red paint. The piece is not slipped. The clay of this vessel fragment is reminiscent of the fabric used in the earlier Middle Bronze Age Cypriot White Painted tradition, and it is likely a Cypriot import. Our final example of a stirrup jar is another shoulder fragment that preserves the opening for the spout and the base of one of the vessel's handles (fig. 5.21.10). The jar is covered with a cream-colored slip and decorated with both red and brown stripes. Next to the handle is a circle filled with a cross motif, the top of a triangle or rhombus is visible in the small part of the upper register preserved below bichrome parallel stripes.

Killebrew defines stirrup jars as Form AS 11 (1998: 185). This Aegean-style vessel type is rare in the earliest monochrome phases at Philistine sites in the southern coastal plain, but becomes more popular in bichrome phases (Killebrew 1998: 185; T. Dothan 1982: 115–25). Stirrup jars are part of the LH IIIC repertoire on Cyprus and further west in the Aegean. Well-preserved LH IIIC Middle stirrup jars have been found at both Tell Keisan in Level 13, the earliest phase of the Iron IA, and Beth Shean in early Level VI, or the Iron IA, along with two stirrup jar fragments (Warren and Hankey 1989: 163–65; table 5.1). Coincidently, both of the stirrup jars from Tell Keisan and Beth Shean are decorated in their upper registers with horizontal bands of linked hatched rhomboids, or lozenges (Warren and Hankey 1989: 163–65; Burdajewicz 1995: pl. 13.18; see another parallel from Byblos, Salles 1980: 33, pl. 12.6). The broad decorative stripes on the handles from the Beth Shean stirrup jar are reminiscent of the decoration on the Akko Area H stirrup jar handle fragment (169/3) (fig. 5.21.9). The vessel from Beth Shean has been determined to be an import from Cyprus or Rhodes, based on visual inspection, while NAA on the jar from Tell Keisan have matched its clay to a Cypriot source (Warren and Hankey 1989: 164; Humbert 1993: 864). At Tel Nami, a similar stirrup jar dating to the LB IIC, has been tested by means of NAA and found to be of Cypriot provenance (Artzy 2006a). Based on the similarity of the decorative use of monochrome linked hatched rhomboids, and the absence of this decoration type in monochrome phases in Philistia, we would identify our decorated piece from Akko as an Aegean-style stirrup jar fragment of a vessel imported from Cyprus. M. Dothan has already published a similar observation based on other monochrome stirrup jars and Aegean-style vessel fragments from other excavation areas at Akko. He says these further examples from Akko are not of the monochrome tradition found at Ashdod in Philistia, which he excavated and knew intimately, but rather are closer to the LH IIIC tradition on Cyprus and in the Aegean (M. Dothan 1989: 60).

Amphoriskoi

Piriform-Shaped Amphoriskoi with Carinated Shoulders: Two virtually identical small jars, or amphoriskoi, were found together in the same pit, Locus 17 (fig. 5.22.1–5.22.2). Each amphoriskos has a slightly thickened upright rim, necks of medium height, angled carinated shoulders, thin piriform bodies, and a rounded toe. One of the jars shows a hint of a button base (fig. 5.22.1). Both examples have two vertical loop handles attached from the shoulder carination at the top.

These amphoriskoi are clearly miniature versions of the Canaanite storage jar type with carinated shoulders, Killebrew's storage jar Form CA 22, just as the other two primary amphoriskoi forms defined for this period imitate other forms of larger storage jars (Killebrew 1998: 131–32). The amphoriskos type with carinated shoulders, however, is extremely rare. One of the few parallels we have been able to identify is an amphoriskos from Stratum XI, Iron I middle, at Tel Qasile (Mazar 1985: 60, fig. 30.9; table 5.1). Mazar defines this amphoriskos as Type AM 2a, a unique find at Qasile. In a later phase of the Iron I, Stratum X, a slightly larger jar was discovered which in outward appearance matches the typology of the carinated shoulder amphoriskoi (Mazar 1985: 58, fig. 47.11). The extreme thickness of the walls of the body, however, differentiates this larger vessel from the amphoriskoi, and Mazar suggests that this unusual vessel may have been used in some sort of industry. Further parallels of amphoriskoi with carinated shoulders are found at Tell Keisan in the last phase of the Iron I at the site, Level 9a–b, and much further south at Tel Masos in Area H, House 314, Stratum II phased to the early Iron IB (Briend and Humbert 1980: pl. 57.3; Fritz and Kempinski 1983: 84, pl. 141.8). These appear, however, in a much later time period than the one associated with Stratum 5.

Ovoid-Shaped Amphoriskos: Our third example of a small jar or amphoriskos comes from the same context as the two detailed above. The rim and neck is missing from the jar, the body of the vessel is ovoid, with a slightly flattened base (fig. 5.22.3). The stumps of the two vertical loop handles remain, the tops of which were attached at the shoulder of the vessel.

Killebrew defines this ovoid-shaped amphoriskos as Form CA 32 (1998: 132). The type comes into use at the end of the LB IIB and is found more frequently in Iron I contexts (table 5.1). Killebrew notes that the form is mainly found at sites in southern Canaan, but is also present at settlements in the Beth Shean and Jezreel valleys (1998: 132).

Jugs

Jugs with High Flared Thin Necks: Two small sherds are flared rims, one simple and one triangular, of high thin-necked jugs (fig. 5.22.4–5). The piece with the simple rim (fig. 5.22.5), has a remnant of the stub of the upper part of the handle, indicating that it would have started at the rim and presumably gone to the shoulder of the vessel. This same vessel was covered on both sides with a self-slip.

The best parallels for this type of high-necked jug come from Tel Qasile (Mazar 1985: 61–63). Our example from Akko with the handle remnant at its rim would fit in Mazar's Type JG 1, which is found in Stratum XI–X, the middle to late Iron I phases at the site. Mazar notes comparable jugs in LB II–Iron I contexts at sites throughout Canaan (1985: 61; table 5.1). Our second example lacks any indication for placement of the handle; thus it could be either Qasile Type JG 1 or JG 2, since a major differentiation between these two jug forms is the location of the upper part of the handle (JG 1 has handles from rim to shoulder while JG 2 has handles from the middle of the neck to the shoulder) (Mazar 1985: 61–63). Type JG 2 is found in Qasile Stratum X, the late Iron I, and Mazar notes parallels for this jug form in Iron I levels at Megiddo, Stratum VII and VI, and Beth Shean, Stratum VI.

Jug with High Thin Straight Neck: Our one example of this jug type, 255/3 (fig. 5.22.6), has an upright simple rim and the upper part of a high thin neck, which is more or less straight. The sherd indicates that the vessel was covered with a self-slip.

This form is best matched by examples of jugs in Mazar's Type JG 2 (1985: 63), although we cannot tell where the top of the handle attached on the piece from Akko. As detailed above, Type JG 2 is from Qasile Stratum X, with parallels at Megiddo VII–VI and Beth Shean VI (table 5.1). One major difference between the Akko piece and the parallels from Qasile is in decoration, as a majority of the Qasile tall-necked jugs are decorated with red slip, some are burnished, and some have black painted bands on top of the red slip (Mazar 1985: 63). It is possible that the cream slipped jug fragment from Akko marks an earlier decorative style, as the red slip tradition does not take hold until the final major phase of the Iron I at Qasile, Stratum X.

Flared Neck Jug: One rim and neck fragment was preserved from a globular or piriform jug (fig. 5.22.7). Its simple rim is gently flared, and the incurved short neck is preserved. A stump from the base of the top of the vertical handle is preserved just below the rim. The vessel fragment is covered inside and out with a self-slip.

Killebrew defines this jug type as her Form CA 16, globular to piriform jugs (1998: 100). It is differentiated from the forms described above by a much wider neck, among other features. This jug type has a broad distribution throughout Canaan mostly in LB II contexts (Killebrew 1998: 100; table 5.1).

Flat and Disklike Bases of Ovoid or Globular Jugs: Two base fragments were found in the same basket in a Stratum 5 context. One is a flat base, decorated on its exterior with red slip (fig. 5.22.8). This piece had smudge marks on its edges, which indicates its reuse as a lamp (utilizing an MB IIA fragment?).

The second jug base has a slight rise to its flat base creating a disklike base (fig. 5.22.9). Shallow grooves on the bottom of the base, radiating in arcs from is center, indicate that the base was sting cut.

Similar bases have been found at Sarepta, and divided into two types by Anderson (1988: 236–37). The example of the flat base fits his type B-5, which Anderson attributes to an ovoid or globular jug form and notes its presence in Stratum L–E, or the MB IIC–Iron IB (table 5.1). The disklike base, Anderson's type B-6, is attributed to a jug or a small jar form (1988: 236–37). Significantly, at Sarepta the majority of these disklike bases were string cut, like the Akko example, and were found in Stratum H–D, LB IIA–Iron IIA, with almost half coming from Stratum G, LB IIB phase at the site (Anderson 1988: 236–37).

Strainer-Spout Jugs: The spouts of two strainer-spout jugs were found in Area H, one in situ and one not. The in situ example, 619/4 (fig. 5.22.11), is quite short and is decorated with red painted stripes. The larger example was found out of context, but is decorated similarly to other Stratum 5 pieces described so far, with a self-slip and red painted stripes on the edge of the spout (fig. 5.22.10).

It is not clear whether the strainer-spout jug is a local, Canaanite form or is an Aegean-style form produced locally. Its earliest appearance in Syria-Palestine is in Tyre Stratum XV and Sarepta Stratum G1, which date to the LB IIB and late LB IIB respectively (Bikai 1978: 34, 41; Anderson 1988: 562). LH IIIC:Ib examples of the form are also found at several sites on Cyprus (T. Dothan 1982: 154–55). Since LH IIIC:Ib pottery on Cyprus spans the LC IIB–IIIB it is possible that the Cypriot examples are more or less contemporaneous with those from Tyre and Sarepta. The question then becomes who inspired whom, and we are not sure if that query is possible to answer at this point. T. Dothan views the origin of Philistine bichrome decorated strainer-spout jugs in the LH IIIC:Ib examples found on Cyprus, and in a few examples found further west in the Aegean and on the Greek mainland (1982: 154–55). Furumark and Gjerstad see the form's origins in Palestine and believe the type was adopted by LH IIIC potters (T. Dothan 1982: 154–55). Regardless, the discovery of an example in Stratum 5 fits in with the pottery assemblage of late LB IIB–Iron IA for the region (table 5.1; examples are found in Levels 12 and 10 at Tell Keisan, Burdajewicz 1995: 63). Stratum 5 seems an appropriate level for the attribution of the unstratified piece, as well. Both examples from Area H appear to be locally manufactured.

Juglets

Dipper Juglets: Two fragmentary remains from dipper juglets in Stratum 5. One piece preserves the upright rim and the top of the vertical loop handle of the juglet (fig. 5.23.3), while the other piece is the shoulder of the vessel and the stump of the lower part of the circular handle (fig. 5.23.4). Thus most of the diagnostic characteristics on which to base a typological comparison are missing.

These examples of dipper juglets agree, in a very general sense, with Killebrew's categorization of the type Form CA 15 (1998: 98–100). As the primary differentiation between Killebrew's dipper juglet subforms CA 15a, b, and c comes from variations in body shape and style of neck, we are at a loss to pinpoint the Akko examples. In general, however, Killebrew notes that the dipper juglets of the period are a continuation of the Canaanite Bronze Age tradition, stretching all the way back into the Middle Bronze Age, but with a date ranging between the LB IIB–Iron I and a wide distribution throughout Canaan (Killebrew 1998: 98–100; table 5.1). While in the LB IIC, there are a few Cypriot White Shaved dipper juglets at Tel Nami, others originated in one or more local centers of manufacture (Artzy 2006a).

Container Juglets: A flared rim and incurving neck of one juglet, and a small ring base that may belong to the same juglet type, represent this form in Area H (fig. 5.23.1–2). The rim fragment is decorated on the inside of the rim and neck with red slip, which is unusual and it may be the case that the red slip on the outside of the piece has worn off.

This juglet type appears to be rare in the LB IIB–Iron I pottery assemblage (table 5.1). We have found a parallel in a rim fragment from Deir el-Balah (Killebrew 1998, ill. II.36.8), although this piece has a handle which is a feature lacking from the Akko example, and at Tell Keisan in Level 12b (Burdajewicz 1995: pl. 17.30). These are LB IIB and Iron I contexts.

Pilgrim Flasks

Globular Pilgrim Flask: One example of a pilgrim flask was uncovered in Area H (fig. 5.23.5). Although a body sherd, there are several diagnostic features to the piece: it preserves the curvature of the body of the vessel, which is globular and not lentoid, and it is decorated with concentric circles painted in red.

This type of flask is defined by Killebrew as Form CA 30, a globular flask with two handles (1998: 130–31). We can only guess at the configuration of the handles and the neck and rim; however, the roundness, or globular shape of the body of the vessel differentiates this pilgrim flask type from LB II types which have lentoid bodies (Killebrew 1998: 124–31). This form of flask, CA 30, is primarily found in Iron I levels of sites in northern Canaan (Killebrew 1998: 131; table 5.1).

Lamps

Saucer Lamp: Only one sherd from a lamp was discovered in Stratum 5 in Area H (fig. 5.23.6). The remains of a base broken off of a jug was reused as a lamp, as is clear from smudge marks left by the wick; this example is discussed above under the section for jugs. Our one lamp fragment is a piece from the spout of the vessel, showing a fairly pinched spout but not much else (fig. 5.23.6). In profile the bowl of the lamp seems to be of medium depth, and it appears that it had a rounded base although this is a bit conjectural. The lamp is covered on both sides with a self-slip.

Saucer lamps, Killebrew's Form CA 37, are related to a Middle Bronze type whose spout narrows over time (1998: 136–38). It is difficult to distinguish LB IIA from LB IIB lamp forms, and the typical LB II saucer lamp with narrowly pinched spout continues to be used through the Iron I period (table 5.1). There are two basic forms differentiated by their bases, either flat or round. The saucer lamp with a round base is the most common type in the LB II–Iron I and is found throughout Canaan (Killebrew 1998: 136–38).

Decorated Sherds

Representative samples of decorated sherds are included to show their relative abundance in this phase in Area H. Our first example (fig. 5.23.7) has a cream-colored fabric, which is not local to the Akko region, and is decorated with a red stripe. The thickness of the wall of the vessel suggests that it is from a large form. It is possible that this is an import. The next four sherds (fig. 5.23.8–11) are all decorated with a cream-colored slip and red, horizontal stripes. They are thick and likely from large forms. The final sherd is thinner and is decorated with dark brown, vertical stripes (fig. 5.23.12).

The four sherds decorated with cream-colored slip and red horizontal stripes, and the sherd with brown vertical stripes, are pieces from vessels carrying on the decorative tradition of LB II Canaanite pottery (fig. 5.23.8–12). Looking through Killebrew's typology it is clear that many different Canaanite forms from the LB IIB–Iron I, bowls, kraters, goblets, jugs, storage jars, krater pithoi, pilgrim flasks, amphoriskoi, and imitation imports, have painted decoration.

Imported Pottery

The number of imported ceramics in good contexts in Stratum 5 is limited. The pottery plates showing typical Late Bronze Age imported wares from Cyprus, the Aegean, Anatolia, and Egypt are not meant to be misleading as many of the pieces were found mixed in later contexts, as detailed above, but are included in this discussion because there is very little of Late Bronze Akko published so far. We know from historical sources, such as Egyptian annals, Ugaritic texts, and the Amarna letters that the site was a major trading center; however, the multiple phases of Late Bronze Age Akko so far are best represented only in a narrow exposure in Area C in the middle of the site, while the rest of the excavation areas ringed the edges of the settlement and produced scanty Late Bronze Age remains (M. Dothan 1976).

Cypriot Wares: While it is usually very easy to identify sherds belonging to the Cypriot fine wares of the Late Bronze Age (fig. 5.24.1–28), there are sherds that belong to ceramic families that are not usually identified as Cypriot. We included some of these with their designated typological counterparts above, such as in the case of the pithoi. Another Cypriot ware family that has been newly identified as imported to sites in the southern Levant is that of the Plain White Wheel Made ware (PWWM), described with its local counterparts above. Similar PWWM have now been identified in Area PH at Akko, as well (Zagorski 2004). These simple wares arrived aboard ships to the port of Akko as they did to the anchorage of Tell Abu Hawam, where numerous examples of the Plain White Wheel Made (PWWM) wares have been found, especially in the anchorage (Artzy 2005: 356; 2006a: 54–55; 2016; 2019). It is quite likely that some of the wares identified as Mycenaean (Myc. IIIB2/IIIC) are also of Cypriot provenience (Artzy and Zagorski 2012). The visual attribution of several of these pieces from Area H to Cyprus by the authors is supported by Sherratt's visual identification of previously published monochrome Aegean-style pottery from Akko also to the island of Cyprus (1998: 304, n. 24). Because of the small size of the fragments, a sherd identified as Myc. IIIC was mistakenly attributed to an Aegean provenience by D'Agata et al. (2005). Stockhammer identified it as belonging to an earlier Myc. II ware (personal communication). White Slip Ware sherds are well within the milieu of the LB IIB–C types associated with the Late Bronze and the end of the Late Bronze Age, bearing only straight line decoration and little slip or grey slip (fig. 5.24.1–12). Base Ring Ware sherds appeared in only a few good contexts. These include 163/2 and 189/1 (fig. 5.24.14, 17), and both belong to Base Ring bowls. A piece of a Base Ring I closed vessel with a plastic decoration (fig. 5.24.26) as well as two jug handles (fig. 5.24.23, 18) were found in Area H. Additional bowl fragments were found in questionable contexts as was a single horn of a bull (fig. 5.24.28). These pieces agree well with the changes in the trade pattern of Base Ring Ware in the end of the Late Bronze Age (Artzy 2001: 107–15).

There are very few pieces of Cypriot Monochrome Ware (fig. 5.24.19, 21, 25) and they are all from the same context, Locus 930. Monochrome Ware appears both in the earlier segment of the Late Bronze or in the later part of it. It is tempting to assign these sherds to robbed graves, similar to those discussed in chapter 4. It should be mentioned, however, that a later type of Monochrome Ware existed and was imported, as can be clearly be discerned at Tell Abu Hawam (Golan 2004).

There is at least one example of PWWM of Cypriot provenance and a likely Cypriot cooking pot from Area H. The large shallow Plain White Wheel Made bowl, 269/1, has an incurved, thickened, rounded rim that extends from the wall of the bowl (fig. 5.25.3). The cooking pot is fragmentary; however, it is distinguished by its upright, triangular rim; its size, which is much larger than the local cooking pots; and its distinct cream-colored fabric (fig. 5.25.4). Parallels for both vessels have been found in the anchorage excavation at Tell Abu Hawam (Artzy 2006a: figs. 8.10, 9.1; 2016).

The presence of Cypriot White Slip II, Monochrome, and Base Ring II Wares together with Myc. IIIC pottery occurs on Cyprus in both the LC IIC and LC IIIA periods (Kling 1991: 182). Perhaps more significantly, Cypriot handmade pottery types occur together with wheel-made Myc. IIIC pottery vessels (origin undetermined) at Tyre in Stratum XIV (Bikai 1978: pls. XLI.10–18, XXXIX.14, 20). Several possibilities arise: the Cypriot White Slip II, Monochrome, and Base Ring Wares II could have been from earlier, strictly LB IIB contexts and were mixed in LB IIB–Iron IA phases; Cypriot handmade Bronze Age pottery types were traded, and utilized, at the same time as Cypriot Myc. IIIC pottery; or Cypriot handmade Bronze Age pottery was still in circulation in the earliest phases of the Iron IA in Palestine, although it ceased to be imported at the end of the LB IIB. A finer division of the Late Bronze II period and the early Iron I should be considered and will be discussed in the conclusion. We suggest here to subdivide the LB IIB into two distinct historic phases. Namely, our LB IIB stops around ca. 1230; and the final several decades, which we consider the LB IIC, extends through the period of the final fall of Ugarit, ca. 1185 BCE. These two subperiods, LB IIB and IIC are represented in the remains from the anchorage of Tell Abu Hawam and Tel Nami (Artzy 2006a; 2013; Martín Garcia and Artzy 2018).

Mycenaean and/or Aegean-style Cypriot and local wares: There are very few examples of clearly Mycenaean sherds in Area H. Two, 620/9 and 46/1 seem to be Myc. IIIA2/B (fig. 5.25.6–7). Another small body sherd, 69/3 (fig. 5.25.8), could well belong to the Myc. IIIB family of which we have examples originating in Nichoria and Messinia, to which the Mycenaean wares found at the Akko Persian Garden were attributed (Gunneweg and Michel 1999; Artzy 2005: 357–58). One piece, 169/3 (fig. 5.21.9), is attributed to Myc. IIIB2 local or other coastal production. Similar pieces were found at Tel Nami as well as in Ugarit. Bowl fragments 226/2 (fig. 5.25.5), 269/2 (fig. 5.25.1), 116/11 (fig. 5.4.9) and handle 304/1 (fig. 5.25.2) are likely Myc. IIIC or IIIB originating on Cyprus.

Anatolian Wares: There are two possible Anatolian Tan Ware bowl rim sherds found in Area H, 612/2 and 116/10 (figs. 5.1.10, 5.25.11); and two Anatolian Grey Ware body sherds, one with incised decoration likely from a krater (fig. 5.25.10) and one from a small carinated bowl (fig. 5.25.12). One further Anatolian Grey Ware fragment from an unidentified vessel was found in a mixed context (fig. 5.25.13).

The earliest appearance of Anatolian wares in our region seems to be at Tell Abu Hawam, where an almost complete dark Grey Ware krater was found in the anchorage excavation. Its origin was established by Neutron Activation Analysis to be in the vicinity of Troy and compares well to the Troy VIg–h shapes. It appears alongside Anatolian Tan ware in the anchorage (Artzy 2006a: 55; 2019). A krater from Miqne-Ekron shows similar properties, although in its case it seems to have more inclusions, is decorated with horizontal incised lines on its upper body, and is of a slightly later date, possibly Troy VIh or VIIa (Heuck Allen 1991). Similar examples from Lachish are dated to Troy VIIa (Yannai 2004). There are not many examples of Anatolian Grey Ware in the southern Levant: it appears at Tell Abu Hawam, Dan, Lachish, Miqne-Ekron, and a single example at Tel Zippor; and the ware is usually associated with true Mycenaean imports (Artzy 2019).

Egyptian Ware: One rim fragment from Area H is from an Egyptian imported vessel, 56/3 (fig. 5.25.9). It is detailed above in the *Stratum 5 pottery from later contexts or stratigraphically floating baskets* section (fig. 5.13.3).

Typological Conclusions

Most of the pottery types from this phase in Area H have a long temporal range, as is evident in the detailed discussion presented above. All of the forms, however, exist in either the LB IIB, LB IIC, or the very early Iron IA periods (table 5.1). This supports our earlier attribution of this phase to the transition from the last part of the LB IIB to the early Iron IA. Probably the shortest lived types are those from the Aegean-style repertoire, which in Area H and elsewhere at Akko are limited mainly to four forms: semihemispherical bowls with flared rims, hemispherical ("bell-shaped") bowls, hemispherical ("bell-shaped") kraters, and stirrup jars. Aegean-style (Myc. IIIB2 and IIIC; LH IIIC) pottery is manufactured locally at sites in Syria-Palestine (Cilicia, Ras Ibn-Hani, Philistia) in the very beginning phases of the Iron IA and on Cyprus in the LC II–IIIB periods (Artzy and Zagorski 2012). LH IIIC pottery appears as imports to Tyre (Stratum XIV), Tell Keisan (Level 13–12b, and mixed in Level 10–9), and Beth Shean (Stratum VI) in their Iron IA phases; and at Sarepta at the very end of the

LB IIB and beginning of the Iron I (Stratum G1–F). LH IIIC imports to Byblos are in a tomb context and thus contribute little to refining the chronological framework of their exchange (Salles 1980: 30–35). Chemical analysis and visual inspection of the Aegean-style ceramics in Area H attributes them mainly to local, coastal production; and the decorated stirrup jar to Cyprus. There are none of the Aegean-style ceramics that can be attributed to the southern coast, namely Philistia. The vast majority of the ceramic assemblage presented above, besides the few Aegean-style types, is simply a continuation of the local northern coastal Late Bronze Age pottery tradition.

In our stratigraphic discussion of Stratum 5 (see above chapter 2), we noted the possibility of several subphases within the stratum. This may be borne out, as well, in the ceramic evidence. Verifying this observation requires further refined stratigraphic excavation at the site. It should be noted that sites such as Tell Keisan, Megiddo, Qiri, and Beth Shean and especially the coastal site of Dor, all have multiple phases within their Iron I horizons. The ceramic evidence from Stratum 5 may span several phases from the end of the LB IIB and the very early Iron IA at Akko, a period we attribute to LB IIC.

However poor, the Stratum 5 occupation in Area H marks a shift in habitation pattern on the tell. It seems to have been the periphery of the occupied area, not a previously location of habitation as it was the location of the city's defenses in the MB IIA, burials in the MB IIB–IIC, and then followed by a gap in the LB I–IIB. This phenomenon is also attested in the same phase in excavation Areas AB, F, and PH that ring the site of Akko (Artzy 2006b). In his survey of the hinterland around Akko, synthesized together with other surveys in the greater region, G. Lehmann has noted that the greatest shift in settlement patterns throughout the Akko Plain and nearby Galilee foothills occurs in the transition from the end of the Late Bronze Age to the beginning of the Iron Age I (2001: 74–75, 78, 81). The emphasis of settlement and population in the Late Bronze Age was located in the coastal plain with Tel Akko as the largest urban site, dominant over the region. In the Iron I, nearly half of the sites in the coastal plain were no longer settled and there is a dramatic increase of contemporary village settlements in the nearby hill country (Lehmann 2001: 74–75, 78, 81). Tell Keisan, just a few kms east of Tel Akko in the plain, exhibits a thick layer of Iron I habitation (Briend and Humbert 1980), a phenomenon not equaled at Tel Akko. While at Tel Akko a layer of clear Iron I remains seems to have been found, especially in Area K excavated by the German expedition headed by D. Conrad, its deposition does not seem to equal that of Tell Keisan.

The shift in settlement on Tel Akko itself during this transition period is clear in Area H. Whether these newly founded habitation areas at Akko represent inhabitants moving from the center of the site itself to its periphery, or settlers from other neighboring sites moving to the central settlement of Tel Akko is not known. It is likely that at least some of the inhabitants hearkened from coastal contexts, possibly Tell Abu Hawam which was undergoing a change due, in part, to the silting of its anchorage. In general, however, it can be remarked that the majority of the assemblage of ceramic types show continuity with the Late Bronze Age local pottery tradition. There does appear to be continued contact with Cyprus, both in the form of a very limited number of imports and possible local emulation of ceramic traditions from the island (Artzy 2006b: 121). The appearance of ship graffiti on a portable altar discovered in Area H also has parallels on Cyprus where ship graffiti have been found in varied contexts in Kition's sacred precinct (Basch and Artzy 1985), as well as in the vicinity of Tel Nami, on the cliffs of the Carmel Ridge (Artzy 2003). A similar set of ceramic connections to Cyprus has been observed at Tel Dor in phases of the Iron IA (Gilboa 2005: 65–67). Thus at Akko and at Tel Dor the transition from the end of the Late Bronze Age to the beginning of the Iron Age IA is better explained by indigenous processes with limited contacts to Cyprus, and not by an invasion, destruction, and settlement of the enigmatic Sea Peoples.

TABLE 5.1 Comparison of Area H Stratum 5 ceramic types with presence in comparative LB–Iron Age phasing

	LB IIA	LB IIB	IR IA	IR IB	IR IIA	IR IIB
Rounded semi-hemispherical bowls with simple rims	■	■	■			
Shallow to semi-hemispherical bowls with folded rims		■				
Semi-hemispherical bowls with flared rim		■				
Semi-hemispherical bowls with cyma profile		■	■			
Carinated semi-hemispherical bowl		■				
Carinated shallow bowl						
Carinated deep bowl			■			
Hemispherical "bell-shaped" bowl			■			
Chalices						

TABLE 5.1 Comparison of Area H Stratum 5 ceramic types with presence (*cont.*)

	LB IIA	LB IIB	IR IA	IR IB	IR IIA	IR IIB
High-neck krater with everted rim		■	■	■		
Krater bowl		■	■	■		
Circular rimmed krater-pithos		■	■	■		
Bichonical amphora-krater	■	■	■			
Hemispherical "bell-shaped" kraters		■	■	■		
Cooking pot with everted rim	■	■				
Cooking pot with vertical to inverted triangular rim		■	■	■		
Low-necked cooking jar		■	■	■		
Pithoi with flared thickened rim		■	■	■		
Pithoi with upright externally thickened rim	■	■	■	■		
Pithoi with upright profiled rim		■	■	■		
Handled piriform-shaped storage jars with carinated shoulders	■	■	■			
Jar with flared pendent rim		■				
Jar with wide neck		■	■	■		
Stirrup jars		■	■			
Piriform-shaped amphoriskoi with carinated shoulder	■	■	■			
Ovoid-shaped amphoriskoi		■				
Jugs with high flared thin necks	■	■	■			
Jug with high thin straight neck	■	■	■			
Flared neck jug	■	■				
Strainer-spout jugs		■	■	■		
Dipper juglets	■	■	■	■		
Container juglets		■	■			
Globular pilgrim flask		■	■	■		
Lamps	■	■	■	■		

Square J/6, basket 632

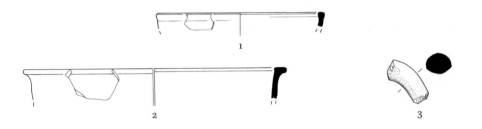

Square J/6, basket 619

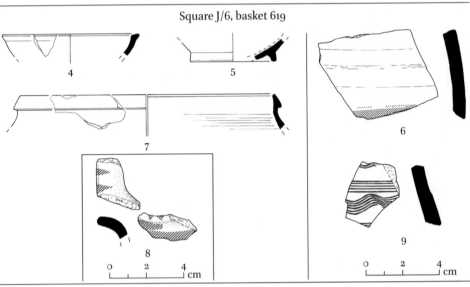

Square J/6, basket 612

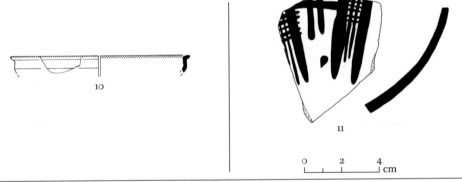

Square K/7

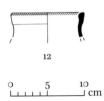

FIGURE 5.1

THE POTTERY OF STRATUM 5

Figure No.	Shape/object	Reg. No.	Locus/Pottery Basket	Description (color of exterior/interior/core; inclusions; decorations; etc.)
5.1.1	Bowl	AK X 1984 H J/6 b. 632/2	632/2	Red/red/red; many small white inclusions
5.1.2	Krater	AK X 1984 H J/6 b. 632/1	632/1	Red/grey/grey; many small white inclusions
5.1.3	Storage jar?	AK X 1984 H J/6 b. 632/3	632/3	Red/red/grey; medium number of small to medium sized white and grey inclusions
5.1.4	Bowl	AK X 1984 H J/6 b. 619/6	619/6	Pink/pink/light grey; few small white inclusions
5.1.5	Bowl or krater	AK X 1984 H J/6 b. 619/2	619/2	Red brown/inside surface gone/grey; few medium sized white inclusions
5.1.6	Body sherd from krater?	AK X 1984 H J/6 b. 619/5	619/5	Pink/pink/light grey; many small white inclusions; red painted stripe
5.1.7	Cooking pot	AK X 1984 H J/6 b. 619/1	619/1	Light brown/light brown/light brown; many small white and quartz inclusions
5.1.8	Jug	AK X 1984 H J/6 b. 619/4	619/4	Pink/pink/pink; few small white inclusions; red painted stripes
5.1.9	Body sherd from krater?	AK X 1984 H J/6 b. 619/3	619/3	Light grey/light grey/light grey; few small white and micaceous inclusions; burnished inside and outside, incised wavy lines; Anatolian Grey Ware
5.1.10	Bowl	AK X 1984 H J/6 b. 612/2	612/2	Pink/pink/pink; medium number of small to medium size white inclusions; red slipped band on top of rim; Anatolian Tan Ware?
5.1.11	Bowl	AK X 1984 H J/6 b. 612/1	612/1	Red/red/dark grey; few small white inclusions; brown paint on poor white slip; Cypriot White Slip Ware
5.1.12	Jar	AK VII 1980 H K/7 b. 299/2	299/2	Pink/pink/pink; many miniscule brown inclusions; dark brown stripe on rim

Square L/7, Locus 750, basket 304

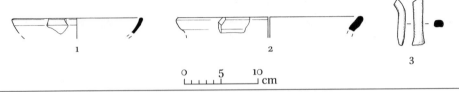

Square L/7, Locus 750, basket 308

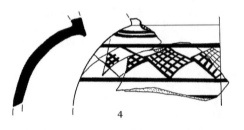

Square L/7, basket 289

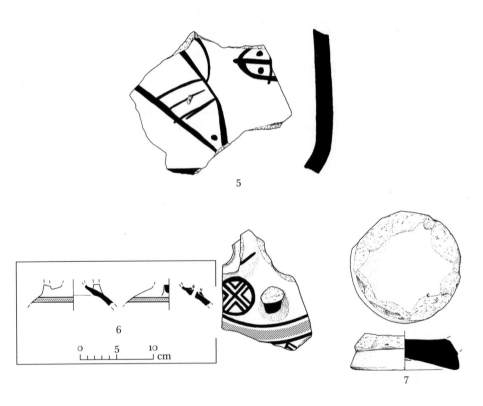

FIGURE 5.2

THE POTTERY OF STRATUM 5

Figure No.	Shape/ object	Reg. No.	Locus/ Pottery Basket	Description (color of exterior/interior/core; inclusions; decorations; etc.)
5.2.1	Bowl	AK VII 1980 H L/7 b. 304/3	Loc. 750	Pink/pink/pink; medium amount of small white inclusions
5.2.2	Bowl	AK VII 1980 H L/7 b. 304/2	Loc. 750	Buff pink/buff pink/pink; medium amount of small brown and grey inclusions
5.2.3	Handle	AK VII 1980 H L/7 b. 304/1	Loc. 750	Pink/pink/pink; few small brown inclusions; Cypriot
5.2.4	Stirrup jar	AK VII 1980 H L/7 b. 308/1	Loc. 750	No fabric description. Painted stripes and rhomboids with net pattern
5.2.5	Krater	AK VII 1980 H L/7 b. 289/1	289/1	Pink/pink/pink; few, small to medium white inclusions; dark brown fish/dolphin, circle with cross and dots; stripe
5.2.6	Stirrup jar	AK VII 1980 H L/7 b. 298/1	298/1	Red/pink/pink; few, medium white inclusions; red and brown paint on cream slip
5.2.7	Stopper	AK VII 1980 H L/7 b. 289/2	289/2	No fabric description

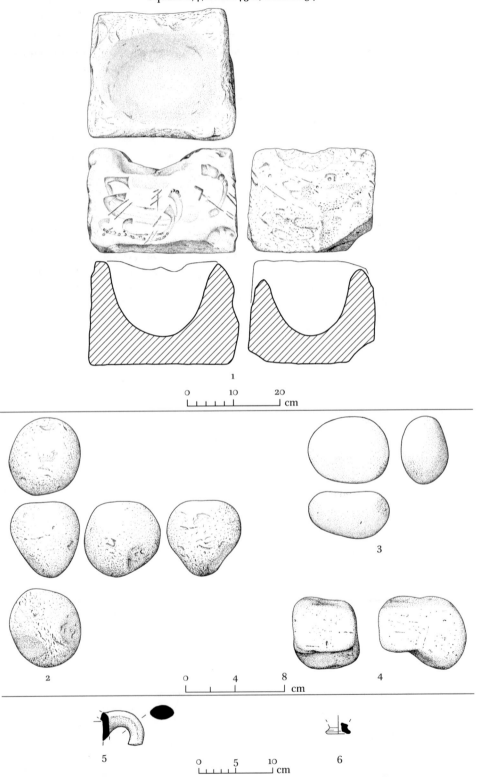

FIGURE 5.3 Fig. 5.3.1 left center (front of altar)
DRAWN BY RACHEL POLAK

Figure No.	Shape/ object	Reg. No.	Locus/ Pottery Basket	Description (color of exterior/interior/ core; inclusions; decorations; etc.)
5.3.1	Ship altar	AK VII 1980 H L/7 b. 254/3	Loc. 731b	limestone; mortar-like bowl, with graffiti of ships on one long side
5.3.2	Pebble	AK VII 1980 H L/7 b. 254/4	Loc. 731b	Quartz; boat and fish motifs
5.3.3	Pebble	AK VII 1980 H L/7 b. 254/5	Loc. 731b	Stone; fish motif
5.3.4	Pebble	AK VII 1980 H L/7 b. 254/6	Loc. 731b	stone
5.3.5	Jar or storage jar	AK VII 1980 H L/7 b. 254/2	Loc. 731b	Pink/pink/grey; medium number of small white and medium grey inclusions
5.3.6	Juglet	AK VII 1980 H L/7 b. 254/1	Loc. 731b	Pink/pink/pink; many small brown inclusions

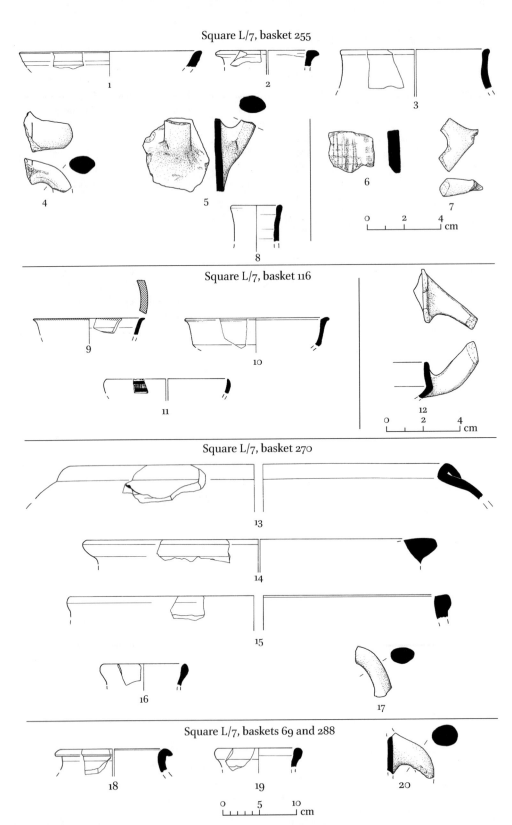

FIGURE 5.4

THE POTTERY OF STRATUM 5

Figure No.	Shape/object	Reg. No.	Locus/Pottery Basket	Description (color of exterior/interior/core; inclusions; decorations; etc.)
5.4.1	Bowl	AK VII 1980 H L/7 b. 255/4	255/4	Pink/pink/grey; small amount, small white inclusions
5.4.2	Krater	AK VII 1980 H L/7 b. 255/2	255/2	Pink/pink/grey; many small brown inclusions
5.4.3	Jar	AK VII 1980 H L/7 b. 255/6	255/6	Pink to grey/buff/light brown; low number, small white inclusions
5.4.4	Storage jar	AK VII 1980 H L/7 b. 255/7	255/7	Pink/pink/grey brown; medium number of small white and medium sized grey inclusions
5.4.5	Storage jar	AK VII 1980 H L/7 b. 255/8	255/8	Pink/buff/dark grey; medium number of small to medium white and light grey inclusions
5.4.6	Body sherd	AK VII 1980 H L/7 b. 255/1	255/1	Cream/cream/cream; few medium to large brown inclusions; dark brown painted stripes
5.4.7	Bowl	AK VII 1980 H L/7 b. 255/5	255/5	Dark brown/dark brown/dark grey; few, small white inclusions; no slip; Cypriot
5.4.8	Jug	AK VII 1980 H L/7 b. 255/3	255/3	Pink/pink/pink to grey; medium number of small white, few large white inclusions; Cypriot?
5.4.9	Bowl	AK VII 1980 H L/7 b. 116/11	Loc. 731b	Cream/cream/cream; low number, small brown inclusions; dark brown painted stripe
5.4.10	Bowl	AK VII 1980 H L/7 b. 116/10	Loc. 731b	Buffish pink/buff to light grey/buffish pink; few, small dark brown inclusions; Anatolian Tan Ware
5.4.11	Bowl	AK VII 1980 H L/7 b. 131/1	Loc. 731b	Red/red/red; few small white inclusions; Cypriot White Slip Ware; creamy, ivory white slip inside and outside, burnished inside; dark brown ladder design on outside
5.4.12	Bowl	AK VII 1980 H L/7 b. 116/5	Loc. 731b	Pink/pink/grey; few, small white inclusions; Cypriot Base Ring Ware
5.4.13	Krater-pithos	AK VII 1980 H L/7 b. 270/4	270/4	Pink/pink/grey; many, medium grey, quartz, and white inclusions
5.4.14	Pithos	AK VII 1980 H L/7 b. 270/5	270/5	Pink/pink/brown; many, small white and brown inclusions
5.4.15	Pithos	AK VII 1980 H L/7 b. 270/2	270/2	Pink/pink/red to grey; numerous small to medium white, small to medium grey, small to medium quartz inclusions; low fired; flared rim
5.4.16	Storage jar	AK VII 1980 H L/7 b. 270/3	270/3	Red/pink/grey; low number, small white inclusions
5.4.17	Storage jar	AK VII 1980 H L/7 b. 270/1	270/1	Pink/pink/grey; numerous, small grey, small to medium black inclusions; handle fragment
5.4.18	Jar	AK VIII 1982 H L/7 b. 69/1	69/1	Pink/pink to buff/grey; medium amount of medium white and grey inclusions
5.4.19	Storage jar	AK VIII 1982 H L/7 b. 69/2	69/2	Pink/pink/light grey; large amount of small dark brown inclusions
5.4.20	Storage jar	AK VII 1980 H L/7 b. 288/1	288/1	Red/red/dark grey; medium amount of small to medium white and dark grey inclusions

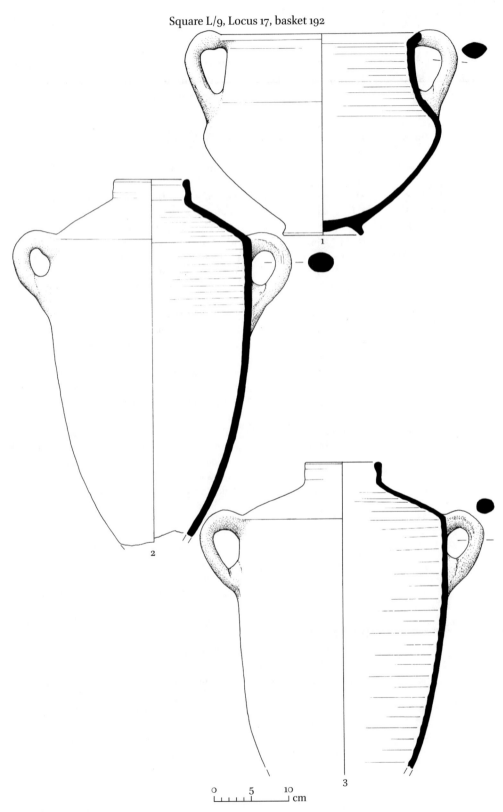

FIGURE 5.5

Figure No.	Shape/ object	Reg. No.	Locus/ Pottery Basket	Description (color of exterior/interior/ core; inclusions; decorations; etc.)
5.5.1	Krater	AK VI 1979 H L/9 b. 192/1	Loc. 17	Orange red/orange red/grey
5.5.2	Storage jar	AK VI 1979 H L/9 b. 186/1	Loc. 17	Orange pink/brown/grey; medium number of small white inclusions
5.5.3	Storage jar	AK VI 1979 H L/9 b. 186/2	Loc. 17	Orange pink/orange pink/ grey; medium number of small white inclusions

Square L/9, Locus 17, basket 192 (cont.)

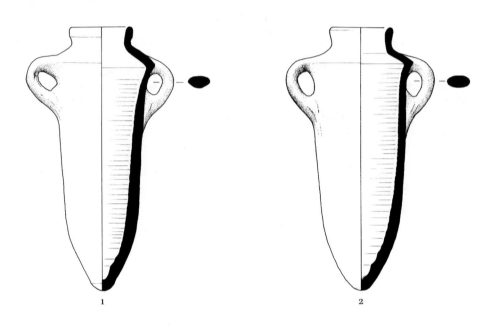

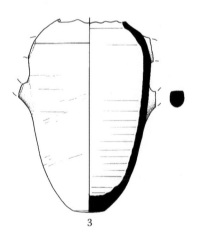

FIGURE 5.6

Figure No.	Shape/ object	Reg. No.	Locus/ Pottery Basket	Description (color of exterior/interior/ core; inclusions; decorations; etc.)
5.6.1	Amphoriskos	AK VI 1979 H L/9 b. 191/1	Loc. 17	Pink to buff/pink/no core; few small white inclusions
5.6.2	Amphoriskos	AK VI 1979 H L/9 b. 193/1	Loc. 17	Pink to buff/pink/grey; few small white inclusions
5.6.3	Amphoriskos	AK VI 1979 H L/9 b. 197/1	Loc. 17	Pink buff/pink buff/pink

Square L/9, Locus 17, baskets 169, 190, and 200

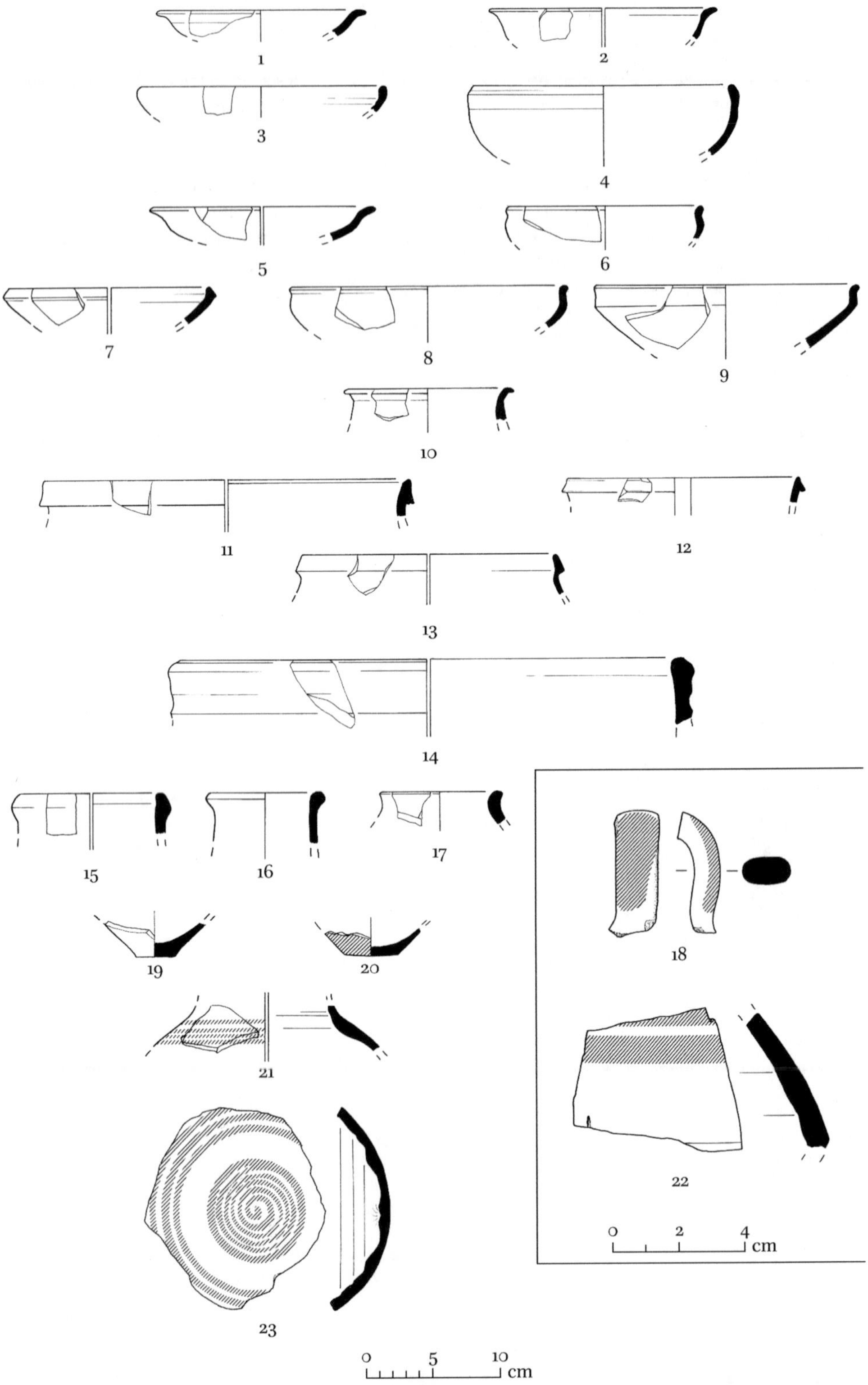

FIGURE 5.7

THE POTTERY OF STRATUM 5

Figure No.	Shape/object	Reg. No.	Locus/Pottery Basket	Description (color of exterior/interior/core; inclusions; decorations; etc.)
5.7.1	Bowl	AK VI 1979 H L/9 b. 200/1	200/1	Reddish pink/reddish pink/reddish pink to light grey
5.7.2	Bowl	AK VI 1979 H L/9 b. 200/2	200/2	Brown/brown/grey brown; small white inclusions
5.7.3	Bowl	AK VI 1979 H L/9 b. 200/3	200/3	Orangey pink/orangey pink/light grey; small white inclusions
5.7.4	Bowl	AK VI 1979 H L/9 b. 169/1	169/1	Pink/pink/red; many white inclusions
5.7.5	Bowl	AK VI 1979 H L/9 b. 190/1	190/1	Pink/pink/pink to grey; medium amount of small to medium white inclusions
5.7.6	Bowl	AK VI 1979 H L/9 b. 169/4	169/4	Pink/pink/pink; many small brown inclusions
5.7.7	Bowl	AK VI 1979 H L/9 b. 190/2	190/2	Pink/pink/pink; medium number of small white inclusions
5.7.8	Bowl	AK VI 1979 H L/9 b. 190/3	190/3	Pink/pink/pink to grey; many small white inclusions
5.7.9	Bowl	AK VI 1979 H L/9 b. 169/5	169/5	Pink/pink/pink to light grey; many small white inclusions
5.7.10	Bowl	AK VI 1979 H L/9 b. 200/4	200/4	Reddish pink/reddish pink/reddish pink
5.7.11	Cooking pot	AK VI 1979 H L/9 b. 200/7	200/7	Orange red/orange red/dark grey; small white inclusions
5.7.12	Cooking pot	AK VI 1979 H L/9 b. 200/8	200/8	Red/red/red; small white inclusions
5.7.13	Cooking pot	AK VI 1979 H L/9 b. 200/9	200/9	Dark brown/orange red/dark grey; many small white inclusions
5.7.14	Pithos	AK VI 1979 H L/9 b. 200/6	200/6	Pink/pink/grey; few small white inclusions
5.7.15	Storage jar	AK VI 1979 H L/9 b. 190/6	190/6	Pink/pink/grey; few small white inclusions
5.7.16	Jar	AK VI 1979 H L/9 b. 169/2	169/2	Pink/pink/pink to light grey; medium amount of small to medium sized white inclusions
5.7.17	Jar	AK VI 1979 H L/9 b. 200/5	200/5	Pink/pink/pink; few small white inclusions
5.7.18	Stirrup jar	AK VI 1979 H L/9 b. 169/3	169/3	Pink/pink/pink; few small brown inclusions; red painted stripe on outside
5.7.19	Jug	AK VI 1979 H L/9 b. 200/10	200/10	Pink/pink/pink to dark grey
5.7.20	Jug	AK VI 1979 H L/9 b. 200/11	200/11	Orangey pink/not preserved/light grey; red slip on outside
5.7.21	Jar	AK VI 1979 H L/9 b. 190/4	190/4	Pink/grey to light brown/grey; few medium white inclusions
5.7.22	Body sherd	AK VI 1979 H L/9 b. 190/5	190/5	Pink/grey/grey; few small white inclusions; red painted stripes
5.7.23	Pilgrim flask	AK VI 1979 H L/9 b. 200/12	200/12	Orangey pink/dark grey/dark grey; red painted stripes

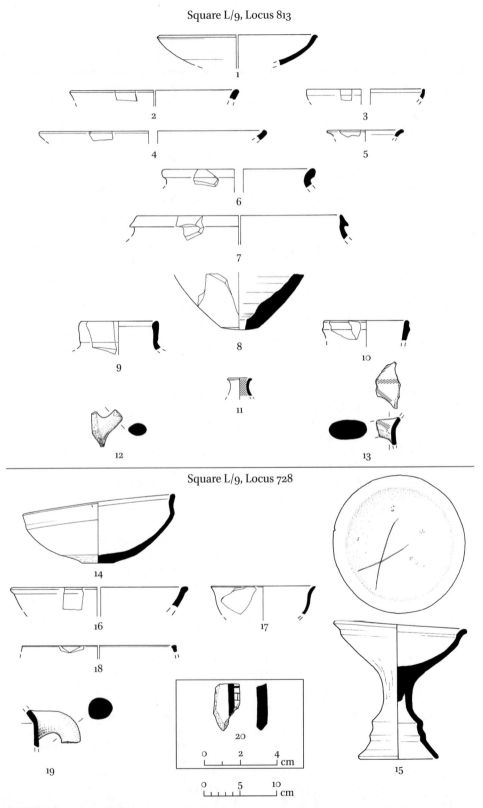

FIGURE 5.8

THE POTTERY OF STRATUM 5

Figure No.	Shape/object	Reg. No.	Locus/Pottery Basket	Description (color of exterior/interior/core; inclusions; decorations; etc.)
5.8.1	Bowl	AK VIII 1982 H L/9 b. 140/1	Loc. 813	Light pink/pink/light pink to light grey; medium number of small to medium white inclusions
5.8.2	Bowl	AK VIII 1982 H L/9 b. 145/1	Loc. 813	Pink/pink/pink; few small white inclusions
5.8.3	Bowl	AK VIII 1982 H L/9 b. 145/2	Loc. 813	Buff/pink/buff; few medium white inclusions
5.8.4	bowl	AK VIII 1982 H L/9 b. 162/2	Loc. 813	Pink/pink/pink; few small white inclusions
5.8.5	Bowl	AK VIII 1982 H L/9 b. 129/1	129/1	Pink/pink/pink; few small white inclusions
5.8.6	Krater	AK VIII 1982 H L/9 b. 129/2	129/2	Pink/pink/grey; few medium white inclusions
5.8.7	Cooking pot	AK VIII 1982 H L/9 b. 145/4	Loc. 813	Light brown/dark brown/dark grey; numerous small white inclusions; lightly fired
5.8.8	Storage jar or pithos	AK VIII 1982 H L/9 b. 129/5	129/5	Red/red/light grey; few medium sized white inclusions
5.8.9	Storage jar	AK VIII 1982 H L/9 b. 162/1 + 3	Loc. 813	Pink/pink/pink; few medium white inclusions
5.8.10	Storage jar	AK VIII 1982 H L/9 b. 129/3	129/3	Pink/pink/pink; few small white inclusions
5.8.11	Juglet	AK VIII 1982 H L/9 b. 145/3	Loc. 813	Pink/pink/pink; small white inclusions; red slip on inside of neck
5.8.12	Jug or jar	AK VIII 1982 H L/9 b. 97/1	Loc. 813	Pink/pink/grey; many small to medium white inclusions
5.8.13	Jug or jar	AK VIII 1982 H L/9 b. 129/4	129/4	Red/red/black; few small white inclusions; painted red stripes
5.8.14	Bowl	AK VII 1980 H L/9 b. 104/1	Loc. 728	Pink/pink/pink to grey; few small white inclusions
5.8.15	Chalice	AK VII 1980 H L/9 b. 29/23	Loc. 728	Orange pink/orange pink/grey; few small white inclusions; X incised inside bowl
5.8.16	Bowl	AK VII 1980 H L/9 b. 72/5	72/5	Pinkish red/pinkish red/pink; medium amount of small white inclusions
5.8.17	Bowl	AK VII 1980 H L/9 b. 72/2	72/2	Pink/pink/pink; few small white inclusions
5.8.18	Bowl	AK VII 1980 H L/9 b. 72/8	72/8	Salmon pink/salmon pink/pink; few small grey inclusions
5.8.19	Storage jar	AK VII 1980 H L/9 b. 72/6	72/6	Tan/pink/tan to pink; few small white and grey inclusions
5.8.20	Bowl	AK VII 1980 H L/9 b. 72/7	72/7	Red/red/red; medium number of small white inclusions; brown stripes on grey/white slip on inside and outside; Cypriot White Slip Ware

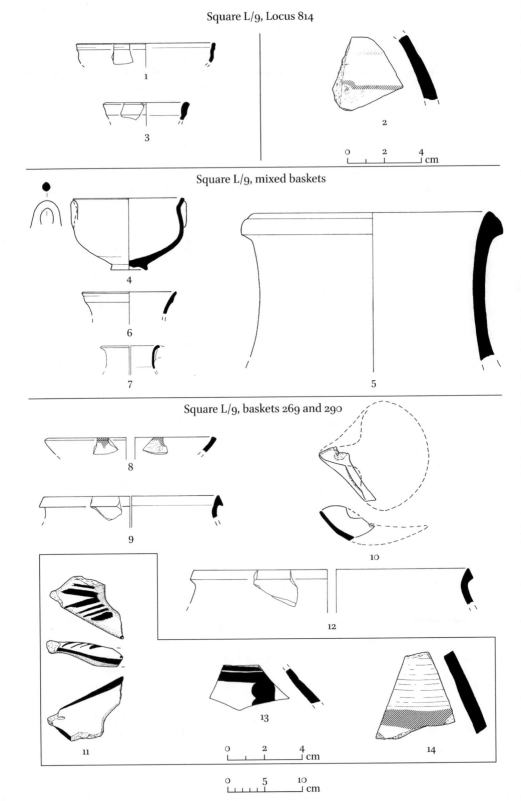

FIGURE 5.9

THE POTTERY OF STRATUM 5

Figure No.	Shape/object	Reg. No.	Locus/Pottery Basket	Description (color of exterior/interior/core; inclusions; decorations; etc.)
5.9.1	Bowl	AK VIII 1982 H L/9 b. 143/1	Loc. 814	Pink/pink/pink to grey; few small white inclusions
5.9.2	Body sherd of closed vessel	AK VIII 1982 H L/9 b. 160/2	Loc. 814	Pink/pink/pink; medium number of small white inclusions; red painted stripe
5.9.3	Storage jar	AK VIII 1982 H L/9 b. 160/1	Loc. 814	Pink/pink/pink; few medium sized white inclusions
5.9.4	Bowl	AK VIII 1982 H L/9 b. 333/1	333/1	Pink to pinkish buff/pink/pink to light brown; few small white inclusions
5.9.5	Pithos	AK VIII 1982 H L/9 b. 238/1	238/1	Orangey pink/red/red; few small white inclusions
5.9.6	Jar or storage jar	AK VIII 1982 H L/9 b. 254/2	254/2	Pink/pink/pink; few small white inclusions
5.9.7	Jug	AK VIII 1982 H L/9 b. 254/1	254/1	Pink/pink/pink; many small brown inclusions
5.9.8	Bowl	AK VIII 1982 H L/9 b. 290/2	290/2	Pink/pink/pink; few small white and grey inclusions; red painted band on inside and outside of rim; burnished inside of vessel (over stripe as well)
5.9.9	Cooking pot	AK VIII 1982 H L/9 b. 290/5	290/5	Red/red/grey; medium number of small white inclusions
5.9.10	Lamp	AK VIII 1982 H L/9 b. 269/1b	Loc. 823	Pink/pink/dark grey; many small white inclusions
5.9.11	Bowl	AK VIII 1982 H L/9 b. 290/1	290/1	Red/red/red; few small white inclusions; cream slip on inside and outside; brown painted decoration; Cypriot White Slip II
5.9.12	Cooking pot	AK VIII 1982 H L/9 b. 290/3	290/3	Cream/cream/cream; large number of small dark brown and white inclusions; Cypriot import
5.9.13	Body sherd	AK VIII 1982 H L/9 b. 269/2	Loc. 823	Buff/buff/buff; very few small white inclusions; brown stripes on burnished background; well levigated, high fired; Mycenaean IIIB, manufactured in Cyprus
5.9.14	Body sherd	AK VIII 1982 H L/9 b. 290/4	290/4	Cream/cream/cream; large number of small dark brown and white inclusions; red painted stripe; Cypriot import

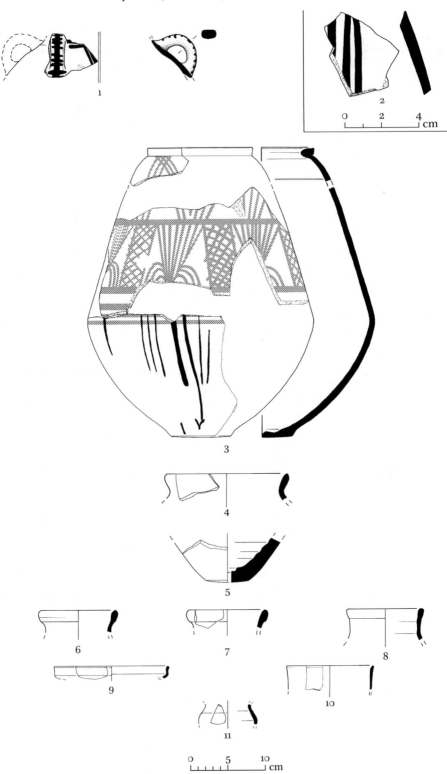

FIGURE 5.10

THE POTTERY OF STRATUM 5

Figure No.	Shape/ object	Reg. No.	Locus/ Pottery Basket	Description (color of exterior/interior/core; inclusions; decorations; etc.)
5.10.1	Amphora-krater	AK VIII 1982 H L/9 b. 212/1	212/1	Pinkish buff/pinkish buff/pinkish buff; few small white inclusions; brown painted stripes
5.10.2	Body sherd, amphora-krater?	AK VIII 1982 H L/9 b. 212/5	212/5	Buff pink/buff pink/buff pink; medium number of small white inclusions; brown painted stripes
5.10.3	Amphora-krater	AK VIII 1982 H L/9 b. 229/1	229/1	Orange pink/orange pink/light grey; many small white inclusions; red painted design, few dark brown vertical stripes
5.10.4	Cooking pot	AK VIII 1982 H L/9 b. 212/2	212/2	Brown/brown/black; many small white inclusions
5.10.5	Storage jar	AK VIII 1982 H L/9 b. 226/5	226/5	Pink/pink/pink; medium number of small to medium white inclusions
5.10.6	Storage jar	AK VIII 1982 H L/9 b. 163/3	163/3	Red/red/grey; few medium white inclusions
5.10.7	Storage jar	AK VIII 1982 H L/9 b. 163/4	163/4	Pink/pink/grey; few small white inclusions
5.10.8	Storage jar	AK VIII 1982 H L/9 b. 163/1	163/1	Pink/pink/pink; many small to medium white inclusions
5.10.9	Bowl	AK VIII 1982 H L/9 b. 163/2	163/2	Pink/pink/light grey; few small white inclusions; brown to red brown slip on outside and inside; Cypriot Base Ring II ware
5.10.10	Bowl	AK VIII 1982 H L/9 b. 226/2	226/2	Cream/cream/cream; medium amount of small brown inclusions; Cypriot Plain White Wheel Made Ware
5.10.11	Bowl	AK VIII 1982 H L/9 b. 212/3	212/3	Dark grey/dark grey/dark grey; few small white inclusions; Anatolian Grey Ware

Square L/9, basket 269

Square L/9, basket 189

Square M/7

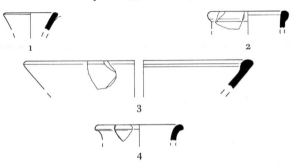
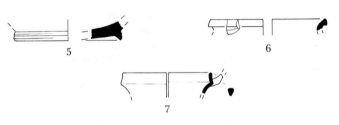

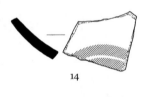
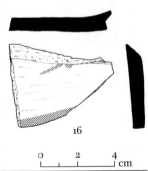
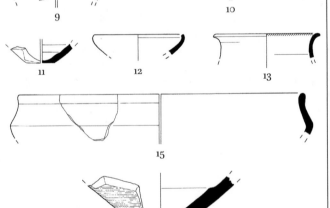
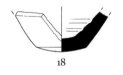

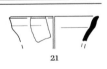
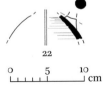

FIGURE 5.11

THE POTTERY OF STRATUM 5

Figure No.	Shape/ object	Reg. No.	Locus/ Pottery Basket	Description (color of exterior/interior/core; inclusions; decorations; etc.)
5.11.1	Jug	AK VII 1980 H L/9 b. 269/3	269/3	Pink/pink/pink; few small white inclusions
5.11.2	Jar	AK VII 1980 H L/9 b. 269/4	269/4	Pink/light pink/pink; medium amount of small brown inclusions
5.11.3	Bowl	AK VII 1980 H L/9 b. 269/1	269/1	Cream/cream/cream; few medium sized white inclusions; Cypriot, Plain White Wheel Made Ware
5.11.4	Jar	AK VII 1980 H L/9 b. 269/2	269/2	Cream/cream/cream; few small brown inclusions; Cypriot Plain White Wheel Made Ware
5.11.5	Large bowl or krater	AK VII 1980 H L/9 b. 189/4	189/4	Pink/reddish brown/grey; few small to medium sized white inclusions
5.11.6	Cooking pot	AK VII 1980 H L/9 b. 189/5	189/5	Grey/grey/grey; few small white inclusions
5.11.7	Bowl	AK VII 1980 H L/9 b. 189/1	189/1	Red brown/red brown/grey; many small white inclusions, few small voids; dark brown slip and burnished on exterior and interior; Cypriot Base Ring II Ware
5.11.8	Juglet	AK VII 1980 H L/9 b. 189/7	189/7	Pinkish tan/pinkish tan/light grey; few small to medium sized white inclusions
5.11.9	Bowl	AK VIII 1982 H M/7 b. 258/2	258/2	Light pink/light pink/light pink; many small brown inclusions
5.11.10	Bowl	AK VIII 1982 H M/7 b. 258/3	258/3	Pink/pink/light grey; few medium white and light grey inclusions
5.11.11	Bowl	AK VIII 1982 H M/7 b. 322/3	322/3	Pink/light grey/light grey; medium number of small white inclusions
5.11.12	Bowl	AK VIII 1982 H M/7 b. 287/2	287/2	Red/red/red; medium number of small to medium sized white and light grey inclusions; cream-colored self slip on interior and exterior
5.11.13	Bowl	AK VIII 1982 H M/7 b. 322/4	322/4	Pink/pink/pink; many small white inclusions; red painted stripe on inside of lip
5.11.14	Bowl	AK VIII 1982 H M/7 b. 258/1	258/1	Pink/pink/light grey; few small white inclusions; cream-colored self slip on interior and exterior; red painted stripes on interior
5.11.15	Bowl	AK VIII 1982 H M/7 b. 305/4	305/4	Pink/pink/pink; few medium sized white inclusions
5.11.16	Krater?	AK VIII 1982 H M/7 b. 322/1	322/1	Pink/pink/pink; medium number of small white and grey inclusions; cream-colored self slip on exterior; red painted stripes
5.11.17	Pithos	AK VIII 1982 H M/7 b. 287/3	287/3	Pink/light grey/dark grey; medium number of small and medium sized white inclusions
5.11.18	Storage jar	AK VIII 1982 H M/7 b. 305/5	305/5	Pink/pink/grey; few small white inclusions
5.11.19	Storage jar	AK VIII 1982 H M/7 b. 287/1	287/1	Pink/pink/pink; few medium sized white inclusions

Figure No.	Shape/ object	Reg. No.	Locus/ Pottery Basket	Description (color of exterior/interior/core; inclusions; decorations; etc.)
5.11.20	Storage jar	AK VIII 1982 H M/7 b. 305/2	305/2	Buff/buff/buff; few small white inclusions
5.11.21	Storage jar	AK VIII 1982 H M/7 b. 322/2	322/2	Pink/pink/pink; medium number of small grey inclusions
5.11.22	Juglet	AK VIII 1982 H M/7 b. 305/1	305/1	Pink/buff/light grey; very few medium sized white inclusions

Square M/4, Locus 744

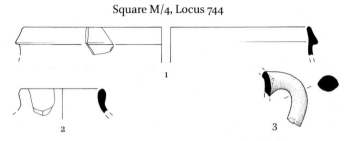

Stratum 5: Pottery from later contexts or stratigraphically floating baskets

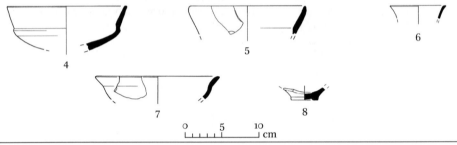

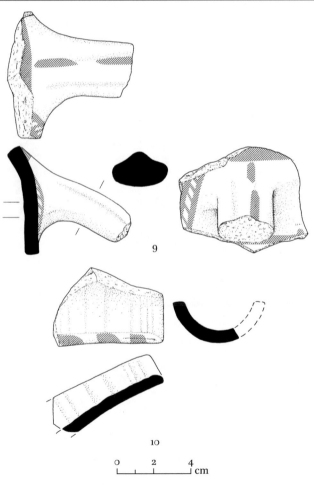

FIGURE 5.12

THE POTTERY OF STRATUM 5

Figure No.	Shape/object	Reg. No.	Locus/Pottery Basket	Description (color of exterior/interior/core; inclusions; decorations; etc.)
5.12.1	Cooking pot	AK VII 1980 H M/4 b. 205/5	Loc. 744	Dark brown/red brown/dark grey; medium number of small white and quartz inclusions
5.12.2	Storage jar	AK VII 1980 H M/4 b. 205/6	Loc. 744	Light pink/light pink/pink; medium number of small brown inclusions
5.12.3	Storage jar	AK VII 1980 H M/4 b. 205/4	Loc. 744	Red/red/dark grey; few small white inclusions
5.12.4	Bowl	AK IX 1983 H L/9 b. 1304/1	1304/1	Buff/buff/light grey; medium amount of small white inclusions
5.12.5	Storage jar	AK IX 1983 H L/9 b. 1304/2	1304/2	Pink/pink/pink to grey; few small white inclusions
5.12.6	Jug	AK IX 1983 H L/9 b. 1304/6	1304/6	Buff/buff/buff; few small brown inclusions
5.12.7	Bowl	AK X 1984 H M/5 b. 509/1	509/1	Brown/brown/brown; many small white inclusions
5.12.8	Bowl	AK X 1984 H M/5 b. 549/2	549/2	Pink/pink/pink; medium number of small brown inclusions
5.12.9	Storage jar	AK VIII 1982 H L/9 b. 178/2	Loc. 818	Pink/pink/red to grey; many small white inclusions; red painted stripes
5.12.10	Jug	AK X 1984 H N/5 b. 528/1	528/1	Pink/pink/pink; medium number of small white inclusions; red stripes on cream slip inside spout

Stratum 5: Pottery from later contexts or stratigraphically floating baskets (cont.)

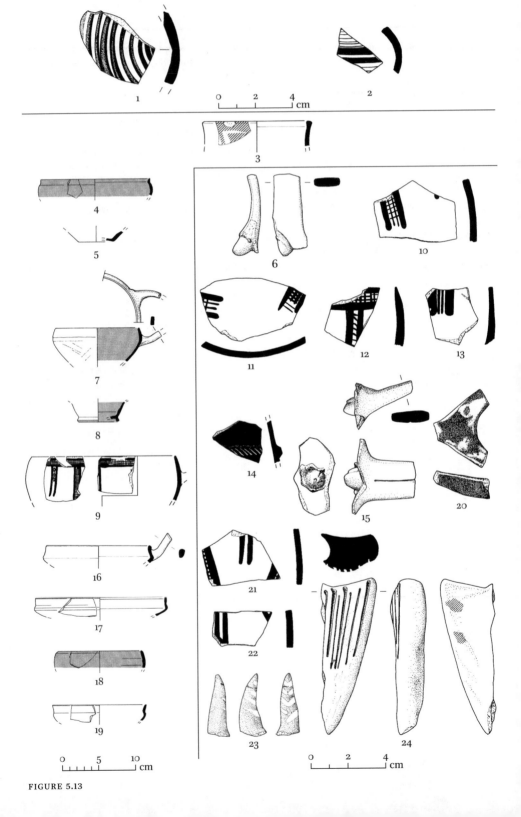

FIGURE 5.13

THE POTTERY OF STRATUM 5

Figure No.	Shape/object	Reg. No.	Locus/Pottery Basket	Description (color of exterior/interior/core; inclusions; decorations; etc.)
5.13.1	Pilgrim flask	AK X 1984 H M/9 b. 620/9	620/9	Buff/buff/buff; burnished exterior with dark brown painted stripes; Mycenaean IIIB Ware
5.13.2	Stirrup jar?	AK VIII 1982 H K/7 b. 46/1	46/1	Buff/buff/buff; few, miniscule brown inclusions; dark brown stripes on highly burnished buff surface; Mycenaean IIIB Ware
5.13.3	Jar	AK VII 1980 H L/8 b. 56/3	56/3	Red/red/dark brown; many small white inclusions; Egyptian, Nile silt, Marl D Ware
5.13.4	Bowl	AK IX 1983 H L/9 b. 1304/3	1304/3	Red/red/red; few small white inclusions; brown slip inside and outside; Cypriot Base Ring Ware
5.13.5	Bowl	AK IX 1983 H L/9 b. 1304/4	1304/4	Red/red/red; few small white inclusions; brown slip inside and outside; Cypriot Monochrome Ware
5.13.6	Bowl	AK IX 1983 H L/9 b. 1304/5	1304/5	Red/red/red; few small white inclusions; Cypriot Monochrome Ware
5.13.7	Bowl	AK IX 1983 H L/9 b. 1304/7	1304/7	Red/red/red; few small white inclusions; brown slip inside and outside; Cypriot Base Ring Ware
5.13.8	Bowl	AK IX 1983 H L/9 b. 1304/8	1304/8	Pink/grey/grey; few small white inclusions; brown slip inside and outside; Cypriot Base Ring Ware
5.13.9	Bowl	AK IX 1983 H L/9 b. 1304/9	1304/9	Grey/grey/grey; few small white inclusions; greyish-white slip on inside and outside; dark brown painted decoration; Cypriot White Slip Ware
5.13.10	Bowl	AK IX 1983 H L/9 b. 1304/10	1304/10	Light grey/light grey/light grey; few small white inclusions; greyish-white slip inside and outside; brown painted decoration; Cypriot White Slip Ware
5.13.11	Bowl	AK IX 1983 H L/9 b. 1304/11	1304/11	Light grey/light grey/light grey; greyish-white slip inside and outside; brown painted decoration; Cypriot White Slip Ware
5.13.12	Bowl	AK IX 1983 H L/9 b. 1304/12	1304/12	Red/red/red; few small white inclusions; cream slip on inside and outside; dark brown painted decoration; Cypriot White Slip Ware
5.13.13	Bowl	AK IX 1983 H O/5 b. 1238/1	1238/1	Red/red/grey; few small white inclusions; brown stripes, white slip and burnished on inside and outside; Cypriot White Slip Ware
5.13.14	Closed vessel	AK VII 1980 H L/8 b. 50/2	50/2	Light brown/light brown/light grey; very few small white inclusions; dark brown slip on exterior; raised rope design; Cypriot Base Ring I
5.13.15	Jug	AK VII 1980 H L/8 b. 50/4	50/4	Buff/buff/light grey; very few small white inclusions; brown slip and burnished exterior; Cypriot Base Ring I
5.13.16	Bowl	AK VII 1980 H L/8 b. 56/1	56/1	Red brown/red brown/grey; many small white inclusions, few small voids; dark brown slip and burnished on exterior and interior; Cypriot Base Ring II Ware
5.13.17	Bowl	AK X 1984 H N/5 b. 529/1	529/1	Red/grey/red to grey; few small white inclusions; dark brown slip inside and outside; Cypriot monochrome
5.13.18	Bowl	AK X 1984 H M/9 b. 625/1	625/1	Pink/pink/pink; no inclusions, well levigated; high fired; dark brown slip on interior and exterior; Cypriot Monochrome Ware

Figure No.	Shape/ object	Reg. No.	Locus/ Pottery Basket	Description (color of exterior/interior/core; inclusions; decorations; etc.)
5.13.19	Bowl	AK X 1984 H M/9 b. 625/2	625/2	Light brown/light brown/grey; few small white inclusions; light to dark brown slip and burnished interior and exterior; Cypriot Monochrome Ware
5.13.20	Bowl	AK VII 1980 H L/7 b. 222/3	Wall 729	Pink/pink/pink; dark grey slip; Cypriot White Slip Ware
5.13.21	Bowl	AK VIII 1982 H M/7 b. 241/1	241/1	Grey/grey/grey; few small white inclusions; brown stripes, white slip and burnished on inside and outside; Cypriot White Slip Ware
5.13.22	Body fragment	AK VIII 1982 H M/7 b. 320/1	320/1	Grey/grey/grey; few small white inclusions; brown stripes on white-grey slip and burnished on inside and outside; Cypriot White Slip Ware
5.13.23	Zoomorphic vessel	AK VIII 1982 H L/9 b. 171/1	171/1	Orange/orange/orange; no inclusions; buff painted stripes; Cypriot Base Ring II
5.13.24	Figurine	AK X 1984 H M/5 b. 594/5	594/5	Pink/pink/grey; medium number of small white inclusions; handmade; red painted stripes, incised lines

LB IIB-Iron IA transition typology

Bowls with simple and folded rims

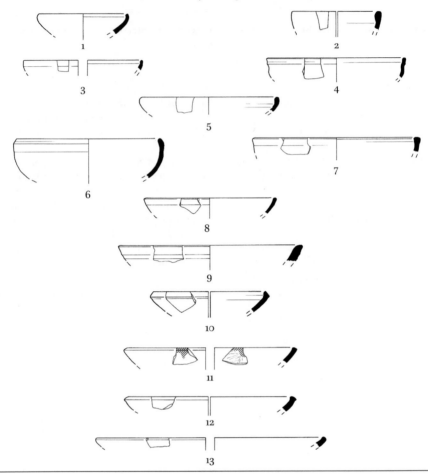

Bowls with flared rim and "cyma" profile

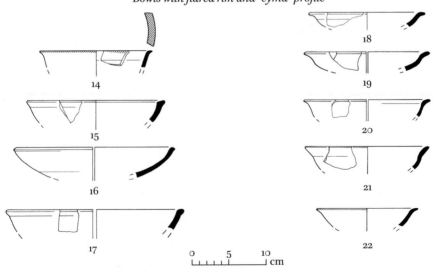

FIGURE 5.14

THE POTTERY OF STRATUM 5

Figure No.	Shape/ object	Reg. No.	Locus/ Pottery Basket	Description (color of exterior/interior/core; inclusions; decorations; etc.)
5.14.1	Bowl	AK VIII 1982 H M/7 b. 287/2	287/2	Red/red/red; medium number of small to medium sized white and light grey inclusions; cream-colored self slip on interior and exterior
5.14.2	Bowl	AK X 1984 H M/10 b. 258/2	258/2	Light pink/light pink/light pink; many small brown inclusions
5.14.3	Bowl	AK VIII 1982 H L/9 b. 145/2	Loc. 813	Buff/pink/buff; few medium white inclusions
5.14.4	Bowl	AK VIII 1982 H L/9 b. 143/1	Loc. 814	Pink/pink/pink to grey; few small white inclusions
5.14.5	Bowl	AK VI 1979 H L/9 b. 200/3	200/3	Orangey pink/orangey pink/light grey; small white inclusions
5.14.6	Bowl	AK VI 1979 H L/9 b. 169/1	169/1	Pink/pink/red; many white inclusions
5.14.7	Bowl	AK X 1984 H J/6 b. 632/2	632/2	Red/red/red; many small white inclusions
5.14.8	Bowl	AK VII 1980 H L/7 b. 304/3	Loc. 750	Pink/pink/pink; medium amount of small white inclusions
5.14.9	Bowl	AK VII 1980 H L/7 b. 255/4	255/4	Pink/pink/grey; small amount, small white inclusions
5.14.10	Bowl	AK VI 1979 H L/9 b. 190/2	190/2	Pink/pink/pink; medium number of small white inclusions
5.14.11	Bowl	AK VIII 1982 H L/9 b. 290/2	290/2	Pink/pink/pink; few small white and grey inclusions; red painted band on inside and outside of rim; burnished inside of vessel (over stripe as well)
5.14.12	Bowl	AK VIII 1982 H M/7 b. 258/3	258/3	Pink/pink/light grey; few medium white and light grey inclusions
5.14.13	Bowl	AK VIII 1982 H L/9 b. 162/2	Loc. 813	Pink/pink/pink; few small white inclusions
5.14.14	Bowl	AK VII 1980 H L/7 b. 116/11	Loc. 731b	Cream/cream/cream; low number, small brown inclusions; dark brown painted stripe
5.14.15	Bowl	AK X 1984 H J/6 b. 619/6	619/6	Pink/pink/light grey; few small white inclusions
5.14.16	Bowl	AK VIII 1982 H L/9 b. 140/1	Loc. 813	Light pink/pink/light pink to light grey; medium number of small to medium white inclusions
5.14.17	Bowl	AK VII 1980 H L/9 b. 72/5	72/5	Pinkish red/pinkish red/pink; medium amount of small white inclusions
5.14.18	Bowl	AK VI 1979 H L/9 b. 200/1	200/1	Reddish pink/reddish pink/reddish pink to light grey
5.14.19	Bowl	AK VI 1979 H L/9 b. 169/4	169/4	Pink/pink/pink; many small brown inclusions
5.14.20	Bowl	AK VI 1979 H L/9 b. 200/2	200/2	Brown/brown/grey brown; small white inclusions
5.14.21	Bowl	AK X 1984 H M/5 b. 509/1	509/1	Brown/brown/brown; many small white inclusions
5.14.22	Bowl	AK VII 1980 H L/9 b. 72/2	72/2	Pink/pink/pink; few small white inclusions

LB IIB-Iron IA transition typology (cont.)

Carinated bowls

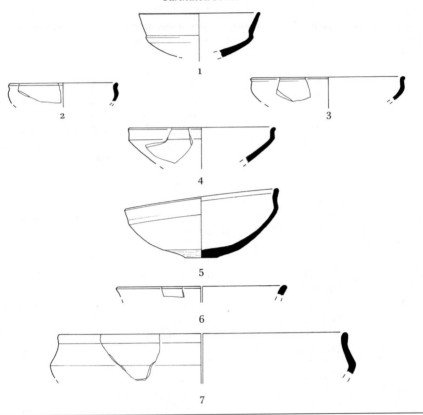

"Bell-shaped" bowls

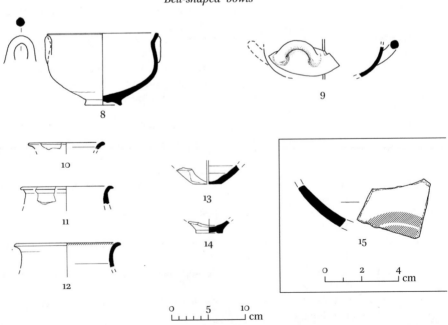

FIGURE 5.15

THE POTTERY OF STRATUM 5

Figure No.	Shape/object	Reg. No.	Locus/Pottery Basket	Description (color of exterior/interior/core; inclusions; decorations; etc.)
5.15.1	Bowl	AK IX 1983 H L/9 b. 1304/1	1304/1	Buff/buff/light grey; medium amount of small white inclusions
5.15.2	Bowl	AK VI 1979 H L/9 b. 190/1	190/1	Pink/pink/pink to grey; medium amount of small to medium white inclusions
5.15.3	Bowl	AK VI 1979 H L/9 b. 190/3	190/3	Pink/pink/pink to grey; many small white inclusions
5.15.4	Bowl	AK VI 1979 H L/9 b. 169/5	169/5	Pink/pink/pink to light grey; many small white inclusions
5.15.5	Bowl	AK VII 1980 H L/9 b. 104/1	Loc. 728	Pink/pink/pink to grey; few small white inclusions
5.15.6	Bowl	AK VIII 1982 H L/9 b. 145/1	Loc. 813	Pink/pink/pink; few small white inclusions
5.15.7	Bowl	AK VIII 1982 H M/7 b. 305/4	305/4	Pink/pink/pink; few medium sized white inclusions
5.15.8	Bowl	AK VIII 1982 H L/9 b. 333/1	333/1	Pink to pinkish buff/pink/pink to light brown; few small white inclusions
5.15.9	Bowl	AK VII 1980 H L/9 b. 70/1	Loc. 728	Pink/pink/pink to grey; few small white inclusions
5.15.10	Bowl	AK VIII 1982 H L/9 b. 129/1	129/1	Pink/pink/pink; few small white inclusions
5.15.11	Bowl	AK VI 1979 H L/9 b. 200/4	200/4	Reddish pink/reddish pink/reddish pink
5.15.12	Bowl	AK VIII 1982 H M/7 b. 322/4	322/4	Pink/pink/pink; many small white inclusions; red painted stripe on inside of lip
5.15.13	Bowl	AK VIII 1982 H M/7 b. 322/3	322/3	Pink/light grey/light grey; medium number of small white inclusions
5.15.14	Bowl	AK X 1984 H M/5 b. 549/2	549/2	Pink/pink/pink; medium number of small brown inclusions
5.15.15	Bowl	AK VIII 1982 H M/7 b. 258/1	258/1	Pink/pink/light grey; few small white inclusions; cream-colored self slip on interior and exterior; red painted stripes on interior

LB IIB-Iron IA transition typology (cont.)

Chalice

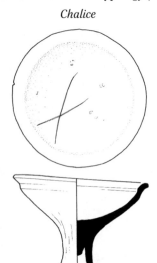

Kraters

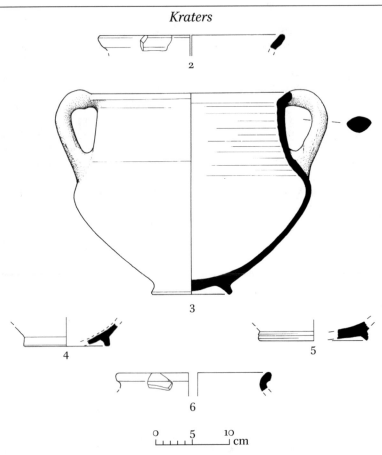

FIGURE 5.16

Figure No.	Shape/ object	Reg. No.	Locus/ Pottery Basket	Description (color of exterior/interior/ core; inclusions; decorations; etc.)
5.16.1	Chalice	AK VII 1980 H L/9 b. 29/23	Loc. 728	Orange pink/orange pink/grey; few small white inclusions; X incised inside bowl
5.16.2	Krater	AK VII 1980 H L/7 b. 304/2	Loc. 750	Buff pink/buff pink/pink; medium amount of small brown and grey inclusions
5.16.3	Krater	AK VI 1979 H L/9 b. 192/1	Loc. 17	Orange red/orange red/grey
5.16.4	Bowl or krater	AK X 1984 H J/6 b. 619/2	619/2	Red brown/inside surface gone/grey; few medium sized white inclusions
5.16.5	Large bowl or krater	AK VII 1980 H L/9 b. 189/4	189/4	Pink/reddish brown/grey; few small to medium sized white inclusions
5.16.6	Krater	AK VIII 1982 H L/9 b. 129/2	129/2	Pink/pink/grey; few medium white inclusions

LB IIB-Iron IA transition typology (cont.)

Krater-pithos

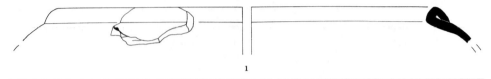

Amphora-kraters and hemispherical ("bell-shaped") kraters

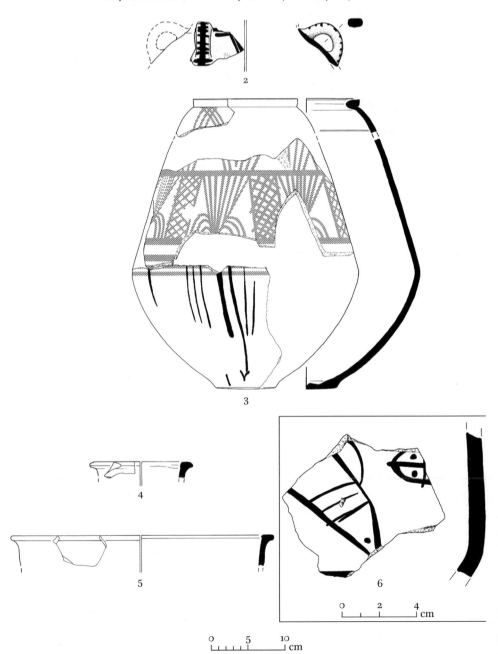

FIGURE 5.17

Figure No.	Shape/object	Reg. No.	Locus/Pottery Basket	Description (color of exterior/interior/core; inclusions; decorations; etc.)
5.17.1	Krater-pithos	AK VII 1980 H L/7 b. 270/4	270/4	Pink/pink/grey; many, medium grey, quartz, and white inclusions
5.17.2	Amphora-krater	AK VIII 1982 H L/9 b. 212/1	212/1	Pinkish buff/pinkish buff/pinkish buff; few small white inclusions; brown painted stripes
5.17.3	Amphora-krater	AK VIII 1982 H L/9 b. 229/1	229/1	Orange pink/orange pink/light grey; many small white inclusions; red painted design, few dark brown vertical stripes
5.17.4	Krater	AK VII 1980 H L/7 b. 255/2	255/2	Pink/pink/grey; many small brown inclusions
5.17.5	Krater	AK X 1984 H J/6 b. 632/1	632/1	Red/grey/grey; many small white inclusions
5.17.6	Krater	AK VII 1980 H L/7 b. 289/1	289/1	Pink/pink/pink; few, small to medium white inclusions; dark brown fish/dolphin, circle with cross and dots; stripe

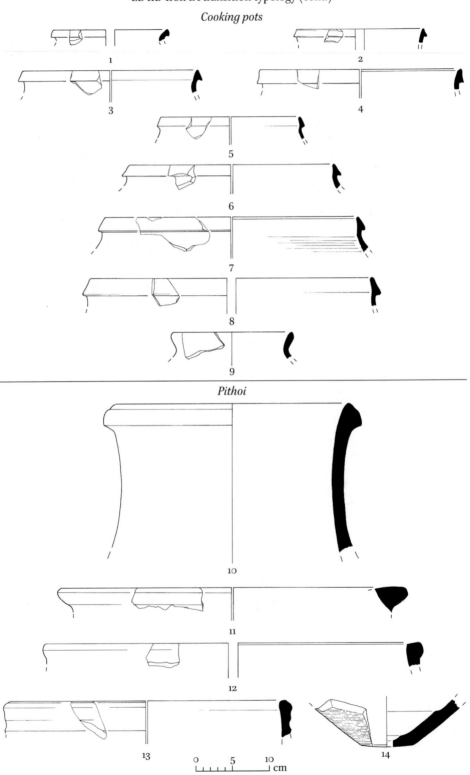

FIGURE 5.18

Figure No.	Shape/object	Reg. No.	Locus/Pottery Basket	Description (color of exterior/interior/core; inclusions; decorations; etc.)
5.18.1	Cooking pot	AK VII 1980 H L/9 b. 189/5	189/5	Grey/grey/grey; few small white inclusions
5.18.2	Cooking pot	AK VI 1979 H L/9 b. 200/8	200/8	Red/red/red; small white inclusions
5.18.3	Cooking pot	AK VIII 1982 H L/9 b. 290/5	290/5	Red/red/grey; medium number of small white inclusions
5.18.4	Cooking pot	AK VI 1979 H L/9 b. 200/7	200/7	Orange red/orange red/dark grey; small white inclusions
5.18.5	Cooking pot	AK VI 1979 H L/9 b. 200/9	200/9	Dark brown/orange red/dark grey; many small white inclusions
5.18.6	Cooking pot	AK VIII 1982 H L/9 b. 145/4	Loc. 813	Light brown/dark brown/dark grey; numerous small white inclusions; lightly fired
5.18.7	Cooking pot	AK X 1984 H J/6 b. 619/1	619/1	Light brown/light brown/light brown; many small white and quartz inclusions
5.18.8	Cooking pot	AK VII 1980 H M/4 b. 205/5	Loc. 744	Dark brown/red brown/dark grey; medium number of small white and quartz inclusions
5.18.9	Cooking jar	AK VIII 1982 H L/9 b. 212/2	212/2	Brown/brown/black; many small white inclusions
5.18.10	Pithos	AK VIII 1982 H L/9 b. 238/1	238/1	Orangey pink/red/red; few small white inclusions
5.18.11	Pithos	AK VII 1980 H L/7 b. 270/5	270/5	Pink/pink/brown; many, small white and brown inclusions
5.18.12	Pithos	AK VII 1980 H L/7 b. 270/2	270/2	Pink/pink/red to grey; numerous small to medium white, small to medium grey, small to medium quartz inclusions; low fired; flared rim
5.18.13	Pithos	AK VI 1979 H L/9 b. 200/6	200/6	Pink/pink/grey; few small white inclusions
5.18.14	Pithos	AK VIII 1982 H M/7 b. 287/3	287/3	Pink/light grey/dark grey; medium number of small and medium sized white inclusions

LB IIB-Iron IA transition typology (cont.)
Storage jars

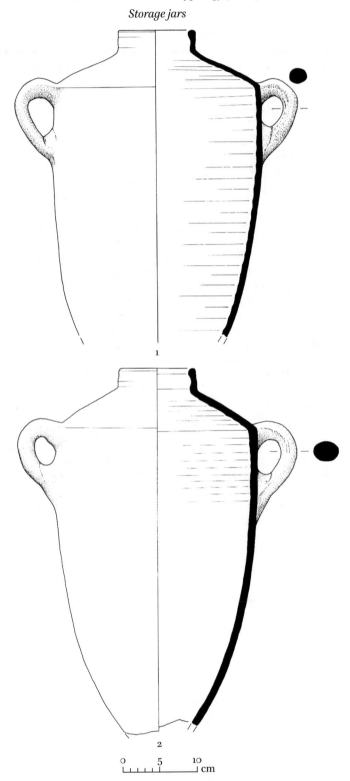

FIGURE 5.19

Figure No.	Shape/object	Reg. No.	Locus/Pottery Basket	Description (color of exterior/interior/core; inclusions; decorations; etc.)
5.19.1	Storage jar	AK VI 1979 H L/9 b. 186/2	Loc. 17	Orange pink/orange pink/ grey; medium number of small white inclusions
5.19.2	Storage jar	AK VI 1979 H L/9 b. 186/1	Loc. 17	Orange pink/brown/grey; medium number of small white inclusions

LB IIB-Iron IA transition typology (cont.)

Storage jars (cont.)

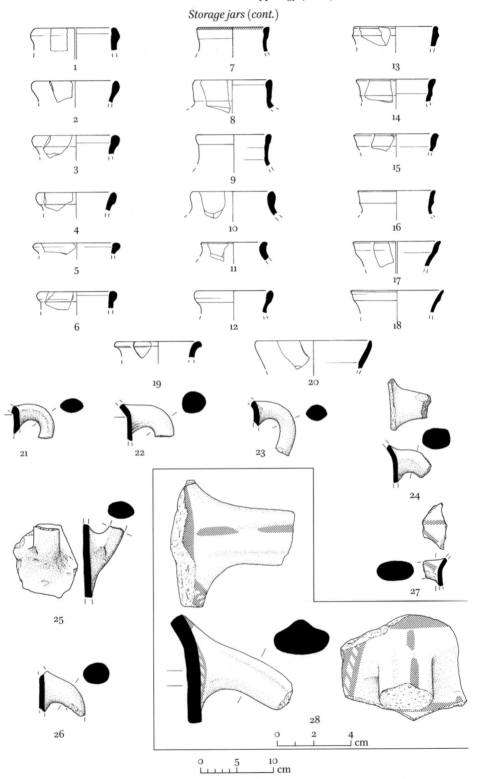

FIGURE 5.20

THE POTTERY OF STRATUM 5

Figure No.	Shape/object	Reg. No.	Locus/Pottery Basket	Description (color of exterior/interior/core; inclusions; decorations; etc.)
5.20.1	Storage jar	AK VI 1979 H L/9 b. 190/6	190/6	Pink/pink/grey; few small white inclusions
5.20.2	Storage jar	AK VII 1980 H L/7 b. 270/3	270/3	Red/pink/grey; low number, small white inclusions
5.20.3	Storage jar	AK VIII 1982 H L/7 b. 69/2	69/2	Pink/pink/light grey; large amount of small dark brown inclusions
5.20.4	Storage jar	AK VIII 1982 H L/9 b. 163/4	163/4	Pink/pink/grey; few small white inclusions
5.20.5	Storage jar	AK VIII 1982 H L/9 b. 245/2	245/2	Pink/pink/grey; few small white inclusions
5.20.6	Jar	AK VII 1980 H L/9 b. 269/3	269/3	Pink/light pink/pink; medium amount of small brown inclusions
5.20.7	Jar	AK VII 1980 H K/7 b. 299/2	299/2	Pink/pink/pink; many miniscule brown inclusions; dark brown stripe on rim
5.20.8	Storage jar	AK VIII 1982 H L/9 b. 162/1 + 3	Loc. 813	Pink/pink/pink; few medium white inclusions
5.20.9	Storage jar	AK VIII 1982 H L/9 b. 163/1	163/1	Pink/pink/pink; many small to medium white inclusions
5.20.10	Storage jar	AK VII 1980 H M/4 b. 205/6	Loc. 744	Light pink/light pink/pink; medium number of small brown inclusions
5.20.11	Jar	AK VI 1979 H L/9 b. 200/5	200/5	Pink/pink/pink; few small white inclusions
5.20.12	Storage jar	AK VIII 1982 H L/9 b. 163/3	163/3	Red/red/grey; few medium white inclusions
5.20.13	Storage jar	AK VIII 1982 H L/9 b. 129/3	129/3	Pink/pink/pink; few small white inclusions
5.20.14	Storage jar	AK VIII 1982 H M/7 b. 287/1	287/1	Pink/pink/pink; few medium sized white inclusions
5.20.15	Storage jar	AK VIII 1982 H L/9 b. 160/1	Loc. 814	Pink/pink/pink; few medium sized white inclusions
5.20.16	Storage jar	AK VIII 1982 H M/7 b. 305/2	305/2	Buff/buff/buff; few small white inclusions
5.20.17	Storage jar	AK VIII 1982 H M/7 b. 322/2	322/2	Pink/pink/pink; medium number of small grey inclusions
5.20.18	Jug	AK VIII 1982 H L/9 b. 254/2	254/2	Pink/pink/pink; many small brown inclusions
5.20.19	Jar	AK VII 1980 H L/9 b. 269/2	269/2	Cream/cream/cream; few small brown inclusions; Cypriot Plain White Wheel Made Ware
5.20.20	Storage jar	AK IX 1983 H L/9 b. 1304/2	1304/2	Pink/pink/pink to grey; few small white inclusions
5.20.21	Jar or storage jar	AK VII 1980 H L/7 b. 254/2	Loc. 731b	Pink/pink/grey; medium number of small white and medium grey inclusions
5.20.22	Storage jar	AK VII 1980 H L/9 b. 72/6	72/6	Tan/pink/tan to pink; few small white and grey inclusions

Figure No.	Shape/ object	Reg. No.	Locus/ Pottery Basket	Description (color of exterior/interior/core; inclusions; decorations; etc.)
5.20.23	Storage jar	AK VII 1980 H M/4 b. 205/4	Loc. 744	Red/red/dark grey; few small white inclusions
5.20.24	Storage jar	AK VII 1980 H L/7 b. 217/1	217/1	Pink/pink/dark grey; medium amount of small white and grey inclusions
5.20.25	Storage jar	AK VII 1980 H L/7 b. 255/8	255/8	Pink/buff/dark grey; medium number of small to medium white and light grey inclusions
5.20.26	Storage jar	AK VII 1980 H L/7 b. 288/1	288/1	Red/red/dark grey; medium amount of small to medium white and dark grey inclusions
5.20.27	Jug or jar	AK VIII 1982 H L/9 b. 129/4	129/4	Red/red/black; few small white inclusions; painted red stripes
5.20.28	Jug	AK VIII 1982 H M/4 b. 178/2	Loc. 818	Pink/pink/red to grey; many small white inclusions; red painted stripes

LB IIB-Iron IA transition typology (cont.)

Jars and storage jars (cont.)

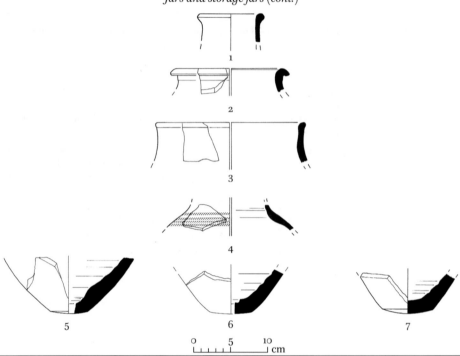

Stirrup jars

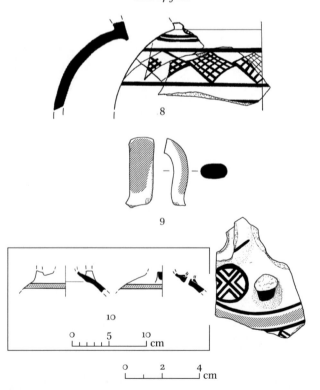

FIGURE 5.21

THE POTTERY OF STRATUM 5

Figure No.	Shape/ object	Reg. No.	Locus/ Pottery Basket	Description (color of exterior/interior/core; inclusions; decorations; etc.)
5.21.1	Jar	AK VI 1979 H L/9 b. 169/2	169/2	Pink/pink/pink to light grey; medium amount of small to medium sized white inclusions
5.21.2	Jar	AK VIII 1982 H L/7 b. 69/1	69/1	Pink/pink to buff/grey; medium amount of medium white and grey inclusions
5.21.3	Jar	AK VII 1980 H L/7 b. 255/6	255/6	Pink to grey/buff/light brown; low number, small white inclusions
5.21.4	Jar	AK VI 1979 H L/9 b. 190/4	190/4	Pink/grey to light brown/grey; few medium white inclusions
5.21.5	Storage jar or pithos	AK VIII 1982 H L/9 b. 129/5	129/5	Red/red/light grey; few medium sized white inclusions
5.21.6	Storage jar	AK VIII 1982 H L/9 b. 226/5	226/5	Pink/pink/pink; medium number of small to medium white inclusions
5.21.7	Storage jar	AK VIII 1982 H M/7 b. 305/5	305/5	Pink/pink/grey; few small white inclusions
5.21.8	Stirrup jar	AK VII 1980 H L/7 b. 308/1	Loc. 750	No fabric description. Painted stripes and rhomboids with net pattern
5.21.9	Stirrup jar	AK VI 1979 H L/9 b. 169/3	169/3	Pink/pink/pink; few small brown inclusions; red painted stripe on outside
5.21.10	Stirrup jar	AK VII 1980 H L/7 b. 298/1	298/1	Red/pink/pink; few, medium white inclusions; red and brown paint on cream slip

LB IIB-Iron IA transition typology (cont.)

Amphoriskoi

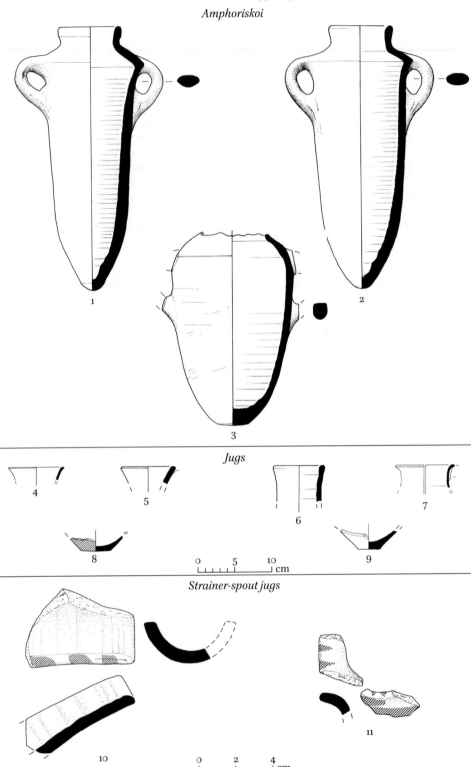

FIGURE 5.22

Figure No.	Shape/object	Reg. No.	Locus/Pottery Basket	Description (color of exterior/interior/core; inclusions; decorations; etc.)
5.22.1	Amphoriskos	AK VI 1979 H L/9 b. 191/1	Loc. 17	Pink to buff/pink/no core; few small white inclusions
5.22.2	Amphoriskos	AK VI 1979 H L/9 b. 193/1	Loc. 17	Pink to buff/pink/grey; few small white inclusions
5.22.3	Amphoriskos	AK VI 1979 H L/9 b. 197/1	Loc. 17	Pink buff/pink buff/pink
5.22.4	Jug	AK IX 1983 H L/9 b. 1304/6	1304/6	Buff/buff/buff; few small brown inclusions
5.22.5	Jar	AK VII 1980 H L/9 b. 269/4	269/4	Pink/pink/pink; few small white inclusions
5.22.6	Jug	AK VII 1980 H L/7 b. 255/3	255/3	Pink/pink/pink to grey; medium number of small white, few large white inclusions; Cypriot?
5.22.7	Jug	AK VIII 1982 H L/9 b. 254/1	254/1	Pink/pink/pink; many small brown inclusions
5.22.8	Jug	AK VI 1979 H L/9 b. 200/11	200/11	Orangey pink/not preserved/light grey; red slip on outside
5.22.9	Jug	AK VI 1979 H L/9 b. 200/10	200/10	Pink/pink/pink to dark grey
5.22.10	Jug	AK X 1984 H N/5 b. 528/1	528/1	Pink/pink/pink; medium number of small white inclusions; red stripes on cream slip inside spout
5.22.11	Jug	AK X 1984 H J/6 b. 619/4	619/4	Pink/pink/pink; few small white inclusions; red painted stripes

LB IIB-Iron IA transition typology (cont.)

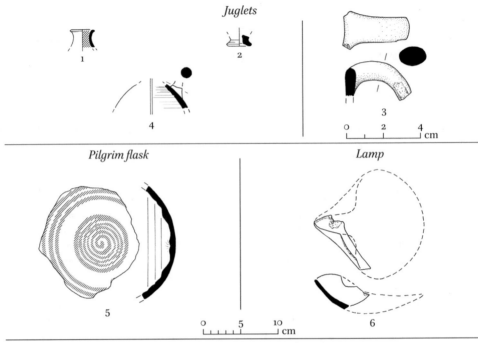

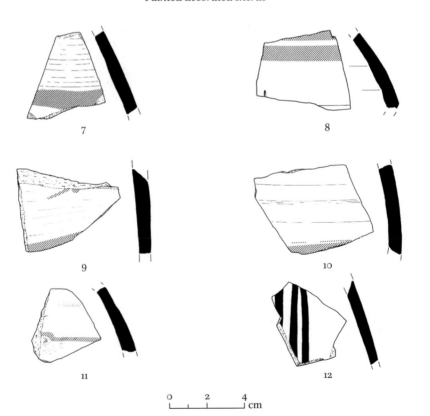

FIGURE 5.23

THE POTTERY OF STRATUM 5

Figure No.	Shape/ object	Reg. No.	Locus/ Pottery Basket	Description (color of exterior/interior/core; inclusions; decorations; etc.)
5.23.1	Juglet	AK VIII 1982 H L/9 b. 145/3	Loc. 813	Pink/pink/pink; small white inclusions; red slip on inside of neck
5.23.2	Juglet	AK VII 1980 H L/9 b. 254/1	Loc. 731b	Pink/pink/pink; many small brown inclusions
5.23.3	Juglet	AK VII 1980 H L/9 b. 189/7	189/7	Pinkish tan/pinkish tan/light grey; few small to medium sized white inclusions
5.23.4	Juglet	AK VIII 1982 H M/7 b. 305/1	305/1	Pink/buff/light grey; very few medium sized white inclusions
5.23.5	Pilgrim flask	AK VI 1979 H L/9 b. 200/12	200/12	Orangey pink/dark grey/dark grey; red painted stripes
5.23.6	Lamp	AK VIII 1982 H L/9 b. 269/1	Loc. 823	Pink/pink/dark grey; many small white inclusions
5.23.7	Body sherd	AK VIII 1982 H L/9 b. 290/4	290/4	Cream/cream/cream; large number of small dark brown and white inclusions; red painted stripe; Cypriot import
5.23.8	Body sherd	AK VI 1979 H L/9 b. 190/5	190/5	Pink/grey/grey; few small white inclusions; red painted stripes
5.23.9	Krater?	AK VIII 1982 H M/7 b. 322/1	322/1	Pink/pink/pink; medium number of small white and grey inclusions; cream-colored self slip on exterior; red painted stripes
5.23.10	Body sherd from krater?	AK X 1984 H J/6 b. 619/5	619/5	Pink/pink/light grey; many small white inclusions; red painted stripe
5.23.11	Body sherd of closed vessel	AK VIII 1982 H L/9 b. 160/2	Loc. 814	Pink/pink/pink; medium number of small white inclusions; red painted stripe
5.23.12	Body sherd, amphora-krater?	AK VIII 1982 H L/9 b. 212/5	212/5	Buff pink/buff pink/buff pink; medium number of small white inclusions; brown painted stripes

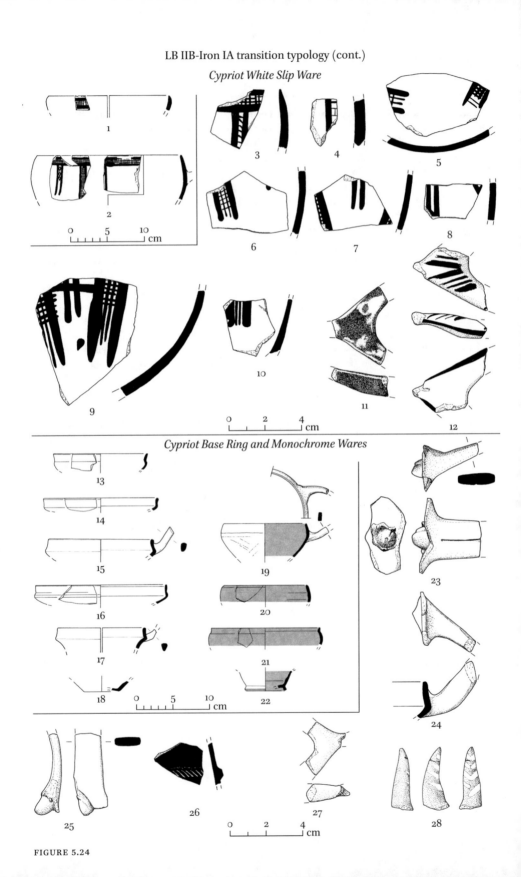

FIGURE 5.24

THE POTTERY OF STRATUM 5 431

Figure No.	Shape/ object	Reg. No.	Locus/ Pottery Basket	Description (color of exterior/interior/core; inclusions; decorations; etc.)
5.24.1	Bowl	AK VII 1980 H L/7 b. 131/1	Loc. 731b	Red/red/red; few small white inclusions; Cypriot White Slip Ware; creamy, ivory white slip inside and outside, burnished inside; dark brown ladder design on outside
5.24.2	Bowl	AK IX 1983 H L/9 b. 1304/9	1304/9	Grey/grey/grey; few small white inclusions; greyish-white slip on inside and outside; dark brown painted decoration
5.24.3	Bowl	AK IX 1983 H L/9 b. 1304/12	1304/12	Red/red/red; few small white inclusions; cream slip on inside and outside; dark brown painted decoration; Cypriot White Slip Ware
5.24.4	Bowl	AK VII 1980 H L/9 b. 72/7	72/7	Red/red/red; medium number of small white inclusions; brown stripes on grey/white slip on inside and outside; Cypriot White Slip Ware
5.24.5	Bowl	AK IX 1983 H L/9 b. 1304/11	1304/11	Light grey/light grey/light grey; greyish-white slip inside and outside; brown painted decoration; Cypriot White Painted Ware
5.24.6	Bowl	AK IX 1983 H L/9 b. 1304/10	1304/10	Light grey/light grey/light grey; few small white inclusions; greyish-white slip inside and outside; brown painted decoration; Cypriot White Painted Ware
5.24.7	Bowl	AK VIII 1982 H M/7 b. 241/1	241/1	Grey/grey/grey; few small white inclusions; brown stripes, white slip and burnished on inside and outside; Cypriot White Slip Ware
5.24.8	Body fragment	AK VIII 1982 H M/7 b. 320/1	320/1	Grey/grey/grey; few small white inclusions; brown stripes on white-grey slip and burnished on inside and outside; Cypriot White Slip Ware
5.24.9	Bowl	AK X 1984 H J/6 b. 612/1	612/1	Red/red/dark grey; few small white inclusions; brown paint on poor white slip; Cypriot White Slip Ware
5.24.10	Bowl	AK IX 1983 H O/5 b. 1238/1	1238/1	Red/red/grey; few small white inclusions; brown stripes, white slip and burnished on inside and outside; Cypriot White Slip Ware
5.24.11	Bowl	AK VII 1980 H L/7 b. 222/3	Wall 729	Pink/pink/pink; dark grey slip; Cypriot White Slip Ware
5.24.12	Bowl	AK VIII 1982 H L/9 b. 290/1	290/1	Red/red/red; few small white inclusions; cream slip on inside and outside; brown painted decoration; Cypriot White Slip Ware
5.24.13	Bowl	AK X 1984 H M/9 b. 625/2	625/2	Light brown/light brown/grey; few small white inclusions; light to dark brown slip and burnished interior and exterior; Cypriot Monochrome Ware
5.24.14	Bowl	AK VIII 1982 H L/9 b. 163/2	163/2	Pink/pink/light grey; few small white inclusions; brown to red brown slip on outside and inside; Cypriot Base Ring II ware
5.24.15	Bowl	AK VII 1980 H L/8 b. 56/1	56/1	Red brown/red brown/grey; many small white inclusions, few small voids; dark brown slip and burnished on exterior and interior; Cypriot Base Ring II Ware
5.24.16	Bowl	AK X 1984 H N/5 b. 529/1	529/1	Red/grey/red to grey; few small white inclusions; dark brown slip inside and outside; Cypriot monochrome

Figure No.	Shape/object	Reg. No.	Locus/Pottery Basket	Description (color of exterior/interior/core; inclusions; decorations; etc.)
5.24.17	Bowl	AK VII 1980 H L/9 b. 189/1	189/1	Red brown/red brown/grey; many small white inclusions, few small voids; dark brown slip and burnished on exterior and interior; Cypriot Base Ring II Ware
5.24.18	Bowl	AK IX 1983 H L/9 b. 1304/4	1304/4	Red/red/red; few small white inclusions; Cypriot Monochrome Ware
5.24.19	Bowl	AK IX 1983 H L/9 b. 1304/7	1304/7	Red/red/red; few small white inclusions; brown slip inside and outside; Cypriot Base Ring Ware
5.24.20	Bowl	AK X 1984 H M/9 b. 625/1	625/1	Pink/pink/pink; no inclusions, well levigated; high fired; dark brown slip on interior and exterior; Cypriot Monochrome Ware
5.24.21	Bowl	AK IX 1983 H L/9 b. 1304/3	1304/3	Red/red/red; few small white inclusions; brown slip inside and outside; Cypriot Monochrome Ware
5.24.22	Bowl	AK IX 1983 H L/9 b. 1304/8	1304/8	Pink/grey/grey; few small white inclusions; brown slip inside and outside; Cypriot Base Ring Ware
5.24.23	Jug	AK VII 1980 H L/8 b. 50/4	50/4	Buff/buff/light grey; very few small white inclusions; brown slip and burnished exterior; Cypriot Base Ring I
5.24.24	Bowl	AK VII 1980 H L/7 b. 116/5	Loc. 731b	Pink/pink/grey; few, small white inclusions; Cypriot Base Ring Ware
5.24.25	Bowl	AK IX 1983 H L/9 b. 1304/5	1304/5	Red/red/red; few small white inclusions; Cypriot Monochrome Ware
5.24.26	Closed vessel	AK VII 1980 H L/8 b. 50/2	50/2	Light brown/light brown/light grey; very few small white inclusions; dark brown slip on exterior; raised rope design; Cypriot Base Ring I
5.24.27	Bowl	AK VII 1980 H L/7 b. 255/5	255/5	Dark brown/dark brown/dark grey; few, small white inclusions; no slip; Cypriot
5.24.28	Zoomorphic vessel	AK VIII 1982 H L/9 b. 171/1	171/1	Orange/orange/orange; no inclusions; buff painted stripes; Cypriot Base Ring II

LB IIB-Iron IA transition typology (cont.)

Misc. other Cypriot imports

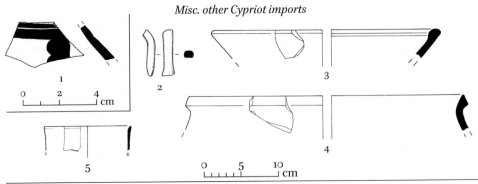

Mycenaean and/or "Myceanized" Cypriot and local wares

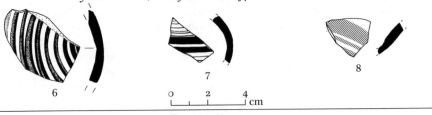

Egyptian import

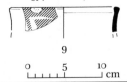

Anatolian imports

Figurine

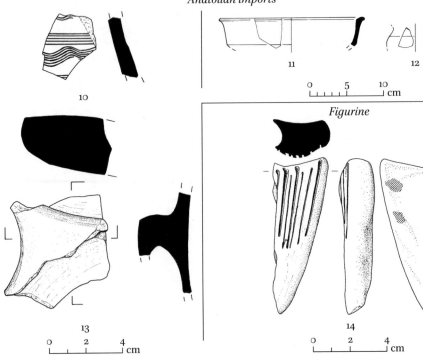

FIGURE 5.25

THE POTTERY OF STRATUM 5

Figure No.	Shape/ object	Reg. No.	Locus/ Pottery Basket	Description (color of exterior/interior/core; inclusions; decorations; etc.)
5.25.1	Body sherd	AK VIII 1982 H L/9 b. 269/2	Loc. 823	Buff/buff/buff; very few small white inclusions; brown stripes on burnished background; well levigated, high fired; Mycenaean IIIB, manufactured in Cyprus
5.25.2	Handle	AK VII 1980 H L/7 b. 304/1	Loc. 750	Pink/pink/pink; few small brown inclusions; Cypriot
5.25.3	Bowl	AK VII 1980 H L/9 b. 269/1	269/1	Cream/cream/cream; few medium sized white inclusions; Cypriot, Plain White Wheel Made Ware
5.25.4	Cooking pot	AK VIII 1982 H L/9 b. 290/3	290/3	Cream/cream/cream; large number of small dark brown and white inclusions; Cypriot import
5.25.5	Bowl	AK VIII 1982 H L/9 b. 226/2	226/2	Cream/cream/cream; medium amount of small brown inclusions; Cypriot Plain White Wheel Made Ware
5.25.6	Pilgrim flask	AK X 1984 H M/9 b. 620/9	620/9	Buff/buff/buff; burnished exterior with dark brown painted stripes; Mycenaean IIIB Ware
5.25.7	Stirrup jar?	AK VIII 1982 H K/7 b. 46/1	46/1	Buff/buff/buff; few, miniscule brown inclusions; dark brown stripes on highly burnished buff surface; Mycenaean IIIB Ware
5.25.8	Body sherd	AK VIII 1982 H L/7 b. 69/3	69/3	Buff/buff/buff; red painted stripes; Mycenaean IIIB Ware
5.25.9	Jar	AK VII 1980 H L/8 b. 56/3	56/3	Red/red/dark brown; many small white inclusions; Egyptian, Nile silt, Marl D Ware
5.25.10	Body sherd from krater?	AK X 1984 H J/6 b. 619/3	619/3	Light grey/light grey/light grey; few small white and micaceous inclusions; burnished inside and outside, incised wavy lines; Anatolian Grey Ware
5.25.11	Bowl	AK VII 1980 H L/7 b. 116/10	Loc. 731b	Buffish pink/buff to light grey/buffish pink; few, small dark brown inclusions; Anatolian Tan Ware
5.25.12	Bowl	AK VIII 1982 H L/9 b. 212/3	212/3	Dark grey/dark grey/dark grey; few small white inclusions; Anatolian Grey Ware
5.25.13	unknown vessel type	AK VIII 1982 H O/I b. 224/9	224/9	Grey/grey/grey; few small white inclusions; Anatolian Grey Ware
5.25.14	Figurine	AK X 1984 H M/5 b. 594/5	594/5	Pink/pink/grey; medium number of small white inclusions; handmade; red painted stripes, incised lines

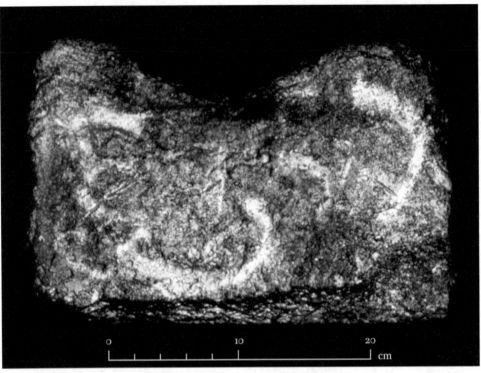

PHOTO 5.1   Locus 253, altar with ship motifs photographed in blue light
PHOTO: M. ARTZY

THE POTTERY OF STRATUM 5

PHOTO 5.2 Locus 253, altar with ship motifs photographed in natural light
PHOTO: R. STIDSING

PHOTO 5.3   Pebbles from altar
PHOTO: M. ARTZY

THE POTTERY OF STRATUM 5

PHOTO 5.4 Pit Locus 17, assemblage of ceramic vessels
PHOTO: R. STIDSING

PHOTO 5.5   Locus 728, chalice
PHOTO: R. STIDSING

CHAPTER 6

The Pottery of Stratum 4 (Iron IIA–IIB Transition)

Aaron Brody and Michal Artzy

Although the exposure of architectural remains from this phase in Area H is very limited (fig. 2.9), the repertoire of ceramics is quite rich. Some problems may arise because later builders in the Persian and Hellenistic periods at the tell mined out areas of the destroyed or abandoned Iron II levels of the city, robbed stones from earlier strata, and moved large quantities of Iron II layers to use as leveling fills throughout the mound. Thus one finds baskets with pure Iron II pottery in perfectly good Persian period or Hellenistic contexts, which extends a note of caution. In addition, on the southern section of Area H, a Crusader castle called Toron was constructed in the 12th–13th century CE (Artzy 2015) and indeed from time to time a glazed sherd was noted in the field diary. There is no doubt that the Crusader builders excavated deeply in order to construct the foundations of their buildings, thus disturbing earlier remains, leaving some undisturbed, disconnected, and spotty Iron II areas of habitation. Remnants of the Templar's Toron is clearly seen in Square M/1. We will not be dealing with these Crusader remains in this volume, which include ceramics.

The Iron II architecture in Area H is concentrated south of the rampart slope from the line of Squares M/1, O/1, and P/1 (fig. 2.9). Unfortunately, the decision to open only half squares in a north south direction, namely M/4, M/3, M/2, and M/1 limits a better understanding of the Iron II occupation in the area. The discussion of the ceramics from the stratified contexts of Stratum 4 will be presented first according to context, in the order in which the stratigraphy is summarized in chapter 2 above, followed by typology.

Stratum 4 Pottery

Square M/4: Only half of Square M/4 was excavated as a probe; thus the 2 × 4 m exposure revealed limited Stratum 4 architecture. A mudbrick floor Locus 742 was exposed (fig. 2.9). The pottery from this phase is presented in its relationship to this surface, beginning with finds beneath the floor and working up following the stratigraphic matrix reconstruction (fig. 2.31). The lowest Iron II remains were found in basket 178 containing a variety of open and closed forms. Open vessels include small and large bowls with incurved rims (fig. 6.1.1–3); a large bowl with an upright rim and a gentle carination (fig. 6.1.4); the base of a vessel (possibly a bowl or jar) which is somewhere between a disk and a ring base (fig. 6.1.5); one cooking pot with a pendent rim (fig. 6.1.6) and a fragment of a baking tray (fig. 6.1.7). Closed vessels are represented by several types of storage jars with upright rims (fig. 6.1.8–11), and an almost complete Cypriot bichrome barrel jug (photo 6.1 and 6.2) with a horizontal ovoid body, a central spout (rim missing), and painted concentric circular bichrome decoration along with a pendent filled with a net pattern (fig. 6.1.12).

Above basket 178 is the mudbrick floor, Locus 742; further Iron II pottery was discovered in the mudbrick fill above the surface, in baskets 182 and 184. Open vessels from these baskets include two large bowls with both gentle and sharp carinations (fig. 6.2.1–2); a ring base, perhaps from a bowl or krater (fig. 6.2.3); the large, flared rim of a krater or basin (fig. 6.2.4); and the upright triangular rim of a small cooking pot or cooking jug (fig. 6.2.5). Closed vessels are represented by three variations of upright rims from storage jars (fig. 6.2.6, 8–9); rim fragments from jars (fig. 6.2.7, 10); the disk base of a plain jug (fig. 6.2.11); and an almost complete Phoenician monochrome jug with a depressed ring base and painted decorations of concentric circles and a typical "ribbon" design (fig. 6.2.12). One small body fragment of Cypriot Black-on-Red ware was also found in basket 182 (fig. 6.2.13).

Basket 183 was excavated next to baskets 182 and 184, and contains similar pottery. Open forms include three carinated bowls with upright rims (fig. 6.3.1–3), two of which are decorated on their interiors with red and dark brown painted stripes; a ring base, which may have been from a bowl (fig. 6.3.4); and four different types of cooking pots, one with handles and a direct rim (fig. 6.3.5), one with handles and an upright triangular rim (fig. 6.3.6), and two with pendent rims without handles(fig. 6.3.7–8). Closed vessels include a variety of upright rim forms of storage jars (fig. 6.3.9–13); holemouth jar (183/10); and the part of the neck from a decorated Phoenician bichrome jug (fig. 6.3.15).

Iron II pottery is present in baskets 153 and 157. Their exact stratigraphic relationship to the baskets so far described in square M/4 is impossible to determine; therefore they must be treated as deriving from much less secure contexts. Open vessels include a large bowl with a bevelled upright rim (fig. 6.3.16) and the base of a large basin or bin (fig. 6.3.17). Closed vessels are represented by two upright rim fragments (fig. 6.3.18–19), the rounded shoulder and handle (fig. 6.3.20), and knobbed base (fig. 6.3.21) from storage jars; a rim fragment from a large holemouth jar (fig. 6.3.22); and a painted body fragment of a possible jug (fig. 6.3.23).

Square M/3: It is difficult to ascertain sound contexts for this phase in this square, as it was investigated only in a narrow probe; therefore, the pottery will be presented with the caveat that it may well represent materials from later fills (figs. 2.9, 2.30). Still, since there are not many Iron II remains published so far from Tel Akko, we will present the ceramics here.

The lowest stratigraphic baskets of this square lie beneath Wall 743, thus predating its construction. Open vessels from baskets 201 and 206 include small, shallow bowls with everted rims (fig. 6.4.1–2); the incurved and everted rim sherds of large bowls (fig. 6.4.3–4); the bases of indeterminate vessels (fig. 6.4.5–6); and the upright rim and vertical loop handle of a cooking jar (fig. 6.4.7). Closed vessels include the upright rims of several storage jars (fig. 6.4.8–10) and storage jar toes (fig. 6.4.11–12); a body sherd from a jug, with incised decorative lines (fig. 6.4.13). One lamp fragment with a disk base was found (fig. 6.4.14), and the direct rim of a small Cypriot Black-on-Red bowl (fig. 6.4.15). Above baskets 201 and 206 but still underneath Wall 743 is basket 200, containing very few diagnostic sherds. A fragment of an incised baking tray (fig. 6.4.17) originates in this context, alongside the handle of an Iron II Phoenician storage jar (fig. 6.4.16).

The finds associated with Wall 743 originate from five pottery baskets; their ceramics will be presented together here. Bowls are represented by a variety of shapes and sizes: small bowls with incurved, upturned, everted, and direct rims (fig. 6.5.1–9); and several bases may be from bowl or jug forms (fig. 6.5.10–13). Chalices are represented by two fragmentary examples with high stems (fig. 6.5.14–15), and kraters by a fragment of a type with a thickened, rounded rim (fig. 6.5.16), and a carinated example with a bevelled rim (fig. 6.5.17). Cooking pots include examples with a variety of rim types, with and without handles (fig. 6.5.18–22). Storage jars are represented by several rim types (fig. 6.6.1–11), and the carinated shoulder and vertical loop handle of another piece (fig. 6.6.12). Three rim fragments appear to be from holemouth jars (fig. 6.6.13–15). Jugs and juglets include the base of a typical Iron II juglet (fig. 6.6.16), and the rim fragment of a jug whose handle has painted decoration with one vertical stripe and six perpendicular, parallel stripes (fig. 6.6.17). One fragment of a lamp was found in basket 190 (fig. 6.6.18). Several typical Phoenician forms come from this context, which may or may not be locally manufactured (193/1 appears to be made from a non-local fabric, fig. 6.6.19, and 177/1; fig. 6.6.20), as well as fragments of Cypriot wares (fig. 6.6.21–24).

Square O/1: The pottery repertoire of square O/1 is rich in diagnostic ceramics from the Iron II period. We will present the pottery from this square by pottery basket, from stratigraphically earliest to the latest (fig. 2.39), which represent the ceramics from over .80 m of accumulation from the destruction of the building. This may provide clues to the existence of an upper story and feasibly the type of room activities within the structure.

The stratigraphically lowest materials came from baskets 354 and 336, which were separated by Wall 831 and may have been associated with floor levels in the building on either side of this wall. Pottery basket 354 contained an almost complete Phoenician monochrome pilgrim flask, decorated with a cream-colored slip (barely preserved) and concentric circles painted in red (fig. 6.7.1). Basket 336 had a wide variety of vessel forms, although none was complete. Open vessels include small and large bowls with a variety of rim types (fig. 6.7.2–7), one of which is decorated with red slip on its interior and exterior and is burnished (fig. 6.7.8). Two bases, one ring base and one flat, may be from bowl or jug forms (fig. 6.7.9–10). The basket included a fragment of an upright rim from a carinated krater (fig. 6.7.11). Fragments of several large handmade vats or tubs were also found, with different rim forms and two different types of base (fig. 6.8.1–5). One of these fragments is of a base (fig. 6.8.5), which had part of a hole preserved at the edge of the sherd made before firing; the hole is very close to the lowest part of the vessel and tilted downward, likely for drainage. These vats or tubs may indicate some sort of industrial use of the building or suggest household industry, although there were no wear patterns or staining to indicate for what purpose the large vessels were used. Only one cooking pot fragment came from this basket, with an upright pendent-shaped rim (fig. 6.8.6). Closed vessels are represented by several forms of upright rims of storage jars (fig. 6.8.7–10), one example of a direct rim (fig. 6.8.11), and a fragment that preserves the carinated shoulder of the vessel and its ovoid loop handle (fig. 6.8.12). Two fragments of holemouth jars with flared rims are preserved (fig. 6.9.1–6.9.2). A handle fragment (fig. 6.9.3), with remnants of a dark brown painted stripe at its base, appears to be from a jug; while a rim fragment (fig. 6.9.4) is from the pouring spout of a jug or juglet. Three fragments of Phoenician pottery (perhaps four if you include the already mentioned red slipped and burnished bowl, 336/16; fig. 6.7.8), the depressed ring base of a red slipped jug (fig. 6.9.5), a fragment of a highly burnished, or polished, jug strainer spout (fig. 6.9.6), and the ridged neck of a jug decorated with red slip and burnish and a black stripe (fig. 6.9.7), come from this context alongside a Cypriot Black-on-Red Ware small bowl fragment (fig. 6.9.8).

Pottery baskets 330 and 319 represent the next level in our sequence. Open forms include two small bowls, one of which has an interior decorated with painted stripes (fig. 6.9.9–10). One ring base, decorated on the exterior of the vessel with dark brown slip, may have belonged to a bowl (fig. 6.9.11). One well-preserved chalice with a high trumpet stem and a shallow bowl with a slightly flared rim came from basket 330 (fig. 6.9.12). Krater forms include two examples with upright rounded rims (fig. 6.9.13–14), one of which has its exterior covered in a cream-colored slip; a third krater with a thickened, rounded rim (fig. 6.9.15); and a very large vessel with an everted rim, covered in a cream-colored slip on its interior and exterior (fig. 6.9.16). Only one cooking pot fragment was found in the two baskets, 330/8; the vessel has an unusual upright triangular rim (fig. 6.9.17). Closed vessels include storage jars, represented by varying upright rim types (fig. 6.10.1–5). Holemouth jar forms include two examples with relatively straight walls and upright rounded and tapered rims (fig. 6.10.6–7). One pinch-mouthed jug, with a vertical handle attached at the rim, covered in a cream-colored slip, was uncovered (fig. 6.10.8), along with a depressed ring base likely from the same vessel (fig. 6.10.9). A handle painted with horizontal red stripes was from a jug (fig. 6.10.10). Juglets include several types: one with a globular body, direct rim, and vertical loop handle attached from the lip of the vessel to the shoulder (fig. 6.10.11); an ovoid body (fig. 6.10.12); and a cylindrical body with a rounded base (fig. 6.10.13). One body fragment of a Phoenician vessel was uncovered (fig. 6.10.14), decorated with the typical red stripe and burnished to a fine polish; and one possible Cypriot vessel (fig. 6.10.15) is represented by the neck and partial handle of a jug whose well-levigated tan-colored fabric appears to be from Cyprus.

Above baskets 319 and 330 was pottery basket 300. This basket had a wide variety of bowl forms, including small and large bowls, and ones with painted and incised decoration (fig. 6.11.1–8). Of special note are the bowls with incised grooves around their rims (fig. 6.11.5–6): the decoration and vessel form of 300/5 is a hallmark of southern Palestine (fig. 6.11.5); while the fabric of 300/6 is Egyptian (fig. 6.11.6), with a good parallel for this imported bowl found in Beersheba Stratum II (Singer-Avitz 1999: 44–46, fig. 13.1–2). The small bowl with an everted rim decorated with a cream slip on its exterior and red and dark brown stripes (fig. 6.11.9) is unusual. There are possible parallels at Keisan; however, the form and matt decoration stands out from the typical Phoenician-style painted bowls (fig. 6.11.3, 7), and may be an import from outside the region (Syria?). A more typical Phoenician vessel is the shallow bowl with wide everted rim, covered on its interior and exterior with a tan slip and highly burnished (6.11.8). A ring base, likely from a bowl, was also uncovered in basket 300 (fig. 6.11.10). The stem of a chalice, with red slip and burnished outside and some red slip on its inside (fig. 6.11.11) was found, along with the upright, rounded and thickened, rims of two kraters (fig. 6.11.12–13). One cooking pot (fig. 6.11.14), with an upright triangular rim, was uncovered. Closed vessels include several storage jar rim fragments (fig. 6.11.15–16) and a vertical loop handle that preserves a small part of the gentle carination of the shoulder of the vessel (fig. 6.11.17). A body sherd, painted with brown and red stripes, is from a jug (fig. 6.11.18); and a cylindrical body, with pointed base, is from a juglet (fig. 6.11.19). A small fragment of the spout of a lamp was found, highly pinched and showing smudges from its use (fig. 6.11.20). Imports include a large body sherd of a nicely decorated Cypriot Black-on-Red bowl with the bottom of one of its horizontal loop handles preserved (fig. 6.11.21), and the upright rounded rim of a large pithos with a cream-colored slip on its interior and exterior that may be East Greek (fig. 6.11.22) (Niemeier and Niemeier 2002: 235–37, 239) or Cypriot.

Basket 297 was excavated above 300. Its open forms are represented by the upright triangular rims of handleless cooking pots (fig. 6.11.1–2). Closed vessels include a vertical loop handle of a storage jar with a small indicator of its carinated shoulder (fig. 6.12.3), the direct rim of a Phoenician red slipped and polished jug (fig. 6.12.4), and the neck of a jug with a remnant of a vertical loop handle beginning at the base of the neck (fig. 6.12.5), whose well-levigated tan fabric appears non-local to Akko. Special items include remnants of a cup-and-saucer (fig. 6.12.6) and two jar stoppers (fig. 6.12.7–8). Imports are represented by a body sherd from a Cypriot jar, decorated with a cream-colored slip on its outside and dark brown stripes (fig. 6.12.9).

The next level above basket 297 is comprised of pottery baskets 281 and 292. Bowl forms are quite varied: small bowls include a rounded bowl, decorated on its inside and outside with red slip (fig. 6.13.1), a shallow bowl with an upright rim decorated with dark brown painted stripes with a burnished interior (fig. 6.13.2), a simple direct rim of a red-slipped and burnished bowl (fig. 6.13.3), a fragment of a pendent rim of a typical Phoenician bowl form decorated with red slip on its interior and the exterior of its lip (fig. 6.13.4), and a body sherd from a highly polished Phoenician bowl with red-striped decoration, of the so called "Samaria Ware" (fig. 6.13.5). Larger bowls include forms with varying rim types, carinations, and decorations with painted stripes or red slip (fig. 6.13.7–10). Two disk bases may be from bowl forms (fig. 6.13.11–12). Two shallow bowls with flared rims are likely the bowls of chalices (fig. 6.13.13–14). There are also remnants of the stems of a plain and a red slipped and polished chalice (fig. 6.13.15–16). Only one krater was found in this level (fig. 6.13.6). Cooking pot forms are varied in rim form, size, and even fabric as several examples have unusual crystalline inclusions. Significantly, all the cooking pot types lack handles (fig. 6.14.1–4, 6) except for one rim fragment with a possible, although questionable, stub from the base of a handle (fig. 6.14.5). One baking tray fragment was uncovered with typical incised ridges (fig. 6.14.7). Storage jars are represented by two rim fragments, one an upright rim vessel with an unusual groove on its interior (fig. 6.14.8, 6.14.11), and by the vertical loop handles and carinated shoulders of two other jars (fig. 6.14.9–10). The rim of a jar was uncovered (fig. 6.14.12), as well as the rim of the cup from a three-handled jar with a cup-like spout attached to hold a dipper juglet, also called a pillar-handled jar (fig. 6.14.13). Jug remnants include a flared rim fragment (fig. 6.14.14) and the neck and globular body of a Phoenician type, decorated with a pink-colored slip and burnished, with traces of a dark brown painted circle, presumably from a design of concentric circles, and a vertical handle stretching from its neck to its shoulder with a central depression (fig. 6.14.15). Juglets are represented by a cylindrical body with a pointed base (fig. 6.14.16), and the high loop handle and flared rim of a Phoenician type (fig. 6.14.17). One fragment of the tubular neck and handles of a red slipped pilgrim flask was uncovered (fig. 6.14.18), along with one small fragment of a lamp (fig. 6.14.19). Two ceramic jar stoppers were found (fig. 6.14.20–21). Imports include a body sherd and ring base from Cypriot Black-on-Red bowls (fig. 6.14.22–23), the upright rim of a large pithos (fig. 6.14.24), a body fragment from a "Samaria Ware" or Phoenician fine ware bowl (fig. 6.36.1), and the base from a Phoenician red-slipped and polished lid, or cover, decorated with horizontal, dark brown painted stripes (fig. 6.14.25).

The uppermost basket in our Stratum 4 sequence from Square O/1 is pottery basket 279. Open vessels are varied, including a wide range of bowl types: undecorated types (fig. 6.15.1–3); a plain bowl of a Phoenician type with everted rim (fig. 6.15.4); and bowls of varying types decorated in varying manners with red slip and burnish of a fabric type which is foreign to Akko (fig. 6.15.5–7), including the particular Phoenician hallmark shape with a pendent rim (fig. 6.15.8). Bowl 279/8 may have been a part of a chalice; its rim is decorated with a red painted stripe and shows evidence of smudges that suggest that it may have been used in the burning of incense or as a lamp (fig. 6.15.9). One large, plain bowl (279/7), with an upright rounded rim, was used in cooking as its fabric is typical for cooking pots and there were smudges preserved from a fire on the outside of the vessel (fig. 6.15.10). Other, more traditional, cooking pots include examples of a variety of rim fragments from handleless pots (fig. 6.15.11–16). Closed vessels are represented by the incurved rim fragment of a storage jar (fig. 6.15.17); the vertical loop handle fragment of a jar, decorated with three parallel red stripes on the top part of the handle, whose fabric appears foreign to Akko (fig. 6.15.18); and the neck and handle stubs of a small pilgrim flask of typical Phoenician shape (fig. 6.15.19). Two ceramic jar stoppers were also discovered (fig. 6.15.20–21), along with fragments of Cypriot imported vessels, including fragments of Black-on-Red bowls (fig. 6.15.22–23) and a Cypriot Bichrome Ware painted sherd from the neck of a pithos (fig. 6.15.24).

Iron I–II pottery from later or mixed contexts: The following is a discussion of Iron Age pottery from later or mixed contexts which includes types not already presented from better stratified contexts and a broader spectrum of pottery forms representative of earlier and later traditions than the majority of the materials defining Stratum 4, that is late Iron IIA–early Iron IIB pottery.

We are including earlier Iron IB and later Iron IIB–IIC forms in this discussion as very little Iron Age material has otherwise been published from Akko (M. Dothan 1976: fig. 15, 17.13–14, 17.16, 24; Conrad 1993). We will not categorize this material by period but will present this broad sweep of Iron Age pottery by type.

A small carinated bowl with an everted rim (fig. 6.16.1), and several examples of bar-handled bowls were uncovered (fig. 6.16.2–3), one of which was decorated with a red slip and patterned hand burnishing (fig. 6.16.4). Other bowl types decorated with red slip and burnish or painted stripes are Phoenician and local forms (fig. 6.16.5–13), including two fragments from "Samaria Ware" Phoenician bowls (fig. 6.16.14–15). Krater forms include a vessel with a globular body and a rectangular upright rim, whose high fired ware appears to be non-local (fig. 6.16.16); a shallow carinated krater with a flanged rim and a vertical loop handle from its lip to its carination (fig. 6.16.17); and a straight-walled krater with an everted rim, decorated on its exterior and top of its rim with red slip and burnish (fig. 6.16.18).

Several types of Phoenician storage jars were uncovered in mixed baskets which were not represented among stratified finds: one with a bag-shaped body, pinched waist, and vertical loop handle from its shoulder to waist (fig. 6.16.19), and two examples with upright ridged rims (fig. 6.16.20–21). Jug forms are varied: only one example was uncovered with an upturned rim and globular body with vertical loop handle attached from the neck to the shoulder of the vessel, typical of the Iron II (fig. 6.17.1); several fragments of monochrome and bichrome decorated strainer jugs (fig. 6.17.2–4); Phoenician-type jugs include the globular body of a jug decorated with bichrome horizontal stripes (fig. 6.17.5), and the rim from a red slipped and polished mushroom lipped jug (fig. 6.17.6). Two small pilgrim flasks were found in later contexts, one with concentric dark brown stripes (fig. 6.17.7) similar to vessels already detailed in examples discussed above, and another covered in red slip and burnished (fig. 6.17.8), a decorative technique not yet detailed for pilgrim flasks.

Imports from unstratified or mixed contexts are from Cyprus and East Greece. The majority of Cypriot imports are from the family of Black-on-Red pottery, as already indicated from stratified remains. Forms from later contexts include a variety of bowl forms, and several bowl fragments (figs. 6.17.9–6.18.1); as well as juglet fragments, including a body sherd, a trefoil spout, and a flared-rim mouth (fig. 6.18.2–4). Other Cypriot imports include a White Painted I Bell Shaped bowl with a horizontal loop handle, decorated both inside and outside with broad dark brown stripes painted over a cream-colored slip (fig. 6.18.5); the shoulder of a jar with horizontal parallel stripes painted in dark brown (fig. 6.18.6); and a fragment of the neck of a Cypriot pithos or large jar covered with a tan slip and painted with vertical stripes around cross hatched pendants and one squiggly line in dark brown paint (fig. 6.18.7). Four fragments of East Greek bowls were found in mixed contexts: two simple bowls, one covered inside and out with a metallic black slip and burnish (fig. 6.18.8), the other is slipped and burnished on its inside with metallic black and decorated on its burnished buff exterior with black painted vertical lines and a pendent motif (fig. 6.18.9); two Ionian cups, one with a flared rim, straight walls, and the stub of a horizontal handle, covered inside and out with a metallic black slip (fig. 6.18.10), and another with an upright rim, carinated body, stub of a horizontal handle, metallic black slip and burnish on the inside, with black and buff (the color of the fabric) horizontal stripes on its exterior and lip (fig. 6.18.11).

Stratum 4 Typology

Despite the fact that the Iron II stratigraphic exposure in Area H was quite limited, the variety of ceramic remains is rich. Nearby sites, such as Tell Keisan, Horbat Rosh Zayit, and the anchorage at Tell Abu Hawam provide the best comparative evidence (Aznar 1996; Briend and Humbert 1980; Gal and Alexandre 2000; Herrera and Gomez 2004). There is no question that the closest comparables are those from the anchorage site of Tell Abu Hawam, which renewed its extensive maritime contacts during the Iron II, as was noted in finds from Hamilton's Stratum III. Iron II Tell Abu Hawam includes many forms of imported, especially Cypriot, ceramics. Tel Mevorakh provides further parallels,[1] as do the pottery studies from Tyre (Bikai 1978), Sarepta (Anderson 1988), Tel Qiri (Hunt 1987), and Tel Qasile (Mazar 1985). We have utilized Amiran's typology as a convenient summary of earlier excavated sites, especially the Iron II ceramics from Megiddo and Hazor (1969).[2] We have consulted Gitin's work on Iron II and later pottery from Gezer (1990), Mazar and Panitz-Cohen's study on the Iron II ceramics from Tel Batash (2001), and Ortiz's work on Stratum IV ceramics from Tel Miqne and the Aijalon Valley region (2000). In general, however, there are few parallels with ceramic types

---

1 At the time of research, the important work on the ceramics of Iron II Yoqne'am was unavailable to the authors. For a robust Iron IIA–IIB transitional sequence see Zarzecki-Peleg et al. 2005.
2 Unfortunately, it was too late in the preparation of this volume to add material from the 2015 publication of the *Pottery of Israel and its Neighbors* edited by Semour Gitin. In it, the Iron Age II period is well represented in the chapters by A. Gilboa (2015) and G. Lehmann (2015), which deal with ceramics from the northern and Carmel Coasts as well as the northern Coastal Plain, and provide numerous comparisons for our materials.

from southern Palestine. This supports Amiran's general separation between northern and southern Iron Age ceramics developed decades ago. To it should be added ceramics from coastal sites and their hinterland, which have their own distinctions from inland, contemporary sites.

Bowls

Pointed rim bowls: The small, carinated bowl type is well represented in Area H's Stratum 4 ceramic repertoire with seven examples of slightly varying sizes. The rims are simple and taper to a rounded point. The stance of the rim can be slightly turned out as in our first three examples (fig. 6.19.1–3), or upright as in the next four vessels (fig. 6.19.4–7). The bodies of this bowl type are shallow, and the carination is gradual ending in a short upper wall. No bases are preserved, but comparative evidence suggests these bowls would have had ring bases. One vessel (fig. 6.19.1) is decorated with a red painted stripe along the inside of its lip, which extends over the top of the rim to the exterior of the bowl.

At Sarepta, a broader group of small bowls with a "simple, or slightly thickened, upturned rim," bowl type X-28, characterizes this form (Anderson 1988: 160). It is phased in Area II,Y between Stratum G2–D1, or the LB IIB–Iron IIB (Anderson 1988: 423, 471); however, the overwhelming majority are found clustered between Stratum E–D2, or the Iron IB–Iron IIA. Amiran includes pointed rim bowls as one of her Iron IIA–IIB forms lumped in a wider category of carinated bowls from the northern part of the region of Palestine (1969: 195). These carinated bowls have a variety of rim types and are grouped together by Amiran by the shape of their bodies. At Tel Qiri, this bowl type occurs infrequently enough to be included in a larger category of "bowl varia," which means it was not found in significant numbers at the site (Hunt 1987: 191, fig. 38.4). The type is part of the Bowl BIII category, "medium bowls with simple rim," from Horbat Rosh Zayit's Strata IIb–IIa (Iron IIA–IIB), where it is noted that the pointed, simple rim is a frequent variation of the more inclusive type (Gal and Alexandre 2000: 36). At Keisan, pointed rim bowls are found in Levels 11–4, or the Iron I–IIC phases at the site (Briend and Humbert 1980: pl. 30.6, 6a; 35.8; 41.11, 11a; 52.6, 8; 55.9, 9a–c; 80.3, 3a; 81.16, 16a; table 6.1).

Incurved rim bowls: This bowl form is well represented in Stratum 4 with seven examples (fig. 6.19.8–14). All have a simple rim, incurved from the body of the vessel, and shallow, hemispherical bodies. None of our examples have their base preserved, though comparable bowls have disk bases. Six of our bowls are small in size, with little variance; however, the seventh bowl (fig. 6.19.14) is much larger and deeper.

Comparisons are best found at Sarepta, where Anderson defines this type as bowl X-29 (1988: 161). The form is quite common, with a range from Stratum G1–B, or the LB IIB–Persian period (Anderson 1988: 423, 471; table 6.1). The type also has parallels at Tell Keisan, where it appears in Level 9 and 7, or the Iron IB to IIA–IIB (Briend and Humbert 1980: pl. 51.10; 66.4b, 4d).

Rounded bowls: This type of simple bowl ranges in size and decoration among the six examples from Area H Stratum 4 (fig. 6.19.15–20). All of the bowls have simple, rounded rims that are mostly upright or slightly incurved from the rounded curve of the vessel's body. No bases are preserved. Decoration is varied, with one bowl covered on its interior and exterior with red slip (fig. 6.19.15), another with a cream-colored slip (279/9; 6.19.17), and a third with red horizontal stripes on the inside and outside of the bowl (fig. 6.19.19).

Parallels abound, as Amiran lists this type of rounded bowl as "one of the commonest forms" for Iron IIA–IIB bowls in the north of Palestine (1969: 195; table 6.1). The examples she illustrates are from Hazor Stratum VIII–IX (Amiran 1969: pl. 62.12–15). Rounded bowls at Tel Qiri, Hunt's Type BIa:Simple or BIIa:Simple, are more common in Iron I levels and begin to taper off in number from the Iron IIA onward (1987: 191). These are the same periods that they appear in at Tell Keisan, where the rounded bowl type is found in Levels 9c–4, or the Iron I–IIC (Briend and Humbert 1980: pl. 29.10; 30.5, 41.9; 52.2; 66.4; 79.14). At Tyre the form, Bikai's Plate (bowl) 11, is found in every phase at the site, but flourishes in Stratum XIII-2 through VII or the Iron IIA–IIC (1978: 24–25).

Straight sided bowls: There are four examples of this bowl type from Stratum 4 in Area H (fig. 6.19.21–6.19.24). All have simple rims that are almost straight extensions from the walls of the body of each vessel. One vessel has a disk base (fig. 6.19.24), this form is also known to have ring bases (Amiran 1969: 195).

As Amiran notes, this vessel type is not very widely spread but is found at several sites in the northern region of Palestine in their Iron IIA–IIB phases (1969: 165). Parallels are best represented at the coastal sites of Sarepta, Tyre, and Tell Abu Hawam. At Sarepta, the form is defined as bowl type X-11, "direct rim with triangular-shaped exterior thickening" (Anderson 1988: 150). Bowl X-11 appears in Stratum E–B, Iron IB–Persian period, with a majority concentrated in Stratum D1–C1, or the Iron IIA–IIC (Anderson 1988: 423, 470; table 6.1). At Tyre, the type corresponds to Bikai's Plate (bowl) 8, which has a range from Stratum XI–I, or the Iron IIB–IIC (1978: 21, 23–24).

Grooved rim bowls: Two bowl fragments with grooved rims were found in the same pottery basket in Area H. One is a small round bowl with an upright pointed rim, grooved on its exterior. The vessel is covered inside and out with red wash (fig. 6.20.1). Our second example is a larger round bowl with a slightly incurved flat rim with three grooves on its exterior (fig. 6.20.2). Though only a small rim fragment is preserved, it likely originates from a deep bowl as is indicated by the stance of the sherd, and by a comparable vessel from Tell es-Safi (Maeir 2001: pl. 6.11).

This bowl type is typically found in Iron IIA–B levels at sites in the southern part of the region (Amiran 1969: 199; table 6.1). At Tel Qasile the form is defined as bowl Type BL5 and is found in Stratum XI–X, or the Iron IB levels at the site (Mazar 1985: 38). The example from Qasile Stratum XI is a direct parallel to our 300/6, including the decorative use of red slip, although the bowl at Qasile had one line of burnishing (Mazar 1985: fig. 22.2). Further parallels are found in Beersheba Stratum II, and were made from Nile silt clay originating in Egypt (Singer-Avitz 1999: 44–46, fig. 13.1–2). Although not analyzed, the fragment from Tel Akko's Area H has a red-colored ware (fig. 6.20.1), which suggests that it too is an Egyptian import. This is not surprising given parallels from Dor, which is a center of Egyptian imports in the Iron II period (Waiman-Barak et al. 2014). Two examples of grooved rim bowls have been found at Tell Abu Hawam Stratum III, or the Iron IIA period at the site (Aznar 1996: 18, fig. 3.39–40).

Everted horizontal rim bowls: Several small, shallow bowls form a group because of their distinct everted horizontal rims (fig. 6.20.3–8). The exact form of the rim varies slightly with each example, from the simply rounded (fig. 6.20.3), to slightly thickened (fig. 6.20.4), to one with an interior ridge (fig. 6.20.5), and others which are more angular in profile (fig. 6.20.6, 8). None of our Akko examples has its base preserved, and comparative evidence shows a variety of types from a low ring or disk base to a flat base (Anderson 1988: 147).

At Sarepta, Anderson subdivides this bowl type into several different forms based on the specifics of the rim shape (1988: 143). Those from Akko would fit the categories of bowl types X-1, X-4, and X-5, all three of which have fairly similar distributions from Stratum D2/D1–B, or the Iron IIA–Persian period (Anderson 1988: 143–44, 146–47, 423, 470; table 6.1). The same form at Tyre, Bikai's Plate 2, has a shorter life as it is found in Stratum IV–I, or the Iron IIC phases at the site (1978: 22). Hunt notes that this bowl type, his bowl BIVb:plate, is rare at Tel Qiri (1987: 191). He relates that the type is well represented, however, from the mid-Iron II forward in the Iron Age pottery repertoire at neighboring Yoqne'am. At Keisan, everted horizontal rim bowls seem limited to Level 5, an Iron IIC phase at the site (Chambon 1980: 166–68). Given the form's presence primarily at coastal sites in northern Palestine and Lebanon, as well as at sites as far afield as Tarsus in Cilicia and Trayamar in Spain, it is fair to call this a Phoenician bowl type (Chambon 1980: 166–68). Concluding whether or not they were locally made or imported from the Lebanese coast requires scientific sourcing, using provenience studies; however, the fabric appears to the eye to be local in all instances.

Painted bowls with flared rim: One example of this rare bowl type was uncovered in Stratum 4 (fig. 6.20.9). The flared rim is fairly flat on top and triangular in profile. The bowl is small, and has a deep semi-circular body. The base is missing. Most notable is the matt-painted decoration on the exterior of the vessel, which was first covered in a cream-colored slip and then painted with broad red horizontal stripes alternating with three thin parallel dark brown stripes.

The only comparisons we have been able to find are from Tell Keisan. Chambon places his examples in the category of Phoenician painted pottery, but admits that this painted bowl type is extremely rare (1980: 171, pl. 42:2). We have not succeeded in finding any parallels in the standard publications from Phoenician sites or of Phoenician pottery, so perhaps this rare bowl type is limited to the Akko Plain? The two examples which were found in stratified contexts at Tell Keisan were from Level 5, a phase from the Iron IIC at the site (Chambon 1980: 171; table 6.1). At Akko, our example was found together with Cypriot Black-on-Red wares that would suggest an earlier date than the comparable bowls at Keisan.

Medium sized bowls with bichrome decoration: Several bowls with flaring and upright rims have been grouped together because of their decoration, despite the variation in their overall shape or stance (fig. 6.20.10–14). Two are carinated bowls with flared rims, and red and cream or red and black horizontal stripes on their lips and the interiors of the vessel (fig. 6.20.10–11). Another example is also a carinated vessel, but one with an upright, slightly thickened rim (fig. 6.20.12). It is decorated with a cream-colored slip on its exterior, and a band of black and red at the carination inside of the vessel. No bases are preserved.

This group of bichrome decorated bowls has been noted as an Iron IIA–B type from Phoenician and northern Palestinian sites by Amiran, with the exact origin left open to this greater region at large (1969: 209–211). Further studies seem to confirm these observations in general, with Anderson noting the majority of bichrome decorated bowls appearing in Stratum D at Sarepta, or the Iron IIA–B (1988: 325). At Rosh Zayit, bichrome bowls are concentrated in Stratum IIb, one of the Iron IIA phases at the site (Gal and Alexandre 2000: 38). At Tell Keisan the type is most prevalent in Level 7, Iron IIA–B, although it is also found in Levels 4 and 5, Iron IIC (Briend and Humbert 1980: pl. 30.10; 41.14–16; 53.1, 4–7; table 6.1). Hunt notes that bichrome wares in general are rare at Tel Qiri and Yoqneʻam (1987: 201). Further examples of bichrome bowls from Tel Akko have been published from Area A, which suggests that the type is both more varied and more common than our sample from Area H (M. Dothan 1976: 23). A visual examination of the fabric of the examples from Area H would suggest that these bowls were locally manufactured.

Bar handled bowls: Three bowls with varying rim types are categorized together because of their shared common feature of the horizontal bar handle. One bowl has a flared rim and a shallow, carinated body (fig. 6.20.15). A second example has an upright rim, high carination, and semi-hemispherical body (fig. 6.20.17). It is covered both inside and out with red slip and hand burnished. The final example has an incurved rim on a carinated body, and a much larger handle than our other two (fig. 6.20.16).

Since none of our examples were found in stratified contexts in Area H, comparative phasing with other sites is not warranted; nonetheless, they do appear at coastal sites, such as Tell Abu Hawam (Herrera and Gomez 2004: 298). Given the punctuated sequence in Area H, it seems likely that they would have originated in a Stratum 4 context.

Fine ware bowls of various types: We have grouped together several varying bowl types because of a similarity of surface treatment, decoration, fineness of their walls, and skill of manufacture (fig. 6.21.1–9). The unifying surface treatment and decoration is a red slip that is highly burnished, some examples are so well burnished they appear polished. The superior quality of manufacture is seen not only in the burnished decoration, but also in the thin walls of these vessels, the artistry of their production, and their firing at a high temperature. Vessel types include a small bowl with a simple incurved rim with tapered lip (fig. 6.21.1); a shallow bowl with a direct rim (fig. 6.21.2); a small globular bowl with flared rim and tapered lip (fig. 6.21.3); a small carinated bowl with externally thickened direct rim (fig. 6.21.4); two examples of pendent rim bowls with tapered lips (fig. 6.21.5–6); a larger bowl with upturned rim with T-shaped thickening (fig. 6.21.8); and a bowl with a flared rim and tapered lip (fig. 6.21.9). In addition to the red slip and burnish, 138/15 has four horizontal red painted stripes on its shoulder and 279/14 has a dark brown stripe on the edge of its lip (fig. 6.21.3, 9). A visual inspection of the ceramic wares suggests that 279/12–14 are not made from local clays (fig. 6.21.4, 8–9).

The variety of shapes in this group of bowls is mirrored by the variety of terminology used in the typology of the individual bowl forms. Sometimes the same type will be placed under the heading "Phoenician," "Samaria Ware," "fine ware," or "local ware," depending on the excavation report or typological study. The note of caution that Amiran applied to the definition of a "Phoenician" group of pottery in many ways still rings true decades after her study was translated into English, despite the fact that since then we have the publication of ceramic sequences from the heartland of Phoenicia at Tyre, Sarepta, and Beirut (Amiran 1969: 272). At Tyre the vast majority of these decorated fine ware bowls "appear suddenly" in Stratum V–IV, which dates to the early part of the Iron IIC (Bikai 1978: 26). At Sarepta the decorative technique has a longer life, being found on fine ware bowls from Stratum G–B, or the LB IIB–Persian period (Anderson 1988: 344–46; table 6.1). The heyday of red slipped and burnished bowls, however, is Stratum D1–C, or the Iron IIB–IIC. Probably the best group for comparisons comes from the variety of red slipped and burnished bowls at Tel Mevorakh in Stratum VII, the Iron IIA (Stern 1978: fig. 12). There are parallels among these Iron IIA bowls from Mevorakh for all of the Akko examples except for 138/15 and 279/13 (fig. 6.21.3–4). In shape, 138/15 (fig. 6.21.3) has parallels in bowls found at Tell Keisan in Level 5, Iron IIC; however, their decoration scheme is different from our Akko example (Briend and Humbert 1980: pl. 42.2). No parallels were found for a small carinated bowl with externally thickened rim, 279/13 (fig. 6.21.4).

Deep bowls with incurved rims: Two examples of this bowl type were uncovered in Area H (fig. 6.21.10–11). Both rims exhibit a slight thickening and have squared off edges in profile. Both bowls have a very high carination. Neither one preserves any of the body of the bowl or its base.

At Sarepta, Anderson has defined this deep bowl type as DB-5, "incurved rim with interior-bevelled lip" (1988: 172). The form spans Stratum D2–C1, or the Iron IIA–IIC phases at the site (Anderson 1988: 423, 480; table 6.1). The type is also found in quantity at Tyre, where it is labeled Plate (bowl) 6 (Bikai 1978: 23). It is found in Tyre Stratum IV–II, all phases of the Iron IIC. At Rosh Zayit we have been able to find one parallel, which dates to Stratum IIa, or the early Iron IIB at the site (Gal and Alexandre 2000: fig. III.82.3).

Deep bowls with rim with T-shaped thickening: Both examples have rims with T-shaped thickening, slanted toward the interior of each vessel (fig. 6.21.12–13). One preserves a very high, very slight carination, and the majority of its semi-hemispherical body. Neither vessel preserves its base.

This deep bowl form, DB-1, has a long life at Sarepta (Anderson 1988: 170–71; table 6.1). It is found in Stratum E–B, or the Iron IB–Persian period, though it is most abundant in the phases of Stratum C, or the Iron IIB–IIC (Anderson 1988: 423, 481). At Rosh Zayit a parallel type with interior red slip and burnish is found in Stratum IIb, or the Iron IIA (Gal and Alexandre 2000: fig. III.77.2). At Tell Keisan the form appears to be limited to Level 5, one phase of the Iron IIC at the site (Briend and Humbert 1980: pl. 41.6).

Deep bowl with "cyma" profile and upright rim: One example of this deep bowl type was uncovered in Area H (fig. 6.21.14). The upright rim of the vessel is slightly thickened, and its carination is high. A red painted stripe covers the lip of the bowl, extending slightly to the interior and exterior of the vessel.

The best discussion of this bowl type, along with the best comparative material, is found in Mazar's treatment of the pottery from Tel Qasile (1985: 39–41). He defines the form alongside a smaller version of the same bowl type as bowl BL 8, thus it is difficult to judge if Mazar's conclusions can be applied to Akko as they may primarily refer to the smaller bowl form. The phasing of the larger "cyma" bowl is presented independently of the smaller vessels, and spans Stratum XII–IX, or the Iron IB–IIA (table 6.1). There are no good parallels at the sites we have been turning to for comparisons, which are situated primarily in the Akko Plain, Jezreel Valley, and Lebanese coast. This suggests that this deep bowl type might be a southern form.

Shallow carinated bowls of medium size: Four medium sized bowls have been categorized together because of the similarity in form and shallowness of their bodies (fig. 6.22.1–4). Otherwise there is variation in their flared rims. No bases are preserved. One example is decorated with a red wash on the exterior of the vessel (fig. 6.22.3).

Mazar has similarly grouped varied bowls from Tel Qasile in his Family D, flat bowl category (1985: 43). The best parallels are found at Rosh Zayit among the bowl type B1, "medium sized carinated bowls with flat thickened rims," which spans Stratum IIb–IIa, phases of the Iron IIA–IIB (Gal and Alexandre 2000: 34–35; table 6.1). This bowl form at Rosh Zayit is a combination of vessels with a variety of rim forms, wall thickness, and decoration, but is unified by size and overall similarity of their bodies. One direct parallel for our 292/6, is found at Rosh Zayit with bichrome stripes on its interior, and is thus categorized with other bichrome decorated bowls (Gal and Alexandre 2000: fig. III.79.9).

Bases: A wide variety of bases were uncovered in Area H's Stratum 4, which were likely from bowl forms (fig. 6.22.5–14). The group combines primarily ring and disk bases. From our examples from the numerous bowl forms already discussed above, only one vessel, 279/6 (fig. 6.15.1), was preserved from rim to base. Given the tendency for individual bowl types in this period with identical rims and body forms to have varying bases, it is not possible to attribute our bases to specific bowl types.

Chalices

Chalices with flared rim and stepped trumpet base: A number of chalice fragments of this type were discovered in Stratum 4, attesting to the relative popularity of the form (fig. 6.23.1–9). The best preserved example, 330/7 (fig. 6.23.1), has a flared rim, gentle high carination and shallow bowl on top of a stepped, trumpet base. The majority of the remaining fragments belong to this type of chalice, with variations in the bowl size, flare of the rim, and decorative red stripe on the lip of the vessel (fig. 6.23.2–9). It is possible that 281/2 is a bowl (fig. 6.23.7), and not the bowl of a chalice; this distinction is difficult to make without a whole form. Two of our examples, 158/2 and 158/3 (fig. 6.23.2, 4), are covered on their exteriors with a cream-colored slip; while two are red slipped and burnished, detailed below (fig. 6.23.8–9).

This chalice type has its origins in the Iron I or even earlier, in the LB IIB, and continues into the Iron IIA–B in both the north and south of the region (Amiran 1969: 213; table 6.1). It is the most common chalice form at Tel Qiri throughout the Iron Age (Hunt 1987: 198–99). At Qasile, the type, Type CH 2, is found in Stratum XI–IX, or the Iron IB–IIA (Mazar 1985: 48–49). The only decoration found on this chalice form at Qasile is a red stripe on the rim, like our example 279/8 (fig. 6.23.6). There are parallels in Iron IIA–IIB Stratum IIB–IIA at Rosh Zayit, despite the fact that chalices are rare at the site (Gal and Alexandre 2000: 39). It also appears at Tell Abu Hawam (Herrera and Gomez 2004: 299–300).

Red slipped and burnished or polished chalices: Two chalice fragments differ from those described above in their decoration. What remains are the stems of two chalices (fig. 6.23.8–9). Both pieces are covered in red slip; 300/19 is burnished (fig. 6.23.8), 281/11 is so well burnished it is polished (fig. 6.23.9).

Normally we would consider the red slip and burnish, especially polishing, a Phoenician or Phoenicianizing decorative trait. We have not been able to find any parallels, however, at Iron Age sites in the Phoenician heartland in Lebanon. The chalices we did find, such as one from Tyre and a group from Phoenician tombs, are all undecorated (Bikai 1978: pl. XXXI.14; Chapman 1972: fig. 22.220–222). This is true for an example from a Phoenician shipwreck of the 8th century BCE as well (Ballard et al. 2002: fig. 9.2). At closer sites in the Jezreel valley, namely Megiddo Stratum VA–IV and Tel Qiri, chalices are decorated with red slip and red and black paint but none seem to be burnished (Loud 1948: pl. 90.8, 91.12; Hunt 1987: 198–99). Red slipped and burnished decoration is popular on chalices from Stratum III at Tel Batash, which dates to the Iron IIB (Mazar and Panitz-Cohen 2001: 56; table 6.1).

Kraters

Carinated kraters with flanged rim: Two examples of this krater type were uncovered in Stratum 4, and one was found mixed with material in a later phase (fig. 6.23.10–12). All three fragments have a flanged rim; two preserve a high carination, and indications of a large bowl of varying depth. Our piece from a later context also has the typical loop handle, attached from the rim of the vessel to the carination, with a slight angle to the handle's verticality. The one highly fragmentary piece, 201/3, is covered on its exterior with a cream-colored slip (fig. 6.23.11).

This krater form is similar to Amiran's Iron IIA–B krater type 4, out of the six types she categorizes for northern kraters of this period (1969: 217–19).

Type 4 kraters are related to Amiran's Type 1, "kraters with pronounced carinations," but are marked by a distinctive "forked" (flanged) rim. The example that Amiran illustrates is from Hazor Stratum VIII, an Iron IIB phase at the site (1969: pl. 71:5). Parallels are found among Mazar's krater Type KR 1, "carinated krater with two loop handles," at Tel Qasile (1985: 45). This form, which spans Stratum XII–VIII, or the Iron IB–IIC, is defined by its body shape and handles and incorporates vessels with rims that are everted or flat on top, as well as flanged (Mazar 1985: 45; table 6.1). Tell Keisan has comparable vessels in Level 4–5, the Iron IIC phases at the site (Briend and Humbert 1980: pl. 28.12; 33.1, 45.4).

Carinated kraters with bevelled rim: Two small rim fragments represent this vessel type, which makes discerning details difficult (fig. 6.23.13–14). Both rims are bevelled toward the interior of the vessel. One is decorated with red paint on its exterior from the carination downward (fig. 6.23.14).

These kraters belong in a very general sense to Amiran's krater type 6, "kraters without handles," from the Iron IIA–B north (1969: 217). The best parallels come from Tel Qiri, where Hunt places similar forms in his krater "Group Va: simple rim" (1987: 195). This type is rare, and occurs in very small quantities in Strata IX, VIII, and VI/V, or the Iron IB and IIC levels at the site (table 6.1). Hunt notes that similar kraters are equally rare at Yoqne'am, except in the Iron IIA when they jump above five percent of the repertoire of kraters (Hunt 1987: 195).

Carinated kraters with simple upright rims: This vessel type is represented by four examples from Area H. Three have upright, slightly thickened simple rims, which vary slightly in the angle of their stance (fig. 6.24.1–3). These three vessels have short necks, one preserves a fairly sharp carination, and a medium sized body. Our largest example, 178/10, also has a slight variation of rim form, with the simple rim flaring slightly (fig. 6.24.4). Its neck is even shorter than the other three examples. None preserve their base.

This carinated krater form falls into Amiran's general category of Iron IIA–B northern kraters without handles (1969: 217). The particular type had gone out of use by the Iron IB at both Sarepta and Tel Qasile (Anderson 1988: 176; Mazar 1985: 47). It is still found at Tell Keisan in Level 6, however, which dates to the Iron IIA–B, suggesting that the form had a longer life in the Akko Plain than it did elsewhere (Briend and Humbert 1980: pl. 49.5; table 6.1).

Carinated kraters with thickened rounded rims: Four rim fragments of this form were found in Stratum 4 levels in Area H (fig. 6.24.5–8). They vary slightly in the thickness of the oval cross section of their upright rims; otherwise the vessels show a similarity in size. It is difficult to comment on other aspects of this form at Akko since the sherds are barely preserved below the rim.

The krater type is defined as CIIb:Oval b (concave) at Tel Qiri, and is part of a larger krater group II at the site (Hunt 1987: 194). Group II kraters dominate the repertoire of kraters at the site in all phases of the Iron Age. At Qasile the form is labeled subtype KR 3a, "krater with carinated body and thickened rim," and is found in Stratum XI–X, both phases of the Iron IB (Mazar 1985: 47). Similarly, at Tell Keisan the form is found in Level 9a–b, or the Iron IB (Briend and Humbert 1980: pl. 64.1, 6, 8). Several parallels are found at Rosh Zayit, where the type is called K II, "kraters with thickened rounded rims," and appears in Stratum IIb–IIa, or the Iron IIA–IIB (Gal and Alexandre 2000: 40; table 6.1).

Krater with a flared, thickened rim: One rim fragment of a very large vessel was discovered in Area H that we are defining as a krater (fig. 6.24.9). Since very little is preserved beyond the flared, thickened rim it is difficult to pinpoint the type, although the small projection on the interior of the rim may help.

Anderson defines his krater type K-9 as having a "flared, thickened rim with interior projection" (1988: 179–80). This form of krater has a long life at Sarepta, from Stratum L–D2, or the MB IIC–Iron IIA at the site (Anderson 1988: 422–23, 483; table 6.1). It is likely that our Akko example is part of this group of kraters. Further parallels are rare, though the type is found in Level 9c at Keisan, or the Iron IB (Briend and Humbert 1980: pl. 78.1).

Basins

We have chosen to include basins in our discussion of open form vessels since they are representative of a ceramic type and they are an open form. Generally, basins are placed in the "varia" section of pottery presentations, perhaps since their handmade forms vary. We have three different rim types on basins all found in the same context in Area H: one is folded out to form an externally thickened, rounded, flared rim (fig. 6.25.2); a second is a direct rim, which has a rounded profile, thickened by an additional layer of clay placed around the rim (fig. 6.25.3); and the third is folded over and inward to form an internally thickened rim which is flat on top and triangular in section (336/10; fig. 6.25.4). A fragment of a base from pottery basket 336/24 (fig. 6.25.1) matches with the rim fragment 336/9 (fig. 6.25.2); even though they do not join they are clearly made from the same fabric and are very likely from the same vessel. The basin has a hole in its side, almost at the base of the vessel, made before firing. Presumably this hole was used in draining a liquid from the basin. Another base fragment was found in pottery basket 336 /11 (fig. 6.25.5), which may have belonged to basin 336/8 (fig. 6.25.3).

Basins, and variations with an interior feature called "footbaths," are common at sites throughout Palestine in the Iron Age II. Basins from Tel Batash, where they are found in Stratum IV–II, Iron IIA–IIC, are discussed along with comparisons from Iron II levels at Ashdod, Hazor, and Samaria (Mazar and Panitz-Cohen 2001: 139; table 6.1). Basins are also found at Megiddo in Stratum IV–II, or the Iron IIB–IIC (Lamon and Shipton 1939: pl. 25.60; 26.81–82). The type does occur earlier at Tell Keisan, where basins are found in Level 9c, or the Iron IB (Briend and Humbert: pl. 73.12–13). Basins were also found at Sarepta in Lebanon, primarily in Stratum C, an Iron IIB–IIC phase at the site (Anderson 1988: 234). What exactly they were used for is not certain; it is suggested that basins at Tel Batash were used in "food preparation, or perhaps some other function such as laundry or a portable water trough for domestic animals" (Mazar and Panitz-Cohen 2001: 139).

Cooking Pots

Cooking pots with triangular pinched rims: This vessel type represents the majority of cooking wares in Stratum 4. The rims are upright and are shaped like a pinched triangle in profile (figs. 6.26–6.27). The necks of these vessels are generally upright or convex, and some examples preserve the carination of the body of the vessel. None of the rounded bases, known from comparative evidence, are preserved. Three of these vessels have thinner walls than the rest (fig. 6.27.6–8), and three others have shortened triangular pinched rims (fig. 6.27.9–11).

Amiran has noted that this cooking pot form is dominant at northern sites in the Iron IIA–B (1969: 227). Features which differentiate the type from Iron I predecessors include shorter rims and longer necks. She also notes that all Iron IIC cooking pot forms in the north have handles (Amiran 1969: 227). At Qiri, the type, CP Group II: Pinched, is the most frequent cooking pot form at the site and is found in almost equal amounts in all phases of the Iron I and II (Hunt 1987: 183; table 6.1). Unlike Amiran, Hunt does not differentiate among cooking pot types by neck length or presence/absence of handles, but bases his conclusions strictly on the rim type. Mazar defines the form at Qasile as Type CP 1b, "cooking pot with shallow, carinated body and elongated concave rim," (1985: 52). This type occurs in Qasile Stratum XII–VIII, or the Iron IB–IIA. At Rosh Zayit, the type is a subset of "cooking pots with triangular rim" CP 1 (Gal and Alexandre 2000: 40). It is noted that those with "pinched triangular rims" occur primarily in Stratum IIa, or the early Iron IIB. Further examples of this cooking pot type from Akko are found in Area A, Stratum 7 (M. Dothan 1976: 23).

Small cooking pot with upright triangular rim and bag-shaped body: Only one fragment of this vessel type was found in Stratum 4 in Area H (fig. 6.28.1). An upright, triangular rim, a short neck, and a bag-shaped body mark the type.

This type is rare at Tel Qiri, as it is at Akko, and is defined by Hunt as part of the cooking pot varia ("CP Varia, A: Triangular") (1987: fig. 34:6). A nice parallel is found in Stratum V Megiddo, although this vessel has handles (Lamon and Shipton 1939: pl. 40.21). At Tyre it is labeled cooking pot type Cp. 4, which spans Stratum XIII-2–IX, or the Iron IB–IIB (Bikai 1978: 50–51). At Sarepta the form is called CP-1, and is found in Stratum D2–B, the Iron IIA–Persian period (Anderson 1988: 221, 423, 500; table 6.1). The form seems much more common at sites along the Lebanese coast, and may be considered a Phoenician type.

Cooking pot with incurved rim with exterior thickening: Two rim fragments of this type were uncovered (fig. 6.28.2–3). Both have distinctly incurved rims with lips that are "turned slightly upwards," to borrow terminology from parallels at Sarepta (Anderson 1988: 226). Each example has a short neck, flared toward the exterior where it meets with the exterior thickening of the rim. One fragment preserves a vertical loop handle, which starts just below the lip and ends on the shoulder of the vessel (fig. 6.28.3). Neither vessel has its body or base preserved, but comparisons suggest that the form has a globular body and rounded base.

Parallels are rare. Similar types appear at Tell Abu Hawam Stratum III (Herrera and Gomez 2004: 305). At Tyre the form is CP 1, which is found in Stratum IV–II, both phases of the Iron IIC (Bikai 1978: 50–51, pl. XII.24). The type has a slightly longer life at Sarepta, where it is called CP-15B and spans Stratum D1–C1, or the Iron IIB–IIC (Anderson 1988: 226, 423, 501, pl. 33.15; table 6.1).

Cooking pot with inverted rim with exterior thickening: Two examples of this vessel type were uncovered in Area H. Both are rim fragments, with typical rounded triangular profiles, with their lip slightly inverted (fig. 6.28.4–5). Each has a long neck for a cooking pot, flared gently toward the interior of the vessel. 281/7 preserves its sharp carination and an indication of its hemispherical body below the carination; its base is not preserved (fig. 6.28.4).

Anderson includes this cooking pot form in his CP-15 group (1988: 266), along with the previous cooking pot type just described above. This subtype is labeled CP-15A, and is found in small quantities at Sarepta in Stratum D1–C1, or the Iron IIB–IIC levels in Area II,Y. We have separated the two types as distinct since their rims appear to be quite different stylistically. Parallels are also found in Level 5 at Tell Keisan, which dates to the Iron IIC (Briend and Humbert 1980: pl. 46.7). At Tel Qiri the form is combined with all cooking pots with overlapping triangular rims, Hunt's CPIa:Overlapping, which have a range from the Iron I through the Iron IIB (1987: 182). Similar examples were discovered in Stratum VII at Tel Mevorakh, which dates to the Iron IIA period (Stern

1978: 49). The form thus appears to have a chronological range from the Iron I through the Iron IIC period (table 6.1).

Cooking pot with ridged rim: Two rim fragments of this cooking pot type were discovered in the same pottery basket. One example has a much longer neck (fig. 6.28.6), in the other the rim itself basically forms the neck of the vessel (fig. 6.28.8). There are indications on this second fragment that the cooking pot had handles, although not even a stub of a handle is preserved.

This cooking pot type is more common in the northern part of the region in the Iron II (Amiran 1969: 227). Cooking pots with ridged rims are found in the Iron IIA–IIB, but are much more common in IIC strata (Tabl 6.1). They do not appear in Iron II contexts at Tyre or Sarepta; however, the type is found in number at Rosh Zayit in Iron IIB contexts in Areas A and C, and in smaller number in earlier Iron IIA–IIB phases from the Fort Area (Gal and Alexandre 2000: 43, 157–58, 192). This appears to be the case, as well, for the appearance of ridged rim cooking pots at Keisan, where they are found in Level 7, Iron IIA–B, but are more common in Levels 4 and 5, Iron IIC (Briend and Humbert 1980: pl. 34.10, 46.4, 52.15).

Cooking pot with externally thickened upright rim and tapered lip: This cooking pot type, as defined through comparisons with Sarepta, is rare at Akko. The one example, 183/18 (fig. 6.28.7), has an upright rim that is flared slightly toward the exterior of the vessel, and the stump of a handle whose top attached just below the rim.

Comparative material is found in Stratum D2–B, or the Iron IIA–Persian period at Sarepta, and is defined by Anderson as type CP-1 (1988: 221; table 6.1). Parallels exist at Tyre, in Stratum XIV–VI, or the Iron I–beginning of the Iron IIC (Bikai 1978: 51–52). We have not found any other comparisons with sites in the southern Levant, which may point to this form as a Phoenician type.

Cooking jar with low neck: One example of a cooking jar or jug was preserved in Stratum 4 in Area H (fig. 6.28.9). The vessel has a flared, rounded rim, a low neck, and the top of its carination preserved around halfway down its body. A vertical loop handle connects from the rim of the vessel to just above the carination. It is not clear from comparative evidence whether this type would have had a second handle or just have had the one (Hunt 1987: 183; Gal and Alexandre 2000: 42–43).

The best parallels for this type are found in Iron Age phases at Tel Qiri. Hunt has defined it as CP Ivb, a low-necked cooking jar (1987: 183). Cooking jars in general, including high-necked versions, make up around seven percent of the repertoire of cooking pots in all of the Iron Age levels at the site (Hunt 1987: 183; table 6.1). Cooking jars or jugs are also found at Rosh Zayit; however, all of the examples have a high neck and different rim types from our example from Akko (Gal and Alexandre 2000: 42–43).

Cooking jar with high neck?: 206/7 represents a possible second fragment of a cooking jar (fig. 6.28.10). This upright, rounded rimmed vessel, with a vertical loop handle connecting from the rim down, is hard to define because the piece preserved is so small. It is clear, however, that it has a slightly inward flaring neck.

We define the type as a cooking jar based on one parallel we have found at Tell Keisan. The Tell Keisan cooking jar has a very similar thin upright, rounded rim and inward flaring neck (Briend and Humbert 1980: pl. 46.3). They have reconstructed a single loop handle for the vessel, attached at the top of the lip, which is also similar to the Akko vessel fragment. This cooking jar is from Level 5 at Tell Keisan, which dates to the Iron IIC period.

Baking trays: Three fragments from baking trays were discovered in Stratum 4 in Area H. One preserves its bevelled rim (fig. 6.28.11), and is scored with numerous grooves on the upper surface of the vessel. The other body fragments, but show the scoring and small round indentations typical of baking trays (fig. 6.28.12–13).

Parallels abound at Iron Age sites. Hunt developed a typology for the baking trays from Tel Qiri, based on their rim types (1987: 199). Our one example with its rim preserved would match with Type BTe: Bevelled. All of the various baking tray types are found in limited numbers throughout the Iron Age levels at Qiri. Baking trays are found at Sarepta in Stratum F–B, or the Iron IA–Persian period (Anderson 1988: 227; table 6.1). At Tyre, baking trays are more limited in their chronological distribution, as they are found in Stratum XII–VI, or the Iron IIA–IIC (Bikai 1978: 50). Bikai does not differentiate between various forms of baking trays, as Hunt does for the Qiri material. She presents all types of baking trays together in one category, Cooking Ware 5, and notes parallels of baking trays from Iron Age strata at Megiddo VI–III and Hazor X–V (Bikai 1978: 50). Baking trays of various types are found in Stratum IIa, an early Iron IIB phase, at Rosh Zayit (Gal and Alexandre 2000: 67–68). They are also present in multiple phases at Tell Keisan, Levels 9c–5, or the Iron IB–IIC (Briend and Humbert 1980: pl. 46.8, 52.16, 63.3, 77.6).

Cooking bowl or lid?: This vessel represents an unusual form of a cooking pot (fig. 6.28.14). It is a hemispherical bowl (or a lid, if one turns it in the opposite direction) with a direct, rounded rim. We are defining this type as a cooking vessel based on its fabric, which is typical of cooking pots and baking trays: the clay is red brown in color on its interior and exterior, with a darker core, and typical white quartz inclusions. The exterior of the vessel has soot smudges, showing that it has been used over a fire. These smudges also suggest that the proper stance for the vessel is that of a bowl, since if this had been used as a very steep sided baking tray the soot from cooking fires would have been on the interior of the vessel. Alternatively, it may have been used as a domed lid, perhaps being set down on its top in the cooking fire when lifted off of the cooking pot it was covering. Parallels from Tel Kabri are defined as lids (Lehmann 2002: 188, 200), and the vessel is of optimal size to cover the cooking pots with triangular pinched rims described above.

The closest parallels for this cooking bowl are from Tell Keisan and Qiri. A bowl defined as a baking tray, with a hemispherical body with a slightly flared rim, was uncovered in Level 9c, an Iron IB phase at the site (Briend and Humbert 1980: pl. 77.6; table 6.1). At Qiri, the baking tray type with an inturned rim is a possible parallel, although the depth (or height, since it is presented with the stance of a tray) is not as pronounced as our example from Akko (Hunt 1987: fig. 41.13). It may be the case that this Akko cooking bowl should be presented with its stance inverted as a steep sided baking tray. Given the presence of soot on the exterior of the vessel, as described above, it appears to have been put in the fire as a bowl at least in its final utilization.

Pithoi

Pithoi with wide mouths and everted rims: A rim fragment from a very large vessel is the only find from Stratum 4 that may have come from a local type of pithos (fig. 6.29.1). Its everted rim is flattened at the lip, its neck flares inward, and the vessel is covered on its exterior and interior with a cream-colored slip. The diameter of the vessel is over 60 cm.

No direct parallel for this vessel has been found. The search process has been hampered by the fragmentary nature of the piece. One pithos was uncovered in Stratum IIa at Rosh Zayit (Gal and Alexandre 2000: 53). This Iron IIB pithos is not a great comparison as it has a different rim form and its mouth is about half the diameter of the Akko example. Large-mouthed vessels, over 50 cm in diameter, were discovered at Tel Batash in Stratum II, the Iron IIC, and at Ashdod (Mazar and Panitz-Cohen 2001: 74; M. Dothan and Porath 1982: fig. 31.1; table 6.1). At Batash excavators have categorized this vessel as a krater, while at Ashdod it is called a pithos. In both cases, the vessels' large folded over rim is quite different than the example from Akko.

Storage Jars

No complete or reconstructable storage jars were uncovered in Stratum 4. Given the wide variety of storage jar types for the Iron II in general, and the observation in pottery studies from Tel Qiri and Rosh Zayit that identical complete jar forms have two different rim types, we are presenting the following material from Akko's Area H with some caution (Hunt 1987: 189; Gal and Alexandre 2000: 44). The fact that two rim forms belong to identical, contemporary vessel types is a warning against putting too much dependence on rim sherds for the study of pottery forms in general.

Storage jar with simple upright rim: The majority of storage jar rims from Stratum 4 have a simple, upright stance with a rounded lip (fig. 6.29.2–25). There are variations in thickness of the rim, some of the necks flare outward slightly, and a few of the rims show a bit of interior modeling. Several examples have slightly longer necks than the rest that are short-necked.

This rim type occurs throughout the Iron Age I and II levels at Tel Qiri (Hunt 1987: 186–89; table 6.1). Simple rims are attributed to four different storage jar types at Qiri, Group I: high-necked; Group II: oval body profile; Group III: shouldered body profile; and Group III: sausage body profile, which again highlights the difficulty in discerning actual jar types based on rims alone. At Rosh Zayit, where numerous whole vessels were discovered, two main storage jar types have simple upright rims, SJ II and SJ III (Gal and Alexandre 2000: 48–51). One of the differentiations between the two types is based on whether the vessel has a short or high neck, two categories which we have combined together for the Akko material. Storage jar type SJ II is found in Stratum IIB–IIA, and SJ III in Stratum IIb–I, which represent ranges from the Iron IIA–IIB. Tell Keisan shows the same variations in storage jar types that have identical body and handle forms but differing rims (Briend and Humbert 1980: pl. 26, 27, 47, 48, 50, 59). Simple upright storage jar rims are found on examples from Level 9a–b through Level 4, or the Iron IB–IIC. Several different storage jar rim types defined at Sarepta, SJ 11, SJ 12, and SJ 14, which fit in the broader category we have defined for the Akko material (Anderson 1988: 195–97). Each has a slightly different range, SJ 11 is found in Stratum F–D1, Iron IA–IIB; SJ 12 in Stratum G1–C1, LB IIB–Iron IIC; and SJ 14 in Stratum D2–B, Iron IIA–Persian period. If we combine the chronological evidence for all three types together, they span many levels at Sarepta from the LB IIB–Persian period.

Storage jar with inturned flattened rim: One example of this type was found in Area H, 279/22 (fig. 6.29.26). The jar also has a short neck. Parallels are found at Rosh Zayit among a variety of rim forms from the SJ II, storage jars with short neck, type (Gal and Alexandre 2000: 48–49, fig. III.87.1, 3). This jar type, regardless of rim form, dates to Rosh Zayit Stratum IIb–IIa at the site, which are phases of the Iron IIA–early Iron IIB (table 6.1).

Storage jar with upright rim with interior thickening and short necks: This group of storage jar rims, 281/10–177/12, is by no means uniform as is seen in the slight variations represented in all five examples (fig. 6.30.1–5). All have upright rims, most of which are rounded although fig. 6.30.4 is more angular than the rest. All show some thickening on the interior of the rim, although the degree of this thickening varies dramatically. All have short straight necks of very similar diameter.

The best comparisons for this rim type in the region are found at neighboring Tell Keisan. Although rare, examples of this form of storage jar rim come from Level 8 and 5, Iron IIA–IIC phases at the site (Briend and Humbert 1980: pl. 54.2, 48.1b; table 6.1). Better parallels appear at sites in the Shephelah and Philistia. At Tel Batash comparable rim forms are found on storage jar types SJ 7a, 7b, and 7d (Mazar and Panitz-Cohen 2001: 97–100). Types 7a and 7b are from Stratum III–II, Iron IIB–IIC, and Type 7d is limited to Stratum II, Iron IIC. Similar types are found in Iron IIB levels from Gezer and Iron IIC contexts at Tel Miqne and Ashdod (Gitin 1990: pl. 17.4–6, 1998: fig. 5.4; M. Dothan and Porath 1982: fig. 22.1, 3, 4). These fragments from Akko appear to be from southern storage jars, suggesting maritime contact with the southern coastal plain.

Storage jar with upright rim with rounded lip and interior bulge: Five examples of this type were found in Area H (fig. 6.30.6–10). The type is marked by a distinct profile of an almost semi-circular interior bulge, and an upright, very short neck.

This rim type, form SJ 13, has its longest chronological range at Sarepta, where it is spans from Stratum F–B, or the Iron IA–Persian period (Anderson 1988: 196; table 6.1). At Tell Keisan it appears in Level 5–3, the Iron IIC–Persian period (Briend and Humbert 1980: pl. 18.1, 2, 3, 25.2, 3, 26.1, 8, 9, 47.6). The form has a similar time span at Tyre, where Bikai designates it as Storage Jar 2 (1978: 47–49). Tyre's Storage Jar 2 is found in Stratum I–II, which are both phases of the Iron IIC. Bikai does not include Persian phases from Tyre in her study, but she mentions that Storage Jar 2 is the ancestor of a type that continues in use through the Roman period.

Storage jar with thickened rim without a ridge: This terminology has been borrowed from the Tel Qiri classification system as it seems the best fit for a varied group of storage jar rims (Hunt 1987: 187). What the examples from Area H, 300/16–183/12 (fig. 6.30.11–18), have in common is that they all have rims that are externally thickened. The exact stance of the rim and its profile differ slightly among the entire group.

Thickened rims are found on three different storage jar types, SJ IB, SJ IIB, and SJ IIIB, from Tel Qiri (Hunt 1987: 187, fig. 35.1, 2, 6, 8). Again this highlights the difficulty of assigning a specific jar type based solely on rim fragments. This rim type was found throughout the Iron I and II levels at Qiri (table 6.1).

Storage jar rim type not found in Area H: Storage jars with externally thickened rims and ridged necks are completely absent from our finds in Stratum 4 in Area H. Amiran names the type as one of the most prevalent in northern Palestine in the Iron IIA–IIB (1969: 238). Two forms of storage jar with this rim type, SJ Ia hippo jars and Ib, have been defined at Rosh Zayit (Gal and Alexandre 2000: 44–48). The hippo jar is a very specific type found with a chronological range basically limited to the end of the Iron IIA (Gal and Alexandre 2000: 44–48). According to Gal and Alexandre, hippo jars are not found at sites in the Akko Plain, while they appear at Rosh Zayit in quantity and at sites in the Jezreel, northern hill country, and Jordan Valley. SJ Ib at Rosh Zayit has a much longer chronological range, as it is found in the Fortress area Stratum IIB–I, Iron IIA–IIB, and in Area B and C, which date to the Iron IIC. The externally thickened ridged rim type is also prevalent at Tel Qiri. Defined by Hunt as type SJ 1/c, the rim form is found in abundance in the Iron I, and its numbers drop off rapidly beginning in the Iron IIA but it continues through the Iron IIC (Hunt 1987: 187). It is possible that the distribution of this diagnostic rim type, whether on the very short-lived hippo jar or the more common jars with ridged necks, marks some sort of cultural boundary between the northern part of Palestine and the Akko Plain in the Iron II, or between the northern Israelite kingdom and Phoenicia.

Carinated shoulders and loop handles: Several body fragments from storage jars have diagnostic indicators of carinated shoulders (figs. 6.30.20–21, 6.31.2–6). All of these fragments preserve a vertical loop handle that connects from the carination to a point lower on the ovoid body of the vessel. Although this jar type is clearly a descendant of the Late Bronze Age Canaanite storage jar (see also the examples previously described for the LB IIB–Iron I transition phase Stratum 5 in Area H), the handles used in the Iron Age are squatter and the hole formed by the handle is smaller than in Bronze Age predecessors.

Like the quandary of individual rim types belonging to multiple storage jar forms described above, carinated shoulders are not a marker specific to any one type of storage jar in the Iron Age. At Rosh Zayit, four different storage jar types, SJ II–V, have carinated shoulders and similar vertical loop handles (Gal and Alexandre 2000: 50–53). Bikai defines only one type of storage jar with a carinated shoulder (besides the distinct sausage jars); however, SJ 9 occurs in every stratum from her excavation area, XVII–I, or the LB–Iron IIC (1978: 45–46). Probably the most instructive comparison comes from the neighboring site of Tell Keisan, where storage jars with similar carinated shoulders and squat handles are found in Level 8–5, Iron IIA–C (Briend and Humbert 1980: pl. 47.7, 8, 48.1, 4, 5, 50.1, 3, 5, 54.1, 4; Tabel 6.1).

Storage jar handles: The storage jar handles from Akko Area H fit into several categories, H-4, H-5, and H-6 (figs. 6.30.20–21, 6.31.2–6), established by Anderson for the finds from Sarepta (1988: 252–53). These three handle types have broad ranges, although they cluster in the Iron IIB–Persian period phases: H-4 is found in Stratum G1–B, LB IIB–Persian period; H-5 in Stratum E–B, Iron IB–Persian period; and H-6 in Stratum D1–B, Iron IIB–Persian period (Anderson 1988: 478; table 6.1).

Rounded shoulder with high loop handle: One fragment of this type was found in Area H (fig. 6.30.19). Although the rim was missing, the stance of this piece was clear from the wheel marks on the interior of the vessel, which show a storage jar with a gently rounded shoulder, and a vertical loop handle placed high up on the shoulder.

Parallels are rare. One possible comparison is a storage jar from Tyre's Stratum VIII–IX, Iron IIB (Bikai 1978: pl. XXI.11). This jar, however, has a carinated shoulder and the handles do not appear to be as high up as in the Akko example. Rounded shoulders with high loop handles are common features on storage jars from Phoenician sites in the western Mediterranean from the end of the 8th century to the end of the 7th, or the Iron IIB–IIC in Syro-Palestinian chronological terms (Bartoloni 1999: 572, 574; table 6.1). It is possible that this one example from Akko is an import from the west, a typological observation that should be further examined with scientific testing.

Rounded shoulder and pinched waist: The only example of this type was found mixed in a later Persian period context in Area H (fig. 6.31.1). The shoulder of this storage jar is rounded, its waist is pinched, and its lower body is unfortunately missing. The handle connects from the shoulder to the pinch in the waist. The ware of this vessel is tan on its inside, outside, and core and is clearly not local to the Akko region.

The best parallel we have found is from Rosh Zayit, in Stratum IIa of the fortress, a phase of the early Iron IIB (Gal and Alexandre 2000: fig. III.87.6; table 6.1). Gal and Alexandre include this pinched waist storage jar among their category SJ III jars; however, the profile of its body and position of its handles are quite different from the typical SJ III jar (for comparisons see the jars on either side of the pinched waist jar, Gal and Alexandre 2000: fig. III.87.5, 7). The origin of this jar type is not clear. We cannot discern any other direct parallels besides the one from Rosh Zayit; it is unlikely that it is local because of the ware type and the rarity with which it is found in the region.

Storage jars with painted handle: One fragment of the upper part of a vertical loop handle from a storage jar was found with red painted decoration (fig. 6.31.5). The salmon-colored fabric of this vessel does not appear to be local to the Akko region. There are possible parallels in painted jars found at Hazor in Stratum VIII, early Iron IIB, and at Qiri (Amiran 1969: pl. 79.6–7; Hunt 1987: fig. 34.14).

Knoblike protruded storage jar base: Three knoblike bases from storage jars were found in Stratum 4 in Area H. All three examples vary slightly in breadth or the depth of their protrusion (fig. 6.31.7–9).

Usually this type of base is associated with Late Bronze storage jars; however, the feature continues on Iron Age descendants of the Canaanite jar. According to Bikai, at Tyre the majority of this type of base, defined as Base 20, is found in Stratum XIV–VIII, or the Iron I–IIB (1978: 46). At Sarepta this storage jar base, B-14, is found in Stratum K–D1, or the LB I–Iron IIB (Anderson 1988: 240–41; table 6.1). The life of this base type is extended at Tell Keisan where it appears on jars from Level 9–5, or the Iron IB–IIC (Briend and Humbert 1980: pl. 47.7, 8; 48.1, 4, 5; 50.1, 3, 5; 54.1, 4; 59; 60; 67).

Holemouth Jars

Holemouth jars with externally thickened rims: Five examples of this holemouth jar type were uncovered (figs. 6.32.1–3, 6.32.5–6). All five differ slightly in rim profile and thickness, although all are upright rims that are externally thickened. Four have rounded lips and one has a tapered lip, 330/6 (fig. 6.32.2). Their bodies are fairly straight sided with a slight flare toward the inside.

No direct parallels for this vessel type were found. It is possible that they are actually krater forms, since we are missing the majority of the bodies of these vessels and their bases; however, we prefer to categorize them as holemouth jars given their general resemblance to known flared-rim holemouth jars that we will discuss below. A similar jar type has been defined at Sarepta as SJ 19, "externally thickened, rectangular rim of holemouth jar or krater" (Anderson 1988: 199–200). This holemouth type is found in Stratum D1–B, or the Iron IIB–Persian period (table 6.1). The rectangular profile of the Sarepta form differs from those from Akko; however, its general size, externally thickened rim, and body shape is quite similar.

Holemouth jar with flared rim: The fragments of this pottery type have flared, rounded rims that are externally thickened (fig. 6.32.4, 7–9). All preserve just a small portion of the neck, which we know from comparative evidence sat on a vertical ovoid body.

Amiran notes that holemouth jars of this type are an innovation in the northern part of Palestine in the Iron IIA, and continue in small numbers through to the Iron IIC (1969: 238, 241; table 6.1). She illustrates nice parallels to the Akko flared rim holemouth jars from Megiddo V and Hazor VIII–VII (Amiran 1969: pl. 79.11, 12; 81.12). Parallels are also found in Stratum IIB–IIA, Iron IIA–IIB, at Rosh Zayit, although the defined type has a more everted rim as is noted by the excavators (Gal and Alexandre 2000: 53–54).

Holemouth jar with inturned rim: Only one fragment of this type was found in Area H, 292/17 (fig. 6.32.11). It is around half the size of the two holemouth forms described so far. This vessel type is found in Iron II levels at Qiri and Yoqne'am, where it is called SJ Vb: Hole-mouth (Hunt 1987: 187; table 6.1). It is also prevalent in Area B at Rosh Zayit, which is dated to the Iron IIB (Gal and Alexandre 2000: 174).

Holemouth jar with upright tapered rim: There is one example of this holemouth jar from Stratum 4, with an upright rim that is tapered externally (fig. 6.32.12). It has a body size similar to the holemouth jar with inturned rim just described. Comparisons are found in the Iron II levels at Qiri, where the type is defined as the SJ Vc: Globular (Hunt 1987: 187; table 6.1).

Holemouth jar with simple rim: Our final holemouth type has a simple upright rim that is internally tapered (fig. 6.32.13). At Qiri, Hunt has defined this vessel type as a krater, C Group V a: Simple rim (1987: 195), while we prefer to categorize this vessel type as a holemouth jar. Hunt notes that the form is related to decorated examples in the Bichrome ware family. Bichrome decorated parallels are found in Stratum IIB–IIA, Iron IIA–IIB, at Rosh Zayit, where the form is called a bowl (Gal and Alexandre 2000: 38; table 6.1). It is possible given this link to Bichrome ware that the type is Phoenician; however, no parallels are found at either Tyre or Sarepta which have the best Iron Age exposures from sites in the heartland of Phoenicia.

Three-Handled Jar with Cup-Like Spout (*Pillar-Handled Jar*)

Three-handled jar with cup-like spout: The one fragment of this vessel type, also referred to as a pillar-handled jar, is a rim fragment from the cup-like spout (fig. 6.32.10). These cups are small and shallow, the example from Akko has an incurved rim.

Amiran places this jar type in the Iron IIC at sites in the north (1969: 241). The discovery of a fragment from this form in a secure Iron IIB context at Gezer, and Gitin's comprehensive typological discussion of the type in both the north and south of the region, demonstrates that three-handled jars are found in Iron IIB levels at several sites and continue in use through the Iron IIC (1990: 137–40; table 6.1). Gitin notes that there are some examples that suggest a beginning for the type in the Iron IIA; however, none of the evidence is from stratigraphically sound contexts. Our fragment comes from a context in Square O/1 that is solidly dated to the Iron IIA–IIB as it is low down in a sequence of pottery baskets replete with Cypriot Black-on-Red ceramics and other hallmarks of the period. It is unfortunate that our example is so fragmentary, since it is harder to base firm conclusions on a single sherd as opposed to a whole vessel.

Jugs

The repertoire of jug forms from Area H is fairly limited and highly fragmentary. This observation changes slightly when one includes jug types discussed below under the headings of Phoenician and Cypriot imports to Akko. Wide-necked jugs, a common category at the nearby sites of Rosh Zayit and Qiri, are not represented at all among our small group of jug fragments (Gal and Alexandre 2000: 54–56; Hunt 1987: 197).

Painted jug with horizontal band decoration: One body sherd and a handle fragment of this type was found in Stratum 4, 336/30 and 300/17 (fig. 6.33.1–2). The complete body of a third example, 126/10 (fig. 6.33.9), was found in a later context; it also preserves its small disk base and a tiny fragment of the base of its vertical handle. The bichrome decoration is on the shoulder of the globular jug, 300/17 (fig. 6.33.2), and slightly lower on the body of the smaller globular form of 126/10 (fig. 6.33.9). In both instances the decoration follows the typical pattern of a broad central red stripe bordered by two thinner dark brown to black stripes; in the fragment the central stripe and lower stripe overlap while the stripes on the other jug are evenly spaced with a small equal distance separating the central stripe from the border stripes. Only the uppermost black horizontal stripe is preserved on the sherd with the lower half of the vertical loop handle.

A. Gilboa has studied this decorative schema, with a focus on well-stratified finds from Tel Dor (1999: 12). The use of bichrome horizontal stripes on the shoulders and bodies of globular jugs is phased to the Iron IB–IIA at Tel Dor, with parallels at sites in the heartland of Phoenicia (table 6.1). This type of bichrome jug is defined at Rosh Zayit as JIIIb, and is found in Stratum IIB, an Iron IIA phase at the site (Gal and Alexandre 2000: 60).

Narrow neck jug: Neck and rim fragments of four of these vessels were preserved (fig. 6.33.3–6). Both rims are flared with flattened profiles, 292/19 and 336/22 (fig. 6.33.4, 6); however, the first example is on a narrow ridged neck, while the second appears to be on a straight neck and is pinched to form a simple spout (this may also be from a juglet). Another narrow ridged neck is evident in 297/9 (fig. 6.33.3), with the stump of the upper part of the handle connecting just below the ridge. A narrow straight-necked jug fragment is found in 319/5 (fig. 6.33.5), which also preserves the upper part of its vertical handle.

Jugs of this type, or types, are common at Iron Age sites in the region. They form one of two basic groups of jugs at Qiri, and the ridged-necked type is found frequently in Stratum IIb–IIa, Iron IIA–IIB, at Rosh Zayit (Hunt 1987: 259; Gal and Alexandre 2000: 57). At Tyre, narrow-necked jugs are defined as

Jug 9, the type is found in Stratum XV–VI, or the LB IIB–Iron IIC (Bikai 1978: 37–40; table 6.1).

Pinched-mouth jug: Only one example of this jug type was found in Area H; fortunately its rim, neck, and base were preserved (fig. 6.33.7–8). The rim is simple, rounded, incurved, and pinched to form a spout for the vessel. The upper part of the vertical handle is preserved, actually folded over and surrounding the rim of the jug. The neck is relatively wide and flares gently down to the globular body, which is mostly missing. The vessel has a depressed ring base.

The best parallels for this jug type come from Sarepta. Although the rim type is different, the pinched-mouth jug at Sarepta, DJ-12, has a very similar mouth and neck (Anderson 1988: 210). Anderson also notes the typical cream-colored slip on this vessel type, a decoration which is also found on the upper half of our Akko example. Pinched-mouth jugs are found in Sarepta Stratum D2-B, or the Iron IIA–Persian period (table 6.1).

Strainer-spout jug: Just a fragment of a spout from a strainer-spout jug remains of this jug type in Stratum 4 (fig. 6.35.15). The fragment is covered in a thick, orangey-pink-colored slip on both sides and is so highly burnished that it is polished. The fact that this jug fragment is the only piece with this kind of decoration in Area H at Akko suggests that it was not locally produced. We have described the type above as Phoenician, and perhaps should have included it in our discussion below on typical Phoenician types; however, we have found no typological indications that this kind of decoration was more common in the heartland of Phoenicia than in the northern part of Palestine.

Amiran notes that strainer-spout jugs are on the decline by the Iron IIA–B, although the type continues into the Iron IIC (1969: 256, 259; table 6.1). The form is rare enough at Qiri and Yoqne'am to merely warrant mention, and is called "negligible" at Rosh Zayit (Hunt 1987: 206; Gal and Alexandre 2000: 60). The type seems to have been more popular at Tyre, where it is defined as Jug 11, and has a distribution in Stratum XV–VIII, V, and I (Bikai 1978: 41). Despite the gaps of the appearance of this form in Stratum VII–VI and IV–III, it still has a chronological range from the LB IIB–Iron IIC (table 6.1).

Jug Bases

Out of the base sherds presented, two types definitely belong to jug forms, the depressed ring base and the flat base of ovoid or globular jugs (fig. 6.33.10–15). The rest are either too fragmentary or too generic to assign to specific types, but are of the general size and shape to belong to a form of jug.

Depressed ring base: Our two examples, 336/22 and 177/15 (fig. 6.33.10, 13), vary slightly in diameter and the depth of the depression in the center of the ring base. The red slip and burnish on the outside of 336/28 is typical of decorated Iron II jugs of several rim, mouth, and neck types in northern Palestine and Phoenicia.

The best evidence for this jug base type is from Sarepta, where Anderson has defined it as Base 9 (1988: 238–39). The type is associated with several jug types, trefoil mouth, ridge-necked, and mushroom lip, at the site and has a distribution from Stratum F–B, or the Iron IA–Persian period (table 6.1). Amiran's typology also shows this base type to be common among numerous other jug forms in the Iron IIC north, and among Phoenician red-slipped and bichrome wares (1969: pl. 88:1–3, 5–9, 10, 11, 13; 92:5, 7, 8, 10–14).

Flat base of ovoid or globular jug: One fragment of this distinctive flat base was found in Area H (fig. 6.33.14). At Sarepta it is defined as Base 5, and has a lengthy distribution primarily early on in Stratum L–E, the MB IIC–Iron IB; however, Anderson notes that the form occurs in smaller numbers in Stratum D–C2, or the Iron IIA–IIB (1988: 236; table 6.1).

Juglets

Studies of Iron Age pottery have established two broad categories of juglets for the period, dipper and container juglets (Hunt 1987: 203–204; Gal and Alexandre 2000: 61). Dipper juglets providing the utilitarian function of transferring small quantities of liquid from larger storage jars and pithoi to more manageable sized pouring and drinking vessels, while container juglets were used to hold and store minute amounts of precious liquids, like perfumed or spiced oils, or medicines.

Among our juglet fragments in Area H, there are no container juglets. Two Black-on-Red container juglets will be detailed below in the section on Cypriot import ceramics, so it is possible that this vessel type was mostly represented at Akko by vessels imported for their contents and the beauty of the containers themselves.

Flared rim dipper juglets with arch-shaped loop handle: Our one example of this juglet type, 292/23 (fig. 6.33.16), displays the typical simple, rounded, flared rim. The handle is not as exaggerated in its arch shape as most parallels; however, it is possible that this is an early, and less developed, version of this loop handle type.

Amiran had already specified this juglet type as Phoenician before the form had been uncovered at sites in the heartland of Phoenicia (1969: pl. 92:15, 16). Her examples were from Iron IIC tombs at Achziv. The form is defined at Sarepta as J 1, and is found in Stratum D1–C1, or the Iron IIB–IIC (Anderson 1988: 217–18; table 6.1). A similar distribution is found at Tyre, where Bikai's Juglet 2 has a range from Stratum IX–VIII, VI–III, Iron IIB–IIC. The form continues into the Persian period at Keisan, Level 3, and is also found in the Iron IIC Level 4 (Briend and Humbert 1980: pl. 19.7; 28.11).

Dipper juglets with externally thickened rims: This juglet fragment, 330/15 (fig. 6.33.17), preserves its externally thickened rim, short neck and the upper part of its globular body. The vertical loop handle attaches from the rim of the vessel to its shoulder, and is circular in cross section.

It is difficult to pinpoint parallels for this juglet, since comparative studies base their typologies mostly on the profile of the body of the vessel. Probably the best comparison is "Rounded Dipper Juglet" type from Rosh Zayit, a single example of which comes from a Stratum IIa, early Iron IIB context at the site (Gal and Alexandre 2000: 64; table 6.1).

Dipper juglets with simple flared rims: Only the simple flared rim and neck of this vessel were preserved (fig. 6.33.18). It is distinguished by its decoration with red slip and burnish on the outside of the neck and interior of the rim, but lack of slip and burnish on its lip.

The best parallels for red slip and burnish decorated juglets are at Tel Qiri (Hunt 1987: 204). Hunt's type JT Ia: Cylindrical has a similar rim profile, though the one illustrated example is more upright than the flared find from Akko (Hunt 1987: fig. 40.14). It is noted that this dipper juglet type is often decorated with red slip and burnish, as are subtypes JT Ib and Ic, and is found in all the Iron Age phases in Area D, or the Iron I–II (table 6.1).

Dipper juglets with cylindrical and ovoid bodies: Five dipper juglet bodies were preserved in Area H, which are cylindrical and ovoid in profile (fig. 6.33.19–23). This is typical for Iron Age dipper juglets in general, and cannot be assigned to a specific type since often times juglets defined by identical rim types have variations in their body profiles including cylindrical, ovoid, globular, and even piriform shape (Hunt 1987: 204).

Pilgrim Flasks

Small burnished or decorated pilgrim flask with tubular neck: The remnants of four pilgrim flasks were found in situ in Area H (fig. 6.34.1–4), and two nearly complete flasks were found in later contexts (fig. 6.34.5–6). Only one rim fragment was preserved among these six examples, 279/23, a direct rim with a tapered lip (fig. 6.34.4). Most have the typical thin, tubular neck, likely formed around a dowel or wooden stick, or perhaps a reed that burned away in the firing (Anderson 1988: 214). Of the four vessels with complete, or nearly complete, lenticular bodies, three are 5.9–6.9 cm in diameter (fig. 6.34.2, 5–6) and the fourth has a diameter of 9.0 cm (fig. 6.34.1). Dual handles attach to the neck below the rim (although most rims are not preserved) and to the shoulders of each vessel.

The decoration varies slightly on each pilgrim flask. The largest vessel, 354/1 (fig. 6.34.1), was covered in a cream-colored slip and painted with red concentric circles. 177/1 is covered with a tan slip and has dark brown concentric circular stripes (fig. 6.34.2), and 210/1 has similar dark brown painted concentric stripes but no slip (fig. 6.24.6). 292/21 is covered with a red slip (fig. 6.34.3); 266/1 is red slipped and burnished (fig. 6.34.5).

Amiran notes that the number of pilgrim flasks is generally in decline by the Iron IIA–B, an observation that is repeated in the pottery studies from Tel Qiri, Rosh Zayit, and Tyre where the amount of Iron II pilgrim flasks is negligible (Amiran 1969: 276; Hunt 1987: 205; Gal and Alexandre 2000: 33). The finds at Sarepta, however, were plentiful enough to define the pilgrim flask type, PF 1, which is found in Stratum F–C1, the Iron IA–IIC (Anderson 1988: 213–14; table 6.1). Avner Raban excavated a feature filled with similar small pilgrim flasks in Area F at Akko (on view in the Hecht Museum, University of Haifa). They also appear at Tell Abu Hawam (Herrera and Gomez 2004: 307–309) as well as Tel Dor (Gilboa 1999). This particular type is found in quantity exported to Cyprus (Bikai 1987: 10).

Lamps

Only four lamp fragments were discovered in Area H's Stratum 4, which makes generalizations about the forms difficult (fig. 6.35.1–4). Two preserve the everted flanged rim of the lamps, 190/11 and 292/24, with 190/11 showing part of the vessel's rounded base (fig. 6.35.1–2). One piece is simply the spout of the lamp, 300/22 (fig. 6.35.4), which shows the pronounced lip of the form but nothing else. And the last fragment is a short disk base from a lamp; however, we are missing the rim and spout of this vessel (fig. 6.35.3).

Studies on Iron Age lamps seem to contradict each other, which illustrates the difficulties of basing typological conclusions on this pottery form. Amiran's observation that Iron IIA–IIB lamps tend to have a "more pronounced lip" than earlier types is negated by Hunt's findings from Qiri and Yoqne'am where this lip type is found in equal number in all phases of the Iron Age (Amiran 1969: 291; Hunt 1987: 204–205). While the finds are numerous from Rosh Zayit, with over forty whole or reconstructable lamps found in the fortress at the site, the lamps are all of one type with everted flanged rim and round base (Gal and Alexandre 2000: 67). This lack of variation and lack of lamps from earlier or later strata at Rosh Zayit makes typological differentiation by phase impossible. Bikai does not fully discuss her Lamp 1 type because it is so ubiquitous throughout the Bronze and Iron Age levels at Tyre (1978: 18–19). However, examples of Lamp 1 with short disk bases, like our 206/5 (fig. 6.35.3), are illustrated in Stratum XII and X-2, or the Iron IIA–IIB (Bikai 1978: pl. XXVI.9–10;

XXXI.9). Anderson's is probably the best study differentiating typologically between lamp forms from the Bronze and Iron Ages (1988: 228–32). Sarepta's lamp type L-7 has a "short, thickened flange" rim very similar to our 190/11 and 292/24 (Anderson 1988: 231; fig. 6.35.1–2). L-7 is found in Stratum G1–D2, or the LB IIB–Iron IIA at Sarepta (table 6.1). The short disk base on lamps, base B-31 at Sarepta, is found in Stratum G2–D2, or the LB IIB–Iron IIA (Anderson 1988: 249). This is comparable to our 206/5 (fig. 6.35.3). Rounded bases on lamps, like our 190/11 (fig. 6.35.1), are much more prevalent at the site, where base B-30 is found in Stratum L–D1, or the MB IIC–Iron IIB (Anderson 1988: 249).

Cup and Saucer

One example of a cup-and-saucer vessel was discovered in Area H (fig. 6.35.5). Since the rim of the cup was not preserved the piece cannot be compared with Hunt's typology of this vessel type (1987: 205). The use of cup-and-saucer vessels is not fully understood; some believe they were utilized in religious ritual activities while others think they functioned as lamps. Find spots are varied (Mazar 1985: 79). The form is found in LB II–Iron II contexts (table 6.1), such as LB IIC Tel Nami, and according to Stern it is distributed primarily at sites in northern Palestine (1978: 51). Cup-and-saucer vessels are also found further north at Sarepta, in Stratum G1 and E, or the LB IIB and Iron IB (Anderson 1988: pl. 28.18; 31:20).

Phoenician Pottery

In many ways a separate category for Phoenician pottery is a misnomer for ceramics from Akko, since the site is widely considered to be a southern Phoenician settlement in the Iron II period. Although we are only dealing with a fragmentary picture of the Iron II ceramics, and the picture will be broadened when further material is published from other areas excavated on the site, it is significant to note the small amount of pottery in Area H classically considered Phoenician. Ceramics such as monochrome and bichrome decorated jugs and pilgrim flasks, red slipped wares, and "Samaria Ware," also known as Phoenician fine ware, are quite limited. Perhaps this is reflective of a typical percentage of decorated wares versus undecorated, or perhaps there were more influences from local potting traditions in the Akko Plain or northern Israel on the ceramic repertoire of Akko, rather than impacts coming from a site closer to the heartland of Phoenicia, such as Tyre or Sarepta. In many ways the Akko Plain was a boundary region between Phoenicia and northern Israel, and this can be seen in the ceramics at the site that reflect influences coming from both the north and the east as well as local traditions carried forward from earlier phases, even in a study solely focused on materials from Area H.

It should be noted, as well, that the examples chosen for this category of Phoenician pottery are only partial. Types such as everted horizontal rim bowls, various bowls and jugs decorated with bichrome horizontal stripes, small cooking pots with upright triangular rims and bag-shaped bodies, cooking pots with externally thickened upright rims and tapered lips, small decorated pilgrim flasks, or undecorated juglets with arch looped handles are northern coastal, or Phoenician, ceramic types. One site with a large collection of ceramics attributed to the Phoenician pottery group, whether produced on Cyprus or along the southern Levantine coast, is Tell Abu Hawam. Tell Abu Hawam was a coastal site with geographical features, like its proximity to a bay and a river, which made it an active anchorage. The publications of the Stratum III at Tell Abu Hawam appeared already in the 1930s following Hamilton's excavation there (Hamilton 1935). Aznar's work followed with her MA thesis on its ceramics in the 1990s, and Herrera and Gomez's reevaluation of the stratum in 2004 (Aznar 1996; Herrera and Gomez 2004). As Ruth Amiran noted over four decades ago, "petrographical analysis should also prove helpful, if not a decisive, instrument in these investigations (in determining differentiations between Phoenician and northern Israelite ceramics)" (1969: 272). Such studies have been carried out by N. Schreiber in her volume focusing on Cypro-Phoenician pottery (2003); as well as A. Gilboa (1999), Gilboa and Goren (2015), and others. Thus, a combination of material science provenience studies of the ceramics; future excavation of stratified Iron Age sites in coastal Lebanon, Syria, northern Israel, and Cyprus; and typological and seriation studies on ceramics will all aid in further differentiating and refining these ceramic categories.

Various decorated jugs: Fragments of Phoenician jugs are presented together, demonstrating the variety in decorative techniques. Certain features stand out, like the central depression on the handle of 292/20 (fig. 6.35.6), which is found on Phoenician jugs at Tel Dor, Sarepta, and on some examples exported to Cyprus (Gilboa 1999: fig. 11.3, 8; Anderson 1988: pl. 36.9; Bikai 1987: pl. III.17, 19, IV.32, V.49, 60, 72). The shoulder of a jug (fig. 6.35.7) with three parallel horizontal bands incised into the vessel is likely a Phoenician type. Comparisons to this decoration, however, are typically found on red-slip jugs of varying types while the piece from Akko lacks any surface decoration (Amiran 1969: pl. 92.4, 7, 10). The one mushroom-lip rim (fig. 6.35.8) was found mixed in a later context, and is included here just to illustrate the existence of the type at Akko. The ridged neck of a jug (fig. 6.35.9), decorated with red slip and burnish and a black painted stripe on the ridge, may have belonged to a mushroom-lip jug or several other types of Phoenician decorated ridged-neck jugs (fig. 6.35.10). Similarly, it is difficult to pinpoint the exact jug type that the decorated handles, 330/19 and 158/4 (fig. 6.35.13–14), belonged to, although the technique is typically Phoenician (see numerous examples of painted handles on various jug and flask forms in Bikai 1987: pl. III–IX).

An almost complete Phoenician globular jug was uncovered in Area H (fig. 6.35.17). The depressed ring base is also nicely preserved, along with the typical designs of vertical concentric circles mirrored on both sides of the vessel, with a "ribbon" painted between the circles on the side opposite the handle. All of the painted decoration is done in black. The decoration of concentric circles painted on a globular jug has a long life at Tyre where the type, defined as Jug 10, is found in Stratum XVII–II, or the LB I–Iron IIC (Bikai 1978: 40–41; table 6.1). Bikai does not differentiate between monochrome, red or black, and bichrome, red and black, decoration on this vessel type. While a monochrome decoration scheme has been differentiated at Tel Dor for the earliest phase of Phoenician pottery in the Iron IA, it must be noted that designs of monochrome concentric circles on globular jugs have a long life at Sarepta where this design scheme is found on vessels in Stratum G1–C1, or the LB IIB–Iron IIC (Gilboa 1999: 1–2; Anderson 1988: 541). The majority of these decorated jugs from Sarepta are found clustered in Stratum D2–D1, or the Iron IIA–IIB. It should also be noted that the depressed ring base type, B-9, is found in Sarepta Stratum F–B, or the Iron IA–Persian period, with the greatest number found in Stratum D1 or the Iron IIB (Anderson 1988: 238–39).

Finally, the body sherd likely from a jug, 330/20 (fig. 3.36.2), is decorated on its exterior with a wide red stripe, and the vessel is so highly burnished that it is polished. This fine burnishing, or polishing, is another decorative technique typically assigned to Phoenician potters (Amiran 1969: 272; Anderson 1988: 337–43).

"Samaria Ware" bowls: Only one body fragment of this ware, better termed Phoenician fine ware, was discovered in situ in Stratum 4 (fig. 6.36.1). Its red slip on one side and red stripe on the other, and high degree of burnishing, or polishing, on both sides of the piece define it as Phoenician. A second fragment, 46/2 (fig. 6.36.3), was found in Area H mixed in a later context. It has a red-slipped and polished interior, and a polished exterior with a red stripe with four parallel incised bands.

In general, these fine wares, red-slipped and highly burnished bowls are found primarily at sites in Phoenicia and northern Israel, and are dated from the Iron IIA–IIC (Amiran 1969: 207; Hunt 1987: 201–202; Gal and Alexandre

2000: 37; table 6.1). Anderson properly warns against the use of the term "Samaria Ware," or any of its variants, preferring calling the class Phoenician fine ware (1988: 355). Phoenician fine ware decorated bowls have an even longer life at Sarepta, where they are introduced in Stratum F and are found all the way into Stratum B, a range from the Iron IA–Persian period (Anderson 1988: 547).

Lid or cover: Our one example of this Phoenician type, 292/1 (fig. 6.35.11), has horizontal, dark brown stripes and is so highly burnished it is polished. The best parallel is found at the cemetery at Achziv, but comparable lids or covers come from Phoenician sites in Lebanon, Cyprus, and Tunisia and are typically associated with urn burials (Dayagi-Mendels 2002: 135 fig. 5.12.15).

Cypriot Imports

As is typical of Iron II northern sites, and especially coastal sites, there are a number of Cypriot imported wares that are found in Area H in Stratum 4 (figs. 6.36.4–10, 6.37.1–15). In a study focused on Black-on-Red wares, but including data on White Painted and Bichrome ceramics, Schreiber concludes that the Akko Plain and neighboring Carmel were a focus of Cypriot Iron Age commerce (2003: 75). This is upheld by the material we will present from Area H, and will be further elucidated by the forthcoming Total Archaeology Project's publication of other excavation areas at Tel Akko.

White Painted Wares: Our first example, 297/7 (fig. 6.36.5), is the shoulder of a jar decorated with a cream-colored slip and a broad horizontal dark brown stripe above four parallel thin brown stripes. In the White Painted family, as defined by Gjerstad, this vessel type is presented as an amphora, with parallels in decoration found among the smaller amphoras in the White Painted I, III, and IV groups (1948: figs.V.15; XX.2, 5; XXIX.13, 14; XXX.1–3).

Another fragment of White Painted Ware is part of a large strap handle, covered with a cream-colored slip and decorated with dark brown painted parallel stripes and a dark brown border around the sides and end of the handle (fig. 6.36.6). Judging by the stance of strap handles, found on White Painted amphoras, this is the bottom of the handle. Painted strap handles are found on White Painted I–IV amphoras; unfortunately the details of the design on the face of the handle are rarely given; thus we cannot determine if the three parallel stripes are of chronological significance (Gjerstad 1948: figs.VI.4; XIV.6–7; XX.5; XXX.2–3).

A body fragment from a White Painted bowl is not detailed enough to identify either the vessel type or family (fig. 6.36.4). The fact that it was decorated both on its interior and exterior with dark brown paint helps to identify this small piece as being from an open form.

The final piece of White Painted ware is the neck of a pithos (fig. 6.37.2), found in a later context with mixed Iron II–Persian period ceramics. The outside of the vessel is covered in a tan-colored slip, and painted with a typical dark brown horizontal band, vertical lines, latticed triangles and lozenges, and a squiggly line. Variations on this design scheme are found on the necks of White Painted I–III amphoras/pithoi (Gjerstad 1948: figs.VI.3; XIV.7; XX.3).

Gjerstad's absolute dates are considered by most archaeologists working in the southern Levant as problematic (Schreiber 2003: 225–30). For comparative dating we will turn to evidence from Syro-Palestinian sites, which have already been presented for ceramic parallels above. White Painted Wares, which have a long life on Cyprus, are found in multiple phases at Tyre and Sarepta. The group, in general, termed Import 5, is found in Stratum XIII/2–II, or the Iron IB–Persian period at Tyre (Bikai 1978: 53). At Sarepta White Painted pottery is found in Stratum E–C2, or the Iron IB–IIB (Anderson 1988: 517). A White Painted III amphora was uncovered in Tyre Stratum XI–XII, or the Iron IIA–IIB (Bikai 1978: pl. XXX.2), and four fragments of White Painted I and II–III amphoras were found in Sarepta Stratum E–D1, or the Iron IB–Iron IIB (Anderson 1988: 275–76; table 6.1). Further to the north, a variety of White Painted amphoras are found at Al Mina. The majority of these Cypriot imported amphoras were found in Al Mina Level VIII, 8th century BCE or Iron IIB, with a few dating to Level VI, 7th century BCE or Iron IIC (Taylor 1959: 71, 91–92). A well-preserved White Painted amphora was found in a Stratum IIb, Iron IIA context at Rosh Zayit (Gal and Alexandre 2000: 80).

Cypriot Bichrome Wares: A body fragment from a Cypriot Bichrome jug was found in pottery basket 151 alongside two White Painted pieces described above (fig. 6.36.7). The piece is made from well-levigated tan clay. Its exterior is burnished and decorated with partially preserved red parallel (concentric?) stripes and small dark brown concentric circles.

Jugs with similar bichrome decoration are found in the repertoire of Cypriot Bichrome III–IV (Gjerstad 1948: figs. XX.11; XXXIII.9, 13; XXXIV.5, 8). The application of small concentric circles as a decorative motif on Bichrome jugs appears to be limited to these two groups. We have not found any direct parallels for this imported jug type in the southern Levant; however, it is so fragmentary that pinpointing a comparable piece is difficult. A Cypriot Bichrome fragment from a spherical or barrel jug was found in Stratum C2 at Sarepta, Iron IIB; however, the piece is not illustrated (Anderson 1988: 277).

A well-preserved barrel jug was discovered in Stratum 4. Its rim, handle, and part of its body, however, are missing (fig. 6.36.8). The decorative schema consists of a buff-colored slip over the outside of the vessel, concentric bichrome circles on the two barrels with broad red stripes flanked by three parallel thin black to dark brown stripes, black to dark brown horizontal stripes on the neck of the jug, and remnants of a dark stripe on the two handle stubs. In the open field opposite the handle is a typical design in black/dark brown of a pendent filled with a net pattern.

The Akko Bichrome barrel jug is nicely paralleled by two examples from the Bichrome III family (Gjerstad 1948: fig. XXII.7–8). Both of these examples from Cyprus have similar bichrome concentric circle designs featuring a broad red stripe surrounded by parallel thin black one, a wider ridge neck than the Bichrome I or II barrel jugs, and one has a pendent filled with a net pattern. We have not found many good parallels for Bichrome barrel jugs in southern Levantine contexts. A fragment from a Cypriot Bichrome barrel or spherical jug was found in Sarepta Stratum C2, Iron II; however, the piece is not illustrated (Anderson 1988: 277), and there are some from Tell Abu Hawam. Several White Painted barrel jugs have been discovered, which likely served a similar export need/function as the Bichrome barrel jug. Amiran publishes one White Painted barrel jug from Tell Jemmeh among her typology of Iron IIA–IIB Cypriot imports, and an example was found in Stratum IIb, Iron IIA, in the fortress at Rosh Zayit (1969: pl. 97.29; Gal and Alexandre 2000: 79–80). In Lebanon, two nicely preserved examples were found at Tyre in Stratum X-2, and one from Sarepta Stratum D1; both of these strata date to the Iron IIB (Bikai 1978: pl. XXVIII.1–2; Anderson 1988: pl. 34.17). There are parallels from the northern Levant, where fragments of both Bichrome and While Painted barrel jugs were found at Al Mina in Level VIII and VI (Taylor 1959: 66–67). Taylor dated these levels to the 8th and 7th century BCE, Iron IIB and IIC, respectively, primarily through comparisons with southern Levantine sites (table 6.1).

The last piece of Cypriot Bichrome ware is a decorated fragment from the neck of an amphora (fig. 6.37.1). The decoration consists of a pink cream-colored slip on the outside of the vessel and broad red horizontal stripe flanked by three thinner dark brown stripes. Below the lower brown stripes one can just make out the tops of two vertical brown stripes, and the rest of the decoration is lost; above the upper brown stripes is a field nicely decorated with sets of three vertical brown stripes surrounding triangles and lozenges filled with net patterns or painted solid dark brown.

Probably the best comparable example for this piece is in the Bichrome III group of amphoras, although the designs are not the same (Gjerstad 1948: fig. XXIII.16–18). An imported Bichrome II amphora was found in Stratum VA, Iron IIA, at Megiddo (Amiran 1969: pl. 97.26), although it is not an exact parallel to this the Akko example. Tell Abu Hawam has similar, yet not exact, examples as well (Herrera and Gomez 2004).

In general, Cypriot Bichrome Ware has a long history of export to the Levant. At Tyre examples of the ware, termed Import 2, are found in Stratum XII–II, or the Iron IIA–Persian period (Bikai 1978: 53; table 6.1). Sarepta has a more limited chronological range for the ware, as it is found in Stratum D2–C2, or the Iron IIA–IIB (Anderson 1988: 517).

Cypriot Plain White Wares (?): The rims of two large pithoi were found in Stratum 4, likely manufactured outside the Akko region. One is an upright rim, rounded, and folded over on a straight neck (fig. 6.36.9), the other is a direct rim, externally thickened with a rounded profile and a broad flared neck (fig. 6.36.10). The ware of the first piece, 292/16 (fig. 6.36.9), is orangey pink in color on the interior of the vessel to tan on its exterior. The ware of the second vessel, 300/14 (fig. 6.36.10), is tan in color with many small brown and white inclusions, and is covered by a cream-colored slip on its interior and exterior.

It is difficult to pinpoint the vessels' types precisely. No exact parallels for 292/16 (fig. 6.36.9) were found. As can be seen from the illustration, however, it is of the same approximate diameter as the White Painted and Bichrome neck fragments (fig. 6.37.1–2). The fabric appears to be foreign to the Akko region, so perhaps it belongs to a Cypriot vessel. Our second, larger-necked vessel has a possible parallel in an "amphora" in the Cypriot Plain White I family (Gjerstad 1948: fig. XI.13). The Cypriot vessel illustrated has a similar wide, flared neck. No clear view of the rim's profile is provided in Gjerstad's illustration, unfortunately. Another possible parallel is found in pithos type RR-2 at Sarepta, which has a very similar rim but a straight neck (Anderson 1988: 186–87). This pithos type is found in Stratum J/H–D1, or the LB IIA–Iron IIB, at Sarepta (table 6.1). Both of these pithoi rims should be tested to help determine their provenience. It should be noted, however, that it would not be surprising for foreign pithoi to appear in a port city as ships commonly carried these large vessels for storage of goods or food (Artzy 2006a: 52).

Black-on-Red Wares: Now that an authoritative study on this ware type has been published, we may say with confidence that Black-on-Red ceramics were a Cypriot ware of which certain types were exported to the Levantine coast in the Iron IIA–IIB periods (Schreiber 2003: 307–312; see also Gal and Alexandre 2000: 69–70). Nine fragments of Black-on-Red decorated vessels were found in situ in Stratum 4 contexts in Area H, while four fragments were found in later Persian and Hellenistic levels (fig. 6.37.3–15). All of the stratified examples are from bowls decorated with typical red to red-orange slip, highly burnished, and black painted vertical stripes and concentric circles, as are two of the unstratified vessels. Both Black-on-Red juglet fragments were found in later contexts. This is unfortunate, because the diagnostic pieces from the stratified group, 206/8, 300/9, and 281/15 (fig. 6.37.3–4, 7), are not particularly helpful in differentiating between the three phases of Black-on-Red ceramics established by Schreiber (2003: 271). The internally thickened rim, 206/8 (fig. 6.37.3), ring base, 281/15 (fig. 6.37.7), and gently carinated body, 300/9 (fig. 6.37.4), are not specific enough to differentiate internal phasing, and Schreiber's work has shown that the groups set up by Gjerstad do not hold chronological significance, which does away with attempts to link his decorative schema to certain phases (2003, Appendix III). Therefore, the presence of small concentric circles on bowls, attributed by Gjerstad to vessels in his Black-on-Red II and III, is not necessarily late in the sequence. Bowls found at Tell Keisan, Rosh Zayit, and Megiddo that have horizontal lines and small concentric circles in their design demonstrate this; they were found in well-stratified Iron IIA contexts, and are therefore attributed by Schreiber to her earliest Phase 1 (2003, Appendix III). Two of the unstratified Area H pieces match those from Schreiber's Phase 1, which she tentatively dates to 940–880 BCE, or the end of the Iron IIA/beginning of the Iron IIB (2003: 271). The trefoil-lipped squat juglet, 86/1 (fig. 6.37.15), is found only in Phase 1, with parallels found in Megiddo VA–IVB, Hazor IX, and Rosh Zayit IIa (Schreiber, Appendix III: 333–34; Gal and Alexandre 2000: 77). The medium bowl with ridged neck (termed medium bowl with carinated body by Schreiber) found at Akko, 267/5 (fig. 6.37.13), has a direct parallel at Tell Keisan in Level 8, Iron IIA (Briend and Humbert 1980: pl. 56.2; Schreiber 2003: 153). The only other example of a Black-on-Red medium bowl with carinated body comes from Tyre Stratum II, and has been dated by Schreiber to her Phase 3, ca. 800–730 or the end of the Iron IIB (2003: 206–208, 309). Stylistically, however, the bowl from Tyre it is not a direct match with either example from Akko or Tell Keisan since it lacks the diagnostic ridge on the neck of the vessel (Bikai 1978: pl. XIA.21). Therefore both of these unstratified Black-on-Red vessels from Area H, the trefoil lipped squat juglet and ridged neck bowl, can be placed in the earliest phase of this Cypriot pottery type to be exported to the Levant. Unfortunately since they were found in later contexts they can only hypothetically be grouped with the stratified Black-on-Red pottery from Area H, whose diagnostic features cannot be differentiated by phase. Regardless, Schreiber groups all of the Black-on-Red pottery into an absolute time frame between 940–730 BCE, or the end of the Iron IIA to the end of the Iron IIB (table 6.1).

Egyptian Imports

A small fragment of the incurved rim of a large bowl was found in Square M/3 in a Stratum 4 context (fig. 6.38.2). The fabric of this vessel is red on the exterior and interior surface and gray to dark brown in its core. There are many small white inclusions, and the vessel is covered outside and inside with a thick cream-colored slip that at times appears almost yellow.

This fabric and slip is definitely foreign to the Akko region. The fabric type is common in Egypt, and likely belongs to the Nile D group (Aston 1996: 5). We base this attribution on the fact that Nile D fabrics have "conspicuous limestone inclusions," and the match of the Akko piece with Nile D ceramics' typical red and brown coloration (Aston 1996: 5). The creamy white-colored slip is common on ceramics from the Late New Kingdom through the Third Intermediate Period (12th–7th century BCE), and is found on several shallow bowl types from the Saite period at Tell el-Maskhuta (Aston 1996: 81; Paice 1986/87: 99). None of the bowl forms from Maskhuta, however, is similar to the Akko example typologically, although they are a good match in terms of the fabric, described at Maskhuta as "a red-brown ware, very well fired, with some lime inclusions," and decorated with "a heavy white slip inside and out" (Aston 1996: 81; Paice 1986/87: 99). The closest typological match is with a bowl from Qantir (Aston 1996: figs. 36.3; 189.c). The Qantir bowl, however, is much smaller, with a diameter of 25.6 cm compared to the 42.5 cm diameter of the Akko bowl. While the treatment of the rim is very similar on both bowls, the stance on the Qantir example is much more shallow, while the fragment from Akko indicates a deeper bowl.

The Akko bowl fragment appears in the same pottery basket as a fragment of a Cypriot Black-on-Red bowl (206/8), a lamp with a short disk base (206/5), and two examples of knoblike protruded storage jar bases (206/3, 12), which are all forms that cluster in the late Iron IIA (see details above, and fig. 6.4). Therefore we consider this large bowl to be an Egyptian import from the late Iron IIA, and look forward to further excavations in Egypt from this time period to help elucidate Egyptian ceramics and their export, as well as further attention in Syria-Palestine to the possibility of utilitarian Egyptian imports in the Iron II, like the study of Egyptian imports to Tel Dor in the early Iron Age (Waiman-Barak et al. 2014). High-value items exported from Tanite Egypt, such as statues, are already known from finds at Phoenician sites along the Lebanese coast, and the Egyptian stylistic influence on Phoenician artistic vocabulary is well documented (Redford 1992: 334–35). A few examples of Egyptian imports have been identified in 7th century BCE levels at Ashkelon, and one Egyptian bowl was discovered among the ceramics sampled from two 8th century BCE shipwrecks of Phoenician origin found in deep waters in the southeastern corner of the Mediterranean (Master 2003: 55; Ballard et al. 2002: 161–62). Two grooved rim bowls from Beersheba Stratum II have been scientifically tested and determined to be manufactured of Nile silt clay (Singer-Avitz

1999: 44–46). A direct parallel of a grooved rim bowl from Area H, 300/6 (fig. 6.38.1) detailed above, is also likely made of Nile silt, which suggests that there are at least two Egyptian imported ceramics in the repertoire for this phase at Akko. A site with a large Egyptian ceramic presence in the early Iron Age is Dor, as noted by Waiman-Barak et al. (2014); Egyptian ceramic imports to the southern Levant are rare but are found in the early Iron IIA and late Iron IIB, at northern coastal sites like Dor, Atlit, and Achziv, but more commonly at sites in the southern coastal plain, Shepelah, and northern Negev (Ben Dor Evian 2011: 110).

Typological Conclusions

The rich variety of Stratum 4 ceramics is attested in the numerous ceramic types we have established for this phase, as the pottery has been divided into over sixty categories (table 6.1). Each one of these categories has a chronological range, which we have determined based on comparative evidence since the sequence in Area H is not continuous.

Out of these sixty-six ceramic categories, only three types do not occur in Iron IIA or Iron IIB levels at sites in Phoenicia, and northern or southern Palestine (table 6.1). This confirms a date of Stratum 4 to the transition period between the end of the Iron IIA and the beginning of the Iron IIB. The three types not represented in the Iron IIA–IIB—painted bowl with flared rim, cooking jar with high neck, and cooking bowl—are all extremely rare at Akko in Area H as each type is represented by only one vessel fragment. The types are also extremely rare at other Iron Age sites, which may have skewed the dating of each of these ceramic categories.

Other factors which may have skewed the dating of ceramic types in Stratum 4 is the low absolute dates used in the Iron Age strata at Tyre (Bikai 1978: 68; Schreiber 2003: 207–208). This low chronology was established based on Cypriot finds at the site, and the low absolute dates assigned in Gjerstad's classic typology of Cypriot Iron Age ceramics. Our translation of Bikai's dates for the strata at Tyre into Iron Age phases (i.e., Stratum XII=Iron IIA, Stratum XI–VIII=Iron IIB, Stratum VII–I=Iron IIC) was based on simply equating her absolute dates with those traditionally assigned to the various phases of the Iron Age in Palestine (Mazar 1990: 372–73, table 7). We do not think, however, that revising the attribution of Iron Age phasing to the strata at Tyre would change the basic conclusions arrived at in this chapter.

The absolute dating of the Iron IIA has been called into question, in the so called great debate over the 10th century (Bruins, et al. 2003; see collected works in Levy and Higham 2005). At this stage the ceramic repertoire from Area H at Akko cannot add any specific information regarding the absolute dates at the site. The repertoire of pottery can add to the general picture of the transitional phase at the end of the Iron IIA and beginning of the Iron IIB in the Akko Plain. The rich assemblage of finds from Stratum 4 suggests that further excavation at Akko will add valuable data in the ongoing effort to work out the absolute dates assigned to phases of the Iron IIA and early Iron IIB, with the use of ^{14}C dating on a sequence of well-stratified short-lived samples from good archaeological contexts combined with refined ceramic seriation. Until then, this chapter has presented what we have determined to be the late Iron IIA/early Iron IIB pottery from Area H, and we will leave the absolute date of this phase open.

Within Area H, the concentration of Iron II material was found mainly in the southern part of the area. The focus of finds is primarily in excavation squares in horizontal line 1, namely M/1, O/1 and P/1. These are situated on the inner depression of the rampart, below its inner structure. On the rampart itself, in squares further north, little or no Iron II remains were noted. The graves of the mid-2nd millennium, Stratum 6, were not disturbed until the Persian period, Stratum 3, as described above in chapters 2 and 4. The location of Stratum 4 stratified remains in Area H in its southeasternmost squares suggests that the Iron IIA-IIB settlement at Akko was primarily located to the south and east, and was concentrated in the acropolis area of the site.

TABLE 6.1   Comparison of Area H Stratum 4 ceramic types with presence in comparative MB–Persian period phasing

	MB IIC	LB IA	LB IB	LB IIA	LB IIB	Iron IA	Iron IB	Iron IIA	Iron IIB	Iron IIC	Pers.
Pointed rim bowl											
Incurved rim bowl											
Rounded bowl											
Straight sided bowl											
Groove rim bowl											
Everted horizontal rim bowl											
Painted bowl, flared rim											
Medium bowl, bichrome decoration											

TABLE 6.1 Comparison of Area H Stratum 4 ceramic types with presence (*cont.*)

	MB IIC	LB IA	LB IB	LB IIA	LB IIB	Iron IA	Iron IB	Iron IIA	Iron IIB	Iron IIC	Pers.
Fine ware bowl						■	■	■	■	■	
Deep bowl, incurved rim							■		■		
Deep bowl, rim with t-shaped thickening							■	■	■		
Deep bowl, cyma profile & upright rim							■	■			
Shallow carinated bowl							■				
Chalice flared rim & stepped base							■	■			
Chalice red slipped & burnished								■			
Carinated krater, flanged rim							■	■			
Carinated krater, bevelled rim							■	■			
Carinated krater, simple upturned rim				■	■	■		■			
Carinated krater, thickened rounded rim							■	■			
Krater, flared, thickened rim	■	■	■	■	■	■	■				
Basin							■	■	■		
Cooking pot, triangular pinched rim						■	■				
Small cooking pot, upright triangular rim & bag body							■	■	■		
Cooking pot, incurved rim, interior thickening									■		
Cooking pot, inverted rim, exterior thickening						■	■	■			
Cooking pot, ridged rim							■	■			
Cooking pot externally thickened upright rim & tapered lip						■	■	■			

TABLE 6.1 Comparison of Area H Stratum 4 ceramic types with presence (*cont.*)

	MB IIC	LB IA	LB IB	LB IIA	LB IIB	Iron IA	Iron IB	Iron IIA	Iron IIB	Iron IIC	Pers.
Cooking jar, low neck						▓	▓	▓	▓		
Cooking jar, high neck											
Baking tray						▓	▓	▓	▓		
Cooking bowl							▓				
Pithos, wide mouth									▓	▓	
Storage jar, simple upright rim						▓	▓	▓	▓	▓	
Storage jar, inturned flattened rim											
Storage jar, upright rim, interior thickening & short neck							▓	▓	▓		
Storage jar, upright rim, rounded lip & exterior bulge						▓	▓	▓	▓	▓	
Storage jar, thickened rim no ridge							▓	▓	▓	▓	
Storage jar, carinated shoulder, loop handle						▓	▓	▓	▓	▓	
Storage jar, rounded shoulder, high loop handle									▓		
Storage jar, rounded shoulder, pinched waist									▓		
Storage jar, painted handle									▓		
Storage jar, knob-like protruded base		▓	▓	▓	▓	▓	▓	▓	▓		
Holemouth jar, externally thickened rim								▓	▓		
Holemouth, flared rim							▓	▓			
Holemouth, inturned rim											
Holemouth, upright tapered lip								▓			
Holemouth, simple rim								▓			

TABLE 6.1 Comparison of Area H Stratum 4 ceramic types with presence (*cont.*)

	MB IIC	LB IA	LB IB	LB IIA	LB IIB	Iron IA	Iron IB	Iron IIA	Iron IIB	Iron IIC	Pers.
3 handled jar w/ cup-like spout									■	■	
Painted jug w/ horizontal band decoration							■	■			
Narrow-necked jug						■	■	■			
Pinched mouth jug								■	■		
Strainer spout jug				■	■						
Jug, depressed ring base					■						
Flat base, ovoid/globular jug	■	■	■								
Flared rim juglet, arch-shaped loop handle									■		
Dipper juglet, externally thickened rim									■		
Dipper juglet, simple flared rim						■	■	■			
Small burnished/ decorated flask						■	■	■			
Lamps											
Cup & saucer		■	■	■	■						
Phoenician jugs		■	■	■	■						
"Samaria ware"					■		■	■			
Cypriot white painted amphoras						■	■				
Cypriot barrel jug								■			
Cypriot bichrome wares								■	■		
Cypriot Black-on-Red ware								■	■		

Square M/4, basket 178

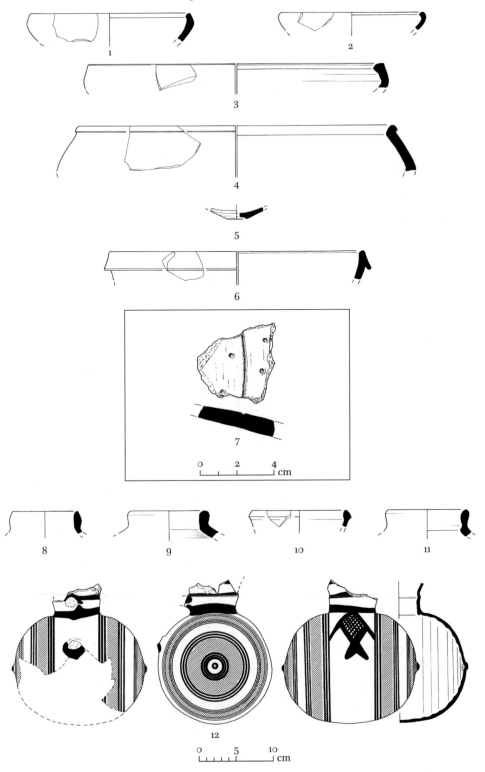

FIGURE 6.1

THE POTTERY OF STRATUM 4

Figure No.	Shape/object	Reg. No.	Locus/Pottery Basket	Description (color of exterior/interior/core; inclusions; decorations; etc.)
6.1.1	Bowl	AK VII 1980 H M/4 b. 178/6	178/6	Orangey pink/orangey pink/orangey pink to light grey
6.1.2	Bowl	AK VII 1980 H M/4 b. 178/9	178/9	Orangey pink/orangey pink/orangey pink; few small to medium sized white inclusions
6.1.3	Bowl	AK VII 1980 H M/4 b. 178/15	178/15	Salmon/salmon/core not visible; few small white inclusions
6.1.4	Bowl	AK VII 1980 H M/4 b. 178/10	178/10	Light brown/light brown/light brown to darker brown; few small to medium sized white inclusions
6.1.5	Bowl or jug	AK VII 1980 H M/4 b. 178/19	178/19	Salmon/salmon/salmon to light grey; few small white inclusions
6.1.6	Cooking pot	AK VII 1980 H M/4 b. 178/5	178/5	Red brown/red brown/red brown to dark grey; medium amount of small white inclusions
6.1.7	Baking tray	AK VII 1980 H M/4 b. 178/8	178/8	Red brown/dark grey/dark grey; medium amount of medium sized white, light grey, and crystalline inclusions
6.1.8	Storage jar	AK VII 1980 H M/4 b. 178/11	178/11	Salmon/salmon/salmon; few medium sized grey inclusions
6.1.9	Storage jar	AK VII 1980 H M/4 b. 178/12	178/12	Orangey pink/orangey pink/orangey pink; few small brown inclusions
6.1.10	Storage jar	AK VII 1980 H M/4 b. 178/13	178/13	Brown/brown/core not visible; few small white inclusions
6.1.11	Storage jar	AK VII 1980 H M/4 b. 178/14	178/14	Salmon/salmon/salmon to light grey; few small brown inclusions
6.1.12	Jug	AK VII 1980 H M/4 b. 178/2	178/2	Pink/pink/pink; few small brown inclusions; buff slip and red and black painted decorations; Cypriot Bichrome Ware

Square M/4, baskets 182 and 184

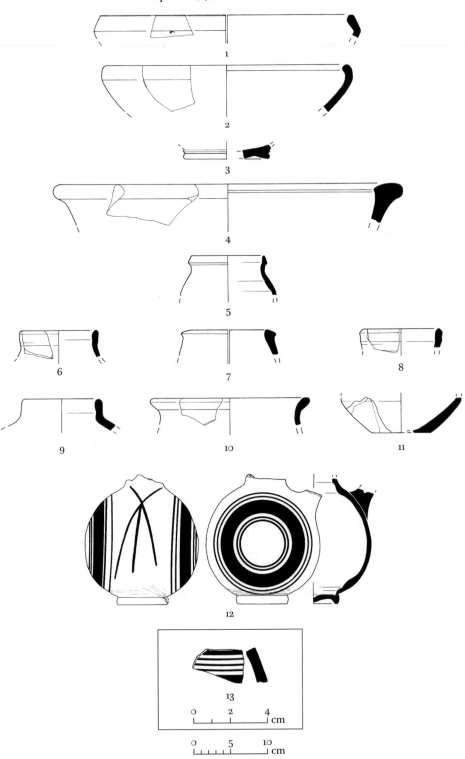

FIGURE 6.2

THE POTTERY OF STRATUM 4

Figure No.	Shape/object	Reg. No.	Locus/Pottery Basket	Description (color of exterior/interior/core; inclusions; decorations; etc.)
6.2.1	Bowl	AK VII 1980 H M/4 b. 182/2	182/2	Pink/pink/light grey; few small to medium sized light brown inclusions
6.2.2	Bowl	AK VII 1980 H M/4 b. 182/1	182/1	Orangey pink/tan pink/light grey; many small white inclusions
6.2.3	Bowl or krater	AK VII 1980 H M/4 b. 182/10	182/10	Red pink/red pink/red pink; many small white inclusions; cream-colored slip on exterior and interior
6.2.4	Krater or basin	AK VII 1980 H M/4 b. 182/6	182/6	Orangey pink/orangey pink/ orangey pink; many small black, and a medium amount of large white and light grey, inclusions
6.2.5	Cooking jug	AK VII 1980 H M/4 b. 182/3	182/3	Red brown/red to dark brown/grey; many small white inclusions
6.2.6	Storage jar	AK VII 1980 H M/4 b. 182/7	182/7	Red pink/red pink/red pink; many small to medium sized white inclusions; cream-colored slip on exterior and interior
6.2.7	Storage jar	AK VII 1980 H M/4 b. 182/4	182/4	Tan/tan/light grey; small to large sized white and grey inclusions
6.2.8	Storage jar	AK VII 1980 H M/4 b. 182/9	182/9	Pink/pink/light grey; few small white inclusions
6.2.9	Jar	AK VII 1980 H M/4 b. 182/8	182/8	Salmon/salmon/salmon; many small to large sized red pink inclusions; cream-colored slip on exterior and interior
6.2.10	Jar	AK VII 1980 H M/4 b. 182/5	182/5	Orangey pink/orangey pink/light grey; many small white inclusions
6.2.11	Jug	AK VII 1980 H M/4 b. 182/11	182/11	Pink orange/pink to tan/tan; many small brown inclusions
6.2.12	Jug	AK VII 1980 H M/4 b. 184/1	184/1	Pink/pink/pink; few small white and miniscule brown inclusions; cream slip on exterior, and black painted concentric circles on both sides, with black painted ribbon decoration opposite the handle
6.2.13	Body sherd	AK VII 1980 H M/4 b. 182/12	182/12	Tan/tan/tan; many small voids; burnished exterior, brown painted stripes on exterior; Cypriot Black-on-Red Ware

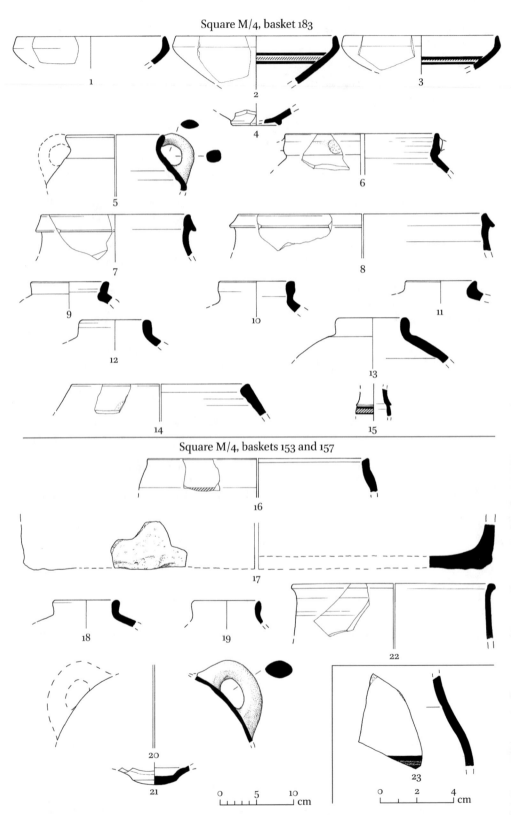

FIGURE 6.3

THE POTTERY OF STRATUM 4

Figure No.	Shape/ object	Reg. No.	Locus/ Pottery Basket	Description (color of exterior/interior/core; inclusions; decorations; etc.)
6.3.1	Bowl	AK VII 1980 H M/4 b. 183/20	183/20	Salmon/salmon/core not visible; very few small white inclusions
6.3.2	Bowl	AK VII 1980 H M/4 b. 183/3	183/3	Orange pink/orange pink/grey to tan; few small white inclusions, few small voids; red and brown painted stripes on interior
6.3.3	Bowl	AK VII 1980 H M/4 b. 183/6	183/6	Pink/pink/light grey; many small to medium sized brown, and a few large white, inclusions; red and dark brown painted stripes on interior
6.3.4	Bowl?	AK VII 1980 H M/4 b. 183/21	183/21	Buff/salmon/light grey; few small white inclusions
6.3.5	Cooking pot	AK VII 1980 H M/4 b. 183/19	183/19	Red brown/red brown/dark grey; few small to medium sized white inclusions; soot smudges on handle
6.3.6	Cooking pot	AK VII 1980 H M/4 b. 183/18	183/18	Red brown/red brown/dark grey; medium amount of small to medium sized white inclusions
6.3.7	Cooking pot	AK VII 1980 H M/4 b. 183/16	183/16	Red brown/red brown/core not visible; few medium sized white and quartzite inclusions
6.3.8	Cooking pot	AK VII 1980 H M/4 b. 183/17	183/17	Red brown/red brown/core not visible; few small white and quartzite inclusions
6.3.9	Storage jar	AK VII 1980 H M/4 b. 183/5	183/5	Salmon/salmon/tan to salmon; few small brown inclusions
6.3.10	Storage jar	AK VII 1980 H M/4 b. 183/12	183/12	Salmon/salmon/light grey; very few small white inclusions
6.3.11	Storage jar	AK VII 1980 H M/4 b. 183/13	183/13	Salmon/salmon/light grey; many small brown inclusions
6.3.12	Storage jar	AK VII 1980 H M/4 b. 183/14	183/14	Salmon/tan/core not visible; very few small white inclusions
6.3.13	Storage jar	AK VII 1980 H M/4 b. 183/15	183/15	Salmon/salmon/light grey; many small to large white inclusions
6.3.14	Jar	AK VII 1980 H M/4 b. 183/10	183/10	Pink/pink/light grey; many small to medium sized white, and a few small dark grey, inclusions
6.3.15	Jug	AK VII 1980 H M/4 b. 183/2	183/2	Orange pink/orange pink/orange pink; few small dark pink inclusions; cream slip on exterior above painted red and dark brown stripes; Phoenician type
6.3.16	Bowl	AK VII 1980 H M/4 b. 153/16	153/16	Salmon/salmon/core not visible; few small white inclusions; red painted stripe on exterior below carination
6.3.17	Basin	AK VII 1980 H M/4 b. 153/14	153/14	Red/red/red; many small white inclusions
6.3.18	Storage jar	AK VII 1980 H M/4 b. 157/9	157/9	Pink/pink/pink to light brown; many small white and red inclusions; cream-colored slip on exterior
6.3.19	Storage jar	AK VII 1980 H M/4 b. 157/10	157/10	Tan/tan/light grey; many small dark brown inclusions
6.3.20	Storage jar	AK VII 1980 H M/4 b. 153/15	153/15	Salmon/salmon/light grey; medium amount of small to medium sized white inclusions

Figure No.	Shape/ object	Reg. No.	Locus/ Pottery Basket	Description (color of exterior/interior/core; inclusions; decorations; etc.)
6.3.21	Storage jar	AK VII 1980 H M/4 b. 153/17	153/17	Pinkish tan/light grey/light grey; many small white inclusions; high fired
6.3.22	Jar	AK VII 1980 H M/4 b. 157/8	157/8	Pinkish tan/light brown/light brown; many small white and dark brown, and few large cream-colored inclusions
6.3.23	Jug?	AK VII 1980 H M/4 b. 157/15	157/15	Pinkish buff/pinkish buff/light grey; few small white inclusions; brown painted stripes on exterior; high fired

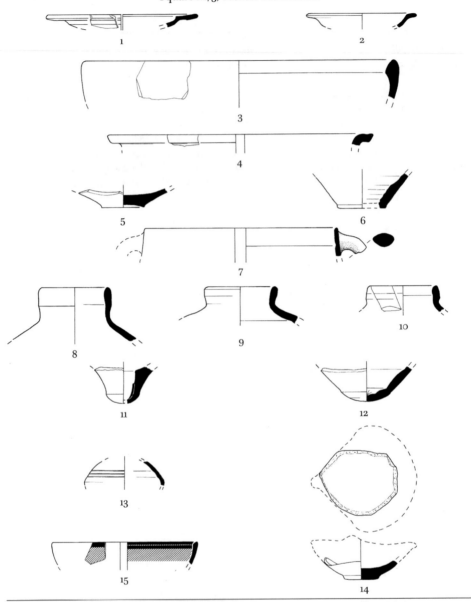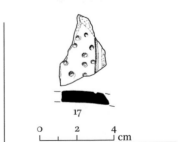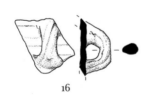

FIGURE 6.4

THE POTTERY OF STRATUM 4

Figure No.	Shape/object	Reg. No.	Locus/Pottery Basket	Description (color of exterior/interior/core; inclusions; decorations; etc.)
6.4.1	Bowl	AK VII 1980 H M/3 b. 201/1	201/1	Pink/pink/pink; few small white inclusions
6.4.2	Bowl	AK VII 1980 H M/3 b. 201/2	201/2	Pink/pink/light grey; many small to medium sized white inclusions
6.4.3	Bowl	AK VII 1980 H M/3 b. 206/9	206/9	Red/red/grey to dark brown; many small white inclusions; thick cream- to yellow-colored slip on exterior and interior; Egyptian import
6.4.4	Bowl	AK VII 1980 H M/3 b. 201/3	201/3	Pink/pink/light grey; medium amount of small white inclusions; cream-colored slip on exterior
6.4.5	Jug? Jar?	AK VII 1980 H M/3 b. 206/10	206/10	Pink/pink/light grey; many small to medium sized white inclusions
6.4.6	Jug? Jar?	AK VII 1980 H M/3 b. 206/11	206/11	Pink/pink/light grey; medium amount of medium sized white inclusions
6.4.7	Cooking jar	AK VII 1980 H M/3 b. 206/7	206/7	Brown/red brown/dark grey; many small to medium sized white inclusions
6.4.8	Storage jar	AK VII 1980 H M/3 b. 206/2	206/2	Pink/tan/light grey; many small to medium sized white, and few small brown, inclusions; cream-colored slip on exterior and interior
6.4.9	Storage jar	AK VII 1980 H M/3 b. 201/4	201/4	Tan/reddish pink/light grey; medium amount of small white inclusions; cream-colored slip on exterior
6.4.10	Storage jar	AK VII 1980 H M/3 b. 201/5	201/5	Pink/pink/light grey; medium amount of small to medium sized white inclusions
6.4.11	Storage jar	AK VII 1980 H M/3 b. 206/3	206/3	Pink/brown/light brown; many small white inclusions; cream- to pink-colored slip on exterior
6.4.12	Storage jar	AK VII 1980 H M/3 b. 206/12	206/12	Tan/light grey/light grey; many small to large sized white inclusions; cream-colored slip on exterior
6.4.13	Jug	AK VII 1980 H M/3 b. 201/6	201/6	Light grey/light grey/light grey; many small white inclusions; incised lines on exterior shoulder
6.4.14	Lamp	AK VII 1980 H M/3 b. 206/5	206/5	Pink/pink/light grey; medium amount of small to medium sized white inclusions
6.4.15	Bowl	AK VII 1980 H M/3 b. 206/8	206/8	Pink/pink/pink; few small white inclusions; red slip and burnished exterior and interior, dark brown painted stripes on exterior from bottom of rim and interior to just below rim; Cypriot Black-on-Red Ware
6.4.16	Storage jar	AK VII 1980 H M/3 b. 200/3	200/3	Salmon/salmon/salmon; very few medium sized grey and white inclusions
6.4.17	Baking tray	AK VII 1980 H M/3 b. 200/4	200/4	Brown/dark brown/brown; medium amount of medium sized white inclusions; incised dimples and line on exterior

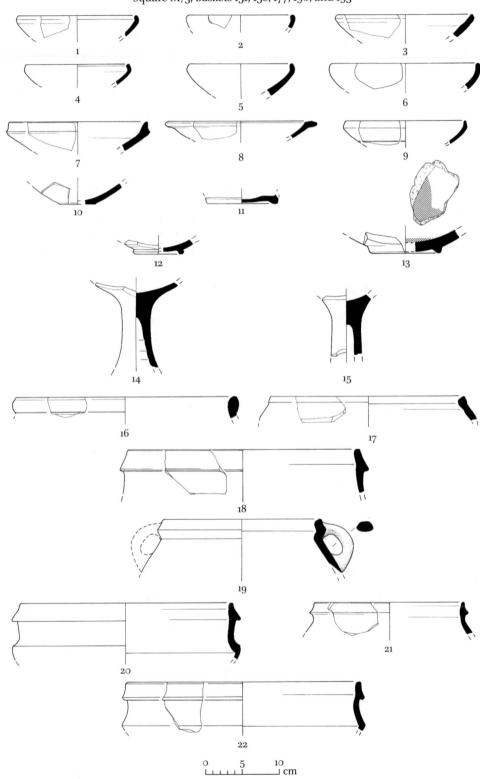

FIGURE 6.5

THE POTTERY OF STRATUM 4

Figure No.	Shape/object	Reg. No.	Locus/Pottery Basket	Description (color of exterior/interior/core; inclusions; decorations; etc.)
6.5.1	Bowl	AK VII 1980 H M/3 b. 193/4	193/4	Pink/pink/tan; medium amount of small white inclusions; cream-colored wash on exterior
6.5.2	Bowl	AK VII 1980 H M/3 b. 190/14	190/14	Pink/pink/light grey; very few small white inclusions
6.5.3	Bowl	AK VII 1980 H M/3 b. 177/10	177/10	Pink/pink/light grey; small amount of medium sized white inclusions
6.5.4	Bowl	AK VII 1980 H M/3 b. 158/8	158/8	Salmon salmon/tan; many small brown inclusions
6.5.5	Bowl	AK VII 1980 H M/3 b. 158/9	158/9	Pink/pink/light grey; small amount of small white inclusions
6.5.6	Bowl	AK VII 1980 H M/3 b. 158/10	158/10	Pink/pink/light grey to pink; many small to medium sized white inclusions
6.5.7	Bowl	AK VII 1980 H M/3 b. 158/11	158/11	Salmon/brown/light grey; medium amount of small white inclusions
6.5.8	Bowl	AK VII 1980 H M/3 b. 158/12	158/12	Pink/salmon/tan; many small to medium sized white inclusions
6.5.9	Bowl	AK VII 1980 H M/3 b. 151/3	151/3	Salmon/salmon/salmon; few small to large sized white inclusions; high fired
6.5.10	Bowl or jug	AK VII 1980 H M/3 b. 177/14	177/14	Pink/pink/light grey; medium amount of small white inclusions
6.5.11	Jug	AK VII 1980 H M/3 b. 177/15	177/15	Orangey pink/orangey pink/tan; few small white and pink inclusions
6.5.12	Bowl or jug	AK VII 1980 H M/3 b. 177/17	177/17	Pink/pink/light grey; few small white and brown inclusions
6.5.13	Bowl or jug	AK VII 1980 H M/3 b. 158/24	158/24	Salmon/salmon/tan to salmon; many small white inclusions; red paint on interior
6.5.14	Chalice	AK VII 1980 H M/3 b. 158/2	158/2	Reddish pink/reddish pink/grey; many small to large white inclusions; cream-colored slip on exterior
6.5.15	Chalice	AK VII 1980 H M/3 b. 158/3	158/3	Reddish pink/pink/grey; many small to medium sized white inclusions; cream-colored slip on exterior
6.5.16	Krater	AK VII 1980 H M/3 b. 177/6	177/6	Orangey pink/orangey pink/brown; many small white inclusions
6.5.17	Krater	AK VII 1980 H M/3 b. 177/5	177/5	Orangey pink/orangey pink/brown; few small white, medium amount of medium sized pink, and medium amount of large sized dark grey, inclusions
6.5.18	Cooking pot	AK VII 1980 H M/3 b. 193/5	193/5	Red/brown/dark grey; many small crystalline inclusions
6.5.19	Cooking pot	AK VII 1980 H M/3 b. 158/5	158/5	Orangey pink/orangey pink/dark grey; medium amount of small white inclusions
6.5.20	Cooking pot	AK VII 1980 H M/3 b. 158/7	158/7	Red/red/dark grey; many small white and crystalline inclusions
6.5.21	Cooking pot	AK VII 1980 H M/3 b. 158/6	158/6	Reddish brown/reddish brown/grey; many small white inclusions
6.5.22	Cooking pot	AK VII 1980 H M/3 b. 151/2	151/2	Red to brown/brown/dark grey; medium amount of small white inclusions

Square M/3, baskets 151, 158, 177, 190, and 193 (cont.)

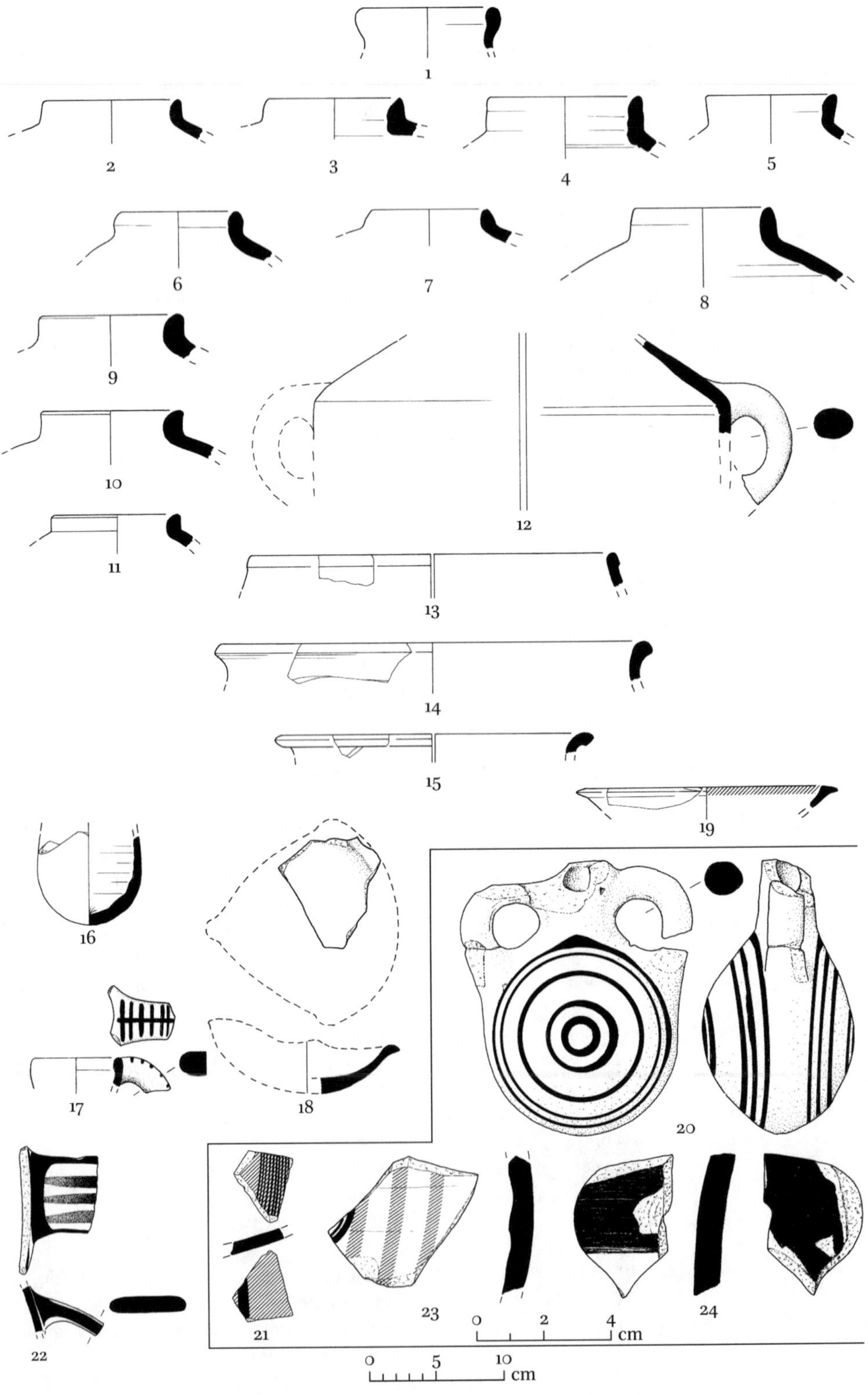

FIGURE 6.6

THE POTTERY OF STRATUM 4

Figure No.	Shape/ object	Reg. No.	Locus/ Pottery Basket	Description (color of exterior/interior/core; inclusions; decorations; etc.)
6.6.1	Storage jar	AK VII 1980 H M/3 b. 193/7	193/7	Salmon/salmon/light grey; few small white inclusions
6.6.2	Storage jar	AK VII 1980 H M/3 b. 177/9	177/9	Pink/pink/pink; many small brown inclusions
6.6.3	Storage jar	AK VII 1980 H M/3 b. 177/11	177/11	Pink/pink/pink; few small to medium sized white, many small pink, inclusions
6.6.4	Storage jar	AK VII 1980 H M/3 b. 177/12	177/12	Pink/pink/light grey; few medium sized white, many small to medium sized pink, inclusions
6.6.5	Storage jar	AK VII 1980 H M/3 b. 177/13	177/13	Pink/pink/tan; few small white inclusions
6.6.6	Storage jar	AK VII 1980 H M/3 b. 158/13	158/13	Salmon/salmon/light grey to salmon; many small brown inclusions
6.6.7	Storage jar	AK VII 1980 H M/3 b. 158/16	158/16	Cream/cream/cream; many small white inclusions; high fired
6.6.8	Storage jar	AK VII 1980 H M/3 b. 151/1	151/1	Salmon/salmon/light grey; small amount of small white inclusions
6.6.9	Storage jar	AK VII 1980 H M/3 b. 193/6	193/6	Salmon/salmon/light grey; few small white inclusions
6.6.10	Storage jar	AK VII 1980 H M/3 b. 158/14	158/14	Salmon/salmon/light grey; many small dark brown inclusions
6.6.11	Storage jar	AK VII 1980 H M/3 b. 158/15	158/15	Cream/cream/cream; many small white, few small grey and red, inclusions; high fired
6.6.12	Storage jar	AK VII 1980 H M/3 b. 158/18	158/18	Pink/pin/light grey; few medium sized white, and many small black, inclusions
6.6.13	Jar	AK VII 1980 H M/3 b. 193/8	193/8	Pink/brown/brown; medium amount of small white inclusions
6.6.14	Jar	AK VII 1980 H M/3 b. 177/4	177/4	Pink/pink/grey; many small, few large, white inclusions
6.6.15	Jar	AK VII 1980 H M/3 b. 193/9	193/9	Red brown/red brown/dark grey (cooking pot fabric); many small to medium sized white inclusions
6.6.16	Juglet	AK VII 1980 H M/3 b. 177/2	177/2	Pink/pink/tan; medium amount of small white inclusions
6.6.17	Jug	AK VII 1980 H M/3 b. 158/4	158/4	Pink/pink/light grey; many small to large sized white inclusions; burnished exterior, brown painted stripes
6.6.18	Lamp	AK VII 1980 H M/3 b. 190/11	190/11	Tan/tan/light grey to tan; many small to medium sized white inclusions
6.6.19	Bowl	AK VII 1980 H M/3 b. 193/1	193/1	Cream/cream/pink; dark brown painted stripe on interior of rim; non-local fabric, Phoenician type
6.6.20	Pilgrim flask	AK VII 1980 H M/3 b. 177/1	177/1	Buff to pink/pink/buff; few small brown and white inclusions; brown painted stripes on burnished exterior
6.6.21	Bowl	AK VII 1980 H M/3 b. 158/17	158/17	Pinkish tan/pinkish tan/pinkish tan; many small brown, and few small white, inclusions; red slip and burnished exterior and interior, dark brown stripes exterior and interior; high fired; Cypriot Black-on-Red Ware

Figure No.	Shape/ object	Reg. No.	Locus/ Pottery Basket	Description (color of exterior/interior/core; inclusions; decorations; etc.)
6.6.22	Jar	AK VII 1980 H M/3 b. 151/4	151/4	Tan/tan/tan; many small white, dark brown, and pink inclusions; cream-colored slip on exterior and interior; dark brown painted stripes on exterior; Cypriot White Painted Ware
6.6.23	Jug? Jar?	AK VII 1980 H M/3 b. 151/7	151/7	Tan/tan/tan; very few small dark brown inclusions; burnished exterior with red and dark brown painted stripes; Cypriot? Phoenician?
6.6.24	Bowl	AK VII 1980 H M/3 b. 151/8	151/8	Pink/pink/pink; very few light brown inclusions; dark brown wash on exterior, dark brown slip on interior; Cypriot White Painted Ware

Square O/1, basket 354

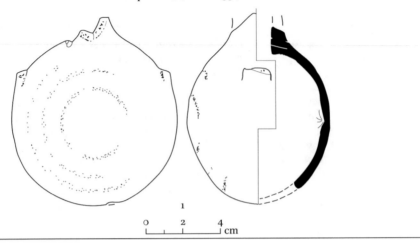

Square O/1, basket 336

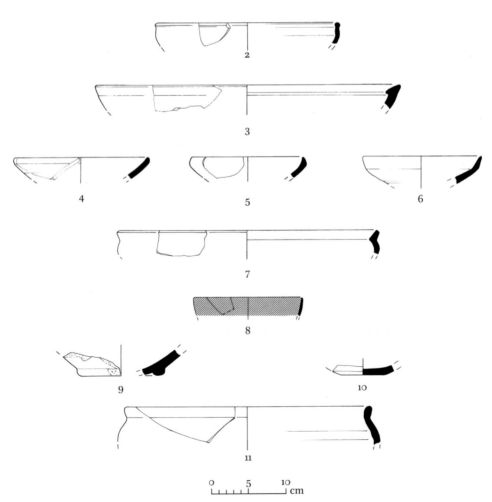

FIGURE 6.7

THE POTTERY OF STRATUM 4

Figure No.	Shape/object	Reg. No.	Locus/Pottery Basket	Description (color of exterior/interior/core; inclusions; decorations; etc.)
6.7.1	Pilgrim flask	AK VIII 1982 H O/1 b. 354/1, 341	354/1	Light grey/orangey pink/orangey pink to grey; few small white inclusions; cream slip and red painted stripes on exterior
6.7.2	Bowl	AK VIII 1982 H O/1 b. 336/3	336/3	Pink/pink/light grey; few small to medium sized light grey inclusions
6.7.3	Bowl	AK VIII 1982 H O/1 b. 336/12	336/12	Orangey pink/orangey pink/light brown; few medium sized white and light grey inclusions
6.7.4	Bowl	AK VIII 1982 H O/1 b. 336/13	336/13	Pink/pink/light grey; few small white inclusions
6.7.5	Bowl	AK VIII 1982 H O/1 b. 336/14	336/14	Pink/tan/pink; few medium sized light brown inclusions
6.7.6	Bowl	AK VIII 1982 H O/1 b. 336/15	336/15	Orangey pink/orangey pink/light grey; few small white inclusions
6.7.7	Bowl	AK VIII 1982 H O/1 b. 336/17	336/17	Orangey pink/orangey pink/grey; many small and medium sized white inclusions
6.7.8	Bowl	AK VIII 1982 H O/1 b. 336/16	336/16	Tan/tan/tan; few small white inclusions; red slip and burnished exterior and interior
6.7.9	Bowl or jug	AK VIII 1982 H O/1 b. 336/25	336/25	Tan/pink/light grey to tan; few small white inclusions
6.7.10	Jug	AK VIII 1982 H O/1 b. 336/27	336/27	Orangey pink/orangey pink/orangey pink; many small white inclusions
6.7.11	Krater	AK VIII 1982 H O/1 b. 336/18	336/18	Pink/pink/light grey; medium amount of small to medium sized white inclusions

Square O/1, basket 336 (cont.)

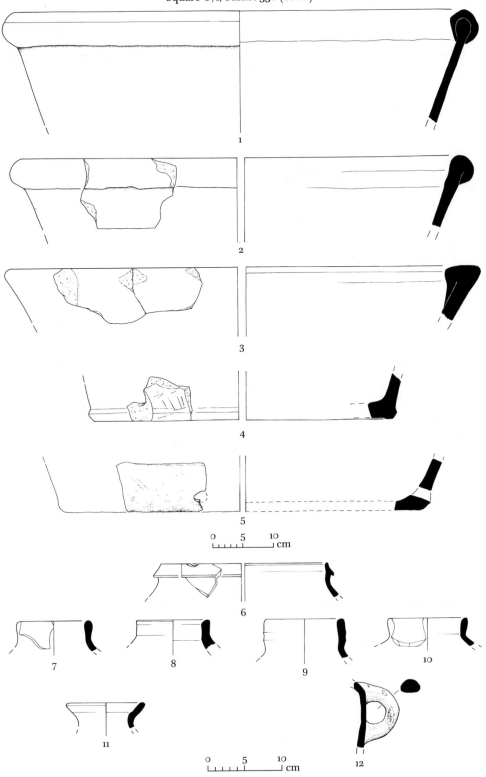

FIGURE 6.8

THE POTTERY OF STRATUM 4

Figure No.	Shape/ object	Reg. No.	Locus/ Pottery Basket	Description (color of exterior/interior/ core; inclusions; decorations; etc.)
6.8.1	Basin	AK VIII 1982 H O/1 b. 336/8	336/8	Pink/pink/dark grey; many small to large white, pink, and tan inclusions
6.8.2	Basin	AK VIII 1982 H O/1 b. 336/9	336/9	Pink/pink/dark grey; many small to medium sized white inclusions
6.8.3	Basin	AK VIII 1982 H O/1 b. 336/10	336/10	Pink/pink/dark grey; many small white inclusions, many small to large voids
6.8.4	Basin	AK VIII 1982 H O/1 b. 336/11	336/11	Pink/cream/dark grey; many small to large voids
6.8.5	Basin	AK VIII 1982 H O/1 b. 336/24	336/24	Pink/pink/dark grey; many small to medium sized white and light grey inclusions; hole in side just above base; hand made
6.8.6	Cooking pot	AK VIII 1982 H O/1 b. 336/19	336/19	Red/red/light brown; medium amount of small white inclusions
6.8.7	Storage jar	AK VIII 1982 H O/1 b. 336/6	336/6	Pink/pink/light grey; few small to medium sized white inclusions
6.8.8	Storage jar	AK VIII 1982 H O/1 b. 336/7	336/7	Salmon/salmon/tan; few small dark brown inclusions
6.8.9	Storage jar	AK VIII 1982 H O/1 b. 336/20	336/20	Pink/pink/light grey; many small to large sized white inclusions
6.8.10	Storage jar	AK VIII 1982 H O/1 b. 336/21	336/21	Pink/pink/dark grey; few small white inclusions, medium amount of small voids
6.8.11	Storage jar	AK VIII 1982 H O/1 b. 336/26	336/26	Tan/tan/tan; many small dark grey inclusions
6.8.12	Storage jar	AK VIII 1982 H O/1 b. 336/29	336/29	Pink/pink/pink; many small white, light grey, and pink inclusions

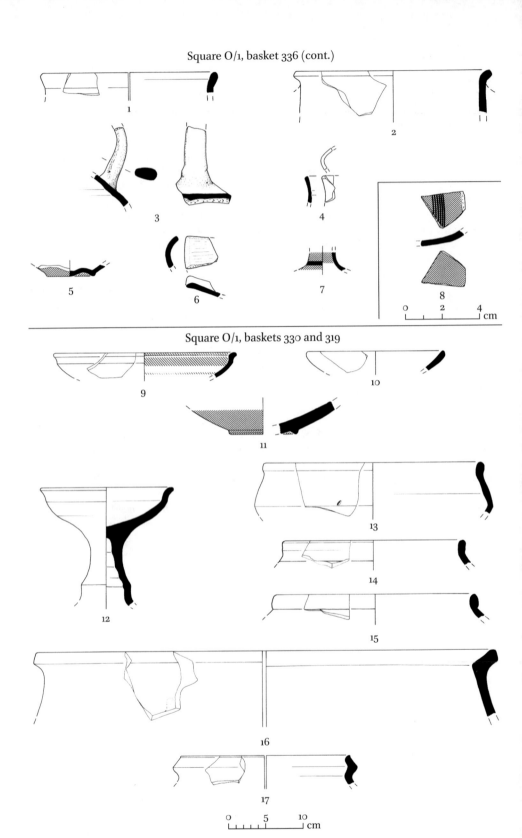

FIGURE 6.9

THE POTTERY OF STRATUM 4

Figure No.	Shape/ object	Reg. No.	Locus/ Pottery Basket	Description (color of exterior/interior/core; inclusions; decorations; etc.)
6.9.1	Jar	AK VIII 1982 H O/1 b. 336/4	336/4	Pink/pink/light grey; few small white inclusions
6.9.2	Jar	AK VIII 1982 H O/1 b. 336/5	336/5	Pink/pink/ grey; many small to medium sized white inclusions; high fired
6.9.3	Jug	AK VIII 1982 H O/1 b. 336/30	336/30	Pink/pink/pink; many small white and light grey inclusions; dark brown painted stripe below handle
6.9.4	Jug or juglet?	AK VIII 1982 H O/1 b. 336/22	336/22	Pink/pink/light grey; few small brown inclusions
6.9.5	Jug	AK VIII 1982 H O/1 b. 336/28	336/28	Tan/red/grey; many small to medium sized white inclusions; red slip on exterior; Phoenician type
6.9.6	Jug	AK VIII 1982 H O/1 b. 336/2	336/2	Orangey pink/orangey pink/light grey; polished (so highly burnished); Phoenician type
6.9.7	Jug	AK VIII 1982 H O/1 b. 336/23	336/23	Pink/pink/tan; few small brown inclusions; red slip and burnished exterior, red slipped interior to bottom of neck; painted dark brown stripe on neck; Phoenician type
6.9.8	Bowl	AK VIII 1982 H O/1 b. 336/1	336/1	Pinkish tan/pinkish tan/pinkish tan; very few small white and red inclusions; red slip and burnished exterior and interior; dark brown painted stripes; Cypriot Black-on-Red Ware
6.9.9	Bowl	AK VIII 1982 H O/1 b. 330/2	330/2	Orangey red/orangey red/light grey; many small white and dark grey inclusions; cream-colored slip on exterior and interior, dark brown painted stripes on interior
6.9.10	Bowl	AK VIII 1982 H O/1 b. 330/3	330/3	Pink/pink/pink; few medium sized white inclusions
6.9.11	Bowl?	AK VIII 1982 H O/1 b. 319/4	319/4	Pink/pink/light grey; many small voids, many medium sized, and a few large, white inclusions; dark brown slip on exterior, not well preserved
6.9.12	Chalice	AK VIII 1982 H O/1 b. 330/7	330/7	Tan/tan/tan; many small white inclusions
6.9.13	Krater	AK VIII 1982 H O/1 b. 330/4	330/4	Pink/pink/light grey to pink; many small white, and medium sized light grey, inclusions
6.9.14	Krater	AK VIII 1982 H O/1 b. 319/2	319/2	Pink/pink/grey to light grey; many small to medium sized white inclusions; cream-colored slip on exterior
6.9.15	Krater	AK VIII 1982 H O/1 b. 319/3	319/3	Pink/pink/tan; few small to large sized white inclusions
6.9.16	Krater	AK VIII 1982 H O/1 b. 319/1	319/1	Reddish pink/reddish pink/light grey; many small to medium sized white and light grey inclusions; cream-colored slip on exterior and interior
6.9.17	Cooking pot	AK VIII 1982 H O/1 b. 330/8	330/8	Red/red/grey; many small white and dark grey inclusions

Square O/1, baskets 330 and 319 (cont.)

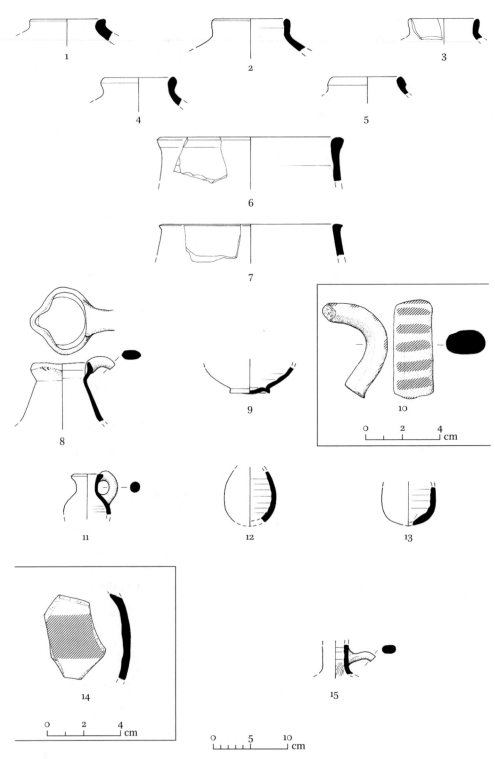

FIGURE 6.10

THE POTTERY OF STRATUM 4

Figure No.	Shape/ object	Reg. No.	Locus/ Pottery Basket	Description (color of exterior/interior/core; inclusions; decorations; etc.)
6.10.1	Storage jar	AK VIII 1982 H O/1 b. 330/9	330/9	Pink/pink/light grey to tan; many small white and medium sized light grey inclusions and voids
6.10.2	Storage jar	AK VIII 1982 H O/1 b. 330/10	330/10	Pink/pink/pink; medium amount of medium sized white inclusions
6.10.3	Storage jar	AK VIII 1982 H O/1 b. 330/11	330/11	Pink/pink/pink; many small brown inclusions
6.10.4	Storage jar	AK VIII 1982 H O/1 b. 330/12	330/12	Orangey pink/orangey pink/grey; many small white inclusions, few small voids
6.10.5	Storage jar	AK VIII 1982 H O/1 b. 330/13	330/13	Orangey pink/orangey pink/orangey pink; few small white inclusions and voids
6.10.6	Jar	AK VIII 1982 H O/1 b. 330/5	330/5	Pink/pink/light grey; many small and medium sized white, and medium dark grey, inclusions; cream-colored slip on exterior below lip
6.10.7	Jar	AK VIII 1982 H O/1 b. 330/6	330/6	Pink/pink/pink; few small white inclusions
6.10.8	Jug	AK VIII 1982 H O/1 b. 330/14	330/14	Salmon/salmon/salmon; many small light grey, and few small pink, inclusions; cream slip on exterior
6.10.9	Jug	AK VIII 1982 H O/1 b. 330/18	330/18	Tan/orangey pink/grey; few small white inclusions
6.10.10	Jug	AK VIII 1982 H O/1 b. 330/19	330/19	Orangey pink/orangey pink/orangey pink; few small white inclusions; red painted stripes on exterior of handle
6.10.11	Juglet	AK VIII 1982 H O/1 b. 330/15	330/15	Tan/tan/tan; few small white inclusions
6.10.12	Juglet	AK VIII 1982 H O/1 b. 330/16	330/16	Pink/pink/grey; few small white inclusions
6.10.13	Juglet	AK VIII 1982 H O/1 b. 330/17	330/17	Pink/pink/light grey; many small to medium sized white, and many small to medium sized dark grey inclusions
6.10.14	Jug? Bowl?	AK VIII 1982 H O/1 b. 330/20	330/20	Pinkish tan/pinkish tan/pinkish tan; many small voids; polished (so highly burnished) with red painted striped on exterior; Phoenician type
6.10.15	Jug	AK VIII 1982 H O/1 b. 319/5	319/5	Tan/tan/tan; many small dark grey, white, and pink inclusions; Cypriot

Square O/1, basket 300

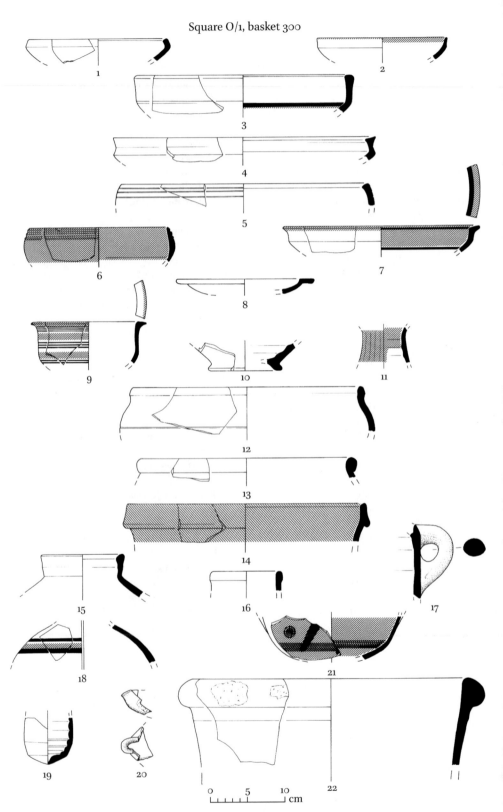

FIGURE 6.11

THE POTTERY OF STRATUM 4

Figure No.	Shape/ object	Reg. No.	Locus/ Pottery Basket	Description (color of exterior/interior/core; inclusions; decorations; etc.)
6.11.1	Bowl	AK VIII 1982 H O/1 b. 300/1	300/1	Pink/pink/light grey; few medium sized white inclusions
6.11.2	Bowl	AK VIII 1982 H O/1 b. 300/2	300/2	Orangey pink/orangey pink/grey; few small white inclusions; red painted stripe on interior and top of rim
6.11.3	Bowl	AK VIII 1982 H O/1 b. 300/3	300/3	Orangey pink/orangey pink/light grey; medium amount of small to medium sized white inclusions; cream slip exterior and interior; brown and red painted stripes on interior
6.11.4	Bowl	AK VIII 1982 H O/1 b. 300/4	300/4	Orangey pink/orangey pink/grey; few small to medium sized white inclusions
6.11.5	Bowl	AK VIII 1982 H O/1 b. 300/5	300/5	Pink/pink/light grey; many small to medium sized white inclusions; three incised grooves below rim on exterior
6.11.6	Bowl	AK VIII 1982 H O/1 b. 300/6	300/6	Red/red/light grey; medium amount of small white inclusions; red wash on exterior and interior; Egyptian import
6.11.7	Bowl	AK VIII 1982 H O/1 b. 300/7	300/7	Orangey pink/orangey pink/light grey; few small to medium sized white inclusions; red and dark brown painted bands on interior, top of rim, and just below exterior of rim
6.11.8	Bowl	AK VIII 1982 H O/1 b. 300/8	300/8	Pinkish tan/pinkish tan/pinkish tan; few small white inclusions; tan slip and burnished exterior and interior
6.11.9	Bowl	AK VIII 1982 H O/1 b. 300/10	300/10	Pink/pink/pink; many small white inclusions; cream-colored slip on exterior; red and dark brown painted stripes on exterior; Syrian?
6.11.10	Bowl?	AK VIII 1982 H O/1 b. 300/21	300/21	Pink/pink/grey to pink; many small white inclusions
6.11.11	Chalice	AK VIII 1982 H O/1 b. 300/19	300/19	Orangey pink/orangey pink/light grey; few small, medium, and large white inclusions; red slip and burnished exterior, red slipped interior
6.11.12	Krater	AK VIII 1982 H O/1 b. 300/11	300/11	Tan/tan/tan; medium amount of small to medium sized white inclusions
6.11.13	Krater	AK VIII 1982 H O/1 b. 300/12	300/12	Salmon/salmon/light grey; medium amount of small to medium sized white inclusions
6.11.14	Cooking pot	AK VIII 1982 H O/1 b. 300/13	300/13	Brown/red brown/dark grey; medium amount of small to medium sized grey inclusions
6.11.15	Storage jar	AK VIII 1982 H O/1 b. 300/15	300/15	Salmon/salmon/light grey; many small white inclusions
6.11.16	Storage jar	AK VIII 1982 H O/1 b. 300/16	300/16	Pink/pink/pink; many small white and light grey inclusions
6.11.17	Storage jar	AK VIII 1982 H O/1 b. 300/18	300/18	Tan/pink/light grey; few medium sized white inclusions
6.11.18	Jug	AK VIII 1982 H O/1 b. 300/17	300/17	Light grey/tan/light grey; medium amount of medium sized white inclusions; brown and red painted stripes on exterior
6.11.19	Juglet	AK VIII 1982 H O/1 b. 300/20	300/20	Red/red/red; many small white, and medium sized light and dark grey, inclusions

Figure No.	Shape/ object	Reg. No.	Locus/ Pottery Basket	Description (color of exterior/interior/core; inclusions; decorations; etc.)
6.11.20	Lamp	AK VIII 1982 H O/1 b. 300/22	300/22	Tan/pink/grey to light grey; few small white inclusions; smudge marks from use
6.11.21	Bowl	AK VIII 1982 H O/1 b. 300/9	300/9	Pink/pink/light pink; very few small white inclusions; red slip and burnished exterior and interior; dark brown stripes and painted decorations on exterior and stripes on interior; Cypriot Black-on-Red Ware
6.11.22	Pithos	AK VIII 1982 H O/1 b. 300/14	300/14	Tan/tan/tan; many small brown and white inclusions; cream-colored slip on exterior and interior; well fired; East Greek? Cypriot?

Square O/1, basket 297

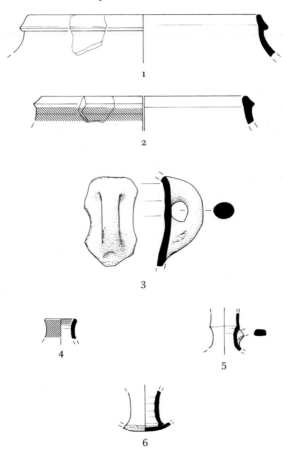

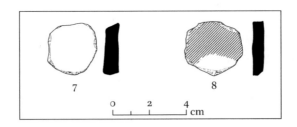

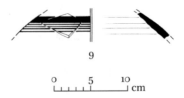

FIGURE 6.12

Figure No.	Shape/ object	Reg. No.	Locus/ Pottery Basket	Description (color of exterior/interior/core; inclusions; decorations; etc.)
6.12.1	Cooking pot	AK VIII 1982 H O/1 b. 297/4	297/4	Red/red/light grey; many small to medium sized white inclusions and a few small crystalline inclusions
6.12.2	Cooking pot	AK VIII 1982 H O/1 b. 297/5	297/5	Red/brown/dark brown; many small white inclusions
6.12.3	Storage jar	AK VIII 1982 H O/1 b. 297/8	297/8	Pink/pink/light grey; many small white inclusions
6.12.4	Jug	AK VIII 1982 H O/1 b. 297/10	297/10	Pink/pink/pink; few small white inclusions; red slip and burnished exterior, red slip on interior to bottom of rim
6.12.5	Jug	AK VIII 1982 H O/1 b. 297/9	297/9	Tan/tan/tan; few small white inclusions and few small voids; non-local
6.12.6	Cup-and-saucer	AK VIII 1982 H O/1 b. 297/1	297/1	Orangey pink/orangey pink/orangey pink; few small to medium sized white inclusions
6.12.7	Stopper	AK VIII 1982 H O/1 b. 297/2	297/2	Pink/pink/pink
6.12.8	Stopper	AK VIII 1982 H O/1 b. 297/3	297/3	Pink/pink/pink
6.12.9	Jar	AK VIII 1982 H O/1 b. 297/7	297/7	Pink/pink/pink; many small white, grey, and red inclusions; cream-colored slip on exterior, and dark brown painted stripes; Cypriot

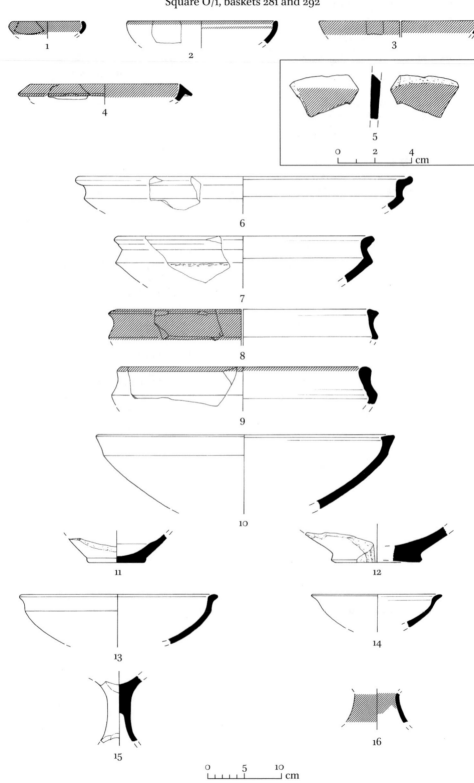

FIGURE 6.13

THE POTTERY OF STRATUM 4

Figure No.	Shape/object	Reg. No.	Locus/Pottery Basket	Description (color of exterior/interior/core; inclusions; decorations; etc.)
6.13.1	Bowl	AK VIII 1982 H O/1 b. 292/12	292/12	Pink/pink/pink; few small to medium sized white inclusions; red slip on exterior and interior
6.13.2	Bowl	AK VIII 1982 H O/1 b. 292/9	292/9	Salmon/salmon/salmon; few small white inclusions and small voids; burnished interior, brown painted stripes on interior and brown and red stripes on exterior
6.13.3	Bowl	AK VIII 1982 H O/1 b. 281/3	281/3	Salmon/salmon/salmon; medium amount of small white inclusions; red slip and burnished on exterior and interior; high fired
6.13.4	Bowl	AK VIII 1982 H O/1 b. 292/11	292/11	Orangey pink/orangey pink/orangey pink; many small white inclusions; red slip on exterior lip and interior; Phoenician type
6.13.5	Bowl	AK VIII 1982 H O/1 b. 292/25	292/25	Pink/pink/pink; small brown inclusions; red slip and polished exterior, painted red strip and polished interior; Samaria Ware or Phoenician fine ware
6.13.6	Krater	AK VIII 1982 H O/1 b. 292/5	292/5	Red brown/red brown/brown; few small white inclusions
6.13.7	Bowl	AK VIII 1982 H O/1 b. 292/6	292/6	Red/red/light grey; numerous small white, grey, and red inclusions
6.13.8	Bowl	AK VIII 1982 H O/1 b. 292/7	292/7	Orangey pink/orangey pink/light grey; few medium to large sized white inclusions; red wash on exterior
6.13.9	Bowl	AK VIII 1982 H O/1 b. 292/8	292/8	Pink/pink/light grey to tan; many small brown inclusions; red painted stripe on top of rim
6.13.10	Bowl	AK VIII 1982 H O/1 b. 281/1	281/1	Pink/pink/grey; many small to medium sized white inclusions
6.13.11	Bowl?	AK VIII 1982 H O/1 b. 281/13	281/13	Tan/tan/light grey; medium amount of small to medium sized white inclusions
6.13.12	Bowl?	AK VIII 1982 H O/1 b. 281/14	281/14	Pink/pink/grey; medium amount of medium to large sized white inclusions
6.13.13	Bowl	AK VIII 1982 H O/1 b. 281/2	281/2	Pink/pink/light grey; medium amount of small white and pink inclusions
6.13.14	Chalice	AK VIII 1982 H O/1 b. 292/10	292/10	Pink/pink/light grey; many small to medium sized white inclusions
6.13.15	Chalice	AK VIII 1982 H O/1 b. 292/22	292/22	Pink/pink/light grey; medium amount of small to medium sized white inclusions
6.13.16	Chalice	AK VIII 1982 H O/1 b. 281/11	281/11	Orangey tan/orangey tan/orangey tan; many small grey and white inclusions; red slipped on exterior and interior, polished (so highly burnished) on exterior

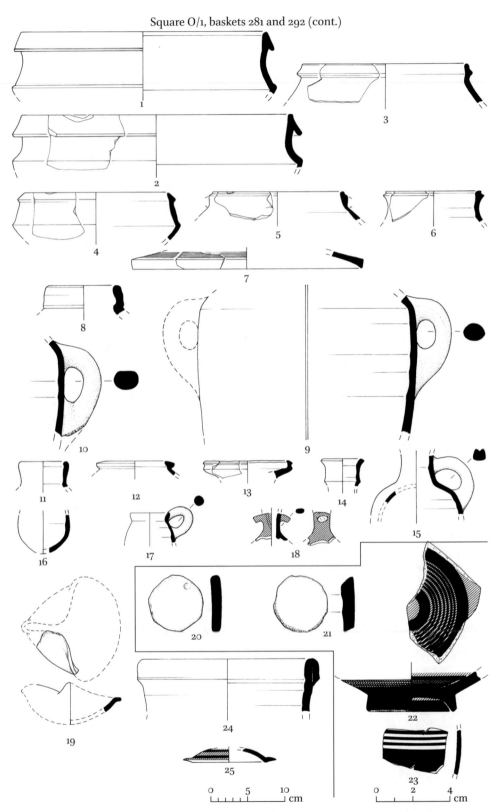

FIGURE 6.14

Figure No.	Shape/ object	Reg. No.	Locus/ Pottery Basket	Description (color of exterior/interior/core; inclusions; decorations; etc.)
6.14.1	Cooking pot	AK VIII 1982 H O/1 b. 281/4	281/4	Red/red/grey; many small white and crystalline inclusions
6.14.2	Cooking pot	AK VIII 1982 H O/1 b. 281/5	281/5	Red/red/grey; many small white and crystalline inclusions
6.14.3	Cooking pot	AK VIII 1982 H O/1 b. 281/6	281/6	Red brown/brown/dark grey; many small white inclusions
6.14.4	Cooking pot	AK VIII 1982 H O/1 b. 281/7	281/7	Red brown/brown/grey; many small white inclusions
6.14.5	Cooking pot	AK VIII 1982 H O/1 b. 292/14	292/14	Red/red/red; many small white inclusions
6.14.6	Cooking pot	AK VIII 1982 H O/1 b. 292/15	292/15	Red/brown/brown; many medium sized white inclusions
6.14.7	Baking tray	AK VIII 1982 H O/1 b. 292/2	292/2	Brown/red brown/dark grey; many small white inclusions; incised ridges on exterior
6.14.8	Storage jar	AK VIII 1982 H O/1 b. 281/10	281/10	Salmon/salmon/salmon; many small brown inclusions
6.14.9	Storage jar	AK VIII 1982 H O/1 b. 281/8	281/8	Orangey tan/orangey pink/grey; many small, medium, and large sized white inclusions
6.14.10	Storage jar	AK VIII 1982 H O/1 b. 281/9	281/9	Salmon/salmon/grey; many small to medium sized white inclusions
6.14.11	Storage jar	AK VIII 1982 H O/1 b. 292/18	292/18	Reddish brown/reddish brown/reddish brown; many small to medium sized white inclusions
6.14.12	Jar	AK VIII 1982 H O/1 b. 292/17	292/17	Pink/pink/light grey; few small white inclusions
6.14.13	Three-handled jar	AK VIII 1982 H O/1 b. 292/13	292/13	Brown/reddish brown/reddish brown; few small white inclusions
6.14.14	Jug	AK VIII 1982 H O/1 b. 292/19	292/19	Pinkish tan/pinkish tan/brown to tan; many small white, few large brown, white, and light grey, inclusions
6.14.15	Jug	AK VIII 1982 H O/1 b. 292/20	292/20	Pink/grey/grey; many small to medium sized white inclusions; pink-colored slip and burnished exterior, painted dark brown stripe; unusual handle with groove
6.14.16	Juglet	AK VIII 1982 H O/1 b. 281/12	281/12	Pink/pink/tan; medium amount of small white and brown inclusions
6.14.17	Juglet	AK VIII 1982 H O/1 b. 292/23	292/23	Orangey pink/orangey pink/orangey pink; many small white inclusions
6.14.18	Pilgrim flask	AK VIII 1982 H O/1 b. 292/21	292/21	Brown/red/grey; many small white inclusions; red slip on exterior
6.14.19	Lamp	AK VIII 1982 H O/1 b. 292/24	292/24	Pink/pink/light grey to pink; many small white inclusions; cream-colored slip on exterior and interior; smudge marks
6.14.20	Stopper	AK VIII 1982 H O/1 b. 292/3	292/3	Pink/pink/pink
6.14.21	Stopper	AK VIII 1982 H O/1 b. 292/4	292/4	Pink/pink/pink

Figure No.	Shape/ object	Reg. No.	Locus/ Pottery Basket	Description (color of exterior/interior/core; inclusions; decorations; etc.)
6.14.22	Bowl	AK VIII 1982 H O/1 b. 281/15	281/15	Pink/pink/pink; numerous small voids; thick buff-colored slip on exterior and interior, dark brown painted stripes on exterior and interior; Cypriot Black-on-Red Ware
6.14.23	Bowl	AK VIII 1982 H O/1 b. 281/16	281/16	Pink/pink/pink; few small white inclusions; buff slip and painted brown stripes on exterior; Cypriot Black-on-Red Ware
6.14.24	Pithos	AK VIII 1982 H O/1 b. 292/16	292/16	Orangey pink/orangey pink/tan; many small white inclusions; import, Cypriot?
6.14.25	Lid or cover	AK VIII 1982 H O/1 b. 292/1	292/1	Pink/pink/tan; many small voids; red slip and polished (so highly burnished) exterior, dark brown painted stripes; Cypriot fabric, Phoenician type

Square M/10, basket 279

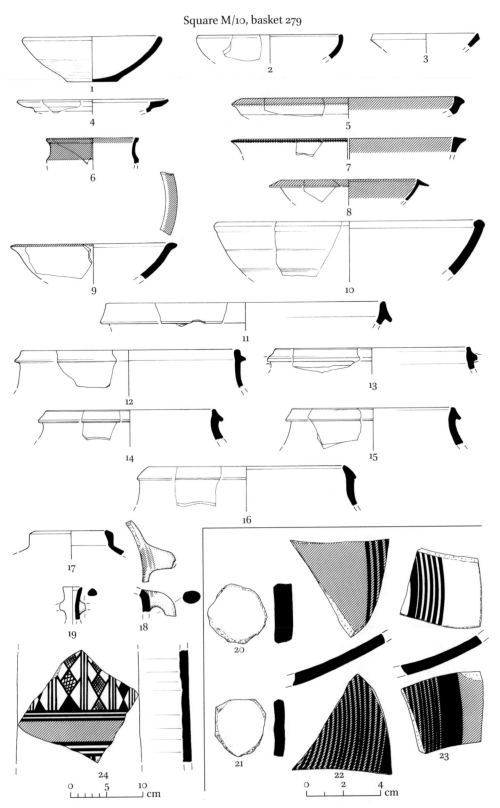

FIGURE 6.15

THE POTTERY OF STRATUM 4

Figure No.	Shape/ object	Reg. No.	Locus/ Pottery Basket	Description (color of exterior/interior/core; inclusions; decorations; etc.)
6.15.1	Bowl	AK VIII 1982 H O/1 b. 279/6	279/6	Red/red/grey; few small to medium sized white inclusions
6.15.2	Bowl	AK VIII 1982 H O/1 b. 279/9	279/9	Orangey pink/orangey pink/grey; many small white inclusions; pink to cream-colored slip on exterior and interior
6.15.3	Bowl	AK VIII 1982 H O/1 b. 279/15	279/15	Pink/pink/light grey; few small white inclusions
6.15.4	Bowl	AK VIII 1982 H O/1 b. 279/11	279/11	Dark tan/dark tan/dark tan; many small white inclusions; Phoenician type
6.15.5	Bowl	AK VIII 1982 H O/1 b. 279/12	279/12	Salmon/salmon/light grey; medium amount of small dark grey and white inclusions; red slipped exterior over lip and interior; non-local fabric
6.15.6	Bowl	AK VIII 1982 H O/1 b. 279/13	279/13	Salmon/salmon/light grey to salmon; medium amount of small white inclusions; red slipped exterior to carination, and interior to bottom of rim; high fired; non-local fabric
6.15.7	Bowl	AK VIII 1982 H O/1 b. 279/14	279/14	Pink/pink/light pink; medium amount of small grey inclusions; red slip and polished interior and rim, dark brown painted strip on rim; non-local fabric
6.15.8	Bowl	AK VIII 1982 H O/1 b. 279/10	279/10	Salmon/salmon/salmon; few medium sized white inclusions; red slip and burnished exterior of lip, and interior; high fired; non-local fabric, Phoenician type
6.15.9	Chalice	AK VIII 1982 H O/1 b. 279/8	279/8	Orangey pink/orangey pink/pink; many small to large sized white inclusions; red painted stripe on top of rim; soot smudges around edge of rim
6.15.10	Cooking bowl	AK VIII 1982 H O/1 b. 279/7	279/7	Red brown/red brown/dark brown to red brown; medium amount of medium sized white inclusions; fire smudges on exterior of bowl
6.15.11	Cooking pot	AK VIII 1982 H O/1 b. 279/16	279/16	Red/brown/dark grey; many small white and grey inclusions
6.15.12	Cooking pot	AK VIII 1982 H O/1 b. 279/17	279/17	Brown/brown/light grey; many medium sized white inclusions
6.15.13	Cooking pot	AK VIII 1982 H O/1 b. 279/18	279/18	Red brown/brown/dark grey to brown; many small to medium sized white and light grey inclusions
6.15.14	Cooking pot	AK VIII 1982 H O/1 b. 279/19	279/19	Red brown/brown/dark grey to brown; many small to medium sized white inclusions
6.15.15	Cooking pot	AK VIII 1982 H O/1 b. 279/20	279/20	Reddish brown/brown/dark grey; many medium to large sized white inclusions
6.15.16	Cooking pot	AK VIII 1982 H O/1 b. 279/21	279/21	Red brown/red brown/light grey; medium amount of medium sized white inclusions

THE POTTERY OF STRATUM 4

Figure No.	Shape/object	Reg. No.	Locus/Pottery Basket	Description (color of exterior/interior/core; inclusions; decorations; etc.)
6.15.17	Storage jar	AK VIII 1982 H O/1 b. 279/22	279/22	Dark pink/dark pink/light pink; many small white and light grey inclusions
6.15.18	Jar	AK VIII 1982 H O/1 b. 279/24	279/24	Tan/salmon/light grey; many small dark grey, few small white, inclusions; red stripes painted on handle; non-local fabric
6.15.19	Pilgrim flask	AK VIII 1982 H O/1 b. 279/23	279/23	Salmon/salmon/salmon; many small brown inclusions; non-local fabric
6.15.20	Stopper	AK VIII 1982 H O/1 b. 279/4	279/4	
6.15.21	Stopper	AK VIII 1982 H O/1 b. 279/5	279/5	
6.15.22	Bowl	AK VIII 1982 H O/1 b. 279/2	279/2	Salmon/salmon/salmon; medium amount of small white inclusions; orangey pink slip and burnished exterior and interior, dark brown painted stripes on exterior and interior; Cypriot Black-on-Red Ware
6.15.23	Bowl	AK VIII 1982 H O/1 b. 279/3	279/3	Salmon/salmon/salmon; orangey pink slip and burnished exterior, orangey red slip and burnished interior, dark brown painted stripes on exterior and interior; Cypriot Black-on-Red Ware
6.15.24	Pithos	AK VIII 1982 H O/1 b. 279/1	279/1	Orangey red/orangey red/grey; many small, and few large, white inclusions; pinky cream slipped exterior, red and dark brown painted stripes and decorations; Cypriot Bichrome Ware

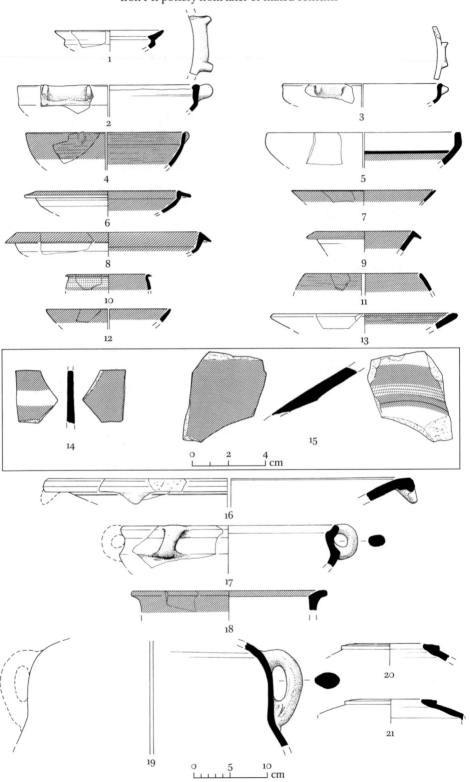

FIGURE 6.16

THE POTTERY OF STRATUM 4

Figure No.	Shape/ object	Reg. No.	Locus/ Pottery Basket	Description (color of exterior/interior/core; inclusions; decorations; etc.)
6.16.1	Bowl	AK VI 1979 H L/9 b. 190/7	190/7	Tan/tan/tan; few small orange inclusions
6.16.2	Bowl	AK VII 1980 H M/3 b. 138/5	138/5	Pink/pink/light grey; few small white inclusions
6.16.3	Bowl	AK X 1984 H N/4 b. 590/5	590/5	Orange pink/orange pink/grey; many small voids
6.16.4	Bowl	AK X 1984 H N/5 b. 522/2	522/2	Orange pink/orange pink/light grey; many small white inclusions; red slip and patterned hand burnishing on exterior and interior
6.16.5	Bowl	AK VIII 1982 H O/1 b. 252/1	252/1	Pink/pink/tan; many small brown, few large white, inclusions; salmon-colored slip and rough hand burnishing on exterior and interior, dark brown and red stripes on interior below the carination; Phoenician type
6.16.6	Bowl	AK VIII 1982 H O/1 b. 252/10	252/10	Pink orange/pink orange/pink orange; many small white and orange inclusions; red slip on exterior on lip and interior; dark brown stripe on interior of rim; Phoenician type
6.16.7	Bowl	AK VIII 1982 H O/1 b. 252/11	252/11	Pink tan/pink tan/pink tan; very few small orange inclusions; red slip and burnished exterior, red slip polished interior; dark brown painted stripe on exterior of rim; Phoenician type
6.16.8	Bowl	AK VIII 1982 H O/1 b. 267/4	267/4	Orangey pink/orangey pink/orangey pink; medium amount of small white inclusions; red slipped on exterior to bottom of rim and interior; Phoenician type
6.16.9	Bowl	AK VII 1980 H M/3 b. 138/10	138/10	Tan/tan/tan; few small brown and pink inclusions; red slip and burnished exterior on lip and interior; burnished exterior below lip; Phoenician type
6.16.10	Bowl	AK VII 1980 H M/3 b. 138/15	138/15	Light pink/light pink/tan; few small white inclusions; red slip and burnished exterior and interior, red slip stripes on exterior; Phoenician type
6.16.11	Bowl	AK VII 1980 H M/3 b. 138/18	138/18	Pink/pink/pink; few small white inclusions; red slip and burnished exterior and interior; Phoenician type
6.16.12	Bowl	AK IX 1983 H P/4 b. 1269/1	1269/1	Pink tan/pink/tan to light grey; few small white inclusions; red slip and burnished exterior and interior
6.16.13	Bowl	AK IX 1983 H L/9 b. 1160/1	1160/1	Pink/pink/light grey; few small white inclusions; red slip and burnished interior
6.16.14	Bowl	AK X 1984 H P/4 b. 507/1	507/1	Buff/buff/buff; no inclusions; red slip and burnished exterior and interior; Samaria Ware or Phoenician fine ware
6.16.15	Bowl	AK VIII 1982 H K/7 b. 46/2	46/2	Tan/tan/tan; no inclusions; polished (so highly burnished), red painted stripes, and 4 incised stripes on exterior, re slip and polished (so highly burnished) interior; Samaria Ware or Phoenician fine ware
6.16.16	Krater	AK VII 1980 H M/3 b. 138/6	138/6	Light pink/cream/light pink; few small to medium sized white inclusions; non-local fabric

THE POTTERY OF STRATUM 4

Figure No.	Shape/ object	Reg. No.	Locus/ Pottery Basket	Description (color of exterior/interior/core; inclusions; decorations; etc.)
6.16.17	Krater	AK VIII 1982 H O/1 b. 267/6	267/6	Red/red/light grey to red; many small grey and white inclusions
6.16.18	Krater	AK VII 1980 H L/9 b. 118/1	118/1	Pink/pink/pink; red slip and burnished exterior and top of lip
6.16.19	Storage jar	AK VII 1980 H M/3 b. 138/23	138/23	Tan/tan/tan; many small to medium sized white inclusions; non-local, Phoenician type
6.16.20	Storage jar	AK VIII 1982 H O/1 b. 267/8	267/8	Tan/tan/tan; many small white inclusions; high fired
6.16.21	Storage jar	AK VIII 1982 H O/1 b. 267/9	267/9	Pink/pink/pink; medium amount of small white and red inclusions; cream slip on exterior

Iron I-II pottery from later or mixed contexts (cont.)

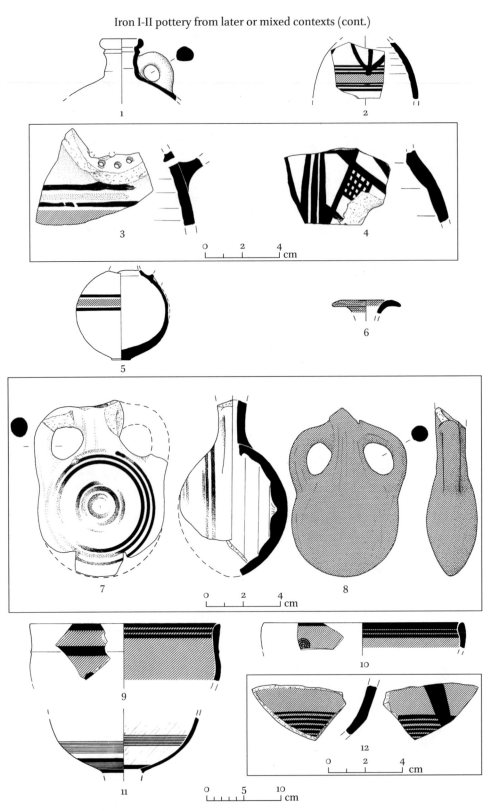

FIGURE 6.17

THE POTTERY OF STRATUM 4

Figure No.	Shape/ object	Reg. No.	Locus/ Pottery Basket	Description (color of exterior/interior/core; inclusions; decorations; etc.)
6.17.1	Jug	AK IX 1983 H O/1 b. 1090/1	1090/1	Red brown/red brown/grey; few small white inclusions
6.17.2	Jug	AK X 1984 H M/9 b. 620/1	620/1	Orange pink to tan/orange pink/light grey; many small black and white inclusions; burnished exterior, red and black painted stripes and decoration
6.17.3	Jug	AK VIII 1982 H L/9 b. 22/1	22/1	Orange pink/orange pink/grey; many small white inclusions; red and dark brown painted stripes below strainer spout
6.17.4	Jug	AK VII 1980 H L/9 b. 49/1	49/1	Pink/pink/pink; few small and medium white inclusions; dark brown painted stripes and checkerboard pattern
6.17.5	Jug	AK VI 1979 H L/9 b. 126/1	126/10	Pink/pink/pink; few medium amount of small to medium white and grey inclusions; red painted stripe on exterior
6.17.6	Jug	AK IX 1983 H O/1 b. 1042/2	1042/2	Orange tan/orange tan/orange tan; many small brown inclusions; red slip and polished (so highly burnished) exterior and interior to bottom of rim; Phoenician type
6.17.7	Pilgrim flask	AK VII 1980 H M/1 b. 210/1	210/1	Pink orange/dark grey/dark grey; many small, medium, and large sized white inclusions; some burnishing, and dark brown painted stripes, on exterior
6.17.8	Pilgrim flask	AK VII 1980 H K/7 b. 266/1	266/1	Pink/pink/pink; few small white inclusions; red slip and burnished exterior
6.17.9	Bowl	AK VIII 1982 H O/1 b. 267/5	267/5	Orangey pink/orangey pink/orangey pink; few small white and pink inclusions; red slip and burnished, and dark brown painted decorations, on exterior and interior; Cypriot Black-on-Red Ware
6.17.10	Bowl	AK X 1984 H N/5 b. 536/7	536/7	Pink orange/pink orange/tan; many small brown and orange inclusions; red slip and burnished, and dark brown painted decoration, exterior and interior; Cypriot Red-on-Black Ware
6.17.11	Bowl	AK VII 1980 H M/1 b. 235/1	235/1	Tan/tan/tan; few small brown and white inclusions; pink-tan slip and burnished, dark brown painted stripes, exterior and interior; Cypriot
6.17.12	Bowl	AK VIII 1982 H O/1 b. 73/1	73/1	Pink orange/pink orange/pink orange; few small orange inclusions; red slip and burnished, painted brown stripes, exterior and interior; Cypriot Black-on-Red Ware

Iron I-II pottery from later or mixed contexts (cont.)

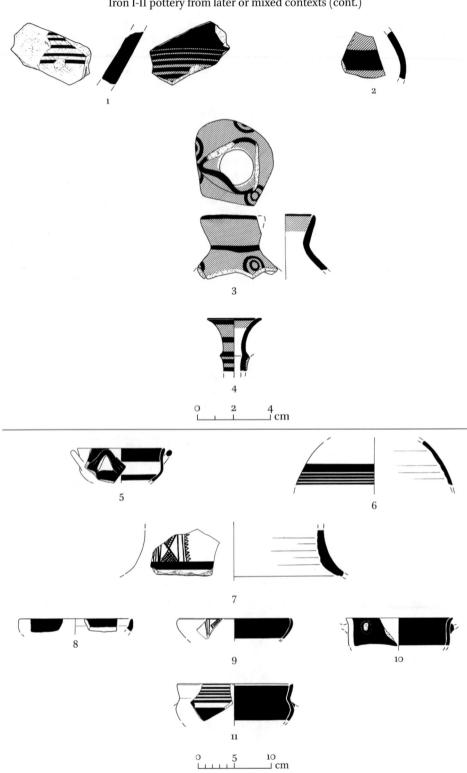

FIGURE 6.18

THE POTTERY OF STRATUM 4

Figure No.	Shape/object	Reg. No.	Locus/Pottery Basket	Description (color of exterior/interior/core; inclusions; decorations; etc.)
6.18.1	Bowl	AK X 1984 H M/9 b. 620/10	620/10	Pink orange/pink orange/pink orange; few small orange inclusions; red slip and burnished exterior, red slip interior, dark brown painted stripes on exterior and interior; Cypriot Black-on-Red Ware
6.18.2	Juglet	AK VIII 1982 H O/1 b. 267/14	267/14	Tan/tan/tan; very few small white inclusions; red slip and burnished exterior, brown painted stripe on exterior; Cypriot Black-on-Red Ware
6.18.3	Juglet	AK VII 1980 H M/3 b. 86/1	86/1	Tan/tan/tan; medium amount of small brown inclusions; red slip, dark brown painted decoration on exterior; Cypriot Black-on-Red Ware
6.18.4	Juglet	AK VIII 1982 H M/7 b. 103/5	103/5	Light grey/light grey/light grey; very few small white inclusions; red slipped, dark brown painted stripes on, exterior, and red slip to bottom of rim and dark brown painted stripe on rim interior; Cypriot Black-on-Red Ware
6.18.5	Bowl	AK IX 1983 H K/8 b. 1256/1	1256/1	Pink/pink/pink; few small brown inclusions; dark brown stripes on cream slip; Cypriot White Painted I
6.18.6	Jar	AK VII 1980 H K/7 b. 296/3	Loc. 753	Pink/cream/pink; many small brown inclusions; dark brown painted stripes on exterior; very high fired; Cypriot
6.18.7	Pithos	AK VII 1980 H M/4 b. 139/7	139/7	Tan/tan/pinkish tan; many small dark brown inclusions; tan slipped exterior with dark brown painted design; Cypriot
6.18.8	Bowl	AK VII 1980 H M/3 b. 138/14	138/14	Tan/tan/tan; few white inclusions; black metallic slip and burnished exterior and interior; East Greek
6.18.9	Bowl	AK VII 1982 H O/5 b. 243/1	243/1	Tan/tan/tan; very few small white inclusions; metallic black slip and burnished interior, burnished exterior with black painted decorations; East Greek
6.18.10	Cup	AK X 1984 H P/4 b. 512/2	512/2	Pink/pink to tan/pink; no inclusions; black slip and burnished exterior and interior; high fired, well levigated; Ionian
6.18.11	Cup	AK VIII 1982 H O/1 b. 252/2	252/2	Tan/tan/tan; very few small white inclusions; metallic black slip and burnished interior, burnished metallic black stripes on exterior; Ionian

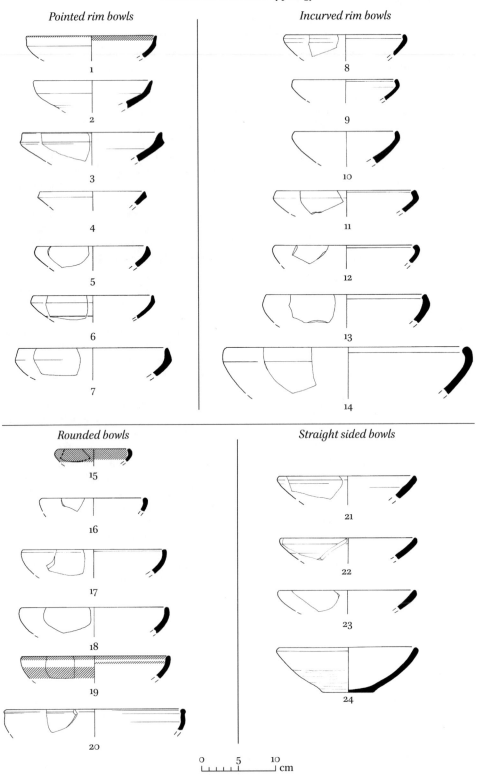

FIGURE 6.19

THE POTTERY OF STRATUM 4

Figure No.	Shape/ object	Reg. No.	Locus/ Pottery Basket	Description (color of exterior/interior/core; inclusions; decorations; etc.)
6.19.1	Bowl	AK VIII 1982 H O/1 b. 300/2	300/2	Orangey pink/orangey pink/grey; few small white inclusions; red painted stripe on interior and top of rim
6.19.2	Bowl	AK VIII 1982 H O/1 b. 336/15	336/15	Orangey pink/orangey pink/light grey; few small white inclusions
6.19.3	Bowl	AK VII 1980 H M/3 b. 158/11	158/11	Salmon/brown/light grey; medium amount of small white inclusions
6.19.4	Bowl	AK VIII 1982 H O/1 b. 279/15	279/15	Pink/pink/light grey; few small white inclusions
6.19.5	Bowl	AK VIII 1982 H O/1 b. 336/14	336/14	Pink/tan/pink; few medium sized light brown inclusions
6.19.6	Bowl	AK VII 1980 H M/3 b. 151/3	151/3	Salmon/salmon/salmon; few small to large sized white inclusions; high fired
6.19.7	Bowl	AK VII 1980 H M/4 b. 183/20	183/20	Salmon/salmon/core not visible; very few small white inclusions
6.19.8	Bowl	AK VII 1980 H M/3 b. 193/4	193/4	Pink/pink/tan; medium amount of small white inclusions; cream-colored wash on exterior
6.19.9	Bowl	AK VII 1980 H M/3 b. 158/8	158/8	Salmon salmon/tan; many small brown inclusions
6.19.10	Bowl	AK VII 1980 H M/3 b. 158/9	158/9	Pink/pink/light grey; small amount of small white inclusions
6.19.11	Bowl	AK VIII 1982 H O/1 b. 300/1	300/1	Pink/pink/light grey; few medium sized white inclusions
6.19.12	Bowl	AK VII 1980 H M/4 b. 178/9	178/9	Orangey pink/orangey pink/orangey pink; few small to medium sized white inclusions
6.19.13	Bowl	AK VII 1980 H M/4 b. 178/6	178/6	Orangey pink/orangey pink/orangey pink to light grey
6.19.14	Bowl	AK VII 1980 H M/4 b. 182/1	182/1	Orangey pink/tan pink/light grey; many small white inclusions
6.19.15	Bowl	AK VIII 1982 H O/1 b. 292/12	292/12	Pink/pink/pink; few small to medium sized white inclusions; red slip on exterior and interior
6.19.16	Bowl	AK VII 1980 H M/3 b. 190/14	190/14	Pink/pink/light grey; very few small white inclusions
6.19.17	Bowl	AK VIII 1982 H O/1 b. 279/9	279/9	Orangey pink/orangey pink/grey; many small white inclusions; pink to cream-colored slip on exterior and interior
6.19.18	Bowl	AK VII 1980 H M/3 b. 158/10	158/10	Pink/pink/light grey to pink; many small to medium sized white inclusions
6.19.19	Bowl	AK VIII 1982 H O/1 b. 292/9	292/9	Salmon/salmon/salmon; few small white inclusions and small voids; burnished interior, brown painted stripes on interior and brown and red stripes on exterior
6.19.20	Bowl	AK VIII 1982 H O/1 b. 336/3	336/3	Pink/pink/light grey; few small to medium sized light grey inclusions

Figure No.	Shape/ object	Reg. No.	Locus/ Pottery Basket	Description (color of exterior/interior/core; inclusions; decorations; etc.)
6.19.21	Bowl	AK VII 1980 H M/3 b. 177/10	177/10	Pink/pink/light grey; small amount of medium sized white inclusions
6.19.22	Bowl	AK VIII 1982 H O/1 b. 336/13	336/13	Pink/pink/light grey; few small white inclusions
6.19.23	Bowl	AK VIII 1982 H O/1 b. 330/3	330/3	Pink/pink/pink; few medium sized white inclusions
6.19.24	Bowl	AK VIII 1982 H O/1 b. 279/6	279/6	Red/red/grey; few small to medium sized white inclusions

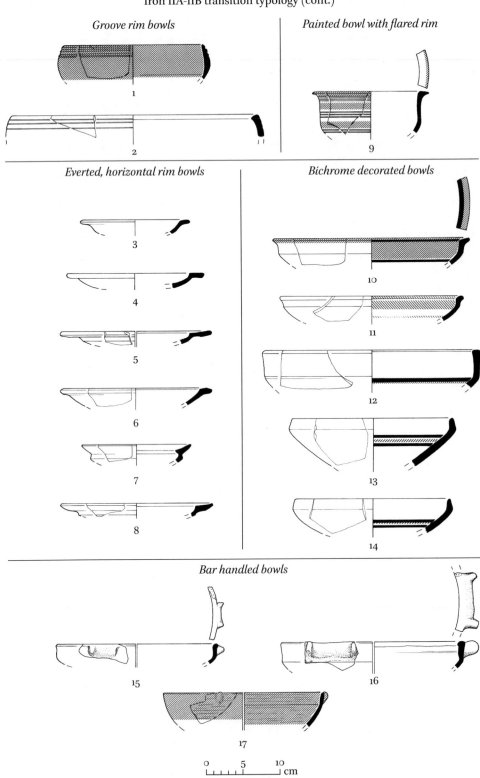

FIGURE 6.20

THE POTTERY OF STRATUM 4

Figure No.	Shape/ object	Reg. No.	Locus/ Pottery Basket	Description (color of exterior/interior/core; inclusions; decorations; etc.)
6.20.1	Bowl	AK VIII 1982 H O/1 b. 300/6	300/6	Red/red/light grey; medium amount of small white inclusions; red wash on exterior and interior; Egyptian import
6.20.2	Bowl	AK VIII 1982 H O/1 b. 300/5	300/5	Pink/pink/light grey; many small to medium sized white inclusions; three incised grooves below rim on exterior
6.20.3	Bowl	AK VII 1980 H M/3 b. 201/2	201/2	Pink/pink/light grey; many small to medium sized white inclusions
6.20.4	Bowl	AK VIII 1982 H O/1 b. 300/8	300/8	Pinkish tan/pinkish tan/pinkish tan; few small white inclusions; tan slip and burnished exterior and interior
6.20.5	Bowl	AK VII 1980 H M/3 b. 201/1	201/1	Pink/pink/pink; few small white inclusions
6.20.6	Bowl	AK VII 1980 H M/3 b. 158/12	158/12	Pink/salmon/tan; many small to medium sized white inclusions
6.20.7	Bowl	AK VI 1979 H L/9 b. 190/7	190/7	Tan/tan/tan; few small orange inclusions
6.20.8	Bowl	AK VIII 1982 H O/1 b. 279/11	279/11	Dark tan/dark tan/dark tan; many small white inclusions; Phoenician type
6.20.9	Bowl	AK VIII 1982 H O/1 b. 300/10	300/10	Pink/pink/pink; many small white inclusions; cream-colored slip on exterior; red and dark brown painted stripes on exterior; Syrian?
6.20.10	Bowl	AK VIII 1982 H O/1 b. 300/7	300/7	Orangey pink/orangey pink/light grey; few small to medium sized white inclusions; red and dark brown painted bands on interior, top of rim, and just below exterior of rim
6.20.11	Bowl	AK VIII 1982 H O/1 b. 330/2	330/2	Orangey red/orangey red/light grey; many small white and dark grey inclusions; cream-colored slip on exterior and interior, dark brown painted stripes on interior
6.20.12	Bowl	AK VIII 1982 H O/1 b. 300/3	300/3	Orangey pink/orangey pink/light grey; medium amount of small to medium sized white inclusions; cream slip exterior and interior; brown and red painted stripes on interior
6.20.13	Bowl	AK VII 1980 H M/4 b. 183/3	183/3	Orange pink/orange pink/grey to tan; few small white inclusions, few small voids; red and brown painted stripes on interior
6.20.14	Bowl	AK VII 1980 H M/4 b. 183/6	183/6	Pink/pink/light grey; many small to medium sized brown, and a few large white, inclusions; red and dark brown painted stripes on interior
6.20.15	Bowl	AK X 1984 H N/4 b. 590/5	590/5	Orange pink/orange pink/grey; many small voids
6.20.16	Bowl	AK VII 1980 H M/3 b. 138/5	138/5	Pink/pink/light grey; few small white inclusions
6.20.17	Bowl	AK X 1984 H N/5 b. 522/2	522/2	Orange pink/orange pink/light grey; many small white inclusions; red slip and patterned hand burnishing on exterior and interior

Iron IIA-IIB transition typology (cont.)

Fine ware bowls

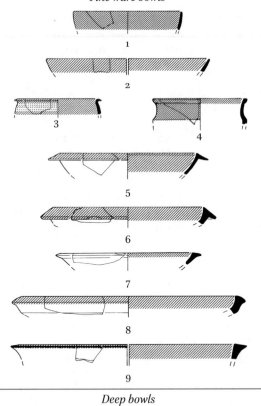

Deep bowls

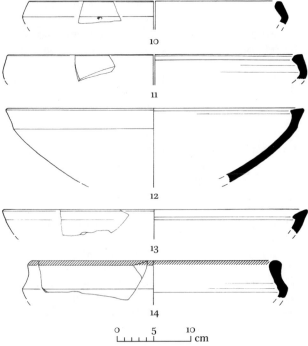

FIGURE 6.21

Figure No.	Shape/ object	Reg. No.	Locus/ Pottery Basket	Description (color of exterior/interior/core; inclusions; decorations; etc.)
6.21.1	Bowl	AK VIII 1982 H O/1 b. 336/16	336/16	Tan/tan/tan; few small white inclusions; red slip and burnished exterior and interior
6.21.2	Bowl	AK VIII 1982 H O/1 b. 281/3	281/3	Salmon/salmon/salmon; medium amount of small white inclusions; red slip and burnished on exterior and interior; high fired
6.21.3	Bowl	AK VII 1980 H M/3 b. 138/15	138/15	Light pink/light pink/tan; few small white inclusions; red slip and burnished exterior and interior, red slip stripes on exterior; Phoenician type
6.21.4	Bowl	AK VIII 1982 H O/1 b. 279/13	279/13	Salmon/salmon/light grey to salmon; medium amount of small white inclusions; red slipped exterior to carination, and interior to bottom of rim; high fired; non-local fabric
6.21.5	Bowl	AK VIII 1982 H O/1 b. 279/10	279/10	Salmon/salmon/salmon; few medium sized white inclusions; red slip and burnished exterior of lip, and interior; high fired; non-local fabric, Phoenician type
6.21.6	Bowl	AK VIII 1982 H O/1 b. 292/11	292/11	Orangey pink/orangey pink/orangey pink; many small white inclusions; red slip on exterior lip and interior; Phoenician type
6.21.7	Bowl	AK VII 1980 H M/3 b. 193/1	193/1	Cream/cream/pink; dark brown painted stripe on interior of rim; non-local fabric, Phoenician type
6.21.8	Bowl	AK VIII 1982 H O/1 b. 279/12	279/12	Salmon/salmon/light grey; medium amount of small dark grey and white inclusions; red slipped exterior over lip and interior; non-local fabric
6.21.9	Bowl	AK VIII 1982 H O/1 b. 279/14	279/14	Pink/pink/light pink; medium amount of small grey inclusions; red slip and polished interior and rim, dark brown painted strip on rim; non-local fabric
6.21.10	Bowl	AK VII 1980 H M/4 b. 182/2	182/2	Pink/pink/light grey; few small to medium sized light brown inclusions
6.21.11	Bowl	AK VII 1980 H M/4 b. 178/15	178/15	Salmon/salmon/core not visible; few small white inclusions
6.21.12	Bowl	AK VIII 1982 H O/1 b. 281/1	281/1	Pink/pink/grey; many small to medium sized white inclusions
6.21.13	Bowl	AK VIII 1982 H O/1 b. 336/12	336/12	Orangey pink/orangey pink/light brown; few medium sized white and light grey inclusions
6.21.14	Bowl	AK VIII 1982 H O/1 b. 292/8	292/8	Pink/pink/light grey to tan; many small brown inclusions; red painted stripe on top of rim

Iron IIA-IIB transition typology (cont.)
Shallow carinated bowls

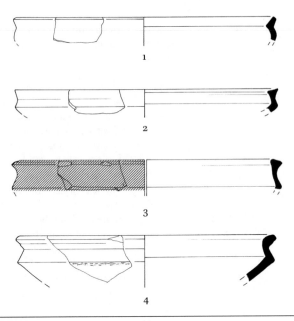

Bowl bases

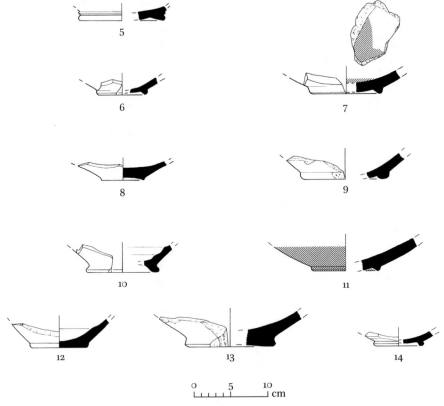

FIGURE 6.22

THE POTTERY OF STRATUM 4

Figure No.	Shape/object	Reg. No.	Locus/Pottery Basket	Description (color of exterior/interior/core; inclusions; decorations; etc.)
6.22.1	Bowl	AK VIII 1982 H O/1 b. 336/17	336/17	Orangey pink/orangey pink/grey; many small and medium sized white inclusions
6.22.2	Bowl	AK VIII 1982 H O/1 b. 300/4	300/4	Orangey pink/orangey pink/grey; few small to medium sized white inclusions
6.22.3	Bowl	AK VIII 1982 H O/1 b. 292/7	292/7	Orangey pink/orangey pink/light grey; few medium to large sized white inclusions; red wash on exterior
6.22.4	Bowl	AK VIII 1982 H O/1 b. 292/6	292/6	Red/red/light grey; numerous small white, grey, and red inclusions
6.22.5	Bowl or krater	AK VII 1980 H M/4 b. 182/10	182/10	Red pink/red pink/red pink; many small white inclusions; cream-colored slip on exterior and interior
6.22.6	Bowl?	AK VII 1980 H M/4 b. 183/21	183/21	Buff/salmon/light grey; few small white inclusions
6.22.7	Bowl or jug	AK VII 1980 H M/3 b. 158/24	158/24	Salmon/salmon/tan to salmon; many small white inclusions; red paint on interior
6.22.8	Jug? Jar?	AK VII 1980 H M/3 b. 206/10	206/10	Pink/pink/light grey; many small to medium sized white inclusions
6.22.9	Bowl or jug	AK VIII 1982 H O/1 b. 336/25	336/25	Tan/pink/light grey to tan; few small white inclusions
6.22.10	Bowl?	AK VIII 1982 H O/1 b. 300/21	300/21	Pink/pink/grey to pink; many small white inclusions
6.22.11	Bowl?	AK VIII 1982 H O/1 b. 319/4	319/4	Pink/pink/light grey; many small voids, many medium sized, and a few large, white inclusions; dark brown slip on exterior, not well preserved
6.22.12	Bowl?	AK VIII 1982 H O/1 b. 281/13	281/13	Tan/tan/light grey; medium amount of small to medium sized white inclusions
6.22.13	Bowl?	AK VIII 1982 H O/1 b. 281/14	281/14	Pink/pink/grey; medium amount of medium to large sized white inclusions
6.22.14	Bowl or jug	AK VII 1980 H M/3 b. 177/17	177/17	Pink/pink/light grey; few small white and brown inclusions

Iron IIA-IIB transition typology (cont.)

Chalices

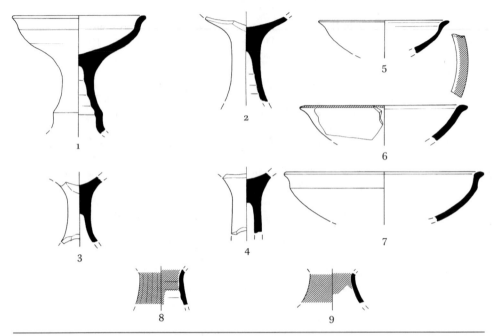

Carinated kraters with flanged rims

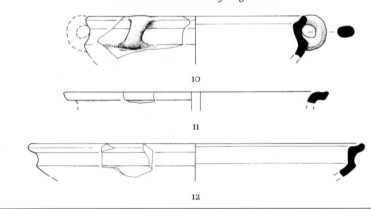

Carinated kraters with bevelled rims

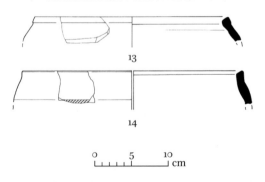

FIGURE 6.23

THE POTTERY OF STRATUM 4

Figure No.	Shape/ object	Reg. No.	Locus/ Pottery Basket	Description (color of exterior/interior/core; inclusions; decorations; etc.)
6.23.1	Chalice	AK VIII 1982 H O/1 b. 330/7	330/7	Tan/tan/tan; many small white inclusions
6.23.2	Chalice	AK VII 1980 H M/3 b. 158/2	158/2	Reddish pink/reddish pink/grey; many small to large white inclusions; cream-colored slip on exterior
6.23.3	Chalice	AK VIII 1982 H O/1 b. 292/22	292/22	Pink/pink/light grey; medium amount of small to medium sized white inclusions
6.23.4	Chalice	AK VII 1980 H M/3 b. 158/3	158/3	Reddish pink/pink/grey; many small to medium sized white inclusions; cream-colored slip on exterior
6.23.5	Chalice	AK VIII 1982 H O/1 b. 292/10	292/10	Pink/pink/light grey; many small to medium sized white inclusions
6.23.6	Chalice	AK VIII 1982 H O/1 b. 279/8	279/8	Orangey pink/orangey pink/pink; many small to large sized white inclusions; red painted stripe on top of rim; soot smudges around edge of rim
6.23.7	Bowl	AK VIII 1982 H O/1 b. 281/2	281/2	Pink/pink/light grey; medium amount of small white and pink inclusions
6.23.8	Chalice	AK VIII 1982 H O/1 b. 300/19	300/19	Orangey pink/orangey pink/light grey; few small, medium, and large white inclusions; red slip and burnished exterior, red slipped interior
6.23.9	Chalice	AK VIII 1982 H O/1 b. 281/11	281/11	Orangey tan/orangey tan/orangey tan; many small grey and white inclusions; red slipped on exterior and interior, polished (so highly burnished) on exterior
6.23.10	Krater	AK VIII 1982 H O/1 b. 267/6	267/6	Red/red/light grey to red; many small grey and white inclusions
6.23.11	Bowl	AK VII 1980 H M/3 b. 201/3	201/3	Pink/pink/light grey; medium amount of small white inclusions; cream-colored slip on exterior
6.23.12	Krater	AK VIII 1982 H O/1 b. 292/5	292/5	Red brown/red brown/brown; few small white inclusions
6.23.13	Krater	AK VII 1980 H M/3 b. 177/5	177/5	Orangey pink/orangey pink/brown; few small white, medium amount of medium sized pink, and medium amount of large sized dark grey, inclusions
6.23.14	Bowl	AK VII 1980 H M/4 b. 153/16	153/16	Salmon/salmon/core not visible; few small white inclusions; red painted stripe on exterior below carination

Iron IIA-IIB transition typology (cont.)

Carinated kraters with simple, upright rims

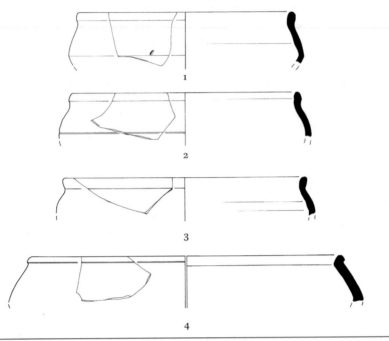

Carinated kraters with thickened, rounded rims

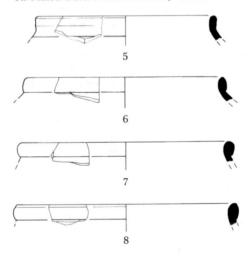

Krater with flared, thickened rim

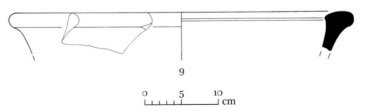

FIGURE 6.24

Figure No.	Shape/object	Reg. No.	Locus/Pottery Basket	Description (color of exterior/interior/core; inclusions; decorations; etc.)
6.24.1	Krater	AK VIII 1982 H O/1 b. 330/4	330/4	Pink/pink/light grey to pink; many small white, and medium sized light grey, inclusions
6.24.2	Krater	AK VIII 1982 H O/1 b. 300/11	300/11	Tan/tan/tan; medium amount of small to medium sized white inclusions
6.24.3	Krater	AK VIII 1982 H O/1 b. 336/18	336/18	Pink/pink/light grey; medium amount of small to medium sized white inclusions
6.24.4	Bowl	AK VII 1980 H M/4 b. 178/10	178/10	Light brown/light brown/light brown to darker brown; few small to medium sized white inclusions
6.24.5	Krater	AK VIII 1982 H O/1 b. 319/2	319/2	Pink/pink/grey to light grey; many small to medium sized white inclusions; cream-colored slip on exterior
6.24.6	Krater	AK VIII 1982 H O/1 b. 319/3	319/3	Pink/pink/tan; few small to large sized white inclusions
6.24.7	Krater	AK VIII 1982 H O/1 b. 300/12	300/12	Salmon/salmon/light grey; medium amount of small to medium sized white inclusions
6.24.8	Krater	AK VII 1980 H M/3 b. 177/6	177/6	Orangey pink/orangey pink/brown; many small white inclusions
6.24.9	Krater or basin	AK VII 1980 H M/4 b. 182/6	182/6	Orangey pink/orangey pink/orangey pink; many small black, and a medium amount of large white and light grey, inclusions

Iron IIA-IIB transition typology (cont.)

Basins

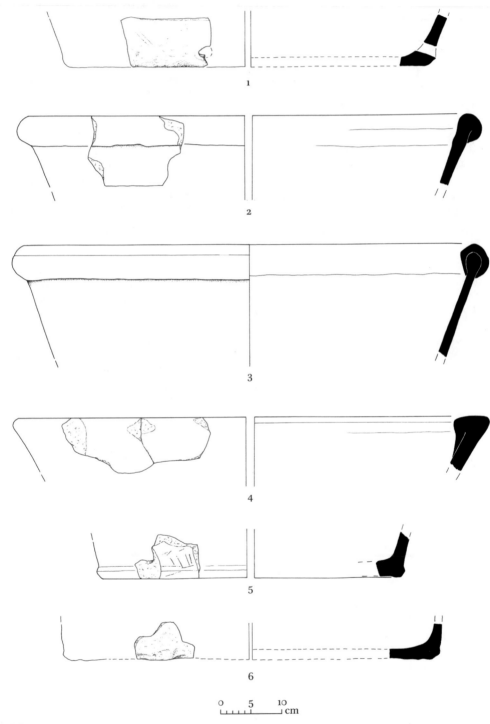

FIGURE 6.25

Figure No.	Shape/object	Reg. No.	Locus/Pottery Basket	Description (color of exterior/interior/core; inclusions; decorations; etc.)
6.25.1	Basin	AK VIII 1982 H O/1 b. 336/24	336/24	Pink/pink/dark grey; many small to medium sized white and light grey inclusions; hole in side just above base; hand made
6.25.2	Basin	AK VIII 1982 H O/1 b. 336/9	336/9	Pink/pink/dark grey; many small to medium sized white inclusions
6.25.3	Basin	AK VIII 1982 H O/1 b. 336/8	336/8	Pink/pink/dark grey; many small to large white, pink, and tan inclusions
6.25.4	Basin	AK VIII 1982 H O/1 b. 336/10	336/10	Pink/pink/dark grey; many small white inclusions, many small to large voids
6.25.5	Basin	AK VIII 1982 H O/1 b. 336/11	336/11	Pink/cream/dark grey; many small to large voids
6.25.6	Basin	AK VII 1980 H M/4 b. 153/14	153/14	Red/red/red; many small white inclusions

Iron IIA-IIB transition typology (cont.)
Cooking pots with triangular, pinched rims

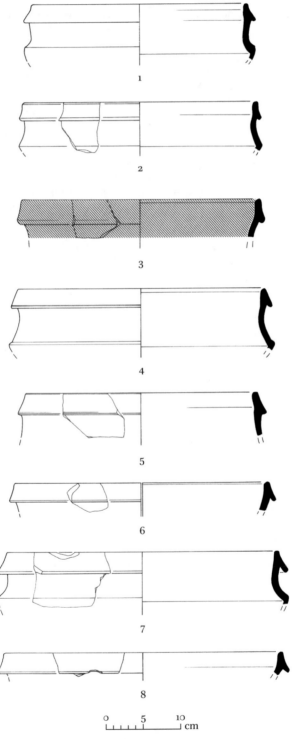

FIGURE 6.26

Figure No.	Shape/ object	Reg. No.	Locus/ Pottery Basket	Description (color of exterior/interior/core; inclusions; decorations; etc.)
6.26.1	Cooking pot	AK VII 1980 H M/3 b. 158/7	158/7	Red/red/dark grey; many small white and crystalline inclusions
6.26.2	Cooking pot	AK VII 1980 H M/3 b. 151/2	151/2	Red to brown/brown/dark grey; medium amount of small white inclusions
6.26.3	Cooking pot	AK VIII 1982 H O/1 b. 300/13	300/13	Brown/red brown/dark grey; medium amount of small to medium sized grey inclusions
6.26.4	Cooking pot	AK VIII 1982 H O/1 b. 281/4	281/4	Red/red/grey; many small white and crystalline inclusions
6.26.5	Cooking pot	AK VII 1980 H M/3 b. 193/5	193/5	Red/brown/dark grey; many small crystalline inclusions
6.26.6	Cooking pot	AK VII 1980 H M/4 b. 178/5	178/5	Red brown/red brown/red brown to dark grey; medium amount of small white inclusions
6.26.7	Cooking pot	AK VIII 1982 H O/1 b. 281/5	281/5	Red/red/grey; many small white and crystalline inclusions
6.26.8	Cooking pot	AK VIII 1982 H O/1 b. 279/16	279/16	Red/brown/dark grey; many small white and grey inclusions

Iron IIA-IIB transition typology (cont.)
Cooking pots with triangular, pinched rims (cont.)

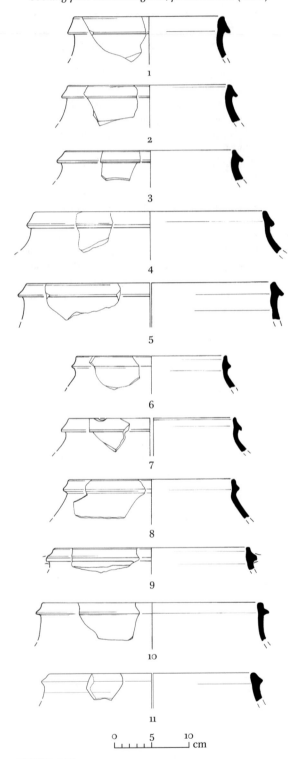

FIGURE 6.27

THE POTTERY OF STRATUM 4

Figure No.	Shape/ object	Reg. No.	Locus/ Pottery Basket	Description (color of exterior/interior/core; inclusions; decorations; etc.)
6.27.1	Cooking pot	AK VII 1980 H M/4 b. 183/16	183/16	Red brown/red brown/core not visible; few medium sized white and quartzite inclusions
6.27.2	Cooking pot	AK VIII 1982 H O/1 b. 279/20	279/20	Reddish brown/brown/dark grey; many medium to large sized white inclusions
6.27.3	Cooking pot	AK VIII 1982 H O/1 b. 279/19	279/19	Red brown/brown/dark grey to brown; many small to medium sized white inclusions
6.27.4	Cooking pot	AK VIII 1982 H O/1 b. 297/4	297/4	Red/red/light grey; many small to medium sized white inclusions and a few small crystalline inclusions
6.27.5	Cooking pot	AK VII 1980 H M/4 b. 183/17	183/17	Red brown/red brown/core not visible; few small white and quartzite inclusions
6.27.6	Cooking pot	AK VII 1980 H M/3 b. 158/6	158/6	Reddish brown/reddish brown/grey; many small white inclusions
6.27.7	Cooking pot	AK VIII 1982 H O/1 b. 336/19	336/19	Red/red/light brown; medium amount of small white inclusions
6.27.8	Cooking pot	AK VIII 1982 H O/1 b. 281/6	281/6	Red brown/brown/dark grey; many small white inclusions
6.27.9	Cooking pot	AK VIII 1982 H O/1 b. 279/18	279/18	Red brown/brown/dark grey to brown; many small to medium sized white and light grey inclusions
6.27.10	Cooking pot	AK VIII 1982 H O/1 b. 279/17	279/17	Brown/brown/light grey; many medium sized white inclusions
6.27.11	Cooking pot	AK VIII 1982 H O/1 b. 297/5	297/5	Red/brown/dark brown; many small white inclusions

Iron IIA-IIB transition typology (cont.)

Cooking pot with with upright, triangular rim and bag shaped body

Cooking pots with incurved rim with exterior thickening

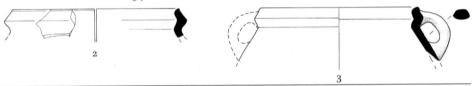

Cooking pots with inverted rim with exterior thickening

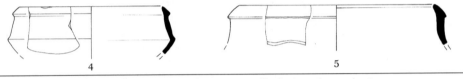

Cooking pots with ridged rim, externally thickened, upright rim and tapered lip, and cooking jugs

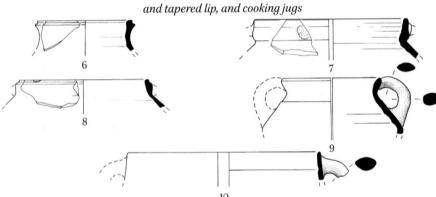

Baking trays

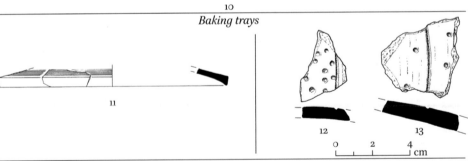

Cooking bowl

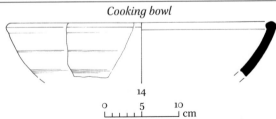

FIGURE 6.28

Figure No.	Shape/object	Reg. No.	Locus/Pottery Basket	Description (color of exterior/interior/core; inclusions; decorations; etc.)
6.28.1	Cooking pot	AK VII 1980 H M/4 b. 182/3	182/3	Red brown/red to dark brown/grey; many small white inclusions
6.28.2	Cooking pot	AK VIII 1982 H O/1 b. 330/8	330/8	Red/red/grey; many small white and dark grey inclusions
6.28.3	Cooking pot	AK VII 1980 H M/3 b. 158/5	158/5	Orangey pink/orangey pink/dark grey; medium amount of small white inclusions
6.28.4	Cooking pot	AK VIII 1982 H O/1 b. 281/7	281/7	Red brown/brown/grey; many small white inclusions
6.28.5	Cooking pot	AK VIII 1982 H O/1 b. 279/21	279/21	Red brown/red brown/light grey; medium amount of medium sized white inclusions
6.28.6	Cooking pot	AK VIII 1982 H O/1 b. 292/15	292/15	Red/brown/brown; many medium sized white inclusions
6.28.7	Cooking pot	AK VII 1980 H M/4 b. 183/18	183/18	Red brown/red brown/dark grey; medium amount of small to medium sized white inclusions
6.28.8	Cooking pot	AK VIII 1982 H O/1 b. 292/14	292/14	Red/red/red; many small white inclusions
6.28.9	Cooking jar	AK VII 1980 H M/4 b. 183/19	183/19	Red brown/red brown/dark grey; few small to medium sized white inclusions; soot smudges on handle
6.28.10	Cooking jar	AK VII 1980 H M/3 b. 206/7	206/7	Brown/red brown/dark grey; many small to medium sized white inclusions
6.28.11	Baking tray	AK VIII 1982 H O/1 b. 292/2	292/2	Brown/red brown/dark grey; many small white inclusions; incised ridges on exterior
6.28.12	Baking tray	AK VII 1980 H M/3 b. 200/4	200/4	Brown/dark brown/brown; medium amount of medium sized white inclusions; incised dimples and line on exterior
6.28.13	Baking tray	AK VII 1980 H M/4 b. 178/8	178/8	Red brown/dark grey/dark grey; medium amount of medium sized white, light grey, and crystalline inclusions
6.28.14	Cooking bowl	AK VIII 1982 H O/1 b. 279/7	279/7	Red brown/red brown/dark brown to red brown; medium amount of medium sized white inclusions; fire smudges on exterior of bowl

Iron IIA-IIB Transition Typology (cont.)
Pithos

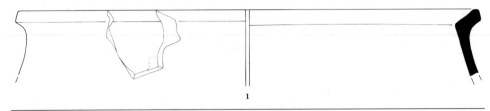

Storage Jars

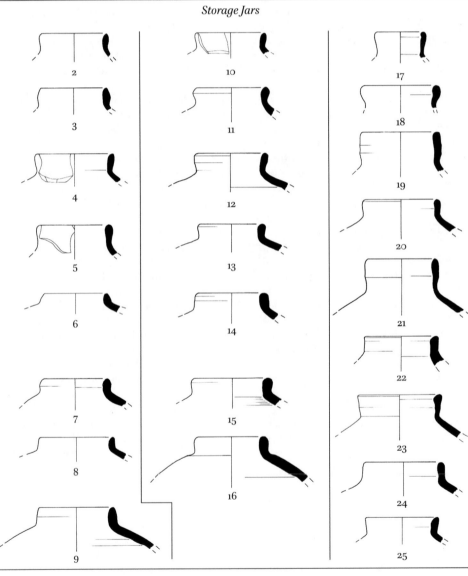

FIGURE 6.29

THE POTTERY OF STRATUM 4

Figure No.	Shape/object	Reg. No.	Locus/Pottery Basket	Description (color of exterior/interior/core; inclusions; decorations; etc.)
6.29.1	Krater	AK VIII 1982 H O/1 b. 319/1	319/1	Reddish pink/reddish pink/light grey; many small to medium sized white and light grey inclusions; cream-colored slip on exterior and interior
6.29.2	Storage jar	AK VII 1980 H M/4 b. 157/10	157/10	Tan/tan/light grey; many small dark brown inclusions
6.29.3	Storage jar	AK VII 1980 H M/4 b. 178/11	178/11	Salmon/salmon/salmon; few medium sized grey inclusions
6.29.4	Storage jar	AK VIII 1982 H O/1 b. 336/21	336/21	Pink/pink/dark grey; few small white inclusions, medium amount of small voids
6.29.5	Storage jar	AK VIII 1982 H O/1 b. 336/6	336/6	Pink/pink/light grey; few small to medium sized white inclusions
6.29.6	Storage jar	AK VII 1980 H M/3 b. 158/16	158/16	Cream/cream/cream; many small white inclusions; high fired
6.29.7	Storage jar	AK VII 1980 H M/3 b. 158/13	158/13	Salmon/salmon/light grey to salmon; many small brown inclusions
6.29.8	Storage jar	AK VII 1980 H M/3 b. 177/9	177/9	Pink/pink/pink; many small brown inclusions
6.29.9	Storage jar	AK VII 1980 H M/3 b. 151/1	151/1	Salmon/salmon; light grey; small amount of small white inclusions
6.29.10	Storage jar	AK VIII 1982 H O/1 b. 330/11	330/11	Pink/pink/pink; many small brown inclusions
6.29.11	Storage jar	AK VIII 1982 H O/1 b. 330/12	330/12	Orangey pink/orangey pink/grey; many small white inclusions, few small voids
6.29.12	Storage jar	AK VII 1980 H M/3 b. 201/4	201/4	Tan/reddish pink/light grey; medium amount of small white inclusions; cream-colored slip on exterior
6.29.13	Storage jar	AK VII 1980 H M/4 b. 157/9	157/9	Pink/pink/pink to light brown; many small white and red inclusions; cream-colored slip on exterior
6.29.14	Storage jar	AK VII 1980 H M/4 b. 183/14	183/14	Salmon/tan/core not visible; very few small white inclusions
6.29.15	Storage jar	AK VII 1980 H M/4 b. 178/12	178/12	Orangey pink/orangey pink/orangey pink; few small brown inclusions
6.29.16	Storage jar	AK VII 1980 H M/4 b. 183/15	183/15	Salmon/salmon/light grey; many small to large white inclusions
6.29.17	Storage jar	AK VIII 1982 H O/1 b. 292/18	292/18	Reddish brown/reddish brown/reddish brown; many small to medium sized white inclusions
6.29.18	Storage jar	AK VII 1980 H M/3 b. 193/7	193/7	Salmon/salmon/light grey; few small white inclusions
6.29.19	Storage jar	AK VIII 1982 H O/1 b. 336/20	336/20	Pink/pink/light grey; many small to large sized white inclusions
6.29.20	Storage jar	AK VIII 1982 H O/1 b. 330/10	330/10	Pink/pink/pink; medium amount of medium sized white inclusions
6.29.21	Storage jar	AK VII 1980 H M/3 b. 206/2	206/2	Pink/tan/light grey; many small to medium sized white, and few small brown, inclusions; cream-colored slip on exterior and interior
6.29.22	Storage jar	AK VIII 1982 H O/1 b. 336/7	336/7	Salmon/salmon/tan; few small dark brown inclusions

Figure No.	Shape/ object	Reg. No.	Locus/ Pottery Basket	Description (color of exterior/interior/core; inclusions; decorations; etc.)
6.29.23	Storage jar	AK VIII 1982 H O/1 b. 300/15	300/15	Salmon/salmon/light grey; many small white inclusions
6.29.24	Storage jar	AK VII 1980 H M/4 b. 182/4	182/4	Tan/tan/light grey; small to large sized white and grey inclusions
6.29.25	Storage jar	AK VII 1980 H M/3 b. 177/13	177/13	Pink/pink/tan; few small white inclusions
6.29.26	Storage jar	AK VIII 1982 H O/1 b. 279/22	279/22	Dark pink/dark pink/light pink; many small white and light grey inclusions

Iron IIA-IIB transition typology (cont.)
Storage jars (cont.)

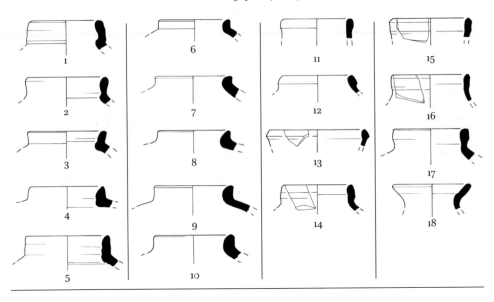
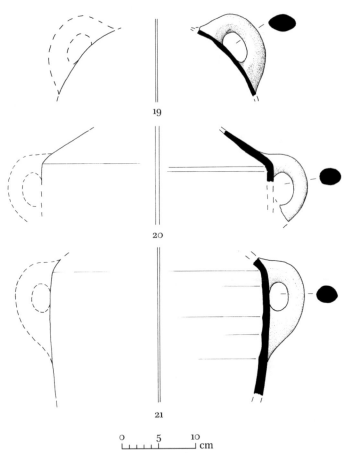

FIGURE 6.30

THE POTTERY OF STRATUM 4

Figure No.	Shape/object	Reg. No.	Locus/Pottery Basket	Description (color of exterior/interior/core; inclusions; decorations; etc.)
6.30.1	Storage jar	AK VIII 1982 H O/1 b. 281/10	281/10	Salmon/salmon/salmon; many small brown inclusions
6.30.2	Storage jar	AK VII 1980 H M/4 b. 178/14	178/14	Salmon/salmon/salmon to light grey; few small brown inclusions
6.30.3	Storage jar	AK VII 1980 H M/4 b. 183/5	183/5	Salmon/salmon/tan to salmon; few small brown inclusions
6.30.4	Storage jar	AK VII 1980 H M/3 b. 177/11	177/11	Pink/pink/pink; few small to medium sized white, many small pink, inclusions
6.30.5	Storage jar	AK VII 1980 H M/3 b. 177/12	177/12	Pink/pink/light grey; few medium sized white, many small to medium sized pink, inclusions
6.30.6	Storage jar	AK VII 1980 H M/3 b. 158/15	158/15	Cream/cream/cream; many small white, few small grey and red, inclusions; high fired
6.30.7	Storage jar	AK VIII 1982 H O/1 b. 330/9	330/9	Pink/pink/light grey to tan; many small white and medium sized light grey inclusions and voids
6.30.8	Storage jar	AK VII 1980 H M/4 b. 183/13	183/13	Salmon/salmon/light grey; many small brown inclusions
6.30.9	Storage jar	AK VII 1980 H M/3 b. 158/14	158/14	Salmon/salmon/light grey; many small dark brown inclusions
6.30.10	Storage jar	AK VII 1980 H M/3 b. 193/6	193/6	Salmon/salmon/light grey; few small white inclusions
6.30.11	Storage jar	AK VIII 1982 H O/1 b. 300/16	300/16	Pink/pink/pink; many small white and light grey inclusions
6.30.12	Storage jar	AK VIII 1982 H O/1 b. 330/13	330/13	Orangey pink/orangey pink/orangey pink; few small white inclusions and voids
6.30.13	Storage jar	AK VII 1980 H M/4 b. 178/13	178/13	Brown/brown/core not visible; few small white inclusions
6.30.14	Storage jar	AK VII 1980 H M/3 b. 201/5	201/5	Pink/pink/light grey; medium amount of small to medium sized white inclusions
6.30.15	Storage jar	AK VII 1980 H M/4 b. 182/9	182/9	Pink/pink/light grey; few small white inclusions
6.30.16	Storage jar	AK VII 1980 H M/4 b. 182/7	182/7	Red pink/red pink/red pink; many small to medium sized white inclusions; cream-colored slip on exterior and interior
6.30.17	Storage jar	AK VII 1980 H M/4 b. 183/12	183/12	Salmon salmon/light grey; very few small white inclusions
6.30.18	Storage jar	AK VIII 1982 H O/1 b. 336/26	336/26	Tan/tan/tan; many small dark grey inclusions
6.30.19	Storage jar	AK VII 1980 H M/4 b. 153/15	153/15	Salmon/salmon/light grey; medium amount of small to medium sized white inclusions
6.30.20	Storage jar	AK VII 1980 H M/3 b. 158/18	158/18	Pink/pin/light grey; few medium sized white, and many small black, inclusions
6.30.21	Storage jar	AK VIII 1982 H O/1 b. 281/8	281/8	Orangey tan/orangey pink/grey; many small, medium, and large sized white inclusions

Iron IIA-IIB transition typology (cont.)

Storage jars (cont.)

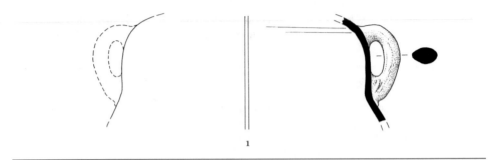

Storage jar handles

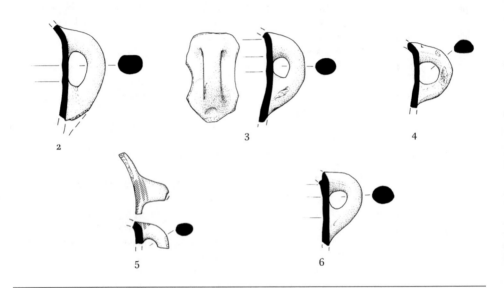

Storage jar bases

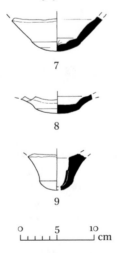

FIGURE 6.31

Figure No.	Shape/object	Reg. No.	Locus/Pottery Basket	Description (color of exterior/interior/core; inclusions; decorations; etc.)
6.31.1	Storage jar	AK VII 1980 H M/3 b. 138/23	138/23	Tan/tan/tan; many small to medium sized white inclusions; non-local, Phoenician type
6.31.2	Storage jar	AK VIII 1982 H O/1 b. 281/9	281/9	Salmon/salmon/grey; many small to medium sized white inclusions
6.31.3	Storage jar	AK VIII 1982 H O/1 b. 297/8	297/8	Pink/pink/light grey; many small white inclusions
6.31.4	Storage jar	AK VIII 1982 H O/1 b. 336/29	336/29	Pink/pink/pink; many small white, light grey, and pink inclusions
6.31.5	Jar	AK VIII 1982 H O/1 b. 279/24	279/24	Tan/salmon/light grey; many small dark grey, few small white, inclusions; red stripes painted on handle; non-local fabric
6.31.6	Storage jar	AK VIII 1982 H O/1 b. 300/18	300/18	Tan/pink/light grey; few medium sized white inclusions
6.31.7	Storage jar	AK VII 1980 H M/3 b. 206/12	206/12	Tan/light grey/light grey; many small to large sized white inclusions; cream-colored slip on exterior
6.31.8	Storage jar	AK VII 1980 H M/4 b. 153/17	153/17	Pinkish tan/light grey/light grey; many small white inclusions; high fired
6.31.9	Storage jar	AK VII 1980 H M/3 b. 206/3	206/3	Pink/brown/light brown; many small white inclusions; cream- to pink-colored slip on exterior

Iron IIA-IIB transition typology (cont.)
Holemouth jars and three-handled jar

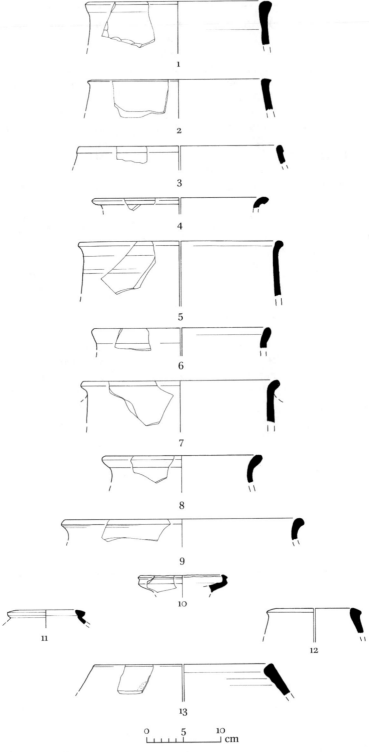

FIGURE 6.32

THE POTTERY OF STRATUM 4

Figure No.	Shape/object	Reg. No.	Locus/Pottery Basket	Description (color of exterior/interior/core; inclusions; decorations; etc.)
6.32.1	Jar	AK VIII 1982 H O/1 b. 330/5	330/5	Pink/pink/light grey; many small and medium sized white, and medium dark grey, inclusions; cream-colored slip on exterior below lip
6.32.2	Jar	AK VIII 1982 H O/1 b. 330/6	330/6	Pink/pink/pink; few small white inclusions
6.32.3	Jar	AK VII 1980 H M/3 b. 193/8	193/8	Pink/brown/brown; medium amount of small white inclusions
6.32.4	Jar	AK VII 1980 H M/3 b. 193/9	193/9	Red brown/red brown/dark grey (cooking pot fabric); many small to medium sized white inclusions
6.32.5	Jar	AK VII 1980 H M/4 b. 157/8	157/8	Pinkish tan/light brown/light brown; many small white and dark brown, and few large cream-colored inclusions
6.32.6	Jar	AK VIII 1982 H O/1 b. 336/4	336/4	Pink/pink/light grey; few small white inclusions
6.32.7	Jar	AK VIII 1982 H O/1 b. 336/5	336/5	Pink/pink/ grey; many small to medium sized white inclusions; high fired
6.32.8	Jar	AK VII 1980 H M/4 b. 182/5	182/5	Orangey pink/orangey pink/light grey; many small white inclusions
6.32.9	Jar	AK VII 1980 H M/3 b. 177/4	177/4	Pink/pink/grey; many small, few large, white inclusions
6.32.10	Three-handled jar	AK VIII 1982 H O/1 b. 292/13	292/13	Brown/reddish brown/reddish brown; few small white inclusions
6.32.11	Jar	AK VIII 1982 H O/1 b. 292/17	292/17	Pink/pink/light grey; few small white inclusions
6.32.12	Jar	AK VII 1980 H M/4 b. 182/8	182/8	Salmon/salmon/salmon; many small to large sized red pink inclusions; cream-colored slip on exterior and interior
6.32.13	Jar	AK VII 1980 H M/4 b. 183/10	183/10	Pink/pink/light grey; many small to medium sized white, and a few small dark grey, inclusions

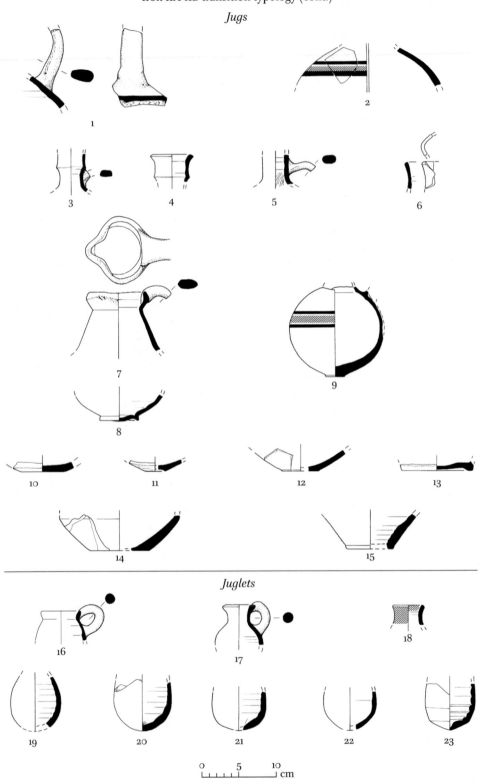

FIGURE 6.33

THE POTTERY OF STRATUM 4

Figure No.	Shape/object	Reg. No.	Locus/Pottery Basket	Description (color of exterior/interior/core; inclusions; decorations; etc.)
6.33.1	Jug	AK VIII 1982 H O/1 b. 336/30	336/30	Pink/pink/pink; many small white and light grey inclusions; dark brown painted stripe below handle
6.33.2	Jug	AK VIII 1982 H O/1 b. 300/17	300/17	Light grey/tan/light grey; medium amount of medium sized white inclusions; brown and red painted stripes on exterior
6.33.3	Jug	AK VIII 1982 H O/1 b. 297/9	297/9	Tan/tan/tan; few small white inclusions and few small voids; non-local
6.33.4	Jug	AK VIII 1982 H O/1 b. 292/19	292/19	Pinkish tan/pinkish tan/brown to tan; many small white, few large brown, white, and light grey, inclusions
6.33.5	Jug	AK VIII 1982 H O/1 b. 319/5	319/5	Tan/tan/tan; many small dark grey, white, and pink inclusions; Cypriot
6.33.6	Jug or juglet?	AK VIII 1982 H O/1 b. 336/22	336/22	Pink/pink/light grey; few small brown inclusions
6.33.7	Jug	AK VIII 1982 H O/1 b. 330/14	330/14	Salmon/salmon/salmon; many small light grey, and few small pink, inclusions; cream slip on exterior
6.33.8	Jug	AK VIII 1982 H O/1 b. 330/18	330/18	Tan/orangey pink/grey; few small white inclusions
6.33.9	Jug	AK VI 1979 H L/9 b. 126/1	126/10	Pink/pink/pink; few medium amount of small to medium white and grey inclusions; red painted stripe on exterior
6.33.10	Jug	AK VIII 1982 H O/1 b. 336/27	336/27	Orangey pink/orangey pink/orangey pink; many small white inclusions
6.33.11	Bowl or jug	AK VII 1980 H M/4 b. 178/19	178/19	Salmon/salmon/salmon to light grey; few small white inclusions
6.33.12	Bowl or jug	AK VII 1980 H M/3 b. 177/14	177/14	Pink/pink/light grey; medium amount of small white inclusions
6.33.13	Jug	AK VII 1980 H M/3 b. 177/15	177/15	Orangey pink/orangey pink/tan; few small white and pink inclusions
6.33.14	Jug	AK VII 1980 H M/4 b. 182/11	182/11	Pink orange/pink to tan/tan; many small brown inclusions
6.33.15	Jug? Jar?	AK VII 1980 H M/3 b. 206/11	206/11	Pink/pink/light grey; medium amount of medium sized white inclusions
6.33.16	Juglet	AK VIII 1982 H O/1 b. 292/23	292/23	Orangey pink/orangey pink/orangey pink; many small white inclusions
6.33.17	Juglet	AK VIII 1982 H O/1 b. 330/15	330/15	Tan/tan/tan; few small white inclusions
6.33.18	Jug	AK VIII 1982 H O/1 b. 297/10	297/10	Pink/pink/pink; few small white inclusions; red slip and burnished exterior, red slip on interior to bottom of rim
6.33.19	Juglet	AK VIII 1982 H O/1 b. 330/16	330/16	Pink/pink/grey; few small white inclusions
6.33.20	Juglet	AK VII 1980 H M/3 b. 177/2	177/2	Pink/pink/tan; medium amount of small white inclusions
6.33.21	Juglet	AK VIII 1982 H O/1 b. 330/17	330/17	Pink/pink/light grey; many small to medium sized white, and many small to medium sized dark grey inclusions
6.33.22	Juglet	AK VIII 1982 H O/1 b. 281/12	281/12	Pink/pink/tan; medium amount of small white and brown inclusions
6.33.23	Juglet	AK VIII 1982 H O/1 b. 300/20	300/20	Red/red/red; many small white, and medium sized light and dark grey, inclusions

Iron IIA-IIB transition typology (cont.)

Pilgrim flasks

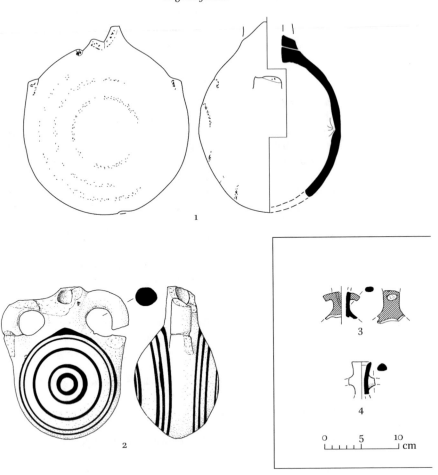
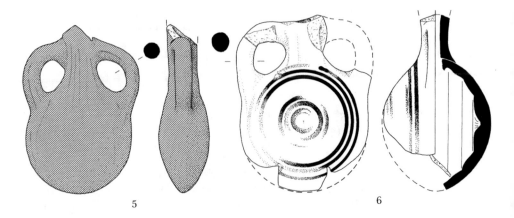

FIGURE 6.34

THE POTTERY OF STRATUM 4

Figure No.	Shape/ object	Reg. No.	Locus/ Pottery Basket	Description (color of exterior/interior/ core; inclusions; decorations; etc.)
6.34.1	Pilgrim flask	AK VIII 1982 H O/1 b. 354/1, 341	354/1	Light grey/orangey pink/orangey pink to grey; few small white inclusions; cream slip and red painted stripes on exterior
6.34.2	Pilgrim flask	AK VII 1980 H M/3 b. 177/1	177/1	Buff to pink/pink/buff; few small brown and white inclusions; brown painted stripes on burnished exterior
6.34.3	Pilgrim flask	AK VIII 1982 H O/1 b. 292/21	292/21	Brown/red/grey; many small white inclusions; red slip on exterior
6.34.4	Pilgrim flask	AK VIII 1982 H O/1 b. 279/23	279/23	Salmon/salmon/salmon; many small brown inclusions; non-local fabric
6.34.5	Pilgrim flask	AK VII 1980 H K/7 b. 266/1	266/1	Pink/pink/pink; few small white inclusions; red slip and burnished exterior
6.34.6	Pilgrim flask	AK VII 1980 H M/1 b. 210/1	210/1	Pink orange/dark grey/dark grey; many small, medium, and large sized white inclusions; some burnishing, and dark brown painted stripes, on exterior

Iron IIA-IIB transition typology (cont.)

Lamps

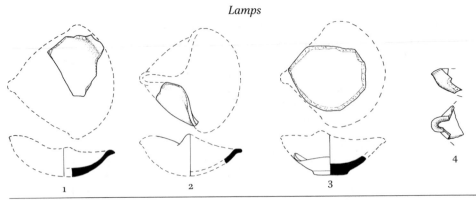

Cup-and-saucer

Phoenician vessels

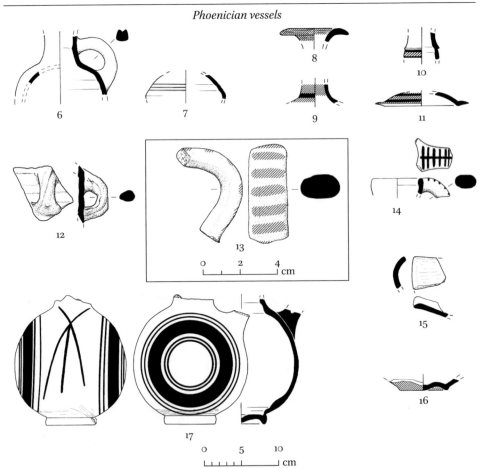

FIGURE 6.35

THE POTTERY OF STRATUM 4

Figure No.	Shape/object	Reg. No.	Locus/Pottery Basket	Description (color of exterior/interior/core; inclusions; decorations; etc.)
6.35.1	Lamp	AK VII 1980 H M/3 b. 190/11	190/11	Tan/tan/light grey to tan; many small to medium sized white inclusions
6.35.2	Lamp	AK VIII 1982 H O/1 b. 292/24	292/24	Pink/pink/light grey to pink; many small white inclusions; cream-colored slip on exterior and interior; smudge marks
6.35.3	Lamp	AK VII 1980 H M/3 b. 206/5	206/5	Pink/pink/light grey; medium amount of small to medium sized white inclusions
6.35.4	Lamp	AK VIII 1982 H O/1 b. 300/22	300/22	Tan/pink/grey to light grey; few small white inclusions; smudge marks from use
6.35.5	Cup-and-saucer	AK VIII 1982 H O/1 b. 297/1	297/1	Orangey pink/orangey pink/orangey pink; few small to medium sized white inclusions
6.35.6	Jug	AK VIII 1982 H O/1 b. 292/20	292/20	Pink/grey/grey; many small to medium sized white inclusions; pink-colored slip and burnished exterior, painted dark brown stripe; unusual handle with groove
6.35.7	Jug	AK VII 1980 H M/3 b. 201/6	201/6	Light grey/light grey/light grey; many small white inclusions; incised lines on exterior shoulder
6.35.8	Jug	AK IX 1983 H O/1 b. 1042/2	1042/2	Orange tan/orange tan/orange tan; many small brown inclusions; red slip and polished (so highly burnished) exterior and interior to bottom of rim; Phoenician type
6.35.9	Jug	AK VIII 1982 H O/1 b. 336/23	336/23	Pink/pink/tan; few small brown inclusions; red slip and burnished exterior, red slipped interior to bottom of neck; painted dark brown stripe on neck; Phoenician type
6.35.10	Jug	AK VII 1980 H M/4 b. 183/2	183/2	Orange pink/orange pink/orange pink; few small dark pink inclusions; cream slip on exterior above painted red and dark brown stripes; Phoenician type
6.35.11	Lid or cover	AK VIII 1982 H O/1 b. 292/1	292/1	Pink/pink/tan; many small voids; red slip and polished (so highly burnished) exterior, dark brown painted stripes; Cypriot fabric, Phoenician type
6.35.12	Storage jar	AK VII 1980 H M/3 b. 200/3	200/3	Salmon/salmon/salmon; very few medium sized grey and white inclusions
6.35.13	Jug	AK VIII 1982 H O/1 b. 330/19	330/19	Orangey pink/orangey pink/orangey pink; few small white inclusions; red painted stripes on exterior of handle
6.35.14	Jug	AK VII 1980 H M/3 b. 158/4	158/4	Pink/pink/light grey; many small to large sized white inclusions; burnished exterior, brown painted stripes
6.35.15	Jug	AK VIII 1982 H O/1 b. 336/2	336/2	Orangey pink/orangey pink/light grey; polished (so highly burnished); Phoenician type
6.35.16	Jug	AK VIII 1982 H O/1 b. 336/28	336/28	Tan/red/grey; many small to medium sized white inclusions; red slip on exterior; Phoenician type
6.35.17	Jug	AK VII 1980 H M/4 b. 184/1	184/1	Pink/pink/pink; few small white and miniscule brown inclusions; cream slip on exterior, and black painted concentric circles on both sides, with black painted ribbon decoration opposite the handle

Iron IIA-IIB transition typology (cont.)

Phoenician vessels (cont.)

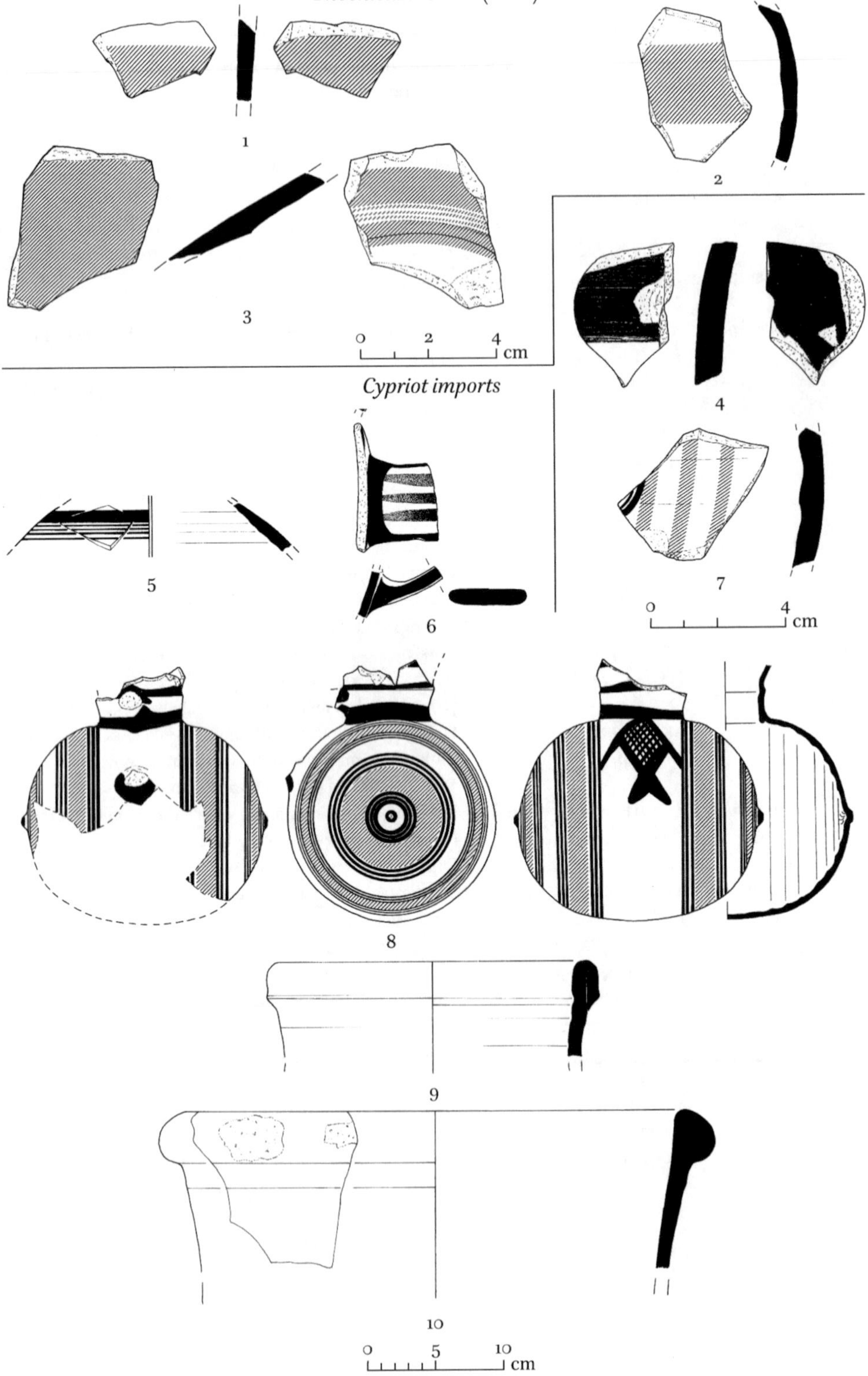

Cypriot imports

FIGURE 6.36

THE POTTERY OF STRATUM 4

Figure No.	Shape/object	Reg. No.	Locus/Pottery Basket	Description (color of exterior/interior/core; inclusions; decorations; etc.)
6.36.1	Bowl	AK VIII 1982 H O/1 b. 292/25	292/25	Pink/pink/pink; small brown inclusions; red slip and polished exterior, painted red strip and polished interior; Samaria Ware or Phoenician fine ware
6.36.2	Jug? Bowl?	AK VIII 1982 H O/1 b. 330/20	330/20	Pinkish tan/pinkish tan/pinkish tan; many small voids; polished (so highly burnished) with red painted striped on exterior; Phoenician type
6.36.3	Bowl	AK VIII 1982 H K/7 b. 46/2	46/2	Tan/tan/tan; no inclusions; polished (so highly burnished), red painted stripes, and 4 incised stripes on exterior, re slip and polished (so highly burnished) interior; Samaria Ware or Phoenician fine ware
6.36.4	Bowl	AK VII 1980 H M/3 b. 151/8	151/8	Pink/pink/pink; very few light brown inclusions; dark brown wash on exterior, dark brown slip on interior; Cypriot White Painted Ware
6.36.5	Jar	AK VIII 1982 H O/1 b. 297/7	297/7	Pink/pink/pink; many small white, grey, and red inclusions; cream-colored slip on exterior, and dark brown painted stripes; Cypriot
6.36.6	Jar	AK VII 1980 H M/3 b. 151/4	151/4	Tan/tan/tan; many small white, dark brown, and pink inclusions; cream-colored slip on exterior and interior; dark brown painted stripes on exterior; Cypriot White Painted Ware
6.36.7	Jug? Jar?	AK VII 1980 H M/3 b. 151/7	151/7	Tan/tan/tan; very few small dark brown inclusions; burnished exterior with red and dark brown painted stripes; Cypriot? Phoenician?
6.36.8	Jug	AK VII 1980 H M/4 b. 178/2	178/2	Pink/pink/pink; few small brown inclusions; buff slip and red and black painted decorations; Cypriot Bichrome Ware
6.36.9	Pithos	AK VIII 1982 H O/1 b. 292/16	292/16	Orangey pink/orangey pink/tan; many small white inclusions; import, Cypriot?
6.36.10	Pithos	AK VIII 1982 H O/1 b. 300/14	300/14	Tan/tan/tan; many small brown and white inclusions; cream-colored slip on exterior and interior; well fired; East Greek? Cypriot?

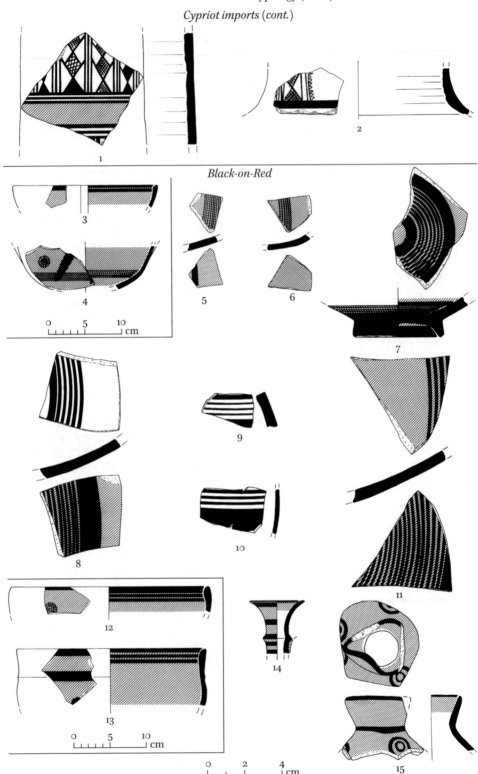

FIGURE 6.37

THE POTTERY OF STRATUM 4

Figure No.	Shape/object	Reg. No.	Locus/Pottery Basket	Description (color of exterior/interior/core; inclusions; decorations; etc.)
6.37.1	Pithos	AK VIII 1982 H O/1 b. 279/1	279/1	Orangey red/orangey red/grey; many small, and few large, white inclusions; pinky cream slipped exterior, red and dark brown painted stripes and decorations; Cypriot Bichrome Ware
6.37.2	Pithos	AK VII 1980 H M/4 b. 139/7	139/7	Tan/tan/pinkish tan; many small dark brown inclusions; tan slipped exterior with dark brown painted design; Cypriot
6.37.3	Bowl	AK VII 1980 H M/3 b. 206/8	206/8	Pink/pink/pink; few small white inclusions; red slip and burnished exterior and interior, dark brown painted stripes on exterior from bottom of rim and interior to just below rim; Cypriot Black-on-Red Ware
6.37.4	Bowl	AK VIII 1982 H O/1 b. 300/9	300/9	Pink/pink/light pink; very few small white inclusions; red slip and burnished exterior and interior; dark brown stripes and painted decorations on exterior and stripes on interior; Cypriot Black-on-Red Ware
6.37.5	Bowl	AK VII 1980 H M/3 b. 158/17	158/17	Pinkish tan/pinkish tan/pinkish tan; many small brown, and few small white, inclusions; red slip and burnished exterior and interior, dark brown stripes exterior and interior; high fired; Cypriot Black-on-Red Ware
6.37.6	Bowl	AK VIII 1982 H O/1 b. 336/1	336/1	Pinkish tan/pinkish tan/pinkish tan; very few small white and red inclusions; red slip and burnished exterior and interior; dark brown painted stripes; Cypriot Black-on-Red Ware
6.37.7	Bowl	AK VIII 1982 H O/1 b. 281/15	281/15	Pink/pink/pink; numerous small voids; thick buff-colored slip on exterior and interior, dark brown painted stripes on exterior and interior; Cypriot Black-on-Red Ware
6.37.8	Bowl	AK VIII 1982 H O/1 b. 279/3	279/3	Salmon/salmon/salmon; orangey pink slip and burnished exterior, orangey red slip and burnished interior, dark brown painted stripes on exterior and interior; Cypriot Black-on-Red Ware
6.37.9	Body sherd	AK VII 1980 H M/4 b. 182/12	182/12	Tan/tan/tan; many small voids; burnished exterior, brown painted stripes on exterior; Cypriot Black-on-Red Ware
6.37.10	Bowl	AK VIII 1982 H O/1 b. 281/16	281/16	Pink/pink/pink; few small white inclusions; buff slip and painted brown stripes on exterior; Cypriot Black-on-Red Ware
6.37.11	Bowl	AK VIII 1982 H O/1 b. 279/2	279/2	Salmon/salmon/salmon; medium amount of small white inclusions; orangey pink slip and burnished exterior and interior, dark brown painted stripes on exterior and interior; Cypriot Black-on-Red Ware
6.37.12	Bowl	AK X 1984 H N/5 b. 536/7	536/7	Pink orange/pink orange/tan; many small brown and orange inclusions; red slip and burnished, and dark brown painted decoration, exterior and interior; Cypriot Red-on-Black Ware
6.37.13	Bowl	AK VIII 1982 H O/1 b. 267/5	267/5	Orangey pink/orangey pink/orangey pink; few small white and pink inclusions; red slip and burnished, and dark brown painted decorations, on exterior and interior; Cypriot Black-on-Red Ware
6.37.14	Juglet	AK VIII 1982 H M/7 b. 103/5	103/5	Light grey/light grey/light grey; very few small white inclusions; red slipped, dark brown painted stripes on, exterior, and red slip to bottom of rim and dark brown painted stripe on rim interior; Cypriot Black-on-Red Ware
6.37.15	Juglet	AK VII 1980 H M/3 b. 86/1	86/1	Tan/tan/tan; medium amount of small brown inclusions; red slip, dark brown painted decoration on exterior; Cypriot Black-on-Red Ware

Iron IIA-IIB transition typology (cont.)
Egyptian imports

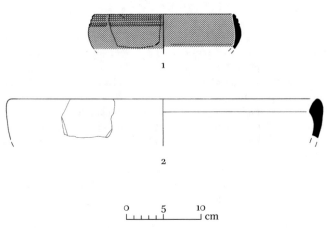

FIGURE 6.38

Figure No.	Shape/ object	Reg. No.	Locus/ Pottery Basket	Description (color of exterior/ interior/core; inclusions; decorations; etc.)
6.38.1	Bowl	AK VIII 1982 H O/1 b. 300/6	300/6	Red/red/light grey; medium amount of small white inclusions; red wash on exterior and interior; Egyptian
6.38.2	Bowl	AK VII 1980 H M/3 b. 206/9	206/9	Red/red/grey to dark brown; many small white inclusions; thick cream- to yellow-colored slip on exterior and interior; Egyptian

PHOTO 6.1 Square M/4, Cypriote Bichrome barrel jug
PHOTO: R. STIDSING

PHOTO 6.2 Squares M/10 jug (a), Square M/4 jug (b), Square K/7 pilgrim flask (c), Square L/9 jug (d)
PHOTO: R. STIDSING

CHAPTER 7

Discussion and Conclusions

Michal Artzy and Aaron Brody

Tel Akko is the most prominent ancient site in the Akko Plain. The settlement commands both the northern and southern regions of the plain, and the international sea lanes that connected the southern Levant with Cyprus, the Aegean, western Anatolia, and the northern Levant with Egypt. The tell is situated north of the Na'aman (Belos) River, ca. 1.5 km east of the coastline today, within the expanding boundaries of the modern city. Additionally, the position of the tell allows for a panoramic view of coastal maritime traffic as well as a vista over the terrestrial routes, especially those leading toward the southern Akko Plain and Jezreel Valley. These networks lead from Akko to the Jezreel Valley and Lower Galilee, and further to the Jordan Valley (Dorsey 1991: 78), and then north to Damascus, thus connecting the northern part of the southern Levant to Mediterranean trade networks. A study (Artzy 2019) shows that the route from the Jezreel Valley linked with Beth Shean, and utilized Akko's anchorage for Egyptian interests in the LB, and not those of Megiddo. The Na'aman River, with its outlet to the sea just south of the site and the modern city, provided a steady source of fresh water. Agricultural produce was grown in the surrounding plain. It was suggested in the past that the site's economic hinterland was connected via several routes, depending on the Na'aman River's flow, around the swamps in the plain.

The coast was closer to the site in the second and first millennia BCE (Artzy 2012; Morhange et al. 2016; Giaime et al. 2018), but the exact locations of the anchorages in the various periods of its habitation are still being studied. Raban suggested that there was a Bronze Age inner anchorage in the southern confines of the tell (Raban 1991). Recent work, however, shows that the bedrock is far too high to allow boats or barges to enter that area. Presently, research is being carried out to establish the boundaries of the changes in the sea's incursion into confines of the bay, so as to determine the size of the bay in the millennia in which Tel Akko was inhabited. These changes affected the Middle Bronze, Late Bronze, Iron Age, and Persian period anchorages' positions, which changed their location in tandem with the vicissitudes of the bay and the river. Using analyses of coring (Morhange et al. 2016; Giaime et al. 2018.) and Ground Penetrating Radar carried out by Jol, Salmon, and students (personal communication), the likely Bronze Age anchorage was located south of the inner depression, claimed by Raban as an inner anchorage (see fig. 7.1).

A likely Iron Age anchorage is currently being searched for just outside the southwestern boundaries of the tell, based on ancient locations of the bay and the estuary of the Na'aman River as part of a more extensive geological study of the area.[1]

Tel Akko was settled and urbanized at least since the early 2nd millennium BCE, if not earlier (Artzy and Beeri 2010). The human impact on the ecology of the area due to urbanization has been noted in several studies (Kaniewski et al. 2013, Kaniewski et al. 2014). Akko could have been self sustaining because of its size, its environs, including water and arable land, and its vicinity to the Haifa/Akko bay and the Na'aman River, which allowed for continuous international maritime connections. Sands added to Akko's economy with the production of glass, for which the area was famous. Other industries included the purple dye production derived from murex shells and, as noted lately, the production of iron which followed the recycling of bronze on the summit of the tell.

The peculiar shape of the site, a banana or crescent moon, has usually been explained as the result of robbing of tell's soil carried out by the British Mandate authorities to combat the swamps caused by the Na'aman River. A study shows that although the British might have caused some damage to the site in the Mandate period, the shape of the tell was there well before the mid-1940s (Artzy and Quartermaine 2014) already during the 5th–4th centuries BCE (Artzy and Quartermaine 2014; Killebrew et al. 2016). Archaeological remains show that the tell was abandoned by the mid-2nd century BCE (Abu Hamid 2016) when a movement of habitation toward the peninsula, now known as the Old City of Akko, occurred. During that period, a harbor was constructed in the bay, ca. 1.6 km from the tell, to accommodate maritime military vessels and trade of the period (Artzy 2013; Gambash 2012; Sharvit et al. 2013). Akko is also known by the misnomer Acre, a name shortened from Saint Jean d'Acre, based on an incorrect identification of the site by the Crusaders (Artzy 2015).

Investigations began at the ancient site of Akko in 1973 under the directorship of M. Dothan. Twelve dig seasons took place over the next seventeen years with the final season occurring in 1989. Excavations in Area H, the focus of this study, started in 1979 and continued for five seasons total under the supervision of M. Artzy (figs. 1.2, 7.1). In that time, twenty-five 5 × 5 m squares were explored in this northwestern edge of the tell, with finds ranging from the Middle Bronze Age to the Hellenistic period. Seven phases were defined for the area, with localized Stratum 7 the earliest and Stratum 1 the latest. Stratum 7 was the last construction phase of the city's rampart, also revealed

---

[1] Artzy wishes to thank the Binational Science Foundation for the grant awarded to Harry Jol of the University of Wisconsin at Eau Claire and herself.

DISCUSSION AND CONCLUSIONS 585

in Area A, AB, B, and K (figs. 1.2, 7.1), and dates to the MB IIA period. In the subsequent phase, Stratum 6, Area H was the location of MB IIB–IIC burials. Middle Bronze burials were also found just to the northeast in Area AB. A gap follows these burials until Stratum 5, which is phased to the transition from the end of the LB IIB–beginning of the Iron IA. Stratum 5 features in Area H reveal a poor settlement made up primarily of beaten earth floors, pits, and scrappy walls. Another gap follows until the southeastern part of the area is resettled in Stratum 4, the transition period between the end of the Iron IIA and the beginning of the Iron IIB. No Iron IIC remains are present in Area H; Stratum 3 is dated to the Persian period and consists of several structures, pits, animal burials, and one human burial. Stratum 2 is phased to the early Hellenistic period and Stratum 1 to the late Hellenistic period. Both Hellenistic strata are comprised of a series of households with industrial installations; the orientation of the architecture of these houses shifts between the two phases.

Remains from Area H display a narrative of the tell's habitation pattern. Area H is located in the north-central part of the tell, combining the tell's northern edge, the flat surface of the human-made MB IIA rampart, its subsequent repairs as well as the bowl-like rampart's inward incline. The utilization of the area over the millennia bears witness to Akko's importance as a center of maritime and terrestrial routes and the trade associated with them. Remains associated with Akko's military importance appear in at least six periods: the Middle Bronze Age, the Persian, the Hellenistic, the Crusader period of the 12th and 13th centuries CE, Napoleon's incursion in the last years of the 17th century CE, and the middle of the 20th century CE.

The impressive MB IIA rampart, discussed in chapters 2 and 3, was constructed in the early part of the 2nd millennium BCE as part of Tel Akko's urbanization and gave the site its height vis-à-vis the surrounding coastal plain at ca. 30 meters above MSL at its summit on its northern side in Area AB (fig. 1.2). The view from the summit includes the Mediterranean Sea from the Carmel Ridge to the Ladder of Tyre and of course, the Haifa/Akko bay, as well as the east-west route leading to the Akko Plain. The height of the rampart in Area H is only 2–4 meters higher than that of Area F, which is situated southwest of Area H and where an MB IIA brick and stone gate, called the Sea Gate, was excavated by Raban (fig. 1.2; M. Dothan and Raban 1980). Meanwhile the rampart in Area AB to the northeast is noticeably higher by at least ten or more meters, although the addition of an MB IIB building should be taken into consideration. The possibility exists that at some point there were stairs leading to the summit of the tell, a part of which we assume to be the acropolis.

Imported Cypriot pottery, mainly White Painted III, was found in Area H Stratum 7 among other material goods, and is favorably compared to the well-stratified examples from Tel Nami (Artzy and Marcus 1992). Possible imports from the Syro-Lebanese coast, including Levantine Painted Ware, can also be compared to the finds at Nami, although there are very few examples of this ware in Area H or on the tell for that matter. This could mean that the rampart, where these ceramics were found, was constructed at a slightly later stage of the MB IIA than Tel Nami or the earlier phases in Tell el-Ifshar. The possibility of different networks reflected in the different stages in the rampart's construction, however, should also be considered. Different coastal sites, such as Beirut and Byblos that were active during the period, were not necessarily on the same trade network as Akko, even if they are situated on the same Mediterranean coast. They, could have been in contact with different sites in the Syro-Lebanese coast and Cyprus and thus, the near absence of particular types of ceramics, in this case, Levantine Painted Ware, could be attributed to minor regional differences and variations in trade networks. The same differences in assemblages are true of other periods and subperiods, which cannot be assumed to be temporal and spatial monoliths. A loom weight with an insignia found at Tel Nami (Marcus and Artzy 1995) as well as ^{14}C readings from MB IIA phases at Tell el-Ifshar and Tel Nami give absolute dates to phases comparable to Aphek Phase three, and Area H's Stratum 7, at approximately 1850/1795–1750 BCE (Marcus 2003). The same is true of the Egyptian bullae from fills in the Phase 13 MB IIA moat at Ashkelon (table 7.1; Stager 2002: 357, fig. 22; Marcus 2003).

The only human signs of intervention in the immediate period following the construction of the MB II rampart in Area H are areas of repair carried out in later periods, possibly as late as the LB II. The first signs of utilization were for burials in the MB IIB–IIC phase as discussed in chapter 4. Three different burials, of two types, make up Stratum 6 in Area H. The three burials are: Locus (grave) 727, a cist burial with an adult and child; and Loci (tombs) 829 and 932, both constructed chamber tombs with multiple burials and numerous grave goods. It is difficult to pinpoint a narrow time frame for the chamber tombs since they were likely used for an extended period; however, they generally range in use over the late MB IIB and MB IIC, and possibly the transition to LB IA.

The two built graves, 829 and 932, are dated to the MB IIB–IIC period, while the cist grave, 727, can be dated slightly earlier to the MB IIB period. This division agrees with the graves in Area AB on the summit of the tell where the cist graves tend to be slightly earlier than a built one found there. The time frame is concurrent with the scarabs present in the two chamber tombs in Area H, which have been phased by O. Keel to the 13th–15th Dynasties; following his absolute chronology these date to 1759–1527 BCE (table 7.1). Only slightly disturbed, the two tombs, Loci 829 and 932, are situated ca. 15 meters from each other with a possibility of a slight temporal difference between them. There is, however, a disparity between the two, and not only in the style of the construction. Tomb 829 shows a clear association with Egypt. While the ceramics are of local Canaanite manufacture with none originating in Egypt itself, amethyst scarabs with gold bezels point toward Egypt, as do the alabaster juglets. It is possible that the tomb was used by a Canaanite merchant family involved in trade with Egypt. Tomb 932, also a multiple burial grave, on the other hand, is quite different, including its shape and construction. Its contents, the skeletons and the grave goods, were not disturbed by water entering, so the last to be buried were found in an articulated manner. Local Canaanite ceramics are the majority of the assemblage, yet there are imported ceramics, both from Cyprus and the Syro-Lebanese coast or even Anatolia. A more important find points to the central Levant, rather than Egypt; these are large water smoothed stones in Tomb 932, whose origins are in the Troodos Mountains on Cyprus. Both in shape and color, they are similar to ones originating in the Kouris River often used as ballast stones on seagoing vessels. In the grave they are in secondary use as headrests under the skeleton's heads, a practice alluded to in the Hebrew Bible in the story of Jacob, the ladder, and the angels in which the patriarch placed a stone under his head before sleeping (Genesis 28:11).

There are surprisingly very few Cypriot imports in these graves as well as others at Tel Akko. Only very few examples of Cypriot Bichrome Ware were found at the tell, which is curious considering the coastal position and the anchorage capabilities of the site. This is a phenomenon paralleled by the limited number of imports from Cyprus in this particular period in much of the northern coast of Israel and Lebanon. The dearth of Proto-White Slip I, Base Ring I, Bichrome ware and other imports in the northern coast is notable when compared to the southern coastal area around Tell el-'Ajjul. It is only later, mainly in the LB II, especially LB IIB–IIC, that the number of Cypriot imports increases in the northern coast of Israel and Syria-Lebanon. This is apparent at the site of Tell Abu Hawam, located on the southern side of the same bay as Akko (Artzy 2016a).

M. Dothan proposed that a defensive wall should be found on the tell, stretching from the summit of the site, Area AB, along the northern rampart in Area H to the rampart and city gate in Area F (fig. 1.2). His reasons for the assumption were based on Ramses II's depiction of the conquest of Akko. The two graves, however, are positioned so there is not a wide enough space to allow for a city wall, and no remnants of a wall were uncovered constructed on top of the MB II rampart in the excavated remains in Area H. In a north-south probe parallel to Area AB, conducted by a mechanical backhoe, no remains of an LB wall were found either, thus corroborating the finds in Area H. The Middle Bronze Age rampart remained as the main defensive element in the Late Bronze period. In addition, absolutely no remains of contemporaneous habitation were found in the general vicinity of the graves. In other words, the top of the rampart was not utilized for habitation during the Middle Bronze and Late Bronze I, IIA, or IIB periods and was left as void until the Late Bronze IIC, the period of the end of the Late Bronze II and the transition to the early Iron Age I (Artzy 2006b).

The second part of the Late Bronze Age, Stratum 5, is mainly represented in Area H by goods attributed to the Late Bronze IIC, the transition period between the Late Bronze II and the beginning of the Iron Age. This phase in Area H follows the overall picture of the excavations which have so far been undertaken at Tel Akko, where a dearth of Late Bronze I and II period remains has been noted. The limited finds dating to this transitional period, noted mainly in Area C and in Area P (figs. 1.2, 7.1), are an enigma, since Akko is mentioned in the Amarna letters by two kings, a father and his son, both of whom wrote letters to the Egyptian Pharaohs, Amenhopis III and his son, Amenhopis IV Akhenaton; the site is also listed in other, contemporary written sources (Artzy 2018).

Stratum 5 is a phase typified by beaten earth floors, pits, stone lined pits, and very few, if any, walls. It should be taken into consideration, however, that the later Late Persian–Early Hellenistic activity in the area was devastating and the robbing of stones for recycling was a common practice. This ephemeral Stratum 5 building phase is matched by a scrappy repertoire of ceramics, as only a few groups of vessels were found buried in the numerous pits or smashed on the floors of the stratum. We assign these ceramics to the LB IIC, or the end of the LB II–early Iron I (table 7.1). Besides a wide variety of local pottery forms, several Aegean-style types, such as semi-hemispherical bowls with flared rims, "bell-shaped" bowls, "bell-shaped" kraters, and stirrup jars are found in this phase in Area H and in other areas at Tel Akko. No clear decorated Aegean imports dating to the period were found in the area, or the rest of the site for that matter. The Aegean-style ceramics were either produced on Cyprus or were localy made (Artzy and Zagorski 2012). There are imports originating in the Aegean, the Myc. IIIA2–B1 ceramics, but these are fragments from earlier disturbed contexts and are not contemporary with the Stratum 5 assemblage. The Aegean-style pottery, also referred to as LH IIIC:IB or Myc. IIIC:Ib in the literature, comprises only a very small percentage of the ceramics found at Akko, and are better viewed as imports to the site, or local copies, rather than material evidence of a Sea Peoples group settling at Akko in this transitional period. Akko lacks an assemblage of material culture types attributed to the early Sea Peoples material culture. As discovered in the Iron

Age IA levels at Ashdod, Tel Miqne-Ekron, and Tel Ashkelon, this assemblage includes bi-metallic knives with ivory handles, unfired clay spool loom weights, incised animal scapulae, hearths, megaron type buildings, and unusual bins. The Aegean-style ceramics from Area H, also, are only represented by several of the hallmark types, and not the full Aegean-style repertoire of pottery forms, as is discussed in chapter 5.

Aegean-style pottery in the southern Levant has many labels, including Mycenaean (Myc.) IIIC:1, Late Helladic (LH) IIIC:1, Philistine Monochrome, and Sea Peoples Monochrome. In past studies of these ceramic types from Akko, a few were labeled "Shardanu" in association with the group of Sea Peoples thought to have conquered the settlement at the end of the Late Bronze Age (M. Dothan 1986; 1989). Since M. Dothan's publications in the late 1980s, it has been shown that there was no overall destruction at Tel Akko in this transitional period. We prefer to utilize the more neutral term Aegean-style to label the ceramics (see Killebrew 1998: 168–69). It has been shown through fabric analysis on samples from Aegean-style forms from other excavation areas at Tel Akko, as well as a stirrup jar found in the neighboring Tell Keisan, that these ceramics originated on Cyprus (Gunneweg and Perlman 1994; Burdajewicz 1995; D'Agata et al. 2005; Artzy and Zagorski 2012).

There is another problem associated with these samples from Akko, and not necessarily only from Area H. M. Dothan attributed several sherds to this Aegean-style family, which he called LH IIIC, found in several areas of excavation at Tel Akko. These, however, were a mixed bag. Not all of them are members of the same family, either in ware or in decoration. Furthermore, Dothan associated a sherd he attributed to the LH IIIC to a feature he called a ceramic kiln in Area AB (M. Dothan 1993). This so called kiln was actually a furnace used for the recycling of metal, as is made clear by the crucibles with metal remains found in association with the feature (Artzy 2006a). This is not the only problem, however, associated with these attributions. Following material science analyses both by Neutron Activation Analysis and thin section petrography, it became clear that a group of Aegean-style ceramics was manufactured on Cyprus, which are often mistaken as true Myc. IIIA2–B1 imports from Greece, the Myc. IIIB Cypriot wares (Artzy and Zagorski 2012). This particular group is not to be mistaken with the Cypriot imports defined as Myc. IIIC/LH IIIC, or, as S. Sherratt called them, White Painted Wheelmade III Ware (Sherratt 1992). They are also different from the ones produced in the eastern part of Cyprus that appeared at Tel Nami (Artzy 2006a) and can easily be distinguished from those named Myc. IIIC/LH IIIC at Akko. Besides, some sherds that were labeled Myc. IIIC1 were locally produced. At least one sherd, mistakenly published by D'Agata et al. (2005) as an Aegean Myc. IIIC, was later declared to be a member of the Myc. II family (Stockhammer, personal communication). Another decorated sherd called "Shardanu" by M. Dothan is of a porous ware and a blurred decorative line and unlikely to have originated in the Aegean, or Cyprus for that matter. Unfortunately, only a drawing of it exists. Stockhammer has addressed the problem of the nomenclature and identification of the types of the ceramics named Mycenaean (forthcoming). His view is that of an Aegean specialist who now studies wares of the period in the Levant, and helps to clarify all of these intricacies, identifications, and misidentifications.

Instead of Shardanu, as Dothan would have it, our understanding of this Aegean-style IIIC:IB pottery is as evidence of sea trade between Cyprus and the descendants of the Bronze Age Canaanite inhabitants of Akko. This exchange system was much diminished from its height in the Late Bronze Age, yet continued into the transition LB IIC (LB IIB–early Iron Age) period. If any foreign groups entered the area, they were, no doubt, mixed with coastal Canaanites (Artzy 2006b). One other possible explanation of the continuity of limited maritime trade, marked by the few Cypriot imports during this transitional period, might be the situation in the Haifa/Akko Bay during the LB IIC period. The termination of use of the anchorage of Tell Abu Hawam in the mid-13th century BCE, or slightly later, might well have influenced the site of Akko, which, continues to show signs of limited contact with Cyprus. The move would explain the appearance of the later White Slip II bowls, ones bearing the hallmarks of origins in Sanidha on Cyprus, and others. We venture to suggest the possibility that the new settlers on the Akko ramparts originated from Tell Abu Hawam. They utilized open areas at Tel Akko to rebuild their lives, namely in locales delineated by the defunct MB rampart in various spaces around the site not inhabited previously (Artzy 2006b). Those settling on the rampart, in Area AB or Area H, were involved in industry, such as metal recycling or the production of purple dye, and had clear maritime connections as indicated by the ship altar and the decorated stones associated with it found in Area H and presented in chapter 5. The type of boat, appearing for the first time on the altar, is the same as the graffiti and ex votos appearing on the walls of Temple I and the altar of Temple IV at Kition as well as on the Carmel Ridge (Basch and Artzy 1985; Artzy 2003).

The ceramics of Stratum 4, dated to the end of the Iron IIA–beginning of the Iron IIB, are both rich and varied, despite the limited presence of this phase in Area H. Most remains from Stratum 4 originate in the southeastern corner of the excavation area, which may indicate that the Iron II city is focused east of Area H, on the acropolis of the site in Areas A/AB, and K, which are more densely populated during the Iron II. Sixty-six categories of pottery types were differentiated in the typology from this stratum, which shows characteristics related to the ceramics of both northern Palestine and Lebanon, as well as local developments from earlier traditions. The Akko Plain's role was that of a borderland between ancient northern Israel and the heartland of Phoenicia. Among the ceramics found in Area H, there are a few types that are more common at southern sites; however, these are very rare. Imports from this phase include pottery from Cyprus, Lebanon, East Greece, and Egypt. The transition from the end of the Iron IIA to the Iron IIB is typically placed around 840/830 BCE, so we can tentatively date this phase in Area H through its ceramic phasing comparisons to the last half of the 9th century or around 850–800 BCE (table 7.1; Bruins, et al. 2003: table S2; Levy and Higham 2005).

The first attempt to understand the layout of the inner city was carried out in Area H in 1980. In order to cover a wider area north-south, the excavation was carried out in alternate squares, where only a half square was opened, either the western or the eastern side (fig. 1.2). In all the half squares, only smatterings of floors and walls were noted. Most of the ceramics originated in fills, likely due to later building activities. During the 13th century CE, a fortress, attributed to the Templars, named Toron was constructed in Area H. Toron is the name the Crusaders called the tell, as well. It was a major building project, which included deep trenching to construct the foundations of the fortress as well as overall robbing of any available stones for building. This might also explain the spotty areas where Iron Age II architecture was noted. The Crusaders' interest on the tell extended to other areas, such as Area G, where evidence of their vineyards and stone robbing were noted (fig. 1.2; Artzy 2015). It is likely that they used the soil, including the sherds which were abundant, as fills to level what now looks like the flat top of Tel Akko, possibly for their gardens. The area on the foot of the southwestern portion of the tell and its southern side, between the tell and the Na'aman River, including area T4 (fig. 1.2), was tilled by Pisans as fruit orchards (Artzy 2015). Recent excavation there shows an attempt to fill and flatten the area with sherds.

The havoc befalling Area H did not stop with the Crusaders. Once the Crusaders were defeated, their buildings were looted and the stones were transported to the Old City of Akko, to be reused in the Ottoman walls. The tell remained in the hands of the Turks. When Napoleon attempted to conquer Akko, he did not have the advantageous heights of the tell on which to place his guns, despite the folklore attributed to Napoleon and the popular name of the site, which today is called "Napoleon's Hill." The levelling of the top of the tell carried out by the Crusaders in the 13th century CE, was, in turn, useful for agricultural tilling of these parts of the tell, which continued until 1972 when M. Dothan's archaeological project started.

The role of Tel Akko as a significant port site is suggested by imported material in all of the phases in Area H from the MB IIA through the Iron IIA–IIB, as well as in the Persian and Hellenistic periods, whose ceramics were not detailed in this volume. In Area H, Strata 3–1, the unusual amount of imported pottery is staggering, as in most of the other excavation areas on the tell. In the 5th and 4th centuries BCE, the Persian army chose Akko as its maritime base in its attempt to conquer Egypt, and eventually Persia defeated the rebellions in Egypt. Greek, Cypriot, and Phoenician mercenaries joined the Persians. Only later, in the Hellenistic period, following the silting of the Na'aman River did the center shift from the tell to the peninsula, the Old City of modern Akko. A harbor was constructed west of the tell, either by the Seleucids or the Ptolemies, possibly Ptolemy II the builder of the harbor in Alexandria. At this point the tell, and with it Area H, become peripheral.

We have shown Area H's position within maritime and international contexts during the different periods at Tel Akko. Nevertheless, there are no clear archaeological signs of LB I–LB IIB phases in Area H, and scanty evidence in other excavation contexts on the tell. Yet, there is plenty of documentary evidence for Akko's position as an international site and even harbor city (Artzy 2018). To conclude our report on Area H we propose a possible scenario as to where this international LB settlement is hidden. We have indicated that the flat tops of the ramparts were, at least in the case of Area H, utilized for burials, but no habitational remains were noted there. This was true of the transitional period between the MB and LB period as well as in the Persian period, where one human burial and two dog burials were found. Some Iron Age remains of the Iron II survived the later land works, destructions, and building material robbing dating from the Persian-Phoenician period to the Crusaders, the Ottomans, and even modern times. In the excavations of Area C (fig. 1.2), excavated by J. Gunneweg in Dothan's 1974 campaign, continual phases dated to the LB I–II were found (table 2.1; M. Dothan 1976: 17–20). More work on the archives needs to be carried out in order to ascertain if there are some architectural remains from these four LB phases, local Stratum 9–12, in Area C (fig. 7.1; table 2.1).

Another area where clear LB remains were found is Area P, excavated by Raban (1991; fig. 7.1). There seems to be a built stone gate which was dated by Raban to the MB II period. The majority of the ceramic remains, however, can be dated to the LB II period, including many imports from Mycenaean Greece, Crete, Cyprus, and Egypt (Marcus, personal communication; Ben-Shlomo et al. 2011). These LB imports could be divided into local, coastal, and Cypriot production of Mycenaean types, as has been shown in a previous study (Artzy and Zagorski 2012). Imports are to be expected since the anchorage of the Bronze Age is located in the vicinity, as has been established in several studies (Morhange et al., 2016; Giaime et al. 2018). The Area P gate seems to have continued to function in the Iron I, and remains from this period were found there (Beeri, personal communication). When this Area P gate went out of use is a topic for another study, but we assume that it was part of the stone rampart noted in the inner part of the "crescent" (Artzy and Quartermaine 2014). According to Raban, there were structures west of the Area P gate, which he dated to the LB, although he does not state to which part of the period he phases them (Raban 1991). This might be of interest considering that the remains of Area PH, situated in the vicinity of Area P (fig. 1.2), include several pits in which ceramics dating to the LB IIC, the transition between the LB and the Iron Ages, were positioned in rampart material (Zagorski 2004). There were some remains from the LB IIB found in Area PH, but they could not be associated with any architecture and could have well been a fill robbed from another area in the vicinity.

The tops of the ramparts were devoid of habitation until the LB IIC; they continued to be used as defensive elements during the LB I and especially the LB IIB, when Akko was the main harbor in the north for the Egyptians (fig. 7.1). That city should thus be searched for just south of Area H; as far west as Area G; as far south as Area C, including some parts of the higher slope; and as far east as Area A, and possibly further east (fig. 7.1). Area P and its gate constituted the entrance from the anchorage to the LB city. Stairs from the harbor works area could have led to the Area P gate, and from there with a slight, comfortable slope to the west of Area P, to arrive at the southern excavation squares in Area H, south of the later location of the Crusader castle (fig. 7.1).

The setting of Tel Akko at a site of natural harborage, close to fresh water from the Na'aman River, natural resources from the Mediterranean, and the agricultural bounty of the Akko Plain gave livelihood to the community throughout its settlement history from the MB IIA through the Hellenistic period, and later further to the west in the current location of the Old City of Akko from the Hellenistic through to current times. The settlements' locations at the hub of overland routes from the Lower and Upper Galilee, Jezreel, Jordan, and Hulah Valleys, and along sea routes connecting the northern Levantine coast with Egypt and the Akko Plain with Cyprus, the Aegean, and further west in the Mediterranean guaranteed their importance from the MB IIA until the present day.

TABLE 7.1 Absolute dates for Area H Bronze & Iron Age local phases

Area H local phase	Periodization	Absolute dates based on comparative stratigraphy	Absolute dates based on evidence from Area H
Stratum 4	Iron IIA–IIB transition	850–800**	
Stratum 5	LB IIB–Iron IA transition	1200–1160*	
Stratum 6	MB IIB–IIC		1759–1527 (scarabs)
Stratum 7	MB IIA, 3rd rampart phase at Akko	1850/1795–1750	

* Absolute dates for this time of transition are highly debated; we prefer a slightly revised traditional chronology placing the end of the LB IIB and the beginning of the Iron IA in the early part of the 12th century, approximately 1200–1160 BCE (Bruins, et al. 2003: Table S2; Gilboa 2005: 52; Levy and Higham 2005).

** The transition from the end of the Iron IIA to the Iron IIB is typically placed around 840/830 BCE, so we can tentatively date this phase in Area H to the last half of the 9th century or around 850–800 BCE (Bruins, et al. 2003: Table S2; Levy and Higham 2005).

DISCUSSION AND CONCLUSIONS

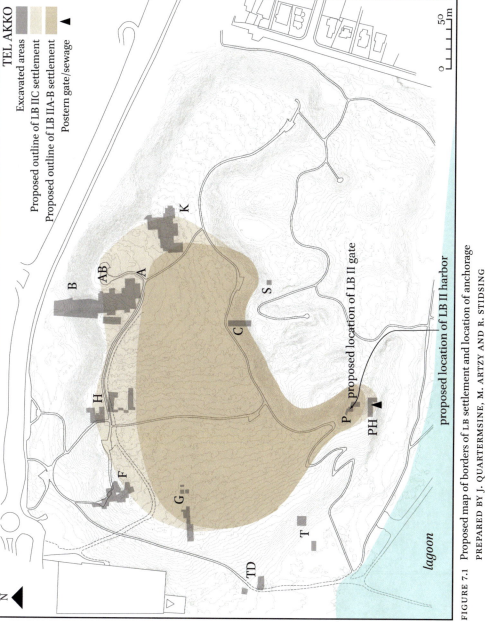

FIGURE 7.1 Proposed map of borders of LB settlement and location of anchorage
PREPARED BY J. QUARTERMSINE, M. ARTZY AND R. STIDSING

APPENDIX 1

The Ground Stone Artifacts from Area H, Akko

Jennie R. Ebeling

A small assemblage of 55 identifiable ground stone artifacts and 18 fragments was unearthed during the excavations in Area H at Akko and retained for analysis and publication. For the purposes of this study, ground stone artifacts include tools whose primary function was to process various materials to a finer texture, as well as objects like ballast and perforated stones that functioned in different ways. The artifacts are discussed below according to type, which is based on both tool morphology and macroscopic evidence of use wear. A sample of the typical artifact forms is illustrated.

As one would expect from this coastal site, the types of stone represented in the assemblage include locally available materials, including limestone and basalt,[1] as well as stones that may have reached the site through maritime activities. A small assemblage of ballast stones was found in Area H, and several are of special interest: one was reused to fashion an axe or similar hafted implement, and four were intentionally deposited in Tomb 932. The origin of the ballast stones may be Cyprus.

Vessels and Mortars: n = 7

Although stone vessels are formally distinguished from mortars based on wall thickness, exterior surface finishing, and other factors (Wright 1992: 75), traces of use wear on the interiors of all the bowls and mortars found in Area H attest to their use in processing activities. Rim, leg, and body sherds from five different stone bowls were found, along with one large, complete mortar (fig. app. 1.2.1) and a second mortar with engraved images of boats that may have also functioned as an altar (fig. app. 1.2.2).

Tripod Bowls n = 2

Leg and body fragments from two different tripod bowls were recovered (table App. 1.1; fig. app. 1.1.1–2). The fragment from basket 80 is a typical example of the tripod bowls with three freestanding legs found in quantity at sites in the Levant with Middle

---

[1] In the text, "V. Basalt" refers to vesicular basalt and "D. Basalt" refers to dense or fine grain basalt.

Bronze and later remains (Sparks 2007: 13; see also Elliott 1991 for published parallels; fig. app. 1.1.1). The example from basket 58 is unusual for the carved decoration on the outer surface of its single preserved leg (fig. app. 1.1.2); similar treatment is seen on a tripod fragment found on a Stratum IV floor at Hazor (Yadin et al. fig. LXXI.28; see Buchholz 1963: abb. 14 for Iron Age parallels from sites in Syria).

Bowls n = 3

Sherds from three different basalt vessels were found in diverse contexts in Area H, and their fragmentary nature makes reconstructing their original forms difficult (table App. 1.2; fig. app. 1.1.3). The everted bowl found in Tomb 727 may have been a gift or functioned in the mortuary cult in some other way, but it is unclear why only a fragment of this vessel was preserved.

Mortars n = 2

A large, intact mortar was found among the grave goods in Tomb 829 (table App. 1.3; fig. app. 1.2.1). A minimally modified limestone boulder, this mortar features a large, smooth-ground central depression with chipping damage along its edge. Although the wear on the interior of the depression suggests that it was used as a mortar sometime during its life history, this object may also have been used as a container for foodstuffs or liquids in its final resting place. Found upside down in the tomb and thus, perhaps, ritually "killed" (Parker Pearson 1999: 26), this mortar may have served a special function related to the mortuary cult practiced by the inhabitants of this site.

A second mortar that is roughly square in profile with engraved representations of boats was unearthed in Area H (table App. 1.3; fig. app. 1.2.2). This object has evidence for burning in its smooth-ground interior and contained several incised pebbles; Artzy believes that it was used as a portable altar (1987: 75).

Grinding Slabs: n = 4

Grinding slabs comprise the lower components of the grinding machine used in the Levant throughout antiquity. Four worked basalt fragments from Area H could be identified as grinding slabs with some certainty based on the grinding wear on their surfaces and their preserved thickness (table App. 1.4). The slab from basket 1198 has a closed, flat edge and saddle-shaped profile characteristic of complete examples of this type known from other sites (Ugarit: Elliott 1991: fig. 6.13; Hazor: Yadin 1958: CCVI.18,

CCCXLV.17; Megiddo: Sass 2000: fig. 12.6.4; Sass and Cinamon 2006: fig. 18.6.71, 76). The other three could not be identified as querns or flat slabs with certainty. Small grinding slab fragments are also surely represented in the large assemblage of Ground Stone Fragments detailed below.

Olynthus Mill: n = 1

One possible fragment of the lower stone of an Olynthus mill was found at Akko (table App. 1.5; fig. app. 1.3.1). These grinding machines represented an intermediate stage in technological development between the grinding slabs of earlier periods and the rotary, or Roman, mills introduced into the Levant during the Late Republican period. Grain was poured through a slot in a mobile upper stone that was moved over a lower stone using an attached wooden rod. The grinding surfaces of both upper and lower stones featured grooves incised in various patterns that allowed for more efficient grinding. The earliest appearance of this type of mill in Israel may be the 4th century (at Tel Michal); the Hellenistic context of the Akko fragment is in keeping with the date of the majority of the published examples from the region (Frankel 2003: 7). This small end fragment features the diagonal grooves that are characteristic of this type of grinding machine.

Handstones: n = 11

Handstones, which appear in various shapes, sizes, and raw materials, were used to grind various materials to a finer texture with a grinding slab or other stationary surface. Eight of the handstones found in Area H are of an elongated type usually made of vesicular basalt, while the remaining three vary in form and raw material (table App. 1.6; fig. app. 1.3.2–3).

Elongated Handstones n = 8
The elongated handstone known in quantity from sites in the Levant is usually planoconvex in section. The length of the tools is often equal to or slightly greater than the width of the grinding slab with which it was used (see Elliott 1991; Hovers 1996; and Milevski 1998 for published parallels). The two illustrated examples are end fragments of this type.

Other Handstones n = 3
The handstone in basket 257 is a bifacial grinding tool with some chipping damage on its rounded short edges (fig. app. 1.4.1). The tool in basket 143 features two adjacent

grinding surfaces on an otherwise unmodified flint nodule (fig. app. 1.4.2). The amorphous sandstone (?) handstone in basket 24 has one clearly ground, flat surface (table App. 1.7).

Pestles: n = 3

Pestles were also used in various processing activities in conjunction with mortars, bowls, or flat surfaces. All three pestles in the assemblage are conical in shape and have a rounded "top," a convex use surface, and a circular section (table App. 1.8; fig. app. 1.5.1–3); all are examples of Elliott's Pestle Type 1 (Elliott 1991: 16). In addition to the clear wear damage on their larger "bases," the tops of all three pestles feature pecking and pounding wear. The pestle from basket 526 is also ground flat and smooth on one of its long sides (fig. app. 1.5.3), suggesting that it functioned as a handstone as well.

Pounders: n = 7

Pounders also functioned as small, handheld processors, but unlike the more uniformly shaped pestles, pounders appear in a wide variety of shapes and sizes (table App. 1.9; fig. app. 1.6.1–3). The example from basket 305 features natural holes that seem to have been slightly enlarged, but not enough to form a complete perforation (fig. app. 1.6.1). The pounders from baskets 1245 and 186 are ovoid in shape with damage on their short ends (fig. app. 1.6.2–3), and are examples of Elliott's Pounder Type 3 (Elliott 1991: 21). The other pounders in the assemblage feature various patterns of pounding and chipping damage on their short ends.

Pecking Stones: n = 2

Two small, roughly spherical objects have battering damage on their surfaces and slightly pointed ends (table App. 1.10; fig. app. 1.7.1–2). They may have been used to peck or roughen other stone objects to create a better grinding surface or they may have been used in a number of other activities.

Polishers: n = 4

Four thin, oval pebbles feature clear abrasion damage along their edges and some scratching on their highly polished surfaces (table App. 1.11; fig. app. 1.7.3–4); they may have been used in a variety of activities that required gentle abrasion. These artifacts have not yet been clearly reported in publications from sites in the Levant, but some parallels have been reported from sites on Cyprus (Elliott 1991: 22–23).

Perforated Objects: n = 6

Six objects feature natural holes, drilled holes, or a combination of the two. Except for the very large example from basket 224, all of the perforated objects are rather small and lightweight, and could have been used as suspended weights in fishing or other activities (table App. 1.12; fig. app. 1.8.1–2). The ad hoc nature of all but the examples from baskets 620 and 127—both of which feature one intentionally drilled perforation—suggests that the inhabitants of Akko collected beach pebbles with natural holes and enlarged them to form suspended weights (as in the examples from baskets 69; 1278, fig. app. 1.8.1; and 224). There is some evidence of battering damage on the object from basket 1278, which indicates that it was also used as a pounder.

Ballast Stones: n = 7

Seven irregularly shaped boulders and pebbles made of a non-local material should probably be identified as ballast stones, brought to Akko through maritime activities (table App. 1.13; fig. app. 1.9.1–3). Although several are broken or chipped, there is no evidence that they were intentionally damaged or otherwise modified for use as tools. Four of these ballast stones, including the two largest examples, were found in Tomb 932.

Axe: n = 1

One hafted tool, perhaps an axe, was found in a fair state of preservation. It has clear chipping damage on both of its short ends, as well as wear that may have resulted from hafting on both faces (table App. 1.14; fig. app. 1.8.3). It appears to be made of the same material as the ballast stones, which suggests that it is a ballast stone in reuse. A similar hafted object found at Tel Mor was made of non-local igneous stone (Ebeling 2007: 227–28, Object A717/11).

Varia: n = 2

Two small stone objects were clearly modified, but do not appear to have been used as tools (table App. 1.15). The object in basket 100 is roughly square, but quite fragmentary. The object in basket 134 is roughly square with one broken edge, and two of its sides seem to be ground flat. Both seem to be made of the same material as the ballast stones, and thus might be pieces of ballast stones that were worked for an unknown purpose.

Ground Stone Fragments: n = 18

These small basalt fragments feature some evidence of grinding wear on their preserved surfaces, and could be the remains of grinding slabs, handstones, and other tools. They are so fragmentary that their lengths and widths cannot be distinguished; the final measurement listed is the object's maximum preserved thickness (table App. 1.16).

Conclusions

The variety of ground stone tools excavated in Area H, and their diffusion in diverse contexts, demonstrates the important roles these implements played in everyday activities at Tel Akko. Although a contextual analysis of the tools is not a focus of this study, the presence of a number of different ground stone artifacts in tombs suggests that certain objects had ritual functions as well as more "mundane" ones. Future publication of the other ground stone artifacts excavated at Akko will hopefully reveal more information about the functions and geological origins of the ground stone tools that will allow for more detailed analysis.

TABLE APPENDIX 1.1   Tripod bowls

Square	Basket	Stratum	Material	Figure	Measurements	Notes
O/1	80		D. Basalt	1.1.1	–	Somewhat rough interior
L/9	58	2	D. Basalt	1.1.2	–	Interior ground smooth

TABLE APPENDIX 1.2   Bowls

Square	Basket	Stratum	Material	Figure	Measurements	Notes
L/9	T272 B173	6	D. Basalt	1.1.3	–	Interior ground smooth
P/5	1132	Pit	D. Basalt?	–	Th 2.5	Very small rim fragment
P/4	261	1	D. Basalt	–	11.5 × 6.1, Th 3.6	Body fragment

TABLE APPENDIX 1.3   Mortars

Square	Basket	Stratum	Material	Figure	Measurements	Notes
L9/M9	T829	6	Limestone	1.2.1	–	Interior ground smooth
K/8		5	Limestone	1.2.2	–	Engraved boats

TABLE APPENDIX 1.4   Grinding slabs

Square	Basket	Stratum	Material	Figure	Measurements	Notes
M/10	1198	5	V. Basalt	–	L20 W16 Th9.2	Saddle quern
L/9	1304	5	V. Basalt	–	L12.5 W12.4 Th4.2	–
K/8	1263	3	V. Basalt	–	L12.2 W6 Th5.2	–
N/4	557	1	V. Basalt	–	L10 W9.3 Th4	–

TABLE APPENDIX 1.5   Olynthus mill

Square	Basket	Stratum	Material	Figure	Measurements	Notes
M/7	44	2	V. Basalt	1.3.1	–	Diagonal grooves

TABLE APPENDIX 1.6   Handstones

Square	Basket	Stratum	Material	Figure	Measurements	Notes
M/10	622	6	V. Basalt	–	L 7.1 W 13.3 Th 6	Grinding wear
L/9	129	5, pit	V. Basalt	1.3.2	–	–
L/9	117	5, pit	V. Basalt	–	L 15 W 11 Th 6	–
L/9	103	4, W723	V. Basalt	–	L 23.5 W 11.5 Th 6.4	Grinding wear
L/9	92	4, W723	V. Basalt	–	L 15.5 W 9.2 Th 5.6	Grinding wear
K/8	1316	3	V. Basalt	1.3.3	–	Grinding wear
L/8	2	Surface	V. Basalt	–	L 16.5 W 10.3 Th 4.2	–
P/4	1260	Surface	V. Basalt	–	L 12.2 W 10.1 Th 5.6	–

TABLE APPENDIX 1.7   Other handstones

Square	Basket	Stratum	Material	Figure	Measurements	Notes
L/9	257	5	Unknown	1.4.1	L 7.1 W 13.3 Th 6	Bifacial grinding tool
L/9	143	5, pit	Flint	1.4.2	–	Bifacial grinding tool
K/7	24	Surface	Sandstone?	–	7.6 × 4.6	One grinding surface

TABLE APPENDIX 1.8   Pestles

Square	Basket	Stratum	Material	Figure	Measurements	Notes
L/9	200/14	5, pit	D. Basalt	1.5.1	–	–
L/9	200/13	5, pit	Limestone	1.5.2	–	Heavy wear on base
N/5	526	3	D. Basalt	1.5.3	–	Multi-use tool

TABLE APPENDIX 1.9   Pounders

Square	Basket	Stratum	Material	Figure	Measurements	Notes
M/7	305/9	5	Limestone	1.6.1	–	Incomplete perforation
L/9	200	5, pit	Limestone	–	11.9 × 8.5 × 6.2	Damage on end; chipping
K/8	1245	3	Limestone	1.6.2	–	Damage on short ends; striations
N/4	636	3?	Limestone	–	–	Damage on end; chipping
P/5	186	2	Limestone	1.6.3	–	Damage on preserved short end
O/5	132	1	Limestone	–	4.2 × 3.8 × 2.9	Damage on short ends
M/7	98	1	Limestone	–	4.4 × 3.6 × 3	Damage on short ends

TABLE APPENDIX 1.10   Pecking stones

Square	Basket	Stratum	Material	Figure	Measurements	Notes
K/8	1316	3	–	1.7.1	–	One pointed end
O/1	217	2	Limestone	1.7.2	–	One slightly pointed end

TABLE APPENDIX 1.11   Polishers

Square	Basket	Stratum	Material	Figure	Measurements	Notes
J/6	632	5	–	–	L 6.9 W 3.5 Th 3.8	Abraded most of edges
K/8	1222	3	–	1.7.3	–	Abraded 75% of edges
O/5	514	3	–	1.7.4	–	Some chipping damage
L/8	4	3	–	–	L 7.1 W 5.9 Th 3.2	Abraded 50% of edges

TABLE APPENDIX 1.12   Perforated objects

Square	Basket	Stratum	Material	Figure	Measurements	Notes
M/7	305/7	5	Limestone	–	6 × 4.5	Natural holes
K/9	69	Probe 2	Limestone	–	6.7 × 4.4 × 3.1	Enlarged perforation
K/8	1278	3	Limestone	1.8.1	–	Multi-use tool
M/9	620	2	Limestone	–	6.6 × 3.2 × 3.1	Artificial perforation
O/1	224	2	Limestone	–	L24; Hole Diam 3.7–4.3	Enlarged perforation
K/7	127	Surface	Limestone	1.8.2	–	Artificial perforation

TABLE APPENDIX 1.13   Ballast stones

Square	Basket	Stratum	Material	Figure	Measurements	Notes
P/5	T932	6	–	1.9.1	–	–
P/5	T932	6	–	1.9.2	–	–
P/5	T932	6	–	1.9.3	–	Chipped
L/9	T932	6	–	–	L18.5 W11 Th8.8	Chipped
N/4	636		–	–	L13 W8.9 Th5.2	Chipped
M/9	610	2	–	–	L9.2 W4.7 Th3	Some scratches on edges
L/9	306/1	5	–	–	L18.5 W12.5 Th10	–

TABLE APPENDIX 1.14   Axe

Square	Basket	Stratum	Material	Figure	Measurements	Notes
M/7	305	5, pit	–	1.8.3	–	Chipped on ends

TABLE APPENDIX 1.15   Varia

Square	Basket	Stratum	Material	Figure	Measurements	Notes
J/7	100	1	–	–	–	Roughly square; broken
L/9	134	Surface	–	–	4.5 × 4 × 3.8	Roughly square

TABLE APPENDIX 1.16   Ground stone fragments

Square	Basket	Stratum	Material	Figure	Measurements	Notes
M/10	626	6	V. Basalt	–	5.2 × 4.6 × 3.3	–
M/10	613	6	V. Basalt	–	5.2 × 3.6 × 3.8	–
M/10	1161	3	V. Basalt	–	6.2 × 3.9 × 2.7	–
N/4	627		D. Basalt	–	8.5 × 6.3 × 4.6	–
K/8	1278	3	V. Basalt	–	7.2 × 6.6 × 4	–
M/9	620	2	V. Basalt	–	5.2 × 3.4 × 3.4	–
N/4	589	2	V. Basalt	–	7 × 5 × 5.2	–
M/9	1068	2	V. Basalt	–	5 × 2.6 × 3.7	–
O/5	1069	2	V. Basalt	–	7.2 × 6.3 × 3.3	–
O/5	303	2	D. Basalt	–	6.9 × 3.5 × 3.7	–
O/1	155	2	V. Basalt	–	4 × 2.8 × 3.2	–
O/1	155	2	V. Basalt	–	6.3 × 5.7 × 4.6	–
O/1	155	2	V. Basalt	–	7.5 × 6.2 × 3.7	–
O/1	155	2	D. Basalt	–	8 × 7.6 × 7.7	–
P/5	76	2?	V. Basalt	–	6.5 × 4.6 × 4.4	–
O/5	195	1	V. Basalt	–	5.9 × 5.3 × 2.9	–
P/5	152	1	V. Basalt	–	4.8 × 3.9 × 2.8	–
L/7	109	Surface	V. Basalt	–	9.5 × 8.3 × 3	–

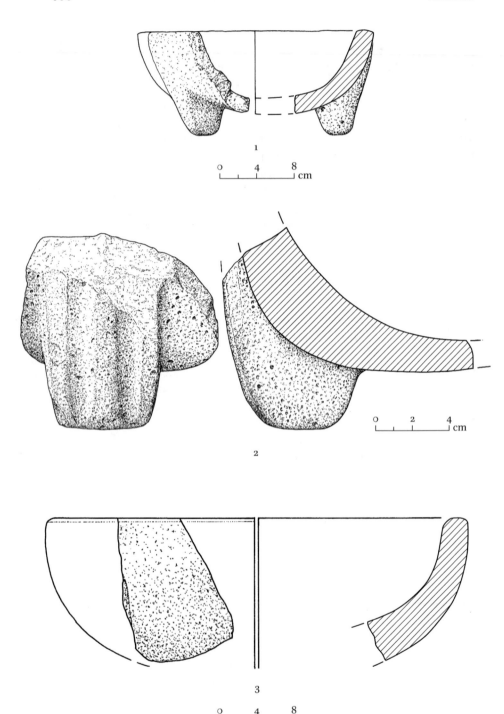

FIGURE APPENDIX 1.1   Tripod bowls, bowls

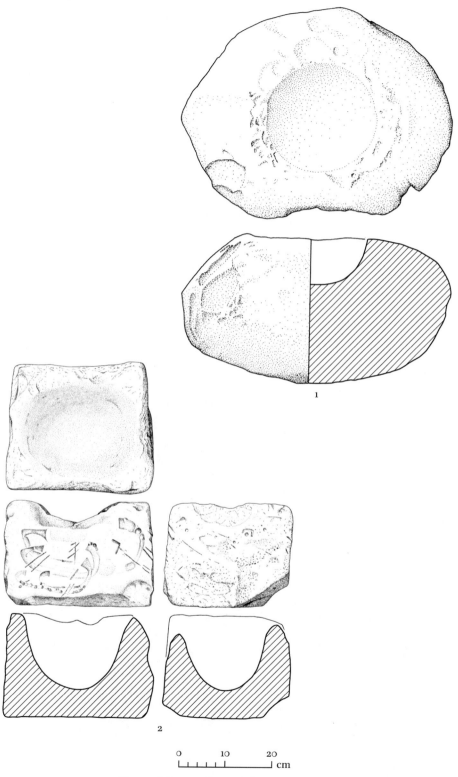

FIGURE APPENDIX 1.2 Fig. 1.2.2 left center (front of altar)
DRAWN BY RACHEL POLAK

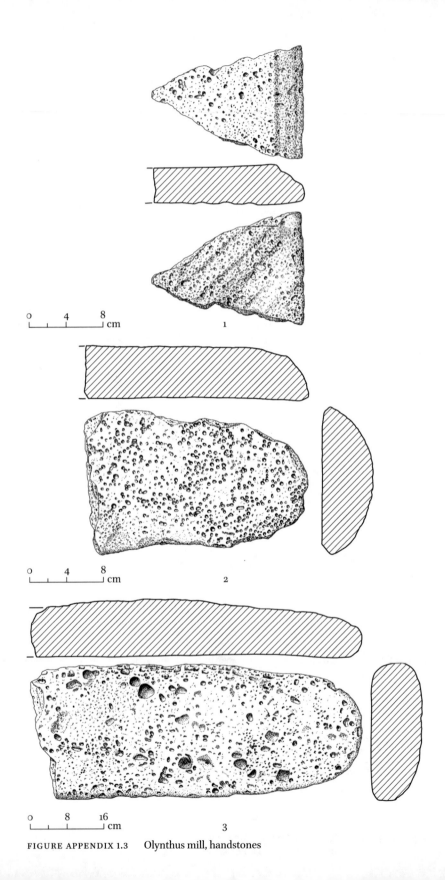

FIGURE APPENDIX 1.3   Olynthus mill, handstones

THE GROUND STONE ARTIFACTS FROM AREA H, AKKO

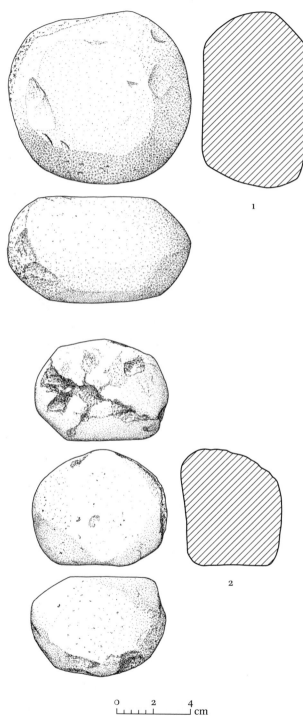

FIGURE APPENDIX 1.4 Other handstones

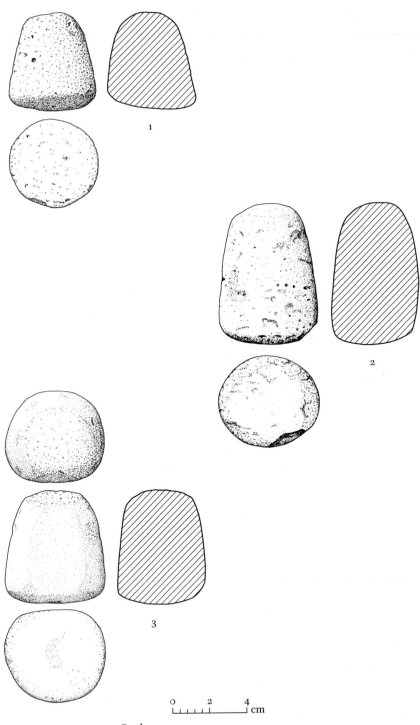

FIGURE APPENDIX 1.5 Pestles

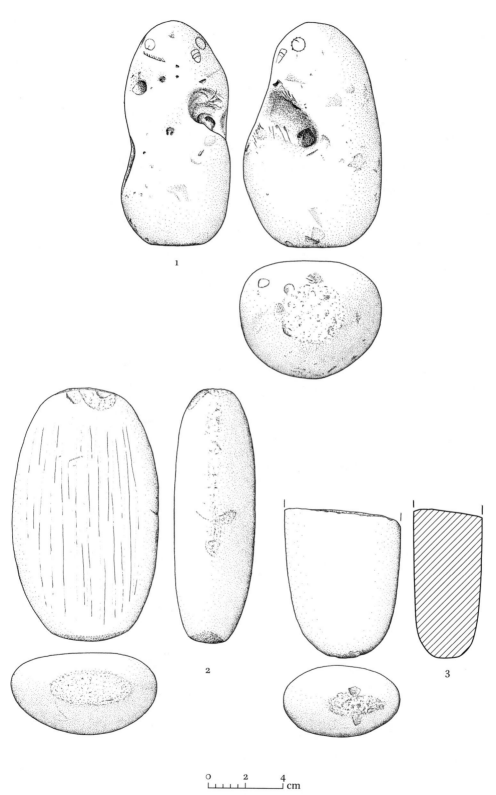

FIGURE APPENDIX 1.6 Pounders

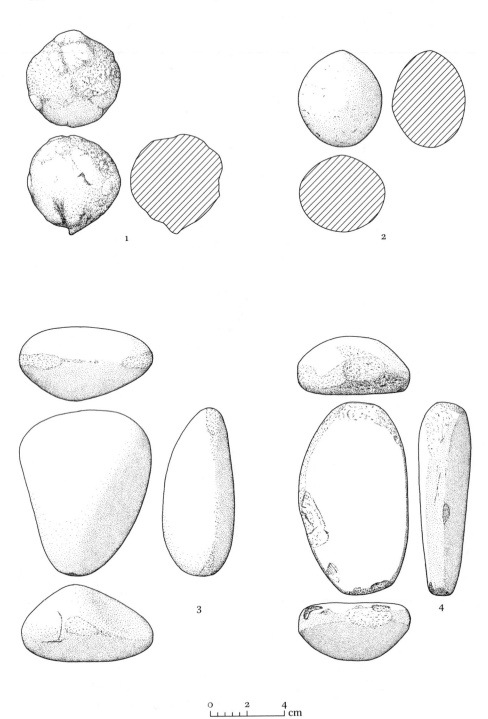

FIGURE APPENDIX 1.7 Pecking stones, polishers

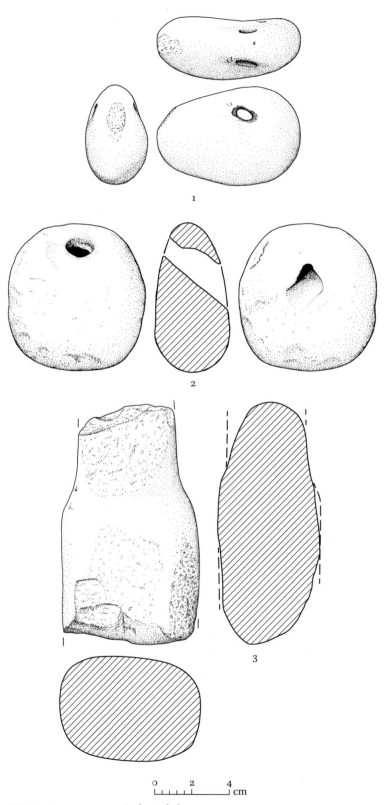

FIGURE APPENDIX 1.8   Perforated objects, axe

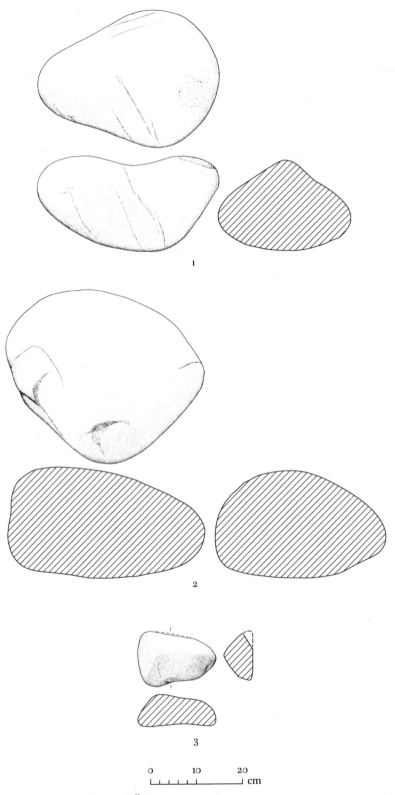

FIGURE APPENDIX 1.9   Ballast stones

APPENDIX 2

Analysis of the Lithic Assemblage from Area H at Tel Akko

Jeffrey Rose

Summary and Description[1]

The chipped stone assemblage from area H at Tel Akko is comprised of 89 pieces manufactured from both flint and limestone. Of this material, 23 artifacts are tools, 44 are classified as debitage, 17 fall into the category of debris, and 5 are cores (table App. 2.1). The lithics are generally in pristine condition; only two pieces appear to be significantly older, exhibiting evidence of heavy patination, rounding, and edge damage.

Two general categories of raw material are present in the Area H lithic assemblage. The first and most prevalent (90 percent of the total assemblage) is a fine grained flint ranging from light to deep brown in color. This material is almost always opaque, typically with few inclusions. In some cases the flint exhibits banding. The raw material originates in the Eocene and Upper Cretaceous formations to the east of the site in the Galilee hills, and nodules were carried to the vicinity of Tel Akko via westward-flowing drainage systems.

The second type of raw material is a hard limestone that can be found throughout the local hills. The limestone is characterized as rough grained and is typically either light beige or gray in color. Only nine limestone pieces were collected, comprising just 10 percent of the total assemblage. No tools were manufactured from this material.

Debitage and Debris

The total lithic assemblage is divided into four main categories: tools, cores, debitage, and debris. Tools are defined as any piece exhibiting retouch; that is, deliberate secondary modification (Tixier et al. 1980: 59). Cores are classified based on the presence of at least one striking platform and more than one removal across the working surface. Debitage consists of the refuse produced during core reduction.

---

1 This paper was initially written in 2004 and does not consider the more current scholarship on historic period lithic assemblages from the Levant.

The category of debris is made up of chunks and chips: amorphous pieces lacking standardized features. Chips are arbitrarily defined as any piece less than 2 cm in maximum dimension, chunks greater than 2 cm. Debris is often the result of shatter during tool production, or from breakage due to excessive heat (Rosen 1997: 30–31). Nine pieces were classified as chunks. The percentage of chips within an assemblage is typically a function of collection techniques. In a fully sieved sample, chips will comprise 80–90 percent of the excavated debris. There are eight chips recovered from Area H, accounting for 9 percent of the total lithic assemblage. This frequency suggests a collection bias toward larger, more clearly reworked artifacts.

The category of debitage constitutes the largest portion of the Area H lithic assemblage: 49 percent of all recovered material (table App. 2.3). For the purposes of this study, debitage was divided into five subgroups: ad hoc flakes, sickle flakes (blades that have been truncated specially for the manufacture of Large Geometric sickles), primary elements, blades/bladelets, and core trimming elements. Flakes constitute 66 percent of the total debitage category, while just one Large Geometric flake was recovered, suggesting sickle segments were neither produced nor resharpened in Area H. Similarly, decortification flakes make up 18 percent of the debitage group, indicating there was little primary reduction carried out in this area.

There were four blades—defined as any blank twice as long as it is wide along the technology axis at midpoint—accounting for just 9 percent of the debitage. Of these pieces, two are bladelets (<14 mm in width), one is an unretouched Canaanean blade, and the other is a ridge blade suggesting core modification. The assemblage also included three core trimming elements, which are diagnostic indicators of core preparation and maintenance.

Cores

Five relatively small cores were recovered from Area H at Tel Akko, with maximum dimensions ranging between 4.1 and 6.4 cm. Three of these are globular in shape and show multiple alternating platforms characteristic of an ad hoc flaking strategy. There was also a naviform-shaped core with bidirectional bladelet removals across the working surface, more likely from EB–MB I phases at the site. The final specimen is clearly intrusive: a heavily weathered and patinated preferential centripetal Levallois core. There do not appear to be any recent removals on this piece, ruling out the possibility of secondary usage. In general, Area H exhibits an extremely low ratio of cores in relation to the number of tools recovered, a trend typical of historic lithic assemblages. Similar findings were reported at Gezer, Tel Yin'am, Tel Qiri, and Beth Shemesh (Rosen 1986; 1987; Rosen and Rose 2004; n.d.). This trend suggests tools were manufactured off site at specialized workshop localities.

Tools

The category of tools accounts for 26 percent of the total lithic assemblage (table App. 2.4), all manufactured from the fine grained Late Mesozoic/Early Tertiary flint found in the limestone formations that make up the Galilee range. Nine of these are sickle segments—the only tool type within historic lithic assemblages that allows for a general chronological attribution. The diagnostic characteristic of sickle segments is the presence of sickle gloss, caused by the accumulation of plant silica on the working edge of the piece (Witthoft 1967; Unger-Hamilton 1984). In addition, the working edge commonly exhibits serrated resharpening. These tools are divided into three subcategories based on the type of blank from which they are constructed: Canaanean blade (Rosen 1983), simple blade, and Large Geometric.

Among the sickles from Area H, three are classified as Large Geometric, a specific type produced from the MB II through Iron II (Rosen 1997: 59–60). This form is typically constructed on large flake-blades with truncated ends, abrupt or semi-abrupt backing, and a serrated working edge (Rosen 1982: 142). Four sickle segments are made from Canaanean blades, a prismatic blade technology associated with the EB–MB I periods. Distinctive features on these pieces include two parallel ridges that run down the length of the dorsal surface, giving the blades their hallmark trapezoidal cross section. The final two sickles consist of a plain blade and a fragment of indeterminate age (table App. 2.2). These mixed typological features suggest either the lithic assemblage comes from a mixture of upper and lower strata, or the EB–MB I tools were reused during subsequent periods of occupation.

Two bifacial pieces were also identified among the tools, including a bifacial celt and handaxe. Notably, they do not bear any sign of patination or water wear, suggesting they are heavy duty tools contemporary with the rest of the assemblage. Of the three backed pieces from Area H, all were made on regular blades and exhibit abrupt lateral retouch. Clearly intrusive based on its technology and weathering, the final formal tool is a Middle Palaeolithic Levallois point with typical faceted striking platform and unidirectional-convergent dorsal scar pattern.

The remaining tools from Area H can be described as ad hoc—expedient implements produced on site for some immediate purpose. Among these were two sidescrapers constructed on thick transverse flakes with steep retouch on the distal end, as well as a notched piece and two denticulates. Finally, there were four retouched pieces, referring to any miscellaneous flake or chunk that does not fit any formal typology, yet shows clear evidence of continuous retouch along one or more edges.

Discussion

Examination of lithic assemblages from historic period sites indicate there were complex systems of specialized production and exchange from the Early Bronze to the Iron II, responsible for disseminating well-crafted flint sickles throughout the Levant. Sickle manufacture is thought to have occurred in three stages. First, the material was quarried and prepared for flaking. In this phase, cortex is removed from the flint nodule and the core is specially trimmed in order to produce the specific flake-blades required in constructing sickle elements. In the second stage, the flake-blade blanks are truncated on both ends in order to produce the geometric shape for which these sickles are named. They are then transported away from the production site to be exported throughout the region. Upon reaching their destination the sickles are further retouched to craft a cutting edge, and finally hafted onto a bone or wood shaft (Rosen 1986: 262).

Several caches attesting to these primary manufacture sites were unearthed in the 12th and 11th century BCE strata at Gezer (Rosen 1986). The caches, all found within the northeast house and lacking any usewear or sickle gloss, are believed to represent the second stage of sickle production, and thus suggest that Gezer served as a specialized center for secondary sickle production. This is based on the observations that sickle caches were not found in any other architectural unit, no other flint tool type was discovered in the house, and the frequency of debitage types indicates specialized production.

Although problematic in its recovery methodology, the Area H assemblage upholds Rosen's sickle exchange model. Based on the low ratio of cores to other flint pieces, as well as the lack of a blade technology necessary for the production of Large Geometric sickle segments, it seems there was no specialized industry at the site, suggesting that Akko was on the receiving end of a similar sickle exchange network. Pieces that would be common within the assemblage if primary production were occurring (e.g., core trimming elements, primary elements, or sickle flakes) are rare. Rather, the debitage and core patterning instead points to the on-site production of ad hoc tools. The possibility that flint working activities at Tel Akko were conducted away from Area H cannot be discounted. Indeed, all of these conclusions should be approached with caution due to the lack of systematic collections, poor chronological control, and bias toward recovering tools.

Comparative analyses of the Area H sickle collection in relation to other Large Geometric assemblages in Israel reveal a degree of standardization that was probably the result of off-site production and exchange. Figures App. 2.1 and App. 2.2 illustrate the range of variability within sickle widths and the derived width/thickness ratio at four separate sites dated to roughly the same time periods. Statistical analyses of variance indicate that Tel Akko, Ein Zippori, and Tel Yin'am are similar in metric distribution, while the Beth Shemesh sickle assemblage is significantly different from the other three (tables App. 2.5 and App. 2.6).

This standardization in size may cluster around geographic or sociopolitical boundaries. The three related assemblages come from sites located in the north of Israel, with Tel Akko on the northern coastal plain, and Ein Zippori and Tel Yin'am located in the hinterland. Beth Shemesh, on the other hand, is situated on the western flanks of the Hill Country in the central southern Levant, within the Philistine sphere of influence during the Iron Age. Perhaps the metric distribution of Large Geometric sickle segments differs at Beth Shemesh due to its involvement in an alternate exchange network from the sickle trade system occurring in the Galilee. Other factors that may affect sickle width include raw material type, degree of resharpening and reuse, and type of haft.

The model for sickle exchange presented above necessitates a high degree of specialization, demanding skilled laborers. Rosen (1989: 107) traces the rise of craft specialization within lithic industries as far back as the Early Bronze Age. This trend toward craft specialization is marked by an increase in standardization and thus can be measured statistically. Standardization is expressed through greater imposed form on whatever tool type is being specially produced, manifested by a decrease in the variability of metric attributes (Arnold 1984).

This trajectory toward greater standardization can be traced at Tel Akko from the blade sickles of the EB–MB I periods to subsequent Large Geometric sickle segments. Figures App. 2.3, 2.4, and 2.5 demonstrate the variability in metric attributes between blade and Large Geometric sickle technology. A chi-square test of homogeneity was employed to determine the coefficient of variation between these two sickle categories. This test was used in order to indicate if there is a significance difference in the degree of standardization between the type of sickle technologies. Analysis of the width/thickness derived ratio yielded a p-value of .02, indicating that Large Geometrics are significantly more homogenous than the preceding Canaanean blade sickle industries.

TABLE APPENDIX 2.1   Categories of lithic material

Category	Frequency	Percent
Debris	17	19.1
Debitage	44	49.4
Tools	23	25.8
Cores	5	5.6
Total:	89	100.0

TABLE APPENDIX 2.2   Sickle type

Sickle type	Frequency	Percent
Large Geometrics	31	68.9
Canaanean Blades	6	13.3
Blades	7	15.6
Fragments	1	2.2
Total:	45	100.0

TABLE APPENDIX 2.3   Debitage type

Debitage type	Frequency	Percent
Flakes	29	65.9
Sickle Flakes	1	2.3
Primary Flakes	8	18.2
Canaanean Blades	1	2.3
Ridge Blades	1	2.3
Bladelets	2	4.5
Core Trimming Elements	2	4.5
Total:	44	100.00

TABLE APPENDIX 2.4   Tool type

Toole type	Frequency	Percent
Sickles	9	39.1
Scrapers	2	8.7
Notches	1	4.3
Denticulates	2	8.7
Celts	1	4.3
Retouched Blades	3	13.0
Retouched Pieces	4	17.4
Handaxes	1	4.3
Total:	23	100.0

TABLE APPENDIX 2.5   Analysis of variance for sickle widths at four sites

(I) SITE	(J) SITE	Mean Difference (I–J)	Std. Error	Sig.	95% Confidence Interval Lower Bound	Upper Bound
Tel Akko	Ein Zippori	2.903E-02	1.6280	0.986	−3.1851	3.2431
	Beth Shemesh	−4.0785*	1.3293	0.003	−6.7028	−1.4542
	Tel Yinam	0.1149	1.9730	0.954	−3.7803	4.0102
Ein Zippori	Tel Akko	−2.9032E-02	1.6280	0.986	−3.2431	3.1851
	Beth Shemesh	−4.1075*	1.3293	0.002	−6.7318	−1.4832
	Tel Yinam	8.589E-02	1.9730	0.965	−3.8094	3.9811
Beth Shemesh	Tel Akko	4.0785*	1.3293	0.003	1.4542	6.7028
	Ein Zippori	4.1075*	1.3293	0.002	1.4832	6.7318
	Tel Yinam	4.1934*	1.7347	0.017	0.7686	7.6182
Tel Yinam	Tel Akko	−0.1149	1.9730	0.954	−4.0102	3.7803
	Ein Zippori	−8.5887E-02	1.9730	0.965	−3.9811	3.8094
	Beth Shemesh	−4.1934	1.7347	0.017	−7.6182	−0.7686

* The mean difference is significant at the .05 level.
DEPENDENT VARIABLE: WIDTH
LSD

TABLE APPENDIX 2.6   Analysis of variance for sickle width/thickness ratio at four sites

(I) SITE	(J) SITE	Mean Difference (I–J)	Std. Error	Sig.	95% Confidence Interval Lower Bound	Upper Bound
Tel Akko	Ein Zippori	−1.70E-02	0.29	1.000	−0.76	0.72
	Beth Shemesh	−0.73*	0.23	0.010	−1.34	−0.13
	Tel Yinam	−0.14	0.35	0.977	−1.04	0.75
Ein Zippori	Tel Akko	1.70E-02	0.29	1.000	−0.72	0.76
	Beth Shemesh	−0.72*	0.23	0.012	−1.32	−0.11
	Tel Yinam	−0.13	0.35	.984	−1.02	0.77
Beth Shemesh	Tel Akko	0.73*	0.23	0.010	0.13	1.34
	Ein Zippori	0.72*	0.23	0.012	0.11	1.32
	Tel Yinam	0.59	0.31	0.216	−0.20	1.38
Tel Yinam	Tel Akko	0.14	0.35	0.977	−0.75	1.04
	Ein Zippori	0.13	0.35	0.984	−0.77	1.02
	Beth Shemesh	−0.59	0.31	0.216	−1.38	0.20

* The mean difference is significant at the .05 level.
DEPENDENT VARIABLE: WDTH_THK
TURKEY HSD

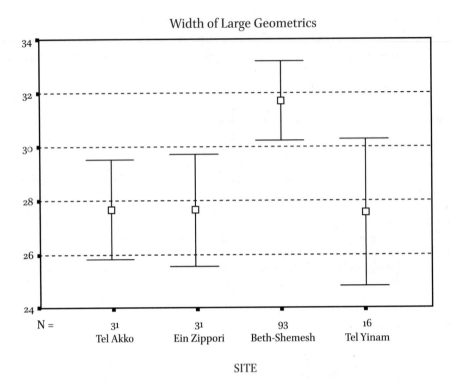

FIGURE APPENDIX 2.1   Range of variability within sickle widths at four sites

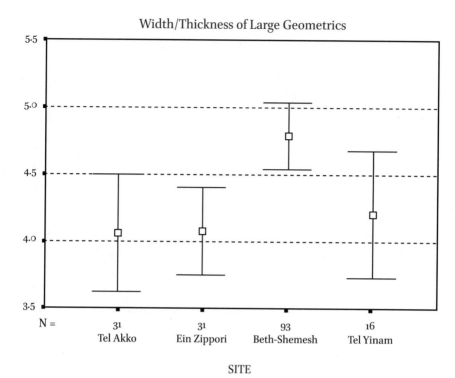

FIGURE APPENDIX 2.2   Range of variability within sickle derived width/thickness ratio at four sites

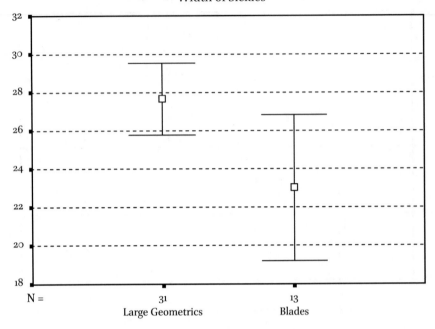

FIGURE APPENDIX 2.3　Variability in metric attributes between blade and large geometric sickle technology

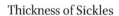

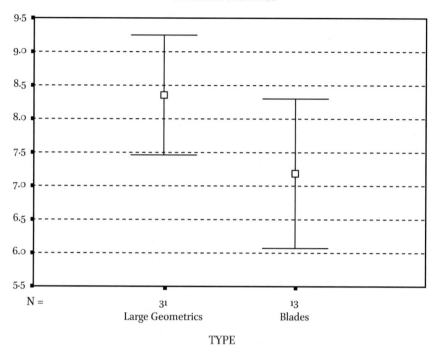

FIGURE APPENDIX 2.4   Variability in metric attributes between blade and large geometric sickle technology

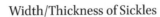

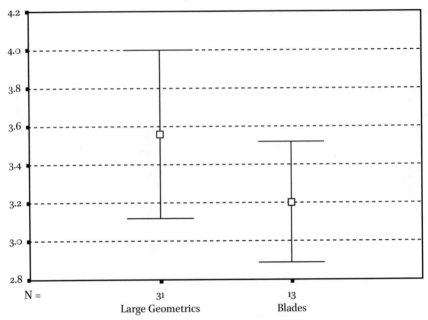

FIGURE APPENDIX 2.5　Variability in metric attributes between blade and large geometric sickle technology

APPENDIX 3

Middle Bronze Age Mortuary Animal Offerings from Akko

Edward F. Maher

The 1983 excavations in squares L9/M9 from Area H at Akko uncovered a small mortuary assemblage from a rectangular stone lined burial chamber designated as Tomb 829 (2.92 × 1.78 m interior base level; 3.92 × 2.26 m exterior base level; depth 1.14–1.46 m) from Stratum 6 dating to the MB IIB–IIC. The tomb, lying in an east-west orientation with a west side entrance, was partially cut into an earlier MB IIA rampart from Stratum 7. For a more detailed description of Tomb 829 and its associated stratigraphy and finds see chapters 2 and 4 above in this volume. Since Tomb 829 received interments on multiple occasions throughout different phases of the MB II period, determining the precise date of the introduction of the animal offerings is problematic. In addition to the zooarchaeological evidence, one field photograph (photo App. 3.1) was consulted to further assess the nature of the mortuary customs at Akko involving animal offerings. The photographic evidence is particularly important since there is very little actual zooarchaeological material available for analysis. The animal bones shown in photo App. 3.1 were not available for first hand study by the author.

The Middle Bronze Age funerary sample from Tomb 829 at Akko further expands the evidence for animals as mortuary offerings in antiquity. The remains of animals, dominated by domestic species, have been found in several contemporaneous and penecontemporaneous tomb contexts (e.g., Bate 1938; Cornwall 1965; Grosvenor-Ellis 1960; Grosvenor-Ellis and Westley 1965; Horwitz 1987; 1989; 1996; 1997; 2007; 2010; Horwitz and Garfinkel 1991; Isserlin 1950; Petrie 1931; Sukenik 1948).

The faunal sample from Tomb 829 (Locus 829 basket 1072/B) available for zooarchaeological analysis consists of a total of six bones. Field recovery strategies did not employ a sifting program as the remains were hand collected. General excavation strategies and practice are addressed in greater detail in chapter 1 above in this volume. At present it is unknown if so few bones reflect an authentic aspect of the local mortuary customs or if this small collection is all that survived of a once larger funerary faunal assemblage. Considering the passage of millennia separating the bone's original time of deposition until their discovery, combined with the decades elapsed between their excavation and storage until the present analysis, it is probable that a portion of the assemblage may have been lost through a combination of perthotaxic agents (animal disturbance), taphonomic processes (mechanical and chemical alteration of buried bone), anataxic variables that reexpose buried bones (such as archaeological excavation), and sullegic factors (recovery procedures employed during excavation). The manner in which the excavated fauna was curated and processed (trephic processes) would have also contributed to the limited survivorship of the mortuary faunal remains.

Of the six bones from Tomb 829 (table App. 3.1) two are identified as fish while two others belong to domestic stock. Two additional fragments could only be identified as belonging to a mammal of medium body size. None of the bones bore any evidence of burning, butchery, pathology, or carnivore access (gnawing or partial digestion). The spatial arrangement of the bones within the tomb as they relate to architectural features, human remains, or other mortuary items is not possible to assess based on the original excavation records.

Mammal Remains

Two of the animal bones from Tomb 829 are identified as domestic sheep (*Ovis aries*) or goat (*Capria hircus*). Each of these bones yields relatively little meat, and as such, they have limited nutritional value. The orbital is a cranial section that forms a portion of the animal's face near the eye, while the third phalanx is a hoof-sheathed toe bone. The other two bone fragments from a medium sized mammal(s) represent meatier areas (scapula and rib). Given their size and general morphology these bones may also belong to domestic sheep or goats.

A field photograph (photo App. 3.1) shows a collection of animal bones discovered in Locus 934 lying approximately one meter north of the northeastern exterior corner of Tomb 829. Their proximity to the tomb suggests their association with one of the interments received in Tomb 829. Although the clarity of the image prohibits definitive assessments regarding taxonomic identity, some observations can be made. The bones represent parts of three distinct limb segments of a ruminant (e.g., cattle, sheep/goat, equid) lying in similar orientation relative to one another. The uppermost limb (nearest the scale) is a lower fore or hind leg (metatarsal or metacarpal) which articulates with a proximal phalanx (toe bone) on its distal (left) end. The middle limb segment is also a lower fore or hind leg (metatarsal or metacarpal) which articulates with a tarsal/carpal bone (perhaps a naviculo-cuboid) on its proximal (left) end and two consecutive phalanxes (toe bones) on its distal (right) end. Although the lowermost limb bone (furthest from the scale) is more difficult to identify, it too may be a lower leg bone and seems to articulate with another long bone. Articulated animal bones from Middle Bronze Age tombs have been documented at Jericho (Grosvenor-Ellis and Westely 1965), Jebel Qa'aqir and Sasa (Horwitz 1987), Nahal Refaim and Yoqne'am (Horwitz 2001: 81), and Gesher (Horwitz 2007). Animal joints associated with funerary areas from the Late Bronze Age include Gezer (Legge and Zeder 1988), Azor (Maher 2012), and Tel Shaddud (Van den Brink et al. 2017: 124–25).

Fish Remains

Two fish bones were found in Tomb 829. One vertebra is from the caudal (tail) portion of an unidentified fish. The upper jaw, or pre-maxilla (fig. app. 3.1) from the right side of the mouth is identified as a member of the Sparidae family known as the common sea-bream (*Pagrus* sp.). Naturally restricted to the open sea as well as salt water lakes, Sparidae inhabit murky sand laden bottoms and are found in relatively shallow water (Reese 1981: 238). Their dietary regime has led to the development of specialized oral anatomies with enlarged flattened molars for grinding calcareous items regularly encountered in their natural habitat (Lernau 2000a: 466). Such distinct morphological developments facilitate their taxonomic classification. Sparidae can achieve a size of 70 cm in length, but most average lengths occur between 20–40 cm (Lernau 2000b: 235). The meat of Sparidae has been prized since ancient times and these fish can be captured in nets or by angling (Lepiksaar 1995: 187).

Although the most common member of the Sparidae family reported from archaeological contexts in Israel is the gilthead sea-bream (*Sparus aurata*), *Pagrus* sp. remains are known from multiple sites of various dates indicating their ease of capture, general appeal, and popularity. For example, *Pagrus* remains were uncovered from Pre-Pottery Neolithic A levels at Hatoula (Van Neer et al. 2004: 112), Iron Age contexts at Ḥorbat Rosh Zayit (Lernau 2000b: 236), the Ophel excavations at Jerusalem (Lernau and Lernau 1992: 131–48) and at the Byzantine fortress from Upper Zohar (Lernau 1995: 100).

The use of fish as funerary offerings accompanying the deceased has been noted in different periods, cultures, and environmental settings. Bone fragments of gray mullet (Mugilidae) are known from an Early Bronze Age tomb at Tel Kabri (Lernau 2002: 422). Middle Bronze Age burials yielding fish bones include Nile catfish (*Clarias gariepinus*) and Nile perch (*Lates niloticus*) from Sasa (Horwitz 1987; Lernau, personal communication); common sea-bream (*Pagrus pagrus*), cichlids (Cichlidae), sea bass (Serranidae), greater amberjack (*Seriola dumerili*), white sea-bream (*Diplodus* sp.) and Nile perch (*L. niloticus*) from Tel Kabri (Lernau 2002: 422); and unidentified fish remains from Tel Dan (Horwitz 1996: 270–71). Sparidae, Serranidae, and *Argyrosomus* sp. were recovered from Middle Bronze Age tombs from Megadim (Lernau, personal communication). Fish from Late Bronze Age mortuary contexts include Nile perch (*L. niloticus*) from Tel Dothan (Lev-Tov and Maher 2001), Tel Shaddud (van den Brink 2017: 125), and unidentified fish bones from Tel Dan (Horwitz 2002: 219). A unique find of preserved scaled skin of a sea bass (Serranidae) was a Late Bronze Age introduction to Zone N of Cave 1.10A at Gezer (David 1988: 149). One Sparidae vertebra was collected in a 7th century BCE grave at Megiddo (Lernau 2000a: 473). Twelve of the seventeen bowls from Tomb 79 at Salamis, located on the east coast of Cyprus and dating to the Iron II, contained the bones of Nile catfish (*C. gariepinus*) (Greenwood and Howes 1973), which most likely came from the Nile (Van Neer et al. 2004: 130). Tombs from Kalavasos, in southern Cyprus, contained *S. aurata* and other species of Sparidae (Lernau, personal communication).

Discussion

Understanding the motivation for including animal remains in a mortuary context is not as obvious as one may suspect. The animal parts may have been intended to symbolically feed the deceased or a local divinity. They may also reflect the deceased's avowed or achieved social status in the community or the mourner's idealized perception of the social standing of the deceased. Such mortuary offerings may even represent remnants of a communal meal partaken by mourners of the deceased and/or officiants of the ceremony. Whatever the reason for their interment, mortuary goods are culturally understood symbols that effectively convey the mourner's suite of beliefs and attitudes (Pearson 2000: 10). The species associated with Tomb 829 (sheep/goat, unidentified grazing animal [possibly domesticated] and fish) were selected not because they were special or particularly difficult to acquire. In fact these animal specimens were taken directly from readily available resources through local shepherds and fishermen. Presumably funerary deposits yielding uncommon or exotic specimens, such as the felid bones from a MB II burial (Tomb T4663) at Tel Dan tentatively identified as an adult lion (*Panthera leo*) (Horwitz 1996: 270), held specific symbolic significance fundamentally and categorically distinct from the offerings of common animal stock.

An additional aspect of the mortuary faunal assemblage from Akko was tentatively revealed through a study of the archived photographic evidence showing the in situ position of articulated animal limb segments lying near, but external to, Tomb 829. Each limb segment must have been buried relatively quickly to preserve their articulated state as human traffic and carnivore interest would have ensured their scattered placement had the bones remained exposed on the surface for too long. Given such considerations, it appears that the rapid burial of limb joints may have been an important act relevant to ceremonial funerary observances.

Conclusion

The Middle Bronze Age offerings from Tomb 829 at Akko include a very small collection of animal bones. That animals were considered as acceptable funerary gifts expands our recognition of this ancient rite. The animals selected were unlikely to evoke unique symbolism or imagery as they were not special or rare in any manner and could be acquired with relative ease by local workers from nearby sources. Their inclusion in the tomb rather demonstrates resources readily accessible and exploitable. Offerings that included limb bone segments outside of Tomb 829 may have served as actual sustenance for the mourners or ritual officials or symbolic provisions for the deceased.

Acknowledgments

I would like to thank Aaron Brody for inviting me to study the mortuary faunal assemblage from Akko, and both Omri Lernau and Arlene Fradkin for their assistance in identifying the fish remains. I also extend my gratitude to Marina Zeltser for her illustrations of the fish bone.

TABLE APPENDIX 3.1   Faunal composition of Tomb 829 at Akko

Species	Bone	Measurements*
Sheep/Goat (*Ovis/Capra*)	orbital	–
Sheep/Goat (*Ovis/Capra*)	third phalanx	–
Fish, common sea-bream (*Pagrus* sp.)	pre-maxilla	Pm 1: 25.1 mm
Medium sized mammal	scapula	–
Medium sized mammal	rib	–
Unidentified fish	caudal vertebra	GL: 70 mm

* Key: Pm 1 = pre-maxillary length (after Wheeler 1981), GL = greatest length

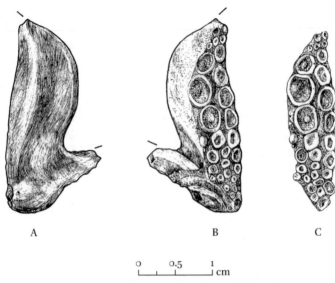

FIGURE APPENDIX 3.1   Three views of a pre-maxilla from the common sea-bream (*Pagrus sp.*) from Tomb 829.
A: lateral; B: medial; C: ventral
DRAWN BY MARINA ZELTSER

PHOTO APPENDIX 3.1   Animal limb bone articulations lying near external corner of Tomb 829
PHOTO: M. ARTZY

Bibliography

Abu Hamid, A. 2016. Akko Area W. *Contract Archaeology Reports VI*, ed. M. Artzy. Haifa: University of Haifa Press.

Amiran, R. 1969. *Ancient Pottery of the Holy Land*. Jerusalem: Massada Press.

Anderson, W. P. 1988. *Sarepta I: The Late Bronze and Iron Age Strata of Area II, Y*. Beirut: Département des publications de l'Université libanaise.

Arnold, J. E. 1984. Economic Specialization in Prehistory: Methods of Documenting the Rise of Lithic Craft Specialization. Pp. 37–58 in *Lithic Resource Procurement: Proceedings of the Second Conference on Prehistoric Chert Exploitation*, ed. S. C. Vehik. Carbondale, IL: Center for Archaeological Investigations, Southern Illinois University Press.

Artzy, M. 1984. Unusual Late Bronze Age Ship Representations from Tel Akko. *Mariner's Mirror* 70: 59–64.

Artzy, M. 1987. On Boats and Sea Peoples. *Bulletin of the American Schools of Oriental Research* 266: 75–84.

Artzy, M. 2001. White Slip Ware for Export? The Economics of Production. Pp. 107–15 in *The White Slip Ware of Late Bronze Age Cyprus: Proceedings of an International Conference Organized by the Anastasios G. Leventis Foundation, Nicosia in Honour of Malcolm Wiener, Nicosia 29th–30th October 1998*, ed. V. Karageorghis. Contributions to the Chronology of the Eastern Mediterranean 2. Denkschriften der Gesamtakademie 20. Vienna: Verlag der Österreichischen Akademie der Wissenschaften.

Artzy, M. 2003. Mariners and Their Boats at the End of the Late Bronze and the Beginning of the Iron Age in the Eastern Mediterranean. *Tel Aviv* 30: 232–46.

Artzy, M. 2005. Emporia on the Carmel Coast? Tel Akko, Tell Abu Hawam and Tel Nami of the Late Bronze Age. Pp. 355–62 in *Emporia: Aegeans in the Central and Eastern Mediterranean I*, eds. R. Laffineur and E. Greco. Aegaeum 25. Belgium: Kliemo.

Artzy, M. 2006a. The Carmel Coast during the Second Part of the Late Bronze Age: A Center for Eastern Mediterranean Transshipping. *Bulletin of the American Schools of Oriental Research* 343: 45–64.

Artzy, M. 2006b. Filling in the Void: Observations on the Habitation Pattern at Tel Akko at the End of the Late Bronze Age. Pp. 115–22 in *"I Will Speak the Riddle of Ancient Times:" Archaeological and Historical Studies in Honor of Amihai Mazar on the Occasion of His Sixtieth Birthday*, eds. A. M. Maeir and P. de Miroschedji. Winona Lake, IN: Eisenbrauns.

Artzy, M. 2013. The Importance of the Anchorages in the Carmel Coast in the Trade Networks during the Late Bronze Period. *Michmanim* 24: 7*–24*.

Artzy, M. 2015. What Is in a Name? 'Akko-Ptolemais-'Akka-Acre. *Complutum* 26: 201–12.

Artzy, M. 2016. Distributers and Shippers: Cyprus and the Late Bronze II, Tell Abu Hawam Anchorage. Pp. 97–110 in *Maritime Transport Containers in the Bronze–Iron Age Aegean and Eastern Mediterranean*, eds. S. Demesticha and A. B. Knapp. Studies in Mediterranean Archaeology and Literature PB 183. Uppsala, Sweden: Åströms Förlag.

Artzy, M. 2018. From Akko/Acco to Beit She'an/Beth Shan in the Late Bronze Age. *Ägypten und Levante* 28: 85–98.

Artzy, M. 2019. Late Bronze Age II Anatolian Imports. Pp. 381–82 in *The Ancient Pottery of Israel and Its Neighbors*, vol. 3, ed. Seymour Gitin. Jerusalem: Israel Exploration Society.

Artzy, M., and Asaro, F. 1979. Origin of Tell el-Yahudiyah Ware Found in Cyprus. *Report of the Department of Antiquities of Cyprus*: 135–50.

Artzy, M., and Beeri, R. 2010. Tel Akko. Pp. 15*–24* in *One Thousand Nights and Days: Akko through the Ages*, eds. A. E. Killebrew and V. Raz-Romeo. Haifa: Hecht Museum.

Artzy, M., and Marcus, E. 1992. Stratified Cypriote Pottery in MBIIa Context at Tel Nami. Pp. 103–10 in *Studies in Honour of Vassos Karageorghis*, ed. G. C. Ioannides. Nicosia: Hetaireia Kypriakōn Spoudōn.

Artzy, M., and Quartermaine, J. 2014. How and When did Tel Akko get its Unusual Banana Shape? Pp. 11–22 in AΘYPMATA: *Critical Essays on the Archaeology of the Eastern Mediterranean in Honour of E. Susan Sherratt*, eds. Y. Galanakis, T. Wilkinson, and J. Bennet. Oxford: Archaeopress.

Artzy, M., and Zagorski, S. 2012. Cypriot "Mycenaean" IIIB Imported to the Levant. Pp. 1–12 in *All the Wisdom of the East; Studies in Near Eastern Archaeology and History in Honor of Eliezer D. Oren*, ed. S. Aḥituv, M. Gruber, G. Lehmann and Z. Talshir. Fribourg: Academic Press.

Aston, D. A. 1996. *Egyptian Pottery of the Late New Kingdom and Third Intermediate Period (Twelfth–Seventh Centuries BC): Tentative Footsteps in a Forbidding Terrain*. Studien zur Archäologie und Geschichte Altägyptens 13. Heidelberg: Heidelberger Orientverlag.

Åström, P. 1957. *The Middle Cypriote Bronze Age*. Lund: Håkan Ohlssons Boktryckeri.

Aznar, C. 1996. *El impacto Asirio en la expansion de los Fenicios hacia Occidente. El caso de Tell Abu Hawam (Haifa, Israel): la rampa septentrional*. Master's thesis, Universidad Complutense Madrid.

Ballard, R. D.; Stager, L. E.; Master, D. M.; Yoerger, D.; Mindell, D.; Whitcomb, L. L.; Singh, H.; and Piechota, D. 2002. Iron Age Shipwrecks in Deep Water off Ashkelon, Israel. *American Journal of Archaeology* 106: 151–68.

Barber, E. J. W. 1991. *Prehistoric Textiles*. Princeton: Princeton University Press.

Bartoloni, P. 1999. Pottery. Pp. 562–78 in *The Phoenicians*, ed. S. Moscati. New York: Rizzoli.

Basch, L. and Artzy, M. 1985. Ship Graffiti at Kition. Pp. 562–78 in *Excavations at Kition: The Pre-Phoenician Levels*, V, eds. V. Karageorghis and M. Demas. Cyprus: Department of Antiquities.

Bate, D. M. A. 1938. Animal Remains. Pp. 209–13 in *Megiddo Tombs*, eds. P. L. O. Guy and R. Engberg. The University of Chicago Oriental Institute Publications 33. Chicago: University of Chicago Press.

Beck, P. 1985. The Middle Bronze Age IIA Pottery from Aphek, 1972–1984: First Summary. *Tel Aviv* 12: 181–203.

Beck, P. 2000a. Area A: Middle Bronze Age IIA Pottery. Pp. 173–238 in *Aphek-Antipatris I: Excavation of Areas A and B, The 1972–1976 Seasons*, eds. M. Kochavi, P. Beck, and E. Yadin. Tel Aviv: Emery and Claire Yass Publications in Archaeology.

Beck, P. 2000b. Area B: Pottery. Pp. 93–133 in *Aphek-Antipatris I: Excavation of Areas A and B, The 1972–1976 Seasons*, eds. M. Kochavi, P. Beck, and E. Yadin. Tel Aviv: Emery and Claire Yass Publications in Archaeology.

Beeri, R. 2003. *The Middle and Late Bronze Graves from Tel Akko (Area AB)*. Master's thesis, University of Haifa (in Hebrew).

Beeri, R.; Motro, H.; Gerstel-Raban, N.; and Artzy, M. 2020. Burials of Domesticated Animals in the Middle Bronze Age Rampart at Tel 'Akko in Light of the Archaeological Finds in the Levant and Ceremonies from the Ancient Near East. Pp. 54–68 in *Nomads of the Mediterranean: Trade and Contact in the Bronze and Iron Ages, Studies in Honor of Michal Artzy*, ed. A. Yassur-Landau and A. Gilboa. Leiden: Brill.

Ben-Ami, D. 2001. The Iron Age I at Tel Hazor in Light of the Renewed Excavations. *Israel Exploration Journal* 51: 148–70.

Ben-Dor, I. 1945. Palestinian Alabaster Vases. *Quarterly of the Department of Antiquities in Palestine* 11: 93–112.

Ben Dor Evian, S. 2011. Egypt and the Levant in the Iron I–IIA: The Ceramic Evidence. *Tel Aviv* 38: 94–119.

Ben-Shlomo, D., Nodarou, E. and Rutter, J. B. 2011. Transport Stirrup Jars from the Southern Levant: New Light on Commodity Exchange in the Eastern Mediterranean. *American Journal of Archaeology* 115: 329–53.

Ben-Tor, A., and Portugali, Y. 1987. *Tell Qiri: A Village in the Jezreel Valley*. Qedem 24. Jerusalem: Institute of Archaeolgy, Hebrew University of Jerusalem.

Bietak, M. 1991. *Tell el-Dab'a V*. Österreichische Akademie der Wissenschaften Denkschriften der Gesamtakademie 9. Vienna: Österreichische Akademie der Wissenschaften.

Bikai, P. M. 1978. *The Pottery of Tyre*. Warminster: Aris & Phillips.

Bikai, P. M. 1987. *The Phoenician Pottery of Cyprus*. Nicosia: A. G. Leventis Foundation.

Biran, A. 1989. The Collared-rim Jars and the Settlement of the Tribe of Dan. Pp. 71–96 in *Recent Excavations in Israel: Studies in Iron Age Archaeology*, eds. S. Gitin and

W. G. Dever. Annual of the American Schools of Oriental Research 49. Winona Lake, IN: Eisenbrauns.

Biran, A. 1994. *Biblical Dan*. Jerusalem: Israel Exploration Society.

Boessneck, J. 1976. Verteilung der Tierknochenfunde über die Flächen und Gräber. Pp. 9–18 in *Tell el-Dab'a III*. Österreichische Akademie der Wissenschaften Denkschriften der Gesamtakademie 5. Vienna: Österreichische Akademie der Wissenschaften.

Briend, J., and Humbert, J.-B. 1980. *Tell Keisan (1971–1976): Une cité phénicienne en Galilée*. Orbis Biblicus et Orientalis Series Archaeologica 1. Fribourg: Éditions Universitaires Fribourg Suisse.

Brody, A. J. 2008. Late Bronze Age Canaanite Mortuary Practices. Pp. 515–32 in *Ashkelon I: Introduction and Overview 1985–2000*, eds. L. E. Stager, J. D. Schloen, and D. M. Master. Winona Lake, IN: Eisenbrauns.

Bruins, H. J.; van der Plicht, H. J.; and Mazar, A. 2003. ^{14}C Dates from Tel Rehov: Iron-Age Chronology, Pharaohs, and Hebrew Kings. *Science* 300: 315–18.

Buchholz, H.-G. 1963. Steinerne Dreifussschalen des ägäischen Kulturkreises und ihre Beziehungen zum Osten. *Jahrbuch des Deutschen Archäologischen Instituts* 78: 1–77.

Buchholz, H.-G. 1993. A Mycenaean Fish Krater from Akko. Pp. 41–55 in *Studies in the Archaeology and History of Ancient Israel in Honour of Moshe Dothan*, eds. M. Heltzer, A. Segal, and D. Kaufman. Haifa: Haifa University Press.

Burdajewicz, M. 1995. *La céramique palestinienne du Fer I. La contribution de Tell Keisan, site de la Galilée maritime*. Doctoral dissertation, Warsaw University.

Chambon, A. 1980. Le niveau 5 (Fer IIC). Pp. 157–79 in *Tell Keisan (1971–1976): Une cité phénicienne en Galilée*, eds. J. Briend and J.-B. Humbert. Orbis Biblicus et Orientalis Series Archaeologica 1. Fribourg: Éditions Universitaires Fribourg Suisse.

Chapman, S. V. 1972. A Catalogue of Iron Age Pottery From the Cemeteries of Khirbet Silm, Joya, Qrayé and Qasmieh of South Lebanon. *Berytus* 21: 55–194.

Cole, D. P. 1984. *Shechem I: The Middle Bronze IIB Pottery*. Winona Lake, IN: American Schools of Oriental Research.

Conrad, D. 1993. The Akko Ware: A New Type of Phoenician Pottery with Incised Decoration. Pp. 127–42 in *Studies in the Archaeology and History of Ancient Israel in Honour of Moshe Dothan*, eds. M. Heltzer, A. Segal, and D. Kaufman. Haifa: Haifa University Press.

Cornwall, I. W. 1965. Appendix K.ii: Collections of Animal Bones from Tombs of E.B.–M.B. Outsize Type. Pp. 702–703 in *Excavations at Jericho II*, ed. K. M. Kenyon. London: The British School of Archaeology in Jerusalem.

D'Agata, A. L.; Goren, Y.; Mommsen, H.; Schwend, A.; and Yasur-Landau, A. 2005. Imported Pottery of LH IIIC Style from Israel. Style, Provenance, and Chronology. Pp. 371–79 in *Emporia: Aegeans in the Central and Eastern Mediterranean*, vol. I, eds. R. Laffineur and E. Greco. Aegaeum 25. Belgium: Kliemo.

David, L. 1988. Fish Scales. Pp. 148–49 in *Gezer V: The Field I Caves*, eds. J. D. Seger and H. D. Lance. Jerusalem: Nelson Glueck School of Biblical Archaeology.

Dayagi-Mendels, M. 2002. *The Akhziv Cemeteries: The Ben-Dor Excavations, 1941–1944*. IAA Reports 15. Jerusalem: Israel Antiquities Authority.

Dikaios, P. 1969. *Enkomi: Excavations 1948–1958*. Mainz am Rhein: Philipp von Zabern.

Dothan, M. 1976. Akko: Interim Excavation Report First Season, 1973/4. *Bulletin of the American Schools of Oriental Research* 224: 1–48.

Dothan, M. 1979. 'Akko, 1979 (Notes and News). *Israel Exploration Journal* 29: 227–28.

Dothan, M. 1986. Šardina at Akko? Pp. 105–15 in *Sardinia in the Mediterranean*, ed. M. S. Balmuth. Studies in Sardinian Archaeology 2. Ann Arbor: University of Michigan Press.

Dothan, M. 1989. Movements of the Early "Sea Peoples." Pp. 59–70 in *Recent Excavations in Israel: Studies in Iron Age Archaeology*, eds. S. Gitin and W. G. Dever. Annual of the American Schools of Oriental Research 49. Winona Lake, IN: Eisenbrauns.

Dothan, M. 1993. Acco. Pp. 16–23 in *The New Encyclopedia of Archaeological Excavations in the Holy Land*, vol. 1, ed. E. Stern. New York: Simon and Schuster.

Dothan, M., and Porath, Y. 1982. *Ashdod IV, Excavation of Area M*. 'Atiqot 15. Jerusalem: Israel Exploration Society.

Dothan, M. and Raban, A. 1980. The Sea Gate of Ancient Akko. *The Biblical Archaeologist* 43: 35–39.

Dothan, T. 1982. *The Philistines and Their Material Culture*. Jerusalem: Israel Exploration Society.

Dothan, T. 1989. The Arrival of the Sea Peoples: Cultural Diversity in Early Iron Age Canaan. Pp. 1–14 in *Recent Excavations in Israel: Studies in Iron Age Archaeology*, eds. S. Gitin and W. G. Dever. Annual of the American Schools of Oriental Research 49, Winona Lake, IN: Eisenbrauns.

Ebeling, J. R. 2007. Groundstone Objects. Pp. 223–28 in *Tel Mor—A Late Bronze Age Egyptian Outpost in Southern Canaan: The Excavations Directed by Moshe Dothan 1959–1960*, ed. T. J. Barako. IAA Reports 32. Jerusalem: Israel Antiquities Authority.

Elliott, C. 1991. The Ground Stone Industry. Pp. 9–100 in *Ras Shamra-Ougarit VI: Arts et Industries de la pierre*, ed. M. Yon. Paris: Éditions Recherche sur les Civilisations.

Finkelstein, I. 1996. The Stratigraphy and Chronology of Megiddo and Beth-Shan in the 12th–11th Centuries B.C.E., *Tel Aviv* 23: 170–84.

Finkelstein, I. 2003. City-States to States: Polity Dynamics in the 10th–9th Centuries B.C.E. Pp. 75–83 in *Symbiosis, Symbolism, and the Power of the Past*, eds. W. G. Dever and S. Gitin. Winona Lake, IN: Eisenbrauns.

Fitzgerald, M. A. 1997. Uluburun. Pp. 430–32 in *Encyclopedia of Underwater and Maritime Archaeology*, ed. J. P. Delgado. New Haven: Yale University Press.

Frankel, R. 2003. The Olynthus Mill, Its Origin, and Diffusion: Typology and Distribution. *American Journal of Archaeology* 107/1: 1–21.

Friend, G. 1996. *The Loom Weights*. Tell Taannek 1963–1968, vol. 3/2. Birzeit, Palestine: Palestinian Institute of Archaeology, Birzeit University.

Fritz, V., and Kempinski, A. 1983. *Ergebnisse der Ausgrabungen auf der Hirbet el-Msas (Tel Masos) 1972–1975*. Abhandlungen des Deutschen Palästinavereins 1–2. Wiesbaden: Otto Harrassowitz.

Gal, Z., and Alexandre, Y. 2000. *Horbat Rosh Zayit, An Iron Age Storage Fort and Village*. IAA Reports 8. Jerusalem: Israel Antiquities Authority.

Gambash, G. 2012. Between Persia and Egypt—Literary Evidence for Achaemenid Activity in Akko. *Recanati Institute for Maritime Studies Newsletter* 37: 15–18.

Gershuny, L. 1985. *Bronze Vessels from Israel and Jordan*. Prähistorische Bronzefunde 2/6. Munich: C. H. Beck.

Gerstenblith, P. 1983. *The Levant at the Beginning of the Middle Bronze Age*. ASOR Dissertation Series 5. Winona Lake, IN: Eisenbrauns.

Giaime, M.; Morhange, C.; Marriner, N.; López-Cadavid, G. I.; and Artzy, M. 2018. Geoarchaeological Investigations at Akko, Israel: New Insights into Landscape Changes and Related Anchorage Locations since the Bronze Age. *Geoarchaeology* 33: 641–60.

Gilboa, A. 1999. The Dynamics of Phoenician Bichrome Pottery: A View from Tel Dor. *Bulletin of the American Schools of Oriental Research* 316: 1–22.

Gilboa, A. 2005. Sea Peoples and Phoenicians along the Southern Phoenician Coast—A Reconciliation: An Interpretation of Sikila (SKL) Material Culture. *Bulletin of the American Schools of Oriental Research* 337: 47–78.

Gilboa, A. 2015. Iron Age IIC Northern Coast, Carmel Coast, Galilee and Jezreel Valley. Pp. 301–26 in *The Ancient Pottery of Israel and Its Neighbours*, vol. 1, ed. Seymour Gitin. Jerusalem: Israel Exploration Society.

Gilboa, A. and Goren, Y. 2015. Early Iron Age Phoenician Networks: An Optical Mineralogy Study of Phoencian Bichrome and Related Wares in Cyprus. *Ancient West and East* 14: 73–110.

Gilboa, A., and Sharon, I. 2003. An Archaeological Contribution to the Early Iron Age Chronological Debate: Alternative Chronologies for Phoenicia and Their Effects on the Levant, Cyprus, and Greece. *Bulletin of the American Schools of Oriental Research* 332: 7–80.

Gilboa, A.; Waiman-Barak, P.; and Sharon, I. 2015. Dor, the Carmel Coast and Early Iron Age Mediterranean Exchanges. Pp. 85–111 in *The Mediterranean Mirror: Cultural Contacts in the Mediterranean Sea between 1200 and 750 BC*, eds. A. Babbi, F. Bubenheimer-Erhart, B. Marín Aguilera, and S. Mühl. Mainz: Schnell and Steiner.

Gitin, S. 1990. *Gezer III: A Ceramic Typology of the Late Iron II, Persian and Hellenistic Periods at Tell Gezer*. Jerusalem: Hebrew Union College.

Gjerstad, E. 1948. *The Cypro-Geometric, Cypro-Archaic and Cypro-Classical Periods*. The Swedish Cyprus Expedition 4/2. Stockholm: The Swedish Cyprus Expedition.

Golan, D. 2004. *Monochrome Ware from Tell Abu Hawam*. Master's thesis, Department of Maritime Civilizations, University of Haifa (in Hebrew).

Gonen, R. 1992a. *Burial Patterns and Cultural Diversity in Late Bronze Age Canaan*. ASOR Dissertation Series 6. Winona Lake, IN: Eisenbrauns.

Gonen, R. 1992b. Structural Tombs in the Second Millennium B.C. Pp. 151–60 in *The Architecture of Ancient Israel From the Prehistoric to the Persian Periods*, eds. A. Kempinski and R. Reich. Jerusalem: Israel Exploration Society.

Greenwood, P. H., and Howes, G. 1973. Fish Remains. Pp. 259–68 in *Excavations in the Necropolis of Salamis III*, ed. V. Karageorghis. Salamis 5. Nicosia: Zevallis.

Grosvenor-Ellis, A. 1960. Appendix C: The Equid in the Shaft of Tomb J3. Pp. 535–36 in *Excavations at Jericho I*, ed. K. M. Kenyon. London: The British School of Archaeology in Jerusalem.

Grosvenor-Ellis, A., and B. Whestley 1965. Appendix J: Preliminary Report on the Animal Remains in the Jericho Tombs. Pp. 694–703 in *Excavations at Jericho II*, ed. K. M. Kenyon. London: The British School of Archaeology in Jerusalem.

Gunneweg, J., and Michel, H. V. 1999. Does the Different Layout of the Late Bronze Age Tombs at Laish/Dan and Akko in Northern Canaan Reflect Different Trade Relations? An Instrumental Neutron Activation Study on Mycenaean Pottery. *Journal of Archaeological Science* 26: 989–95.

Gunneweg, J. and Perlman, I. 1994. The Origin of the Mycenaen IIIC: I Stirrup Jar from Tell Keisan. *Revue Biblique* 101: 559–61.

Guy, P. L. O. 1938. *Megiddo Tombs*. The University of Chicago Oriental Institute Publications 33. Chicago: University of Chicago Press.

Hallote, R. S. 1995. Mortuary Archaeology and the Middle Bronze Age Southern Levant. *Journal of Mediterranean Archaeology* 8/1: 93–122.

Hamilton, R. W. 1935. Excavations at Tell Abu Hawam. *The Quarterly of the Department of Antiquities in Palestine* 4: 1–69.

Hammond, N. 1993. Matrices and Maya Archaeology. Pp. 139–52 in *Practices of Archaeological Stratigraphy*, ed. E. C. Harris, M. R. Brown III, and G. J. Brown. London: Academic Press.

Harris, E. C. 1975. The Stratigraphic Sequence: A Question of Time. *World Archaeology* 7/1: 109–21.

Harris, E. C. 1989. *Principles of Archaeological Stratigraphy*. Orlando: Academic Press.

Herrera, M. D. and Gomez, F. 2004. *Tell Abu Hawam (Haifa, Israel)*. Huelva: University of Huelva Press.

Heuck Allen, S. 1991. Late Bronze Age Grey Wares in Cyprus. Pp. 151–67 in *Cypriot Ceramics: Reading the Prehistoric Record*, eds. J. A. Barlow, D. R. Bolger, and B. Kling. University Museum Monograph 74. Philadelphia: A. G. Leventis Foundation.

Hocking, N. R. 2001. Lessons from the Kiln: Reduction Firing in Cypriot Iron Age Pottery. *Near Eastern Archaeology* 64/3: 132–39.

Horwitz, L. K. 1987. Animal Offerings from Two Middle Bronze Age Tombs. *Israel Exploration Journal* 37: 251–55.

Horwitz, L. K. 1989. Sedentism in the Early Bronze IV: A Faunal Perspective. *Bulletin of the American School of Oriental Research* 275: 15–25.

Horwitz, L. K. 1996. Animal Bones from the Middle Bronze Age Tombs at Tel Dan. Pp. 268–77 in *Dan I: A Chronicle of the Excavations, the Pottery Neolithic, the Early Bronze Age & the Middle Bronze Age Tombs*, eds. A. Biran, D. Ilan and R. Greenberg. Jerusalem: Nelson Glueck School of Biblical Archaeology.

Horwitz, L. K. 1997. The Animal Bone Assemblage from the Middle Bronze II Tomb (T1181, Area L) at Hazor. Pp. 344–47 in *Hazor V*, eds. A. Ben-Tor and R. Bonfil. Jerusalem: Israel Exploration Society.

Horwitz, L. K. 2001. Animal Offerings in the Middle Bronze Age: Food for the Gods, Food for Thought. *Palestine Exploration Quarterly* 133: 78–90.

Horwitz, L. K. 2002. The Animal Remains. Pp. 219–21 in *Dan II: A Chronicle of the Excavations and the Late Bronze Age "Mycenaean" Tomb*, eds. A. Biran and R. Ben-Dov. Jerusalem: Nelson Glueck School of Biblical Archaeology.

Horwitz, L. K. 2007. The Faunal Remains. Pp. 125–29 in *The Middle Bronze Age IIA Cemetery at Gesher: Final Report*, eds. Y. Garfinkel and S. Cohen. Annual of the American Schools of Oriental Research 62. Boston: American Schools of Oriental Research.

Horwitz, L. K. 2010. Animal Bone Remains from Fassuta. *'Atiqot* 62: 51–52.

Horwitz L. K. and Y. Garfinkel. 1991. Animal remains from the site of Gesher, Central Jordan Valley. *Journal of the Israel Prehistoric Society* 24: 64–76.

Hovers, E. 1996. The Groundstone Industry. Pp. 171–92 in *Excavations at the City of David IV, 1978–85, Directed by Y. Shiloh*, eds. A. de Groot and D. T. Ariel. Qedem 35. Jerusalem: Institute of Archaeology, Hebrew University of Jerusalem.

Humbert, J.-B. 1993. Keisan, Tell. Pp. 862–67 in *The New Encyclopedia of Archaeological Excavations in the Holy Land*, vol. 3, ed. E. Stern. New York: Simon and Schuster.

Hunt, M. 1987. The Pottery. Pp. 139–223 in *Tell Qiri, A Village in the Jezreel Valley*, eds. A. Ben-Tor and Y. Portugali. Qedem 24. Jerusalem: Institute of Archaeology, Hebrew University of Jerusalem.

Ilan, D. 1996. The Middle Bronze Age Tombs. Pp. 161–329 in *Dan I: A Chronicle of the Excavations, the Pottery Neolithic, the Early Bronze Age & the Middle Bronze Age Tombs*, eds. A. Biran, D. Ilan, and R. Greenberg. Jerusalem: Nelson Glueck School of Biblical Archaeology.

Ilan, D. 1999. Rural Archaeology—Tel Dan During the Iron Age I (Hebrew). Pp. 51–66 in *Material Culture, Society and Ideology: New Directions in the Archaeology of the Land of Israel, Conference Proceedings*, eds. A. Faust and A. Maeir. Ramat-Gan: Bar-Ilan University Press.

Isserlin, B. S. J. 1950. On Some Possible Early Occurrences of the Camel in Palestine. *Palestine Exploration Quarterly* 82/1: 50–53.

Jidejian, N. 1968. *Byblos Through the Ages.* Beirut: Dar el-Machreq.

Johnson, P. 1982. The Middle Cypriote Pottery Found in Palestine. *Opuscula Atheniensia* 14: 49–72.

Kaniewski, D.; Van Campo, E.; Morhange, C.; Guiot, J.; Zviely, D.; Shaked, I.; and Artzy, M. 2013. Urban Impact on Mediterranean Coastal Environments. *Nature Scientific Reports*: 1–5.

Kaniewski, D.; Van Campo, E.; Morhange, C.; Guiot, J.; Zviely, D.; Le Burel, S.; Otto, T.; and Artzy, M. 2014. Vulnerability of Mediterranean Ecosystems to Long-Term Changes along the Coast of Israel. *Plos One* 9/7: 1–9.

Kaplan, M.; Harbottle, G.; and Sayre, E. 1982. Multi-Disciplinary Analysis of Tell el Yahudiyeh Ware. *Archaeometry* 24/2: 127–42.

Karageorghis, V. 2003. The Cult of Astarte in Cyprus. Pp. 215–21 in *Symbiosis, Symbolism, and the Power of the Past*, eds. W. G. Dever and S. Gitin. Winona Lake, IN: Eisenbrauns.

Karageorghis, V., ed. 2001. *The White Slip Ware of Late Bronze Age Cyprus: Proceedings of an International Conference Organized by the Anastasios G. Leventis Foundation, Nicosia in Honour of Malcolm Wiener, Nicosia 29th–30th October 1998.* Contributions to the Chronology of the Eastern Mediterranean 2. Denkschriften der Gesamtakademie 20. Vienna: Verlag der Österreichischen Akademie der Wissenschaften.

Keel, O. 1997. *Corpus der Stempelsiegel-Amulette aus Palästina/Israel, Von den Anfängen bis zur Perserzeit, Katalog Band I: Von Tell Abu Farag bis 'Atlit.* Orbis biblicus et Orientalis Series Archaeologica 13. Göttingen: Vandenhoeck and Ruprecht.

Kempinski, A. 1992. The Middle Bronze Age. Pp. 159–210 in *The Archaeology of Ancient Israel*, ed. A. Ben-Tor. New Haven: Yale University Press.

Kempinski, A., ed. 2002. *Tel Kabri: The 1986–1993 Excavation Seasons.* Tel Aviv: Emery and Claire Yass Publications in Archaeology.

Kenyon, K. M. 1969. The Middle and Late Bronze Age Strata at Megiddo. *Levant* 1: 25–60.

Kenyon, K. M., and Holland, T. A. 1982. *The Pottery Type Series and Other Finds.* Excavations at Jericho IV. London: The British School of Archaeology in Jerusalem.

Khalifeh, I. A. 1988. *Sarepta II: The Late Bronze and Iron Age Periods of Area II, X.* Beirut: Département des publications de l'Université libanaise.

Killebrew, A. 1998. *Ceramic Craft and Technology during the Late Bronze and Early Iron Ages: The Relationship Between Pottery Technology, Style, and Cultural Diversity.* Doctoral dissertation, Hebrew University of Jerusalem.

Killebrew, A. E.; Quartermaine, J.; Kaelin, O.; and Mathys, H. P. 2016. Total Archaeology@ Tel Akko (The 2013 and 2014 Seasons): Excavation, Survey, Community Outreach and New Approaches to Landscape Archaeology in 3D. Pp. 491–502 in *Proceedings of the 9th International Congress on the Archaeology of the Ancient Near East*, vol. 3. Wiesbaden: Harrassowitz.

Kling, B. 1991. A Terminology for the Matte-Painted, Wheelmade Pottery of Late Cypriot IIC–IIIA. Pp. 181–84 in *Cypriot Ceramics: Reading the Prehistoric Record*, eds. J. A. Barlow, D. R. Bolger, and B. Kling. University Museum Monograph 74. Philadelphia: A. G. Leventis Foundation.

Koehl, R. B. 1988. *Sarepta III: The Imported Bronze and Iron Age Wares from Area II, X*. Beirut: Département des publications de l'Université libanaise.

Lamon, R. S., and Shipton, G. M. 1939. *Megiddo I*. Chicago: University of Chicago Press.

Legge, A. J., and Zeder, M. A. 1988. Animal Remains. P. 147 in *Gezer V: The Field I Caves*, eds. J. D. Seger and H. D. Lance. Jerusalem: Nelson Glueck School of Biblical Archaeology.

Lehmann, G. 2001. Phoenicians in Western Galilee: First Results of an Archaeological Survey in the Hinterland of Akko. Pp. 65–112 in *Studies in the Archaeology of the Iron Age in Israel and Jordan*, ed. A. Mazar. Journal for the Study of the Old Testament Supplement Series 331. Sheffield: Sheffield Academic.

Lehmann, G. 2002. Pottery V: Iron Age. Pp. 178–222 in *Tel Kabri: The 1986–1993 Excavation Seasons*, ed. A. Kempinski. Tel Aviv: Emery and Claire Yass Publications in Archaeology.

Lehmann, G. 2015. Iron Age IIA–B: Northern Coastal Plain. Pp. 115–34 in *The Ancient Pottery of Israel and Its Neighbours*, vol. 1, ed. Seymour Gitin. Jerusalem: Israel Exploration Society.

Lepiksaar, J. 1995. Fish Remains from Tel Hesban, Jordan. Pp. 169–210 in *Hesban 13*, eds. O. S. LaBianca and A. von den Driesch. Berrien Springs, MI: Andrews University Press.

Lernau, H., and Lernau, O. 1992. Fish Remains. Pp. 131–48 in *Excavations at the City of David 1978–1985: Final Report vol. III*, eds. A. De Groot and D. T. Ariel. Qedem 33. Jerusalem: Institute of Archaeology, Hebrew University of Jerusalem.

Lernau, O. 1995. The Fish Remains from Upper Zohar. Pp. 99–111 in *Upper Zohar: An Early Byzantine Fort in Palestina Tertia: Final Report from Excavations in 1985–86*, ed. R. P. Harper. Oxford: Oxford University Press.

Lernau, O. 2000a. Fish Bones. Pp. 463–77 in *Megiddo III: The 1992–1996 Seasons*, eds. I. Finkelstein, D. Ussishkin, and B. Halpern. Tel Aviv: Emery and Claire Yass Publications in Archaeology.

Lernau, O. 2000b. Fish Bones from Horbat Rosh Zayit. Pp. 233–37 in *Horbat Rosh Zayit, an Iron Age Storage Fort and Village*, eds. Z. Gal and Y. Alexandre. IAA Reports 8. Jerusalem: Israel Antiquities Authority.

Lernau, O. 2002. Fish Bones. Pp. 409–27 in *Tel Kabri: The 1986–1993 Excavation Seasons*, ed. A. Kempinski. Tel Aviv: Emery and Claire Yass Publications in Archaeology.

Lev-Tov, J. S. E., and Maher, E. F. 2001. Food in Late Bronze Age Funerary Offerings. *Palestine Exploration Quarterly* 133: 91–110.

Levy, T. E., and Higham, T. 2005. *The Bible and Radiocarbon Dating. Archaeology, Text and Science.* London: Equinox.

Liebowitz, H. A. 1977. Bone and Ivory Inlay from Syria and Palestine. *Israel Exploration Journal* 27/2–3: 89–97.

Loud, G. 1948. *Megiddo II.* Chicago: University of Chicago Press.

Lucas, A., and Harris, J. R. 1962. *Ancient Egyptian Materials and Industries.* London: Edward Arnold.

Maeir, A. M. 2001. The Philistine Culture in Transformation: A Current Perspective based on the Results of the First Seasons of Excavations at Tell es-Safi/Gath (Hebrew). Pp. 111–29 in *Settlement, Civilization and Culture, Proceedings of the Conference in Memory of David Alon,* eds. A. M. Maeir and E. Baruch. Ramat-Gan: Bar Ilan University.

Maher, E. F. 2012. Mortuary Animal Offerings from Azor. Pp. 195–98 in *The Cemetery of Azor, Moshe Dothan's Excavations (1958, 1960),* ed. David Ben-Shlomo. IAA Reports 50. Jerusalem: Israel Antiquities Authority.

Marcus, E. S. 2003. Dating the Early Middle Bronze Age in the Southern Levant: A Preliminary Comparison of Radiocarbon and Archaeo-Historical Synchronizations. Pp. 95–110 in *The Synchronisation of Civilizations in the Eastern Mediterranean in the Second Millennium B.C.: Contributions to the Chronology of the Eastern Mediterranean II,* ed. M. Bietak. Denkschriften der Gesamtakademie 29. Vienna: Österreichische Akademie der Wissenschaften.

Marcus, E. S. and Artzy, M. 1995. A Loom Weight from Tel Nami with a Scarab Seal Impression. *Israel Exploration Journal* 45: 136–49.

Marcus, E. S.; Porath, Y.; and Paley, M. 2008. The Early Middle Bronze Age IIa Phases at Tel Ifshar and their External Relations. *Ägypten und Levante* 18: 221–44.

Martin, M. 2004. Egyptian and Egyptianizing Pottery in Late Bronze Age Canaan. Typology, Chronology, Ware Fabrics and Manufacture Techniques. Pots and People? *Ägypten und Levante* 14: 265–84.

Martín Garcia, J. M., and Artzy, M. 2018. Cultural Transformations Shaping the End of the Late Bronze Age. Pp. 97–106 in *Proceedings of the 10th International Congress on the Archaeology of the Ancient Near East,* ed. B. Horejs et al. Wiesbaden: Harrassowitz.

Master, D. M. 2003. Trade and Politics: Ashkelon's Balancing Act in the Seventh Century B.C.E. *Bulletin of the American Schools of Oriental Research* 330: 47–64.

Mazar, A. 1985. *Excavations at Tell Qasile, Part Two, The Philistine Sanctuary.* Qedem 20. Jerusalem: Institute of Archaeology, Hebrew University of Jerusalem.

Mazar, A. 1988. Israeli Archaeologists. Pp. 109–28 in *Benchmarks in Time and Culture,* eds. J. F. Drinkard, Jr., G. L. Mattingly, and J. M. Miller. Atlanta: Scholars Press.

Mazar, A. 1990. *Archaeology of the Land of the Bible, 10,000–586 B.C.E.* New York: Doubleday.

Mazar, A., and Panitz-Cohen, N. 2001. *Timnah (Tel Batash) II, The Finds from the First Millennium BCE*. Qedem 42. Jerusalem: Institute of Archaeology, Hebrew University of Jerusalem.

Merrillees, R. S. 1983. The Early Local Cypriote Pottery. Pp. 25–33 in *Excavations at Athienou, Cyprus 1971–1972*, eds. T. Dothan and A. Ben-Tor. Qedem 16. Jerusalem: Institute of Archaeology, Hebrew University of Jerusalem.

Milevski, I. 1998. The Groundstone Tools. Pp. 61–77 in *Villages, Terraces, and Stone Mounds: Excavations at Manahat, Jerusalem, 1987–1989*, eds. G. Edelstein, I. Milevski and S. Aurant. Jerusalem: Israel Antiquities Authority.

Millek, J. M. 2019. *Exchange, Destruction, and a Transitioning Society: Interregional Exchange in the Southern Levant from the Late Bronze Age to the Iron I*. RessourcenKulturen 9. Tübingen: Tübingen University Press.

Morhange, C.; Giaime, M.; Marriner, N.; Abu Hamid, A.; Honnorat, A.; Kaniewski, D.; Magnin, F.; Portov, A. V.; Wente, J.; Zviely, D.; and Artzy, M. 2016. Geoarchaeological Evolution of Tel Akko's Ancient Harbor. *Journal of Archaeological Science: Reports* 7: 71–81.

Negbi, O. 1989. Bronze Age Pottery. Pp. 43–63 in *Excavations at Tel Michal, Israel*, eds. Z. Herzog, G. Rapp, Jr., and O. Negbi. Minneapolis: The University of Minnesota Press.

Niemeier, B., and Niemeier, W.-D. 2002. Archaic Greek and Etruscan Pottery. Pp. 223–42 in *Tel Kabri: The 1986–1993 Excavation Seasons*, ed. A. Kempinski. Tel Aviv: Emery and Claire Yass Publications in Archaeology.

Niemeier, W.-D. 1998. The Mycenaeans in Western Anatolia and the Problem of the Origins of the Sea Peoples. Pp. 17–65 in *Mediterranean Peoples in Transition, Thirteenth to Early Tenth Centuries BCE*, eds. S. Gitin, A. Mazar, and E. Stern. Jerusalem: Israel Exploration Society.

Oren, E. D. 1975. The Pottery from the Achzib Defence System, Area D: 1963 and 1964 Seasons. *Israel Exploration Journal* 25/4: 211–25.

Ortiz, S. M. 2000. *The 11/10th Century B.C.E. Transition in the Aijalon Valley Region: New Evidence from Tel Miqne-Ekron Stratum IV*. Doctoral Dissertation, University of Arizona.

Paice, P. 1986/87. A Preliminary Analysis of Some Elements of the Saite and Persian Period Pottery at Tell el-Maskhuta. *Bulletin of the Egyptological Seminar* 8: 95–107.

Paice, P. 1991. Extensions to the Harris Matrix System to Illustrate Stratigraphic Discussions of an Archaeological Site. *Journal of Field Archaeology* 18: 17–28.

Paley, S. M., and Porat, Y. 1997. Early Middle Bronze Age IIA Remains at Tell el Ifshar, Israel: A Preliminary Report. Pp. 369–78 in *The Hyksos: New Historical and Archaeological Perspectives*, ed. E. D. Oren. Philadelphia: The University Museum, University of Pennsylvania Press.

Parker Pearson, M. 1999. *The Archaeology of Death and Burial*. Phoenix Mill, United Kingdom: Sutton.

Petrie, F. 1931. *Ancient Gaza I*. London: British School of Archaeology in Egypt.

Pulak, C. 1997. Cape Gelidonya Wreck. Pp. 84–86 in *Encyclopedia of Underwater and Maritime Archaeology*, ed. J. P. Delgado. New Haven: Yale University Press.

Raban, A. 1991. The Port City of Akko in the MBII. *Michmanim* 5: 17*–34*.

Redford, D. B. 1992. *Egypt, Canaan, and Israel in Ancient Times*. Princeton: Princeton University Press.

Reese, D. S. 1981. Notes on the Fish Identified from the Cisterns. Pp. 238–41 in *Excavations at Carthage 1977 Conducted by the University of Michigan, VI*, ed. J. H. Humphrey. Ann Arbor: University of Michigan Press.

Rey, E. G. 1889. Supplément à l'étude sur la topographie de la ville d'Acre au XIIIe siècle. *Mémoires de la Société nationale des antiquaires de France*, t. XLIX. Nogent-le-Rotrou, France: Daupeley-Gouverneur.

Rosen, S. A. 1982. Flint Sickle Blades of the Late Proto-historic and Early Periods in Israel. *Tel Aviv* 9: 139–45.

Rosen, S. A. 1983. The Canaanean Blade and the Early Bronze Age. *Israel Exploration Journal* 33: 15–29.

Rosen, S. A. 1986. The Gezer Flint Caches 1970–71. Pp. 259–63 *in Gezer IV*, ed. W. G. Dever. Jerusalem: Nelson Glueck School of Biblical Archaeology.

Rosen, S. A. 1987. The Lithic Assemblage of the Iron Age Strata. Pp. 246–48 in *Tell Qiri, A Village in the Jezreel Valley*, eds. A. Ben-Tor and Y. Portugali. Qedem 24. Jerusalem: Institute of Archaeology, Hebrew University of Jerusalem.

Rosen, S. A. 1989. The Origin of Craft Specialization: Lithic Perspectives. Pp. 107–14 in *People and Culture in Change: Proceedings of the Second Symposium on Upper Palaeolithic, Mesolithic, and Neolithic Populations of Europe and the Mediterranean Basin*, ed. I. Hershkovitz. BAR International Series 508. Oxford: British Archaeological Reports.

Rosen, S. A. 1997. *Lithics After the Stone Age: A Handbook of Stone Tools from the Levant*. Walnut Creek, CA: AltaMira Press.

Rosen, S. A., and Rose, J. I. 2004. Chipped Stone Assemblage. Pp. 211–19 in *Tel Yin'am I: The Late Bronze Age. Excavations at Tel Yin'am 1976–1989*, ed. H. J. Liebowitz. Studies in Archaeology 42. Austin: Texas Archaeological Research Laboratory.

Rosen, S. A., and Rose, J. I. n.d. The Lithic Material from Ein Zippori, 1993–1994. Unpublished report.

Salles, J.-F. 1980. *La nécropole "K" de Byblos*. Boulogne: Maison de l'Orient.

Saltz, D. L. 1984. Imported Cypriot Pottery from the Middle Bronze Age Strata. Pp. 58–59 in *Excavations at Tel Mevorakh (1973–1976), Part Two: The Bronze Age*, ed. E. Stern. Qedem 18. Jerusalem: Institute of Archaeology, Hebrew University of Jerusalem.

Sass, B. 2000. The Small Finds. Pp. 349–423 in *Megiddo III: The 1992–1996 Seasons, vol. II*, eds. I. Finkelstein, D. Ussishkin and B. Halpern. Tel Aviv: Emery and Claire Yass Publications in Archaeology.

Sass, B. and Cinamon, G. 2006. The Small Finds. Pp. 353–425 in *Megiddo IV: The 1998–2002 Seasons, vol. I*, eds. I. Finkelstein, D. Ussishkin, and B. Halpern. Tel Aviv: Emery and Claire Yass Publications in Archaeology.

Schreiber, N. 2003. *The Cypro-Phoenician Pottery of the Iron Age*. Culture and History of the Ancient Near East 13. Leiden: Brill.

Sharvit, J.; Planer, D.; and Buxton, B. 2013. Preliminary Findings from Archaeological Excavations along the Foot of the Southern Seawall of Akko, 2008–2012. *Michmanim* 24: 39–52 (in Hebrew with English abstract).

Sherratt, S. 1992. Immigration and Archaeology: Some Indirect Reflections. Pp. 316–47 in *Acta Cypria. Acts of an International Congress on Cypriote Archaeology Held in Goteborg on 22–24 August, 1991*, Part II. Jonsered: P. Åstrom.

Sherratt, S. 1998. "Sea Peoples" and the Economic Structure. Pp. 292–313 in *Mediterranean Peoples in Transition, Thirteenth to Early Tenth Centuries BCE*, eds. S. Gitin, A. Mazar, and E. Stern. Jerusalem: Israel Exploration Society.

Singer-Avitz, L. 1999. Beersheba—A Gateway Community in Southern Arabian Long-Distance Trade in the Eighth Century BCE. *Tel Aviv* 26/1: 3–75.

Sparks, R. 2007. Stone Vessels in the Levant. *Palestine Exploration Fund Annual VIII*. London: Maney.

Stager, L. E. 2002. The MB IIA Ceramic Sequence at Tel Ashkelon and Its Implications for the "Port Power" Model of Trade. Pp. 353–62 in *The Middle Bronze Age in the Levant*, ed. M. Bietak. Denkschriften der Gesamtakademie 26. Vienna: Österreichische Akademie der Wissenschaften.

Stern, E. 1978. *Excavations at Tel Mevorakh (1973–1976), Part One: From the Iron Age to the Roman Period*. Qedem 9. Jerusalem: Institute of Archaeology, Hebrew University of Jerusalem.

Stern, E. 1984. *Excavations at Tel Mevorakh (1973–1976), Part Two: The Bronze Age*. Qedem 18. Jerusalem: Institute of Archaeology, Hebrew University of Jerusalem.

Stern, E. 2001. *Archaeology of the Land of the Bible, vol. II, The Assyrian, Babylonian, and Persian Periods (732–332 B.C.E.)*. New York: Doubleday.

Stockhammer, P. W. In preparation *Materielle Verflechtungen—Zur lokalen Einbindung fremder Keramik in der ostmediterranen Spätbronzezeit*. Vorgeschichtliche Forschungen 26. Rahden: Marie Leidorf.

Sukenik, E. L. 1948. Archaeological Investigations at Affula. *Journal of the Palestine Oriental Society* 21: 1–78.

Taylor, J. du Plat 1959. The Cypriot and Syrian Pottery from Al Mina, Syria. *Iraq* 21: 62–92.

Tixier, J.; Inizan, M. -L.; and Roche, H. 1980. *Préhistoire de la Pierre taillée I: Terminologie et technologie*. Paris: Cercle de Recherches et d'Etude Préhistorique.

Tschegg, C.; Ntaflos, T.; and Hein, I. 2009. Thermally Triggered Two-Stage Reaction of Carbonates and Clay During Ceramic Firing—A Case Study on Bronze Age Cypriot Ceramics. *Applied Clay Science* 43/ 1: 69–78.

Unger-Hamilton, R. 1984. The Formation and Use-Wear Polish on Flint: Beyond the "Deposit Versus Abrasion" Controversy. *Journal of Archaeological Science* 11: 91–98.

Ussishkin, D. 1985. Levels VII and VI at Tel Lachish and the End of the Late Bronze Age in Canaan. Pp. 213–30 in *Palestine in the Bronze Age: Papers in Honour of Olga Tufnell*, ed. J. N. Tubb. London: Institute of Archaeology.

Ussishkin, D. 1995. The Destruction of Megiddo at the End of the Late Bronze Age and Its Historical Significance. *Tel Aviv* 22: 240–67.

Van den Brink, E. C. M. 1982. *Tombs and Burial Customs at Tell el-Dab'a*. Beiträge zur Ägyptologie 4. Cairo: Berichte des Österreichischen Archäologischen Institutes.

Van den Brink, E. C. M.; Beeri, R.; Kirzner, D.; Bron, E.; Cohen-Weinberger, A.; Kamaisky, E.; Gonen, T.; Gershuny, L.; Nagar, Y.; Ben-Tor, D.; Sukenik, N.; Shamir, O.; Maher, E. F.; and Reich, D. 2017. A Late Bronze Age II Clay Coffin from Tel Shaddud in the Central Jezreel Valley, Israel: Context and Historical Implications. *Levant* 49: 105–35.

Van Neer, W.; Lernau, O.; Friedman, R.; Mumford, G.; Poblóme, J.; and Waelkens, M. 2004. Fish Remains from Archaeological Sites as Indicators of Former Trade Connections in the Eastern Mediterranean. *Paléorient* 30: 101–48.

Waiman-Barak, P.; Gilboa, A.; and Goren, Y. 2014. A Stratified Sequence of Early Iron Age Egyptian Ceramics at Tel Dor, Israel. *Ägypten und Levante* 24: 317–41.

Warren, P., and Hankey, V. 1989. *Aegean Bronze Age Chronology*. Bristol: Bristol Classical.

Wheeler, A. 1981. The Fish Remains. Pp. 231-37 in *Excavations at Carthage 1977 Conducted by the University of Michigan*, VI, ed. J. H. Humphrey. Ann Arbor: University of Michigan.

Witthoft, J. 1967. Glazed Polish on Flint Tools. *American Antiquity* 32: 383–89.

Wolff, S. R. 2002. Mortuary Practices in the Persian Period. *Near Eastern Archaeology* 65/2: 131–37.

Wright, K. I. 1992. A Classification System for Ground Stone Tools from the Prehistoric Levant. *Paléorient* 18/2: 53–81.

Yadin, Y.; Aharoni, Y.; Amiran, R.; Dothan, T.; Dunayevsky, I.; and Perrot, J. 1958. *Hazor I: An Account of the First Season of Excavations, 1955*. Jerusalem: Magnes Press, Hebrew University.

Yannai, E. 2004. The Northwest Anatolian Grey Ware. Pp. 1273–79 in *The Renewed Archaeological Excavations at Lachish (1973–1994): The Pre-Bronze Age and Bronze Age Pottery and Artefacts*, Vol. 3, ed. D. Ussishkin. Tel Aviv: Emery and Claire Yass Publications in Archaeology.

Yellin, J. 1984. Provenance of Selected LBA and MBA Pottery from Tel Mevorakh by Instrumental Neutron Activation Analysis. Pp. 87–103 in *Excavations at Tel Mevorakh*

(*1973–1976*), *Part Two: The Bronze Age*, ed. E. Stern. Qedem 18. Jerusalem: Institute of Archaeology, Hebrew University of Jerusalem.

Yoselevich, N. 2004. *The Utilization of Chalices as Incense Burners on Boats and Coastal Sites*. Master's thesis, University of Haifa (in Hebrew).

Zagorski, S. 2004. *Tel Akko (Area PH) during the Late Bronze IIB Period until the Iron IA Period*. Master's thesis, University of Haifa (in Hebrew).

Zarzecki-Peleg, A.; Cohen-Anidjar, S.; and Ben-Tor, A. 2005. Pottery Analysis. Pp. 235–344 in *Yoqne'am II: The Iron Age and the Persian Period, Final Report of the Archaeological Excavations (1977–1988)*, eds. A. Ben-Tor, A. Zarzecki-Peleg, and S. Cohen-Anidjar. Jerusalem: Institute of Archaeology, Hebrew University.

Zevulun, U. 1990. Tell el-Yahudiyah Juglets from a Potter's Refuse Pit at Afula. *Eretz-Israel* 20: 174–90.

Index

'Ajjul, Tell el-   275, 277, 287, 587
'Akka   50
Abu Hawam, Tell   28, 345, 347*n*, 349, 362, 364, 372–74, 376, 449, 451–2, 454, 457, 461, 475, 477, 481–2, 587, 590
Acre   11, 50, 584
Aegean-style ceramics/pottery   29, 288–90, 344*n*, 346, 348, 350, 375
Alabaster   20, 24, 27, 79, 101, 266, 270, 278–97, 299, 334, 587
Altar   3, 28, 30–31, 210, 347–8, 376, 382–3, 436–8, 590, 597–8, 609
Anatolia/Anatolian   105, 266, 278, 344, 346, 348–9, 351, 371, 374, 379, 385, 397, 435, 583, 587
Anatolian Tan ware   346, 349, 374, 379, 385, 435
Animal bones   5, 17, 20, 22, 24, 38, 42, 71, 73, 75, 99, 274–5, 630, 632–33
Antiochus IV Epiphanes   52
Aphek-Antipatris, Tel   223–31, 586
Ashkelon, Tel   19, 22*n*, 39*n*, 484, 586, 589,
Athienou   289

Ballast stones   24, 26, 94–5, 267, 279–80, 315, 587, 597, 601–2, 606, 616
Beads   20, 22, 24, 65, 77, 80–1, 83, 101, 266–7, 269–70, 272–74, 277, 305, 307, 335, 339
Belos River   51, 583
Beth Shean, Tel   266, 271, 353, 360, 365–68, 374–5, 583
Bone inlays   20, 22, 80, 77, 337, 343
British Mandate   27, 50, 584
Bronze Balance scale pans   79, 267, 270–1, 297, 333
Bronze jewelry   18–20, 24, 65, 81, 101, 270, 273, 339
Bronze recycling   3, 584, 589–90
Bronze weapons and tools   24, 101, 242, 278, 313
Byblos   277, 287, 366, 375, 586

Canaanite   18, 354–5, 362–64, 367, 369–71, 467, 469, 587, 590
Carmel Coast   345, 354, 449*n*

Ceramic loom weight   24, 267, 277, 586, 589
Chamber tomb   20–1, 24–5, 36–7, 268, 275, 286–7, 629
Chocolate on White ware   280, 315
Cilicia   358, 362, 374, 452
Crete   278, 281, 592
Crusaders   iii, 3, 25, 50–52, 441, 584–5, 591–93
Cypriot Base Ring ware   344, 353, 372–3, 385, 397, 399, 405, 407, 432–3, 587
Cypriot Bichrome ware (Bronze Age)   280, 289, 317, 329, 587
Cypriot Bichrome ware (Iron Age)   361, 442, 453, 470, 473, 480–82, 489, 491, 529, 577
Cypriot Monochrome ware   346, 352–3, 372–3, 407, 431, 433, 405
Cypriot Red on Black, Red on Red, ware   27*n*, 107, 288, 290, 317, 329, 446, 489, 499, 453, 503, 511, 517, 529, 525, 535, 537, 579
Cypriot White Painted ware (Bronze Age)   219, 221, 223, 229–30, 233, 239, 241, 243, 245, 249, 265, 277, 288–9, 329, 345*n*, 431
Cypriot White Painted ware (Iron Age)   290, 448, 479–82, 489, 505, 537, 577, 589
Cypriot White Slip ware   105, 220, 225, 280, 344–5, 348*n*–9, 351–53, 372–3, 385, 393, 395, 405, 407, 431, 587, 590

Dan, Tel   17*n*, 19, 21, 28, 32, 281, 283–4, 360–63, 632
Dog burial   51, 38, 214, 592
Dor, Tel   39*n*, 230, 345, 354, 358, 375–6, 452, 471, 475, 477–8, 484, 485, 583
Dothan, Moshe   1–4, 12, 15, 21, 30, 33, 230, 344–47*n*, 361, 369, 372, 448, 584–5, 589–592, 631

Egyptian import   352–54, 452, 483–85, 499, 515, 543

Fish bone   20, 22, 24, 27, 71, 279, 630–33
Fukhar, Tell el   1, 50

Gold   20, 77, 80–1, 270, 272, 274, 297, 305, 335, 587
Graffiti of ships   28, 373, 383, 590

Ifshar, Tell   223–25, 227, 230, 586

Jericho   227, 283, 287, 288, 630

Kabri, Tel   21, 464, 631
Keisan, Tell   344*n*, 354*n*, 357–62, 364–67, 368, 370, 374–75, 444, 449–53, 455, 458–67, 469, 474, 483, 589
Killebrew, Ann   1–2*n*, 344*n*, 353–62, 354*n*, 364–68, 368–9, 370–1, 584, 589
Kythera   278

Late Helladic   29–30, 344*n*, 347*n*, 358, 589
Lead   36, 81, 247, 270, 274, 297

Megiddo, Tel   16, 21, 224–27, 229–231, 275, 277, 282, 284–289, 345, 353, 357, 361, 368, 375, 449, 457, 460–61, 463, 469, 481, 483, 583, 599, 632
Metal   5, 22, 27, 259, 266, 268, 272, 276–7, 344*n*, 449, 537, 589–90
Mevorakh, Tel   284, 289, 449, 455, 461
Michal, Tel   284, 289, 599
Miletus   278
Minoan   267, 278, 313, 318, 362
Mortar   20, 22, 28, 36, 81, 270–21, 299, 336, 383, 597, 598, 600, 603
Murex shells   32, 43–4, 584
Mycenaean (Myc.) ware   344*n*–5*n*, 347, 349, 351–53, 372–74, 588, 590

Na'aman River   1, 50–1, 218*n*, 583–4, 591–2
Nami, Tel   230, 231, 345, 347*n*–8*n*, 354, 366, 370, 373, 376, 347, 586, 589
Napoleon   15*n*, 50, 585, 591
Napoleon's Hill   50, 591

Ocher   77, 103, 280
Ostrich eggshell   24, 27, 101 279, 315
Ottoman   50, 591–92

Philistia   347, 354–56, 361–2, 366, 374–5, 466
Plain White Wheelmade ware (PWWM)   345, 348, 372–3, 351, 482, 577

Qasile, Tel   354, 364, 367–8, 449, 452, 456–60
Qiri, Tel   28, 354, 359–62, 375, 449–53, 457–72, 474–5, 618
Quadruped   23
Quartermaine, Jamie   1, 3, 9, 27, 51, 584, 593

Rampart   15–18, 23–4, 28–9, 31–34, 36, 38, 44, 51–56, 206, 218*n*, 222–24, 230–1, 259, 266, 282–3, 352, 486, 584–588, 590–92
Ramses II   15, 27, 51, 587
Rhodes   366

Samaria ware   446–48, 454, 476, 478–9, 489, 521, 531, 577
Sarepta   28, 354–60, 362–64, 369, 374, 449, 463, 465–67, 469–70, 472–3, 475–82
Scarab   20, 22, 24, 27, 80, 101, 266, 272, 277–8, 297–8, 305, 313, 315, 337, 338, 343, 586–7, 594
Sea Gate   2, 231, 585
Shardanu   344, 347, 589–90
Shechem   281, 282, 283–85, 288
Silver   20, 24, 80, 101, 270, 277–8, 297, 305, 313

Tell el-Yahudiyeh ware   229
Templar castle   50, 441
Toron   3, 50, 441, 591
Total archaeology   x, 2, 7, 51, 280, 479
Tyre   28, 345, 354–5, 357–60, 362, 364, 369, 373, 374, 449, 451–52, 455, 457, 461–63, 466, 468–73, 475–6, 478, 480–82, 485, 585

Weights   20, 22, 80, 266, 269, 271, 274, 333, 607

Printed in the United States
by Baker & Taylor Publisher Services